112

The Continuum Companion to Existentialism

Also available from Continuum

The Continuum Companion to Aesthetics, edited by Anna Christina Ribeiro
The Continuum Companion to Continental Philosophy, edited by Beth Lord and John Mullarkey
The Continuum Companion to Epistemology, edited by Andrew Cullison
The Continuum Companion to Metaphysics, edited by Robert Barnard and Neil A. Manson
The Continuum Companion to Philosophical Logic, edited by Leon Horsten and Richard Pettigrew
The Continuum Companion to Philosophy of Mind, edited by James Garvey
The Continuum Companion to the Philosophy of Language, edited by Manuel Garcia-Carpintero and Max Kolbel
The Continuum Companion to the Philosophy of Science, edited by Steven French and Juha Saatsi

The Continuum Companion to Existentialism

Edited by

Felicity Joseph,

Jack Reynolds

and

Ashley Woodward

continuum

Continuum International Publishing Group

The Tower Building	80 Maiden Lane
11 York Road	Suite 704
London SE1 7NX	New York NY 10038

www.continuumbooks.com

British Library Cataloguing-in-Publication Data
A catalogue record for this book is available from the British Library.

ISBN: 978-0-826-4-38454 (hardcover)

Library of Congress Cataloging-in-Publication Data
A catalog record for this book is available from the Library of Congress

Typeset by Newgen Imaging Systems Pvt Ltd, Chennai, India
Printed and bound in Great Britain

Contents

Contributors   vii

1 Introduction   1
   Felicity Joseph, Jack Reynolds and Ashley Woodward

2 Existentialism, Phenomenology and Philosophical Method   15
   Felicity Joseph and Jack Reynolds

Part I – Current Research and Issues   37

3 Existentialism, Metaphysics and Ontology   39
   Christian Onof

4 Existentialism and Politics   62
   David Sherman

5 Existentialism, Psychoanalysis and Psychotherapy   83
   Douglas Kirsner

6 Existentialism and Ethics   98
   Debra Bergoffen

7 Existentialism and Religion   117
   George Pattison

8 Existentialism and Literature   138
   Colin Davis

9 Existentialism, Feminism and Sexuality   155
   Marguerite La Caze

10 Existentialism and the Emotions   175
   Suzanne L. Cataldi

11 Existentialism, Authenticity and the Self   198
   Christopher Macann

12 Existentialism and Latin America   215
   Roberto Domingo Toledo

Contents

Part II – New Directions   239

13 Existentialism and Cognitive Science   241
    Michael Wheeler and Ezequiel Di Paolo

14 Existentialism and Poststructuralism:
    Some Unfashionable Observations   260
    Jack Reynolds and Ashley Woodward

15 Recent Developments in Scholarship on Key Existentialists   282
        I. Kierkegaard   282
            William McDonald

       II. Nietzsche   290
            Keith Ansell-Pearson

      III. Heidegger   300
            Andrew J. Mitchell

       IV. Sartre   305
            Peter Gratton

        V. De Beauvoir   310
            Laura Hengehold

Part III – Resources   323

16 A–Z Glossary   325

17 A Chronology of Key Events, Texts and Thinkers   373

18 Research Resources in Existentialism   380

19 Annotated Guide to Further Reading   384

Index   401

Contributors

Keith Ansell-Pearson is Professor of Philosophy at Warwick University. He is the author of several books, including *Nietzsche contra Rousseau* (1990), *Viroid Life: Perspectives on Nietzsche and the Transhuman Condition* (1997), *Germinal Life: The Difference and Repetition of Deleuze* (1999), *Philosophy and the Adventure of the Virtual: Bergson and the Time of Life* (2002) and *How to Read Nietzsche* (2005). He has also edited various books on Nietzsche, Bergson and Deleuze.

Debra Bergoffen is Emerita Professor of Philosophy, George Mason University and Bishop Hamilton Lecturer of Philosophy, American University. She is the author of *The Philosophy of Simone de Beauvoir: Gendered Phenomenologies, Erotic Generosities* (1997).

Suzanne L. Cataldi is Professor of Philosophy at Southern Illinois University at Edwardsville. She is author of *Emotion, Depth and Flesh, A Study of Sensitive Space – Reflections on Merleau-Ponty's Philosophy of Embodiment* (1993) and co-editor of *Merleau-Ponty and Environmental Philosophy: Dwelling on the Landscapes of Thought* (2007), along with various articles.

Colin Davis is Professor of French at Royal Holloway College, University of London. His most recent books are *Scenes of Love and Murder: Renoir, Film and Philosophy* (2009) and *Critical Excess: Overreading in Derrida, Deleuze, Levinas, Žižek and Cavell* (2010).

Ezequiel Di Paolo is Ikerbasque Research Professor in Philosophy at the University of the Basque Country, Spain, and has recently been a Reader at the Centre for Computational Neuroscience and Robotics, University of Sussex. He is interested in various scientific and philosophical aspects of embodied cognitive science, including new approaches to artificial intelligence, evolutionary robotics and artificial life, adaptive behaviour, social cognition and phenomenology. He is the editor-in-chief of the journal *Adaptive Behavior*.

Peter Gratton is Assistant Professor in Philosophy at University of San Diego, author of *The State of Sovereignty: Lessons from the Political Fictions of Modernity* (2011) and co-editor of *Traversing the Imaginary: Richard Kearney and the Postmodern Challenge* (2007) and *Jean-Luc Nancy and Plural Thinking: Expositions of World, Politics, Art, and Sense* (forthcoming). He is working on a manuscript taking up recent philosophical approaches to the world and realism.

Laura Hengehold is Associate Professor of Philosophy at Case Western Reserve University in Cleveland Ohio, USA. She is the author of *The Body Problematic: Foucault and Kant on Political Imagination* (2007), and many articles on de Beauvoir, Foucault, and feminist and psychoanalytic themes in political philosophy.

Felicity Joseph completed her Ph.D. at the University of Melbourne in 2006. Her doctoral research was on the phenomenology of the lived body and explored the philosophies of Husserl, Merleau-Ponty and Marcel, among others. She has tutored and lectured in courses on existentialism and phenomenology at the University of Melbourne and her research interests include embodiment, feminist philosophy and the phenomenology of women's experience.

Douglas Kirsner is Professor of Philosophy and Psychoanalytic Studies at Deakin University, and author of *The Schizoid World of Jean-Paul Sartre and R. D. Laing* (2003) and *Unfree Associations: Inside Psychoanalytic Institutes* (2009, updated edition).

Marguerite La Caze is Senior Lecturer in Philosophy at the University of Queensland. She has research interests and numerous publications in European and feminist philosophy. Her publications include *The Analytic Imaginary* (2002) and *Integrity and the Fragile Self*, with Damian Cox and Michael Levine (2003) and various articles on Sartre, Derrida, de Beauvoir, Le Doeuff, and others.

Christopher Macann is the author of numerous works, including *Kant and the Foundations of Metaphysics* (1981), *Four Phenomenological Philosophers: Husserl, Heidegger, Sartre, Merleau-Ponty* (1993), *Being and Becoming* (2007), *Presence and Coincidence* (1990) and editor of *Martin Heidegger: Critical Assessments* (4 vols, 1992).

William McDonald is Senior Lecturer in Philosophy at the University of New England, translator of Kierkegaard's *Prefaces*, co-editor of *Kierkegaard's Concepts* with Jon Stewart and Steven Emmanuel (forthcoming), and author of various summative pieces on Kierkegaard, including for the *Stanford Encyclopedia of Philosophy*.

Andrew J. Mitchell is Assistant Professor of Philosophy at Emory University. He is author of *Heidegger among the Sculptors: Body, Space, and the Art of Dwelling* (2010) and numerous articles on Heidegger, Nietzsche, Derrida, Joyce and Fassbinder. He is co-translator of *Heidegger's Four Seminars* (2003).

Christian Onof is Honorary Research Fellow in Philosophy at Birkbeck College, University of London. He has published on Kant's ethics and metaphysics (*Kant Studien*, *Kant Yearbook*), on Heidegger and Sartre as well as on the nature of consciousness (*Philosophy and Phenomenological Research*, *Journal of Mind and Behavior*). He is co-founder of the journal *Episteme*, and on the Editorial Board of

Kant Studies Online. He is Senior Lecturer at the Faculty of Engineering, Imperial College London.

George Pattison is Lady Margaret Professor of Divinity at the University of Oxford and a Canon of Christ Church Cathedral. He is author of *Routledge Philosophy Guidebook to the Later Heidegger* (2000), *God and Being: An Enquiry* (2011) and several books on Kierkegaard, including *The Philosophy of Kierkegaard* (2005). He has also translated a selection of Kierkegaard's upbuilding discourses under the title *Kierkegaard's Spiritual Writings* (2010).

Jack Reynolds is Senior Lecturer in the Philosophy Department at La Trobe University. He has written four books: *Chronopathologies: The Politics of Time in Deleuze, Derrida, Analytic Philosophy and Phenomenology* (2011), *Analytic versus Continental: Arguments on the Methods and Value of Philosophy* (2010, with James Chase), *Merleau-Ponty and Derrida: Intertwining Embodiment and Alterity* (2004) and, most relevant to this companion, *Understanding Existentialism* (2006).

David Sherman is Professor in Philosophy at the University of Montana, and is author of *Camus* (2009), *Sartre and Adorno: The Dialectic of Subjectivity* (2007), and co-editor of *Reading Negri* (forthcoming), *The Blackwell Guide to Continental Philosophy* (2003) and *Hegel's Phenomenology of Self-Consciousness* (1999).

Roberto Domingo Toledo is currently finishing his dissertation in the Department of Philosophy at Stony Brook University. His field-based project is titled 'Treating the "Behavior Disorders" of French Ghetto Youth: Technoscientific Racism in French Delinquency Prevention Programs'. Specializing in technoscience, race studies and Latin American philosophy, he has also published in translation studies, religious studies and disability studies. In 2007, he received the American Philosophical Association's prize in Latin American thought for his essay, 'The Authenticity of Indigenous Rebellion in Mexico: Luis Villoro's Critique of Leopoldo Zea's Nationalism'.

Michael Wheeler is Professor of Philosophy at the University of Stirling. His primary research interests are in philosophy of science (especially cognitive science, psychology, biology, artificial intelligence and artificial life) and philosophy of mind. He also works on Heidegger, and is particularly interested in developing philosophical ideas at the interface between the analytic and the continental traditions. His book, *Reconstructing the Cognitive World: the Next Step*, was published in 2005.

Ashley Woodward is a member of the Melbourne School of Continental Philosophy and an editor of *Parrhesia: A Journal of Critical Philosophy*. He is author of *Nihilism in Postmodernity* (2009) and *Understanding Nietzscheanism* (2011), editor of *Interpreting Nietzsche* (2011) and co-editor of *Sensorium: Aesthetics, Art, Life* (2007).

1 Introduction

*Felicity Joseph, Jack Reynolds and
Ashley Woodward*

The general brief for the series of *Continuum Companions* in which this book
appears calls for the coverage of current research and guidance to new
research in the subject area. For many currently working in the academic
humanities, such a prescription would appear to be a non sequitur when
placed in relation to existentialism, a philosophy which for some decades
now has been widely perceived as outmoded. However, we take the commis-
sioning of this book in the series as a fortunate opportunity for us to counteract this all-too-prevalent perception, which in our view is a prejudice of
historical fashion rather than a view with a substantive argumentative basis.
The usual story about existentialism which typically goes unchallenged – but
which we wish to challenge here – is well expressed in the following
comments:

> Existentialism fell out of favour with the rise of structuralism, which explicitly
> attacked the naivety of existential ideas about freedom and consciousness.
> Nevertheless, existentialism is often one of the first forms of continental
> philosophy encountered by readers, and it sheds light on many other
> philosophical traditions, in particular phenomenology and psychoanalysis,
> with their emphasis on questions of meaning and the structure of
> consciousness. (Nina Power in Mullarkey and Lord, 2009, p. 292)

There is an allusion here to the fact that existentialism continues to be taught in
many undergraduate philosophy curricula, and continues to attract the attention of the wider public. The view for many professional philosophers, however, has been that while existentialism is okay for undergraduates or
non-philosophers to grapple with, and makes a useful starting-point for a philosophical education, serious researchers in contemporary philosophy should not
waste their time with it. It is precisely such a view we wish to challenge in this
book, first by charting research that *has* continued to be done in the area, if by a
minority of scholars, and second, by encouraging and indicating paths for new
research in existentialism.

There is, of course, a sense in which existentialism *is* outmoded, and we must draw a distinction here between the *philosophical* existentialism we defend and encourage, and the *cultural* existentialism that was distinctively a phenomenon of the mid-twentieth century. Existentialism, perhaps to an extent unprecedented in the history of philosophy, managed to capture the attention of the general public. Estimations regarding the amount of people at Jean-Paul Sartre's funeral in 1980 vary from 50–100,000, and this was well after his cultural and intellectual heyday. Simone de Beauvoir's famous treatise on the situation of women, *The Second Sex*, has been one of the most widely read non-fiction books of the twentieth century. Existential plays and novels – in particular Sartre's *Nausea* and Albert Camus's *The Outsider* – have been read voraciously and critically acclaimed. Sartre, and his more academically inclined colleague Maurice Merleau-Ponty, were the co-editors of the influential magazine *Les Temps Modernes*, which considered all things philosophical, political and aesthetic, providing an intellectual point of reference for much of France. Friedrich Nietzsche's books continued to sell to a wide-reading public throughout the twentieth century. There are many reasons for this primarily philosophical phenomenon capturing the attention of the public in the way that existentialism did, not least the Second World War and the German occupation of France, which intensified existential concerns with freedom, responsibility and death. The literary manifestations of existentialism also allowed a greater proportion of people to possess at least a tentative grasp of what it meant and certainly a greater grasp than might have been attained through the sometimes obscure philosophy of Heidegger, Sartre, Merleau-Ponty and de Beauvoir. What we can identify as 'cultural' existentialism centred on postwar France, and can be glossed with the image of a young man or woman dressed in a black turtle-neck, smoking a cigarette and reading *L'Être et Le Néant* at the famous 'headquarters of existentialism' at Café de Flore on the boulevard St Germain, or even while listening to jazz in a basement club. While the cultural manifestations of existentialism extended far beyond this stereotype – a stereotype that Sartre and de Beauvoir contributed to by posing for *Vogue* magazine in the United States and generally playing up to this image of the French intellectual (for more on this, see Cotkin, 2002) – it shows the extent to which the view of existentialism as *the* philosophy which sums up the ethos of the current generation *is* an outdated fashion.

Nevertheless, existentialism as a philosophy has continued to capture the attention of students, artists and educated readers well beyond the decline of its cultural and intellectual heyday, far more so than many other forms of philosophy. Why might this be? Arguably all of the existentialist philosophers retain a focus that has not characterized most of the philosophy done in the twentieth and twenty-first centuries, in that they are centrally concerned with questions to do with the meaning of life, how to live well, and a general insistence on philosophy being more than merely an abstract intellectual pursuit. Camus, for example, states in the opening pages of *The Myth of Sisyphus* that the question of whether or not to commit suicide is the only serious philosophical question. Camus indicates here with dramatic flourish the central concern of all existentialist philosophy, the question of what it means to live, and to live well. Of course, such a characterization would apply equally well to figures in the history of philosophy such as Blaise Pascal, most religious thinkers and the entire tradition of Greek philosophy. However, existentialism arguably represents the most significant recent attempt in the history of philosophy to foreground the practical problems of living, to relate these to the historical conditions of modernity, and to think them in a way that is both philosophically sophisticated and practically concrete. It is this connection of philosophical reflection with the problems of life as it is lived in the contemporary world that is, we believe, the reason for existentialism's ongoing appeal and relevance.

Defining Existentialism

What exactly *is* existentialism? This is not a question with a straightforward answer. There is a real question about whether there is any philosophical unity governing the thinkers commonly called existentialist. Indeed, the term 'existentialism' was not initially used by any of these philosophers, and it does not appear in any of the canonical texts of the tradition – it is not in Sartre's *Being and Nothingness*, nor in Heidegger's *Being and Time*. In fact, the term was initially coined by Gabriel Marcel in a 1943 review of Sartre's *Being and Nothingness* as we discuss in the next chapter, and it only came to be accepted by Sartre and de Beauvoir a couple of years later in 1945. Merleau-Ponty never accepted the label wholeheartedly, while Heidegger and Camus vehemently rejected it. Moreover, it was not used as a self-description by early thinkers who in retrospect came to be labelled as existentialist, such as Kierkegaard or Nietzsche. It is hence difficult to argue that existentialism represents a single, unified philosophical movement, although it would be too hasty to conclude from this difficulty that existentialism is, in fact, a term with no real referent and no real philosophical unity.

Following Ludwig Wittgenstein's lead in *Philosophical Investigations*, it is possible loosely to define existentialism in a family resemblance manner, which does not require a single set of necessary and sufficient conditions for every philosopher labelled existentialist. Things may be grouped together in a 'family resemblance' when there are many overlapping traits between the things so grouped, even if there is no single thing they all share in common. In this respect, some of the major overlapping thematic concerns that are associated with existential philosophers include the following:

1. a focus on concrete lived experience as opposed to academic abstraction;
2. freedom;
3. death, finitude and mortality;

4. an interest in first-personal experiences and 'moods', such as anguish (or anxiety), nausea and boredom;
5. an emphasis upon authenticity and responsibility as well as the tacit denigration of their opposites (inauthenticity, bad faith, etc.);
6. a suggestion that human individuality tends to be obscured and denied by the common social mores of the crowd, and, in the work of some, a pessimism about human relations per se;
7. a rejection of any external determination of morality or value, including certain conceptions of God and the emphasis upon rationality and progress that were foregrounded during the Enlightenment;
8. methodologically, as we see in the next chapter, many existentialists are invested in phenomenology and the use of transcendental reasoning.[1]

On this reading, then, existentialism appears as a constellation of overlapping concerns, many but not all of which are treated by any particular thinker labelled an existentialist. The above is not an exhaustive list, but it is worth noting that in addition to the existentialist philosophers already mentioned, an interest in related themes characterizes novelists like Fyodor Dostoevsky, Leo Tolstoy (who influenced Heidegger's understanding of death), Franz Kafka, and others, who have been productively associated with existentialism.

A Brief History of Existential Philosophy

In addition to these topical family resemblance similarities, existentialism may be understood as discernible trajectory in the history of philosophy. If we understand existentialism in a general enough sense, then it is possible – as some have done – to trace existential thought far back through history, to Pascal's 'reasons of the heart', to Aristotle's assertion of the primacy of the particular over the universal, to the understanding of Being as dynamic in pre-Socratic philosophers such as Heraclitus, and even, speculatively, to the first stirrings of wonder at the strangeness of existence with the prehistoric dawning of human self-consciousness (see, for example, Friedman, 1964). However, if we restrict our enquiry to what is meant by *modern* existentialism (i.e. philosophy to which that term has generally been attached, and typified by figures such as Heidegger, Sartre, and others), we find that a more precise understanding can emerge through its identifiable history. This history is not composed of anything like the foundation of a school, but rather of a lineage of interaction between many of the major existentialist philosophers in Europe (and elsewhere, such as Latin America, as we see in Roberto Toledo's chapter in this volume), even if they are sometimes very critical of one another (as Heidegger was of Sartre, for example). They read and cite each other's work, with Kierkegaard, Nietzsche and Jaspers important for French existentialist philosophy, just as they were important for Heidegger (for example).

Although not always recognized, it is arguable that the origins of this existential lineage can be traced back to the late works of F. W. J. von Schelling and the critical reaction to Idealism they contain. Schelling used the old philosophical category of 'existence' in a new way, indicating that which resists subsumption within the kind of totalizing rational systems that idealist philosophers such as Hegel had developed. The Danish philosopher and theological writer Søren Kierkegaard (1813–1855) attended Schelling's lectures and adopted this idea of existence in his own way, to emphasize the singular concreteness of the 'existing individual', which he considered irreducible to any theoretical abstractions (such as systems like Hegel's). Kierkegaard has frequently been cited as the first existentialist.

The second sometime contender for that honour is Friedrich Nietzsche, and together they are often cited as the two nineteenth-century forefathers to twentieth-century existentialism (see, for example, Jaspers, 1955, p. 23). Fritz Heinemann later contended that he was the first person to use the term 'philosophy of existence' (*Existenzphilosophie*) in his 1929 book *New Paths in Philosophy* (*Neue Wege der Philosophie*) (Schnädelbach, 1984, p. 157), to characterize the philosophies of Karl Jaspers (1883–1969) and Heidegger. Notably, Marcel independently developed a notion of 'existence' in the 1920s before having read Kierkegaard or Jaspers, which he later recognized as having close affinities with their use of the concept. Jaspers and Marcel both used the term 'philosophy of existence' to describe their work, before the latter's coining of the term 'existentialism' in 1943, and its adoption by philosophers such as Jean-Paul Sartre (1905–1980), Simone de Beauvoir (1908–1986) and Maurice Merleau-Ponty (1908–1961). 'Existentialism' has since widely been used in relation to all these thinkers, to characterize previous philosophers such as Kierkegaard and Nietzsche, and it has been applied to others who didn't accept this description themselves – most notably Albert Camus (1913–1960) and Martin Heidegger (1889–1976), but also many others, including some of the novelists we have mentioned above.

Research in Existentialism

This book is conceived as a guide to research in existentialism. But what does it mean to 'do research' in existentialism? What does it mean to 'study existence'? And how can we consider existentialism in relation to the usual topics of relevance to research, such as 'methodology'? These issues will be given a fuller consideration in the next chapter. However, we may signal here the important point that in order to arrive at any adequate understanding of these issues, it is first crucial to note the degree of resistances to terms such as 'research' and 'methodology' embedded in much of the existentialist tradition itself, such that the terms themselves need to be carefully and radically understood if not to betray the very spirit and value of the existentialist project.

First, existentialism resists 'research' insofar as that term tends to invoke overtones of the natural sciences. Frequently, existentialists have criticized the application of the models of the natural sciences to the study of human beings (see Douglas Kirsner's chapter on 'Existentialism, Psychoanalysis and Psychotherapy' for more on this) and insisted that the study of human existence requires a special approach. Briefly put, the reason for this resistance to scientific method is that human beings are subjects, not objects; they are dynamic and changing rather than static, and they are points of view on the world, with intellectual, emotional, *'existential'* involvements that significantly constitute what (or more appropriately *who*) they are. Scientific methods cannot capture the special uniqueness of human existence, and thus research into such existence cannot be made using scientific models.

Second, existentialism is itself divided from within on the issue of methodology, and one strand resists any systematic application of a methodology at all, insisting that the only strategy that does justice to existence is 'pointing to the concrete'. On the other hand, however, there is a major strand of existentialism that has made much use of the phenomenological method. This division itself indicates one of the central problems of the thematic unity of existentialism, which Maurice Friedman describes as 'phenomenological analysis of existence versus pointing to the concrete' (1964, p. 547). It is with this problematic division in methodological priorities, Friedman suggests, that 'the greatest actual difficulty lies in understanding what existentialism is and in subsuming under one heading all those who are held to be existentialists' (p. 547). On the former side, he lists Merleau-Ponty, Heidegger, Sartre, Ludwig Binswanger and Paul Tillich, while the latter includes Kierkegaard, Marcel, Camus, Martin Buber and Nikolai Berdyaev (p. 547). The problem, in short, is that the latter group of existentialists often argue that the key feature of 'existence' is precisely that it cannot be analysed or thematized, but is instead an irreducible, concrete singularity. As Kierkegaard famously insisted, there can be no 'existential system'. By way of introduction to the problems and issues discussed in detail throughout this volume, we will briefly outline some of the key aspects of these apparently conflicting issues for research in existentialism below.

Existentialism and 'Existence'

While Heidegger has attempted to trace the origins of the concepts of essence and existence to Aristotle's metaphysical distinction between *dynamis* (potentiality) and *energeia* (actuality) (Heidegger, 1973, p. 68), the terms enter philosophy proper with Aquinas, through an adaptation from Averroes (Tyman,

1999, p. 146). They were used in medieval scholastic philosophy, where 'existence' designated the aspects of the created being (or 'creature') which could not be reduced to its essential features (1999, p. 146). In this sense, and in the general sense that is still often used, essence has been understood as 'what-ness' (*quidditas*) – what a thing, is understood in terms of what it has in common with other things of the same type. Existence has meant the very fact of being, simply *that* a thing is (its 'thatness', or *haecceitas*). In this sense, the 'thatness' of particular things include features not essential to 'what' it is, and these inessen-tial features are covered by the category of 'existence'. As such, the term exist-ence could be said to apply to anything that 'has being', or exists.

For existentialist philosophers, however, the word 'existence' has a special-ized meaning: it refers only to *human* existence, and it indicates that human beings are free individual subjects, with unique qualities which set them apart from other kinds of beings. This uniqueness is most famously and most neatly captured in Sartre's credo of existentialism, 'existence precedes essence', which means that we exist as 'thatness' more primordially than any determination of 'what' we are. This priority of existence over essence means that we are not restricted or determined by a limiting essence and are free to make of ourselves what we will.

'Existence' comes from the Latin *ex-sistere*, which means 'to stand out'. To exist means to stand out against a background, but also to stand outside of oneself (as the term 'ecstasy', from the related Greek term 'ekstasis', implies). John Macquarie suggests that although the suggestion that we 'exist ecstat-ically' might seem like something of a tautology, it tells us something import-ant about the existentialist understanding of existence (Macquarie, 1972, p. 69). While all beings exist in the sense of standing out against a background, it is only human beings who exist ecstatically, that is, outside of ourselves. As Heidegger and Sartre both analyse through what they call the 'ecstases' of time, we stand outside ourselves in the present through our consciousness of the past and of the future. Unlike other beings, we are not fixed in our essence, but are open to possibilities through our ecstatic, dynamic relation to ourselves and the world.

The problem the concept of existence presents for any research methodology is clearly implied by Andrew J. Mitchell in his chapter on new directions in Heidegger studies for this volume. He notes the epistemological corollary of the ontological notion of essence, commenting that:

Across the history of philosophy, essence has served both epistemological and ontological roles. As the 'whatness' or *quidditas* of an object, essence determines 'what' a thing is and what it means to know that thing. This whatness is nothing peculiar to the particular thing in question, how-ever, but something held in common by other things of the same sort.

Epistemologically this means that to know what the thing is one must know its essence. Due to the general nature of this essence, however, one never knows the thing as a particular, but always only comprehends it in its 'essentials'.

As we have seen, existentialism concerns itself precisely with what 'cannot be comprehended in its "essentials"': the uniqueness of the individual that I am. Existentialists thus frequently resist the 'essential' features and structures that have often been thought necessary in order for thought to 'grasp' its object, to identify it and say something meaningful about it. The resistance of many existentialists to methodologies and to conceptual systems stems from the suspicion that they rely precisely on such essential features and thereby overlook significant features of concrete existence. Nevertheless, such existentialists continue to reflect on, and attempt to communicate their findings regarding human existence. The nub of the problem here is then how to say anything philosophically meaningful, communicable and useful about existence – how to analyse or thematize it, for example – while also maintaining its singularity and concreteness.

This problem has led, for some existentialists, to highlight the value of literature over systematic philosophy, or in other ways to insist on the necessity of something like 'indirect communication', to testify to the singularity of concrete existence, to simply 'point to it', rather than try to capture it in thematic analysis. Literature in particular has frequently been used by existentialists in order to evoke and communicate salient features of existence. In this, it may be thought to have a number of advantages over theoretical philosophy: first, it 'shows' the concrete, instead of abstracting and generalizing in theoretical terms; second, the 'art' of literature (as well as other arts) can be understood to consist in breaking the stereotypical linguistic and conceptual structures through which we habitually understand everyday life and experience, allowing us a kind of insight into existence; and third, it appeals to and engages a fuller range of human faculties (emotion, imagination, empathy, etc.) than abstract intellectual theory, and these other faculties are frequently seen by existentialists as essential to existential insight. While literature has been paramount in the history of existentialism, it is by no means a final solution to the problem, and we may well ask: what new methods, mediums or strategies might be invented to study existence in the existentialist sense?

Existentialism and Phenomenology

For many of the post-twentieth-century existentialist philosophers there is an engagement with the work of Edmund Husserl (1859–1938) and the method of phenomenology – roughly the sustained attempt to describe experiences without theoretical speculations – that he founded, or at least was the first to explicitly thematize. Of course, the fact that philosophers as different as Sartre, Merleau-Ponty and Heidegger consider themselves phenomenologists calls into question exactly what the term phenomenology refers to. While we consider such issues in depth in the next chapter, it is important to clarify here, in a preliminary way, the two main components of the phenomenological method. They are usually understood as follows:

1. The negative move consists in suspending judgement on anything that might prevent us attending to the 'things themselves' (the famous *epoché*, or suspension of the 'natural attitude' that assumes, for example, that there is an external world).
2. The positive move involves a 'return' to the specific mode of appearing of the phenomenon and requiring some kind of search for essences (technically called an *eidetic reduction*).

Probably the most important concept to understand in this tradition is what is termed the *phenomenological reduction* (point 1 above). Phenomenology is often characterized as a 'return to the things themselves', or to phenomena as they are experienced *before* the 'natural attitude'. In the so-called natural attitude, we assume that there is an external world and that other people exist. Husserlian phenomenology wants us to abandon these and other presuppositions, and see if such insights are actually given to us in the purity of experience. This problem then will be one regarding how we can actually know that other people exist, for example, based solely upon attending to our own experience. Without answering this question here (but see Reynolds, 2010; Russell and Reynolds, 2011), philosophy has often constructed theories and then returned to experience to see if those theories are true. Phenomenology, however, wants to begin with the experiences themselves, and, secondly, to perform an *eidetic reduction* to see if those experiences have any essential or necessary conditions (point 2 above). In Sartre's work, this is apparent in his consistent use of examples, which appear almost literary in character, but from which he deduces certain essential and necessary conditions – usually that we are free. His use of eidetic analysis also involves attempts to characterize the essence of 'bad faith', as well as to look at one instantiation of an emotion and deduce the essence of the emotion, and indeed of all other emotions, from that.

Two things are worth noting about phenomenology before we go any further. First, phenomenology is not simply a form of introspective subjectivism because it involves a search for essences, or exemplifications, and hence retains a generalizing tendency. In fact, Husserl famously goes so far as to proclaim the opposite; that phenomenology is a rigorous science, although he insisted that it is a science of consciousness rather than of empirical things. This is not surprising given that in Husserl's hands phenomenology began as a critique of both naturalism (which is roughly the idea that everything belongs to the world of nature and can be studied by the methods appropriate to studying that world) and the valorization of science and the scientific method. Phenomenologists tend to argue that the study of consciousness must actually be very different to the study of nature. Indeed, phenomenology does not proceed from the collection of large amounts of data and generalize a theory beyond the data itself (the scientific method of induction). Rather, it aims to look at particular examples without theoretical presuppositions (such as the phenomena of love, of two hands touching each other, etc.), before then discerning what is essential to these experiences, as well as their conditions of possibility. This technique of argument is employed by all of the existential phenomenologists, notwithstanding the criticisms they raise about 'pure' phenomenology and the ideal of a sustained bracketing away – or 'epochal reduction', in Husserl's terms.

To conclude our introductory comments on research and methodology, we may note that there is an obvious sense in which the phrase 'research in existentialism' implies the production of academic papers and monographs, considered as the 'results' of such research. But the existentialist tradition stands this notion on its head (or rather, on its feet, to follow Marx's comment about his own relation to Hegel): it insists that the only meaningful 'results' are those produced in the world and in our lives. If existentialism is to mean anything, it must resist the narrow understanding of research in the abstract and quantifiable scholastic sense. In the light of such an existential imperative, much of what is traditionally and institutionally understood as 'research' becomes all but redundant. Nevertheless, as the tradition has shown, there is the possibility of a productive resonance between existentialist theory and practice, and one of the key lessons of this tradition is that conducting reflective research and actively living life do not need to be disconnected, as they so frequently are.

Existentialism, Contemporary Politics and Feminism

Existentialism is sometimes perceived as an excessively individualist philosophy counter-productive to responsible political engagement. Existentialists of the 1940s focused on the individual because they felt the individual had been lost in the social and political machinations of their world. Things arguably appear very differently today, and there is a sense in which individualism has triumphed in liberal democracies. Superficially, existentialism might seem perfectly suited to the contemporary status quo. However, the *type* of individual – the private consumer – encouraged by typically capitalist liberal societies is very different to that which interested the existentialists. Existentialism reminds us that in order for our freedom to be meaningful, our choices must be existentially relevant – they must profoundly impact on our lives (which the choice between competing brands and consumer products typically does not). Questioning the best kind of life is not just an individual action, but a political one. One of the issues of our contemporary society which most stands in need of critique is the assumption that the 'liberal–consumerist' lifestyle is unquestionably the best form of life (and should be implemented everywhere, by force if necessary). Existentialism contributes to such a critique by reminding us to take stock of what is genuinely valuable in life, and to refuse to be complacent about the kind of world in which we live.

Moreover, one form of the concretizing of philosophy that existentialism offers is an understanding and potential dismantling of the mechanics of oppression, whether colonialist, sexist or racist. The continued enthusiasm among undergraduate students for the ideas of de Beauvoir, for example, occurs against the background of complex intrafeminist debates about what oppression is and how to counteract it. One of de Beauvoir's core contributions to the understanding of women's oppression in her most famous text, *The Second Sex*, is to view it as an *ontological* oppression: an oppression at the level of her being. As Debra Bergoffen points out in her chapter on 'Existentialism and Ethics' in this volume:

> considered from a phenomenological perspective, oppression is not essentially a matter of material depravation, exploitation or physical abuse. From a phenomenological perspective these oppressive tactics are a means to the more fundamental violation of alienating human beings from their meaning-giving and world-making powers.

For the contemporary student of existentialism, de Beauvoir's theory offers an understanding of the sheer difficulty and complexity of the task of achieving equality of being. Current debates within feminism struggle, for example, with the competing claims made by rival cultures. It is often in the interests of first-world countries to stress the more easily measurable indicators of equality such as increased participation in the workforce, while ignoring the issue of a woman's own understanding of her being. This questionable auditing then leads to a programme of action that focuses on identifying elements of a first-world lifestyle to replicate in other countries. In these contemporary debates an existentialist understanding of the meaning of sexual equality will prompt the activist to examine the concrete individual and collective existence of women of other cultures and to seek access to the 'other' woman's self-understanding, to ensure a true rather than counterfeit movement towards equality.

The goals of sexual equality cannot be simply summarized as a certain set of quantifiable achievements (such as rate of participation in a particular industry – although we should note that philosophy in Anglo-American countries is sadly among the poorest of all academic disciplines in this regard). Existentialist feminism calls upon us to look deeply, not superficially, at a society and ask what conditions must be set in place in order that women's 'power to act' is fully realized. The power to act is both internal and external to the subject – legislation in the public sphere can carve out space for women to act and bestow meaning, but no such action can occur without the appropriate belief in herself as *having* such power.

The existentialist concept of self-creation, too, plays a vital explanatory role in the understanding of female oppression: the education of women was not to be merely the acquirement of 'external' knowledge but a changed understanding of her own self, a new vision of a bodily 'I can', in Husserl's famous phrase. This was realized in the popularity of 'consciousness-raising' groups in the 1970s (which, in existentialist terms, bring women to consciousness of their power to bestow meaning upon the world) and various movements to teach women new skills, to realize the power of their body-subject and fully live their 'I can'.

De Beauvoir led the way in choosing to theorize about *how* women are not *what* they are. The replacement of the 'what' with the 'how' of human being has been immensely useful to recent transformations in identity politics, a politics that aims to resist both the imposition of a categorization imposed 'from above' by society and the requirement to pronounce one's identity for oneself once and for all as binding. In her article in this volume, Laura Hengehold explains, 'De Beauvoir proposed that human freedom could only be preserved insofar as people refused to confirm or congeal themselves as *beings* in order, rather, to *disclose* being, including the being of human values.'

Contemporary feminism has conducted a fruitful dialogue between postmodern theorists of identity such as Judith Butler, and de Beauvoir's and Merleau-Ponty's understandings of biology and the lived body. The site of intrafeminist debates is often the female body, variously understood, and de Beauvoir's existentialist feminism continues to offer rich resources for such issues as Marguerite La Caze demonstrates in her discussion in this volume, 'Existentialism, Sexuality and Feminism':

> De Beauvoir is not suggesting that differences between men and women will always entail an oppressive situation for women. What she means is that there are bodily differences between men and women that won't disappear with oppression. Yet how we interpret those differences is up to us.

Thus although the existentialist cannot be an essentialist about existence, she can be a realist about the persistence of the various elements of facticity such as biological sex. The very distinction between facticity and situation (which is facticity bestowed with meaning, a meaning which potentially can be changed) thus can point the way out of essentialist versus anti-essentialist debates and other stalemates that contemporary feminists face today.

The place opened up for ambiguity, variously understood by de Beauvoir and Merleau-Ponty, aids contemporary understanding of ethics as maximizing spaces for action rather than prescribing the actions themselves. This open-endedness extends itself into the tricky sphere of political action. The imperative to know oneself and to align oneself politically with one's self-understanding may not always favour easy and immediate political action, but on the positive side it may safeguard the integrity of any such action. Existentialist thought does not entail political clarity, nor shortcuts to political action. This was a particularly painful lesson for the French existentialists, as David Sherman suggests in his chapter on politics in this *Companion*, with various disagreements about political action (particularly violence) eventually fracturing many of their relationships. Sherman says:

> Theoretically, all would have supported a political arrangement in the vicinity of democratic socialism, or some form of anarcho-syndicalism, but, practically, this was not a viable option, and what actually separated the French existentialists was the complexities of the theory–practice problem (i.e. how to make sense of the relationship between theory and practice for the purpose of forging political *praxis*).

The experience the existentialists faced of a lack of 'viable' options for political representation is one that many of us experience today. Their answer was not *no* political action but *diverse* political action. What will our answer be? Robust contemporary feminist and other political existentialist research should go a long way towards answering that question, both in words and in actions.

Conclusion

This *Companion* will help students and researchers to understand some of the many important and enduring contributions of existentialist thinkers on a variety of key topics – for example, philosophical method, ontology, politics, psychoanalysis, ethics, religion, literature, the emotions, feminism and sexuality, authenticity and the self, and the sometimes neglected significance of existentialism in Latin America. Some of the rich insights of such essays have been summarized in our above introduction and we do not want to dwell further upon this here, other than to recognize that such essays have been written by some of the best existentialist-inspired 'researchers' in the English-speaking world.

In addition to such featured essays, we also have five short chapters that summarize the state of play in the academic reception of canonical existentialist figures – like Kierkegaard, Nietzsche, Heidegger, Sartre and de Beauvoir – and point to new directions that such scholarship is taking. In 'Existentialism and Cognitive Science', Michael Wheeler and Ezequiel Di Paolo also consider the positive use of existentialist-inspired work (largely via the work of Hubert

Dreyfus and Hans Jonas, drawing on Heidegger, Merleau-Ponty and others) in contemporary cognitive science, much of which promises to complicate any too-stark division between the natural sciences and existential phenomenology by seeing each as able to enrich the other. In 'Existentialism and Poststructuralism', Jack Reynolds and Ashley Woodward explore the relation between existentialism and its putative successor on the French scene, poststructuralism, seeking to undermine the too common trajectory in which the latter is thought to show problems with the former that make it untenable for philosophy today.

Finally, we include at the end of the book some resources that we think will be especially useful for students new to existentialism: an A–Z glossary of key terms and thinkers; a timeline of existentialism; a list of further resources (web and otherwise); and an annotated guide to further reading, which, along with this *Companion*, will help the new reader navigate the difficult but rewarding texts that continue to comprise the heart of existentialism today. And, of course, these imposing texts ought to be read seriously, but rather than copied or imbibed as truth, they should also be treated as but various prolegomena, or conduits, to seeing the world anew.

Note

1. These criteria expand upon the account given in Jack Reynolds' *Understanding Existentialism* (Chesham, UK: Acumen 2006). Some other parts of this introduction also rework material that was first published in the introduction of this book.

Bibliography

Cotkin, G. (2002), *Existential America*. Baltimore, MD: Johns Hopkins University Press.
Friedman, M. (ed.) (1964), *Worlds of Existentialism: A Critical Reader*. New York: Random House.
Heidegger, M. (1973), *The End of Philosophy*, trans. J. Stambaugh. New York: Harper & Row.
Jaspers, K. (1955), *Reason and Existence*, trans. W. Earle. New York: Farrar Straus.
Macquarrie, J. (1972), *Existentialism: An Introduction, Guide, and Assessment*. London: Penguin.
Mullarkey, J. and B. Lord (eds) (2009), *The Continuum Companion to Continental Philosophy*. London and New York: Continuum.
Reynolds, J. (2010), 'The Problem of Other Minds: Solutions and Dissolutions in Analytic and Continental Philosophy'. *Philosophy Compass* 5 (4): 326–35.
Russell, M. and J. Reynolds (2011), 'Transcendental Reasoning about Other Minds', *Philosophy Compass*. 6 (5): 300-311.
Schnädelbach, H. (1984), *Philosophy in Germany 1831–1933*, trans. E. Matthews. Cambridge and New York: Cambridge University Press.
Tyman, S. (1999), 'Existence', in H. Gordon (ed.), *Dictionary of Existentialism*. Westport, CT: Greenwood Press.

2 Existentialism, Phenomenology and Philosophical Method

Felicity Joseph and Jack Reynolds[1]

In order to understand the relationship between existentialism and phenomenology we need to be clear on precisely what each of these terms refers to. Unfortunately, this is no easy task because few philosophers unambiguously subscribed to being existentialists, and those that did accept this term (at least for a period of time) disagreed on many core topical and methodological issues. Jean-Paul Sartre and Simone de Beauvoir are among those few who accepted the designation, along with their colleague and sometime friend Maurice Merleau-Ponty. The designation had been bestowed by Gabriel Marcel, who coined the term to describe Sartre's work in a 1943 review of *Being and Nothingness*, while applying the term 'neo-Socratic' to himself. However, Sartre soon after described Marcel as a 'Christian existentialist', a label which would stick. While it is clear that from the late 1930s to the late 1940s these French philosophers understood themselves to be broadly fellow travellers in that they were united by social and political realities (i.e. the Second World War) as much as anything else, and there were many explicit (and implicit) philosophical disagreements between them. In addition, there were not any programmatic manifestoes written by these philosophers that unified (in a compelling manner) their respective concerns. Perhaps Sartre's *Existentialism is a Humanism*, initially given as a public lecture in 1945, attempts something of this sort, but in Merleau-Ponty's reflections on existentialism in essays in *Les Temps Modernes* and subsequently published in *Sense and Nonsense* (see 'The Battle over Existentialism' and 'A Scandalous Author'), it is clear that he understood existentialism rather differently.

On an understanding of existentialism as an individualism concerned with free choice, decisions that require leaps of faith (Kierkegaard), 'limit situations' like suffering and guilt which reveal the lack of an essential self (Jaspers), the de-individualizing significance of social norms and mores (Nietzsche), the importance of *Angst*, death and dread for an authentic life and indeed for philosophy (Kierkegaard, Heidegger, Camus, etc.), existentialism might not seem to be fertile territory for the more austere ambitions of phenomenology. Inaugurated by Edmund Husserl at the beginning of the twentieth century in *Logical Investigations* (1900–1901), phenomenology is the sustained attempt to describe the structures of experience without theoretical speculations. While Husserl's search for a presuppositionless starting-point for philosophy and careful descriptions of the structure of various mental states and acts (like perception, memory, etc.) might seem rather scholastic when compared with some of the standard thematic concerns of existentialism, the phenomenological method also promised to bring philosophy down from the theoretical heavens and to make it more concrete, and this seems to be why Sartre's first encounter with Husserlian phenomenology turned him pale with excitement and emotion (de Beauvoir, 1986, p. 112).

Indeed, what is distinctive about the work of the French existentialists, and the work of Martin Heidegger in *Being and Time* (2004; originally published 1927) that was so significant for them, is that while they share many of the above topical interests that are characteristic of existentialist thinkers, methodologically speaking they are all also significantly indebted to Husserlian and Heideggerian phenomenology. In Heidegger's work of the 1920s (influenced as it was by Kierkegaard, and to a lesser extent Nietzsche and Jaspers), and in the work of the French existentialists from the late 1930s to late 1940s, especially Sartre, de Beauvoir and Merleau-Ponty, these two rich trajectories were brought into fruitful dialogue that we now call existential phenomenology. While the starting-point of existentialism is often claimed to be Kierkegaard's opposition to Hegel's systematizing ambitions and his metaphysics of *Geist* (for ignoring the individual), this opposition is not so apparent in the work of the French existentialists. This is because they were significantly influenced by Alexandre Kojève's interpretations of Hegel in public lectures in Paris from 1933–1939, and also because of their own systematizing aspirations (due largely to their inheritance of phenomenology). This meant that Merleau-Ponty, for example, was able to argue that Hegel is also an existentialist because Hegel first emphasized that 'man is a place of unrest' (1992, p. 66).

There are, of course, some important shared concerns that made the rapprochement between existentialism and phenomenology possible: a suspicion of scientism and objectivism that began with Husserl; an insistence on the irreducibility of the first-person perspective (precisely because embodied) and its philosophical importance; and the general ambition for a philosophy that is adequate to the complexity of lived experience, as opposed to one that simplifies or ignores lived experience, perhaps by considering it as ultimately illusory or as only of psychological (rather than philosophical) interest. While some have maintained, implausibly, that phenomenology was just the vehicle that allowed the existentialists to justify and expand upon their thematic concerns with existence (freedom, self, God, death, anguish, etc.), and it could have been any other method (Earnshaw, 2006, p. 133), in practice we cannot identify any of the thinkers we are concerned with in this essay as chronologically existentialists before they were phenomenologists (or vice versa). Indeed, we cannot even precisely distinguish the phenomenological aspects of their work from the existential aspects, since they are necessarily methodologically connected. If we do want to prise existentialism apart from phenomenology with a panoptic view of the history of philosophy in the nineteenth and twentieth centuries, then we are best served by insisting that with the incorporation of phenomenological methods, existential philosophy (as opposed to existential literature and art) becomes systematic in a way that it had not earlier been. With the existential phenomenology of Heidegger, Sartre, Merleau-Ponty and de Beauvoir, and with the forms of transcendental reasoning that phenomenology had made possible for them, there are various orders of presupposition that naturally are best elaborated on through careful and systematic description.

Despite the existentialists' differing interpretations of phenomenological method, the use of transcendental reasoning would seem to be a uniting factor, with experience as its premise. Although originally associated with Kant, in the twentieth century some form of transcendental reasoning has continued to be frequently deployed in existentialism and phenomenology, albeit in very different ways. Husserl in his systematic phenomenology aims to use transcendental reasoning to reveal *the* transcendental, a whole 'region of being' that was previously unexplored (it is thus both a method and an object of inquiry, as with Kant); Heidegger associates the transcendental project with both phenomenology and hermeneutics; Sartre gives transcendental philosophy an existential turn, as well as a famous phenomenological 'proof' of the existence of the other; Merleau-Ponty offers an account of an omnipresent bodily intentionality seeking equilibria with the world, through the refinement of our 'body-schema' and the acquisition of flexible habits and skills: he presents this as a condition for the subject's encountering a meaningful field of experience rather than fragmented raw sense data.

In the context of existential methodology, of course, transcendental reasoning should not be construed as involving merely formally valid inferences. Such a characterization omits something vital, since for any transcendentally reached conclusion to be a priori true requires some kind of *shifting* to the level of experience. As a result, the thinker needs to be coimplicated with what is thought. This phenomenological (or performative) element thus links all transcendental reasoning that is not merely analytic to a kind of minimal phenomenology, at least in the relation between the propositional content and the speaker/experiencer of such content. While there is certainly a circularity here, it is one that is part of reflection and not something that can be overcome.[2]

Of course, suggesting that phenomenology and the deployment of differing forms of transcendental reasoning constitute a common method, along with the previously mentioned thematic concerns, which loosely unifies the work of the existential phenomenologists still leaves the question of method underdetermined. After all, many philosophers have subscribed to phenomenology while employing quite distinct methods and evincing by their practices very different conceptions of what the return 'to the things themselves' involves (the famous Husserlian motto for phenomenology). As such, one of the key tasks for this essay will be to make perspicuous what is at stake in existential phenomenology. In this respect, it seems to us that Heidegger, Sartre, Merleau-Ponty, de Beauvoir and Marcel all argue for the priority of the pre-reflective domain over the reflective domain, and the task for philosophy is hence to describe this without betraying it through the reflective activity that is philosophy. Moreover, in proposing such a position these philosophers aim to differentiate themselves, to varying extents, from Husserlian phenomenology. In *Being and Time*, Heidegger initially says that rather than have a Cartesian view in which reflective knowledge of ourselves is the foundational starting-point, we need to see the centrality of our ready-to-hand relationship with objects that are available for use, as against the present-at-hand analysis of objects when they are detached from their worldly situation and analysed. Merleau-Ponty argues in *Phenomenology of Perception* that consciousness is not first a matter of 'I think' but of 'I can' (1962, p. 137), and although this idea is itself borrowed from Husserl, Merleau-Ponty rightly claims in 'The Philosopher and His Shadow' to develop such themes in the direction of Husserl's 'unthought' (1964, pp. 159–81). Throughout *Being and Nothingness* and especially in the introduction, Sartre contends that it is on the prejudicative level that what he calls the 'transphenomenality of Being' is made manifest: that is, the reality of Being beyond our conceptual and reflective knowledge of it. As such, there is a kind of 'pragmatism' in the work of these thinkers, notwithstanding their complicated and sometimes labyrinthine philosophical systems; all contend that knowing is a mode of doing and being, and all emphasize the centrality of the pre-reflective cogito or the 'average everydayness' of our ready-to-hand engagements with the things, others and the world.

None of these philosophers have quite the same aspirations for the phenomenological method that Husserl did. In particular, they are wary of the idea that a sustained reduction or bracketing of the natural attitude (common-sense opinions and tacit theories that we take for granted) is possible, as well as the idea that a reflective analysis of conscious experience could both exhaust the mental and establish all of the salient features of our being-in-the-world. We can attend to experience in order to discern necessary or essential conditions, but any kind of sustained bracketing away is impossible, as we are necessarily what Heidegger calls beings-in-the-world, inextricable from our social situation. Moreover, as Mark Wrathall puts the key point, 'existential phenomena may show themselves best when we are not focally aware of them, not reflecting

on them, or not thinking about them' (2009, p. 33). For the existential philosophers, experiences and moods like *Angst* (often translated as anxiety or anguish),
nausea, boredom, and so on, all take on philosophical significance, as does the
manner in which we pre-reflectively cope with things habitually. Sartre and
Merleau-Ponty thus accord sustained attention to the difference between the
lived body (*Leib*) as opposed to the body known as an object (*Körper*). On this
largely shared view, if we treat experience, social understanding, and so on, as
primarily deductive and calculative, a model in which beliefs and desires func-
tionally cause behaviour, then we have a pale imitation of the human being in
the world. While many of these developments were already present in Husserl's work in various forms – sometimes embryonic, sometimes developed (as
with the German distinction between *Leib* and *Körper*) – it remains the case that
the existential phenomenologists have altered the direction of Husserlian phenomenology in important ways. Contrary to a certain view of the history of
philosophy in which existentialism is considered a mere historical curiosity
rather than a serious prospect for contemporary thought, these particular
renewals of the phenomenological method were among the most fruitful of the
twentieth century. They remain of intellectual significance today, relevant to
current debates in philosophy of mind, perception, intersubjectivity, and in cognitive science where reductionist programs seem to be in abeyance (see Gallagher and Zahavi, 2008; Morris, 2010), and continue to exert a significant
influence in art, literature and cinematography.

Heidegger's Hermeneutical Phenomenology: Fundamental Ontology in *Being and Time*

While Heidegger arguably remained a phenomenologist throughout his career, it
is *Being and Time* that is the focus of any interpretation of his work as an existential phenomenologist. Although he carefully avoided using Husserlian terms –
like consciousness, the transcendental ego, the natural attitude, the
phenomenological reduction, intentionality, and so on – and although he had
also come to consider Husserl's project as idealist in a manner that he thought
to be problematic, he also comments in his introduction to this work that 'the
following would not have been possible if the ground had not been prepared by
Edmund Husserl, with whose *Logical Investigations* phenomenology first
emerged' (2004, sec. 7, p. 62/38).[3] Despite the fact that Heidegger elsewhere
extends the origins of phenomenology back to the pre-Socratic philosophers,
his indebtedness to Husserlian phenomenology is clear.

However, Heidegger's relationship to existentialism is more troubled and
complicated than is his relationship to Husserl's phenomenology. First, we
must recognize that his stated aim in *Being and Time* was to reawaken the ques-

tion of the meaning of Being, and his so-called existential analytic in this text was said to be merely the necessary first step before the question of the meaning of Being could be addressed. In these parts of *Being and Time*, as well as in Division 2, he draws heavily on earlier existential insights in Kierkegaard and others, and this material was very important for Sartre's *Being and Nothingness* (Sartre read *Being and Time* during his internment as a prisoner of war). In his 'Letter on "Humanism"', however, Heidegger came to express disdain for the term existentialism and for what he was acquainted with of Sartre's work, as well as Sartre's translation of *Dasein* as 'human reality'. Nonetheless, no account of the relationship between existentialism and phenomenology would be adequate without considering him, and there is perhaps also reason to think that Heidegger protests a little too much about the distortions that 'bad' metaphysical existentialism made of his work.

Many themes from Heidegger's work are important to existentialism, but notable among these are the following: (1) his non-essentialist understanding of human subjectivity (or *Dasein*, literally translated as being-there) as always being-in-the-world; (2) the initial priority that Heidegger accords to 'average everydayness' and what he calls the 'ready-to-hand' as opposed to the 'present-at-hand'; (3) his analyses of authenticity and inauthenticity; (4) his descriptions of fallenness/theyself/*das Man*; (5) his discussion of the philosophical significance of moods like fear, *Angst* and boredom; (6) his interpretation of *Dasein* in terms of temporality, with *Dasein*'s distinctiveness consisting in its orientation to the 'not yet', the future; (7) as well as his famous ruminations on being-towards-death and its ontological significance in Division 2 of *Being and Time*.

We cannot adequately summarize these rich contributions here, but it is worth dwelling on the starting-point of his book, *Dasein*. Heidegger characterizes the mode of Being of *Dasein* as existence, meaning that *Dasein* has no fixed nature. In Heidegger's words, 'the essence of *Dasein* lies in its existence' (2004, sec. 9, p. 67/42). This was clearly an inspiration for Sartre's famous existentialist motto that, for humans, 'existence precedes essence' (Sartre, 1995, pp. 25, 568), even if Heidegger himself would later, in 'Letter on "Humanism"', renounce this Sartrean formulation for being still too metaphysical. Heidegger's point is that *Dasein* stands out from mere immersion in the world, is self-interpreting, and does not have objective attributes or essences that can adequately define it. Heidegger also suggests that there are two other aspects of *Dasein* that are peculiar to it.

First, only *Dasein* can 'understand itself in terms of its existence, in terms of its possibility to be itself or *to not be itself*' (2004, sec. 3, p. 33/12). On Heidegger's view, there is something peculiar about a creature that is capable of not being itself, of being what he calls inauthentic (Sartre also draws attention to this feature of human existence in his discussions of bad faith).

Second, *Dasein* also has the character of what is sometimes translated as 'mineness', basically meaning specificity and individuality but not an enduring sense of personal identity. Rather, the point is that for any particular case of responsibility and for any particular decision, it can be said that it is *my* responsibility, *my* decision and, ultimately, *my* death, which Heidegger argues no one else can undergo for me. *Dasein* names this individuality as it is lived as opposed to objectively described.

It is also worth noting the worldly and externalist conception of meaning that is a large part of *Being and Time*. On Heidegger's view, *Dasein* associates with things first and foremost on a *practical* and immediate basis that he calls the ready-to-hand, which refers to the availability of things for our use and deployment in relation to the completion of tasks. For Heidegger, useful things are necessarily in a situation and are always related to other useful things by a network of association. Heidegger calls this connection between various objects and our potential use of them an 'equipmental totality' (which is basically synonymous with the notion of the world) and he describes it in detail. An interrogation of this kind of practical 'average everydayness' is prioritized in Division 1 of *Being and Time*, because here, Heidegger tells us, things are least distorted by metaphysical abstractions. Of course, these dimensions of existence are usually in the background and not explicitly attended to (not a direct object of consciousness, but more in the order of background conditions for consciousness), and phenomenological descriptions of such dimensions must hence seek to reawaken us to their significance. Indeed, this is one of the reasons why Heidegger associates phenomenology with hermeneutics. All interpretation is guided by some preunderstanding (e.g. a preontological comprehension of the meaning of Being), and this circularity is also characteristic of *Dasein*'s relationship to itself.

Being and Time is also oriented around a prescriptive (if not traditionally moral) distinction between authentic modes of existence and inauthentic ones, and the experience of *Angst* in the face of recognizing one's being-towards-death is central to establishing the anticipatory resoluteness that Heidegger characterizes as authentic. Whether or not one accepts such analyses (and many have contested them, including Emmanuel Levinas, Theodore W. Adorno and Jacques Derrida), his broader project of existential phenomenology remains of significance for any non-reductive attempt to understand being-in-the-world.

Sartre's Existential Phenomenology: From *Transcendence of the Ego* to *Being and Nothingness*

Sartre and Merleau-Ponty were among the first serious interpreters of Husserl in France in the 1930s, and their divergent interpretations of Husserl revealed to each other the richness and depth of his work. As Sartre observed in his moving eulogy for Merleau-Ponty upon the latter's death in 1961: 'Alone, each of us was too easily persuaded of having understood the idea of phenomenology. Together, we were, for each other, the incarnation of its ambiguity' (1965, p. 159). Along with Emmanuel Levinas who translated some of Husserl's main texts into French, they were the major players in making phenomenology so dominant in France either side of the Second World War.

Sartre began to establish a philosophical reputation with his essay of 1937, *Transcendence of the Ego*. This essay was explicitly an engagement with Husserl and the phenomenological method, and Sartre outlines his view of what is wrong with a phenomenology that is oriented around the transcendental ego, as with Husserl's *Ideas*. For Husserl, the sense in which an apple (for example) presents itself from one side as involving others sides, and as a unified object, requires that there be a unifying structure within consciousness itself: the transcendental ego. Sartre and Merleau-Ponty both disagree with such an analysis, albeit for different reasons. Sartre thinks that such an account would entail that the perception of an object would always also involve an intermediary perception – such as some kind of perception or consciousness of the transcendental ego – thus threatening to disrupt the transparency of consciousness. All forms of perception and consciousness would involve (at least) these two components, and there would be a kind of complication and opaqueness to consciousness that is not phenomenologically apparent. Moreover, Husserl's transcendental ego would have to pre-exist all of our particular actions and perceptions, which is something that the existentialist dictum 'existence precedes essence' would seem to be committed to denying. While many would defend Husserl against these charges, Sartre's general claim here is that the notion of a self or ego is not given in experience, but is rather something outside of (or transcendent) to pre-reflective experience. The ego or self is the product of memory and reflection on what was initially pre-reflectively lived (rather than known). This move forms one important part of Sartre's argument for the primacy of pre-reflective consciousness over reflective consciousness, which is central to almost all of the pivotal arguments of *Being and Nothingness*. It is, for example, vital to his criticisms of traditional ways of responding to the 'problem of other minds', as well as his own famous 'solution', which is elucidated through the pre-reflective experience of shame when we hear footsteps, or a door creak open, and are suddenly caught peering through a keyhole (1995, pp. 252–69). Moreover, when Sartre comes to argue in several different registers for our absolute ontological freedom – noting that freedom always has a context, a facticity and situation, and is inconceivable without them – it is never a traditional argument for free will that emphasizes the human ability to deliberately choose on a course of action and be reflectively aware of this. On the contrary, as Sartre provocatively suggests, 'voluntary deliberation is always a deception'

(1995, p. 488). To put his point less provocatively, reflectively weighing up pros and cons is itself a choice, and usually a motivated one.

The other main thesis that Sartre first proffers in *Transcendence of the Ego*, and which is developed in *Being and Nothingness* of 1943, is the metaphysical register that Sartre gives Husserl's thesis of intentionality, which is that all consciousness is consciousness *of* something. In the very dense early parts of *Being and Nothingness*, Sartre suggests that this thesis doesn't merely give us knowledge of essences, or meaning, as Husserl suggests, but rather it gives us the being of the phenomenon (1995, pp. xxiii–xliii): all consciousness is directed at something that is *not* consciousness, we might say at being itself. Sartre seems to give us a thesis of metaphysical realism, notwithstanding his repeatedly expressed reservations regarding traditional formulations of realism. Another way of putting Sartre's point might be to say that rather than simply intuit essences through the phenomenological method, for Sartre we also intuit existence in the failure of our ability to perceive meaning or essences in the Husserlian manner, and, in a related manner, Merleau-Ponty contends that the most important lesson of the phenomenological reduction is the inability to complete it (1962, p. xiv). Some of the most famous and evocative descriptions of this kind of 'failure' are in Sartre's literature, in particular in *Nausea* and Antoine Roquentin's famous encounter with the tree trunk in its brute contingency. While the experience of nausea when confronted with the contingency of the in-itself does not give us conceptual knowledge, Sartre thinks it involves a form of non-conceptual ontological awareness, and our access to brute existence in this respect is argued to be of a fundamentally different order to, and cannot be derived from, our conceptual understanding and knowledge of brute existence.

Merleau-Ponty's *Phenomenology of Perception*

Unlike Sartre, Merleau-Ponty's relationship to Husserl is one that preoccupies him throughout his philosophical career. In terms of his contribution to existential phenomenology, however, Merleau-Ponty's preface to *Phenomenology of Perception* is particularly famous. Here he attempts to show that if the sciences offer an account of perception, thought, and so on, in terms of causal relations between already determinate entities, phenomenology must seek to disclose the original experience of the world that such explanations take for granted. As such, phenomenologists must use methods that differ substantially from two of the dominant philosophical methods. As Merleau-Ponty puts it, 'the demand for a pure description excludes equally the procedure of analytical reflection on the one hand, and that of scientific explanation on the other' (1962, p. ix). Only by avoiding these tendencies, according to him, can we 'rediscover, as anterior to the ideas of subject and object, the fact of my subjectivity and the nascent object, that primordial layer at which both things and ideas come into being' (1962, p. 219). The point here is that starting from the subject–object polarity is to neglect something more fundamental: *l'être au monde* or being-in-the-world.

For Merleau-Ponty, there is an inextricability from our social world or life-world (*Lebenswelt*, again a concept that comes from Husserl) that makes pure phenomenology and the postulation of the transcendental subject impossible, and necessitates a turn to history. Merleau-Ponty therefore argues that phenomenology is essentially, and necessarily, existential philosophy (1962, p. xiv), which is to say that any attempted reduction to the 'things themselves', or experience, will actually end up by revealing the ways in which experience is permeated by the social situation and world that we are in. For Merleau-Ponty this inability to complete the phenomenological reduction does not herald the end of phenomenology – it actually reveals a lot about the human situation, notably our ties to the world. We are constituting (as with Husserl) but also constituted in Merleau-Ponty's dialectical philosophy, and his commitment to 'existential phenomenology' means that the unity of the world is first lived as ready-made or already there, not produced as a conscious judgement as some (unfair) readings of Husserl suggest. Rather than envisage a purification of consciousness of all empirical involvement and the 'natural attitude', existential phenomenology is understood as the reflective effort to disclose our pre-reflective engagement in the world, primarily via a sustained analysis of the body.

In the history of philosophy, Merleau-Ponty will also be remembered for his associated critiques of empiricism and of what he calls intellectualism (which sometimes refers to idealism, sometimes rationalism). He argues that both of these broad theoretical trajectories falsify the phenomenological evidences of perception, understanding it either in terms of sensation or judgement. For Merleau-Ponty, it is no coincidence that empiricists and intellectualists both also understand the body as an object, and hence perpetuate a mind–body dualism that he spent his career attempting to overcome, instead thematizing our ambiguous and paradoxical situation as embodied beings who are of the world but nonetheless are not reducible to it. Although he is often associated with the idea of the 'primacy of perception' (a thesis which is both ontological and epistemological), rather than rejecting scientific and analytic ways of knowing the world, Merleau-Ponty argues that such knowledge is always derivative in relation to the more practical aspects of the body's exposure to the world, notably our bodily intentionality that seeks equilibrium or 'maximum grip' with the world through the refinement of our 'body-schema' and the acquisition of flexible habits and skills (1962, pp. 98–153). For him, these aspects of bodily motility and perception are the transcendental conditions that ensure that sensory experience has the form of a meaningful field rather than being a fragmented relation to raw sense data.

Although he has frequently been associated with existentialism, Merleau-Ponty never propounded quite the same extreme accounts of death, freedom, anguished responsibility and conflicted relations with others for which existentialism became both famous and notorious. Instead, he spent much of his academic career contesting and reformulating many of Sartre's positions, including a sustained critique of what he saw as Sartre's dualist and ultimately Cartesian ontology. Perhaps Merleau-Ponty's most well-known contribution to existentialism was in providing it with an account of freedom that was not as extreme as Sartre's. That said, in his existentialist period, he also defends both Sartre and existentialism, arguing that the merit of the new philosophy, as he calls it, is that it tries, in the notion of existence,

> to find a way of thinking about our condition. In the modern sense of the word, 'existence' is the movement through which man is in the world and involves himself in a physical and social situation which then becomes his point of view on the world. (1992, p. 72)

In *Phenomenology of Perception*, he also associates existentialism with a 'new cogito', one that is not pure Cartesian immanence (Busch, 2008, p. 34), and suggests:

> If we keep, for the *cogito*, the meaning of 'existential experience' and if it reveals to me, not the absolute transparency of thought wholly in possession of itself, but the blind act by which I take up my destiny as a thinking nature and follow it out, then we are introducing another philosophy, which does not take us out *of time*. (1962, p. 374)

This worry about reflective consciousness being able to transparently take possession of itself captures some of the key aspects of what is at stake in the 'shift' from Husserlian to existentialist phenomenology. Merleau-Ponty thus denies the epistemological primacy of our first-personal relationship to ourselves. For the externalist existential phenomenologists, it is possible that other people may know us better than we (reflectively) know ourselves. Moreover, there is a disjunction in Merleau-Ponty's work between the lived and the known, between the pre-reflective and reflective dimensions of experience, that makes for a philosophy of ambiguity, and this is not only in Merleau-Ponty's case, but also in de Beauvoir's philosophy, and perhaps also in Sartre's philosophy in the idea of a 'situation', which refers to the necessary intermingling of facticity and freedom, as well as Sartre's consequent claim that situation and motivation for pursuing certain projects are indistinguishable (1995, p. 487). Ambiguity, for Merleau-Ponty, is a condition of being a perspective on the world and yet being blind to that perspective. Finally, on a metaphilosophical level, Merleau-Ponty makes apparent that the point of existential phenomenology is not to erect forms of 'high-altitude thinking', or nether worlds of thought, but to affirm that philosophical reflection is only useful and of interest to the extent that it makes perspicuous and allows us to experience anew the things themselves. He comments:

> It is true neither that my existence is in full possession of itself, nor that it is entirely estranged from itself, because it is action or doing, and because action is, by definition, the violent transition from what I am to what I intend to be. I can effect the *cogito* and be assured of genuinely willing, loving or believing, provided that in the first place I actually do will, love or believe, and thus fulfill my own existence. (1962, p. 382)

Phenomenological descriptions are thus but a prolegomena to this future seeing that is never attained once and for all. In that sense, they are, as Eugen Fink had earlier suggested (cited in 1962, p. xiv), concerned with awakening the reader (and thinker) to wonder, a theme subsequently given new significances by Heidegger, Sartre and Merleau-Ponty.

De Beauvoir's Interdisciplinary Phenomenology in *The Second Sex*

Much debate surrounds de Beauvoir's categorization as an 'existentialist', in which questions are asked about the presence or absence of an identifiably 'existential' methodology and whether there is a systematic element to be found in her work. De Beauvoir's methodology has been likened, among other things, to the critical method of Descartes in his *Meditations* (Bauer, 2001, to a 'philosophical anthropology' (Mahon, 1997) and to a shift from ontology to ethics or politics (Le Doeuff, 1991). Putting aside her self-characterization as a non-philosopher (Simons, 1989, p. 20), de Beauvoir's extensive autobiographical writings reveal her scholarship and application of phenomenological and other philosophies. This knowledge informs her works, including *The Second Sex*, and makes clear a philosophical genealogy going back to Hegel, with acknowledgements of Husserl, Heidegger and Bergson among others. In addition to deploying in her descriptions some technical terms from these philosophers, de Beauvoir also makes use of Sartrean terms made famous by *Being and Nothingness*, such as being-for-itself and being-for-others. However, these terms and the genealogy they represent were obscured for Anglophone audiences until recently. Contentions that there is no formal phenomenological methodology applied in her work were prematurely formulated upon particular mistranslations of her work. The original translation of *The Second Sex* sometimes obscured or deleted de Beauvoir's use of technical philosophical and phenomenological/ existentialist terms. For instance, Simons points out:

> Rendering the title of Book II, *L'experience vecue* as 'Woman's Life Today' rather than, more accurately, as 'Lived Experience', effectively masks the significance of the work as a phenomenological description. (1983, p. 563)

'Lived experience' is an Husserlian term and is a signal, to the informed reader, of a phenomenological influence. However, to seek to acknowledge the phenomenological and existential methodology in de Beauvoir's work is not to *reduce* it to that. Her interdisciplinary approach, her emphasis on women and her subtle transformation of Sartrean existentialist terms into something that would describe and potentially explain women's experience take her beyond the existentialism contained in *Being and Nothingness*. Nevertheless, it is also important to acknowledge the philosophical scholarship that informs her main work and structures its method.

Existential methodologies tend to start within the realm of the self or subject, albeit variously construed. In *The Second Sex* de Beauvoir's starting-point is specifically the female/feminine self. Did this, of necessity, dictate the methodology that was to be used? Certainly, a questioning of the starting categories was deemed necessary for her investigation. The categories of 'transcendence' and 'immanence' that so structure Sartre's ontology take on a different significance in de Beauvoir's discussion when applied specifically to women. She does not reject outright these all-important categories but finds that the dividing line between them is blurred: her phenomenological descriptions, specifically of women's experience, detail a movement across and through the states of transcendence and immanence. As she famously put it:

> Every time transcendence falls back into immanence, stagnation, there is a degradation of existence into the *'en-soi'*, – the brutish life of subjection to given conditions – and of liberty into constraint and contingence. (1997 p. 29)

The freedom of existence is something which, rather than defining existence, may be degraded by circumstances. Transcendence is something that not only may be denied with regard to oneself (i.e. in bad faith, as Sartre points out), but may be 'denied' on behalf of others (1997, p. 635) – specifically, as de Beauvoir illustrates, denied to women by men.

Methodologically, de Beauvoir finds that she had to draw upon disciplines other than philosophy (biology, sociology, anthropology, etc.) in order to gain access, as it were, to women's experience and render the phenomenological description accurately. Heinämaa traces de Beauvoir's 'empirical' approach back to Husserl: specifically to his 'strong view of the relationship between philosophy and the empirical sciences' (1999, p. 114). De Beauvoir draws upon interdisciplinary sources to produce descriptions that reveal not what must be the case if human beings are free (i.e. as consciousnesses), but what must be the case if human beings are *not* free. Contingency and necessity are mingled in 'situation', for de Beauvoir, and freedom is revealed *not* to be the defining feature of existence. A note of ambiguity emerges. As Heinämaa puts it, 'women's subordination is not a contingent fact nor a necessary structure; its way of appearing, its ontological meaning, is somehow between these two extremes' (1999, p. 126). Thus, a substantial proportion of *The Second Sex* consists in extended descriptions (revealed as even further extended in the new translation – see de Beauvoir, 2009) of women's *un*free existence, the world as a system of constraints rather than tools. In de Beauvoir's words:

> The world does not seem to women 'an assemblage of implements' intermediate between her will and her goals, as Heidegger defines it; it is on the contrary something obstinately resistant, unconquerable; it is dominated by fatality and shot through with mysterious caprices. (1997 p. 609)

In closer focus, we see that de Beauvoir's descriptions are of women's self, this self being existentially understood as a partially self-creating being, a being who 'lives' the identity she creates. The word 'create' is more appropriate than 'chosen' here, for it is de Beauvoir's contention that the women in question do not 'choose' their oppressed identity (although they may collude in it). In the words of Hazel Barnes, who first translated Sartre's *Being and Nothingness* into English, I am 'the story I tell myself about myself' (Barnes, 1997, p. xviii). Hence, what de Beauvoir describes is the woman's self-perception, that is, what it is like to *be* that woman, and what it is like to be that woman 'for others'. Looking for signs of an existential argument form, the steps of de Beauvoir's methodology in *The Second Sex* could be construed as follows:

1. describing women's self-understanding and experience (as 'immanent');
2. describing women's situation (as enclosed in immanence and subject to oppression);
3. arguing what must be the case such that women's self-understanding as immanent beings colludes in their own oppressed situation.

This conforms to the structure of the standard 'transcendental argument', in which it is argued that certain conditions must obtain such that the examples investigated are as they are. Here we find a form of transcendental reasoning still at work in de Beauvoir's writings, but her conclusions about human nature and freedom are markedly different.

Indeed, de Beauvoir's alternative conclusions are sometimes seen to point to a deficiency or error in Sartre's methodology and starting-point. Sartre starts from not a human's perspective but a *male* human's perspective and the contention is that this causes him to understate the extent of restrictions on women's existence. Sartre does not only describe from his own point of view but presumes to know what life is like for others, including women. His notorious example of the 'woman on a date' (Sartre, 1995, p. 55) has been criticized repeatedly (for instance, by Moi, 1994 and Le Doeuff, 1991), although it has its defenders (e.g. Bartok, 2003). These critiques often take the form of questioning Sartre's supposed access to the woman's experience and thus also querying the grounds upon which he attributes bad faith. Although arguably for Sartre's purposes a different example could be substituted, it does raise the question of whether some types of human experience have been overlooked and thus what structures of existence may remain hidden. Indeed, de Beauvoir in *The Second Sex* does hint at the limitations that may govern men's universal theorizing of experience: 'there is a whole region of human experience which the male deliberately chooses to ignore because he fails to *think* it: this experience woman *lives*' (1997 p. 622; her emphases).

For a transcendental argument to work, one has to be taken along by a story of sorts (a description, a genealogy, and so on, of the experience), one has to imagine and reconstruct experiences (from an embodied situation), and one has to critically and sceptically reflect in another moment, using various other devices of argumentation. Both de Beauvoir and Sartre offer stories of – and conclusions about – how women behave in particular situations: which of these competing descriptions we find most compelling will depend on the critical process of empathic reconstruction and a more distanced reflection. This critical response, of course, may be indefinitely ongoing; a final apodicticity and certainty of the Husserlian sort may never be achieved.

Indeed, existential method enacts an expansion of the possible forms of philosophical inquiry. The call to capture experience demands forms other than the traditional academic paper or monograph; the increased emphasis on being 'in *situation*' and in the world requires a description of the dramas of consciousnesses responding to one another and to the world's facticity. Plays, novels, short stories, and the like emerge as just as fruitful, perhaps more so, than any formalized transcendental arguments. De Beauvoir, like Sartre, utilizes the novel form to express philosophical truths. Rather than merely offering up 'examples' of philosophical principles already espoused (as one common understanding of the philosophical novel would have it), she sees this form as only valid if the author does not decide for the reader what conclusions will ultimately be drawn (in Simons, 2004, p. 272). The writing of the novel, then, is itself a philosophical process, a methodological approach that sets fictional constraints in which the gamut of ethical, epistemological and ontological issues may be explored. Far from illustrating an already-worked-out philosophy, de Beauvoir's novels *are* philosophies in action and an alternative method of following through an existential–phenomenological investigation and expressing the new-found ambiguity in existence.

Marcel and 'Existential Certitude'

Marcel, as the originator of the term existentialism, may reveal to us something important about its approach and methodologies. In fact, by the time Marcel wrote his famous review of *Being and Nothingness*, he had already been employing the terms 'existence' and 'existential' with particular intent in his own work for many years. The influence of Husserlian phenomenology was less strong for Marcel than for Heidegger, Merleau-Ponty and Sartre. Marcel firmly rejected any systematic methodology, preferring, as he stated, the 'neo-Socratic' style of dialogue and questioning (two of his most famous published works, *Being and Having* and the *Metaphysical Journal*, take this form). However, he demonstrated a lifelong interest in achieving descriptions of what human existence is really like, and employed at times the word 'phenomenology' – for instance, in his essay 'On the Phenomenology of Having', in which he sets out a detailed description and analysis of various experiences of 'having' a body.

Marcel's use of the word 'existential' functions as a divider between an older systematic phenomenology and a phenomenology that will be faithful to the vagaries of existence. For Marcel, the word 'existential' means principally 'immediate' – he uses it to express the immediacy of experience, the irreducibility of the intensity of first-person experience to third-person terms. The fundamental element of experience, for Marcel, is the 'existential certitude' found in one's basic sensory awareness – a state he terms 'exclamatory awareness' (1951, p. 125). Methodologically, this term separates true philosophical inquiry from pregiven, prejudiced forms of thought. The integrity of philosophical inquiry is safeguarded though a continual returning to the exclaiming of the irreducible self – the certainty of the 'now' and 'here' of experience, the sheer consciousness of being alive. In *The Mystery of Being* Marcel evokes the image of 'the small child who comes up to us with shining eyes, and who seems to be saying: 'Here I am! What luck!' (1951, p. 90)

Exclamatory awareness, expressed in avowals such as 'Here I am!', 'cannot really be separated' (1951, p. 91) from bodily existence itself. To do so would be to rob the subject of its 'proper nature', that is, its self-conscious nature, which Marcel clearly takes to be more intrinsic than Merleau-Ponty considered it to be. But 'self-conscious' here does not mean a staid or ponderous regarding of the self, but an immediate sensuous self-awareness. As he puts in *The Mystery of Being*:

> Separated from that exclamatory self-awareness . . . existence tends to be reduced to its own corpse; and it lies outside the power of any philosophy whatsoever to resuscitate such a corpse. (1951, p. 91)

The challenge, of course, is to investigate existence using the type of reflection which will not render it lifeless. Central to this purpose, Marcel draws a distinction between 'primary' and 'secondary' reflection: primary reflection being a kind of self-distorting reflection, of the kind that scientific inquiry engages in when it puts to one side the issue of its own subjective perspective. This bracketing of the subjective perspective may be appropriate and indeed necessary to the scientific method and to producing the kind of results the natural sciences seek; however, Marcel's contention is that this kind of reflection is fundamentally inappropriate to any kind of inquiry into the self or into the world inclusive of the self, which of course covers philosophical inquiry. Thus primary reflection actually robs existence of its true nature, reducing it to a 'corpse': philosophy's task is not to 'resuscitate' this corpse, that is, not to try and salvage this view of existence, but rather to see through this false understanding of what existence is and reclaim 'exclamatory awareness' as at the heart of it. This would then allow us to investigate *existence itself* rather than our own, flawed, self-reflective representation of existence. However, primary reflection would seem to be built into our language, such that we cannot, although we might wish to, proceed directly to secondary reflection, to a reflection which opens up subjectivity for investigation. When we start to philosophize we must pass through this phase because, Marcel implies, the language immediately available to us is steeped within objectifying and distancing thought. It requires *further* reflection to dismantle this thinking and install a different style of thinking (and different language) in its place. The initial dismantling is required *prior* to the rebuilding of different structures of thought – it is as if we have to clear away the rubble before we build a new edifice, and this 'clearing away' is what secondary reflection achieves.

In his 1930s work *Being and Having* Marcel draws the methodological distinction between 'problem' and 'mystery'. By asserting the category of 'mystery', Marcel is not thereby giving up on what are commonly known as philosophical 'problems', nor espousing a religious rejection of inquiry in the face of some difficult-to-explain phenomenon. Rather he is espousing the philosopher's concern to understand the nature of the inquiry. In inquiry about being, the ontological status of the questioner becomes 'of highest importance' (1949, p. 171). Marcel does not intend this word 'mystery' literally: it could perhaps be renamed more prosaically as an 'internal problem' or as a species of the paradox of self-reference, which he differentiates it from the conventional 'problem' thus:

> A problem is something which I meet, which I find complete before me, but which I can therefore lay siege to and reduce. But a mystery is something in which I myself am involved, and it can therefore only be thought of as 'a sphere where the distinction between what is in me and what is before me loses its meaning and its initial validity'. A genuine problem is subject to an appropriate technique by the exercise of which it is defined; whereas a mystery, by definition, transcends every conceivable technique. (1949, p. 117)

For Marcel, an existentialist methodology could never be reduced to something as impersonal as a 'technique' (and here in particular we find a further fissure opening up between Husserlian phenomenology and its existential consequents). He is far from offering a solution to any traditional philosophical problem; rather, he is concerned to point out the confusion of our thinking and speaking on the topic, the logical errors committed in the course of trying to even state the alleged problem. When certain issues are misrepresented as 'problems' (in his technical sense), the 'therapy'[4] required is, first, to restate the issue carefully, and second, to return to the 'things themselves', paying close attention to our experience and to our discourse about them. This is the familiar phenomenological method of description and language critique, but Marcel perhaps takes it in a more radical direction. He, too, it could be argued, engages in a Merleau-Ponty-style 'hyperdialectic' to clarify the impact of the inquirer upon the subject-matter of the inquiry.

Along with Sartre and de Beauvoir, Marcel found it useful to explore his existential themes through drama as well as academic works. In these he explores the anxieties and moral quandaries of modern human beings, and conveys his regard for the immediacy of experience. In this genre Marcel finds the natural expression of his 'neo-Socratic' approach to philosophy involving open dialogue and repeated questioning: an existentialist philosophy must deal with 'living' existence and take place between subjects in a common world. The kinds of descriptions Marcel proffers emphasize the (potential or actual) connections between persons rather than solitariness – an existential 'communion'. Out of his careful and detailed descriptions of human behaviour emerges a picture of a temporarily lost communion – a contingent dissociation; however, he resists offering such descriptions as the final assessment of the human condition.

Generally, Marcel seems to hold a fairly pessimistic view of the potential for adequate description of any aspect of reality, but especially of the self. His reason for this appears to be that we simply stand in too close a relationship to it, affecting and being affected by it, for the distance necessary for objective description: Husserl's original confidence in philosophy's outcome has been lost, and Marcel asserts:

There is not, and there cannot be, any global abstraction, any final high terrace to which we can climb by means of abstract thought, there to rest forever, for our condition in this world does remain, in the last analysis, that of a wanderer, an itinerant being, who cannot come to absolute rest except by a fiction, a fiction which it is the duty of philosophic reflection to oppose with all its strength. (1951, p. 133)

Phenomenological method as applied by Marcel and the other existentialists has become diffused through an increased variety of genres of communication, the injection of ambiguity and uncertainty, and the emergence of competing phenomenological descriptions from which the important structures of exist-ence will be drawn out. With the contribution of de Beauvoir's investigation of women's existence we find the 'who' of existential inquiry being placed into the realm of controversy. Who investigates and describes? Who draws the line between the contingent and the necessary, the immanent and the transcendent? Existentialist philosophers who sought to shed light on existence using the examples of others find the spotlight turned back upon themselves, and now the situation of the philosopher's own self emerges as the battleground for the ongoing controversy over competing methodologies.

Notes

1. Parts of this work appeared as the essay 'Existentialism', by Jack Reynolds in *The Routledge Companion to Phenomenology*, ed. Sebastian Luft and Søren Overgaard, Routledge (2011). Thanks to Adam Johnson and Routledge for permission to reuse here, albeit in substantially reconfigured form and with a co-author. Thanks also to the editors of that volume for their useful feedback, as well as Steven Churchill.
2. For an in-depth discussion of the fate of transcendental reasoning in the twentieth century, see the chapter on this in James Chase and Jack Reynolds, *Analytic versus Continental: Arguments on the Methods and Value of Philosophy*. Durham: Acumen, 2010. Elements of this account are summarized here.
3. 'The lower number refers to the pagination in the original German edition, which is also given in the margins of the Macquarrie/Robinson translation'.
4. Wittgenstein's term, from the *Philosophical Investigations*: For the clarity we are aiming at is indeed *complete* clarity. But this simply means that the philosophical problems should *completely* disappear . . . There is not *a* philosophical method, but there are indeed methods, like different therapies (1953, sec. 133).

Bibliography

Barnes, H. (2001), *The Story I Tell Myself: A Venture in Existential Autobiography*. Chicago: University of Chicago Press.
Bartok, P. (2003), 'Sexism and Phenomenological Method in Sartre's Analysis of Bad Faith'. Address given to the American Philosophical Association, Spring Meeting.

Busch, T. (2008), 'Existentialism – The New Philosophy', in R. Diprose and J. Reynolds (eds), *Merleau-Ponty: Key Concepts*. Chesham: Acumen.

De Beauvoir, S. (1948), 'Literature and Metaphysics', trans. V. Zaytzeff, in M. Simons (ed.), *Simone de Beauvoir: Philosophical Writings*. Chicago, IL: University of Illinois Press.

— (1986), *The Prime of Life*, trans. P. Green. Harmondsworth: Penguin.

— (1997), *The Second Sex*, trans. H. M. Parshley. London: Vintage.

— (2009), *The Second Sex*, trans. C. Borde and S. Malovany-Chevallier. London: Jonathan Cape.

Earnshaw, S. (2006), *Existentialism: A Guide for the Perplexed*. London: Continuum.

Fulbrook, E. and K. Fulbrook (1998), 'Merleau-Ponty on Beauvoir's Literary-Philosophical Method'. Address given to the Twentieth World Congress of Philosophy, in Boston, MA, 10–15 August: www.bu.edu/wcp/Papers/Lite/LiteFull.htm. Access date 12 November 2002.

Gallagher, S. and D. Zahavi (2008), *The Phenomenological Mind*. London: Routledge.

Grosholz, E. (2009), 'Simone de Beauvoir and Practical Deliberation'. *PMLA* 124 (1): 199–205.

Hanley, K. (1987), *Dramatic Approaches to Creative Fidelity: A Study in the Theater and Philosophy of Gabriel Marcel (1889–1973)*. Boston, MD: University Press of America.

Heidegger, M. (2004), *Being and Time*, trans. J. Macquarrie and E. Robinson. London: Blackwell [1927].

— (2000), 'Letter on Humanism', in D. Krell (ed.), *Martin Heidegger: Basic Writings*. London: Routledge.

Heinämaa, S. (1999), 'Simone de Beauvoir's Phenomenology of Sexual Difference'. *Hypatia* 14 (4): 114–32.

Husserl, E. (1900), *Logical Investigations*, trans. J. N. Findlay. London: Routledge.

— (1913), *Ideas Pertaining to a Pure Phenomenology and to a Phenomenological Philosophy – First Book: General Introduction to a Pure Phenomenology*, trans. F. Kersten. The Hague: Nijhoff.

Le Doeuff, M. (1991), *Hipparchia's Choice*, trans. T. Selous. Oxford: Blackwell.

Mahon, J. (1997), *Existentialism, Feminism and Simone de Beauvoir*. London: Macmillan.

Marcel, G. (1927), *Metaphysical Journal*, trans. B. Wall. London: Rockcliff.

— (1949), *Being and Having*, trans. K. Farrer. Westminster: Dacre Press.

— (1951), *The Mystery of Being*, trans. G. S. Fraser. London: Harvill.

Merleau-Ponty, M. (1962), *Phenomenology of Perception*, trans. C. Smith. London: Routledge.

— (1964), *Signs*, trans. R. McCleary. Evanston, IL: Northwestern University Press.

— (1992), *Sense and Nonsense*, trans. H. Dreyfus and P. Dreyfus. Evanston, IL: Northwestern University Press.

Moi, T. (1994), *Simone de Beauvoir: The Making of an Intellectual Woman*. Oxford: Blackwell.

— (2002), 'While We Wait: The English Translation of *The Second Sex*'. *Signs* 27 (4): 1005–35.

Moran, D. (1992), *Gabriel Marcel: Existentialist Philosopher, Dramatist, Educator*. Boston, MD: University Press of America.

Morris, D. (2010), 'Empirical and Phenomenological Studies of Embodied Cognition', in D. Schmicking and S. Gallagher (eds), *Handbook to Phenomenology and Cognitive Science*. Dordrecht: Kluwer.

Sartre, J-P. (1995), *Being and Nothingness*, trans. H. E. Barnes. London: Routledge.

— (1962), *Transcendence of the Ego*, trans. F. Williams and R. Kirkpatrick. New York: Noonday Press.

— (1965), 'Merleau-Ponty', in *Situations*, trans. B. Eisler. New York: Braziller.

Simons, M. A. (1983), 'The Silencing of Simone de Beauvoir: Guess What's Missing from *The Second Sex?' Women's Studies International Forum* 6 (5): 559–64.

— (1989), 'Two Interviews with Simone de Beauvoir'. *Hypatia* 3 (3): 11–27.

— (1999), *Beauvoir and 'The Second Sex': Feminism, Race, and the Origins of Existentialism*. Lanham, MD: Rowman & Littlefield.

— (2004), *Simone de Beauvoir: Philosophical Writings*. Chicago, IL: University of Illinois Press.

Wittgenstein, L. (1953), *Philosophical Investigations*, trans. G. E. M. Anscombe. Oxford: Blackwell.

Wrathall, M. (2009), 'Existential Phenomenology', in H. Dreyfus and M. Wrathall (eds), *A Companion to Phenomenology and Existentialism*. London: Wiley-Blackwell.

Part I

Current Research and Issues

3 Existentialism, Metaphysics and Ontology[1]

Christian Onof

Existentialism is a broad philosophical current that may be viewed as setting itself in opposition to traditional metaphysics. But in so doing, it takes a stance on certain traditional metaphysical topics and defines new ones. In this paper, I shall illustrate these two aspects of the metaphysics of existentialism. In so doing, I shall deal with the breadth of existentialist philosophy in two ways. First, examining how nineteenth-century existentialist thought emerged in reaction to dominant metaphysical doctrines of the day, I shall identify key topics that characterize the existentialist stance against these doctrines. This will take the paper into an examination of how twentieth-century philosophers dealt with these key topics.

Subjectivity and Truth

Schelling, in his late works, attacks Hegel for his claim that he can account for the whole of reality in the concept (Schelling, 1995; Frank, 1975). The concept cannot, however, account for being. It is not satisfactory to account for being merely in terms of a potentiality that is actualized (Hegel, 2002). This attack on Hegel makes a strong impression on the young Kierkegaard who puts his hopes in Schelling's approach to philosophy. By placing being beyond the reach of the concept, Schelling is establishing a bridge between being as the ground of the subject–object relation according to the earlier Romantics (Hölderlin, Novalis, Schleiermacher, etc.), and the specific form of transcendence which the later Existentialists view as characterizing existence.

What it takes to make the move to the existentialist conception of transcendence is a focus upon a particular way of being which distinguishes itself from others. The grounds for this move are both methodological and axiological. The perceived failure of Hegel's optimistic metaphysics, which secured a place for human flourishing within the coming to self-consciousness of the absolute, had two related consequences. First, philosophy cannot account for the particularity of human existence from the standpoint of the absolute. Second, the value of such existence can no longer be guaranteed by grounding it in an absolute.

When Kierkegaard enthuses in 1842 about Schelling's stance on being, his focus is human existence. That is, his focus is on that particular form of being which is the most mysterious although, or perhaps because, it is that which seeks to make sense of being in general. For Kierkegaard, to exist is to commit oneself with passion, and thereby rise above any determination of oneself in universal terms. Kierkegaard understands this as resulting from a three-stage process. In the first, aesthetic stage, the individual primarily seeks to alleviate boredom by imaginative devices (Kierkegaard, 1992). In the ethical stage, the individual views this way of life as escapist and meaningless. Instead, she chooses to act upon universal moral principles. In this way, however, the individual has not yet come into her own. This happens only through understanding that 'the single individual as the single individual stands in an absolute relation to the absolute' (Kierkegaard, 1983, p. 56). The individuality of the existing human being thus rises above any particular universal determination through this relation to the absolute. This amounts to a notion of transcendence, but one that, for Kierkegaard, is fundamentally defined in relation to an absolute being, God.

This transcendence has the key features that characterize later existential transcendence. That is, it defines the being that transcends any determination, and is thereby nothing. For Kierkegaard, this nothingness is the individual's annihilation in the face of the highest form of existence. However, Kierkegaard is not doing ontology here, but his evaluation of the limitations of other ways of being human amounts to identifying that way of being which is *adequate* to the nature of what it is to be a human individual. The claim is that this way of being is a transcendence of any essentialist universal determination of one's being towards annihilation in relation to God. This claim is normative therefore, and the normativity can be described as that of *subjective* truth. The way of subjective truth is, for Kierkegaard, the way of inwardness, that of the search for the kind of truth that is adequate to that type of being which is existence (Kierkegaard, 1968, p. 23).

In a sense, Kierkegaard proposes a notion of truth that takes Kant's programme, of circumscribing the realm of knowledge to make room for faith, one step further. For Kant, understanding one's duty as a rational being will lead one to postulate certain metaphysical truths such as the existence of God, the immortality of the soul, and so on. Although these lie beyond the bounds of theoretical reason, we have to believe these claims on practical grounds. We thus get a *practical expansion* of the realm of metaphysical truths. For Kierkegaard, there are two important differences. First, the practically normative dimension is changed, and not itself grounded in reason: it is rather the normativity of inwardness as an attitude through which the encounter with God is made possible. Second, the claims made in inwardness are not merely beliefs that one ought to hold. They are *true* in the sense of subjective truth, that is, a notion of truth appropriate for states of affairs that have no place in an objective description of the world. This is not to be understood as a move to endorse relativism: rather, subjective truth has to be experienced in existence. For Kierkegaard, through an understanding of the normativity of the subjective attitude of inwardness (as opposed to the objective attitude) the truth of the existence of God and the absolute bindingness of his command can be understood.

Nietzsche also introduces a notion of subjective truth. This is, however, clearly intended as a relativization: 'The criterion of truth lies in the enhancement of the feeling of power' (1968, p. 284). If Nietzsche does not examine its relation to any notion of objectivity, this is because he can be interpreted as going a step further than Kierkegaard: he wants to do away with the traditional notion of truth altogether. If truth understood subjectively is connected with usefulness (e.g. in relation to the feeling of power), then one may substitute usefulness for a criterion of truth. And Nietzsche finds in the *Twilight of the Idols* that the '"true" world [is] . . . an idea which has become useless and superfluous', and so Nietzsche concludes, '*consequently* a refuted idea' (1998, p. 20). Together with this notion of subjective truth, Nietzsche introduces a notion of transcendence, namely of transcendence of the limiting moral values that are passed on by the tradition. Ultimately, this defines the possibility of overcoming man towards a higher form of humanity, the *Übermensch*. As with Kierkegaard, therefore, this transcendence is no ontological feature of existence, but rather a task (although it is perhaps only reserved for a small elite): 'Overcome, you higher men, the petty virtues, the petty prudences . . . , the "happiness of the greatest number"' (1978, p. 298). More broadly than at the individual level, transcendence is also the constant creation that animates the kind of world Nietzsche outlines as antidote to Schopenhauer's pessimistic picture of a world animated by a will that is never satisfied. Nietzsche's world is, on the contrary, that of 'the eternally self-creating, the eternally self-destroying' (1968, p. 544).

These nineteenth-century thinkers define a core tenet of existentialism: the individual subject transcends objective reality, and thereby has her own subjective truth. This subjectivity may lie in its only being attainable through lived experience (Kierkegaard), or in its being a mere reflection of the agent's interests (Nietzsche). In all cases, this subjective truth is essentially connected with the agent's practice. This notion of truth connected with practice is meant as a reaction to the dominant metaphysics of the earlier part of the century. As such, it constitutes no alternative metaphysical doctrine. Below, we shall examine how the twentieth century provided new directions of thought that enabled an existentialist metaphysics and ontology to integrate these concepts of transcendence and subjective truth.

Freedom

Before that, it is important to take note of the key direction defined by these nineteenth-century thinkers in their understanding of subjectivity. If individuality identifies a notion of truth that is closely bound up with the individual as agent who transcends what can be circumscribed in objective terms, the nature of this agency must be of central importance. Aside from truth and transcendence, we thus find a third key feature of nineteenth-century existentialist thought, namely the central role it assigns to *freedom* as characteristic of human existence. The existentialist notion of freedom distinguishes itself from earlier understandings of this concept in that it is no longer a mere *property* of human beings characterizing their practical dimension. It is rather a *defining* characteristic of human existence and one which has to be *nurtured*. This feature is probably the most fundamental notion of the existentialist tradition.

The importance of freedom for humanity can be gauged by how humans value their freedom. Dostoevsky's protagonist in *Notes from the Underground* aims above all to be free from any constraint, be it natural, rational, selfish or self-interested. As he puts it 'The fact is, gentlemen, it seems there must really exist something that is dearer to almost every man than his greatest advantages . . . for the sake of which a man, if necessary is ready to act in opposition to all laws' (1992, p. 15). For what purpose? For what Dostoevsky describes as 'that fundamental, most advantageous advantage which we have overlooked', namely 'one's own free unfettered choice . . . through which all systems and theories are continually being shattered to atoms' (1992, p. 17).

Aside from the fact that freedom is placed here as highest value, the fact that it appears to be what is most important, points to its being a defining characteristic of human existence. Thus Dostoevsky identifies it as a necessary condition of humanity in a passage which is remarkably relevant in view of current discussion about alleged empirical evidence against free will (Libet, 1985; Crane, 2005): 'if there really is some day discovered a formula for all our desires and caprices' (1992, p. 18), that is, 'the laws of our so-called free will' (p. 19), 'man . . . will at once be transformed from a human being into an organ stop or something of the sort' (p. 18).

But freedom is a characteristic of humanity that is simultaneously axiological, so that to be human is to be free, but also to preserve and nurture this freedom. Because of this normative dimension, this freedom cannot simply be identified with the traditional concept of free will. One ought to nurture and pursue freedom because that is what makes one what one is, that is, a human being. But this is an unusual form of normativity as any norm external to freedom would threaten it, and is therefore rejected. Whether this normativity without any constraint is practically sufficient is questionable, hence Dostoevsky's comment that 'If God is dead, everything is permitted' spoken by Ivan

Karamazov (2004). Raskolnikov's freedom that is contained by no values (Dostoevsky, 2000), echoed in the twentieth century by Camus's outsider who kills an Arab (Camus, 2000), also suggests so much.

Even though an anchoring of the normativity of free action in rationality, as in Kant, is not possible for an existentialist view of humans as transcending all objective determinations, this does not mean that freedom must ignore rationality. Raskolnikov claims to have a grasp of the requirements of universalist ethics (rationalism, utilitarianism), but to be required to contravene their dictates for a higher purpose. To discard ethical claims on the grounds of an overinflated perception of the importance of one's task and purpose would be, for Kierkegaard, not to understand where one's true freedom lies. For Kierkegaard, the religious stage in which the freedom of the individual can be truly expressed is only to be reached after graduating to the ethical stage from the merely aesthetic stage of the pursuit pleasures. That is, the individual who can live the inward way is an individual who has paid the universality of rational ethical norms their due, but understood that his individuality must take him beyond that. This is not Raskolnikov's claim to be above certain universal norms, because of some greater purpose he might be pursuing, or indeed Nietzsche's Superman who has overcome such norms. On the contrary, Kierkegaard's agent in the religious stage views himself as a nothingness that is only defined through its subservience to God and his command. Nevertheless, Kierkegaard's knight of faith may have to act against the commands of universalist ethics, as in the case of Abraham. Such considerations illustrate the problems that existentialist thought encountered in trying to define normative constraints governing free action that do not threaten the integrity of this freedom.

The Twentieth Century

Kierkegaard and Nietzsche's philosophical contributions set out the essential themes of existentialism, but these themes were not woven into a complete body of work that addresses the traditional metaphysical concerns of philosophy. To a large extent, this is not fortuitous, but follows from the very nature of their enterprise that can be seen as reacting against metaphysical systems, in particular Hegel's absolute idealism in Kierkegaard's case, and the Judeo-Christian tradition in Nietzsche's. But a philosophy which champions subjective truth, without properly addressing its relation to objectivity, calls for further developments. And such developments might seem particularly urgent in a climate characterized by the growing status of science. But how could such a development take place? After all, objectivity and subjectivity appeared to be two incompatible perspectives, mutually exclusive domains that could not be integrated into a whole without doing violence to the one or the other.

This is where the key philosophical development of the early twentieth century, that is, the emergence of phenomenology, provided a clue. The slogan of the phenomenological movement, which enjoins a return to 'the things themselves' (Husserl, 1970), invites us to consider our conscious experience as the primary data for philosophical reflection. For Husserl, this means that phenomenology brackets out the issue of the existence of things independently of consciousness. Rather, the object is understood as belonging to a world defined by the intentional reach of consciousness. This object is not a representation or image of some outer reality, since it lies properly beyond the subject which reaches out to it. But it is also not outside the subject independently of its perspective since it is determined in terms of the subject's intentional stance. So, without falling prey of the subjectivism of an empiricist picture that views private sensations as the raw material from which representations of the world are formed, Husserlian phenomenology would appear to give both the objective and the subjective their due by focusing upon 'lived experience', '*Erlebnis*' (Husserl, 1982).

This phenomenological programme does not obviously define a metaphysics of what it is to be human in the world, that is, an ontology of human existence. In fact, Husserl (1982) is committed to a notion of transcendental ego. That is, he understands phenomenological investigation as involving a bracketing of the world and the existence of objects, which leaves him with a transcendental ego as the source of all meaning and as constituting the world (Husserl, 1967). This essentially Cartesian bracketing defines a metaphysics that is broadly in line with Kantian transcendental idealism. But this commitment to a transcendental ego, and the concurrent cognitive orientation of his philosophy, seemed to many of his followers to be a poorly grounded attachment to a residue of traditional metaphysics[2] in an otherwise revolutionary step towards a new philosophical orientation.

It is a dissatisfaction with Husserl's transcendental metaphysics that lies among the motivations for Heidegger's redefining of phenomenology in *Being and Time*. Returning to the Greek roots of the word 'phenomenology', Heidegger understands it as a way of uncovering that from which what shows itself can show itself (*BT*, sec. 7, p. 34). Although entities show themselves, their showing themselves is only possible on the basis of something that does not show itself. In this way, beings are distinguished from Being, which is the light that lets things show themselves. This understanding of phenomenology, therefore, defines it as dealing with the question of Being, that is, of its meaning, and thus as being ontology. And since that which is to be revealed is hidden, the Heideggerian method is essentially one of interpretation, that is, hermeneutic.

But Heidegger's way of doing phenomenology is not the only option for a philosophy which seeks to understand existence phenomenologically, without endorsing Husserlian transcendentalism. That is, this identification of phenomenology with ontology is not uncontroversial. Other ways of developing an ontology of what it is to be human might consist in the following:

1. formulating a basic ontological framework and letting the phenomenological analysis of human existence confirm its appropriateness, and inform its further development;
2. carrying out a phenomenological investigation of how a human being relates to other beings with a view to letting ontological truths emerge from this analysis.

The first of these options was adopted by Sartre. He sets up a basic ontological framework with the reality of the being of non-human entities as its cornerstone. From what we said above, this might seem to preclude the possibility of accounting for subjectivity. But Sartre's onto-phenomenology interprets the fact that there is no place for subjectivity within an objective world by viewing consciousness as a 'nothing' that is added to a world of things. And he takes it that a proper ontology must account for this nothingness and reveal its nature.

The second of these options might, arguably, be viewed as that pursued by Merleau-Ponty towards the end of his life, although he never completed *The Visible and the Invisible*. Although *Phenomenology of Perception* (1962) is a complete phenomenological analysis, it leaves ontological issues open. I shall, therefore, not discuss Merleau-Ponty in the remainder of this paper, other than to note his original contribution to an understanding of subjectivity in terms of embodiment with the notion of the lived body (Merleau-Ponty, 1962, p. 206).

We are therefore left with the Heideggerian path of phenomenology as ontology, and the Sartrean understanding of phenomenology as supporting an ontology. How does ontology thus informed by phenomenology tackle the issues that nineteenth-century thinkers brought to the fore as characteristic of human existence? Such an ontology would have to address the following questions. What is subjectivity and its truth? What is the place and meaning of transcendence in human existence? What is the nature of human freedom? Finally, much as the metaphysics of existentialism ought to give subjective truth its due without ignoring objective truth, the issue of whether reality is ultimately to be understood in subjective or objective terms cannot be avoided: is this an idealist or a realist ontology, or neither? In examining how Heidegger and Sartre tackle these questions, I shall also refer to two other key twentieth-century existentialist philosophers whose views cannot, in the context of this paper, be examined in any detail: Karl Jaspers and Gabriel Marcel.

Heidegger's Being-in-the-world

Truth and *Dasein*

Insofar as Heidegger views phenomenology as defining the only way in which to do ontology (*BT*, sec. 7, p. 35), his understanding of what it is to exist is entirely defined by his understanding of phenomenology. Heidegger rejects traditional notions of subjectivity, such as that of consciousness as characterizing human existence. Heidegger views the phenomenological enterprise as bound up with the forestructure of hermeneutic investigation. That is 'Inquiry, as a kind of seeking, must be guided beforehand by what is sought' (*BT*, sec. 2, p. 5). But rather than see this as a limitation of the scope of the interpretative strategy of hermeneutics, Heidegger views the hermeneutic circle which arises as non-vicious, because 'our questioning really is a kind of light which casts a certain pattern on the phenomenon, while filling in our expectation in a way which allows us to formulate further questions' (Moran, 2000, p. 237). The disclosing of truth can, therefore, no longer be detached from the enquirer who seeks the truth. This is how Heidegger ushers in a notion of truth that replaces the conceptions of subjective truth put forward by Kierkegaard and Nietzsche.

But this disclosure of truth also has implications for the enquirer. Just as it is not incidental that truth is revealed by a particular interpretation carried out by a questioning being, it is not incidental to this being that it asks the question about the meaning of Being. If ontology is to be properly phenomenological, it must let the phenomenon reveal its truth. The questioning stance is what is first encountered as characteristic of that being which is ours, and which Heidegger calls '*Dasein*'. And to be a questioning being is to be a being which has a world that defines a context within which an answer to the question can be meaningful. That is how Heidegger understands intentionality, and this means that *Dasein* is primarily characterized as Being-in-the-world. Thus, Heidegger finds his way out of the problems encountered by the nineteenth-century thinkers who sought to find a place for subjective truth while assuming the notion of subjectivity was clearly understood. Heidegger starts with a notion of truth that arises from his understanding of phenomenology, and lets this be the basis from which the notion of *Dasein* emerges.

Insofar as Heidegger rejects Husserl's assumption that intentionality is to be understood as a feature of consciousness, it also follows that he rejects a tradition that privileges a cognitive relation to the world over other forms of involvement. A proper hermeneutic method must, on the contrary, aim to provide fundamental interpretations to get at the Being of things. What the phenomenon of intentionality reveals is a way of being that is characterized by its worldliness. This worldliness is primarily practical for Heidegger, as entities first of all appear meaningful insofar as *Dasein* understands how they feature with respect to its pursuits. In this way, Heidegger's ontology encompasses the practical at a very fundamental level. We will see the consequences of this point when we examine freedom.

For the moment, let us just note how Heidegger's enterprise relies crucially upon the understanding of the hermeneutic circle as non-vicious. Unlike the romantic roots of Schleiermacher's original work in hermeneutics (1988), the truth of the hermeneutic circle is no longer anchored in an intuition of an ultimate unity, that which underpins both the interpreting subject and the object of his interpretation, and situates the first in the greater scheme of things. As Kierkegaard had done before him, Heidegger cuts loose from such any grounding in something like Hölderlin's primordial unity of being. This does leave it unclear, however, whether, and why, the methodology of the hermeneutic circle, in its Heideggerian form, can attain to the truth.

An answer to the first question lies simply in our finding that Heidegger's methodology in *Being and Time* yields interpretations of *Dasein's* being which echo one's experience of what it is to be human. To address the second point, an account is required of why the hermeneutic method is fruitful. And arguably, such an account is to be found in Heidegger's later views about Being. *Dasein's* destiny is to say the truth of Being: Being reveals itself to *Dasein* in different ways, and it is up to *Dasein* to be open to the truth of Being. One might want to follow Heidegger along this path that leads to poetry as the locus of the revealing of the meaning of Being. But one might also see it as merely replacing the Romantics' notion of an original all-encompassing unity by a mysticism of Being.

Another concern which Heidegger's notion of truth raises is that it apparently has no place for the kind of objective truth informing the traditional epistemological outlook. What does Heidegger tell us about the 'world' of entities considered independently of *Dasein*? That it comes to the fore through an impoverished type of interpretation (*BT*, sec. 33, p. 157), and that 'with the disclosedness of the world, the "world" has in each case been discovered too' (*BT*, sec. 43, p. 203). Whether or not the latter claim assuages epistemological worries about whether we know that there is indeed an objective 'world',[3] the first claim does not do justice to the truth revealed by science in the form of the complexity of the structure of the objective 'world'. At the core of this issue lies the problem flagged by Tugendhat (1970, pp. 333–7; cf. Dahlstrom, 2001, pp. 394–6) who argues that Heidegger's conception of truth is not satisfactory in that it defines no notion of falsehood.

Certainly, Heidegger is right to claim that the bare world of entities sheds little light on what he has singled out as characteristic of *Dasein*. But Heidegger's interpretative stance can be questioned for its sidelining the role of rationality and the rich causal structure governed by universal laws that it identifies (see Cassirer's questions in Heidegger, 1998, pp. 277–8). This interpretative stance has strong roots in the basic struggle against alienation in the universal that characterizes the impetus behind existentialism as we have seen above. But is it possible to provide a satisfactory ontology without paying due attention to the light reason sheds on reality?

Dasein as transcendence

Insofar as *Dasein* is Being-in-the-world, *Dasein's* being is always such that it has its being to be. *Dasein's* worldliness consists in its understanding that it has possibilities which it chooses, and that the range of its possibilities is related to the situation it has been thrown into. In this grasp of its possibilities, *Dasein* always shows some understanding of Being, that is, of that which makes it possible that beings show up (make sense) for *Dasein*. This is *Dasein's* transcendence: in this understanding of Being, *Dasein* goes beyond merely being one among beings in the world. But, unlike traditional notions of transcendence, *Dasein's* transcendence is essentially beyond any being, that is, towards no-thing.

However, *Dasein* always tends to interpret itself in terms of the beings of the world in which it dwells. That is what Heidegger calls *Dasein's* 'falling'. Since Heidegger's investigation in *Being and Time* is essentially transcendental, once Being-in-the-world is in place, the question arises as to how it is possible. That is, what kind of being is it that is thrown into a world projects onto its possibilities and interprets itself in terms of the entities of this world? This introduces a characterization of *Dasein* as 'care' ('Sorge'), which in effect encapsulates these three dimensions together (*BT*, sec. 41, p. 192). But Heidegger points out that this still yields no understanding of the primordial unity of *Dasein* (*BT*, sec. 45, p. 32). A further transcendental investigation leads to the essential connection of *Dasein's* being with time, which was already announced at the start of *Being and Time*, insofar as this was part of the preconception of the whole hermeneutic investigation. *Dasein* is essentially a temporal being: it is ecstatic (*BT*, sec. 65, p. 329). The structure of care can now be interpreted more fundamentally in terms of future, past and present. *Dasein* is always pressing into the future, while carrying a past, and dwelling among entities in the present. Temporality in effect is what opens up a world for *Dasein*.

And this reveals Heidegger's radically novel understanding of time. It is no longer viewed as a sequence of equidistant instants, but the very condition of an opening: the opening up which is the gap created between moments of time is that which enables *Dasein* to be open to Being, and is thus the *condition of its transcendence*.

This shows how radically different Heidegger's understanding of transcendence is from traditional metaphysical notions (*BT*, sec. 10, p. 49). These provide our frail human condition with the solidity of a timeless transcendent being (e.g. a soul in the image of God). *Dasein's* transcendence, on the contrary, is essentially temporal. And it is, therefore, fully in tune with *Dasein's* finitude (*BT*, sec. 65, pp. 329–30).

But Heidegger's later thought suggests that this distinctive notion of transcendence has many parallels with that of human existence in God and that it does not preclude a relationship of faith (Capelle, 1998). It remains an open question to what extent Heidegger's reflections, for example, on the role of poetry in his Hölderlin book, are compatible with an existentially oriented theology (Pattison, 2000, pp. 196–200).

Finally, note that the existentialist philosophies of Jaspers and Marcel provide notions of transcendence which amount to existentialist versions of something like the traditional transcendence towards God. Similarly to Heidegger, Jaspers's notion of transcendence is towards being, but unlike Heidegger's, this involves different types of experience of being as an unconditioned beyond the world (Jaspers, 1956). The philosophical faith Jaspers proposes transcends any particular religion. Marcel's notion of transcendence, on the other hand, is more explicitly directed to a notion of the holy, of God as being (Marcel, 1951b, p. 187).

Dasein's freedom

As we saw in the previous section, *Dasein* tends to interpret itself in terms of the entities it is closest to. This takes on the form of the adoption of ways of being from the ways that 'They' behave (*BT*, sec. 27, p. 126). But there are existential experiences that can show that such interpretations of oneself involve a levelling of anything that is existentially important. As Kierkegaard had already noted, anxiety is such an experience. For Heidegger, anxiety is a state of mind characterizing the encounter of *Dasein* with the world as background of all the involvements that constitute what is meaningful for us (*BT*, sec. 40, pp. 186–7): in anxiety, *Dasein* finds that 'the world has the character of completely lacking significance' (*BT*, sec. 40, p. 186). Insofar as *Dasein* can, in anxiety, no longer interpret itself in terms of the world, anxiety reveals *Dasein's* freedom 'of choosing itself' (*BT*, sec. 40, p. 188).

We are, therefore, free to interpret our situation in different ways. Heidegger distinguishes between two ontologically relevant ways of being we can choose. *Dasein* can be in a way that displays an understanding of what it is to be *Dasein*, or, on the contrary, let its way of being follow the dictates of the 'They'. In both cases, *Dasein* is free, but in the first, authenticity, it chooses to choose (*BT*, sec. 54, pp. 268, 270). The resoluteness to be authentic (*BT*, sec. 59, p. 293) arises as a result of understanding what anxiety reveals, namely our lack of ground (which Heidegger connects with a notion of 'guilt' – *BT*, sec. 57, p. 277). Much of what

Heidegger has to say about authenticity has strong echoes of Kierkegaard, including the notion of 'situation' as the authentic way of being in the present. A key difference is the absence of a deity upon which the authentic attitude would be focused: authenticity involves rather a recognition of our finitude in being-towards-death (*BT*, sec. 53, p. 263). Another difference is that Heidegger is merely describing ways of being and strives to steer clear of any injunction to be authentic.

The first difference amounts to their being no guide as to how to live one's life authentically. There are, of course, conditions for authentic life, for instance, that one live with the certainty of death as that possibility which is one's own and cannot be taken away from one, but the notion of Being-towards-death hardly provides specific content to authenticity.[4]

The second difference is connected with the first: Heidegger is doing ontology, not ethics, and he resists the very possibility of giving ethical rules (which would also determine a specific content for the notion of authenticity); such rules 'would deny to existence nothing less than the very possibility of taking action' (*BT*, sec. 59, p. 294).

The question of whether this leaves any room for a Heideggerian ethics is a controversial one (Hodge, 1995). However, one comes down on this issue, it is clear that what interests Heidegger primarily is the ('existential') difference between authenticity and inauthenticity, insofar as the first reveals an understanding of *Dasein's* being: this difference is *ontologically* relevant. *Ontic* issues relating to the different specific ways ('existentiell') of being under one of these categories must take second place. Famously, of course, it is this order of priority which Levinas disputes, and completely reverses (Levinas, 1979).

The problem of reality

Finally, one may ask how Heidegger's take on reality is to be understood. On the one hand, a number of statements make Being dependent upon *Dasein* (*BT*, sec. 39, p. 183; sec. 43c, p. 212; sec. 69c, p. 365). On the other hand, Heidegger clearly claims that there are entities without *Dasein* (*BT*, sec. 43, p. 207). As a result, it appears difficult to classify Heidegger in either the idealist or realist camp.

Heidegger does, however, state that idealism is always a more promising route (*BT*, sec. 43, p. 207). The main problem with idealism for Heidegger is that, traditionally, it has not explained its understanding of Being. It, therefore, remains open, in principle, to view the light Heidegger sheds upon the understanding of Being as compatible with an idealist position. Thus, insofar as *Dasein's* Being has been interpreted as care in Division 1 of *Being and Time*, and that 'the ontological meaning of "care" is temporality' (*BT*, sec. 69c, p. 365), there is room for an interpretation of Heidegger's position as a temporal idealism (Blattner, 1999). The fact that, in more than one other publication, Heidegger appears to identify *Dasein* itself with time lends additional support to this view (Blattner, 1999, pp. 230–1).

The alternative is to understand Heidegger's position as a realist one, whereby the realism has to be defined carefully, so as to allow for the dependence of Being upon *Dasein*. This avenue has been pursued by a number of recent commentators (e.g. Dreyfus and Spinosa, 1999; Hoffman, 2000). It finds support in Heidegger's wanting to distance himself from the idealism of the neo-Kantian tradition which he took to lead to an unbridgeable gap between questions of validity and questions of being (*BT*, sec. 44a, p. 218; Friedman, 2000, p. 54).

Carman (2003) views Heidegger's investigation as a form of transcendental enquiry into conditions of intelligibility. This does not mean Heidegger is a transcendental idealist, but it does go some way to enabling a realistic interpretation of *Being and Time* to accommodate its claim of a dependence of Being upon *Dasein* (but cf. Onof, 2004, pp. 17–18). As there is no space to discuss this further, let us just observe that, since a reasonable case can be made for both realism and idealism, these traditional categories are arguably not adequate to capture the essence of Heidegger's position.

This brief survey of his ontology has shown how Heidegger takes it in an entirely new direction by returning to the original question of the meaning of Being. In so doing, he gives the first systematic interpretation of what it is to be human as that kind of being which has its being to be. One may question his exclusive focus upon this question of Being, as this arguably led to the neglect of other important issues (e.g. ethics). But his rich interpretation of the nature of *Dasein* is definitive of twentieth-century existentialist philosophy, and influenced both Sartre and Merleau-Ponty.

Sartre's For-Itself

In *Being and Nothingness*, Sartre did not follow Heidegger in identifying ontology with phenomenology: being, 'as phenomenon, requires a foundation which is transphenomenal' (1977, p. xxvi). First, although critical of Husserl's transcendentalization of phenomenology, Sartre did not adopt Heidegger's understanding of phenomenology. That is, on the one hand, Sartre does not adopt Husserl's Cartesian method of bracketing the world or endorse the notion of a transcendental ego constituting its world; and like Heidegger, he sought to move away from transcendental idealism. But, on the other hand, as Sartre's philosophical interests, unlike Heidegger's, were closely connected with psychology, he expands the field of Husserlian phenomenology (Moran, 2000, p. 363) by taking seriously what traditional philosophical systems had ignored as irrelevant, such as a whole range of emotions, anguish, and so on, to shed light on what it is to be a conscious being.

Second, Sartre does not adopt Heidegger's understanding of ontology, but opted for a speculative metaphysics that is, arguably, 'of a very traditional kind' (Moran, 2000, p. 385). He belongs to the broadly Cartesian tradition, which views the cogito as revealing a basic evidence: that I, as consciousness, exist. He explicitly criticizes Heidegger for his abandonment of the concept of consciousness: 'Understanding has meaning only if it is consciousness of understanding' (1977, p. 85). That is, self-consciousness is required for understanding.

Truth and the for-itself

Heidegger had it that, outside the world, there is nothing. But in effect, nothing for Heidegger is of interest as it is the locus of the encountering of Being, which lies beyond things, as a no-thing. Sartre adapts Heidegger's take on nothingness in a highly original way, which provides a cornerstone of his ontology. Nothingness is that which is brought into the world by the human subject.[5] Nothingness will in effect provide a way of introducing a place for subjectivity in the objective world, thereby enabling the traditional understanding of truth as objective, to be extended so as to take 'subjective truth' into account.

Sartre takes it that there are two forms of being. There is being in-itself, which characterizes all entities whose being is unproblematic: they are just what they are. On the contrary, human beings are characterized by the fact that they are a lack of being. Indeed, consciousness is an intentional relation to an object in which the subject is merely characterized as that which *is not* the object. And the imagination expresses this ability to negate by applying it to what is real.

The for-itself is thus characterized primarily through its power of negation, as that being which has Nothingness at its core. This power is manifested through the 'negative realities' ('négatités') that it creates (1977, pp. 9–11). These are, for instance, the absence of Pierre, or the gap between two portions of a straight line. In this way, Sartre shows a way of overcoming the subjective/objective divide by giving the for-itself a key role in defining what is real.

Although Sartre himself criticizes Heidegger for not providing an account of how nothingness comes about (1977, pp. 18–19), one might find Sartre's lack of explanation of why the negating and incomplete for-itself arises out of the inert and complete in-itself unsatisfactory.[6]

The for-itself and transcendence

In the same way as Heidegger views *Dasein* as having its being to be, Sartre's for-itself always transcends its own actuality. If Heidegger's transcendence is manifested in an understanding of Being, and, therefore, ultimately located in Being, Sartre remains faithful to the realist tradition in identifying the object as transcendent: consciousness is a relation to a transcendent object. This transcendence of the object parallels Heidegger's transcendence of the world. Sartre, however, differs from Heidegger in rejecting the notion of an understanding of Being that does not involve consciousness. For Sartre, consciousness, in its pre-reflective form, involves an immediate presence to oneself.

This has an important consequence: for reasons we shall examine below, reflective consciousness then constitutes an object, the ego (or the 'Psyche' in *Being and Nothingness*),[7] as the for-itself's transcendence. The ego, however, is not the for-itself, since it is constituted in reflection: such reflective self-consciousness has an opacity that contrasts with the transparency of the pre-reflective self-consciousness of the for-itself. In thus presenting his theory of the transcendence of the ego in the essay of that name, Sartre at first places himself in the Kantian transcendental tradition,[8] and responds to Husserl's appropriation of it in his transcendental phenomenology. Sartre accepts the Kantian requirement that it be possible for the 'I think' to accompany all my representations (2004, 3–4). But this transcendental condition does not require that a psychological entity, the ego, feature in an empirical consciousness, because it addresses Kant's *Quid juris?* rather than any *Quid facti?* question. That is, it is a justificatory function in accounting for the possibility of knowledge, but does not represent an actual cognitive process. Sartre understands Husserl as introducing a substantial notion of ego that is both at the core of consciousness (immanent), and defines a point of reference for the grasp of an objective reality (transcendent) (2004, pp. 9–11). Sartre wants to purify consciousness of any such notion of ego that would introduce opacity, and thus Sartre's ego transcends consciousness.

The difference between Heidegger and Sartre's understandings of transcendence, is thus that between, on the one hand, an openness that is a transcendence in Being, that is, in no-thing, and, on the other hand, the source of nothingness which transcends itself, and constitutes an object, the ego to hypostatize this transcendence. Both forms of transcendence are essentially temporal, and both view time as ecstatic. For Heidegger, time is primarily a condition for the very openness to Being of that way of being that is care. Sartre takes over the concept of 'projection' that forms one of the dimensions of care, and puts it at the heart of his account of the temporality of the for-itself. But for Sartre, 'this nothingness which separates human reality from itself is at the origin of time' (1977, p. 102). The more primordial role that Sartre gives to nothingness leads to an understanding of the for-itself as a project when this nothingness is viewed in its temporal form.

Sartre can identify the nature of this project (*projet fondamental*) insofar as he has characterized the for-itself as nothingness. As we saw above, this nothingness is experienced as a lack of being. Such a lack is manifested in the duality of facticity and transcendence that characterizes the for-itself (1977, p. 482). The for-itself is always already situated in a world in a way which is out of its control, so that it is not identical with this facticity (1977, p. 79): it *is not* in the mode of being what it is (i.e. the mode of being of the in-itself). The for-itself is also always ahead of itself insofar as it is transcendence (1977, p. 486): it *is* in the mode of not being what it is (i.e. in the mode of being a lack of in-itself). What the for-itself seeks is an identity with itself, that is, to be in the mode of being what it is. So the project characterizing the for-itself, and of which the reflective constitution of the ego is a manifestation (1977, p. 153), aims at the for-itself becoming an impossible for-itself-in-itself, that is, of taking on characteristics which, in traditional metaphysics, accrue to God: a self-grounded existing entity. This impossible identification of the for-itself with an object-ego would provide a substitute for God in traditional metaphysics (1977, p. 90).

Marcel (1951b, p. 183) criticizes this notion of transcendence as, in fact, merely 'horizontal'. For him, Sartrean transcendence is an impoverished form of transcendence, because it is directed to an object, that is, an (impossible) in-itself. As such, Marcel views Sartre's notion of transcendence as characteristic of contemporary thought, namely, its inability to go beyond the divide between a subject of knowledge and an object as studied by science, which for Marcel is characteristic of what he calls 'primary knowledge' (Marcel, 1940, p. 34). This may not be a fair criticism of Sartre,[9] but we shall see in the next section that there may be grounds for viewing the Sartrean notion of transcendence as insufficient even for his own purposes.

The freedom of the for-itself

More than any other twentieth-century philosopher, Sartre does justice to the emphasis of nineteenth-century thought on freedom, by having it as key characteristic of what it is to be a for-itself. For Sartre, the negating spontaneity of consciousness requires that the for-itself not be 'subject to the causal order of the world' (1977, p. 23). This means that the for-itself is free, and it is the awareness of this freedom that constitutes the experience of anguish for Sartre.

The freedom in question is absolute. The ethical consequence is that there are no 'excuses' for choosing any particular way of living one's life, as there are no limits to the individual's freedom. The problem with this notion of freedom is that it is not clear how a free act is to be distinguished from a random choice. Indeed, Sartre does not subscribe to any kind of belief-desire account of action. If we consider an act as motivated by an incentive, as such, it is only relatively free. The focus then shifts to the motivation for the act. For Sartre, such motivation is itself chosen by the agent, and it cannot itself be further motivated without entering a motivational regress. This choice is Sartre's absolute freedom

(1977, p. 450). Sartre exemplifies it by considering, in *Existentialism is a Human-ism*, an individual's choice between fighting for the Free French and looking after his ailing mother. These options are very distinct: on the one hand, enrol-ment in the French armed forces that were loyal to the anti-Nazi French govern-ment seated in London during the Second World War occupation of France; on the other, assistance to a close relative in need. There are, for Sartre, no a priori rules that can guide the individual in her choice: this is ultimately a choice of the values this individual wants to espouse.

There are, at least, negative guidelines for action. These lie in the avoidance of what Sartre singles out as the archetypal form of inauthenticity, *bad faith* (1977, p. 70; Sartre, 1964). Unlike Heidegger's notion of inauthenticity, the free choice of bad faith is morally condemnable (1970, pp. 84–5):[10] the moral dimen-sion of freedom means that it goes hand in hand with responsibility. Since Sar-trean freedom is absolute, this responsibility is complete: there are no excuses for being who I am. And insofar as my choice is a commitment, I am responsible to the whole of humanity (Sartre, 1970, p. 74).

Sartre's notion of freedom may, at first brush, be viewed in analogy to Kant's notion of transcendental freedom, but Kant's freedom finds its place within the duality of the empirical and intelligible perspectives upon action. That is, tran-scendental freedom accounts for action viewed independently of the temporal conditions of the empirical world. From this intelligible perspective, something like a first beginning can be understood (*Critique of Pure Reason*, A544/B572). Sartre does not have access to such a duality of points of view on human agency, and it is, therefore, difficult to reconcile his notion of freedom with our under-standing of the psychology of decision-making.

Sartre would reply that this conception of freedom is ontological, and dis-tinct from the usual empirical notion (1977, p. 483). Rather, freedom is ultim-ately identified with the being of the for-itself: 'To exist as the fact of freedom or to have to be a being in the midst of the world are one and the same thing' (1977, p. 486). This follows from the intimate connection between freedom and nothingness: nothing is the ground of freedom, a nothing that is 'made-to-be by the human being in his relation to himself' (1977, p. 34). It is the contingent necessity of having to be free. If we accept this understanding of freedom, one might still ask how it is possible for the for-itself to be, through its freedom, the ground of value. This is unclear, and this issue prompts another facet of Marcel's criticism of Sartre's notion of transcendence. The question here is that, if the for-itself is nothingness, how can it ground value? (Marcel, 1960, p. 39). For Marcel, Sartre's notion of freedom is rather like a commodity for which supply exceeds demand: it thus has no value. This problem, connected with Sartre's merely 'horizontal' understanding of tran-scendence, may account for Sartre's inability to finalize his reflections upon an existentialist ethics (Sartre, 1992).[11]

One might also observe that this problem is not unrelated to the issue flagged above of the absence of a satisfactory account of how the for-itself emerges from the in-itself. Would such an account of the origin of the for-itself be compatible with conceiving it merely as a nothingness? And if not, this might provide a way to ground for the value of freedom which Sartre places at the centre of his ethical reflection.[12]

The problem of reality

As we have seen above, Sartre's ontology presents characteristics typical of realism, for example, its account of being in-itself. But the Sartrean world also has idealist features in that the subject's spontaneity is constitutive of its negative features. Unlike Heidegger's case, however, the argument for taking Sartre as an idealist is much weaker, and Sartre explicitly claims that 'the for-itself *adds nothing* to being' (1977, p. 209). The primacy of being in-itself which is identical to itself and self-sufficient in its being suggests a form of realism. But Sartre is also dismissive of standard forms of realism (1977, p. 151). If one can talk of realism at all here, it must be of an extended realism that accommodates the subjective dimension of reality that existentialism is keen to put to the fore.

To make sense of how such an extension is possible, we must note that the constitutive role of the for-itself can be understood as Sartre's version of Husserl's constitution of reality by the transcendental Ego. Much as Sartre does away with Husserl's transcendental Ego, the spontaneity of the for-itself is constitutive of reality. This constitution happens at different levels. Unlike the static constitution of the given in Husserl's phenomenology, Sartre's constitution is preobjective, and thus does not define parts of the object (Besnier, 2000). Rather, it defines hierarchically ordered conditions of objectivity. Among them, pre-reflective self-consciousness is most fundamental, and different degrees of its nihilation constitute possibility, value, and so on. Finally, nihilation takes on a temporal form (1977, p. 104). In this way Sartre's realism can, to a certain extent, be understood in the tradition of transcendental philosophy (Gardner, 2009, pp. 80–3), but with an important difference from Heidegger: the primordial role of time in Heidegger's analysis is here replaced by that of nothingness at the heart of the for-itself. For Heidegger, the ultimate horizon for *Dasein* is time. For Sartre, it is his version of the cogito, that is, the nihilating for-itself, that is the basis of the constitution of its world.

Also, unlike Heidegger whose whole investigation in *Being and Time* can more straightforwardly be viewed as a transcendental enquiry, Sartre looks beyond the phenomenon to identify Being in-itself as that which underpins his whole ontology, that is, as that which is nihilated in the for-itself. Rather than transcendental questioning, it is psychological states such as nausea and boredom that reveal this being to us (Cabestan, 2004, p. 327).

Ultimately it should come as no surprise that existentialism, as exemplified in Heidegger and Sartre's writings, should not fit easily under either the idealist or the realist headings. This can be seen from the following brief considerations. Existentialism primarily aims to create a space for subjective truth. This would, prima facie, suggest an affinity with idealism. But idealism involves privileging the subjective viewpoint understood in a narrow sense in terms of the thinking subject. This understanding springs from the epistemological distinction between knowing subject and known object. And as a result, idealism has to deal with the question of how the subject knows there is a world of objects.

Existentialism rebels against this consequence of the epistemological bias of this view of the subject. The existentialist subject is, on the contrary, rooted in a world. For Heidegger, worldliness defines our way of existing, while Sartre starts his existential investigation with the being of things in the world. It is in the tears of the fabric of this being in-itself that consciousness is found. The indisputability of the existence of the world may draw an interpreter to a realist understanding of existentialist metaphysics, as we saw above. But the realist's reality is traditionally defined by fencing off anything subjective. Why? Again, it is the epistemological subject/object framework that is at work here. The object, as that which knowledge is about, is that whereby the subject reaches beyond the confines of his individual perspective. But in so doing, this understanding of reality leaves no room for the individuality of the subjective point of view.

So the epistemological subject/object divide underpinning the traditional dichotomy of realism and idealism is not suited to making sense of the declared ambitions of existentialism. Only a redefinition of these terms can accommodate existentialist metaphysics.

Conclusion

The brief investigation of this chapter has shown how twentieth-century existentialism inherited themes from nineteenth-century existentialist authors, and drew on phenomenology to redefine ontology and metaphysics around these themes. Existentialism wrestled with issues that first arose in post-Kantian philosophy, although without the Romantics' assumption of a notion of being providing a unified ground for both subject and object. The existentialist subject is typically cut loose from any ground, and the truth of its situation is the starting-point for existentialist metaphysics.[13]

While this subjective 'bias' can be questioned for its neglect of the role of rationality in shaping the world, existentialism provides important insights into how to construct an ontology that accommodates our subjectivity. Existentialism's main contribution to metaphysics is the light it has shed on what is characteristic of human existence, as contrasted with a general notion of being

(Schrader, 1967): to be an individual is not to be an instantiation of a type. It is a freedom with its own possibility of transcendence and its subjective truth. How these notions are defined and interrelated varies.

With Being defined as that which makes it possible for beings to appear in the world, Heidegger understands *Dasein* as a temporal openness to Being. Emphasizing being as that which always encompasses the situation we are in, and is, therefore, prior to the division between subject and object, Marcel understands human existence as originally marked by a thirst for being, one which can only be dulled by diverse forms of abstraction. On the contrary, with the being of self-sufficient material substance taken as primary, Sartre understands the for-itself as the source of nothingness, a disturbance in the plenitude of being in-itself that is a freedom seeking to ground itself in such being.

In these relations to being, a notion of truth emerges that lies beyond the traditional notion of objective truth in that human existence has a role in it. The metaphysics of these relations to being define new forms of transcendence that are distinct from the traditional relation to the divine. While freedom becomes a defining characteristic of human existence, it remains an open question to what extent the normative dimension that is minimally found in the requirement to nurture freedom, and maximally represented by ethical commands, can find an anchoring in existentialist ontology.

Notes

1. Insightful comments from Felicity Joseph, Jack Reynolds and Christian Skirke are gratefully acknowledged.
2. Thus Sartre draws attention to the fact that the Ego cannot be viewed as a subject endowed with predicates since, 'every new state produced by the Ego colours and nuances the Ego in the moment the Ego produces it' (Sartre, 2004, pp. 35–6). Sartre will thus propose the view that the Ego is a product of conscious reflection, rather than where it originates.
3. We may want to take a sympathetic stance to Heidegger's claim that scepticism about the external world does not arise as a problem, but nevertheless wonder about how something like the permanence of the 'world' can be accounted for merely through an impoverishment of the interpretative stance in *Dasein's* world (see Onof, 2005, pp. 226–7).
4. Here, there is a question over where the certainty of one's mortality originates, if not in an objective attitude (which Heidegger would consider inauthentic).
5. In so doing, Sartre rejects Heidegger's claim that there is some Being which grounds the fact that entities are (in themselves). Although Sartre recognizes that the being of phenomena is indeed an issue, this being is given with the phenomena, and is not to be considered as defining an ontological domain separate from the ontic. That is, 'the being of the phenomenon cannot be reduced to the phenomenon of being' (1977, p. xxv).

6. Once again, the connection to post-Kantian romantic philosophy is striking: as Gardner (2006) argues, Schelling addresses this very issue in his criticism of Fichte's attempt to derive his whole system from self-consciousness.

7. In *Being and Nothingness*, Sartre refines his theory of the transcendent psychological object (now called 'Psyche'). This is the result of impure reflection (1977, p. 155). Reflection itself is the attempt by the self to grasp itself as a unity (1977, pp. 153–4): this defines the project, as we shall see below. This attempt follows upon the instability of pre-reflective consciousness in which selfhood is, contradictorily, both a primordial unity, and a synthetic unity (1977, p. 77).

8. His understanding of the 'I' of apperception is however distinct from Kant's, and it has to be insofar as he does not endorse transcendental idealism (Sartre, 2004, pp. 5–7). That is, Sartre takes the 'I' to be an infinite contraction of the ego (Sartre, 2004, p. 8). The 'I think' should, for Sartre, now be viewed as impersonal (Sartre, 2004, p. 5). In *Being and Nothingness*, Sartre abandons his references to transcendental philosophy, but the general thesis about the ego remains.

9. This criticism overlooks the important Sartrean contribution to the understanding of consciousness, namely the notion of the transparency of consciousness in its pre-reflective mode; it also amounts to a crude interpretation of the in-itself.

10. Moreover, Sartre accommodates practical rationality, but in such a way that reasons are not prior to, but emerge together with free choice (1977, pp. 445ff.). Reason provides no independent guide to action.

11. Gardner (2009, pp. 195–7) proposes the outline of a proof by elimination that freedom must be the value pursued by beings whose existence is understood as nihilating freedom. Although this broadly Kantian approach is convincing as it stands, it is not clear that it can provide a ground for an ethics without equivocating over the notion of freedom. The argument appears valid if ontological freedom is what is at stake. But for an action guiding value, it seems that a practical notion of freedom, that is, empirical freedom is required.

12. Again, Schelling's thought presents us with an example of such a grounding of the value of freedom (Schelling, 1936, pp. 40, 78–80).

13. From within the existentialist movement itself however, Marcel stressed the need to separate the primary reflection characteristic of a scientific approach to a desubjectivized world, from a secondary reflection in which subject and object are no longer torn apart (Marcel, 1960, p. 93). In this way, Marcel echoes a century and a half later the insights that originally emerged from Hölderlin and Novalis's speculation. Marcel emphasizes the central role of a notion of being, a notion which he similarly characterizes in a preobjective fashion. He refers to the mystery of being (Marcel, 1960): being is something we cannot grasp insofar as we participate in it.

Bibliography

Besnier, B. (2000), 'Le Problème du movement', in J.-M. Mouillie (ed.), *Sartre et la Phénoménologie*. Fontenay-aux-Roses: ENS Editions, Theoria.

Blattner, W. (1999), *Heidegger's Temporal Idealism*. Cambridge: Cambridge University Press.

Cabestan, P. (2004), *L'Etre et la Conscience*. Bruxelles: Ousia.

Camus, A. (2000), *The Outsider*. London: Penguin.

Capelle, P. (1998), *Philosophie et théologie dans la pensée de Martin Heidegger*. Paris: Cerf.

Carman, T. (2003), *Heidegger's Analytic: Interpretation, Discourse and Authenticity in Being and Time*. Cambridge: Cambridge University Press.

Crane, T. (2005), 'Review of "Mind Time: The Temporal Factor in Consciousness"'. *Times Literary Supplement*, January 14.

Dahlstrom, D. O. (2001), *Heidegger's Concept of Truth*. Cambridge: Cambridge University Press.

Dostoevsky, F. (1992), *Notes from the Underground*, ed. Philip Smith, correcting a 1918 translation by Constance Garnett. New York: Dover Publications.

Dostoevsky, F. (2000), *Crime and Punishment*. Ware: Wordsworth Editions.

— (2004), *The Brothers Karamazov*. London: Vintage.

Dreyfus, H. L. (1991), *Being-in-the-World. A Commentary on Heidegger's Being and Time, Division I*. Cambridge, MA: MIT Press.

Dreyfus, H. L. and C. Spinosa (1999), 'Coping with Things-in-Themselves: A Practice-Based Phenomenological Argument for Realism'. *Inquiry* 42 (1): 49–78.

Frank, M. (1975), *Der unendliche Mangel an Sein*. Frankfurt: Suhrkamp.

Friedman, M. (2000), *A Parting of the Ways. Carnap, Cassirer, and Heidegger*. Chicago: Open Court.

Gardner, S. (2006), 'Sartre, Schelling, and Onto-Theology'. *Religious Studies*, 247–71.

— (2009), *Sartre's Being and Nothingness*. London: Routledge.

Hegel, G. W. F. (2002), *Science of Logic*, London: Routledge.

Heidegger, M. (1979), *Nietzsche, Vol. I: The Will to Power as Art*, trans. David F. Krell. New York: Harper & Row

— (1988), *Being and Time*, trans. J. Macquarrie and E. Robinson. Oxford: Blackwell.

— (1996), 'The Question Concerning Technology', in D. F. Krell (ed.), *Basic Writings*. London: Routledge, pp. 311–41.

— (1998), *Kant und das Problem der Metaphysik*. Frankfurt am Main: Vittorio Klostermann.

Hodge, J. (1995), *Heidegger and Ethics*. London: Routledge.

Hoffman, P. (2000), 'Heidegger and the Problem of Idealism'. *Inquiry* 43 (4): 403–11.

Husserl, E. (1967), *Cartesian Meditations*, trans. D. Cairns. The Hague: Nijhoff.

— (1970), *Logical Investigations*, trans. J. N. Finlay. London: Routledge.

— (1982), *Ideas Pertaining to a Pure Phenomenology and to a Phenomenological Philosophy – First Book: General Introduction to a Pure Phenomenology*, trans. F. Kersten. The Hague: Nijhoff.

Jaspers, K. (1956), *Philosophie*. Berlin: Springer.

Kierkegaard, S. (1968), *Concluding Unscientific Postscript*, trans. D. F. Swenson. Princeton: Princeton University Press.

— (1983), *Fear and Trembling. Repetition*, ed. and trans. H. V. Hong and E. H. Hong. Princeton: Princeton University Press.

— (1992), *Either/Or: A Fragment of Life*, ed. and trans. A. Hannay. London: Penguin.

Levinas, E. (1979), *Totality and Infinity: An Essay on Exteriority*. Dordrecht: Kluwer.

— (1995), *The Theory of Intuition in Husserl's Phenomenology*, trans. A. Orianne. Evanston, IL: Northwestern University Press.

Libet, B. (1985), 'Unconscious Cerebral Initiative and the Role of Conscious Will in Voluntary Action'. *Behavioral and Brain Sciences* 8: 529–66.

Marcel, G. (1940), *Du refus à l'invocation*. Paris: Gallimard.

— (1951a), *Homo Viator*, trans. Emma Cranfurd. Chicago: Regnery.

— (1951b), *The Mystery of Being*, vol. II, trans. R. Hague. London: Havill Press.

— (1960), *The Mystery of Being*, vol. I, trans. G. S. Fraser. London: Havill Press.

Merleau-Ponty, M. (1962), *Phenomenology of Perception*, trans. C. Smith. London: Routledge.

— (1968), *The Visible and the Invisible*, ed. and trans. C. Lefort. Evanston, IL: Northwestern University Press.

Moran, D. (2000), *Introduction to Phenomenology*. Abingdon: Routledge.

Nietzsche, F. (1968), *The Will to Power: In Science, Nature, Society and Art*, trans. W. Kaufmann and R. J. Hollingdale. New York: Random House.

— (1978), *Thus Spoke Zarathustra*, trans. R. J. Hollingdale. London: Penguin.

— (1998), *Twilight of the Idols: Or How to Philosophize with a Hammer*, trans. D. Large. Oxford: Oxford University Press.

Onof, C. (2004), 'Review of Taylor Carman's "Heidegger's Analytic"', *Philosophy in Review* 24 (1): 17–19.

— (2005), 'Hermeneutic Conditions and the Possibility of Objective Knowledge', in K. Boudouris and K. Kalimtzis (eds), *Philosophy, Competition and the Good Life*, vol. II. Athens: Iona Publications.

Pattison, G. (2000), *Routledge Philosophy Guidebook to the Later Heidegger*. London: Routledge.

Sartre, J-P. (1964), *Nausea*, trans. L. Alexander and R. Howard. New York: New Directions.

— (1970), *L'Existentialisme est un Humanisme*. Paris: Nagel.

— (1977), *Being and Nothingness*, trans. H. E. Barnes. London: Methuen.

— (1992), *Notebooks for an Ethics*, trans. D. Pellauer. Chicago: Chicago University Press.

— (2004), *The Transcendence of the Ego. A Sketch for a Phenomenological Description*, trans. A. Brown. London: Routledge.

Schelling, F. W. J. (1936), *Of Human Freedom*, trans. J. Gutmann. Chicago: Open Court.

— (1995), *Schelling's Philosophy of Mythology and Revelation*, trans. and reduced by V. C. Hayes. New South Wales: Armidale.

Schleiermacher, F. D. A. (1988), *On Religion. Speeches to Its Cultured Despisers*, trans. R. Crouter. Cambridge: Cambridge University Press.

Schrader, G. A. (ed.) (1967), *Existential Philosophers. Kierkegaard to Merleau-Ponty*. New York: McGraw-Hill.

Tugendhat, E. (1970), *Der Wahrheitsbegriff bei Husserl und Heidegger*. Berlin: De Gruyter.

4 Existentialism and Politics

David Sherman

Delineating the relationship between existentialism and politics is no straight-forward task. Just what 'existentialism' signifies is not entirely clear, who quali-fies as an existentialist is a matter of contention, and the theoretical frameworks of those philosophers most often associated with existentialism substantially differ. Furthermore, none of the 'existentialists' were political philosophers in any classical sense, and to the extent that they wrote about or engaged in polit-ics, their positions ran the gamut from fascism to Marxism.

Despite their many differences, what the existentialists did share, crudely, was a concern with the plight of the individual in the modern age, and the political positions (theoretical or practical) of the existentialists were primarily shaped by the way in which their philosophical frameworks made sense of this defining problem. Now, at first blush, this 'problem' seems to be a false one; after all, modernity's primary concern is (at least nominally) with the individ-ual. Although the rise of the modern individual is only one aspect of modernity – the rise of the nation-state, the market economy and reason (as exemplified by the natural sciences) are all part and parcel of it – each of these commitments relates back, at least ideologically, to the idea of the free, self-determining indi-vidual. The cornerstone of political legitimacy, as it is reflected in social contract theory, is individual consent; the cornerstone of the market economy is the indi-vidual entrepreneur, who seeks his own interest and thereby serves the interest of all, as if, in Adam Smith's words, guided by an 'invisible hand'; and the ground of reason itself, from René Descartes's 'natural light' through Immanuel Kant's subject of pure reason (theoretical or practical) resides, first and fore-most, in the individual. In each of these cases, although the free, self-determin-ing individual is primary, there is also, at least ideally, a seamless reconciliation within the larger whole, whether it be the nation-state, the market economy or the domain of reason itself.

Still, by the middle of the nineteenth century it became increasingly clear that modernity's commitment to the individual was fundamentally problem-atic. The belief that in the end this commitment (at least to the extent that it had played out socio-historically) was ideologically motivated increasingly took hold: although nominally serving as the ground and justification of the nation-state and the market economy, modernity's conception of individuality, many came to suspect, was actually driven by the demands of these massive social institutions, which did not facilitate so much as overwhelm the free, self-determining individual. So, too, it was recognized that by supplanting the religious world-view, which was inherently meaningful and purposive, the scientifically based modern world-view had left this individual in a spiritual quagmire: the question 'free and self-determining for what?' could not be easily answered, as even secularized, humanistic values could not stand up to the rigors of a scientifically based rationality. Finally, it came to be recognized that even as an ideal, the abstract conception of morality that was offered by modernity was incoherent. As G. W. F. Hegel had suggested earlier in the century, whether viewed from an epistemological or ethical standpoint, human beings, as Aristotle had claimed, are *zoon politikon* (political animals) and must be understood, first and foremost, in terms of their social world. It was Hegel's aim to make good this insight and, more broadly, legitimize the social institutions of the modern world, but without sacrificing the uniquely modern commitment to the free, self-determining individual, or what he called 'the right of subjectivity'. Still, although Hegel offered a devastating critique of the excessively abstract notion of individuality that had pervaded modern thought, his effort to make good a more concrete notion of 'the right of subjectivity' was much less successful; the free, self-determining individual was swallowed whole by Hegel's 'system'. At the beginning of the *Phenomenology of Spirit*, the individual is told 'to forget himself, as the nature of Science implies and requires' (1977, p. 45), and in the *Philosophy of Right*, what is demanded of the individual is not even Aristotelian virtue but, rather, rectitude, the fulfilling of one's obligations as dictated by one's station in life and, more broadly, the social institutions of one's world (Hegel, 1952).

Hegel's philosophy is a springboard for existentialism, both negatively and positively. To be sure, his emphasis on the social totality rather than the individual, as well as his putative emphasis on 'knowing' rather than 'existence', provoked both Kierkegaard (directly) and Nietzsche (at least indirectly, by way of Arthur Schopenhauer). Nevertheless, without his attempt to make good, at least in some sense, a notion of concrete subjectivity in response to the abstract conception of individuality offered up by the liberal enlightenment tradition, existentialism might not have come into existence. Kierkegaard insists that, like Hegel, he is a dialectical thinker, and he sets forth an 'existential dialectic'; Nietzsche, like Hegel, asserts that the way in which individuals come to know the world is conditioned by the same set of factors that make them who they are; and, with the exception of Camus, it could be argued that Hegel's thought impacted on all of the twentieth-century existentialists. Crucially, therefore, it must be understood that while the existentialists all looked to redeem the individual in the face of Hegel's system, none simply reverted to the abstract, liberal concept of individuality that Hegel had critiqued. In this sense, notwithstanding the fact that liberalism and existentialism have a shared commitment to the individual, Alasdair MacIntyre's (1997) depiction of existentialism – in particular, his depiction of Kierkegaard, Nietzsche and Sartre – in largely liberal terms is not right. Although the existentialists differed with respect to the significance of such concepts as absurdity, anxiety (*Angst*), authenticity, choice, commitment and responsibility, these are concepts with which they all grappled, and they grappled with these concepts because, in contrast to liberalism, they did aim at a full-blooded conception of the individual.

It is for this reason that the relationship between existentialism and politics is much more problematic than the relationship between liberalism and politics. Although there are significant differences between classical liberalism and contemporary liberalism – not the least of which is the tendency of contemporary liberalism to embrace a thoroughgoing proceduralism grounded in neo-Kantian commitments that would have troubled classical liberals – liberalism *as such* has always been concerned with reconciling individuals both within and to the larger society, with relatively little concern for the substantive nature of that reconciliation. (To put the matter differently, liberals have historically attempted to bracket questions of 'the good' in favour of questions of 'rightness'.) In contrast, as reflected by the constellation of concepts set forth above ('authenticity' perhaps most of all), existentialists have always been concerned with substantive questions concerning the individual, and (with the possible exception of Kierkegaard) the larger society, because they recognize that individuals are largely the stuff of their social world. Crucially, this gives rise to a basic ambiguity: to be 'authentic' is, in some sense, to be self-possessing in the very sort of way that the existentialists' recognition of the social constitution of the self would seem to all but preclude. It is here that a (perhaps *the*) basic tension between existentialism and politics resides: what could it mean for an individual who is the stuff of his social world to assert himself qua *himself* in the face of that world? From what quarter does the stuff of the more authentic self come? If there is a more authentic self, how can the individual epistemically bootstrap himself into a position in which its contours could be glimpsed, much less realized? And, finally, along more explicitly political lines, what could political legitimacy possibly mean if authenticity is the ideal? Isn't the very sort of (relative) unanimity that could confer legitimacy, or, indeed, serve as the polis's condition of possibility, fundamentally at odds with individual authenticity? These are the sorts of questions that play out in complex, and largely problematic, ways among the existentialists.

Kierkegaard, Nietzsche and the Rise of Power Politics

The relationship between Kierkegaard and Nietzsche, who were the nineteenth-century forerunners of existentialism (if not the first existentialists themselves), is an ambivalent one. At first blush, it would appear that the fundamentalist Christian and the self-styled 'Antichrist' had very little in common. As Karl Löwith, among others, has suggested, however, Kierkegaard and Nietzsche shared more than this basic difference suggests: both emphasized 'the individual' in opposition to 'the herd', and both were, more generally, penetrating critics of contemporary society; both privileged the passions in opposition to the rationalism of the German philosophical tradition, from which, nevertheless, both heavily drew; and, finally, notwithstanding their opposing standpoints on Christianity, they basically agreed on the nature of Christianity as it was being practiced by their contemporaries in nineteenth-century Europe, which is to say that both viewed modern Christianity (or what Kierkegaard contemptuously called 'Christendom') as, in essence, a social club for the indolent. Still, when considering the relationship between each of them and politics, from which both abstained (with the possible exception of Kierkegaard's well-known 'Corsair affair'), it is their philosophical differences that are defining, and, sociopolitically, these differences point in different directions.

To be sure, in addition to the affinities set forth above, both Kierkegaard and Nietzsche, at least superficially, had a taste for the conservative, if not downright reactionary, politics of a bygone era. Moreover, both have contemporary advocates who seek to show that, notwithstanding their actual pronouncements on the matter, their politics were more radical than these pronouncements imply, a position that has some merit but can be overdone. Nevertheless, bracketing for a moment the question of whether Kierkegaard and Nietzsche were politically radical, liberal or conservative, which arguably plays into the kind of modern schematization of which both were contemptuous, the fact remains that their differences on the question of subjectivity placed them in diametrical opposition, and, on the political question, these differences are dispositive. Generally speaking, for Kierkegaard, the self-styled 'champion of subjectivity', a religiously inspired 'interior' is to be privileged in opposition to the profane external world (Hegel's putative terrain), and, therefore, the political question is inessential; consequently, at least intrinsically, his thought tends towards political quietism. Conversely, for Nietzsche, who embraced a *Lebensphilosophie* of sorts and, in so doing, viewed such notions as 'subjectivity', 'interiority' and 'depth', with a great deal of suspicion, political questions are essential; nevertheless, because his thought is not up to the task of delineating political objectives, it intrinsically tends towards political decisionism. Still, in the final analysis, although Kierkegaard and Nietzsche asymmetrically move towards opposed standpoints with respect to the question of political praxis, what they shared politically is a nuanced concern for 'the individual' in the face of modern 'power politics', of which both were trenchant critics.

Along these lines, Kierkegaard's contempt for 'power politics' is reflected in the sharp distinction that he draws between 'the quantitative' and 'the qualitative', a distinction that directly tracks the equally sharp distinction that he draws between, on the one hand, the political and economic realms, and, on the other hand, the religious realm. According to Kierkegaard, the political and economic realms are characterized, first and foremost, by the triumph of the purely quantitative, and his antipathy towards these realms arises from the fact that they level the kinds of qualitative distinctions that he takes to be essential and that, in his view, can only be realized in the religious realm. In his battle with the paper the *Corsair*, for example, Kierkegaard laments that 'there is no room for the harmony of category relations but only the rattle of money in the cash box' (Marsh, 1995, p. 203), and in terms of the relationship between the political and religious realms, he declares: 'Political and religious activities have an inverse relation. Political action is concerned with having the masses on its side; religious action attempts to have God on its side and therefore it can disregard the force of number.' Given his own commitments (and the commitments to which he attempts to seduce his readers), he, therefore, reasonably concludes: 'I have to serve a religious cause, and above all, to keep myself away from politics and from political considerations' (quoted in Nicoletti, 1992, p. 184). Although there are many scholars who are loathe to do so, Kierkegaard should be taken at his word here. This is not to say that his religious thought does not have political implications (which, indeed, I shall now discuss); it is to say that these political implications, which must be viewed in terms of his essentially religious comportment, are derivative, or, as suggested above, 'inessential'.

By virtue of his antipathy towards the purely quantitative, or, as he states it, 'the force of number', Kierkegaard may reject the majoritarian principle that underlies liberal democracy, but, crucially, he does not reject straightaway its fundamental principles. The French Revolution's 'liberty, equality, and fraternity' all find some form of expression in his religiously based point of view, and, moreover, the primacy of 'the individual', the nominal touchstone of liberal democracy, is clearly his touchstone as well. What Kierkegaard does reject are the notions of 'liberty, equality, and fraternity', as well as the prerogatives of 'the individual', as they are manifested in liberal democracy. In essence, he believes, the liberal democratic form overrides the religious realm politically as Hegel's system had overridden it ontologically and overrides individuality by levelling it, thus precluding (rather than facilitating) the possibility of individual authenticity. For Kierkegaard, liberty or freedom, the existence of which is attested to by anxiety, should be understood morally and existentially rather than politically; equality, quite simply, should be understood as the equality of all people 'before God'; and fraternity should be understood as the loving of one's Neighbour, but this love, too, which assumes equality, is invariably 'before God'. Finally, even as Kierkegaard privileges 'the single individual', he explicitly rejects the idea that this, his defining category, ought to be viewed in political terms: ' "the individual" is the category of spirit, as opposite to politics as is indeed possible' (quoted in Kirmmse, 1992, pp. 176–7).

To the extent that Kierkegaard's religious point of view abstracts from the everyday particulars that constitute 'the individual' and, moreover, the political society of which 'the individual' is a part (see Mackey, 1962), his approach has a certain affinity with liberalism. But while liberalism eschews all talk of 'the good' in favour of 'rightness', Kierkegaard moves in the other direction (virtually) eschewing all talk of what can at most be only relatively good, the institutions of a profane external world based on purely quantitative considerations, in favour of what is absolutely good, the religious perspective, which is based on purely qualitative considerations. Thus, in contrast to the liberal point of view, Kierkegaard's religious point of view furnishes him with a standpoint of critique with respect to mass culture, power politics and the liberalism of which they are, in some sense, an expression. But furnishing a theoretical space for an ideological critique of some unspecified sort and making good either a political philosophy or some articulable standpoint for the purpose of engaging in political action are entirely different matters, and for this reason I find advocates of the idea that Kierkegaard offers either a political philosophy or at least some basis for political action unpersuasive. The relationship between Kierkegaardian inwardness and a profane external world, the purely qualitative and the purely quantitative, and, ultimately, the religious and the political, is one of radical incommensurability. For this reason, Kierkegaard's interventions, as in 'the *Corsair* Affair', cannot be understood 'politically', if by this we mean an intervention in the external world for the purpose of actually moving it towards religious guideposts; rather, his interventions are basically 'negative' in that they are, and can only be, intended to hold open a space for the radically incommensurable (inwardness, the purely qualitative, and, ultimately, the religious) instead of actually making a political mark.

In the end, there is no basis for religiously informed political action in Kierkegaard's thought because such action invariably does violence to the religious: it sets in motion a dynamic whose ultimate consequence is either Hegel's 'system', in which Spirit is explicitly secularized, or an empty religiosity, in which the religious implicitly takes on the very qualities of the profane world against which it nominally sets itself (consider the way in which religious fundamentalism has manifested itself in American power politics). It is for good reason, then, that Kierkegaard referred to the 'disastrous confounding of politics and Christianity' (Kirmmse, 1990). Of course, the Christian who 'inwardly' sets himself apart is still, in some form or other, of the world and has some view of politics, if only from a distance. What are the politics of this individual? It would seem that this individual would be of the political world. The 'knight of faith', Kierkegaard tells us, could be mistaken for the tax collector: he can fully – indeed, passionately – participate in life just as he finds it because he knows that he will be redeemed in the end, which is where his passion is ultimately directed. Otherwise, the particulars of this life, political and otherwise, are inessential, and to the extent that one dwells on them, the opportunity cost on Kierkegaard's account is, quite literally, infinite.

According to Nietzsche, whose focus is on life as we encounter it, this is the essence of nihilism, and it is the depreciation of this life (even if lived passionately) against which he sets himself. However, just what 'this life' actually means is open to question. To be sure, Nietzsche rejects all 'two-world' philosophies, whether Platonic or Christian, for such philosophies give short shrift to *our* world, or life as such, in favour of a 'true' or 'real' world; much beyond this, however, there are ambiguities concerning how deeply Nietzsche wants to sink us into 'this life'. Nietzsche surely does not mean that each of us must affirm every moment of the lives that we individually live, which a literal interpretation of his doctrine of eternal recurrence would suggest; and, far more significantly, he surely does not mean that we must affirm the general framework of collective life as it is presently constituted, which would also mean affirming that to which he is opposed, modernity, or at least the nihilism that he takes to be intrinsic to its current stage. This problem of distance – that is, the critical standpoint that we assume with respect to life as it is presently constituted – is one with which Nietzsche self-consciously grapples, and it is Zarathustra's most nettlesome problem. In opposition to Kierkegaard, the problem is not justifying an 'infinite' distance but, rather, any distance at all, for a critical, reflective stance pulls one out of the flow of life (as neo-Nietzschean philosophers such as Jean-François Lyotard emphasize).

Like Kierkegaard, Nietzsche is hostile towards power politics – his productive years more or less coincided with the reign of Bismarck's Reich – but the realm that he is concerned with protecting against its encroachment is not religious but, rather, cultural (see Ansell-Pearson, 1994). Intrinsically, the relationship between culture and politics for Nietzsche is much more entangled than the one between religion and politics for Kierkegaard because politics is an unavoidable fact of 'this life', and, invariably, there will be at least some 'confounding' of culture and politics. This is clearly reflected in Nietzsche's 'early' period. (It is generally taken to be the case that Nietzsche's thought traverses three more or less distinct periods: a 'romantic' period; a 'positivistic' period; and a mature period, which includes his most penetrating critiques of morality and reason.) In *The Birth of Tragedy*, which is the heart of his early period, Nietzsche wistfully looks to the ancient (pre-Socratic) Greeks, for whom the relationship between culture and politics was nowhere near as problematic as it is for us. Still under the sway of Schopenhauer's metaphysics, and, therefore, preoccupied with the 'horrors of existence', Nietzsche viewed ancient Greek society as an organic whole that was well positioned to enable its citizens to deal not just with political matters but also with existential matters, which were interrelated to a far greater degree than they were in Nietzsche's time, not to mention today. The culture of the ancient Greeks, Nietzsche claimed, was inspired by a 'pessimism of strength', and tragedy functioned both psychologically and politically: psychologically, it enabled the polis to effectively sublimate life's horrors, whereas, politically, it performed a reconciling function. More importantly for our purposes, because ancient Greek society was hierarchically ordered on the basis of the aristocratic virtues, it was politically structured to enable the very best to flourish, which is a commitment that Nietzsche retained throughout his career. Although he rejected any historical account that smacked of teleology, he thought that the goal of political society *should be* facilitating the achievements of its highest types. Nietzschean individualism is, therefore, of a distinctly illiberal kind.

Although Nietzsche's unswerving commitment to some form of aristocratic individualism conflicts with modernity's liberal socio-political conceptions, he becomes interested in the modern form of the problem of political legitimacy during his middle period, his positivistic period, in which his sympathy for modernity's commitments hits its high point. There are two factors, in particular, that account for this new-found interest. First, Nietzsche comes to view his earlier preoccupation with the ancient Greek polis in nihilistic terms, as it reflects a nostalgia for what is long gone that is not entirely unlike the Christian's eschatologically driven preoccupation with what (allegedly) will be; and, second, Nietzsche comes to genuinely appreciate certain aspects of modernity itself, such as its experimental style, and, more specifically, the type of critical reasoning that inheres in the natural sciences, which he prefers to the dogmatism of the religious world-view that had been supplanted. Accordingly, Nietzsche now aims to make sense of modernity in its own terms, and although he rejects its universalistic pretensions in regard to both the individual and reason itself, he recognizes that these commitments require the justification of political authority in a different way, one in which political authority is neither self-justifying nor justified by its grounding in a larger religious world-view. For this reason, Nietzsche looks at the issue of political legitimacy more thoroughly in his positivistic period than in either his romantic period or his mature period, which is characterized by a more comprehensive disenchantment with the modern project, thus rendering the problem less compelling for him.

Human All Too Human is the most representative of Nietzsche's positivistic works, and in a short chapter of the book titled 'A Glance at the State' he deals more extensively with the justification of political authority than anywhere else in his corpus. In 'A Glance at the State', Nietzsche offers some remarkable insights with respect to the issue of political authority's justification, but these insights are more diagnostic than prescriptive. The principal problem, as Nietzsche sees it, is that political authority can only be justified by religion or, at the very least, a venerable tradition, neither of which have very much traction in modern society. As to the latter, he asserts in a section titled 'Arbitrary Law Necessary' that 'where law is no longer tradition, as is the case with us, it can only be commanded, imposed by constraint . . . so we have to put up with arbitrary law, which is the expression of the necessity of the fact that there has to be law' (Nietzsche, 1986, sec. 459). It is Nietzsche's contention that an impartial, rationally based law is actually more, rather than less, arbitrary for having these features, and that without the imprimatur of a long-standing tradition with which those subject to the law identify, the law itself can have no genuine legitimacy. Of course, Christianity had been the 'tradition' that had dominated European life for more than a millennium, and in a passage titled 'Religion and Government', Nietzsche says that as religious belief subsides the state itself will appear increasingly arbitrary. 'Without the assistance of the priests even now no power can become legitimate', he declares, but as the diversity of opinion intrinsic to democratic principles gets the upper hand, religion will necessarily become a private affair and politicians will factor it less and less into their deliberations, which, in turn, will cause a backlash by the religiously inclined, who will become irreparably hostile to the state. This will lead to a battle for the state, but the damage will have already been done: the state's legitimacy will be undermined from the standpoint of all concerned and it will be absorbed by purely private concerns, which is emblematic of the decay of the state under democratic principles (Nietzsche, 1986, sec. 472).

Despite these gloomy (but rather prescient) prognostications, Nietzsche, as already indicated, does not simply repudiate modern politics during his positivistic period; instead, he only aims to carve out a space for those who are superior to it. In a segment that nicely captures his general attitude towards (what he sees as) 'the demagogic character' of democratic politics, he states that 'there is little to be objected to, always presupposing that this narrow-mindedness does not go so far as to demand that *everything* should become politics in this sense, that *everyone* should live and work according to such a standard' (Nietzsche, 1986, sec. 438). As Nietzsche moves into his last period, however, this tolerance goes by the wayside. What is needed, he comes to believe, is nothing less than a revaluation of all values, and in this regard he sets his sights on the modern project itself, which, in essence, he takes to be a secular continuation of nihilistic Christian principles. During this period, Nietzsche aims to reveal the true content of modernity to itself by examining its highest values, and he does this by demystifying them. Perhaps, the best example of this is *On the Genealogy of Morality*, in which he reveals the less than noble (indeed, slavish) beginnings of morality to show that what we call morality, whether in its religious (Judeo-Christian) or secular (Kantian deontology) form, arises from particular types of people with particular interests, and that it serves these interests to formulate *their* morality (i.e. the morality that best suits their limitations) in universal form. By making clear that there is no 'one size fits all' morality, Nietzsche hopes to open up possibilities for higher types, who should not be constrained by it (which is not to say that he countenances all of the actions that conventional morality proscribes). Ultimately, it is this concern that motivates Nietzsche, and in the service of these higher types he calls for 'a great politics'; but, crucially, he never tells us what the content of this great politics should be. What Nietzsche does continue to discuss are the shortcomings of the political views of his day, most notably socialism, liberalism and nationalism, his posthumous *mis*appropriation by the Nazis notwithstanding. These political forms represent, Nietzsche believes, a deep-rooted, festering resentment that would, at best, level culture in accordance with a vulgar egalitarianism, and, at worst, seek retribution in frighteningly destructive ways.

Heidegger, Nazism and the Crisis of Modernity

While the Nazis sought to appropriate Nietzsche for their purposes, Heidegger, who many regard as the most important philosopher of the twentieth century, sought to appropriate Nazism for his own purposes. Just how to make sense of Heidegger's involvement with the Nazis in the early 1930s is no straightforward matter, and there are many conflicting interpretations. Following the war, there was a push to 'de-Nazify' Heidegger, a push whose spur included some of the leading lights of French existentialism, many of whom had drawn on Heidegger's philosophy and were inclined to vouch for him. As the facts concerning Heidegger's involvement with the Nazis began to come to light, however, maintaining his innocence was no easy task, but many still argued that his philosophy could be insulated from his political transgressions. Yet, by the 1960s, the claim could be heard that Heidegger's personal transgressions could not so easily be separated from his philosophy, as is perhaps best reflected in Theodor Adorno's claim that Heidegger's philosophy is 'fascist in its innermost cells'; and, in the 1980s, with the publication of even more detailed historical works in both France and Germany, Heidegger's unsavoury relationship to the Nazis was brought home even more forcefully (Farias, 1989; Ott, 1994). More recently, however, there has been a push to reassess what has been called 'the Heidegger controversy'. The argument in favour of this reassessment holds that there might have been a rush to judgement, and that with the passage of time we are in a better position to dispassionately make sense of Heidegger's involvement with the Nazis (Sluga, 1993; Young, 1997).

Even those (reputable) scholars who are inclined to reassess Heidegger's relationship to the Nazis do not dispute the factual charges that have been brought against him. What is undisputed is that Heidegger successfully lobbied the Nazis for the rectorship of Freiberg University; that, at least during the

71

mid-1930s, he would regularly curry favour with the Nazi Party; that he would often spout the Nazi line, notoriously telling an assemblage of German students, for example, that 'the *Führer* alone is the present and future German reality and its law' (Wolin, 1991, p. 47); and that he would justify the Nazi program on philosophical grounds that appeared to correspond to his own philosophical commitments, stating, for example, that the Nazi program was 'linked to Being' because the German nation is 'in the center of the Western world' and, therefore, has a 'historical mission' that the Nazis will bring to fruition. The push to reassess the Heidegger controversy, which goes both to the personal and the philosophical dimensions of his relationship to the Nazis, essentially takes the following form: Heidegger's personal involvement was undoubtedly nasty, but he has been unjustly singled out for his involvement when many (non-Jewish) philosophers collaborated with the Nazis, and in far more pernicious ways. Placed in both the historical context and the context of his larger life, Heidegger's personal shortcomings, which ought not be given short shrift, must not be blown out of proportion either. So, too, Heidegger's philosophy, which concerned itself with the question of origins in the face of a rootless modernity, does not stand in a fundamental relationship to Nazism, and it is better understood as the continuation of a long-standing romantic tradition in which a people, their language and their customs are emphasized, a tradition that has strong resonances today in certain forms of communitarianism (see Young, 1997).

Making sense of Heidegger's politics philosophically is complicated. His philosophical works do not explicitly consider political issues, and attempts to tease out their political implications can easily give rise to unwarranted inferential leaps, or at least so his defenders have maintained. However, given both the relative constancy of Heidegger's philosophical problematic and its ongoing influence, it is important to make sense of his politics not only for philosophical reasons, but also for historical reasons. Now, to hold that Heidegger's philosophical problematic remains relatively constant is not to say that he does not embellish different aspects of it for political profit, but it is to say that the central categories of his philosophy remain basically the same. Thus, from his 1927 masterpiece *Being and Time* through such late essays as 'The Question Concerning Technology', 'The Turning' and 'Discourse on Thinking' (all published in the 1950s), Heidegger's primary concern is with recovering 'the meaning of Being', which, he maintains, has been covered over by the Western metaphysical tradition since the pre-Socratics. This commitment remains constant, and the only philosophical concession that Heidegger seems to make to his association with the Nazis, and, indeed, the fact of Nazism more generally, is that he shifts from humankind's forgetfulness of Being in his earlier works to its abandonment by Being in his later works. Of course, for those who seek some acknowledgement by Heidegger (philosophical or otherwise) of the exceptionally malignant nature of Nazism, this philosophical concession comes to little; in fact, by shifting the locus of agency from human beings to Being, Heidegger pardons himself, the Nazis, technocrats and Western meta-physicians in equal measure, which is merely the reverse side of condemning all in equal measure, as he does in a postwar correspondence with his former student, Herbert Marcuse. So, too, although Heidegger subsequently repudi-ated what Nazism had become, he never repudiated his judgement as to its initial promise. In his 1935 lecture 'An Introduction to Metaphysics', he refers to 'the inner truth and greatness of [the National Socialist] movement (namely, the encounter between global technology and modern humanity)' (Heidegger, 2000, p. 213), and he reproduces this passage in its entirety in the work's 1953 publication. Given that what is enclosed within the parentheses *is* one of the staples of both his philosophy and the Nazi platform, and, furthermore, that on philosophical grounds he continued to agree with the Nazis into the mid-1930s, well after they had made clear the general direction of their program, it would certainly seem that there is a disposition in Heidegger's philosophy to fascist politics, and that the real question concerns the strength of this dispos-ition. His philosophy could either entail National Socialism, or some other equally fascistic politics, or it could merely be consistent with a range of polit-ical positions, with Nazism representing only the most virulent extreme. Either way, the most important evidence, I believe, is to be found in *Being and Time*, which is the conceptual core of his corpus.

In *Being and Time*, Heidegger sets forth what he calls an 'existential analytic of *Dasein*' ('being-there'). *Dasein* refers to human beings, and by articulating the deep structures of *Dasein*, which pertain to *Dasein* by virtue of its very existence, Heidegger aims to reveal the fundamental nature of being human, which goes towards revealing the meaning of Being for *Dasein*. Fundamentally, Heidegger maintains, human beings are not subjectivities, and they do not objectify them-selves or their world, as the dualistic subject–object paradigm at the heart of the metaphysical tradition would have it; instead, human beings are always already engaged in the world, which is a unitary phenomenon that he captures with the phrase 'being-in-the-world'. Furthermore, the world of which *Dasein* is a part is a world in which *Dasein* is with others, and this world, the particular community in which an individual is raised ('thrown' in Heidegger's terminology), is consti-tuted in the most elaborate ways by the always already existing rules of these others. For Heidegger, this has positive and negative implications: the rules of the community are the very condition of intelligibility, given that they orient *Dasein* to the world in the most fundamental ways, but they also level individuality, and, therefore the term that he uses to characterize this rule-engendering collective is *das Man*, 'the One', which refers to both everybody and nobody in particular. For *Dasein* to unthinkingly 'do as (the) one does' is to live an inauthentic existence, but for *Dasein* to live an authentic existence, for it to make its life its own, neces-sarily involves some continuing relationship to the community.

73

It is at this juncture that things get tricky, for if authentic *Dasein* is neither a free-floating 'I', as Heidegger puts it, nor one with *das Man*, what is the nature of this relationship? Heidegger says that *Dasein* must resolutely take hold of the situation into which it has been thrown, but towards what end should this resoluteness be geared? The universal objective, of course, is to recover the meaning of Being, but how does this indeterminate imperative translate into a highly determinate political context? This problem, which goes to what has been called the 'heroic voluntarism' of *Dasein*, is a problem of finding adequate criteria for action, and the concern is that without these criteria the end becomes the act of heroic self-assertion itself and, ultimately, the triumph of the will. Now, while Heidegger would reject the very idea of criteria, preferring instead to speak of an openness to the situation and to others, he does see the problem, and towards the end of *Being and Time* he states that the necessary orientation derives from one's heritage. Of course, heritage itself, without more, would appear to be little more than a prior instantiation of *das Man*, and for this reason Heidegger offers up the notion of an *'authentic* historicality', which is not burdened by what is modern and is committed to the resolute 'repetition of the possible'. This orientation still underdetermines matters, however. Even Heidegger's staunch conservatism would not have authentic *Dasein* repeat the past in every way that it possibly could, which means that promoting heritage as a basis for action only pushes the indeterminacy problem back a step. Nevertheless, even if heritage could orient authentic *Dasein*, another problem comes to the fore: Heidegger's emphasis on heritage smacks of a severe cultural and moral relativism. For Heidegger, there is nothing external to the rule structure of a community that can legitimate or delegitimate it. On what basis, then, could the heritage of a community be called into question, even if that heritage entails, or is consistent with, fascism? For Heidegger, reason, 'that most stiff-necked adversary of thought' (Heidegger, 1977, p. 112), is no more up to the task than those who would dissent from the majority's take on what the people's heritage entails.

In *Being and Time*, Heidegger never considers ethics (or, for that matter, politics) in a philosophical way because he believes that ethics (and, presumably, politics) rolls out of the ontology that he offers, a belief that came to be evinced in his own ethico-political commitments. Heidegger was faced with a unique situation in the mid-1930s, and he saw himself as resolutely seizing the moment to take on nothing less than modernity itself so as to reconstitute Germany's cultural heritage. His actions, at least to this extent, find support in his masterpiece. Yet, as his defenders contend, politics for Heidegger should have been subordinated to the cultural imperative, and Heidegger did have the megalomaniacal notion that as the representative of the German cultural tradition he should and would 'lead the leader' (*den Führer zu führen*) (Sluga, 1993, p. 172). Thus, whatever else his reactionary philosophical impulses entail, they do not *directly* entail a totalitarian state. So, too, by all accounts, although Heidegger was a cultural chauvinist, he was not an anti-Semite or racist, and there is nothing in *Being and Time* that suggests this sort of view. But, crucially, just where Jews and other minorities would have fit into his reconstituted German cultural heritage is by no means clear, and where cultural minorities would fit into the fundamental role that a people's heritage plays in *Being and Time* is no clearer. Even Heidegger's staunchest defenders see him as a cultural totalitarian of sorts, and this kind of totalitarianism is in evidence in *Being and Time* (Young, 1997, pp. 47–8). Whether Heidegger's philosophy entails a fascistic politics (if not Nazism as such) or is only consistent with it would thus seem to depend on whether, and to the extent which, cultural totalitarianism entails a totalitarian state.

French Existentialism, Cold War Politics and the Problem of Political Praxis

The French existentialists were a politicized lot. They were all, at least to some extent, involved in the French Resistance (most of all Camus, who editorialized for, and served as editor-in-chief of, the underground Resistance newspaper *Combat*), and they were all involved in a variety of leftist political causes during the postwar era. They were all political essayists, and a magazine founded by Sartre, de Beauvoir and Merleau-Ponty, *Les Temps Modernes*, deals, in no small part, with political matters. Moreover, they all produced books that examined both political theory and contemporary politics. Merleau-Ponty's *Humanism and Terror*, published in 1947, argues that the Soviet Union should be given the benefit of the doubt despite the existence of its labour camps, while *Adventures of the Dialectic*, published in 1955, signifies his withdrawal of this conditional support on both theoretical and practical grounds. Four years earlier, in 1951, Camus had attacked the Soviet Union on both theoretical and practical grounds in *The Rebel*, and this had set off a notorious public battle that put him at odds with much of the French intellectual Left. In 1960, Sartre published the massive *Critique of Dialectical Reason*, which takes up the challenge of Merleau-Ponty's *Adventures of the Dialectic* by trying to comprehend nothing less than the movement of history, and its second volume largely deals with Stalinism and the Soviet Union. And, finally, de Beauvoir's *The Second Sex*, published in 1949, is the seminal work of French feminism, and it came to be one of the most influential works in feminist politics.

Although, theoretically, the French existentialists were all relatively close on the political spectrum, it was the exigencies of *realpolitik* that, with the exception of the relationship between Sartre and de Beauvoir, turned erstwhile friends into enemies. Theoretically, all would have supported a political arrangement in the vicinity of democratic socialism, or some form of anarcho-syndicalism, but, practically, this was not a viable option, and what actually separated the French existentialists was the complexities of the theory–practice problem (i.e. how to make sense of the relationship between theory and practice for the purpose of forging political *praxis*). Indeed, after the War, in a brief historical moment when French intellectuals thought that France might chart its own political destiny, Sartre and Camus joined the Revolutionary Democratic Union, a worker organization that offered a 'third way' (i.e. one that would conform to neither the American capitalist nor Soviet Communist political models); however, the organization was infiltrated by agents on the CIA payroll, equally strong pressure was brought to bear from Soviet supporters, and the organization collapsed under the weight of cold war politics. Much the same could be said of the relationship among the French existentialists.

Even in 1947, Merleau-Ponty acknowledges the deep authoritarian strain implicit within Stalinism (if not Leninism) and, more concretely, the ruthlessness of the Soviet regime in connection with its forced industrialization and political show trials; nevertheless, in *Humanism and Terror*, he takes the position that the Soviet Union is not yet beyond redemption in terms of its animating Marxist goals. The book was occasioned, in no small part, by a former Communist supporter turned hard line anti-Communist, Arthur Koestler, who had published influential literary and political works attacking Soviet communism (most notably *Darkness at Noon* and *The Yogi and The Commissar*). Although Merleau-Ponty disagrees with Koestler's factual conclusions concerning the nature of the Soviet Union, his criticisms focus primarily on the standpoint from which Koestler initiates his critique, the detached standpoint of universal humanism. For Merleau-Ponty, 'universality is only conceived, it is not lived', and universal humanism's endorsement of non-violence merely reinforces the existing institutionalized violence, which accrues to the benefit of the international capitalist order. Humanism, in other words, must be made concrete, and in terms of history this means that 'there is no absolute neutrality or objectivity'. This suggests, moreover, that values, and, indeed, freedom itself, must be understood in terms of our ongoing historical practices (the context in which they arise in the first place) rather than in consciousness or the will, which is in keeping with Merleau-Ponty's view in the *Phenomenology of Perception*. Koestler thus 'forgets what he should have kept from his Communist past – the sense of the concrete – and keeps what he should have forgotten – the disjunction between the inward and the external'. It is Merleau-Ponty's position that it is only when the Soviet Union's 'compromises cease to be Marxist and become opportunistic' (which is to say when its actions are no longer oriented towards the more radical humanism to which Marxism is committed) that support for it should be withdrawn (Merleau-Ponty, 2001, pp. 116, 39, 169, 150).

Merleau-Ponty's willingness to continue to give the benefit of the doubt to the Soviet Union in the mid-1940s infuriated Camus, and an earlier version of

Merleau-Ponty's analysis of Koestler's works, which was published the year before in *Les Temps Modernes*, had occasioned a clash between them. Camus disliked both Soviet communism and American capitalism, and although he also disliked Koestler's anti-Communist line (because the term 'anti-Communist' signified that one was aligned with the United States), he was moving towards a universal humanist position, the very position for which Merleau-Ponty had reproached Koestler. (Camus's view is reflected in the title of the collections of essays on which he was then working, *Neither Victims nor Executioners*.) After this clash, Camus distanced himself from Sartre, de Beauvoir and Merleau-Ponty, and in 1952, when *Les Temps Modernes* harshly reviewed *The Rebel*, Camus's break with his former friends was complete. This break was highly publicized, and in terms of the final confrontation between Camus and Sartre, it was Sartre who was judged to have gotten the better of it at the time. In the light of subsequent historical events, however, there are many who argue that it was Camus who had actually been right.

In *The Rebel*, Camus does not analyse the particulars of Soviet communism so much as the form of institutionalized violence that it exemplifies, and what he finds so striking about this violence (as opposed to, say, the 'irrational' violence of Nazism) is the way that philosophy is used to justify it. For Camus, the modern age is defined by 'crimes of logic' that assume the form not only of rightness but of necessity, murder is rationalized, and judgement thereby becomes clouded. As a result, he seeks to return to first principles, and the first principles that he aims to articulate relate to the question of political action itself, or, as he puts it, whether innocence can act in the pursuit of justice without committing murder. Of course, over 300 years earlier, Descartes had searched for epistemic first principles, and it is no coincidence that Camus does the same in the ethico-political domain; indeed, Camus's earlier philosophical essay, *The Myth of Sisyphus*, had famously put forth the concept of 'The Absurd', which grows out of the Cartesian problematic. As for Descartes at the end of the *Second Meditation*, there is, for Camus, consciousness and the world, but unlike Descartes, who proceeds to bridge the gap between the *cogito* and the world by way of God, Camus, an atheist, leaves the problematic right there: there is nothing to bridge the gap between consciousness and an indifferent world, the meaningfulness of life is thereby called into question, and the crucial philosophical question becomes whether to commit suicide. Rather than choose suicide, however, Camus argues in favour of what he calls 'metaphysical rebellion', a protest at our fate that has existential implications. In *The Rebel*, he shifts from this absurdity-suicide pairing to the rebellion-murder pairing, arguing that it is from the meaninglessness of the Absurd, which (like Descartes' evil genius) wipes the slate clean, that rebellion must first get its bearings. This means that rebellion must find its first principles within itself and that whatever principles it generate must be viewed in terms of the groundlessness engendered by the

Absurd, which calls for ethico-political modesty. Camus's first principle, his *'cogito'*, 'I rebel, therefore we exist', holds that by protesting unjust conditions, the rebel protests in the name of universal human values: 'Man's solidarity is founded on rebellion, and rebellion, in its turn, can only find its justification in this solidarity' (Camus, 1984, p. 22).

Camus goes on to paint with a broad brush, recounting, along separate lines, the histories of both metaphysical and historical rebellion. Crucially, it is Camus's position that 'the death of God', which is at the core of metaphysical rebellion, is also at the core of historical rebellion, and that history reflects humankind's attempt to ascend to His empty throne. He asserts that 'revolution is only the logical consequence of metaphysical rebellion'; that revolutionaries seek God's crown 'in the realm of time, and, rejecting God, choose history with an apparently inevitable logic'; and that revolution, 'which claims to be materialist, is only a limitless metaphysical crusade'. From the perspective of what he calls Mediterranean moderation, Camus attacks (with the exception of Nietzsche) the German philosophical tradition since Hegel for seeking 'totality' in history rather than a more modest 'unity' of human beings, and he argues that Soviet communism is the zenith of this historical drift, in which the ethical is entirely subordinated to the political and thus goes by the boards. Ultimately, then, Camus rejects virtually all murder as inconsistent with rebellion, and what his principle of moderation counsels is 'the mutual recognition of a common destiny and the communication of men between themselves', or more simply the principle of dialogue (Camus, 1984, pp. 105–8, 283).

As was the case with Merleau-Ponty's critique of Koestler, Sartre charges Camus with assuming a standpoint above the fray, but he articulates this standpoint in terms that are particular to Camus's thought rather than in terms of a more indiscriminate universal humanism. According to Sartre, Camus's contention that the Hegelian–Marxist tradition absolutizes history is symptomatic of the eternal standpoint that he privileges, the standpoint of the absent God, and in privileging this standpoint he makes injustice eternal and effectively gives short shrift to all socio-historical injustices, with the exception of those that run afoul of the universal values once underwritten by God. In contrast to Camus's metaphysical standpoint, it is Sartre's position that we are always already immersed in the socio-historical realities, that freedom must, therefore, be understood in immanent rather than transcendent terms, and that the concrete actions we take construct rather than obscure universal values (see Sherman, 2009, pp. 173–84). Ironically, at the very time that Sartre and Camus were engaging in this battle, Merleau-Ponty was coming to the conclusion that the Soviet Union was no longer entitled to the benefit of the doubt, particularly given recent revelations concerning the existence of Soviet labour camps. (Accordingly, he tried to convince the author who reviewed *The Rebel* to moderate his review before its publication.) The final straw for Merleau-Ponty was the

Soviet Union's role in the Korean War, and in *Adventures of the Dialectic* he asserts that his 'wait-and-see Marxism' in *Humanism and Terror* is no longer supported by objective historical conditions, and that he had been wrong in his earlier work to think that Soviet Marxism could remain true as a theoretical critique of capitalism even as its practices violated Marxist precepts: 'This in itself shows well enough that we were not on the terrain of history (and of Marxism) but on that of the apriori and morality'. Merleau-Ponty thus calls for a new non-Communist Left (although where within the objective historical constellation of the time it was to be found is less than clear), and, not unlike Camus in *The Rebel*, he speaks in favour of parliamentary practices, since 'Parliament is the only known institution that guarantees a minimum of opposition and of truth' (Merleau-Ponty, 1973a, pp. 227–32).

In a chapter titled 'Sartre and Ultrabolshevism', which constitutes almost half of *Adventures of the Dialectic*, Merleau-Ponty launches a widespread attack on Sartre's thought. To begin with, he attacks Sartre's *The Communists and the Peace* (which initially appeared in *Les Temps Modernes*) on political grounds. In *The Communists and the Peace*, Sartre asserts that he will maintain his theoretical independence from the Communist Party, but he justifies his continuing support for it along classical vanguardist lines, arguing, in essence, that the Party is indispensable for realizing genuine working-class (and thus human) aims. Since Merleau-Ponty believes that these aims no longer inhere in the existing socio-historical field, however, he takes Sartre's support for the Party to be wholly unjustified by the facts on the ground. Furthermore, although Sartre's philosophical commitment to individual freedom in *Being and Nothingness* is at odds with Soviet vanguardism and its belief in the historical inevitability of communism, he contends that Sartre's subjectivism and Soviet objectivism are equally authoritarian, and thus can converge on means despite their philosophical differences. According to Merleau-Ponty, Sartre's authoritarianism can be traced back to the absolute, asocial freedom that he accords to consciousness, which is able to make of its world what it will. Put rather crudely, much as Sartre had argued that Camus privileged the absent standpoint of God in his Cartesian problematic, which gave rise to his political quietism, Merleau-Ponty argues that Sartre privileges the freedom of the Cartesian *cogito* in its relation to the world, which gives rise to his political actionism. For his part, although also beginning with the Cartesian problematic, Merleau-Ponty emphasizes neither 'men' nor 'things' but what he calls 'the interworld, which we call history, symbolism, truth-to-be-made' (Merleau-Ponty, 1973a, p. 200).

Sartre's distinction between consciousness and the world (natural and social) does constitute the core of his phenomenological ontology in *Being and Nothingness*, and it is the basis for his 'absolute freedom' thesis, namely, that human beings are always free to choose. Yet, crucially, Sartre rejects the Cartesian notion that consciousness is a substance that stands over and against the natural world, and, moreover, he emphasizes that the social world both provides the stuff of our egological commitments and conditions our practical freedom. For this reason, in my view, Merleau-Ponty, along with a host of others, overdoes his attack on Sartre's concept of freedom (Sherman, 2007). What's more, Sartre's philosophy was evolving, and with the publication of *Search for a Method* and, especially, *The Critique of Dialectical Reason* less than five years later, he offers a more mediated framework: praxis (human action), motivated by need and confronting omnipresent scarcity, and the practico-inert (the socio-historical field), comprised of the intended and unintended consequences of all prior praxes, dialectically inform one another in a much more fluid way than the relationship between consciousness and the world in *Being and Nothingness*. Sartre's moves here are, in no small part, prompted by Merleau-Ponty's criticisms, and although he cannot finally make good his attempt to think through the meaning of history itself, he offers, in opposition to the petrified dialectic of Soviet Marxism, a model that can make sense of both the subjective and the individual in history, thereby opening up spaces that harbour the theoretical possibility of historical change. Of course, practically, these changes were not in the cards, and after the Soviet Union's brutal repression of the 1968 uprising in Czechoslovakia, which was unreservedly backed by the French Communist Party, he rejected both. Still, 1968 was also the year of the French student uprisings, and Sartre continued to throw in his lot with Marxism, supporting, in particular, the French Maoists, whom, he thought, rejected Soviet vanguardism in favour of a political approach based on the spontaneity of the masses. Finally, near the end of his life, well after structuralism and poststructuralism had supplanted existentialism in France, Sartre appears to move towards an anarchist position (Sartre, 1981, p. 21), seeing this as the political form most in accord with his commitment to a society of free human beings.

Conclusion

The existentialists had diverse philosophical frameworks and divergent political commitments, which suggests that there is no existentialism *as such* and that there is no essential relationship between existentialism and politics. Although the existentialists were unified by a concern for the plight of the individual in the modern age, they had divergent perspectives on modernity itself, the 'without which not' of existentialism. These perspectives, and the philosophical frameworks in which they were embodied, were dispositive in terms of the politics that each of the existentialists embraced. To comprehend their respective political commitments, therefore, it is necessary to consider how each of their distinctive philosophical frameworks stands in relation to the ideals of modernity itself. Generally speaking, the French existentialists all see modernity as a stalled project that must be brought to fruition through the concretization of these ideals, whose continuing abstractness they take to be the stuff of bourgeois ideology, and what divided them was not their substantive political visions but the fashion in which each deciphered the theory–practice problem in their polarized socio-historical context. Heidegger, in sharp contrast, sees modernity as more or less misguided in the first instance, and whatever relationship his philosophy seems to bear towards modernity's ideals must be interpreted in the light of this more basic rejection: even his commitment to the individual itself is problematic, given his rejection of what Hegel calls 'the right of subjectivity', and it is no accident that his cultural totalitarianism leaves little room for the political privileges accorded to the modern individual, his commitment to the authentic individual notwithstanding. Finally, Kierkegaard and Nietzsche were more or less ambivalent in terms of modernity, either explicitly (Kierkegaard) or implicitly (Nietzsche) embracing 'the right of subjectivity' (which is why Heidegger calls Nietzsche 'the last metaphysician') but otherwise rejecting its political and cultural institutions, given their shared hostility to mass society, which both saw as part and parcel of the modern project. Much more could obviously be said here, but what the existentialists ultimately did share was a commitment to exposing the fundamental aporias of modernity, of which all were penetrating critics.

Bibliography

Ansell-Pearson, K. (1994), *An Introduction to Nietzsche as Political Thinker*. Cambridge: Cambridge University Press.

Camus, A. (1984a), *The Myth of Sisyphus and Other Essays*, trans. J. O'Brien. New York: Vintage Books.

— (1984b), *The Rebel: An Essay on Man in Revolt*, trans. A. Bower. New York: Vintage Books.

De Beauvoir, S. (1973), *The Second Sex*, trans. H. M. Parshley. New York: Vintage Books.

Descartes, R. (1993), *Meditations on First Philosophy*, trans. D. Cress. Indianapolis: Hackett Publishing.

Farias, V. (1989), *Heidegger and Nazism*, trans. P. Burrell and G. Ricci. Philadelphia: Temple University Press.

Hegel, G. W. F. (1952), *Phenomenology of Spirit*, trans. T. M. Knox. Oxford: Oxford University Press.

— (1977), *Phenomenology of Spirit*, trans. A. V. Miller. Oxford: Oxford University Press.

Heidegger, M. (1962), *Being and Time*, trans. J. Macquarrie and E. Robinson. New York: Harper & Row.

— (1977), 'The Word of Nietzsche: God is Dead', in W. Lovett (ed.), *The Question Concerning Technology and Other Essays*. New York: Harper & Row.

— (2000), *Introduction to Metaphysics*, trans. G. Fried and R. Polt. New Haven: Yale University Press.

Kirmmse, B. (1990), '"This Disastrous Confounding of Politics and Christianity": Kierkegaard's Open Letter of 1851', in R. Perkins (ed.), *International Kierkegaard Commentary: The Corsair Affair*. Macon, Georgia (GA): Mercer University Press.

— (1992), 'Call Me Ishmael – Call Everybody Ishmael: Kierkegaard on the Coming-of-Age Crisis of Modern Times', in G. B. Connell and C. S. Evans (eds), *Foundations of Kierkegaard's Vision of Community: Religion, Ethics, and Politics in Kierkegaard*. Atlantic Highlands, New Jersey (NJ): Humanities Press.

MacIntyre, A. (1997), *After Virtue: A Study in Moral Theory*. N University of Notre Dame Press.

Mackey, L. (1962), 'The Loss of the World in Kierkegaard's Ethics'. *The Review of Metaphysics* 15: 4.

Marsh, J. L. (1995), 'Kierkegaard and Critical Theory', in M. J. Matustik and M. Westphal (eds), *Kierkegaard in Post/Modernity*. Bloomington, IN: Indiana University Press.

Merleau-Ponty, M. (1973), *Adventures of the Dialectic*, trans. J. Bien. Evanston, IL: Northwestern University Press.

— (2001), *Humanism and Terror*, trans. J. O'Neill. Boston: Beacon Press.

Nietzsche, F. (1986), *Human All Too Human*, trans. R. J. Hollingdale. Cambridge: Cambridge University Press.

— (1994), *The Birth of Tragedy: Out of the Spirit of Music*, trans. S. Whiteside. Harmondsworth: Penguin.

Nicoletti, M. (1992), 'Politics and Religion in Kierkegaard's Thought: Secularization and the Martyr', in G. B. Connell and C. S. Evans (eds), *Foundations of Kierkegaard's Vision of Community: Religion, Ethics, and Politics in Kierkegaard*. London: Humanities Press.

Ott, H. (1994), *Martin Heidegger: A Political Life*, trans. A. Blunden. London: Fontana Press.

Sartre, J-P. (1956), *Being and Nothingness: An Essay in Phenomenological Ontology*. trans. H. E. Barnes. New York: Washington Square Press.

— (1981), 'Interview with Jean-Paul Sartre', in P. A. Schilpp (ed.), *The Philosophy of Jean-Paul Sartre*. La Salle, IL: Open Court.

— (1991), *Critique of Dialectical Reason: Theory of Practical Ensembles*, vol. 1, trans. A. Sheridan-Smith. New York: Verso.

Sherman, D. (2007), *Sartre and Adorno: The Dialectics of Subjectivity*. Albany, NY: SUNY Press.

— (2009), *Camus*. London: Wiley-Blackwell.

Sluga, H. (1993), *Heidegger's Crisis: Philosophy and Politics in Nazi Germany*. Cambridge, MA: Harvard University Press.

Wolin, R. (1991), *The Heidegger Controversy*. New York: Columbia University Press.

Young, J. (1997), *Heidegger, Philosophy, Nazism*. Cambridge: Cambridge University Press.

5 Existentialism, Psychoanalysis and Psychotherapy

Douglas Kirsner

Existentialism and psychoanalysis are often seen to be in opposition. However, although there are surely differences, existentialism, psychoanalysis and psychotherapy all share a common quest, problematic, and terrain. This shared domain addresses fundamental questions as to the nature of the human condition, including issues such as anxiety, choice, responsibility, alienation, freedom, agency, life, death, relationships, experience and subjectivity. They investigate ethics: the question of how best to live, given the nature of human subjectivity. The existential response to the past century's record of massive and rapid change and unsettling of verities, including religion in the West, meld clearly with the same problems that psychoanalysis and psychotherapy address.

As Rollo May suggested, the attitude that existential analysis was 'an encroachment of philosophy into psychiatry, and does not have much to do with science' was 'partly a hang-over of the culturally inherited scars from the battle of the last of the nineteenth century when psychological science won its freedom from metaphysics' (May, 1958, p. 8). The period around 1913 when Karl Jaspers published his classic *General Psychopathology* reflected a turning point in psychiatry, which had mainly been entrenched in biological paradigms. Now taking account of the 'whole person', psychiatry was becoming 'fundamentally historic and temporal, interpersonally orientated, and affirming of human freedom' (Wertz, 2006, p. 402). The idea that social or sexual maladjustment were no longer deemed sufficient to explain psychological illness was an important seed for the existential psychology movement. This movement arose spontaneously in different parts of Europe with diverse contributors sometimes unaware of each other's work.

R. D. Laing credited Eugène Minkowski (1885–1972) with being the first psychiatrist to have seriously attempted to 'reconstruct the other person's lived experience' (Laing, 1963, p. 207). Minkowski, drawing on Henri Bergson, created the expression 'lived time', which refers to being able to differentiate past, present and future, and of the priority of time over space. He also stressed the importance of meeting reality through 'vital contact', again reflecting Bergson's *élan vital* (see Spiegelberg, 1972, pp. 243–6).

Two main schools of psychotherapy were founded by existentialists: one by followers of Heidegger, and one by followers of Sartre. Swiss psychiatrists Ludwig Binswanger and Medard Boss were the two major Heideggerian figures, while Scottish psychiatrist and psychoanalyst R. D. Laing followed Sartre (although he also drew from other figures including Martin Buber, Rollo May and Heidegger). There was also Logotherapy, an existential therapy founded by Viktor Frankl, highlighted in the title of his well-known 1946 book, *Man's Search for Meaning*, which was an account of his experiences in a Nazi concentration camp where he found a 'will to meaning', which in life was the foremost human urge. According to him this concept went way beyond his Viennese compatriots Nietszche ('will to power') and Freud ('will to pleasure') (Frankl, 2006).

Ludwig Binswanger (1881–1966), the founder of the major approach in existential psychiatry, observed that the existential movement in psychiatry arose from rejecting the idea that psychiatry should deal just with 'mentally ill man' rather than with 'man as such'. It was based on Heidegger's idea that man was not to be explained by any theory, whether mechanistic, biological or psychological (May, 1958, p. 3). It dealt with human nature itself, which meant that illness needed to be understood at least partly in terms of human agency. Some of the main concepts Binswanger adopted from Heidegger were the *Umwelt*, *Mitwelt* and *Eigenwelt* (the physical, social and personal worlds).

Medard Boss (1903–1990) extended Heidegger's concepts of past, present and future as primary Heideggerian 'existential structures'. From this he elaborated his main existential concerns of human space and time (i.e. shared rather than individual existence), the body projecting itself forth, and the use of associations to describe a mood or 'attunement'. He understood dreams as reflective of one's state of being, the way that certain aspects of life are illuminated or not, rather than as representing specific unconscious wishes or archetypes. In general, for Boss, we do not so much interpret the world as have it reveal itself to the light of *Dasein*. Light and darkness are central metaphors: psychopathology is a choice to live in darkness, and therapy brings enlightenment of an aspect of life that has not previously been illuminated.

American psychologist and psychoanalyst Rollo May (1909–1994) made a substantial contribution to the dissemination of existential ideas in the Anglophone world. He introduced English-speaking readers to the ideas of continental thinkers beyond Sartre (who was already known via the route of his novels and plays). In 1958 May, together with Ernest Angel and Henri Ellenberger, edited a landmark book, *Existence*, that introduced the existential–phenomenological psychology of Binswanger, Minkowski and others to the United States. The book included translations of Binswanger's 1946 groundbreaking articles, 'The Existential Analysis School of Thought' (1946) and 'The Case of Ellen West' (1944) (May et al., 1958). May's influence was such that he is often referred to as the father of existential psychotherapy. May's ideas often overlapped with Binswanger, but he wanted to reconcile existential psychology with humanism and Freudian psychoanalysis in the United States. He introduced new and reframed some existing existentialist concepts, as is revealed from the titles of his best-selling books, including *Love and Will*, *Power and Innocence*, *Freedom and Destiny*, *The Courage to Create*, and *The Discovery of Being*.

R. D. Laing (1927–1989) argued for greater social intelligibility of schizophrenia, not for a complete explanation in social terms. Laing preferred the dentist to use his or her scientific 'look' in examining his teeth, but emphasized the inappropriateness of the exclusive use of such a 'look' by a doctor at childbirth. The emphasis on the primacy of experience is as a redress to simply looking at outcomes or effects. As Laing argued in *The Divided Self*, science deals with what is appropriate to it. So the science-based art of dentistry, for example, studies teeth and their relation to the mouth. But the study of a mental illness deals with the attributes of mind, however 'mind' is defined. This does not imply Descartes's total separation of mind and body, which function on different principles. Laing was a psychiatrist who always assumed a role for biology, and was influenced by Maurice Merleau-Ponty's more holistic position that we are 'embodied subjects'.

A science, as Laing pointed out, deals with the area appropriate to it. Understanding human actions properly begins from a standpoint of a 'science of persons', as first outlined in *The Divided Self*. This starting-point is the apprehension of the personal, as a self-acting agent who always chooses, whether he or she likes it or not. Laing's commandment: Always treat a person as an agent, a choosing being, not a thing. The point of view of Martin Buber's 'I–thou' division as opposed to 'I–it' is central in *The Divided Self*, and it continued to underpin Laing's further work. If we treat somebody as a 'thou', they are likely to behave very differently from if we treat them as an 'it'. This view was at the root of Laing's critique of psychiatry, which so often treated persons as processes instead of agents.

Nonetheless, in this, as in so much else, Laing essentially follows Sartre. Laing kept very careful and copious notes on his minutely detailed reading of *Being and Nothingness*. Laing, together with his anti-psychiatry colleague David Cooper, summarized three major later works of Sartre as *Reason and Violence*. Like Sartre, Laing's approach starts from the existential–phenomenological premise that consciousness is always consciousness of something, that it cannot be seen just as an 'in itself', but is always directed and in relation to something or someone. Laing's primary apprehension is that the person cannot be reduced to a thing as the person is always choosing and deciding, while a thing does not. A decision is not causally determined but is the action of an agent. That intuition is shared by both psychoanalysts and existentialists: for psychoanalysts our actions may have an unconscious motivation that might be investigated so as to bring it into conscious control; for existentialists, we may be denying our role in what is happening and need to recognize it.

In *The Schizoid World of Jean-Paul Sartre and R. D. Laing* (Kirsner, 2003), I emphasized how very much both Sartre and Laing centred on context and on situating the problems of acting meaningfully within it. As inherently social beings, we are always in significant relationships with others. Social phenomenology is an application of phenomenology that provides more detailed understanding of social relationships.

Existentialism emphasizes the nature of humans as actively choosing beings born into a world they did not choose. For existentialists generally, we cannot choose not to choose and are responsible for the results of our actions. Generally, we are oriented towards future action; we are agents who cannot avoid choosing futures we often do not see. Existentialists tend to view human beings as operating in continuing crisis, who need to constantly question conventional or received notions of what constitutes the best life. But the best life is not a universally agreed one, nor is it restricted to particular reasonably stable cultures. Philosophies of existence attempt to understand our identity and how we can and how we should act in a social and physical context that is not of our choosing and most often is not benign. These philosophies viewed the human condition as a question that the individual needed to address themselves in their own being without recourse to covering generalizations from either theology or science. There was a new focus on individual experience as connected to the nature of the life-world. There was a particular emphasis on the ethic of the self, how and why we choose our world, what the parameters of choice are, and the nature of authentic and inauthentic action.

For many, including philosophers who had not properly separated philosophy from theology, the source of meaning could be viewed as deriving from God. Others considered God and meaning independent. But atheistic existentialism, of which Sartre was the leading proponent, put them together, holding that values derive from the consequences of there being no God:

> If man as the existentialist sees him is not definable, it is because to begin with he is nothing. He will not be anything until later, and then he will be what he makes of himself. Thus, there is no human nature, because there is no God to have a conception of it. Man simply is. (Sartre, 1975, p. 349)

Thus for the existentialists, there is no intrinsic human nature. Whatever our identities, they are formed by our interactions with the outside world. We are our choices, as Sartre wrote in *Being and Nothingness*. We are judged by actions and not intentions. So for Sartre biology is a foundation but not a determinant of action. Albert Camus held that life is absurd and that there is no transcendent reason for living, though we are condemned to the consciousness and the hopelessness of this situation. The one thing we can do is rebel, to be clear-sighted and not succumb to our fate. Like Sartre, Camus at bottom promotes a Sisyphean freedom of not allowing the self to be dominated and controlled by outside forces. This is the setting or stage on which we act with our freedom, and that we cannot escape. But there is a human condition into which we are 'thrown', as Heidegger asserted, involving the parameters of life and death, of lack of control of a destiny that we nonetheless steer. We dwell in a 'clearing' which is a space that enables experience to be created and to become meaningful (Heidegger, 1962, p. 113).

The existentialist understanding of freedom is both optimistic and pessimistic. On the one hand, it is optimistic insofar as we can make the world or at least ourselves according to our designs. On the other hand, we cannot escape the freedom and thus we bear full responsibility for our actions. Rather than having a given make-up that determines our actions, we make our own essence. It is an active process that is not reducible to external or biological factors. Instead of being *given* meaning, we *create* meaning ourselves. No matter what the arguments or evidence for or against an action, it is ultimately the result of an ineffable decision that we make only on the basis of reasons; our decisions are not *caused* by them. The decision is our responsibility and involves our being-in-the-world: consciousness is always consciousness *of* something and is intentional. A decision implies an intuitive experience which involves phenomenology and not physical reality.

Along with Sartre's concept of *mauvaise foi*, self-deception (sometimes misleadingly translated as 'bad faith'), where people attempted to escape their freedom by treating themselves or others as objects instead of subjects, the nature of Sartre's 'for itself' or 'existence' is that this being is always in question, whether or not we want to admit it. The only restriction on individual freedom is that, as Sartre proposed in *Being and Nothingness*, we are 'condemned to be free', so we are not free not to be free. Deception restricts freedom by not revealing the true situation on which to freely decide upon action. For Sartre, it is essential to endeavour to be clear about what is going on, taking into account the many personal, social and environmental factors that make for this particular situation's occurrence. This involves the fine detail of the settings of the stage upon which actions are undertaken. Understanding particular actions demands that one analyse the biological and social settings within which actions are undertaken.

Sartre developed his own theory of psychotherapy, which he called 'existential psychoanalysis'. Sartre's existential psychoanalysis was based on finding the original choice that a person makes of his or her life, rather than an original trauma (as Sartre would have it that Freud sought). Instead of pursuing how a person was impacted upon by biology, relationships or circumstances, it sought individual meaning in a person's orientation of their actions towards the future as part of a project. Existential psychoanalysis tried to understand the circumstances within which the individual actor then makes a decision in view of his or her own goals. It was an attempt to understand the context in which the ineffable decision-making process takes place by seeing how the individual experiences the situation and acts so as to go beyond it in terms of his or her own goals. For Sartre, we are not lumps of clay, and what is important is not what people have made of us 'but what we ourselves make of what they have made of us' (Sartre, 1964, p. 584).

In the case of the writer Jean Genet, Sartre sought to understand how Genet transcended his situation as an orphan who seemed destined to become a thief when he was discovered stealing something. Sartre surmised that Genet rejected the identity as a thief and decided to become a writer at that moment (Sartre, 1964, p. 2). For Sartre, our freedom was such that we could see it most clearly when we are in chains. During the Algerian War of independence from France in the 1950s, the French–Algerian journalist and political activist Henri Alleg turned the tables on his French Army torturers by refusing to accept that he had to give in at any given moment. For Sartre, who wrote a preface to Alleg's account of his torture, this was an exemplary case of an existential hero because he refused to be what he was defined to be as an essence and rather showed his irreducible existence (see Alleg, 2006).

Existentialism has been a response to, and rejection of, scientistic materialism and mechanistic approaches to the nature of human existence. Nonetheless, the philosophies of existence have acted as *correctives to* reductionist biological or mechanistic understanding of human action, and inevitably these models were based upon the presuppositions of individual freedom and responsibility. They stress the ineffable human element in creating action, particularly each individual's role. Sociological factors may lay the conditions for actions but do not determine them. For existentialists, there is always room for choice, however, little that may be. So they have a model of the human mind that begins with the individual who is not completely subsumed by biological or social factors. Or even where these are paramount, existentialists will follow the role played by individual choice in understanding the particularity of human actions within these contexts, including how human beings can treat themselves as being determined, as having no choices. They focus then on the nature of the human condition.

There was a space where existentialism fitted a need for the insertion of an active individual attitude that was not mechanistic and which recognized individual experience and responsibility. Dominant models for understanding action did not see humans as starting as active, creative beings but instead determined cogs in religious or mechanistic wheels. For all the vagueness of many existential philosophies, the fact that the language used is deliberately humanistic and not mechanistic is a step forward towards truly human psychology. Binswanger was convinced that traditional scientific methods hid rather than revealed what was going on in the patient (May, 1958, p. 8).

Laing argued that a rigorous 'science of persons' was necessary in contrast to natural science medical approaches. As Laing put it in *The Divided Self*:

It seems extraordinary that whereas the physical and biological sciences of it-processes have generally won the day . . . an authentic science of persons has hardly got started by reason of the inveterate tendency to depersonalize or reify persons. People who experience themselves as automata . . . are rightly regarded as crazy. Yet why do we not regard a theory that seeks to transmute persons into automata or animals as equally crazy? (Laing, 1960, p. 23)

Laing always stuck with this theme, and quoted the physicist and theologian C. F. von Weizsacker, who wrote in the last paragraph of his book, *The History of Nature*, that '[t]he scientific and technical world of modern man is the result of his daring enterprise, knowledge without love' (1949, p. 190). To which Laing added: 'Chilling. I cannot see how knowledge without love can yield a knowledge of love; how a heartless method, yielding heartless results can do anything but explain away the heart' (Laing, 1976, pp. 151–2).

In his excellent introduction to the pivotal volume *Existence*, titled, 'The Origins of the Existential Movement in Psychology', May described the issue in this way:

The existentialists are centrally concerned with rediscovering the living person amid the compartmentalization and dehumanization of modern culture, and in order to do this they engage in depth psychological analysis. Their concern is not with isolated psychological reactions in themselves but rather with the psychological being of the living man who is doing the explaining. That is to say, they use psychological terms with an ontological meaning. (May, 1958, pp. 14–15)

Some existential philosophers mistakenly included Freud and psychoanalysis within the mechanistic and scientistic approaches they criticized. Yet, as I shall now argue, psychoanalysis at base investigated the ineffable at least as much as the existentialists did.

An important response to the past century's upheavals and uncertainties came from Sigmund Freud (1856–1939), the founder of psychoanalysis. Psychoanalysis is the first form of psychodynamic psychotherapy and was inaugurated in the dialogue between Freud's colleague, Josef Breuer and the first psychoanalytic patient, 'Anna O', who dubbed the process the 'talking cure'. Psychoanalysis linked unconscious motivation with individual experience and neurosis, mass behaviour, and questions of life and death. Freud attempted to answer similar fundamental philosophical questions about the character of human nature, also focusing on individual experience and identity.

Psychoanalysis was often regarded as scientific or medical on the model of the natural sciences and Freud's models of human beings were seen as reductionistic, mechanistic and medical. On one version of psychoanalysis that was dominant during the rise of existentialism, these involved scientistic models of energy and force, such as hydraulic or economic models of sexual and aggressive impulses vying for fulfilment of pleasure and destruction. The official English translation for the *Standard Edition of the Complete Psychological Works of Sigmund Freud* of Freud's term *trieb* as 'instinct' (instead of the more correct 'drive') indicated the scientistic bent of the translators, as did the mistranslation of ordinary German terms *Das Es*, *Das Ich* and *Das Über-Ich* as the quasi-technical terms 'id', 'ego' and 'superego' (instead of 'it', 'I' and 'over-I') (for more instances, see Kirsner, 2007). By contrast, Lacan rendered Freud's motto, *'wo es war, soll ich werden'* – often translated as 'Where id was ego shall be' – as instead 'Where it was I shall become' (Žižek, 2007). The Latinizations make Freud's intent seem more technical than philosophical. The scientistic bent is in line with the translator, James Strachey's direct comment in the 'General Preface' to the *Standard Edition*:

> The imaginary model which I have always kept before me is of the writings of some English man of science of wide education born in the middle of the nineteenth century. And I should like, in an explanatory and no patriotic spirit, to emphasize the word 'English'. (Strachey, 1966, p. xix)

Thus the translation ills add to the ambiguities that German philosopher Jürgen Habermas labelled as Freud's 'scientistic self-misunderstanding of metapsychology' (Habermas, 1971, p. 246). Metapsychology describes the general abstract theoretical framework of the operation of the psyche. At this level, as a child of his time, Freud did not fully understand his discovery of psychoanalysis as really a hermeneutic inquiry, seeking to understand the meaning of human actions.

Thus, perhaps the important philosophical dimension of Freud's thinking has been obscured by the way he couched his discoveries in the scientific terms of his time. However, many have argued that his discoveries were more in the realm of meanings than of causes (Rycroft, 1966), or that his language combined that of physical energy and that of subjective desires; what he called 'force' and 'meaning' (Ricouer, 1970). This hermeneutic view was in tandem with philosophical traditions, including existentialism. As Canadian psychoanalyst and philosopher Jon Mills asserted:

> in the end, existentialism remains a multitudinous set of precepts, some systematized, but mainly recalcitrant to systematic reduction. But one

irrefutable premise is that we as subjective agents are never static or inert creatures; rather we are a process of becoming, an observation made by the ancients from Heraclitus to Lao-tzu. One could argue that psychoanalysis has always been an existential enterprise, and nowhere do we see this more poignantly realized than in Freud. Freud's entire metapsychology could be said to be an existential treatise on the scope, breadth, and limits to human freedom. Freud was profoundly engaged with the questions of life and death, determinism and choice, self and other, alienation and causality, so much so that his mature model of the mind is none other than a return to the Greek concept of the soul. (2003, pp. 272–3)

From the perspective of 'force', of the quantitative or energetic side of psycho-analysis that gave it a scientific facade and acceptance, it is understandable why psychoanalysis appeared to existentialists as treating human beings as though they were mindless machines. Sartre rejected Freud in terms of his attack on consciousness as pre-eminent, which meant, Sartre thought, that freedom and self-determination were undermined. For their part, such rejection did not endear existentialists to psychoanalysts, especially in the United States (Mills, 2003, p. 272). Existentialism appeared more humanistic and less authoritarian and mechanistic than psychoanalysis, and truer to experience.

If there is no essential or intrinsic human nature that determines our actions, how can this relate to psychoanalysis, which stresses how embedded we are in our natures (e.g. the Oedipus Complex, the Pleasure Principle, sexuality)? Do our drives control us? Are we our drives? One problem here is the way the question is framed. Are we something 'beyond' our biology? Descartes's dual-istic division of consciousness and physical extension, the mind and the body, has bedevilled modern philosophy and extended to some twentieth-century existentialists, particularly Sartre. This approach assumes our wishes and drives are part of our physical biological make-up, whereas our thinking is mental. According to George Lakoff and Mark Johnson, who are influenced by a differ-ent existential thinker, Maurice Merleau-Ponty, this folk theory asserts that since our essence is to think, therefore, our minds are disembodied 'and there-fore what makes us human has nothing to do with our bodies' (1999, p. 401). However, this idea of essences is questionable as it does not see human beings or the world as systems. It can be seen to be part of a 'bewitchment of language' in which words which are used to name things appear to thereby confer some substance of their own. Thus, because we can say the word 'mind', we may assume it refers to real processes. Because we can distinguish 'it' from 'the body' in words, this may convey the appearance of necessarily quite separate entities. Freud did not take this separated view when he understood the way the unconscious mind functioned in relation to the conscious and outer world. Sex-uality was not just a bodily mechanism but was an essential part of being human. The mind/body distinction takes a particular assumption that because we can distance ourselves from a concept, we are, therefore, not part of it – as Descartes did by doubting everything and arriving at the view that 'I think therefore I am'.

Sartre arguably made such an error in criticizing Freudian psychoanalysis as involving 'a lie without a liar': he thought that the idea of the agency of censorship of conscious ideas meant that the person had to know what was being censored in order to censor it. Sartre proposed the idea of *mauvaise foi* to understand why people denied aspects of their own freedom and treated themselves as things rather than as choosing beings. One main form of bad faith involved treating oneself as an object, as a thing that has no choice. Sartre described three main patterns of self-deception that meant that a person was treating himself or herself or others as objects, as though they had no choice. These were ways of trying to evade our inescapable freedom which we cannot escape. For Sartre, we are 'condemned to be free'. According to Sartre, we can be understood as having 'existence' or 'essence' – following Descartes's ideas about the non-mental. This distinction was made in *Being and Nothingness* as between 'being-for-itself' and 'being-in-itself'. Irving Yalom encapsulated Sartre's goals and approach to therapy as 'Sartre considered it his project to liberate individuals from bad faith and to help them assume responsibility' (Yalom, 1980, p. 222).

The norm in nineteenth-century psychiatry was containment in asylums. But psychoanalysis involved a new turn: listening to the patient for meaning instead of simply noting external symptoms. This was because for Freud the mind was not equivalent to consciousness and was the study of the unconscious and its relationships with the rest of the mind and the outer world. Although for Freud unconscious mental activity played a crucial role in human behaviour, this did not imply that choice was not involved.

Insofar as psychoanalysis is about unacknowledged agency and intention, it shares much with existentialism. Unless Freud's theory is viewed as materialistic, it can be seen as being about choice, albeit unconscious. The idea of 'unconscious choice' is a contradiction in terms only if 'choice' is defined from the outset as being necessarily conscious. Freud proposed two hypotheses that were 'an insult to the entire world'. The first was that the psychical is not equivalent to the conscious, and the conscious mind was only a portion of mental processes. The other was that sexual drives play a crucial part in the formation of mental illness (Freud, 1961, pp. 21–2). Psychoanalysis is a means of uncovering what we don't know we know (see Eisold, 2010). This implies a psychodynamic view of mind. Repression involved having blotted out the memory of the memory so that it is inaccessible and seemingly non-existent. Although Freud himself took his sexual aetiology to be the fundamental ground, other schools of psychoanalysis (e.g. Carl Jung, Alfred Adler, Karen Horney, Melanie Klein, Donald Winnicott) adopted different views.

Psychoanalysts did not know the unconscious of their patients. It is not for the analyst to tell the patient what to think. Freud's approach was exploratory. He insisted on continuing to ask questions even when the path appeared to have ended. The meaning or meanings of the unconscious may not be found, especially where the wishes rest in the end on a decision. The term 'decision' comes from the Latin *decidere*, 'to cut off'. Difficulties are resolved 'at a stroke' so that it is a matter of agency, not determination. But that agency is itself individual, both in existentialism and in psychoanalysis. Psychoanalysis was the first systematic psychotherapy to focus upon unconscious action. Freud's German term *Unbewusst* had the sense of what is unbeknown to me; it implies unwitting behaviour. Insight is a desired quality shared by psychoanalysts and existentialists, as is the ultimately unknowable quality of subjective decision-making, as opposed to mechanistic calculation.

As outlined above, Sartre's *Being and Nothingness* worked towards what he labelled 'existential psychoanalysis', as applying the methods of psychoanalysis within the context of beings which are future orientated, because for Sartre psychoanalysis had no concept of the future. Psychoanalysis can be seen as a way of unblocking the influence of the past on the present and the future. It can be a way of liberating the individual from the control of unconscious wishes. The supposed antithesis between psychoanalysis and existentialism is erroneously conceived, as though psychoanalysis is somehow inimical to the idea of the importance of the future because of a focus on the past. But to the contrary, the revelation of the experienced history involves unlocking the patient from being stuck in the past. Freud discussed two patients who, he said,

> give us an impression of having been 'fixated' to a particular portion of their past, as though they could not manage to free themselves from it and were for that reason alienated from the present and the future. They then remained lodged in their illness in the sort of way in which in earlier days people retreated into a monastery in order to bear the burden there of their ill-fated lives. (Freud, 1963, p. 273)

The task of psychoanalysis is to understand the past so as to free the patient from it. The future then becomes possible to experience as a normal conflict between different wishes on the same psychological level instead of being a conflict where neurotic symptoms are expressions of the result of a psychic conflict between unconscious and conscious wishes.

Freud made an important point in defining neurosis:

> people usually overlook the one essential point – that the pathogenic conflict in neurotics is not to be confused with a normal struggle between mental

impulses both of which are on the same psychological footing. In the former case the dissention is between two powers, one of which has made its way to the stage of what is preconscious or conscious while the other has been held back at the stage of the unconscious. For that reason the conflict cannot be brought to an issue; the disputants can no more come to grips than, in the familiar simile, a polar bear and a whale. A true decision can only be reached when they both meet on the same ground. To make this possible is, I think, the sole task of our therapy. (Freud, 1963, p. 433)

In an earlier paper, Freud described the cure for neurosis as 'transforming your neurotic misery into common unhappiness. With a mental life that has been restored to health, you will be better armed against that unhappiness' (1955, p. 305). This marked a change of register from neurosis to normality, as in the normal struggle between two conscious wishes. Health for Freud did not mean happiness but rather the relative absence of neurosis in the sense that pathogenic unconscious wishes were not what were standing in the way of the fulfilment of important conscious goals.

If the unconscious is viewed as an entirely separate domain unlinked to the conscious aspects of the self except through physiological or mechanistic impulses, then there is a point to some existential critiques of Freud for having divided the self into two, wherein an energetic homunculus of the unconscious drives the conscious self. But while Freud emphasized the importance of the unconscious domain, he showed how it was connected with the conscious, how access could be gained via interpretation, free association, understanding of cultural, anthropological, literary and social phenomena, jokes, slips, and so on. Psychoanalysis provides other modes of access to unconscious desires, which are very much 'known unknown' parts of our dynamic selves. Conscious and unconscious are parts of a whole agent who can be more or less aware.

As University of Chicago philosopher and psychoanalyst Jonathan Lear has argued, the reality principle is not just an empirical read-out of reality. It is ethical. Freud is trying to explain 'psychological perturbations' on how neurotics live. Lear explains: 'that is, he sees people who are failing to flourish, and he sets out to give a psychological account of why that is. On his account, neurotics fail to live well because they themselves "turn away from reality"' (2005, p. 10). Lear asserted that for Freud neurotics are gripped by a 'psychologically organized orientation that actively distorts their ability to understand the world and their place in it'. Freud doesn't see pure cases of the pleasure principle or the reality principle at work but instead 'theoretical posits, whose joint and conflicted workings are supposed to explain what he does see: people living structured unhappy lives. The pleasure principle and the reality principle are there to explain why people are doing such a poor job answering the question of how to live' (Lear, 2005, p. 153). Lear asserts that the master-complaint of his patients was 'in my own attempt to figure out how to live, something is going wrong' (p. 10). Lear argued further that:

> Freud was not well-placed to hear this master-complaint. He was a doctor and he conceived himself as engaged in scientific research. Just as a doctor probes for the hidden causes of physical diseases, so Freud took himself to be probing the unconscious for hidden meanings making the patient ill. With the benefit of hindsight, we can now see that a certain clinical brutality flows from this self-understanding . . . It also blinds him to the profound philosophical and ethical significance of his discoveries. (p. 10)

I have elsewhere suggested (Kirsner, 2006) that Freud was essentially ethical, that across the board from clinical to social theory as well as personally, he adopted a stoic approach.

I have been arguing that existential analysis and psychoanalysis are cut from the same cloth of attempting to define a fully personal ethical approach to studying human nature. Moreover, psychoanalysis was also very much part of the scene in the development of existential psychotherapy. Boss, for example, was a Freudian psychoanalyst, while Binswanger joined the Vienna Psychoanalytic Society at Freud's invitation, after Freud's split with Jung. Like psychoanalysis, existential psychiatry and psychology arose in response to a more general need in psychology and psychiatry (May, 1958, p. 4).

Binswanger combined psychotherapy with Heidegger's existentialism. Freud and Binswanger remained long-standing friends for the remainder of Freud's life. As Binswanger wrote to Freud's wife following Freud's death that underlying his admiration for Freud's outstanding scientific achievement,

> I was deeply receptive, over the decades, to the greatness and the indomitable spiritual and moral force of his personality. But underlying all that was my love for him, which from the day of our first meeting in Vienna in 1907 has remained unchanged to this day . . . nothing made me happier than his statement a few years ago that we had kept faith with each other for twenty-five years. (Reppen, 2003, p. 28)

Binswanger was one of two of Freud's most long-standing friends – the other was a fellow Swiss, Oskar Pfister who, like Binswanger, was also connected with Jung (Reppen, 2003, p. 281). Although Freud and Binswanger had their differences – Freud feuded with all but the most devout of his psychoanalytic colleagues – 80-year-old Freud wrote to Binswanger: 'I have always confined myself to the ground floor and of the edifice – you maintain that by changing one's point of view, one can also see an upper story, in which dwell such distinguished guests as religion, art, etc.' (Binswanger, 1957, p. 96).

A comparison of existentialism and psychoanalysis, far from amplifying their differences, shows them to be closer than is often thought as responses to the same social crises and changes with the rise of mass communications, science, the 'death of God' and the focus on the human subject. As Jon Mills concluded:

> Da-sein is the subjective human being who lives in a world composed of multiple dynamic organizations that are psychologically, socially, and temporally realized in relation to the past, the present, and future possibilities. Just as Sartre emphasizes our subjectivity as radical freedom, and psychoanalysis as the pursuit of bringing to light that which lies hidden from our immediate conscious awareness, we exist in relation to what we can become. Ultimately in both the existential and psychoanalytic traditions, we can only become more free through knowledge. (Mills, 2003, p. 278)

Bibliography

Alleg, H. (2006), *The Question*. Lincoln, NE: University of Nebraska Press.

Binswanger, L. (1957), *Sigmund Freud; Reminiscences of a Friendship*, trans. Norbert Guterman. New York: Grune & Stratton.

De Beauvoir, S. (1989), *The Second Sex*, trans. H. M. Parshley. New York: Vintage Books [1949].

Dreyfus, H. and M. Wrathall (eds) (2006), *A Companion to Phenomenology and Existentialism*. Oxford: Blackwell.

Eisold, K. (2010), *What You Don't Know You Know: Our Hidden Motives in Life, Business, and Everything Else*. New York: Other Press.

Frankl, V. (2006), *Man's Search for Meaning*. Boston: Beacon.

Freud, S. (1955), 'The Psychotherapy of Hysteria', in J. Breuer and S. Freud, *Studies on Hysteria*, in J. Strachey (ed. and trans.), *The Standard Edition of the Complete Psychological Works of Sigmund Freud, Volume 2 (1893–1895)*. London: Hogarth [1893–1895].

— (1961), 'Introductory Lectures on Psycho-Analysis', Parts 1 & 2, in J. Strachey (ed. and trans.), *The Standard Edition of the Complete Psychological Works of Sigmund Freud, Volume 15 (1915–1916): Introductory Lectures on Psycho-Analysis (Parts I and II)*. London: Hogarth [1916].

— (1963), 'Introductory Lectures on Psycho-Analysis', Part III, in J. Strachey (ed. and trans.), *The Standard Edition of the Complete Psychological Works of Sigmund Freud, Volume 16 (1916–1917): Introductory Lectures on Psycho-Analysis (Part III)*. London: Hogarth [1917].

Habermas, J. (1971), *Knowledge and Human Interests*, trans. J. J. Shapiro. Boston: Beacon.

Heidegger, M. (1962), *Being and Time*, trans. J. Macquarrie and E. Robinson. New York: Harper & Row.

Kirsner, D. (2003), *The Schizoid World of Jean-Paul Sartre and R. D. Laing*. New York: The Other Press

— (2006), 'Freud, Civilization, Religion and Stoicism'. *Psychoanalytic Psychology* 23: 354–66.

— (2007), 'Fresh Freud: No Longer Lost in Translation'. *Psychoanalytic Psychology* 24: pp. 658–66.

Laing, R. D. (1960), *The Divided Self: An Existential Study in Sanity and Madness*. Harmondsworth: Penguin.

— (1963), 'Minkowski and Schizophrenia'. *Review of Existential Psychology* 9: 195–207.

— (1976), *The Facts of Life: An Essay in Feelings, Facts, and Fantasy*. New York: Pantheon Books.

Lakoff, G. and M. Johnson (1999), *Philosophy in the Flesh: The Embodied Mind and Its Challenge to Western Thought*. New York: Basic Books.

Lear, J. (2005), *Freud*. New York: Routledge.

May, R. (1958), 'The Origins and Significance of the Existential Movement in Psychology', in May et al. (1958).

May, R., E. Angel and H. Ellenberger (1958), *Existence: A New Dimension in Psychiatry and Psychology*. New York: Simon and Schuster.

Mills, J. (2003), 'Existentialism and Psychoanalysis: From Antiquity to Postmodernism'. *Psychoanalytic Review* 90: 269–79.

Reppen, J. (2003), 'Ludwig Binswanger and Sigmund Freud: Portrait of a Friendship'. *Psychoanalytic Review* 90: 281–91.

Ricoeur, P. (1970), *Freud and Philosophy: An Essay on Interpretation*. New Haven: Yale University Press.

Rycroft, C. (1966), 'Causes and Meaning', in C. Rycroft (ed.), *Psychoanalysis Observed*. London: Constable.

Sartre, J-P. (1964), *Saint Genet: Actor and Martyr*, trans. B. Frechtman. New York: George Braziller [1952].

— (1966), *Being and Nothingness: An Essay in Phenomenological Ontology*, trans. H. E. Barnes. New York: Washington Square Press [1943].

— (1975), 'Existentialism and Humanism', in W. Kaufman (ed.), *Existentialism: From Dostoevsky to Sartre*. New York: New American Library [1946].

Spiegelberg, H. (1972), *Phenomenology in Psychology and Psychiatry: A Historical Introduction*. Evanston, IL: Northwestern University Press.

Strachey, J. (1966), 'General Preface', in *The Standard Edition of the Complete Psychological Works of Sigmund Freud*, Volume I (1886–1899): Pre-Psycho-Analytic Publications and Unpublished Drafts. London: Hogarth.

von Weizsacker, C. F. (1949), *The History of Nature*, trans. F. D. Wieck. Chicago: University of Chicago Press.

Wertz, F. (2006), 'Phenomenological Currents in Twentieth Century Phenomenology', in H. Dreyfus and M. Wrathall (eds), *A Companion to Phenomenology and Existentialism*. Oxford: Blackwell.

Yalom, I. (1980), *Existential Psychotherapy*. New York: Basic Books.

Zank, M. (2007), 'Martin Buber', *Stanford Encyclopedia of Philosophy*. http://plato.stanford.edu/entries/buber/

Žižek, S. (2007), 'Introduction' in *How to Read Lacan*. www.lacan.com/zizhowto.html

6 Existentialism and Ethics

Debra Bergoffen

Variations on a Theme

Thinking about existentialism and ethics is much like listening to Mussorgsky's 'Pictures at an Exhibition'. While there is an ongoing recurrent theme, the pieces joined by it are unique. Existentialists record the singularity of their ethical theories in the phrases they use to characterize them and in the situations they identify as ethically exemplary. Simone de Beauvoir speaks of an ethics of ambiguity. The best published insight into Jean-Paul Sartre's ethical thought, or at least the only ethics he was prepared to defend, can be found in his account of the author–reader relationship in *Existentialism and Literature*, originally titled *What is Literature?*. Maurice Merleau-Ponty develops a unique ethics of the 'flesh' and dialogue. Martin Buber describes his ethic of dialogue in terms of the I–Thou. These singular ethical visions are linked by a shared phenomenological understanding of the subject as inherently intersubjective, embodied, fissured and ambiguous: it is intersubjective not only in the sense that our lives though uniquely singular are lived among others, but more importantly in the sense that subjectivity cannot be conceived of solipsistically or in terms of autonomy; it is embodied in the sense that as subjects we are neither pure consciousness nor sheer materiality, but are the interwovenness of mind and body; it is fissured and ambiguous in the sense that as subjects we are not a static, stable or clearly definable reality but an existing openness to the world caught up in the contingencies of being-in-the-world and carrying the responsibility of bearing witness to the world.

Phenomenology was born as a descriptive discipline. The early phenomenologists were interested in deciphering how we encounter and construct a meaningful world, how we distinguish the imagined world from the perceived world and how we experience time. Though they were interested in describing the process of making judgements, they did not ask whether the judgements we made were ethical. In viewing the phenomenological subject as an engaged, acting, willing and desiring being, existential thinkers draw out the ethical implications of earlier phenomenological descriptions of a subject. For them, the fact that we are inherently intersubjective gives rise to the question: What is our responsibility to/for others? The aim of this chapter then is to discern the diverse ways in which existential thinkers have transformed phenomenological descriptions of who we are into existential–phenomenological accounts of how to be faithful to the 'who' of subjectivity.

Simone de Beauvoir: Embodying the Meaning of Intentionality

Friedrich Nietzsche's observation in *On the Genealogy of Morals*, 'man would rather will nothingness than not will' (1989, p. 163), may be seen as setting the existential ethical agenda; for in establishing that we cannot will not to will Nietzsche argues that the how and what of our willing will determine the future of humanity. Hence the importance of ethics – or in Nietzsche's terms, the importance of getting beyond the resentment that poisons the ethics of good and evil. Though de Beauvoir will not follow Nietzsche in rejecting the concept of evil she may be heard as echoing Nietzsche when she argues in *Pyrrhus and Cinéas* that we cannot not act (de Beauvoir 2004, p. 139). Her point, like his, is to establish that since we are determined to act, the question of how to act must be given philosophical priority. De Beauvoir, like other existentialists, calls the impossibility of not willing/acting the fact of human freedom. Sartre was more dramatic: he described us as condemned to be free.

If *Pyrrhus and Cinéas* begins by echoing Nietzsche, *The Ethics of Ambiguity* begins by rewriting Husserl's theory of intentionality. Taking Husserl's watch words of intentionality, 'Consciousness is always consciousness of something', de Beauvoir identifies two moods and moments of intentionality. The first, a moment where consciousness discloses the meanings of the world, is experienced in a mood of joy. The second, a moment where consciousness moves to impose its meanings on the world, is accompanied by a mood of failure; for the world in offering itself to our meaning-giving powers in the first moment of intentionality resists our attempt to dominate it in the second moment of intentionality. This moment's mood of failure, however, is never final. It evokes the desire to try again and throws us back to the world-revealing moment of intentionality and its joy.

De Beauvoir reads this doubled and fluctuating dynamic of intentionality as a pre-reflective enactment of our two-dimensional freedom – the freedom that discloses the world and the freedom that seeks to bring new meaning into the world. As she looks to this pre-reflective dynamic for ethical guidance, she determines that we are ethically obliged to bring meanings to the world that support a future where the pre-reflective freedoms of intentionality can be reflectively fostered. She writes, 'we must disclose the world with the purpose of further disclosure and by the same movement try to free men by means of whom the world takes on meaning' (1948, pp. 71, 74). Ethics, in short, is a matter of consciously fostering the freedom of the pre-reflective freedom of intentionality. This means that we must keep the doubled movement of intentionality

99

alive by resisting the authoritarian temptation of the second moment of intentionality's desire to impose its meaning on the world. Living the ethical life might be described as preserving the failure of the second moment of intentionality – to keep it from solidifying – for by preserving this failure we are returned to the first moment of intentionality's freedom to disclose new meanings of the world, which in turn moves us to give the world new values.

This revision of Husserl's description of intentionality and its translation into an ethical and political injunction threatens the stability of all ethical and political systems; for the act of disclosing already established ethical and political meanings of the world immediately becomes the desire to give the world new meanings. As we cannot will not to will, as we cannot stop the momentum of intentionality, we cannot stop the intentionality of disclosure from becoming an intentionality of critique. The revelation of the way things are always entails the question: Why are things this way rather than that? The realities of the world are always accompanied with their (other) possibilities. From an ethical and political perspective, the joy of disclosing the possibilities of the world is also and necessarily the freedom that opens the world to transformation (de Beauvoir 1948, pp. 20, 27). From this perspective, disclosure is an agency of change.

In providing the ground for de Beauvoir's argument that to exist as a singular subject entails a responsibility to others and the world we share with them (de Beauvoir, 1948, pp. 18, 67, 72), this revision of Husserl's formula of intentionality provides a way of establishing responsibility as a necessary correlate of freedom. This is not, however, de Beauvoir's only ground for the argument that freedom and responsibility are two sides of the same coin. Taking an uncompromising atheistic stand, she also appeals to the fact that God is dead. She rejects Ivan Karamazov's claim in Dostoevsky's *The Brothers Karamazov* that in a world without God everything is permissible. In a world without God, de Beauvoir argues, we are totally responsible for the course of history and the fate of others. Everything is not permissible, because there is no God to undo the effects of our actions. Raising the stakes even higher, she declares that because an atheist existentialist ethic is the only ethic that holds us absolutely responsible for evil, it is the only ethic that takes the problem of evil seriously. There is no God to save us.

Ironically in taking this stand against Dostoevsky's Ivan Karamazov, de Beauvoir may be alerting us to the influence of Søren Kierkegaard, on her thought. She, like Kierkegaard rejects the idea of anchoring ethics in the word of God. Although de Beauvoir severs ethics from belief in God because relying on God allows us to escape responsibility for our choices and actions and Kierkegaard severs ethics from faith to show us that it is only in the act of faith that the paradox of subjectivity is fully lived, their differences should not obscure the fact that they both find that using God to anchor ethics is a way of evading the meaning of subjectivity. Kierkegaard contrasts the figure of Abraham to the figures of Socrates and Agamemnon to make his point. Socrates and Agamemnon are the faces of the ethical subject. In subordinating their existential singularity to the demand of the ethical universal they embody the ambiguity of the human subject. Socrates lives this ambiguity serenely. Agamemnon lives it tragically. He must choose between the competing demands of the universal: the demand to serve the interests of the polity and the demand to protect his daughter. Reason will direct him to subordinate the requirements of paternity to the obligations of state. Because Socrates and Agamemnon experience the paradox of the human condition as an intelligible tension, they do not, according to Kierkegaard, fully experience the paradox of the infinite within the finite that constitutes us as human. This is left to Abraham who abandons the ethical domain entirely. Placing his particularity as an existing individual above the authority of the ethical universal, Abraham is prepared to sacrifice his son in the name of a relationship to God that can neither be explained nor justified. Kierkegaard calls Abraham's decision a leap of faith. In raising the knife to his son, Abraham leaves the realm of rational ethical action. Most of us read the story of Abraham with hindsight. We know that God will send a ram to take Isaac's place. Reading in this way we miss the point. Abraham had no such knowledge. He confronted the infinite in the only way a finite being can confront it – as a subject who announces his singularity in a personal and passionate response to an incomprehensible infinite call.

This expression of existential singularity is rejected by de Beauvoir not so much because it comes through faith (Kierkegaard's God bears no resemblance to the God she refuses) but because it diverts attention from the question of evil. Although the passion of faith is an expression of the ungrounded nature of the freedom through which we must define ourselves, it is not an expression of the relationship between this freedom and our responsibility to others. Abraham does not tell Sara where he is going. In severing faith from ethics de Beauvoir's thought takes a very different direction. We see this in her decision to address the evil of oppression by probing the meaning of being a woman.

The Second Sex frames the abstract question of the relationship between freedom and responsibility raised in *The Ethics of Ambiguity* in terms of the concrete reality of the second sex status of women. De Beauvoir found the condition of women analogous to the condition of slaves. She argued that women like slaves are oppressed (1989, p. 64). Many dismiss this claim, especially when applied to women in the Western world, as hyperbolic. Coming from the analyses of *The Ethics of Ambiguity* we see it is not; for considered from a phenomenological perspective, oppression is not essentially a matter of material depravation, exploitation or physical abuse. From a phenomenological perspective these oppressive tactics are a means to the more fundamental violation of alienating human beings from their meaning-giving and world-making powers. The joys of disclosure and the desires of freedom are our birthright (1948, pp. 32, 34). To be oppressed is to be robbed of these rights. Oppression at its most fundamental level exists wherever people do not/cannot experience themselves as world-disclosing beings who bring meaning and value to life. To be oppressed is to live as the Other in the world of an-other.

When, in the Introduction to *The Second Sex*, de Beauvoir tells us that the world belongs to men, that men determine the truths of the world and that women as the Other must submit to these truths (1989, pp. xxi–xxii), she is identifying patriarchy with this fundamental form of oppression. De Beauvoir describes the process of becoming a woman, the one who sees her oppression as natural; the one who passively receives men's meanings of the world; the one who depends on men for validation; the one who experiences herself as powerlessness; as a matter of becoming habituated to live one's body as fragile, vulnerable and weak – a matter of sabotaging the body's 'I can' powers by learning to 'throw like a girl' (Young, 1990). Becoming a woman is a matter of embodying a specific set of dependency habits and behaviours. Habits, however, can be broken. That is the point of *The Second Sex*.

In taking her ethical and political case to the body, de Beauvoir is again re-reading the phenomenology she inherited from Husserl; for she is teaching us that giving meaning to the world is not the activity of a pure consciousness; it is the work of an embodied being whose experience of its body as having the right to be in the world is essential to affirming the right to its freedom to give the world meaning and value. In detailing the ways our embodiment expresses our humanity, de Beauvoir also looks to the body, specifically the erotic body, as a liberatory force. She identifies it as the site where the hold of oppressive sex/gender ideologies are challenged. In de Beauvoir's words, 'The erotic experience is the one that most poignantly discloses to human beings the ambiguity of their condition; in it they are aware of themselves as flesh and as spirit, as the other and as the subject . . . The dimension of the other still exists but the fact is that alterity no longer has a hostile implication' (1989, pp. 448–9).

Unpacking these words, we discover the ways in which the erotic body, in alerting us to our ambiguity, alerts us to the injustice of patriarchal gender codes; for these codes, like all forms of injustice, transform us from ambiguous beings who cannot be designated either as absolute subjects or abject objects into permanent objects or subjects. In patriarchy this reification of our ambiguity takes the form of positioning man as the subject and woman as his other. By doing this it transforms intersubjectivity from a dynamic responsive relationship into an alienating and oppressive one. De Beauvoir's ethics of ambiguity, originally theorized as an ethic of intentionality, is materialized in the vicissitudes of the body that exists both as a subject for itself and an object for others.

As an object for others the embodied subject is vulnerable to being objectified and exploited by them. As subject for itself, the embodied subject is ethically bound to recognize the other's subjectivity and to respect their freedom. This affirmation of the other's subjectivity may be lived in the ethics of the project where we recognize each other as allies working towards a common goal or the ethics of the gift where 'in the midst of carnal fever [I become] a voluntary gift, an activity [where I] live out . . . the strange ambiguity of existence made body' (1989, p. 163). This gifting activity may best be described as an act of generosity. It can become the ground of an ethics of generosity, a supplement to the ethics of the project where instead of asking you to become my ally for a particular cause I offer you the gift of my ambiguity as the home for yours.

De Beauvoir's turn to the body and the ways in which it can become the instrument of oppression or the site of political liberation and ethical gifting puts her in conversation with Sartre's descriptions of the Look and the Caress, and Merleau-Ponty's descriptions of the reciprocity embedded in acts of perception; but where de Beauvoir's ethical focus remains tied to the sex/gendered materialities and contingencies of embodiment, Sartre's and Merleau-Ponty's do not. They find that as embodied beings we are speaking beings who dwell in language and that the principles of our ethical relationships may be found in the dynamics of speaking, dialogue, writing and reading.

Sartre: Countering the Look with the Caress and the Word

Sartre, like de Beauvoir, flags the atheistic ground of his thinking. The niceties of the centuries old debates concerning the compatibility of human freedom with the existence of an omnipotent and omniscient God are a waste of time and words. If God exists we are determined by His will. Everything about us, however, points to the fact of our freedom – our anxiety in confronting it; our bad faith attempts to escape it; our struggle to secure it. We exist. God does not. So speaks Sartre.

Sartre's *Being and Nothingness* is a phenomenological ontology, not an ethics. Yet its descriptions and arguments cry out for an ethics. Sartre acknowledges this in a footnote at the end of the discussion of bad faith (1956, p. 116), and in the concluding section of *Being and Nothingness* titled 'Ethical Implications'. He promises that an ethic will follow. He recognizes, that his portrayal of the Look compels us to ask whether or not hostility, the original meaning of our being-for-others, is the final word on human relationships; that his account of the caress moves us to ask whether this moment of fleshed recognition must succumb to the dynamics of domination; that his discussions of anxiety in the face of freedom, and his descriptions of the bad faith flights from freedom direct us to consider whether these responses to freedom are inevitable. Though Sartre never delivers on his promise to publish an ethics, several of his other works take up the ethical implications of these questions. *No Exit* provides a bleak set of answers. *Existentialism and Literature* provides more hopeful ones.

Two of Sartre's ethical works, one, 'Existentialism and Humanism' originally delivered as a lecture and then published by him, and the other *Notebooks for an Ethics* published posthumously in 1983 but written in 1947 and 1948, were deemed by him to be unsatisfactory. While today scholars debate Sartre's decision to abandon the *Notebooks,* Gabriel Marcel is clear: the ontology of *Being and Nothingness* precludes the possibility of an ethics. According to Marcel, Sartre cannot develop a satisfactory ethics because his account of freedom precludes the possibility of the openness to God that directs us to the 'we' of humanity. Ethics, according to Marcel, concerns the who, not the what of the subject, but Sartre in erasing the distinction between the who and the what of the individual abandons us to a universe where the space of appropriation smoothers the hope for communion. In short, Marcel accuses Sartre of taking away the value of human beings by making human freedom the foundation of all values. Sartre sees things differently. Freedom, for him, is the source of human dignity.

Sartre understands freedom phenomenologically. To be free is to have the capacity to bring meaning into the world. Sartre makes this point in certain descriptions: his counter-intuitive account of vertigo and in his description of our relationship to the alarm clock. Vertigo, Sartre says, is not a fear of falling, it registers the anxiety we experience when we realize that there is nothing stopping us from jumping (1956, pp. 65–7). It is not the height of the mountain which frightens us, but our power to give this height suicidal meanings. In a similar vein, Sartre tells us that we are free to shut the alarm off when it rings. The alarm clock is an inert thing in the world. It cannot get us out of bed and to work unless we choose to listen to it (1956, p. 76). These vignettes make the point that though we find ourselves born into a world comprised of things and laws – a world where meaning is already given – we are not determined by this world of things or the laws of the other. We are free to bring new meaning to the world and are responsible for doing so.

Sartre is unambiguous about this in *The Flies*. In the final confrontation between Zeus and Orestes, Zeus recognizes that Orestes has discovered the secret the Gods have tried to hide from humanity. They are free; and as free they are dangerous (1989, p. 102). Confronting Zeus and confirming his freedom, Orestes declares, 'What do I care for Zeus? . . . It is right to stamp you out like the foul brute that you are, and to free the people of Argos from your evil influence. It is right to restore to them their sense of human dignity' (1989, p. 103). Orestes is portrayed as responding to his freedom joyfully. Whether he can convince the people of Argos to joyfully embrace their freedom or whether their anxiety will prod them to retreat to their old ways is left undecided.

It is difficult to know how much credence to give to this portrayal of Orestes' joy. Is it a matter of dramatic effect or philosophical import? It certainly has no place in *Being and Nothingness*. There Sartre aligns freedom with moods of dread. Unlike Orestes, who uses his freedom to free others, the people who populate *Being and Nothingness* use their freedom to escape it. The escape routes have many faces but share the same structure. The waiter in the cafe who reduces himself to his professional role to avoid confronting the nothingness of his freedom, the woman in the cafe who becomes a pure intellect to avoid noticing her date's desire for her body, the alcoholic, the homosexual and the gambler who sincerely promise to annihilate their past and become someone else – all of these ploys are versions of what Sartre calls bad faith. Each of these strategies exploits the fact that we are fissured subjects who can never coincide with ourselves by rejecting one or another aspect of our unstable subjectivity. The waiter is not wrong to see himself as a man in the role of a waiter. He is in bad faith when he identifies himself as a waiter. The woman is not wrong in wanting to be recognized for her intellect. She is in bad faith when she rejects her embodiment. Making a promise to change is not wrong. The promise is in bad faith, however, if it is premised on rejecting the reality of the past.

The focus of the analyses of bad faith is our relationship to ourselves. With the discussion of the Look, Sartre's attention shifts. Now he is explicitly focused on our experience of ourselves as an object in another's world. Here, I am not the one trying to escape my freedom, I am the one whose freedom is stolen from me. Far from welcoming this theft, I resist it. I return the other's Look and affirm my freedom. I reclaim the world as mine. Sartre's account of the Look is reminiscent of Hobbes' description of the state of nature as a war of all against all and Hegel's account of the fight to the death that sets the scene for the master–slave relationship. Again, Sartre the playwright dramatizes the phenomenology: 'Hell is other people' (1989, p. 45). The title of the play that contains this outburst, *No Exit*, might be read as describing Sartre's dissatisfaction with Hobbes' social contract and with Hegel's 'Absolute Spirit' resolution of the problem of competing demands of intersubjectivity and freedom. It may also be read as anticipating Sartre's failure to provide a solution of his own.

The discussions of the Look record the discovery that we are embodied subjects whose being for others renders us vulnerable to their power. Interrogating our response to this discovery, Sartre finds that the original meaning of intersubjectivity is conflict (1956, pp. 474–5). The conundrum of intersubjectivity concerns the status of this meaning. As the original meaning of our relationship to the other, is conflict the final word on intersubjectivity?

We might be inclined to turn to the experience of love as a solution to this conundrum. Sartre is not. He describes love as a game of seduction and mirrors, as a series of deceptions in search of an impossible ideal (1956, p. 491). Still, there is a note of hope. The failure of love to transform the original meaning of our relationship to the Other is, like the problem of the Other, marked by the recognition that the Other, like me is free. In the residue of the failure of love there remains an awareness that the Other as an object in the world, is like me, a unique object who cannot, phenomenologically speaking, be reduced to, or treated like, a mere thing. Thus, the failure of love does not shut the door on hope.

Turning from the failure of love to the possibilities of the caress, Sartre suggests that the problem of the other might find its way out of the labyrinth of conflict if we allowed ourselves to be led by the experience of each other as flesh rather than bodies; that is, if we allowed our bodies to become ensnared in the world and clogged by facticity (1956, p. 509). Doing this, our desire to possess the Other's freedom is transformed. It 'appears as a double reciprocal incarnation' (1956, p. 508). Unhappily this reciprocity does not last; for though this reciprocity of incarnation is the goal of desire, desire is 'naturally continued not in the caress but by acts of taking and penetration . . . [where] my body ceases to be flesh and becomes again the synthetic instrument which I am' (1956, p. 516). The call of the flesh is fragile and so it cannot, for Sartre, become the ground of an ethics. In his *Notebooks*, however, Sartre returns to the possibility of the flesh. Here he describes these possibilities in terms of generosity and the gift. Though he does not remind us of his discussions of the caress, his descriptions of the joys of giving that refuse the temptations of possession (1992, pp. 493–5) sound very much like the hope embedded in the caress. Again this hope is abandoned. Where for de Beauvoir the doubled moment of intentionality provided an opening to and a ground for ethics that could be immediately experienced in the erotic drama of the flesh, for Sartre, the doubled demands of freedom that threaten the ethical project cannot be resolved through the caress. He will look to language to provide a more reliable way to navigate the ambiguities of freedom.

Language, Sartre tells us, forms part of the human condition. It is synonymous with the recognition of the other's existence (1956, p. 486). Sartre writes: 'As soon as I express myself, I can only guess at the meaning of what I express . . . The Other is always there, present and experienced as the one who gives to language its meaning . . . The very fact of expression is a stealing of thought since thought needs the cooperation of an alienating freedom in order to be constituted as an object . . . Language reveals the other as the one who listens to me in silence ' It also reveals the other to me as a freedom to be engaged rather than as an object to be used. Sartre finds that, 'The problem of language is exactly parallel to the problem of bodies' (1956, p. 487). In *Being and Nothingness*, the intersubjective promise of bodies is constantly betrayed. In *Literature and Existentialism*, however, Sartre finds that language takes the problem of our being-for-others in a direction where the hope for an ethic can take root.

Literature and Existentialism opens by affirming the parallel between language and embodiment. Language, Sartre writes, 'is our shell and out antennae . . . We are within language as we are within our body' (1964, p. 20). Sounding the phenomenological theme of consciousness as a disclosing activity and, like de Beauvoir, linking the act of disclosure to the act of critique, Sartre characterizes the word as a mode of action and the prose writer as someone who 'has chosen a certain method of secondary action which we may call action by disclosure' (Sartre, 1964, p. 22). This action is both concrete and universal. Concretely, it registers the particular situation of a specific writer and the action that the author takes to reveal its injustices in order to protest them. Universally, the engaged writer forces us to face our responsibility for the world and to others. '[T]he function of the writer', Sartre writes, 'is to act in such a way that nobody can be ignorant of the world and that nobody may say that he is innocent' (1964, p. 24).

According to Sartre, the artist understands that freedom decides on the fate and value of thought (1964, p. 114). The final goal of art, he writes is 'to recover this world by giving it to be seen as it is, but as if it had its source in human freedom' (1964, p. 57). This recovery is neither a solipsistic nor an authoritarian enterprise; for the essence of literature is not just to disclose the world but also and necessarily to will itself as an appeal to the other's freedom (Sartre 1964, p. 150). Here the other is no longer the one who steals my world from me, but the one with whom I build a world. Now, aesthetic joy – freedom experiencing its creative activity of constituting objects – rather than dread is the prevailing mood (Sartre 1964, p. 58).

It is in light of this analysis of the appeal as essential to the relationship between author and reader, and it is in light of the way that this relationship makes us responsible for the world and each other that Sartre finds the moral imperative at the heart of the aesthetic imperative (Sartre, 1964, p. 62). In creating a world 'impregnated always with more freedom', in appealing to the reader's freedom, writing is a certain way of wanting freedom (1964, pp. 63–5).

Merleau-Ponty: The Paradox of Ambiguity, Dialogue and the Possibility of Ethics

Turning from one of Sartre's works to another, it is difficult to know whether or not he believed that it was possible to reconcile the ontology of conflict and domination with an ethics grounded in the reciprocity of literature and the flesh. Merleau-Ponty confronts the matter of the possibility of reconciliation by thinking of this paradox in terms of an ambiguity that makes communication possible and by turning to the phenomenology of communication to ground his existential ethics. Closer to de Beauvoir who aligns intentionality with the mood of joy than to Sartre who associates the immediate experience of freedom with the moods of dread and anxiety, Merleau-Ponty links my experience of myself as the meaning giver to/of the world to the mood of wonder (Merleau-Ponty, 1962, p. xiii). He tells us, that this wonder before the strangeness of the world awakens me to the ways that I am embedded in a network of relationships (1962, p. xx). This network of relationships is cultural and historical. Each age has its own way of being towards others, nature, time and death. Each age has its way of patterning these relationships. Being born into these patterns we must decide whether to adopt or transform them (1962, p. xvii). In *Humanism and Terror* (1969) Merleau-Ponty describes the twentieth-century revolutionary way of patterning the world. In *Signs* (1964b) he provides directives for transforming terrorist patterns into ethical ones.

Merleau-Ponty sees his phenomenological project as probing the unthought in the work of Edmund Husserl (1964b, p. 160). Like the later Husserl, Merleau-Ponty examines the ways in which we, as linguistic beings, exist at the intersection of the particular and the universal. He discerns the ways in which historical contingencies, our embeddedness in a particular language, and our specific modes of embodiment, inscribe us in a world of others that reaches back to a shared prehistorical condition and looks forward towards a shared historical future.

Guided by Husserl's unthought, Merleau-Ponty finds the key to Husserl's enigmatic statement 'Transcendental subjectivity is intersubjectivity' (Merleau-Ponty, 1964b, p. 97). He finds that once we anchor subjectivity in the lived body we encounter the corporeal primordial 'we' embedded in the 'I'. Where de Beauvoir *argues* that I cannot deprive the other of their freedom without necessarily threatening my own, Merleau-Ponty, in his descriptions of perception and speech, *shows* us that your world is necessarily mine and that my world is necessarily yours. Describing the phenomenon of sight and touch, Merleau-Ponty writes: 'between my body looked at and my body looking, my body touched and my body touching, there is an overlapping or encroachment so that we must say that the things pass into us as well as we into things' (1968, p. 123). Describing speech, he says: 'When I speak or understand, I experience that presence of others in myself or of myself in others' (1964b, p. 97). In both speaking and perceiving we experience the same double reference, the simultaneous retiring into oneself and leaving oneself (1968, p. 124) that marks us as ambiguous.

This is not to say that perceiving and speaking can be reduced to each other. Speech and language are unique in that they are the ways that we superimpose human meanings on the world (Merleau-Ponty, 1962, p. 188). Further, 'of all bodily functions they are the most intimately linked with our communal co-existence' (1962, p. 160). This intimacy, this openness to the other happens through language because it is through language that I transport myself into the other person's perspective (Merleau-Ponty, 1973b, p. 19). In transporting myself into the other's perspective, I also become vulnerable to them for, 'Speaking and listening . . . presuppose the capacity to allow oneself to be pulled down and rebuilt again by the other person' (1973b, p. 17). In allowing myself to be vulnerable to the other in this way I embody the freedom to transcend myself towards a new form of behaviour, a new way of being in the world and with others (1973b, p. 20). But, and this will become crucial in Merleau-Ponty's formulation of his new humanism, these new ways of being cannot be predicted. The being of language is a becoming that takes up random factors and transforms them into a meaningful whole where the bond between the subject and the world and the subject and others becomes visible. The meaning-making operation of language is constantly interrupted by accidents and chance. Unlike formal logics that move from a first premise to a final conclusion according to predetermined laws, the logic of language is a logic of contingency. In transforming random factors into meaningful wholes it is inhospitable to the finality of conclusions or the stability of meaning. As a logic of contingency, language reflects the ambiguity of the embodied subject who is both a presence in a pre-constituted world and a spontaneity that interrupts the givenness of the world and gives it new meanings. The challenge of an existential humanist ethics, as Merleau-Ponty sees it, lies in endorsing the spontaneity that renders all ethical demands unstable while validating the ethical universal necessary for intersubjective life.

While he shares contemporary humanists' suspicion of traditional humanism and finds the traditional humanist appeal to the idea of necessary progress a secularized theology that evades the material realities of contingency and chance, Merleau-Ponty determines that there is an affinity between the phenomenological project of recovering the meaning of the speaking subject and the humanist project of discerning the universal within the particular (Merleau-Ponty, 1964b, pp. 40–1). Severing humanism from its metaphysical anchors, he explores the ways that it expresses a desire for a possible future, and the ways that as linguistic, embodied beings it is possible for us to transform an imagined future into one that is concretely real (1964b, p. 241). In endorsing this new humanism, Merleau-Ponty situates himself as both a man of his (our) times and a philosopher. His new humanism expresses the way in which we have patterned our relationship to time – namely, contingency (1964b, p. 239). As a reformulation of the humanism of the Enlightenment, his new humanism performs the philosophical operation of, 'taking over . . . cultural operations begun before our time and pursued in many different ways which we now "reanimate" and reactivate from the standpoint of the present' (Merleau-Ponty, 1973a, p. 101). He writes:

> Even those among us today who are taking up the word 'humanism' again no longer maintain the *shameless humanism* of our elders. What is perhaps

proper to our time is to disassociate humanism from the idea of a humanity fully guaranteed by natural law and not only reconcile consciousness of human values and consciousness of the infrastructures which keep them in existence, but insist upon their inseparability. (1964b, p. 226)

Becoming conscious of human values is a descriptive phenomenological project. Insisting on the inseparability of these values and the infrastructures which keep them in existence leads us into the domains of ethics and politics – the domain of action; for only our actions can establish infrastructures which express human values and only our persistence can ensure their continued existence.

The hope of Merleau-Ponty's new humanism lies in the transformative power of speech and dialogue. Dialogue enacts this reversibility through the power of speech. Here the openness to otherness that is embodied in the reciprocity and doubling of perception is lived as an openness to the other that is encountered in the reversibility of perspectives. With respect to dialogue, however, the metaphors of obverse and reverse (Merleau-Ponty, 1968, p. 140) are misleading; for here, the reversibility is not necessarily complementary. Different perspectives are not necessarily two aspects of the same movement. Although our different perspectives are different ways of constituting the common world to which we belong, as often as not the expression of these differences (e.g. in racism) become venues for tearing the 'we' of the world apart rather than ways of articulating its intersecting dimensions. The ethical work of dialogue may be seen as encountering the differences of our singularity in ways that keep us open to the reversibility of perspectives and the transformative power of language.

Focusing on the ethical and political valence of this transformative power Merleau-Ponty characterizes our relationship to language in terms of 'dwelling' (Merleau-Ponty, 1964b, p. 232). We dwell in language because we are beings who do not coincide with ourselves like things. In Merleau-Ponty's words, 'man is the being who . . . represents himself to himself, sees himself, imagines himself, and gives himself rigorous or fanciful symbols of himself, it is quite clear that in return every change in our representation of man translates a change in man himself' (1964b, p. 225). Dwelling in language we reinvent ourselves; for through language we create new relationships to meaning (1964b, p. 232). In dialogue, the other and I meet through the different ways in which we experience our shared world. We surprise and encroach on each other and in this surprise and encroachment we are mutually transformed (1973b, p. 142). As the transformative power of speech lies in its reality as dialogue, the transformative power of dialogue is captured in the notion of 'trespassing' (1973b, p. 133). In the speech–dialogue situation I throw the other towards what I know and she has not yet understood as she carries me towards what I am still on the way to understanding.

Merleau-Ponty calls this tug and pull of the dialogue situation the 'violence of speech'. It is a violence of change and transformation created by the operation of meaning which comes into being through anticipations, encroachments and transgressions (Merleau-Ponty, 1973b p. 131). What Merleau-Ponty calls the 'violence of speech' bears no relationship to the rivalry usually associated with the phenomenon of violence. In dialogue, violence is synonymous with the effects of surprise and disorientation that are essential for the movement of speech and the coming into being of meaning. (Merleau-Ponty, 1973b p. 141). Unlike the violence of the friend–enemy antagonism which sets the stage for war, the violence of speech, grounded as it is in the common culture of the parties to the dialogue, realizes the 'impossible' agreement between rival totalities by seducing these totalities to engage each other and through this engagement to transform the walls that separate us into passages between us. This vision of transformation is not, Merleau-Ponty insists, a utopian vision. It does not depend on an impossible conversion. It is grounded in the power of speech and in the common world revealed in the dynamics of dialogue. The spontaneous power of speech undermines the active/passive structure of antagonistic rivalry, for as speakers we are also listeners. Further in speaking to each other, however, antagonistic our words may be, the fact that we understand each other is traceable to the fact that our words evoke a common world (1973b pp. 144–5). The hope of the new humanism lies here. According to Merleau-Ponty the rationality or agreement of minds, the ground of the possibility of a shared *moral* world, only requires that 'every experience contains points of catch all for all other ideas and that ideas have a configuration' (1973b p. 143). As the old humanism relied either on a rationality that transformed the contingencies of the human condition into the necessities of a fully realized (already given) human nature, or on the determinism of the dialectic, Merleau-Ponty's hope for a new humanism relies on the existential contingencies and ambiguities that define us. Rationality in the context of this new humanism is understood as a meeting through which shared and changing meanings of the world emerge, not as the imposition of the universal on the particular. The future is considered the time of unanticipated possibilities, not as the realization of an already conceived world.

Merleau-Ponty's ethics of shared meanings and dialogue comes with a warning. We must not let the pursuit of shared meanings obscure the unreachable strangeness of the other or dull the wonder of encountering it. We must not let our humanist hope 'iron out the I and the Thou in an experience shared by a plurality, thus introducing the impersonal into the heart of subjectivity and eliminating the individuality of perspectives' (Merleau-Ponty, 1962, pp. 355–6). Merleau-Ponty leaves this reference to the I and the Thou hanging. It will be left to Martin Buber to engage it.

Martin Buber: The Conversation with God

Martin Buber would not have been surprised at Merleau-Ponty's reference to the I and the Thou of intersubjectivity. From Buber's perspective no account of our relationship to others can avoid speaking of the Thou. He would also understand why Merleau-Ponty's reference is fleeting. Merleau-Ponty is silent on the question of God, and as Buber sees it, this silence deprives him of the resources he needs to address the meaning of the personal Thou that lies at the heart of the intertwining of subjectivity and intersubjectivity. For Buber, the shared personal I and Thou experience of plurality is grounded in an I–Thou encounter with God – the Absolute Person. 'As a Person', Buber writes, 'God gives personal life, he makes us as persons become capable of meeting with Him and with one another' (1958, p. 136). Buber calls this giving of personal life and our response to it a 'conversation with God' that 'penetrates what happens in the life of each one of us and all that happens in the world around us' (1958, p. 136). This conversation as the ground of every Thou relationship is also and necessarily the ground of our ethical life. In Buber's words: 'Happening upon happening, situation upon situation, are enabled and empowered by the personal speech of God to demand of the human person that he take his stand and make his decision' (1958, pp. 136–7).

The God with whom Buber is in conversation and in whose image he says we are made, bears little resemblance to the God rejected by de Beauvoir and Sartre. As images of God, human persons have no predetermined nature that threatens our existential becoming by establishing its boundaries. We can no more determine our essence than we can determine the essence of God. In Buber's words: 'The concept of a personal being is indeed completely incapable of declaring what God's essential being is, but it is both permitted and necessary to say that God is *also* a Person' (1958, p. 135). Though Buber holds to the biblical view that we are created by God, he finds that though as human we are the twoness of the I–Thou I–It relationship, we are images of God only as I–Thou.

One way of understanding Buber's account of the I–It/I–Thou is to see it as radicalizing the phenomenological account of intentionality. Where phenomenology speaks of the subject as existing *in* relationship to the world and others, Buber speaks of the subject *as* a relationship to the world and others. For Buber there are two primary words, I–It and I–Thou. There is no I. He writes: 'The I of the primary word I–Thou is different from that of the primary word I–It. . . . [these primary words] intimate relations . . . [they] do not describe something that might exist independently of them, but being spoken they bring about existence' (1958, p. 3). The I of the I–Thou and the I–It are radically different. The I of the I–Thou describes our unique way of existing as/in relationship to the mysteries of the world, each other and God. The I of the I–It describes our relationship to the world as a realm of objects that can be organized and used.

Understanding Buber's existential ethics requires that we remember that it is we, not God, who create the world's twofold existence (1958, p. 131).

In the beginning, Buber says, there is no I. There is only the Thou. The I emerges through the Thou, and with the emergence of the I of the I–Thou, the primary word I–It is also assembled. Now the world will become populated with objects of perception, useful objects, objects of experience. Watching an infant emerge from the web of its early life to explore the world on its own, we can see the lived realities of the birth of the I–Thou and the I–It. We treat this emergence as growth. Buber treats this coming into being of the I–It as a necessity for which we pay a price. In emerging from the I–Thou, the I–It drains energy from the I–Thou. This I of the I–It is the I of the I–Thou 'shrunk from substance and fullness to a functional point, to a subject which experiences and uses' (Buber, 1958, p. 29) Thus, although we are born into the primordial Thou, 'the exalted melancholy of our fate is that every Thou in our world must become an It' (1958, p. 16). Buber identifies the Thou as the a priori of all relationships. He writes, 'In the beginning is relation' (1958, p. 27). The bodily individual who is born into the world by entering into relations becomes a personal actualized being whose uniquely human Thou relationships are consummated in the life of dialogue – the life of speech and counter-speech, 'the give and take of talk' (1958, p. 103). Buber calls this rhythm of dialogue, 'the real simile of the relationship with God' and identifies 'the sound of the lively and impressive I of Socrates as epitomizing the life of the I 'bodied forth in dialogue' (1958, p. 66).

Although Buber describes the emergence of the I–It as the melancholy of our fate, he does not accuse the It of alienating us from our humanity. The I–It is the source of the ordered, reliable world that sustains us. It establishes the causal connections of space and time. It reveals a measured and conditioned nature (Buber, 1958, pp. 29–30). It has given us the polio vaccine, AIDS medications and the Hubble telescope. So long as this ordered world is open to the Thou which both grounds and dissolves the It, so long as the world remains twofold, humanity will thrive. The health of humanity, however, cannot be guaranteed. It is vulnerable to sickness. The It of smooth causality can rise up till it becomes an oppressive stifling fate (1958, pp. 53–4). Buber reads history as a contest between the poles of the I–It, I–Thou (1958, p. 65). The rise and fall of civilizations follows the rise and fall of the Thou in the life of a people. When a people's will to profit and power (their I–It) is severed from their will to enter into relation (their I–Thou), they will be consumed by the laws of utility and mechanics that characterize this will. As history records the fall of those peoples consumed by the It, it also records the rise of others inspired by their encounter with the Thou. In principle, the domination of our age by the law of the It, however, much it constitutes a crisis for us, should not constitute a crisis for humanity. Buber, however, finds the sickness of our age unprecedented; as unprecedented it is more than of parochial concern. In Buber's words: 'The sickness of our age is like that of no other age, and it belongs together with them all' (1958, p. 55).

Reading Buber's compelling descriptions of the I–Thou, it is difficult to understand how things could have taken this turn. His accounts of the promise of the I–Thou, however, are accompanied by descriptions of the risks of encountering the Thou once we emerge into the world of the It. In meeting the Thou, the reliability of the world of the It and my secure place in the It is disrupted. I am torn 'away to dangerous extremes, loosening the well tried context, leaving more questions than satisfaction behind them, shattering security – in short, uncanny moments we can well dispense with. For since we are bound to leave them and go back into the "world" why not remain in it?' (Buber, 1958, p. 34). In times of sickness we decide the risks are not worth the trouble. Where Nietzsche saw the crisis triggered by the death of God in terms of a world thrown into chaos, Buber sees the crisis precipitated by the end of our conversation with God in terms of the threat of a world held in the stranglehold of the mechanical laws of the It. No longer able to bear witness to the Thou, we ourselves become an It (1958, p. 57).

Neither the I–It nor the I–Thou are in themselves unethical relationships. Ethics is concerned with the balance of power between these ways of expressing the meaning of the world. The I–It gives us a liveable world. The I–Thou ensures that this liveable world is also a human one. 'Without It', Buber writes, 'man cannot live. But he who lives with It alone is not a man' (1958, p. 134). Ethics is a matter of ensuring that the I–It makes a place for the I–Thou. It is a matter of holding us responsible for acting as witnesses to the Thou and for ensuring that the It that gives the world and our lives order does not reject the mystery of the Thou that envelops us in the wonder of the world.

Risking the Ethical Life

In insisting that our ethical stance be anchored in the ground of the Absolute person, Buber challenges the humanist existential project. He finds secular humanism both dangerous and naïve: naïve because it asks too much of human power; dangerous because asking too much of human power opens the way for the domination of the It. Like the humanist existentialists Buber never suggests that he can guarantee the future. He can only hope that we will find our way to the Thou.

In turning to an Absolute Thou, however, and in describing all I–Thou relationships in terms of our conversation with God, Buber alerts us to the limits of an ethics of reciprocal freedom. We cannot reciprocate an act of grace or redemption (Buber, 1958, pp. 11, 120). We cannot guarantee that in meeting the other as a Thou we will be met in return. It is not that the secular existentialists are unaware of the limits of an ethics of reciprocity. De Beauvoir speaks both of an ethics of the project taken up in reciprocity and of an ethics of generosity and the gift. Sartre also speaks of ethics in terms of generosity and the gift. But where de Beauvoir gives little space to this ethics of gifted generosity and where Sartre abandoned the hope of an ethics emerging from the caress and refused to publish his accounts of ethical generosity, Buber puts the ethics of the gift at the centre of his thought. He, however, has little to say about the ethics of the project. Reading these existentialists in conversation with each other, we might find that an ethics that creates a dialogue between the ethics of the project and the ethics of the gift would best express the ambiguities of our doubled way of being in the world.

Bibliography

Buber, M. (1958), *I and Thou*, trans. Ronald Gregor Smith. New York: Charles Scribner's Sons.

De Beauvoir, S. (1948), *The Ethics of Ambiguity*, trans. Bernard Frechtman. New York: Philosophical Library.

— (1989), *The Second Sex*, trans. H. M. Parshley. New York: Vintage Books.

— (2004), 'Pyrrhus and Cineas', trans. Marybeth Timmermann, in M. A. Simons (ed.), *Simone de Beauvoir: Philosophical Writings*. Urbana: University of Illinois Press, pp. 90–141.

Kierkegaard, S. (1954), *Fear and Trembling*, trans. Walter Lowrie. New York: Doubleday.

Marcel, G. (1984), 'Existence and Human Freedom', *The Philosophy of Existentialism*, trans. Manya Harai. Secaucus: Citadel Press, pp. 47–90.

Merleau-Ponty, M. (1962), *Phenomenology of Perception*, trans. Colin Smith. New York: Humanities Press.

— (1964a), 'The Film and the New Psychology', *Sense and Non-Sense*, trans. Hubert L. Dreyfus and Patricia Allen Dreyfus. Evanston, IL: Northwestern University Press, pp. 48–62.

— (1964b), *Signs*, trans. R. McCleary. Evanston, IL: Northwestern University Press.

— (1968), 'The Intertwining – The Chiasm', *The Visible and the Invisible*, trans. A. Lingis. Evanston, IL: Northwestern University Press, pp. 130–55.

— (1969), *Humanism and Terror*, trans. John O'Neill. Boston: Beacon Press.

— (1973a), 'Phenomenology and the Sciences of Man', in M. Natanson (ed.), *Phenomenology and the Social Sciences*. Evanston, IL: Northwestern University Press, 1: 47–108.

— (1973b), *The Prose of the World*, ed. Claude Lefort, trans. John O'Neill. Evanston, IL: Northwestern University Press.

Nietzsche, F. (1989), *On the Genealogy of Morals*, trans. Walter Kaufmann. New York: Vintage.

Sartre, J-P. (1956), *Being and Nothingness*, trans. Hazel E. Barnes. New York: Washington Square Press.

— (1964), *Literature and Existentialism*, trans. Bernard Frechtman. New York: Citadel Press.

— (1989), *The Flies. No Exit and Three Other Plays*, trans. Stuart Gilbert and Lionel Abel. New York: Vintage.

— (1992), *Notebooks for an Ethics*, trans. David Pellauer. Chicago: Chicago University Press.

— (1996), *Hope Now*, trans. Adrian van den Hoven. Chicago: Chicago University Press.

Young, I. M. (1990), *Throwing Like a Girl and Other Essays in Feminist Philosophy and Social Theory*. Bloomington, IN: Indiana University Press.

7 Existentialism and Religion

George Pattison

The question of religion and, more particularly, the question of God is unavoidable in considering the phenomenon of twentieth-century existentialism and its main nineteenth-century predecessors – Kierkegaard, Dostoevsky and Nietzsche. Many commentators saw existentialism itself as little more than a thinly secularized form of religiosity. Helmut Kuhn's *Encounter with Nothingness* states in its 'Introduction' that 'crisis as depicted by the Existentialists is the Christian crisis in caricature', adding that 'the Nothingness which the Existentialist encounters is the shadow of the repudiated God' (Kuhn, 1951, pp. xviii–xix, xxii). Conversely, as Walter Kaufmann claims in introducing his anthology of *Existentialism from Dostoevsky to Sartre*:

> [R]eligion has always been existentialist: it has always insisted that mere schools and bodies of belief are not enough, that too much of our thinking is remote from that which truly matters, and that we must change our lives. It has always been preoccupied with suffering, death, and dread, with care, guilt, and despair. (1956, pp. 49–50)

It is, therefore, not surprising that several of the key figures cited in standard accounts of the genesis of existentialism were in one or other sense 'religious'. Examples would include Blaise Pascal, Søren Kierkegaard and F. M. Dostoevsky – with some commentators extending the story back to Augustine or even to the book of Job. Furthermore, in the period when existentialism was at the height of its cultural impact there were a number of writers who were regarded as religious existentialists. These typically included the Jewish thinkers Martin Buber, Franz Rosenzweig and Lev Shestov, the Catholic philosopher Gabriel Marcel, and the Orthodox lay thinker Nicholas Berdyaev in addition to the explicitly existentialist theologies of the Lutherans Rudolf Bultmann and Paul Tillich (for more on all these figures see Pattison, 1999). There were also strong existentialist elements in the movement of Japanese Buddhist philosophy known as the Kyoto School (see Pattison, 1996, pp. 108–37).

Yet, thanks chiefly to the influence of Jean-Paul Sartre, it is widely assumed that existentialism is inherently and necessarily atheistic. Sartre himself believed passionately that there is a simple and straightforward conflict between divine and human freedom. If God exists, then he is the supreme Other, whose gaze not only reduces me to the status of a mere exterior object but who anticipates my every possibility. To claim the freedom in and by which I become who I am, I have, as it were, to tear it away from God. In his autobiographical memoir *Words*, Sartre gives vivid expression to his own early realization of this situation:

> One day I handed my teacher a French essay on the Passion; it had delighted my family, and my mother had copied it out herself. It won only the silver medal. This disappointment plunged me into impiety . . . For several years longer, I kept up public relations with the Almighty; in private, I stopped associating with Him. Once only I had the feeling that He existed. I had been playing with matches and had burnt a mat; I was busy covering up my crime when suddenly God saw me. I felt his gaze inside my head and on my hands; I turned round in the bathroom, horribly visible, a living target. I was saved by indignation: I grew angry at such a crude lack of tact, and blasphemed, muttering like my grandfather: '*Sacré nom de Dieu de Dieu de nom de Dieu*'. He never looked at me again. (1967, p. 65)

Against the background of this anecdote, we may say that, for Sartre, God is the one who looks at me *when I don't want to be looked at*. As such God is the powerful epitome of the Other who limits, constrains and ultimately frustrates my attempt to become who I am. As Sartre writes elsewhere in *Words*: 'a vast collective power had penetrated me; lodged in my heart, it was keeping watch, it was the faith of others' (1967, p. 155). This 'vast collective power', he acknowledges, was not so easy to throw off as conscious belief in God. Indeed, it continued to hold sway over his early attempts to be a writer. 'It is enough to debaptize and modify superficially its normal object: faith recognized it beneath the disguises which deceived me, threw itself on it and enclosed it in its tendrils. I thought I was giving myself to literature when I was, in fact, taking holy orders.' 'Writing', in other words, was a God substitute, a new and subtle version of 'the Other, the Invisible, the Holy Ghost, he who guaranteed my mandate and dominated my life through great, anonymous and sacred forces, he remained . . . For a long time, writing was asking Death or Religion in disguise to tear my life away from chance. I was of the Church' (p. 156).

This, then, is a very different kind of atheism from the atheism of logical positivists or Neo-Darwinians. The issue is not about the existence of a metaphysical or supernatural entity called 'God' but the meaning that God might and can have for human beings. Sartre clearly believed that God didn't exist in the former sense also, but far more important was that God *shouldn't* exist. It is not just a matter of not believing in God but of refusing to believe in God.

These comments indicate a number of tasks in considering the relationship between religion and existentialism. First, is Sartre correct in his view that human freedom requires the refusal of God or are there ways of modelling human selfhood that either demonstrate the compatibility of human and divine freedom or that give an alternative interpretation of the role of the Other in human self-constitution? But, secondly, is the kind of absolute freedom to which Sartre seemingly aspires itself a legacy from a de-divinized idea of God? As Nietzsche's madman commented in proclaiming the death of God to a crowd of bemused bystanders, we ourselves will have to become gods to be worthy of having killed the God of Christianity and metaphysics (1972, pp. 126–8). And then, more broadly, what are the features of existentialism that it inherited from religious – chiefly Jewish and Christian – traditions and how deeply did they penetrate the formation of existentialism as such? I shall consider these questions in reverse order before turning finally to the issue as to whether there can be a religious existentialism and what it might be like, with reference to some of the figures regularly classified as religious existentialists.

However, one further prefatory remark is in order. It may seem as if I am too simplistically subscribing to the view that there actually is such a thing as 'existentialism' and failing, from the outset, to make the necessary distinctions between, let us say, Heidegger's philosophy of *Existenz* and French existentialism, or between 'existentialism' as expressive of an intellectual mood and existentialism as a distinct body of philosophical views (which possibly never existed and in relation to which we might paraphrase Nietzsche's remark about there only ever having been one Christian, who died on the cross: that there was only ever one existentialist, and he converted to Marxism). All these distinctions – and more – are, of course, important, but this is not the place to argue for any one particular definition of existentialism. In what follows I shall be assuming rather than arguing for a certain view of existentialism, but I hope that in doing so I shall not be perpetrating any kind of subterfuge on the reader and that my assumptions will be more or less transparent. It may, however, be useful to stress now that I am taking the term as applying less to a particular set of philosophical positions and more to a certain current in the history of ideas that first acquires a clear profile in the writings of Søren Kierkegaard and that culminates in the postwar atmosphere of Parisian existentialism.

Existentialism's Religious Inheritance

The back-story of existentialism involves many different threads and invites rather loose speculation as to what is or isn't 'existential'. Rather than attempting a broad overview of all the possible sources and aetiologies, therefore, and given the role of Martin Heidegger in formalizing what would become known as the philosophy of existence, it seems appropriate to begin by looking, briefly, at the role of religious sources in shaping Heidegger's early master-work *Being and Time*. In a 1927 exchange of letters with the New Testament scholar Rudolf Bultmann (who had been charged with writing an encyclopedia article on Heidegger), the philosopher sums up his then current agenda. The basic task, he says, is the radicalizing of classical ontology and rethinking it on the ground of history, thus fulfilling one of the basic aspirations of German Idealism. In pursuit of this task he cites Aristotle, scholasticism and Dilthey as having particular significance, all to be read within the new paradigm of scientific philosophy established by Husserl. However, he also states emphatically that 'Augustine, Luther, Kierkegaard are philosophically essential for the formation of a radical understanding of Dasein' (Heidegger in Großmann and Landmesser, 2009, p. 48). All of these will, in fact, reappear in footnotes in *Being and Time*, footnotes that simultaneously stress their importance for the task in hand but that also – to the chagrin of many theological readers – seemingly subordinate them to Heidegger's more purely philosophical task.

In fact, as a survey of Heidegger's development up to *Being and Time* makes clear, the role of religion is even more prominent than the letter to Bultmann might suggest. Of course, Heidegger does mention scholasticism there, and it is well known that his own early ambition was to enter the Jesuit order and to teach as a Catholic philosopher. Although he would subsequently be extremely critical of scholastic philosophy (referring to it in *Being and Time* itself as an 'ossified tradition'), it remained the focus of much of his work up to and including his *habilitation* thesis on *Duns Scotus' Doctrine of Categories and Meaning* (1916).[1] Although he had plans to follow this up with a further study of medieval mysticism, he is increasingly drawing on wider sources. In 1917 he is reading Schleiermacher's *Speeches on Religion* (Kisiel and Sheehan, 2007, pp. 86–91) and, like many of his contemporaries, finding food for thought in Dostoevsky, Kierkegaard and Luther. In the immediate postwar period his lectures on the phenomenology of religion engage critically with contemporary Protestant theology (von Harnack and Troeltsch) and develop striking new interpretations of St Paul and Augustine in which key elements of *Being and Time* are anticipated. These include the future-oriented structure of temporality, concern or care, being-in-the-world, and an emphasis on the 'how' of the self's engagement with itself and its world rather than on defining the self through its essence. Augustine – with help from Kierkegaard – focuses the scenario of the self that exists in the mode of self-questioning: student notes excitedly record Heidegger's train of thought when, apropos Augustine's search for God, he asks '1. What really is 'seeking'? 2. What do I really seek? [. . .] In searching for God there is something in me that doesn't just come to "expression", but something that constitutes my facticity and my concern [*Bekummerung*] for it [. . .] What does it mean to say I "am"? (It turns on winning an "idea" [*Vorstellung*] of the self, what sort of idea I have of my self. Kierkegaard)' (Heidegger, 1995, p. 192).

These indications of Heidegger's preoccupation with religious sources in the period leading up to *Being and Time* suggest something of the importance of religious experience and religious life in the formation of the kind of self-relation that he would call *Dasein*. But it should also be stressed that he is also throughout this period (and even when he is still referring to himself as a 'theologian') reading his religious sources in the context of a philosophical programme. This becomes especially apparent in *Being and Time* itself. Heidegger's scholastic heritage is apparent in the basic characterization of the question of Being in the 'Introduction' and opening pages and his use of such scholastic terms as *essentia* and *existentia*. However, it is no less apparent that from the very outset he is subverting these terms by suggesting that *Dasein* is characterized by a relationship between essence and existence – cf. '*the essence of Dasein lies in its existence*', Heidegger, 1962, sec. 9, pp. 67/42[2] – that scholasticism reserves for God.[3] With the major exception of the treatment of anxiety, Heidegger's debt to the kind of religious experience found in Augustine, Luther and Kierkegaard is relatively in the background in part I of *Being and Time* (where, arguably, it is Husserl and Aristotle who play the more important role). However, it becomes highly visible in part II, as he moves to the analysis of *Dasein*'s existence as a being-to-wards-death, and of the role of conscience, guilt and nothingness. So too with regard to the time-experience of the self and the description (or is it a postulate?) of a 'moment of vision' in which the dimensions of past-present, and future are synthesized and held together in an act of resolute self-choice on the part of *Dasein*. The repetition of such an act in turn grounds the possibility for *Dasein* to exist across time, living with and even, to use Heidegger's phrase, 'running forward' towards its own ineluctable death. This whole scenario is decidedly Kierkegaardian and, although he himself studied neither Augustine nor Luther in depth, Kierkegaard here pulls together a wide historically attested spectrum of expressions of the Christian view of existence. Before returning to Heidegger, then, let us briefly look at these terms as they are found in Kierkegaard so as better to see how what has a distinctively religious context in the work of the Danish thinker is relocated in the work of the German philosopher.[4]

I begin with anxiety, which Kierkegaard discusses in a work, *The Concept of Anxiety*, devoted to the problem of sin in, as he puts it, a psychological perspective. However, anxiety is not itself sin nor an expression of sinfulness. Indeed, under certain conditions it can play a role in intensifying and furthering human beings' God-relationship. What, then, is it? Essentially, Kierkegaard sees it as the state or condition that is presupposed by sin and, as such, it provides a kind of middle ground between the human being as a merely natural or biological entity, determined by its nature, and the human subject who freely chooses him- or herself by deciding for the good – or for evil. Kierkegaard explains this by retelling the Genesis story of the Fall.

Kierkegaard describes Adam and Eve as living before the Fall in a state of innocence in which, he says, 'the human being does not have the attributes of spirit but has the attributes only of "soulishness" in immediate unity with nature' (1980, p. 41, translation amended). In other words, humanity at this level is almost indistinguishable from an animal existence, with sensation and feeling but without the kind of self-reflection that is a condition for 'spirit', a term he often uses as a near synonym of 'freedom'. However, since Adam and Eve were human beings and not simple animals, they – and, as he makes clear, each human infant – is, qua human, destined to become spirit. However, in Eden – or in each childhood – spirit/freedom is still only 'dreaming' (Kierkeg-aard, 1980, p. 41, translation amended). And this is something different from not existing at all. For, even if I have not yet awoken to my own possibilities for existing as a self-conscious agent, they are, nevertheless, still my possibilities. The child is a human child and not an animal. But its very humanness is, on this account, dependent on a capability that it does not yet have. Kierkegaard, some-what paradoxically, explains:

> In this state there is peace and rest, but at the same time there is something else, which does not disturb the peace or engender conflict, for there is nothing to be in conflict with. What is there then? Nothing. But what effect does nothing have? It gives birth to anxiety. This is the deep secret of innocence, that at the same time it is anxiety. Dreaming, spirit projects its own actuality, but this actuality is nothing, but innocence always sees this nothing outside itself. (1980, p. 41, translation amended)

Anxiety, then, is the child's dream of its own possibility for a kind of existence of which it cannot yet conceive. This existence is 'nothing', a mere possibility, and whether it is ever actualized or realized is not something that will happen by means of any spontaneous biological development but requires the subject's readiness freely to embrace this possibility and enact it. This bears close comparison with Heidegger's view of existence as a question of possibility: '*Dasein*', he writes, 'always understands itself in terms of its existence – in terms of a possibility of itself: to be itself or not itself' (Heidegger, 1962, pp. 41/19).

For Kierkegaard, however, although the story begins again with each individual, it is typically the case that we fail fully to realize our possibilities. The dawning awareness of our not-being-determined and our having to take responsibility for our own existence is too much for us. Cast out from the pleni-tude of Edenic being, we are faced with an empty abyss that engenders a kind of spiritual vertigo in which, characteristically, we 'succumb', as Kierkegaard puts it, and 'grasp at finitude', identifying ourselves with one or other limited, finite goal or purpose. Nevertheless, the fact that even when we are failing to be all that we might be we are still accompanied by anxiety is a reminder of a possibility for spiritual existence that we can never be rid of. Thus anxiety or the fact that we are concerned about the meaning our life as a whole might have also contains the possibility of a religious view of life. It reminds us that we were made for something more than eating, sleeping and reproducing.

This picture is further complicated by our knowledge that we must die. In *Concluding Unscientific Postscript* Kierkegaard seizes on the question of a possible immortality as a decisive counter-instance to the approach of speculative, that is, Hegelian philosophy. The problem, as he puts it, is that no matter how much I know about death, nothing I know can answer the question as to whether, in fact, death is the mere extinction of life or whether I am destined for an eternal blessedness. This is not an issue to be addressed in the spirit of disinterested contemplation since I cannot deny my essential interest in it. It is an essentially and properly subjective question that forces me into a subjective approach to the question of my own identity. The unknowability of death is especially sharply and dramatically emphasized in a discourse titled 'At a Graveside', where Kierkegaard insists that a truly serious approach to death will always recognize its inexplicability. Meditating on death does not make us expert in the art of dying, that is, it yields neither theoretical nor practical consolation. Rather it unsettles our whole manner of living and reveals the questionableness of our lives:

> [T]he inexplicability is not a request to solve enigmas, an invitation to be ingenious, but is death's earnest warning to the living: I need no explanation; but bear in mind, you yourself, that with this decision all is over and that this decision can at any moment be at hand; see, it is very advisable for you to bear this in mind. (Kierkegaard, 1993, p. 101)

Death forces us to decide who we are to be in our lives, how we are to exist, what values we should live by and, this side of the grave, it is only in the power of such a decision that our lives can acquire a certain unity – although, typically, struck down by vertigo, we fail to decide. If such a decision does occur, it will have the character of what Kierkegaard – and, following Kierkegaard, Heidegger – calls 'the moment of vision'. Although – unlike Heidegger – Kierkegaard explains this in terms of the presence of the eternal in time, giving coherence and consistency to a human life in time, there is no way of making this moment effective outside of the total acceptance of our own limitation by time. Thus, it is not the kind of mystical vision of the eternal that suffices to give meaning to life once and for all, but, to use another Kierkegaardian term, it requires 'repetition'. Choosing ourselves for what and as we are is something we must do again and again. And although Kierkegaard quietly drops the term 'repetition' itself after his early novella of that title, the idea is present in, for example, the role he gives to patience and hope in many of his upbuilding writings. Moreover, precisely these features serve to bring out the character of resoluteness involved here. What is at issue is not an arbitrary or gratuitous act of will but a commitment and self-commitment sustained over time. This also includes accepting the guilt for not having lived according to our best possibilities up to the moment of vision itself.

The term 'resoluteness' is especially notable in Kierkegaard's writings in association with the fictional character Assessor Vilhelm, representative of what Kierkegaard calls the ethical point of view. In a passage that has a possibly unintended ironic effect, the Assessor, writing in defence of marriage, insists that the specific quality of a married man is not that he says 'I do', but that he takes up his cross daily! (Kierkegaard, 1987, p. 135). In a later work, the same character speaks of resoluteness as being something more than a merely spontaneous courage; rather, it is a fully self-conscious, passionate, and enduring commitment: it is 'a new immediacy, attained through an exhaustive ideal reflection . . . [It] is not man's strength, it is not man's courage, it is not man's talent . . . but it is a religious starting-point' or, as he also says, it is 'a religious life-view constructed upon ethical postulates' (Kierkegaard, 1940, p. 159). There are extensive debates among Kierkegaard scholars as to how far the Assessor's position can be regarded as fully religious and we shall return to the question as to whether a religious existentialism may not require something more or something other than a simple act of resolute self-commitment.

Returning to Heidegger, what we see emerging here is precisely a model of existence that, within the limits of temporality, allows for what the philosopher calls an 'authentic being-towards-death'. However, this brief detour through Kierkegaard also helps us see the ambivalence of Heidegger's relation not only to Kierkegaard but to other religious figures, such as Augustine and Luther, who played an important role in the genesis of *Being and Time*. Although, as we have seen, Heidegger acknowledged the importance of these thinkers in his thought, he also treats them with a certain reserve. In a much-cited footnote, Heidegger writes of Kierkegaard as 'the man who has gone farthest in analysing the phenomenon of anxiety . . . in the context of a "psychological" exposition of the problem of original sin' (1962, pp. 492/190) and as having 'explicitly seized upon the problem of existence as an existentiell problem, and thought it through in a penetrating fashion' although 'the existential problematic' was 'alien' to him and 'as regards his ontology, he remained completely dominated by Hegel and by ancient philosophy as Hegel saw it'. He also, and intriguingly, adds that 'there is more to be learned philosophically . . . [from Kierkegaard's religious writings] . . . than from his theoretical [works] – with the exception of his treatise on the concept of anxiety' (pp. 494/235). With regard to the moment of vision, he states that Kierkegaard is 'probably the one who has seen the existentiell phenomenon of the moment of vision with the most penetration', although 'this does not signify that he has been correspondingly successful in Interpreting it existentially' (pp. 497/338).

These comments all hinge on a distinction Heidegger draws between the 'existentiell' and the 'existential'. The latter relates specifically to the task of generating a philosophical analysis of existence that would have universal validity. The former relates more to the particular, local experience of existing that each of us, philosophers or not, always have. Thus, while you or I may find ourselves in the situation of having to choose between Christianity and Islam or to choose between the commitment of marriage and continuing to play the field as a committed singleton, what interests the philosopher is the general structure of choice that such specific choices presuppose or reveal. While my interest may be focused on the respective merits of Christianity and Islam or on the virtues of the beloved versus the pleasures of promiscuity, the philosopher zooms in on the striking fact that I find myself having to choose at all and finding my identity in and through my choices. But the philosopher could never have invented the scenario of choice and it is crucial to Heidegger's procedure in *Being and Time* that his existential philosophical analysis is not just an invention or construction, but a genuine interpretation of what is going on in human lives, that is, at the level of the existentiell. As he puts it, the existential analysis needs the testimony of the existentiell. And this is just what religious writers such as Kierkegaard provide. In other words, the possibility of philosophy being able to arrive at a true interpretation of Being is, in a way, dependent on what Kierkegaard would call actual existing human beings proving capable of enacting a decisive and resolute affirmation of life in, for example, marriage or religious faith. Thus, it is not only the general delineation of the human being as anxiously thrown towards its own ineluctable death and nothingness that Heidegger takes from a certain Augustinianism and Kierkegaardianism: it is also, centrally, the possibility of this situation being resolved in a meaningful and non-absurd fashion, that is, the possibility of existing authentically.

This, however, seems to mark a significant difference vis-à-vis Sartre. For Sartre, it is axiomatic that human beings can never establish the ground of their own being. We are necessarily and in every case, a 'failed project'! Our freedom is not the freedom to affirm our lives as a whole, such as Heidegger looks to find in the figure of authentic resoluteness, but the freedom to be as we are in our unfinished, partial and essentially absurd contingency. For Heidegger, it seems, there is the possibility of a genuine openness to Being, whereas, for Sartre, the 'upsurge of nothingness' that we ourselves are disrupts any possible relation to Being from the very start. Again we can see why, for Sartre, allowing the existence of God would seem to undermine such freedom, since the contingency and absurdity of our individual lives would find an absolute and necessary ground in the will of God: in choosing ourselves we would be choosing ourselves and our lives as willed by God.

We have now seen something of how Heidegger's philosophy of existence drew heavily on the religious writer, Kierkegaard, and how, in so doing, he also relied on the religious experience of faith as testifying to the possibility of an authentic existential understanding of Being as such. The Russian religious writer, Lev Shestov, whose book *Kierkegaard and Existential Philosophy* did much to introduce a French readership to Kierkegaard, gave extreme expression to this aspect of Heidegger's undertaking when he wrote that 'Heidegger's whole book consists only of putting [Kierkegaard's] ideas into a Husserlian framework' and that *Being and Time*, far from being a genuine work of phenomenology, was 'the attempt, under the flag of phenomenology to smuggle something non-philosophical into the territory of philosophy, that is, the Biblical account of the fall and of original sin' (Baranova-Shestova, 1983, p. 17).

But Shestov's characteristic one-sidedness does not really do justice to Heidegger's project, since the philosopher wants to insist that qua philosopher he remains neutral to the specific claims of Christianity or any other existentiell attitude or commitment. Philosophy does not simply 'smuggle' a religious content into its own territory, it also interprets it and, in doing so, strips it of whatever is essentially non-philosophical in it.

That, at least, is how Heidegger understood it in *Being and Time*. Sartre, as we have seen, will not yield to religion even the possibility of its serving as an existentiell testimony to authentic existence, not least because he does not think authentic existence is a real possibility![5] Admitting religion on even the limited terms offered by Heidegger would be to admit a Trojan Horse, since, for Sartre, we are obliged to make a clear and irrevocable choice between deity and humanity.

Divine and Human Freedom

In this regard, Sartre is the inheritor of a classic trope of nineteenth-century radical thought. We have already heard Nietzsche's madman warn his listeners that they would have to become gods in order to live up to the greatness of having been the agents of the death of God and the idea persistently resonates throughout Zarathustra's teaching on the superman, creator of his own values, poet of his own life. But Nietzsche's essential idea here had already been anticipated by Dostoevsky. There are several characters in various of Dostoevsky's novels who seek to enact one or other – usually violent – form of self-creation, but perhaps the clearest and most extreme is Kirillov, an idiosyncratic nihilist who is one of the 'demons' analysed in the novel of that name. Kirillov believes that humanity is held back from being master of its own destiny because of its perennial and universal fear of death. However, he argues that the person who has the courage to commit suicide without any reason for doing so will make himself the Man-God. Why? Because whereas a normal suicide is motivated by fear or pain of one kind or another, such a voluntary and unmotivated suicide would demonstrate that human beings have the power to overcome their deepest fear. This is how Kirillov explains his view:

> 'If there is God, then the will is all his, and I cannot get out of his will. If not, the will is all mine, and it is my duty to proclaim self-will.' 'Self-will? And why is it your duty?' 'Because the will has become all mine. Can it be that no one on the whole planet, having ended God and believed in self-will, dares to proclaim self-will as the fullest point? It's as if a poor man received an inheritance, got scared, and doesn't dare go near the bag, thinking he's too weak to own it. I want to proclaim self-will. I may be the only one, but I'll do it . . . To recognize that there is no God, and not to recognize that you have become God, is an absurdity, otherwise you must necessarily kill yourself. Once you recognize it, you are king, and you will not kill yourself but will live in the chiefest glory. But one, the one who is first, must necessarily kill himself, otherwise who will begin and prove it?' (Dostoevsky, 2000, pp. 617–19)

Kirillov has a 'purpose', but it is not (like that of other more political 'demons' in the novel) the utilitarian purpose of a politically motivated murder: it is what we might call the infinite purpose of enacting the death of God and freeing humanity not for anything in particular but merely for its own self-will. As for Sartre, the will is either all on the side of God or all on the side of humanity. Sartre's readiness to dispense with the notion of authenticity may seem to signal that he is further than Heidegger from the scope of religious presuppositions, but, on the other hand, we may also question whether he doesn't, in his own way, remain locked in to a certain dependence on religion: needing religion in order to oppose it. We may recall again Kuhn's comment that 'the Nothingness which the Existentialist encounters is the shadow of the repudiated God' (1951, p. xxii).

But is this simple confrontation between human and divine wills really an adequate account of what Heidegger might call the existentiell possibilities open to human beings? Much as Heidegger drew on various of Kierkegaard's writings (and despite his reference to the importance of the latter's specifically religious works), there were also important aspects of Kierkegaardian faith that Heidegger seems not to have paid much attention to. But we shall begin what we might call a religious response to Sartre's and Kirillov's opposing of divine and human will with Dostoevsky himself.

Like Kierkegaard, Dostoevsky would become one of the main sources of twentieth-century existentialism, even though, unlike Kierkegaard, he rarely wrote in the language of philosophy and is chiefly known for works of fiction. Both figures became especially fashionable in Germany in the period from about 1910 onwards and even Heidegger, who scarcely ever cites the Russian writer directly, set him alongside Kierkegaard as part of the wave of new ideas that shaped his own intellectual formation in the second decade of the twentieth century. In the preface to the second edition of his commentary on Romans, Karl Barth sets Kierkegaard and Dostoevsky side by side as having influenced the development of his thought since the publication of the first edition, writing that 'I have also paid more attention to what may be culled from the writings of Kierkegaard and Dostoevsky that is of importance for the interpretation of the New Testament' (Barth, 1968, p. 4).

Now it has to be said that Dostoevsky (like Kierkegaard) was often significantly misread in this period and made the spokesperson for the kind of nihilism that most contemporary readers would see him as attacking. His portrayal of figures such as Kirillov or Ivan Karamazov seemed, like Milton's Satan, to give them all the best lines, as in Ivan Karamazov's dictum that 'if God does not exist, then everything is permitted' – an alternative espoused by Sartre among others.[6] Whether or to what extent Dostoevsky is properly read as a Christian or theological writer continues to be a controversial question, but it is clear that he was concerned to present a serious alternative to nihilism and the doctrine of the Man-God. In this respect it is characteristic that he titles a major section of *The Brothers Karamazov* 'Pro et Contra' and that it is in this section that he juxtaposes Ivan Karamazov's 'rebellion' against divine injustice and the Satanic Church of the Grand Inquisitor with the holy life and memoirs of the saintly Elder, Zosima.

Ivan's rebellion is a complex and even ambiguous affair, perhaps condensing much of existentialism's love–hate relation to religion. In the chapter titled 'Rebellion' Ivan reads out the charge-sheet against God's mismanagement of the world, focusing in harrowing details on horrific crimes committed against children, all drawn from contemporary examples and, as Dostoevsky emphasizes through Ivan, not just offences committed by enemies of Russia but committed on Russians by Russians themselves and even by Russian parents on their own children. Ivan does not use this litany as evidence against the existence of God in a purely philosophical sense, as in the philosophical treatment of theodicy, but, like Sartre, as an argument for rejecting God and God's plan for the world even if God existed. Even if the sufferings of the present time are to be justified by a future happiness and universal forgiveness in which all, even the victims and their murderers will be reconciled, Ivan wants none of it. As he puts it, 'though all that may come to pass, I don't accept it. I won't accept it' (Dostoevsky, 1912, p. 241). 'I have a Euclidian earthly mind', he tells his brother Alyosha, the novice monk, 'even if parallel lines do meet and I see it myself, I shall see it and say that they've met, but still I won't accept it' (1912, pp. 240–1).

As he sums up, 'it's not God that I don't accept, Alyosha, only I most respectfully return Him the ticket' (p. 251).

The meaning of his next contribution, the so-called Legend of the Grand Inquisitor, is perhaps even harder to penetrate and has been read by many religious readers in an essentially positive vein. However, we should not underestimate the fact that Dostoevsky puts it in the mouth of Ivan, whose stance towards religion is intellectual and sceptical. In brief, the legend tells of Christ's return to earth during the time of the Inquisition. He makes himself known among the crowd by miracles and by the radiance of his presence, but is immediately arrested by the Grand Inquisitor. The latter harangues him for having failed during his life on earth to give people what they needed. This is summed up in the Inquisitor's inversion of the three temptations in the wilderness: people are not capable of living solely by the divine word but need earthly bread; they need the miracle, mystery and authority of religion (or, we might say, ideology); and they need universal world-government, forcing them to live in a peace they cannot give themselves. Christ, however, appealed to and wanted only their freedom. Throughout this, Christ remains silent. At the end he kisses the Inquisitor on his bloodless lips. The latter lets him go, warning him never to return.

The image of Christ is generally experienced by readers as deeply sympathetic and his silence and humility reflect features of what some see as a distinctively Russian Christ figure. Alyosha himself, to whom Ivan narrates the legend, tells his brother that he has revealed that, deep down, he too wants such a Christ. Yet many readers, especially in the first half of the twentieth century, concluded that this Christ is, after all, powerless to effect real change on earth. He is a mere ideal, unable to save. Such an interpretation might be reinforced by the fate of Prince Lev Myshkin, the eponymous hero of *The Idiot*. Myshkin has many Christ-like traits, but, again, he seems unable to save and his presence even exacerbates some of the negative and destructive relationships at play in the novel. Such Christ figures may be beautiful but they are, at best, Quixotic and, at worst, tragic.

In response to Ivan, Dostoevsky goes on to offer us a hagiographical life of the Elder Zosima, Alyosha's spiritual father. Again, this is not a 'response' in the sense of an argument that might carry weight in a debate about the existence of God: it is more a matter of setting one kind of life against another. In fact, we could almost see it in Kierkegaardian terms as setting the stance of intellectual speculation (Ivan) against that of personal involvement, concern and passionate 'interestedness'. Zosima's story comprises what we might call a double-conversion story: not only did he himself convert back to Christianity at a moment in his life when he was preparing to fight a duel, but he also recounts the conversion of his brother, Markel.

Markel is a student of philosophy who regards religion as superstitious nonsense. His story perhaps exemplifies what Kierkegaard called the seriousness of death's decision, since it culminates when he is dying of consumption. At first, he ignores his mother's pleas to take the sacrament until, on the Tuesday of Holy Week, he agrees to go to Church with her – but only for her sake, he insists. Soon, however, it becomes clear that it is for himself and, as he becomes more and more uninhibited in his new-found faith, he tells his mother that 'life is paradise, and we are all in paradise, but we won't see it, if we would, we should have heaven on earth the next day'.[7] In a final rhapsodic confession he declares that:

> [E]very one of us has sinned against all men, and I more than any . . . believe me, everyone is really responsible to all men for all men and for everything . . . why do we quarrel, try to outshine each other and keep grudges against each other? Let's go straight into the garden, walk and play there, love, appreciate, and kiss each other, and glorify life . . . Birds of heaven, happy birds, forgive me, for I have sinned against you too . . . there was such a glory of God all about me; birds, trees, meadows, sky, only I lived in shame and dishonoured it all and did not notice the beauty and glory . . . If I have sinned against everyone, yet all forgive me, too, and that's heaven. Am I not in heaven now? (Dostoevsky, 1912, pp. 297–8)[8]

Likewise Zosima, in his own conversion, discovers a similar will to universal responsibility and a similar vision of God's glory in all things. As a spiritual leader, he shows himself capable of relating to people of all social classes and views of life without prejudice. There seem to be virtually no limits to his capacity for acceptance of others. His freedom in dealing with visitors and the simple, radical directness of his pastoral advice he gives them is regarded with grave suspicion by many others in the monastery. Nor does he attempt to constrain the freedom of his disciple Alyosha. On the contrary, he insists that Alyosha's own way to holiness will require him to leave the monastery and find his own way in the world.

Perhaps, then, Alyosha was right to detect in the silent kiss of Christ a sign of Ivan's proximity to faith, since that too seems to point to an analogous power of total acceptance and unconditional love. Is Dostoevsky, then, teaching that Christian love is the 'answer' to nihilism? Perhaps he is, but he is too good a novelist to state this in any doctrinaire way. Perhaps Zosima's is only one view of life alongside others. Certainly, when the saintly man dies, his body is not miraculously preserved from decomposition as his admirers had hoped and he rots like any other corpse. Perhaps, then, death does, in the end, have the last word? Or, perhaps, Dostoevsky is simply leaving the answer to us, his readers, realizing that how we interpret his novel will depend on how we interpret life itself.

What is crucial, however, is that, as against the Grand Inquisitor and as against Kirillov's, Nietzsche's and Sartre's view that the divine will necessarily requires the suppression of human will, Zosima offers a model of religious faith that, rooted and grounded in love, experiences the grace and beauty of God as liberating him for a totally free relation to himself and to others, a freedom that is not denied by but is consummated in acceptance of his infinite answerability and responsibility in relation to others.

Something similar is argued in more directly philosophical terms in Gabriel Marcel's response to Sartre. For Marcel, like Heidegger and unlike Sartre, human beings do experience the revelation of Being in their lives, above all as it is concretized in their relations to other human beings. In the claims Others make on us, we experience what Marcel called the 'exigency' of Being, when Being, as it were, demands our attention and response. In relation to such an experience of exigency we are empowered to demonstrate what he calls 'fidel-ity' to Being and thereby to testify to the possibility of love being a defining feature of human relationships. Like Zosima's practice of love, this is not so much submission to a heteronomous or alien power, but what Marcel calls *cre-ative* fidelity, involving a free choice of how we wish to be in our lives. Famously, Sartre's view of the Other as necessarily limiting and even destroying my free-dom is summed up in the line from his play *Huis Clos* (*No Exit*) 'Hell is other people'. As Marcel rightly argues, this is an inevitable consequence of an ontol-ogy that defines a human being's way of being for-itself as a radical freedom that annihilates all forms of externally given reality (what Sartre calls being in-itself) that might limit or constrain it. By way of contrast, Marcel suggests that the basic human way of being is neither that of the *en soi* or in-itself (as if it were some natural object) nor that of the *pour soi* or for-itself (i.e. as a simple 'upsurge of nothingness') but as being *chez soi*, that is, living in the world as a readiness to welcome the other, 'to receive [the other] in one's own prepared place of reception' (Marcel, 1950, p. 118). In what might be taken as a gloss on Heide-gger's distinctive expression *Dasein* (often rendered 'being-there') but that also proposes a striking counter-instance to Sartre's account of the humiliation of falling victim to the gaze of the Other, he offers as a primary instance of our relation to Being the picture of a child, gathering flowers in a meadow and run-ning up to its mother shouting 'Look at what *I've* gathered!' In this simple scene Marcel sees both that our sense of self is indeed inseparable from a relation to the other – it is from the other, in this case its mother, that the child seeks recog-nition of its being and identity – but that this relation is one in which the other is approached as a source of affirmation 'resonating and amplifying', as Marcel puts it, its original pleasure (*jouissance*) in its own being (Marcel, 1940, p. 15).

The possibility that love is the real measure of human relationships is also found in a number of other thinkers often seen as religious existentialists, including Martin Buber and Nicholas Berdyaev. Of course, regarding the rela-tion to the other as definitive of the human way of being will not in every case be interpreted in terms of love. Levinas, who certainly took to heart Markel's message of infinite answerability, saw this in terms of an infinite ethical obligation that had the character of commandment rather than what he saw as a sentimental and even orgiastic tendency to extol love. In this regard, he was critical of Buber's explication of the I–Thou relationship in terms of love since, for Levinas, this suggested a kind of reciprocity that weakens and limits the infinity of the ethical demand. Yet, for all these differences Levinas and Buber were at one in thinking both that the relation to the Other was determinative for the individual's existence and that this relation could not finally be understood without reference to the God-relationship.

The Religious Individual

In linking the question of religious individualism to the relation to the Other and to the possibility of fidelity to the revelation of Being-as-love, we may seem to have abandoned what, for many, is one of the basic characteristics of any kind of existentialism, namely, its radical emphasis on the individual. Kierkegaardian faith, for example, is typically portrayed – sometimes by its supporters as well as by its critics – as an example of extreme individualism. Didn't Kierkegaard himself insist that 'the crowd is untruth' and that a necessary precondition for a person to become a Christian was that they should become detached from the crowd and become a 'single individual', since only as such 'single individuals' can we respond to God in faith and, in infinite responsibility before God, practice Christian discipleship? Wasn't it for such reasons that Kierkegaard chose to concentrate so intensely on Abraham as a defining figure of faith, since the ordeal of Abraham, called by God to sacrifice his only beloved son, Isaac, was precisely of a kind that accentuated the radical isolation and singular character of faith? *Fear and Trembling,* very possibly Kierkegaard's most influential book, portrays Abraham as exemplifying the knight of faith and it does so in such a way as to underline the utter solitude that Abraham is forced into. Unlike Agamemnon, whose sacrifice of Iphigenia can be justified for reasons of state and in accordance with generally recognized religious practices, Abraham is not in a position to give a public account of his reasons for doing what he is setting out to do. All he has is the inner assurance of his God-relationship, but there is no one else who hears the voice of God as he does. As Kierkegaard's pseudonym, Johannes de Silentio, insists (and the reference of the pseudonym to silence is by no means accidental!), Abraham has no alternative but to be silent. What he is about to do is against all human and even divine laws, it will destroy his own hopes for being blessed through his posterity, and it is, of course, entirely impossible for him to speak about it either to his wife or to Isaac himself. It is for such reasons that he undertakes his journey to Mount Moriah in 'fear and trembling' and this, it seems, will be so for all subsequent knights of faith.

There is certainly no denying the massive emphasis Kierkegaard places on the individual, nor that this is an emphasis carried forward into philosophical existentialism. Here we might especially note Heidegger's argument that only by facing death as 'my' death and not being distracted by the deaths of others do I really achieve an authentic relation to it; acquiring the courage to face up to death and acquiring the courage to be myself in my unique singularity are two sides of the same coin. The point is underlined in the subtitle of Heidegger's 1929–1930 lectures on *The Fundamental Concepts of Metaphysics* – 'World, Finitude, Solitude'. *Dasein*'s authentic way of being-in-the-world is essentially marked both by finitude and solitude. We have also seen how, for Sartre, it is not only God but also the human Other who in every case poses an insurmountable obstacle to my realization of my own freedom. Is the abandonment of 'the individual', then, tantamount to abandoning what is most decisively existentialist in existentialism?

This, I suggest, is to misconceive the issue. While Kierkegaard undoubtedly stressed the ineluctable role of the individual and the impossibility of a responsible faith that seeks support from external metaphysical, historical or social sources, he was from the beginning clear that, in the Christian scheme of things, 'faith' could never be separated from love. Already in an early journal he notes that 'fear and trembling (cf. Phil 2:12) is not the primus motor in the Christian life, for that is love; but it is what the balance is in a clock – it keeps the Christian life ticking' (Kierkegaard, 2008, p. 9). And, on the same day that he published *Fear and Trembling*, he published a collection of three upbuilding discourses, two of which were on the text 'Love covers a multitude of sins'. This is not the place to begin an exposition of Kierkegaard's writings on love and the exact import of his teaching remains much debated (cf. Ferreira, 2001; Hall, 2002; and Krishek, 2009). Yet it is clear that while faith certainly requires radical individuation, the Christian is also obliged to love the neighbour and to be responsible for how he or she is in relation to the neighbour. Moreover, the religious relation itself is essentially one of love, a point that Kierkegaard makes by his repeated use of the story from Luke 7 of the 'sinful woman' whose many sins were forgiven, because she loved much. Although, as he retells the story, she becomes an icon of self-annihilation, losing herself in utter self-forgetfulness at the feet of the Saviour, there is also a new level of reciprocity established in the love he sees in her and the love he shows her. Thus, as Kierkegaard points out, Christ says her many sins are forgiven *because* she loved much, while she, for her part, will (he speculates) have heard him say 'because he (i.e. Christ) loved much': in love, each attributes love to the other, not to themselves (Kierkegaard, 2010, pp. 262–3).

Love presupposes that each individual who loves is indeed an individual, but love also presupposes or is able to experience – as Sartre cannot – that the presence of the Other is so far from being an obstacle to my existing as a centre of free self-consciousness in the world that it is the Other who, above all, calls me, in the mode of responsible love, to be fully individual.

If this is the case in relations between human beings, what of human beings in relation to God? Surely, even if Sartre is wrong about human others, he is, at one level, right about God? If God exists and is an all-powerful, all-knowing Being whose will is manifest in everything that exists, how can God not mark a limit to human freedom and human possibilities?

One response to this question is offered by Nicholas Berdyaev, who was certainly second to none in insisting on a radical and ungrounded freedom as the basis of human existence. Berdyaev resolutely opposed all forms of ontology that prioritized Being over freedom, including both Thomism and Heidegger. Berdyaev believed we would do better to turn to subjectivity, existence, Spirit, freedom and personality – terms that he uses more or less interchangeably. A philosophy that did this would no longer be a philosophy of Being: 'The philosophy of Spirit should not be a philosophy of being or an ontology, but a philosophy of existence', he wrote: 'Spirit is freedom, creativeness. Spirit exercises a primacy over being, the primacy of freedom' (Berdyaev, 1939, pp. 4, 31). Consequently, 'existential philosophy is not ontological philosophy in the traditional sense of the word' (1939, p. 31). Instead of 'a philosophy which acknowledges the primacy of Being over freedom', Berdyaev prefers a 'philosophy which recognizes the supremacy of freedom over Being' (1943, pp. 75–6). 'Freedom', he says, 'is without foundation; it is not determined by being nor born of it. There is no compact, uninterrupted being. There are breaks, fractions, abysses, paradoxes; there are transcensions. There exist, therefore, only freedom and personality' (1943, p. 76). And of personality, he adds that 'personality is outside of all being. It stands in opposition to being . . . its principle is dissimilarity' (p. 80).

Yet Berdyaev also sees this as being grounded in the revelation of divine freedom. In his view, the realization of creative freedom by human beings is possible and is called for on theological grounds: 'Human nature is creative because it is the image and likeness of God the Creator', he wrote in an early study, *The Meaning of the Creative Act* (1908), that would be determinative for his entire subsequent authorship (Berdyaev, 1955, p. 110). Far from divine and human freedom being in opposition, Berdyaev believes that the higher we value the one, the higher we will also value the other. 'The being of the world is creature; being which has been and continues to be created. And the stamp of the creative act lies on all created being. A thing created, createdness, speaks of the creator. Createdness is creativity. The creation of the world is creative development in God, His emergence from divine solitude; it is the call of divine love' (1955, p. 128). And, as we have seen, 'the creative act is a free and independent force, immanently inherent only in a person, a personality' (1955, p. 135). It is as creative *personality* that the human subject is the true image of God.

If there is to be such a thing as a religious existentialism, then, it would seem that it will be differentiated from secular existentialism in its classic Sartrean form by two decisive and interconnected features. On the one hand, it will – like Sartre – see the human subject as an irreducible centre of freedom, but, on the other, it will not see this as needing to be thought in opposition to divine freedom. Furthermore, it will see relations to human others, whether conceived under the rubric of obligation (Levinas[9]) or love (Dostoevsky, Kierkegaard, Buber, Marcel), as decisive both for the individual's self-relationship and for the same individual's God-relationship. That such a position is still appropriately called 'existentialism' will depend on the extent to which it is able to argue its case by means of the interpretative analysis of what Kierkegaard called actually existing human beings and Heidegger called *Dasein* – rather than deriving its key concepts from some theological a priori. The argument, then, is over which existentialism, atheistic or religious, offers the most adequate account of human existence. Religious existentialism, of course, does not address the further questions that interest many other kinds of philosophers as to whether, for example, God can be shown to exist independently of or without reference to the human–God relationship. Neither the classical theistic proofs nor arguments from biblical or ecclesiastical authority enter into this particular discourse. For non-existentialist philosophers, that may be a fatal weakness and a symptom of existentialism's subjectivism. For the existentialist, secular or religious, it is an obligatory act of intellectual renunciation, since ontological uncertainty is a fundamental feature of the human condition.

Notes

1. The text that was the main focus of this study has subsequently been shown to be by Henry of Erfurt. It should be mentioned that by this time, Heidegger was already working under the influence of neo-Kantianism and of Husserl and was not constrained by the scholastic paradigm.
2. The lower number refers to the pagination in the original German edition, which is also given in the margins of the Macquarrie/Robinson translation.
3. Subsequently, E. Gilson and J. Maritain would argue for a version of Christian existentialism that, as they saw it, was founded precisely in such an 'existential' understanding of God. However, I shall not discuss this particular variant of existentialism further in this article, but will limit myself to those versions of religious existentialism that take their starting-point in the analysis of existing human subjectivity.
4. Notoriously, Heidegger does not give extensive citations for his use of Kierkegaard, although it seems fairly clear that he was familiar with a significant range of Kierkegaard texts, including *The Concept of Anxiety*, *Practice in Christianity*, and some of his 'upbuilding' works, including the discourse 'At a Graveside'.
5. In 'L'existentialism est un humanisme' Sartre appeals to 'strict authenticity' as the sole criterion of morality (1970, p. 85). However, the central argument of *Being and*

Nothingness, that it is impossible for freedom to be the foundation of its own Being and thus occurs solely as nothingness, contradicts Heidegger's claims regarding a possible moment of authentic resoluteness, repeatable through time, in which *Dasein* is held open to its Being.

6. This is called 'existentialism's point of departure' by Sartre (1970, p. 36).
7. This view is also stated by Shestov, in the conclusion of his study of Kierkegaard, representing a position that, he believed, Kierkegaard was himself unable to affirm.
8. The statement that 'everyone is really responsible for [or, as some translations read: guilty before] all men and for everything, and I more than any' is frequently cited by Levinas. It is helpfully discussed in Toumayan (2004). Toumayan uses Bakhtin to formalize Markel's statement as the requirement of unlimited answerability and responsibility.
9. And also, in a sense, Kierkegaard, although doing justice to the manner in which Kierkegaard combines duty and love would require a discussion extending far beyond the limits of this paper.

Bibliography

Baranova-Shestova, N. (1983), *Jiizn' L'va Shestova*, vol. 2. Paris: La Presse Libre.
Barth, K. (1968), *The Epistle to the Romans*, trans. E. C. Hoskyns. Oxford: Oxford University Press.
Berdyaev, N. (1939), *Spirit and Reality*, trans. G. Reavey. London: Geoffrey Bles.
— (1943), *Slavery and Freedom*, trans. R. M. French. London: Geoffrey Bles.
— (1955), *The Meaning of the Creative Act*, trans. D. Lowrie. London: V. Gollanz.
Dostoevsky, F. M. (1912), *The Brothers Karamazov*, trans. C. Garnet. London: Heinemmann.
— (2000), *Demons*, trans. R. Pevear and L. Volokhnosky. London: Everyman.
Ferreira, J. (2001), *Love's Grateful Striving: A Commentary on Kierkegaard's Works of Love*. Oxford: Oxford University Press.
Großmann, A. and C. Landmesser (eds) (2009), *Rudolf Bultmann/Martin Heidegger, Briefwechsel 1925–1975*. Frankfurt am Main: Vittorio Klostermann/Mohr Siebeck: Tübingen.
Hall, A. M. (2002), *Kierkegaard and the Treachery of Love*. Cambridge: Cambridge University Press.
Heidegger, M. (1962), *Being and Time*, trans. J. Macquarrie and E. Robinson. Oxford: Basil Blackwell.
— (1995), *Phänomenologie des Religiösen Lebens. Gesamtausgabe, Vol. 60*. Frankfurt am Main: Vittorio Klostermann.
Kaufmann, W. (1956), 'Introduction' to Kaufmann (ed.), *Existentialism from Dostoevsky to Sartre*. Cleveland, OH: Meridia.
Kierkegaard, S. (1940), *Stages on Life's Way*, trans. W. Lowrie. Oxford: Oxford University Press.
— (1980), *The Concept of Anxiety*, trans. R. Thomte. Princeton: Princeton University Press.
— (1987), *Either/Or Part II*, trans. H. V. Hong and E. H. Hong. Princeton: Princeton University Press.

— (1993), *Three Discourses on Imagined Occasions*, trans. H. V. Hong and E. H. Hong. Princeton: Princeton University Press.

— (2008), *Kierkegaard's Journals and Notebooks, Vol. 2*, ed. and trans. N.-J. Cappelørn et al. Princeton: Princeton University Press.

— (2010), *Kierkegaard's Spiritual Writings: Gift, Creation, Love*, trans. G. Pattison. New York: Harper.

Kisiel, T. and T. Sheehan (2007), *Becoming Heidegger. On the Trail of His Early Occasional Writings, 1910–1927*. Evanston: Northwestern University Press.

Krishek, S. (2009), *Kierkegaard on Faith and Love*. Cambridge: Cambridge University Press.

Kuhn, H. (1951), *Encounter with Nothingness: An Essay on Existentialism*. London: Methuen.

Marcel, G. (1940), 'Moi et Autrui', in *Homo Viator: Prolégomènes à une Métaphysique de l'Espérance*. Paris: Aubier.

— (1950), *The Mystery of Being I: Reflection and Mystery*, trans. G. S. Fraser. London: Harvill Press.

Nietzsche, F. (1972), *Die Fröhliche Wissenschaft* in *Werke II*. Frankfurt am Main: Ullstein.

Pattison, G. (1996), *Agnosis: Theology in the Void*. New York: Palgrave Macmillan.

— (1999), *Anxious Angels: A Retrospective View of Religious Existentialism*. Basingstoke: Macmillan.

Sartre, J-P. (1967), *Words*. Harmondsworth: Penguin.

— (1970), 'L'existentialism est un humanisme'. Paris: Nagel.

Toumayan, A. (2004), ' "I More Than the Others": Dostoevsky and Levinas', in *Yale French Studies* 104 (*Encounters with Levinas*), pp. 55–6.

8 Existentialism and Literature

Colin Davis

Ever since Plato described the ancient quarrel between philosophy and poetry, philosophers have often been mistrustful of literature or indifferent to it. Existentialists, though, have not shared this low evaluation of literature. Works by key precursors such as Kierkegaard's *The Seducer's Diary* (1843) or Nietzsche's *Thus Spoke Zarathustra* (1883–1885) may appear to be, in conventional terms, more literary than philosophical, although they also question how useful such distinctions can be for the new ways of doing philosophy that they anticipate. More recently, Heidegger established the poet as the thinker's equal, finding in great poetry a profound summons to thought. So existentialism came into an intellectual climate that was highly favourable to literature. Its forebears include Dostoevsky and Kafka every bit as much as Hegel and Husserl. Some of the thinkers associated with it combined literary and philosophical writing. Jean Wahl wrote poetry as well as works of philosophy; Jean Grenier, an important influence on Albert Camus, was the author of poetic meditations and two novels; Gabriel Marcel wrote numerous plays that explore ethical and political themes. For such writers, literature contributes to the philosophical project of rethinking the foundations of existence.

This chapter looks in particular at the work of three writers, Jean-Paul Sartre, Simone de Beauvoir and Camus, for whom literature and thought are inseparable. Above all else, Sartre, de Beauvoir and Camus were great writers. De Beauvoir won France's most prestigious literary prize, the Prix Goncourt, for her novel *Les Mandarins/The Mandarins* (1954); Camus won the Nobel Prize for Literature, and Sartre famously declined it. Sartre wrote novels, short stories, plays, a volume of autobiography and film scripts. Camus's first novel *L'Etranger/The Outsider* (1942) remains one of the most read works of twentieth-century fiction, and he went on to produce further novels, short stories and plays. De Beauvoir produced a distinguished body of fiction, and she was also an especially prolific author of autobiographical volumes, beginning with *Mémoires d'une jeune fille rangée/Memoirs of a Dutiful Daughter* (1958). In her autobiographies de Beauvoir charted the development and experiences of a prominent committed intellectual through the twentieth century. For de Beauvoir as for Sartre and Camus, literature probes and challenges philosophical ideas in their relation to lived experience. Rather than merely serving to express well-established theoretical positions, their literary texts often push their thought to its limits, creating productive tensions with their philosophical works. Their writing foreshadows the necessity of finding some philosophical accommodation with the uncertainties of literature. The chapter looks at each of the three authors in turn and finally examines how, for each of them, literature plays a central role in the exploration of ethical issues.

Existentialism, then, is a literary movement at least as much as it is a trend in thought. This is in part not surprising because in France the boundaries between literature and philosophy are less clearly marked than they tend to be in English-speaking countries, so it is less unusual for an individual to achieve success as both a writer and a thinker. The importance of phenomenology for existentialism also contributed to its literary aspects. As the attempt to understand the concrete reality of everyday life, phenomenology lends itself as readily to literature as to philosophy. The question of whether Sartre, de Beauvoir and Camus were writers who dabbled in philosophy or thinkers who dabbled in literature is, then, ultimately unanswerable. For all of them, theoretical and literary writing are different, but vitally bound up with one another. I should stress from the outset, though, that there is no unified view or practice of literature which is shared by the writers being discussed here. Long before his public rift with Sartre, Camus expressed surprise that his name was often linked with Sartre's, and insisted that he should not be called an existentialist. If I include him here alongside Sartre and de Beauvoir it is because there are some resemblances between their work, but as I shall suggest, these resemblances certainly do not exclude fundamental differences.

Existentialism brings with it a set of themes which literature might explore: freedom, contingency, anguish, responsibility, commitment, the hostility of others and death. Some literary techniques are better suited to an existentialist world-view than others. In one of the greatest critical put-downs of all time, Sartre dismissed fellow novelist François Mauriac's fiction because it put the narrator in the position of God and denied human freedom: '[Mr Mauriac] has chosen divine omniscience and omnipotence. But a novel is written by a man for men. In the eyes of God, who sees straight through appearances, there is no novel, there is no art, because art lives on appearances. God is not an artist; neither is Mr Mauriac' (1947a, p. 69; translations from French are my own throughout). All-seeing, all-knowing narrators with perfect insight into their characters have no place in existentialist fiction. Sartre argued that 'a novelistic technique is always related to the novelist's metaphysics' (1947a, p. 86); so literary technique is integral to the work's philosophical significance. In line with this claim, existentialist fiction uses unreliable first-person narrators, journal forms or multiple narrative voices which plunge the reader into the rich, dark ambiguity of lived experience. In the opening lines of Camus's *L'Etranger*, the narrator Meursault seems unaware of the chronology of his own narrative: 'Today mother died. Or perhaps yesterday, I don't know' (1942a, p. 9). The first sentence of de Beauvoir's novel *Le Sang des autres/The Blood of Others* drops us in the middle of the action without even naming its male protagonist:

> When he opened the door, all eyes turned towards him:
> What do you want from me? he said. (1945, p. 11)

Existentialist literature reflects a view of reality as dense, multilayered and bewildering, requiring choices, decisions and interpretations of which the ultimate correctness can never be assured. The chosen forms of fiction convey a world in which meaning has to be made rather than found.

It would be a serious mistake, though, to assume that existentialist literature serves simply to convey a world-view which pre-exists and could be formulated independently of its literary expression. The line 'hell is other people' from Sartre's play *Huis clos/No Exit* illustrates the confusion that can arise if literary context is neglected (1947b, p. 92). The line is frequently cited as if it represented Sartre's own settled view on human relations. It does not; it is spoken by a fictional character who cannot be identified with the author. To take this to be an expression of Sartre's opinion is no better than arguing that Shakespeare didn't like the state of Denmark because he thought there was something rotten in it. To be sure, *L'Etre et le néant/Being and Nothingness* (1943) describes a conflict between self and other which could readily turn into the hell of *Huis clos*. The play depicts what human relations could be and perhaps all too frequently are. But Sartre's political activism rests on the conviction that the human condition can be changed through our own agency. So to ascribe to Sartre the view that hell is other people elides the more optimistic side of his thinking according to which others are also our comrades in the project to improve the world. Although there are obviously connections between Sartre's views and his literary works, they cannot be found merely by extracting a few striking quotations and using them to construct a facile semblance of a literary philosophy. The following sections of this chapter suggests that in fact the literary works of Sartre, de Beauvoir and Camus often test or contradict the views which they express elsewhere.

Sartre and the Vicissitudes of Theory

There is no existentialist theory of literature. There are theories, and elements of theory, but no unified and stable final position. Of the authors discussed here, Sartre was the one who wrote most extensively about literature and literary authors, with substantial works on Baudelaire, Genet, Mallarmé and Flaubert, many other critical essays, and his theoretical treatise *Qu'est-ce que la littérature?/ What is Literature?* (1948). The latter would appear flatly to contradict the claim that there is no existentialist theory of literature since its very title seems to promise that the work will tell us what literature is. The philosopher Jacques Derrida, who was a severe critic of aspects of Sartre's work (cf. Derrida, 1972, pp. 135–8), rejected all questions in the form 'What is . . . ?' because they suggest a belief in unchanging essences. Sartre, though, does not hesitate to pose the question of the nature of literature, breaking it down into three further questions which serve as chapter headings: What is writing? Why write? For whom does one write? In practice, much of Sartre's reply to his own question 'What is literature?' is historical, as he shows that the function of literature changes with its epoch. So to some extent he escapes the charge that he subscribes to belief in an immutable essence of literature. He develops a theory of writing which fits in with his views on freedom and commitment. Key to this is his distinction between prose and poetry. Sartre's committed writer is the author of prose works. In prose, language serves as an instrument which points to and acts on something outside it; it is capable of revealing the world and its meanings. In poetry, on the other hand, language is treated as an end in itself rather than used for its communicative abilities; because of this, Sartre is adamant here that the poet is not a committed writer. Authors of prose, on the other hand, are free subjects and citizens who use language in the service of their responsibility to others and to the society in which they live. By unveiling the world, by revealing it to us as it is, they play a role in changing it. They write from within their freedom and appeal to the freedom of their readers. Reading is thus 'a pact of generosity between the author and the reader; each places his trust in the other, each counts on the other, demands from the other as much as he demands from himself' (1948a, p. 105).

In *Qu'est-ce que la littérature?* the committed writer reveals the world to other free subjects. Sartre's views, though, were continually in a state of flux, so to arrest his thinking at any one point always risks giving a false picture of it. Sartre's 'theory of literature' turns out to be a constantly evolving theoretical reflection which often contradicts itself. So whereas the poet in *Qu'est-ce que la littérature?* could not be a committed writer, by 1960 Sartre could say of Mallarmé that 'his commitment seems to me to be as total as possible: social as much as poetic' (1972, p. 14). Despite what appeared to be his earlier clear-cut distinction between poetry and prose, Sartre argued that poetry might act on the world because of, not despite, the opacity of its language. Meanwhile, the 'pact of generosity' which bound together the respective freedoms of the writer and the reader was mutating into something altogether more conflictual. In his study of Jean Genet, *Saint Genet, comédien et martyr/Saint Genet, Actor and Martyr* (1952), he describes how literature becomes a trap to snare unwary readers, luring them into sharing experiences they would not freely countenance; or in *L'Idiot de la famille/The Family Idiot* (1971–1972), his mammoth study of Gustave Flaubert, he shows how the great nineteenth-century realist used his fiction to demoralize a despised public. Sartre establishes a theory of literature which he also dismantles and contradicts.

One could say, of course, that he merely changed his mind, as he was certainly entitled and prone to do. But it is more in keeping with the characteristic self-contestation of Sartre's thought to regard the contradictions as inherent to the texture of his work; taken together, his texts constitute an oeuvre which is unified, paradoxically, by its restless self-revisions. A good example of this is the tension between the views on humanism expressed in the novel *La Nausée/Nausea* and those seemingly espoused by Sartre himself in later years. In the 1940s, as we have seen, Sartre argued fiercely in favour of commitment; and in the title of a lecture delivered in 1946 he famously declared that 'existentialism is a humanism'. Nearly a decade earlier, *La Nausée* had viciously satirized humanism as an aspect of bourgeois self-mystification. When the protagonist Roquentin is asked what he thinks of the view that 'we are committed', he replies bluntly 'Nothing', while recording in fact that he considers it to be the kind of lie which hypocrites tell to themselves (1938, p. 159). He goes on to mock the Parisian humanists with whom Sartre would later align himself, and refuses to classify himself as either humanist or anti-humanist: 'I *am not* a humanist, that's all' (1938, p. 167; emphasis in original).

In the course of an analysis and repudiation of the humanism he finds in Sartre and others, Derrida refers to this passage of *La Nausée* in a footnote, saying that in it the humanism of Sartre's philosophy is 'very surely and very ironically taken apart' (Derrida, 1972, p. 136). But Derrida seems to be at a loss to know what to make of this contradiction. It does not affect his portrayal of Sartre as a humanist, and appears to be just a moment of lucidity on Sartre's part which merits no more than a footnote. Derrida misses two important points: first, contradiction and self-contestation are essential to Sartre's thought, a fact which endangers any unproblematized presentation of him as, say, humanist, anti-humanist or not humanist; and second, Sartre's literary works are frequently precisely where this self-contestation takes place, providing him with a forum to probe and to question positions he might polemically champion in other contexts. So, while he was insisting on man's absolute capacity to make free choices in all situations, plays such as *Les Mouches/The Flies* (1943) or *Les Mains sales/Dirty Hands* (1948) showed the difficulties and dilemmas which impede our freedom; while asserting in *L'Etre et le néant* that the hostility between self and other does not preclude the possibility of salvation and ethical renewal, the hell of *Huis clos* makes any such renewal seem improbable in practice.

De Beauvoir and the Loss of Voice

Sartre's literary works seem frequently to be ill at ease with his theoretical pronouncements, reflecting them but not endorsing them as fully as one might expect. In the rest of this chapter I want to suggest that this is not just the case for Sartre; it can also be observed in the work of Camus and de Beauvoir, and indeed it is an important factor in the role of literature for the existentialists. De Beauvoir is as interesting as Sartre in this respect. Despite a substantial essay on Sade, and chapters on Montherlant, Claudel, D. H. Lawrence, Breton and Stendhal in *Le Deuxième Sexe/The Second Sex* (1949), de Beauvoir's writing on literature is less extensive than Sartre's; nevertheless, in her contribution to a symposium held in 1964 under the title *Que peut la littérature?/What Can Literature Do?* and her lecture 'Mon expérience d'écrivain'/'My experience as a writer', she sketches a theory of literature which can be contrasted with her actual achievement as an author.

In her contribution to the 1964 symposium, de Beauvoir opposes the avantgarde aesthetics of some of her contemporaries and outlines a conception of literature as communication and commitment. Literature has a role which is distinct from mere information because the world is not a fixed totality which can be known once and for all; rather it is, in a phrase which de Beauvoir acknowledges as Sartre's, a 'detotalized totality' (Beauvoir, 1965, p. 76). What this means is that on the one hand the world is shared and the same for all, but that on the other hand each of us has a unique situation which makes us irreducibly singular, comprising the combination of our class, our past, our condition and our projects. The detotalized totality is the sum of individual situations, each of which is open to all others but not contained by them. Because the world is shared, we can communicate with one another; because each situation is unique, there nevertheless remains something unshareable about our experience which makes it opaque and incommunicable to others.

In *Que peut la littérature?* Beauvoir cites death as an example of that which separates the individual from all others, even if this separation is itself part of our common humanity: 'I will die a death which is absolutely unique for me, but it's the same for everyone' (1965, pp. 78–9). Death is evidently more than one example among others. It is mentioned several times in the course of de Beauvoir's talk as the ultimate marker of our isolation and singularity. Our death is our own and only our own; it cuts us off from others and them from us. But the incommunicability of our singular deaths does not mark the failure of communication as such. We can communicate from within our separation. The use of the first-person pronoun is of paramount importance here: 'I mean that I am a subject who says "I", I am the only subject for myself who says "I", and it's the same for everyone' (1965, p. 78). The self-positing, self-affirming 'I' of 'I am a subject who says "I"' is essential to de Beauvoir's conception of literature and its privileged, unmatched role; and it gives a clue to why autobiography occupies such an important place in her writing. Literature makes available to us the otherwise barred singularity of others because the author, or at least the authentic author, speaks as an individuated, separate subject and allows us to share her world:

> [Literature] is – if it is authentic literature – a means of going beyond separation by affirming it. It affirms it because when I read a book, a book which is important for me, someone speaks to me; the author is part of her book; literature begins only at that moment, at the moment when I hear a singular voice. (1965, p. 79)

Even if the author does not explicitly say 'I', even if she is not the compulsive chronicler of her own life as de Beauvoir was, she is nevertheless the creative source of her writing. What de Beauvoir calls 'authentic literature' is animated by 'a singular voice', which is also a unique style or tone through which the author imposes her presence on the reader. For the reader, the key mechanism which makes the author's world available to us is identification. By identifying with the author as I read, the world of the other becomes temporarily mine: 'I abdicate my "I" in favour of that of the person who is speaking; and yet I remain myself' (1965, p. 82).

The theory that de Beauvoir sketches here depends upon the author's 'singular voice', which makes it possible to communicate with others from within the absolute singularity of the speaking subject. However, some of de Beauvoir's writing dramatizes a *loss* of voice which contrasts starkly with her theoretical views. I will suggest this briefly with reference to her accounts of the deaths of her mother and Sartre, published as *Une mort très douce/A Very Easy Death* (1964) and *La Cérémonie des adieux/Adieux: A Farewell to Sartre* (1981) respectively. In these works, through the encounter with dead or dying others, the singular voice is precisely what her writing comes to forfeit and disown. *Une mort très douce* begins with a sentence in which there are no fewer than six personal pronouns or possessives, as if to prove the statement that 'I am a subject who says "I"'. The text opens, then, with the overwhelming presence of the self-confident subject. However, in the course of the text the narrator will be changed by the imminent death of the mother. We can observe a progressive growing together of the narrating subject and the dying mother, so that each enters more into the perspective of the other. The mother no longer falls so easily into the political and racial prejudices of her class which had previously infuriated her daughter; and the daughter finds that she is acquiring the same likes and dislikes as her mother. The confident first-person singular of the text's opening is in process of becoming a voice that shares in the subjectivity of an other.

This merging of self and (m)other reaches its most dramatic point in a passage which has received considerable critical attention. While spending an evening with Sartre, the narrator bursts into uncontrollable tears:

> All my sorrows, until that night, I had understood them; even when they overwhelmed me, I could recognise myself in them. This time, my despair escaped my control: someone other than me was crying in me. I spoke to Sartre through the mouth of my mother, such as I had seen her in the morning, and through everything that I could see in it: denied greed, almost servile humility, hope, distress, a solitude – that of her death, that of her life – which could not be confessed. And my own mouth, he told me, no longer obeyed me: I had placed mother's mouth on my face and despite myself I imitated its expressions. All her person, all her existence were materialized in it, and compassion tore me apart. (De Beauvoir, 1964, pp. 43–4)

This is not merely a hysterical collapse on the daughter's part. The narrator is first estranged from herself and then possessed, as if her mother's spirit were refusing death, abandoning its dying shell and occupying her daughter's body instead: 'someone other than me was crying in me'. Moreover, it is particularly significant that this possession affects pre-eminently the narrator's mouth, the place where speech emerges from within her body. We can see the full importance of this if we contrast the statement from *Que peut la littérature?*, 'I am a subject who says "I", I am the only subject for myself who says "I"', with what the narrator discovers here: 'I spoke to Sartre through the mouth of my mother'. Someone else speaks out of the narrator's mouth; her voice is usurped, taken over by another. In *Que peut la littérature?* De Beauvoir envisaged, as we saw, that the reader gives up her 'I' by opening herself up to author's world. She did not, though, conceive of the author as *also* abdicating her speaking voice. Moreover, whereas the reader both abdicates her voice and remains herself ('and yet I remain myself'), there is for the narrator here no such self-retention: 'my own mouth [. . .] no longer obeyed me'. The possibility enters the text here that the singular voice, which had seemed so vital to de Beauvoir's conception of literary communication, is precisely what is torn away from the subject in its encounter and identification with the dying other.

The question of the speaking voice, of who is speaking to whom, is raised again in the opening sentence from *La Cérémonie des adieux*: 'This is the first of my books – probably the only one – that you will not have read before it is published' (1981, p. 11). The problem of the addressee is in a sense easy to resolve, since it is clearly intended to be Sartre, whose last ten years of life are recorded in the book. But this identification raises further problems because Sartre is now dead. The book is addressed to someone who cannot read it. De Beauvoir goes on to reconsider the identity of the book's addressee: 'This *you* that I use is a lure, a rhetorical artifice. No one can hear it; I am speaking to no one. In truth, it is Sartre's friends whom I am addressing: those who want to know more about his final years' (1981, p. 11). Faced with the prospect of having no addressee, or no living addressee, de Beauvoir appears to change her mind and direct the book to the living rather than to the dead. But perhaps it is too late; perhaps the dead have already left an indelible mark on the work. Sartre was not the kind of reader to whom *Que peut la littérature?* refers, the reader who abdicates her 'I' in order to encounter the singular voice of the author. De Beauvoir's opening sentence specifies that Sartre read each of her books 'before it [was] published', that is, before it was finalized, with a view to intervening in it. Sartre was de Beauvoir's collaborator, in a sense her co-author, as she was his. During the 1940s a series of articles which appeared under Sartre's name were in fact written by de Beauvoir (see Francis and Gontier, 1979, pp. 48, 127); parts of de Beauvoir's *La Force des choses/Force of Circumstance* (1963) were apparently dictated by Sartre. There is no clear separation between the utterances of the two speakers. Indeed, as de Beauvoir recounts in the Epilogue to *La Force des choses*, she and Sartre would often complete each other's sentences (1963, p. 489). So the absence of Sartre as reader is also the absence of Sartre as collaborator, co-author or partner in discourse. The singular voice of de Beauvoir's writing was in fact always a shared voice; now, it is endangered in its particularity by the death of one of its creative sources.

This perhaps helps to explain the curious flatness of de Beauvoir's prose here. As she refers to Sartre's final years, her tone is matter-of-fact; her language is without colour or affect, as if the search for a singular voice had been relinquished. *Que peut la littérature?* describes how the author should invent a tone or a style which will enable her to communicate with others from within her separation. In the earlier text, the privilege of literature was its ability to communicate the incommunicable, to tell of that which is utterly singular about the individual's world. De Beauvoir now insists bluntly that the voice that has survived bereavement can achieve no such communication: 'It cannot be said, it cannot be written' (1981, p. 11).

The question remains of where this leaves the theory of literature sketched in *Que peut la littérature?* De Beauvoir's aesthetics entail the endeavour to fashion a voice of her own, a 'singular voice' that speaks *from* and speaks *of* the singularity of the subject who says 'I'. Her achievement is precisely the opposite. Her own voice is not uniquely her own because it becomes radically suffused with the presence of others. This entails something different from communicating the incommunicable or embracing intersubjectivity; it is something different from writing with or for the Other. This is rather a subjectivity which finds itself occupied, haunted by the Other, its own voice stolen from it but nevertheless discovering in this loss an access to writing.

Camus and the Nostalgia for Unity

Camus's philosophical essays *Le Mythe de Sisyphe/The Myth of Sisyphus* (1942) and *L'Homme révolté/The Rebel* (1951) both contain lengthy discussions of artistic creation. In the earlier book Camus describes the creator as 'the most absurd of characters' (1942b, p. 124). The work of art immerses the creator and the reader in the experience of the Absurd without trying to explain or to justify it. Rather than a refuge from unsavoury realities, it is the place where such realities can be honestly and lucidly confronted. While arguing for this position, however, Camus's analysis of actual works suggests a rather different picture. In his account, even important precursors such as Dostoevsky and Kafka succumb to the temptation of offering explanations and justifications. Art, it seems, is as much an escape from the Absurd as a place of lucid confrontation with it. This ambivalence is reproduced in the more ambitious discussion of creation in *L'Homme révolté*.

In *L'Homme révolté* Camus describes creation as an activity in which the sensibility of revolt can be observed in its purest form. Indeed, revolt is closely tied to art. Revolt is the demand for unity coupled with the knowledge that it cannot be achieved. The artist knows this and attempts to fabricate a replacement universe which may supply the unity lacking in reality. Art creates enclosed worlds in which 'man can reign and know at last' (1951, p. 306). For Camus, the novel in particular serves as a vehicle for revolt because it protests against the incompleteness of the world. The novel draws on the desire for a better world, but 'better' here does not mean different in detail so much as *unified*. The novel remedies the incompleteness of the world by giving characters a destiny. Life acquires meaning and coherence; great emotions endure rather than fading away with the passing of time. Art, then, is the correction of experience through the lens of man's nostalgia for unity.

Camus is adamant that art should be related to the sensibility of revolt rather than to revolution because, in his account, the rejection of reality which it entails is not an absolute negation. The refusal of the world coexists with an acceptance of its beauty and of the nature of man. The artist's correction of reality is not a revolutionary destruction of it in the name of some abstract idea; it is rather a reconfiguration of experience in the light of the desire for unity. Creation is a revolt against the nonsense of the world, so that, as Camus puts it, 'there is no art of nonsense' (1951, p. 309), or more affirmatively still, 'Literature of despair is a contradiction in terms' (1951, p. 314). Art both rejects the world and tries to save something of value in it from the pure flux of history. Camus's fiction certainly reflects in part this uneasy balance between an awareness of meaninglessness, absurdity, exile and alienation on the one hand and a perception of beauty, belonging and the intensity of sensual experience on the other.

However, it is difficult to see Camus's literature as fully endorsing the view of art as 'corrected creation', resisting the loss of meaning by finding unity in a broken world. It is rather as if Camus were theorizing a literary practice which his own writing would demystify. As we have seen, *L'Etranger* begins by indicating that its narrator has only a weak grasp of time; and anyway, he dismisses the significance of what he is saying with the abrupt words 'That does not mean anything' (1942a, p. 9). This might refer to the conventional expression of condolences in the telegram telling Meursault of his mother's death, or to the death itself, or to the uncertainty as to when it occurred, or to the novel we are reading. The problem of turning this disjointed narrative into a meaningful whole is exemplified by the murder which Meursault commits on the beach. There is evidence in the novel to support a number of quite different accounts of the events leading to the murder. One plausible explanation might suggest that diverse, unrelated factors combine, such as the heat, a series of unplanned encounters with a group of Arabs, and the effects of alcohol; Meursault finds himself by chance facing a man with a knife, whom he shoots without prior motivation. Or alternatively, we might think that, still grieving for the death of his mother, with a strong sense of isolation from those around him, and in an Algeria fraught with racial tensions, the crime is psychologically motivated, as Meursault takes out his anxiety and pain on an Arab assailant. Or again, we might suspect that Meursault's first-person narrative of the event should be distrusted; the sequence of events suggests that the murder is premeditated and deliberate: excluded from an earlier fight, he takes Raymond's revolver, returns to the same spot where he last saw the Arab, and coldly executes him, firing a total of five bullets into his body to make sure the job is done properly. In the second half of the novel the examining magistrate, the defence and prosecution lawyers and the jury endeavour, like the reader, to decide which of these ways of understanding the event is true; but there is simply no decisive solution. Camus's theory makes of art a quest for unity and sense; his practice offers us no prospect of finding either, except at the cost of the most brutal simplification. At the end of *L'Etranger* Meursault awaits his execution, condemned to the guillotine for a crime which remains enigmatic.

Literature as Ethical Investigation

For Sartre, de Beauvoir and Camus, there is a tension between theoretical assertion and literary practices which can unsettle their author's own pronouncements. Their literary texts tend to be too exploratory, uncertain, tentative or just plain opaque to serve as any kind of reliable ancillary to their intellectual positions. Their literature is better understood as a zone of experimentation in which ideas are formed and interrogated without a predetermined sense of where they are leading. This is especially the case when it comes to their ethical aspects. At the very end of his monumental *L'Etre et le néant*, when Sartre raises the question of ethics he teases his reader by promising a subsequent book: 'We will devote a forthcoming work to it' (1943a, p. 722). He never completed the study to which he alludes here, although de Beauvoir did attempt to formulate an existentialist ethics in *Pyrrhus et Cinéas/Pyrrhus and Cinéas* (1944) and *Pour une morale de l'ambiguïté/The Ethics of Ambiguity* (1947). My suggestion here is that the literary writing of the existentialists can be read as their investigation into ethics as it is lived and fought over, replete with unanswerable questions, actions with consequences we cannot predict and, as we saw in the case of *L'Etranger*, impenetrable motives.

Given the violent times in which they lived, it is not surprising that the key ethical question which haunts these writers is violence towards the other, and specifically murder. The killing of the Arab on the beach at the centre of *L'Etranger* is perhaps the twentieth century's most memorable emblem of the face-off between self and other which culminates in murderous violence. Its resonance comes in part from our knowledge that, when the novel was first published in 1942, the Second World War was raging; in the death camps, systematic murder was becoming official policy; and in only a few years more the sunlit world of Algeria in which Camus's novel was set would descend into a vicious War of Independence in which atrocities would be calmly perpetrated on both sides.

De Beauvoir's first novel *L'Invitée/She Came to Stay*, also published during the Second World War, has an epigraph attributed to Hegel: 'Every consciousness pursues the death of the other' (1943, p. 8). It ends with a woman causing the death of her rival by gassing her. Although de Beauvoir cannot have known when writing this ending that at Auschwitz and elsewhere gas was being used to kill on industrial scales, for postwar readers it is hard to avoid the connection. De Beauvoir's second novel, *Le Sang des autres*, has a very different epigraph, from Dostoevsky's *The Brothers Karamazov* (1880): 'Each person is responsible for everything before everyone' (1945, p. 10). The difference between the two epigraphs encapsulates the dilemma of existentialist ethics: it must find some way to reconcile the conflict of consciousnesses with responsibility for others. *Le Sang des autres* is in fact a fine and challenging example of this endeavour. Rooted in the political struggles of the 1930s and 1940s, it describes the different paths by which its central characters come to be involved in the Resistance. Conflict is certainly not overcome. The protagonists are after all engaged in violent acts against the German occupying forces, and strains persist within the Resistance group itself; but their violence has an ethical horizon, even if the Resistants can never be certain that their actions can be justified or will be successful. When de Beauvoir completed the novel, the war was ongoing and its outcome was still in doubt.

The tension between responsibility and murderous hostility towards the other is at the core of much existentialist fiction, in ever-changing, never settled constellations. In Camus's play *Caligula* (1944) the eponymous Roman emperor embarks on a killing spree in order to give his subjects a keener sense of their mortality; in *Le Malentendu/The Misunderstanding* (1944) a man returns incognito to visit his mother and sister only to be murdered and robbed by them; in *L'Etranger* Meursault kills without any sense of guilt or moral transgression; *La Peste/The Plague* (1947) portrays a community which has learned to work together whereas *La Chute/The Fall* (1956) suggests that we are linked to others only in hypocrisy and self-love. Violence or the potential for violence are always present, and the possibilities for overcoming the urge to kill are sketched and discredited in turn.

Sartre's plays are also motored by the anguish of moral choice in a world without rules and absolutes. In *Les Mouches* Oreste kills a tyrannical king in order to liberate the people of Argos; and given that the play was first performed in occupied Paris in 1943, it can readily be seen as a justification of Resistance violence. But the king is also the murderer of Oreste's father, so Oreste's act may be in part an act of revenge which is less free and morally pure than he would like to think; and anyway, it is by no means clear that the people of Argos actually want and will preserve the liberty which Oreste's extreme act may offer them. In the later play *Les Séquestrés d'Altona/The Condemned of Altona* (1960) we discover that the troubled central character Frantz had authorized the use of torture during the Second World War because he thought it might help save Germany from defeat; but it turned out to have no effect, and in any case Germany survived its defeat and flourished once again. Sartre certainly believes that in certain circumstances violent acts are legitimate interventions. However, this creates more problems than it resolves, and his plays explore the ways in which acts and decisions are entangled with the density of lived experience, leaving their motives uncertain and their consequences unpredictable.

The differences between Sartre and Camus on the problem of legitimating violence can be illustrated through two of their plays which deal with similar issues: Camus's *Les Justes/The Just Assassins* (1949) and Sartre's *Les Mains sales*. Both plays are concerned with political assassination. In *Les Mains sales* Hugo, a member of the Communist Party in a fictional Eastern European state towards the end of the Second World War, is entrusted by party leaders with the task of assassinating Hoederer, another Communist leader who advocates compromise with other political parties. Posing as his new secretary, Hugo infiltrates Hoederer's headquarters. He finds himself drawn to Hoederer and his humane pragmatism, and seems to decide to disobey the order to kill him. However, his wife Jessica is also impressed by Hoederer, and when Hugo surprises them in what appears to be a romantic embrace, he shoots and kills his rival. Later, on his release from prison, Hugo claims that he still does not know why he killed Hoederer, but that it would be disrespectful to his victim to claim that it was merely a crime of passion. Meanwhile, though, the policy of the Communist Party has come into line with Hoederer's position, so it now wants his assassination to appear to be the result of a jealous act rather than a political command. Hugo refuses to go along with this, so the play ends with him being killed in turn.

Hugo's intention to murder Hoederer initially seems to be easily justifiable, at least to himself. His decision is freely made, even if it is also ordered by the Party: Hoederer is pursuing policies which betray the Communist cause, so he must be stopped by whatever means are necessary. But as the play progresses this clarity is lost. Is Hugo acting to prove himself to his comrades and to himself rather than out of genuine conviction? Is it so certain that Hoederer is in the wrong? Why does Hugo in fact shoot him? Is he still self-deluded when he refuses to say that it was out of jealousy? And does his effective suicide at the end actually achieve anything worth achieving? When the play's audiences sympathized with Hugo, Sartre insisted that they had misunderstood his work, which was meant to be on the side of Hoederer's mature pragmatism; and he stopped the play from being performed for a period. But Sartre here is confronted with the same reality which Hugo and Frantz from *Les Séquestrés d'Altona* also discover: our acts, including the literary works we might write, always partially escape us; they have meanings and consequences which we may not have intended and which we cannot foresee. The play does not condemn political assassination in itself; Hoederer himself states at one point that he does not in principle oppose political assassination. But *Les Mains sales* makes it palpable that, given the complex interactions of character and situation, no action can be confidently justified in advance or unambiguously explained in retrospect.

Camus's *Les Justes* also deals with political assassination, this time in imperial Russia at the beginning of the twentieth century. The title – and even more so its English translation as *The Just Assassins* – raises its central question: how can killing ever be a just act? Under what circumstances, and at what price, is it legitimate to take the life of another human being? In the play Kaliayev willingly accepts the task of killing the Grand Duke by throwing a bomb at his carriage. When he attempts to do so, however, he sees that his victim is accompanied by his young nephew and niece. He is willing to kill the Grand Duke in the cause of revolution, but not two innocent children. His failure prompts a discussion of ends and means among the revolutionary group. Dora supports Kaliayev and argues that their choice of violence does not remove all ethical constraints: 'Even in destruction there is an order, there are limits' (1960, p. 62). The murder of children will not prevent other children from dying of hunger. The more dogmatic Stepan counters that no moral scruple should stand in the way of the revolution: 'There are no limits. The truth is that you don't believe in revolution' (1960, p. 62). The current régime must be destroyed, at whatever cost, if a better world is to be created. Through all this Kaliayev insists that he will not kill in the name of some future world which might never exist, and which in any case would be tarnished if it were built on the bones of murdered children. In this debate Stepan comes across as an unbending advocate of violence, so most spectators will feel little sympathy for his views. Nevertheless, the discussion of ends and means is not clearly resolved. When Kaliayev sets out for a second time to kill the Grand Duke, the dilemma which prevented him from succeeding on the first occasion has been removed: the Grand Duke is alone, so Kaliayev can throw his bomb with a calmer conscience.

In *Les Mains sales* Hoederer admits that he has 'dirty hands': to be effective involves fully accepting the terms of a compromised world. Camus's Kaliayev, by contrast, wants to retain his moral purity even as he commits murder. In prison, he clings to the belief that the assassination was not a crime but an act of justice. He is a killer, but he is also somehow innocent. A final encounter in prison between him and the Grand Duke's widow tests his self-righteousness. She reveals that the Grand Duke was a man like him who spoke of justice and wanted the best for his people; he had been sleeping calmly in his chair shortly before Kaliayev murdered him; moreover, one of the children he saved was a spoiled, snobbish brat. Kaliayev remains steadfast and happily pays the price for taking a life by accepting his own execution. The question remains, though, of whether he is any less self-deluded, whether he understands his act and his motives any better, than Hugo in *Les Mains sales*. Discordant voices haunt the play. Stepan may be right that moral scruples will only delay the revolution; the police inspector Skouratov may be right when he comments ironically that if the idea for which Kaliayev kills does not justify murdering children, it may not be enough to justify murdering a Grand Duke either; the Grand Duchess briefly weakens Kaliayev's resolve when she insists on her husband's humanity; and in the final act Dora has a moment's doubt when she considers that Kaliayev's sacrifice may serve no purpose: 'And if he died for nothing?' (1960, p. 138). These discordant voices may not prevail in the play, but they do not entirely get eradicated either.

Kaliayev's desire to retain his innocence despite being a killer indicates a resistance to moral compromise even when faced with the most testing situations. Sartre's characters are more willing to accept that we are forced to act irrevocably, possibly mistakenly, in a compromised world. Despite these differences, both plays are mired in the problem of reconciling violence and ethics. The multivoiced nature of drama, with different characters expressing conflicting views, might appear to make it an ideal medium for juxtaposing unresolved positions. In fact, though, this uncertain, open-ended, exploratory impulse persists in existentialist literature in general. Literature is an essential part of the existentialist project, perhaps *the* essential part of the existentialist project, precisely insofar as it resists and unsettles any pre-established knowledge which its authors or its readers might bring to it. It tests the views explicitly espoused by its authors; and it suggests that what may be most interesting about them, and most fruitful for scholars to study, is not so much what they said or thought as the dynamic tensions inherent in the different kinds of texts they produced. Immersed in and fascinated with the opacity of lived experience at extreme moments, existentialist literature reflects a violent century and its still poignant, unsolved dilemmas.

Bibliography

Camus, A. (1942a), *L'Etranger*. Folio edition. Paris: Gallimard.
— (1942b), *Le Mythe de Sisyphe*. Idées edition. Paris: Gallimard.
— (1947), *La Peste*. Paris: Gallimard.
— (1951), *L'Homme révolté*. Idées edition. Paris: Gallimard.
— (1956), *La Chute*. Paris: Gallimard.
— (1958/1944), *Caligula, suivi de Le Malentendu*. Paris: Gallimard.
— (1960), *Les Justes*. Folio edition. Paris: Gallimard.
De Beauvoir, S. (1943), *L'Invitée*. Folio edition. Paris: Gallimard.
— (1944), *Pyrrhus et Cinéas*. Paris: Gallimard.
— (1945), *Le Sang des autres*. Folio edition. Paris: Gallimard.
— (1947), *Pour une morale de l'ambiguïté*. Paris: Gallimard.
— (1949), *Le Deuxième Sexe*. Paris: Gallimard.
— (1954), *Les Mandarins*. Paris: Gallimard.
— (1958), *Mémoires d'une jeune fille rangée*. Paris: Gallimard.
— (1963), *La Force des choses*, vol. 2. Paris: Gallimard.
— (1964), *Une mort très douce*. Folio edition. Paris: Gallimard.
— (1965), *Que peut la littérature?* With Yves Berger, Jean-Pierre Faye, Jean Ricardou, Jean-Paul Sartre and Jorge Semprun. Paris: Union Générale d'Editions.
— (1979), 'Mon expérience d'écrivain', in Claude Francis and Fernande Gontier (eds), *Les Ecrits de Simone de Beauvoir: La Vie – l'écriture*. Paris: Gallimard, pp. 439–57.
— (1981), *La Cérémonie des adieux*. Folio edition. Paris: Gallimard.
— (1985), *A Very Easy Death*. New York: Pantheon.
Derrida, J. (1972), *Marges de la philosophie*. Paris: Minuit.
Dostoevsky, F. (1993), *The Brothers Karamazov*, trans. David McDuff. Harmondsworth: Penguin.
Francis, C. and F. Gontier (1979), *Les Ecrits de Simone de Beauvoir: La Vie – l'écriture*. Paris: Gallimard.
Kierkegaard, S. (1987), *The Seducer's Diary*, in *Either/Or, Part 1*, trans. H. V. Hong and E. H. Hong. Princeton: Princeton University Press, 301–445.
Nietzsche, F. (1961), *Thus Spoke Zarathustra*, trans. R. J. Hollingdale. Harmondsworth: Penguin.

Sartre, J-P. (1938), *La Nausée*. Folio edition. Paris: Gallimard.
— (1943a), *L'Etre et le néant*. Paris: Gallimard.
— (1943b), *Les Mouches*. Paris: Gallimard.
— (1946), *L'Existentialisme est un humanisme*. Paris: Nagel.
— (1947a), *Critiques littéraires (Situations, I)*. Idées edition. Paris: Gallimard.
— (1947b), *Huis clos, suivi de Les Mouches*. Folio edition. Paris: Gallimard.
— (1948a), *Situations, II: Qu'est-ce que la littérature?* Paris: Gallimard.
— (1948b), *Les Mains sales*. Paris: Gallimard.
— (1952), *Saint Genet, comédien et martyr*. Paris: Gallimard.
— (1960), *Les Séquestrés d'Altona*. Paris: Gallimard.
— (1971–1972), *L'Idiot de la famille*. 3 vols. Paris: Gallimard.
— (1972), 'Les Ecrivains en personne' (1960), in *Situations, IX*. Paris: Gallimard, pp. 9–39.

9 Existentialism, Feminism and Sexuality[1]

Marguerite La Caze

The work of existential phenomenologists such as Simone de Beauvoir and Jean-Paul Sartre is distinct from that of other phenomenological thinkers partly through their concentration on sexuality. In this essay I explore their articulations of sexuality and discuss their potential usefulness for feminist philosophy.[2] In Sartre's elaboration of the experience of sexuality in *Being and Nothingness* he presents an apparently timeless, ahistorical account of sexuality. His accounts of bad faith, desire and love are based in his understanding of conscious experience as involving a range of contradictory projects, doomed to failure. Sartre does not make a general distinction between experiences of sexuality according to sex or gender, although in some examples he focuses on women. Furthermore, unlike de Beauvoir, he does not delineate an ideal of authentic relations with others. Sartre's apparently pessimistic thinking about sexuality makes for a significant comparison with de Beauvoir's view and may contain more resources for feminist philosophy than is sometimes thought.

De Beauvoir suggests in *The Second Sex* that a sexuality that is not structured by oppression would be experienced differently. In an oppressive world, women encounter sexuality as passive prey, subject to violation and domination. These aspects of experience are contingent. However, de Beauvoir argues that even if women were no longer oppressed:

> [T]here will always be certain differences between man and woman; her eroticism and therefore her sexual world, have a special form of their own, and therefore cannot fail to engender a sensuality, a sensitivity, of a special nature. This means that her relations to her own body, to that of the female, to that of the male, to the child, will never be identical with those the male bears to his own body, to that of the female, and to the child; those who make much of 'equality in difference' could not with good grace refuse to grant me the possible existence of differences in equality. (1976, II: p. 661; 1983, p. 740)[3]

De Beauvoir's conception of these differences depends on her understanding of authentic relations with others not structured by conflict. Feminist philosophers

155

have debated how to interpret de Beauvoir's account and have developed and applied her insights.

I will begin with Sartre's description of sexual relations, as proceeding in that order will enable a clearer insight into the distinctiveness of de Beauvoir's existential feminism. In the Sartre sections I will show how Sartre used his concepts of freedom, bad faith and the look to illuminate the nature of desire and also how women figured in the development of these concepts. In the sections on de Beauvoir's work I will demonstrate how she established an existential theory of oppression that implies a divergence between how sexuality is experienced under oppression and how a more authentic sexuality might be experienced in the future. My overall aim is to explain both the limitations of Sartre's and de Beauvoir's accounts of sexuality and their potential to inspire further feminist research and understanding of sexuality.

Sartre and Freedom

Sartre argues that we are radically free and does not take oppression as a central category in his early work, including *Being and Nothingness*, where his most extensive discussions of sexuality feature. Sexuality is central to his understanding of human interaction. In his account of love and desire, Sartre claims that these attitudes form the basis for all our associations with others. This account relies on a complex ontology of the self or human reality. In developing his fundamental ontology, Sartre distinguishes between three modes or categories of being. They are Being-in-itself (*être-en-soi*), or the non-conscious, objective features of being; Being-for-itself (*être-pour-soi*), the projection of consciousness beyond Being-in-itself; and Being-for-others (*être-pour-autrui*), the way we are perceived by others.[4] For Sartre, freedom is always experienced in a situation and in relation to facticity. He says facticity or the given 'is *my place, my body, my past, my position* in so far as it is already determined by the indications of Others, finally my *fundamental relation to the Other*' (2003, p. 511). Nevertheless, we are not our facticity. We choose to understand our facticity as we will, but our facticity means that we have to make these kinds of choices. Sartre holds that as conscious individuals, we are able to transcend facticity. Situation consists in both our facticity or the things that are true about us and how we respond to and live that facticity. Sartre uses these concepts to develop his account of bad faith, desire and love. He also uses a range of controversial examples that have led to much criticism by feminist philosophers.[5]

The Bad Faith of Women

The concept of 'bad faith', or lying to oneself, plays a central role for Sartre in explicating the nature of consciousness. Bad faith consists in denying one of the modes of being and its associated features. Thus we may be in bad faith by denying our for-itself and so denying freedom and responsibility or by denying our aspect as an in-itself and, therefore, our facticity, or by confusing the two. Sartre's account of bad faith has been criticized by feminist philosophers for its reliance on sexist examples and indeed, for using examples where someone is denigrated, as in the case of the waiter who is too much a waiter and the homosexual who denies their homosexuality.[6]

Sartre begins by discussing a 'frigid woman', an example assessed in detail by Michèle Le Doeuff in *Hipparchia's Choice* (2007). He finds support for his view that bad faith is a phenomenon of the unity of consciousness – rather than explained by the existence of an unconscious – in Wilhelm Stekel's work. Stekel bases the source of psychosis in the conscious, in *Frigidity in Woman* (1926).[7] For instance, Sartre suggests that a woman may be in bad faith in not enjoying sex because her frigidity is a reaction to her partner's infidelity. He sees a pattern of distraction: women distract themselves in advance from the pleasure they dread, for instance, by thinking of the household accounts during sex. Sartre writes 'Yet if the frigid woman thus distracts her consciousness from the pleasure which she experiences, it is by no means cynically and in full agreement with herself; *it is in order to prove to herself* that she is frigid' (2003, p. 77). He argues that this is a phenomenon of bad faith, since the effort the woman is making to distance herself from the 'experienced pleasure' shows she is experiencing it. Le Doeuff analyses Sartre's claim that women show 'objective signs of pleasure', arguing that such a phrase is a contradiction in itself and against the tenor of his philosophy, as a sign is something that must be interpreted (2007, p. 67). The fundamental problem of this example is that 'The consciousness of the frigid woman is thus faulted by that of her husband, then by that of the psychiatrist, then by that of Sartre, where the argument alleges that the husband, the psychiatrist and Sartre all know what is really going on in women's consciousness' (2007, p. 71). It is this problem that is at the base of feminist criticisms of Sartre's account of women in relation to sexuality.

The problem can be seen in another famous example of bad faith. Sartre asks: What must the being of humanity be like in order for it to be capable of bad faith? To answer this question Sartre turns to a woman on a date:

Take the example of a woman who has consented to go out with a particular man for the first time. She knows very well the intentions which the man who is speaking to her cherishes regarding her. She knows also that it will be necessary sooner or later for her to make a decision. But she does not want to realise the urgency; she concerns herself only with what is respectful and discreet in the attitude of her companion. (2003, p. 78)

On Sartre's reading of what is going on, the woman takes away the sexual background from what the man is saying. He says she does not know what she wants. Furthermore, Sartre finds in the woman a contradictory desire for the man to address both her personality or full freedom and her body as object. When the man takes her hand she has to decide. If she leaves it there, she is flirting; if she withdraws she will ruin the evening, so she postpones the decision. The woman leaves her hand there, but does not notice that she is doing so. She talks of intellectual things: 'And during this time the divorce of the body from the soul is accomplished; the hand rests inert between the warm hands of her companion – neither consenting nor resisting – a thing' (2003, p. 79).

The bad faith of the woman Sartre calls a 'coquette' involves treating the actions of her companion as in the mode of the in-itself, being only what they are (ignoring the fact that they lead to an aim – seduction). But she allows herself to enjoy the desire, and so recognizes her companion's transcendence. Moreover, although she is aware of the presence of her body, she treats herself as not being her own body, as if it were a passive object that events only happen to. Sartre argues that the unity in acts of bad faith 'is a certain art of forming contradictory concepts which unite in themselves both an idea and the negation of that idea. The basic concept which is thus engendered, utilizes the double property of the human being, who is at once a facticity and a transcendence' (2003, p. 79). They should be able to be coordinated, but in bad faith we do not want to do this. Instead facticity is affirmed as transcendence and transcendence as facticity, so that as we grasp one, we face the other. Toril Moi argues that Sartre overlooks the way such a situation is shaped by social and sexual differences (1994, pp. 127–33). More importantly, 'The real problem in this passage is not the woman's interpretation, but Sartre's bland assumption that he knows more than the woman' (1994, p. 130). She imagines an alternative reading where the woman is engaged in a flirtation that is ruined by the man grabbing her hand and forcing her to respond to the man's project of seduction. Max Deutscher provides a nuanced reading of the example, adding that Sartre also assumes we understand the man's desire. He suggests that today a man could be made uncomfortable by a woman taking his hand or the situation could be one 'of sensitivity and care rather than of what had appeared as "bad faith"'(2003, pp. 32–8). Julien S. Murphy defends Sartre's illustrations by noting that they at least show a sensitivity to differentiated gendered experiences (1999, p. 3). Sartre's examples highlight the issues concerning our capacity to understand what others are experiencing and, to a certain extent, conflict between the sexes. In his account of desire and love, Sartre focuses on conflict within relations in general.

The Importance of 'the Look'

To understand Sartre's account of sexuality and desire, we need to examine his famous account of our immediate connection to the Other through 'the look'. He writes 'This relation, in which the Other must be given to me directly as a subject although in connection with me, is the fundamental relation, the very type of my being for others' (2003, p. 277). We perceive others through this elemental relation that we experience in everyday life. The original relation with the other refers to our being perceived by the other: 'if the Other-as-object is defined in connection with the world as the object which *sees* what I see, then my fundamental connection with the Other-as-subject must be able to be referred back to my permanent possibility of *being seen* by the other' (2003, p. 280). The other has to reverse the relation so that I am an object for them. Seeing the other is based on their seeing me, so we have to explain the meaning of the other's look, Sartre argues. To apprehend a look of the other is to be conscious of being looked at. We become aware of the transformation which the consciousness of the Other makes in me, turning me into an object.

Although Sartre uses a number of instances to make this point, the best-known example is that of the listener at the door who experiences shame. Here Sartre describes the phenomenon of shame, where someone stands in a hallway looking through a keyhole into a room. At first the person is not aware of themselves as a physical presence, then they hear the sound of footsteps coming: 'Shame reveals to me that I *am* this being, not in the mode of "was" or of "having to be" but *in-itself*' (2003, p. 286). The sound transforms the relation to the self by revealing the presence of the Other.

This experience makes the person ashamed, and they become what Sartre calls a 'transcendence-transcended' by the presence of the person looking at them. They experience themselves as 'being-seen-by-the-other'. Sartre's idea is that when looking through the keyhole the person is totally involved in the situation, but when they are looked at by the other they are judged. The passer-by may judge the person as a voyeur, as desperate, or as lacking in self-control and pride. Insofar as in these examples I become a means for others, I am in danger, Sartre argues. In the case of shame or pride, we experience ourselves as objects through the subjectivity of the Other. Shame and pride make me *live* the situation of being looked at. In a recent article, Lisa Folkmarson Käll argues that Sartre's account of the look or gaze shows how being seen as belonging to a certain category is part of how I form my identity as a woman (2010).[8] Sandra Lee Bartky adapts Sartre's account of shame to discuss the specificity of the shame women feel (1990, pp. 83–98). Feelings such as fear, shame and pride show that there are other consciousnesses and reveal the character of our consciousness. Other existences are required to account for our feelings of shame. For Sartre, love, desire and other human relations are structured by the look, where one is either subject or object, looker or looked at.

Sartre and Desire

The idea of concrete relations with others, as Sartre calls them, is that 'There is a relation of the for-itself with the in-itself *in the presence of the other*' (2003, p. 361). He focuses on what he sees are the central or basic human relations or attitudes. There are two kinds of relations, Sartre argues: one is to look at the other and transform the other into an object; they are indifference, desire, hate and sadism. The second is to try to integrate the Other's freedom – to make myself an object for them without their freedom being overcome; the attitudes here are love, language and masochism. On Sartre's account, each of the attitudes may easily be converted into another: 'Each attempt is the death of the other; that is, the failure of the one motivates the adoption of the other' (2003, p. 385). He pessimistically suggests that conflict is the meaning of being-for-others as we are always trying to achieve the same projects as the Other, for instance, in the project of 'desire'. I will concentrate on Sartre's theory of desire here.

Desire, for Sartre, is like this: 'My original attempt to get hold of the Other's free subjectivity through his objectivity-for-me is *sexual desire*' (2003, p. 404). According to him, we are fundamentally sexual beings and this is a feature of our relations with others. He points out that sexuality is not tied to adult reproductive sexuality, as children, eunuchs and old people feel desire. Desire is not confined to certain acts, to satisfaction or to a certain period of life. Sartre makes a number of distinctive points concerning the nature of desire, which he sees as discovering the other as a sexed being. First, he says that desire is not desire for the satisfaction of desire through pleasure or by ending pain (2003, p. 406). Desire is not desire for sex as such or any particular act, evidenced by the variety of sexual practices. In contrast to Freud, Sartre argues that desire is not a desire to do something. Desire is for the Other as a transcendent object, he maintains.

Sartre's second point is that desire is not (simply) desire for another body; sexual desire is desire for the other person as a consciousness manifest in and through the body (2003, p. 408). The third point Sartre makes is that desire is trouble, analagous to clouded or muddy water (2003, p. 409). He is trying to convey our experience of consciousness losing its clarity as it is affected by the body. This overwhelming character of sexual desire, Sartre argues, distinguishes it from an appetite like hunger, and he gives lively descriptions of a 'heavy, fainting consciousness [that] slides toward a languor comparable to sleep' (2003, p. 410). Sexual desire is for the other person and I to be wholly in our own bodies. In desire, we passively consent to desire, and consciousness makes itself body.

The description of desire necessitates a further distinction, that between body and flesh. The body is the body in action or in situation, whereas flesh is experiencing body as the *'pure contingency of presence'* (2003, p. 411). Sartre writes that 'in desire I make myself flesh in the presence of the Other in order to appropriate the Other's flesh' (p. 411). In desire, contact is made through the caress, which Sartre sees as an attempt to incarnate the other's body or make them experience themselves as flesh by making myself flesh (p. 412). The possibility of realized desire is double reciprocal incarnation: 'in desire there is an attempt at the incarnation of consciousness . . . in order to realise the incarnation of the Other' (p. 413). Sartre claims that desire is a primitive mode of relations with others. Desire is also an invitation to desire, so that both desirers will have the same aim.

Like all concrete relations with others, desire fails. The first reason, Sartre argues, is that sexual pleasure ends desire, and in focusing on one's own incarnation, one forgets that of the Other. The second reason is that in attempting to possess the Other through desire, one's flesh becomes body again and the reciprocity of incarnation is disturbed in that way (pp. 419–20). These two failures may lead to masochism or sadism, respectively.

The account given here may sound unrelentingly negative, yet Sartre hints that there are other possibilities. There are other attitudes towards the Other (p. 527), but 'they [the basic attitudes] are fundamental, and . . . all of men's complex patterns of conduct toward one another are only enrichments of these two original attitudes . . . Of course examples of concrete conduct (collaboration, conflict, rivalry, emulation, engagement, obedience, etc.) [also maternal love, pity, kindness, etc.] are infinitely more delicate to describe, for they depend on the historic situation and the concrete particularities of each relation of the For-itself with the Other; but they all include as their skeleton – so to speak – sexual relations' (pp. 428–9). They are the primary projects we adopt, and they may be maintained for different lengths of time depending on the character of our bad faith and the situation. However, we can never have a fully stable relation to the Other as all these, including desire, are impossible projects.

Feminist interpretations of Sartre's account of sexuality and desire have been mixed. Naomi Greene focuses on the characters in Sartre's novels, yet she argues that his portrayal of female sexuality is linked to his philosophical concepts: specifically 'the contrast between the *pour-soi* (with its overtones of masculinity, order, hardness and reason) and the *en-soi* (associated with the world of matter, of nature, of flesh and female sexuality)' (Greene, 1980, p. 201). These associations are linked to a valorization of the for-itself and transcendence, she maintains. In contrast, Hazel Barnes defends Sartre's overall account and his use of examples, pointing out that women play a great variety of roles in his cases and some of them, for example, in *Critique of Dialectical Reason II* (1991) challenge male dominance (Murphy, 1999, pp. 26–7).[9] She extols Sartre's account of embodied experience, particularly as he develops it in *Notebooks for an Ethics* (1992).[10] She sees potential in his account of authentic love there and in his account of the possibility of remaking ourselves that is essential for hope in any feminist project. In his later work, Sartre also focuses on oppression, a phenomenon de Beauvoir theorizes in relation to sexuality in *The Second Sex*.

Sexuality under Oppression

In the second volume of *The Second Sex* de Beauvoir provides a phenomenological description of women's development and of women's distinctive situation. In that sense, de Beauvoir is working firmly in the tradition inspired by Husserl and taken up by Heidegger, Sartre, Merleau-Ponty and others. Yet de Beauvoir's approach to phenomenology is distinctive both in the range and nature of the material she uses for description of women's experiences, including letters, diaries as well as empirical research, and in her detailed exploration of the effect of cultural and social factors on experience. In the introduction to this volume 'Lived experience', de Beauvoir explains her mode of proceeding:

> I shall seek to describe how woman undergoes her apprenticeship, how she experiences her position, in what kind of universe she is confined, what modes of escape are vouchsafed her. . . . When I use the words *woman* or *feminine* I obviously refer to no archetype, no changeless essence whatever; the reader must understand the phrase 'in the present state of education and custom' after most of my statements. It is not our concern here to proclaim eternal verities, but rather to describe the common basis that underlies every individual feminine existence. (II: 9/31)

These descriptions are her way of showing how one becomes a woman. This approach has to be kept in mind; yet it does not entirely resolve all the questions that de Beauvoir's complex analysis of sexuality raises.

As has been noted by de Beauvoir scholars, the concept of 'situation' is essential to understanding her conception of women and sexuality.[11] For her, situation includes our embodiment, the place and time we live in, societal mores, and our psychological response to and experience of these elements. Myths and ideologies about women are one important aspect of situation that impacts on consciousness and behaviour. In a patriarchal society, women's situation involves being compelled to live almost exclusively in immanence. Immanence is associated with passivity, repetition and maintenance, whereas transcendence involves human choices and projects that go beyond facticity. Much of the early feminist work on de Beauvoir saw her as influenced by the sexism of Sartre's philosophy and portrayal of female characters in his novels, or by a fundamental phallocentric bias in existentialism itself, through terms such as 'transcendence '(see Greene, 1980; Lloyd, 1984; Gatens, 1991; Allen,

1989). Nonetheless, she argues that 'The fact is that every human existence involves transcendence and immanence at the same time; to go forward, each existence must be maintained, for it to expand towards the future it must integrate the past' (II: pp. 226/449). De Beauvoir contends that woman sees herself and makes her choices not in accordance with her own terms, but as she is defined by 'man' (I: pp. 234/169). This 'Being-for-men' is one of the factors in women's situation, so women come to live the myths of the eternal feminine or myths that are constituted by how men see or imagine women. However, a situation may also open up possibilities, and make action possible. Historically, men have had more opportunity for action and thus in some respects live a privileged situation. Yet situations can be interpreted in different ways, and in describing women's sexuality de Beauvoir aims to be sensitive to this diversity of interpretation and to the possibility that women's situation affords privileged insights and experiences.

De Beauvoir is trying to describe what it is like to live a female body when that body is surrounded by myths. She argues in the section on biology that the traditional social construction of bodies is not entailed by the facts of biology. Nevertheless, de Beauvoir does not believe that there are no relevant differences between the sexes and that bodies could be experienced any way at all. Judith Butler suggests that 'there is nothing in her [de Beauvoir's] account that guarantees that the "one" who becomes a woman is necessarily a female' (Butler, 1990, p. 8). Yet, as I noted earlier, de Beauvoir argues that 'there will always be certain differences between man and woman' (II: pp. 661/740) and connects those differences to the body. De Beauvoir is not suggesting that differences between men and women will always entail an oppressive situation for women. What she means is that there are bodily differences between men and women that won't disappear with oppression. Yet, how we interpret those differences is up to us. The difference between de Beauvoir and Butler is that Butler believes that there are no general differences between the sexes to be interpreted. De Beauvoir is attempting to demonstrate an awareness of the distinctiveness of the female body even in her descriptions of sexual encounters that are overlaid with structures and prohibitions. But she cannot articulate exactly how that distinctiveness might appear in the future, as her description is that of women as subordinated. Like the other existentialists, de Beauvoir believes that sexuality has a special role in our lives, and so is worthy of serious study.[12] Sexuality reveals the ambiguity of the human condition, and makes us aware of ourselves as flesh and spirit, as other and subject. Furthermore, we have to relate sexuality to life in general; for example, women's sexual life has to be understood in terms of women's social and economic situation.

In 'Sexual Initiation' de Beauvoir concentrates on heterosexual sex. This is because she sees heterosexuality as the 'classic solution', the only one 'officially allowed by society' (II: pp. 191/423).[13] Nevertheless, she devotes a chapter to

'The Lesbian', where she argues that many women are inclined to lesbianism as all women begin life in relation to a female and feminine body, a body that she implies is much more appealing than the masculine one for both sexes. De Beauvoir's complex argument allows that lesbianism is a choice made in a certain situation and that the nature of that choice would alter if women were no longer oppressed – different women would be lesbian for different reasons. What matters is that the choice be authentic. In that chapter, she sums up her view: 'The development of feminine eroticism, as we have seen, is a psychological process which is influenced by physiological factors but which depends upon the subject's total attitude towards existence' (II: pp. 194/425). In the next section I will examine the extent to which the details of de Beauvoir's analysis support this summation.

Women's Sexuality

In the following sections I will focus on de Beauvoir's chapter 'Sexual Initiation'. She begins the chapter dramatically by suggesting that women's erotic life can be disastrous and lead to 'suicide or madness' (II: pp. 146/392). The situation is very different for the sexes, de Beauvoir argues – biologically, psychologically and socially – and the possibility of sexual pleasure depends on their lived situation. How de Beauvoir understands biology here is a complex question, as although she believes that becoming a woman involves many myths, she also suggests that there are important differences that cannot be fully attributed to such myths. She details each of these features that will account for many (but not all) the differences in experiences between women and men and also the trauma of sexuality for women. One of the factors in that trauma is that heterosexual sex means a sharp break with a childhood sexuality (focused on the clitoris) for women that there is not for men, who simply extend their desire towards another person. Furthermore, the first erotic experiences have great effects on later life. This is one of the ideas that feature prominently in Stekel's *Frigidity in Woman* (1926), mentioned earlier in connection with Sartre, which is enormously influential on de Beauvoir's understanding of sexuality. Stekel notes that this effect is equally relevant for men: 'But for men too, the first mature experience may be decisive for life' (1926, p. 71). Nevertheless, in both cases their focus is on the sexual trauma of women. While de Beauvoir acknowledges that there is a wide range of individual variations in sexual experience among both sexes, she discerns general patterns that distinguish the sexes.

What de Beauvoir means by the differences between the moral and social situation of men and women's experiences of sexuality is that they are structured around the restrictions on women's lives and the language within which sex is understood. The patriarchal double code accepts that men have sexual freedom whereas women are expected to be abstinent outside marriage. The risk of pregnancy also affects erotic encounters in a number of ways, provoking a fear that may be due to the possibility of illegitimacy, the effect on health or the economic burden a child entails (II: pp. 168/407–8). De Beauvoir argues for better and more reliable contraception, an improvement that has not been fully realized to this day. Furthermore, in her chapter 'The Married Woman', de Beauvoir argues against marriage and thus against the distinction between legitimacy and illegitimacy.

A feature of de Beauvoir's analysis is her demonstration of how the language used to describe sexuality affects the way sexuality is interpreted and experienced. She gives a range of examples where women having sex is constructed as a wrong: 'The sexual act, if not sanctified by the code, by a sacrament, is for her a fault, a fall, a defeat, a weakness: she should defend her honour; if she "yields", if she "falls", she is scorned; whereas any blame visited upon her conqueror is mixed with admiration' (II: pp. 150/395). Sex is associated with sin and guilt and this makes it difficult for women to enjoy it. Women have to entirely and completely accept sex to find it pleasurable, she claims, but the conditions of feminine existence make such acceptance improbable. De Beauvoir maintains that these strictures limit desire: 'An active participation is asked of her in an adventure that is positively desired neither by her virgin body nor by her mind, beset as it is by taboos, prohibitions, prejudices, and exactions' (II: pp. 157/400).

She also details the language surrounding sexuality that constructs it as adversarial, or as she says more precisely, males are inspired by a military vocabulary in discussion of sexuality (II: pp. 151/396). Thus women live sexuality as a defeat, men live it as a conquest or victory. De Beauvoir explains how men will experience women as prey, whereas women experience themselves as passive. Another myth is that the man pollutes the woman in sex, which can be set beside the view that women are impure. Sex is considered a service that women do for men and are rewarded for, which means that the man is the master. Fundamentally, there is a lack of reciprocity in all these understandings of sexuality and so in how sex is lived and this, for de Beauvoir, is the key to changing sexual experience – to develop ethical reciprocity between the couple in that they respect each other and a reciprocity in their expectations of sexuality. (I discuss this point further in the final section).

As I noted, de Beauvoir discusses some aspects of sexuality that may be interpreted as implying that there are differences between the sexes unrelated to myths and restrictions. Some de Beauvoir scholarship emphasizes ambiguity, inconsistency and contradiction in de Beauvoir's work between a constructivist view and a view that accepts biological differences (Fishwick, 2002; Deutscher, 1997). There are points where she implies that there are differences not related to cultural myths or restrictions. For instance, de Beauvoir writes

that men experience their own sexuality as simple and unified, where transcendence and immanence become one.[14] Furthermore, de Beauvoir notes that males
do not give up their independence in sexuality, that they achieve their goals in
sexuality and that the male body retains its integrity.[15] This is how she begins
the chapter, but her later remarks give quite a different picture, suggesting that
this feature of her account of men's sexuality is to some extent tongue-in-cheek.[16]
Another point along these lines is that normally, due to anatomical differences,
men have to consent to sex for it to take place, whereas women do not
(II: pp. 150/395), a point that can be disputed.

Nonetheless, de Beauvoir more strongly and consistently suggests that
'Woman's eroticism is much more complex, and it reflects the complexity of the
feminine situation' (II: pp. 147/393). Women's sexuality is more complicated,
partially, she maintains, due to an opposition between the clitoris and vagina
and the independence of the clitoris from procreation (II: pp. 178–8/393–4). De
Beauvoir argues that this means that women experience sex with men as a kind
of violation. Loss of virginity also plays a role in women's distinctive experience of sexual initiation. The high value placed on virginity means that sex is a
sudden rupture rather than a gradual process. A man 'takes' a girl's virginity
away from her, and losing virginity outside marriage is considered a catastrophe (II: pp. 158/394, 400). The transition, like any change, appears to have an
irreversible character, and this is a particularly dramatic one for women.

Beside these remarks that appear to emphasize biological difference, de
Beauvoir also explains how biological differences are invested with certain
meanings due to social understandings of sexual difference, where men are
thought to be transcendent as they are powerful or sovereign and women are
taken to be passive and have only the properties of being hot or cold (II:
pp. 152/397). This means that women experience sexuality in an atmosphere
very different from that of men.

Women are forced to relinquish many of their own desires, de Beauvoir
argues. First, there is the ambiguity of touch, which has different consequences for men and women. Girls and boys both enjoy softness and deli-
cacy, but women are expected to give their desire for this up. This is partly
due to the fact that both boys and girls first loved their mothers, as they are
the primary care-givers. This is a factor that could change if men were to take
a greater role in childcare. Yet without that change, the situation leads to an
inner tension or conflict for women that does not exist for men. De Beauvoir
sees it as a tension between sexual pleasure and sensuality or the pleasure
that we gain through the senses. Second, women may have an active element
in sexuality but they are expected to develop a passive sexuality.[17] Rather
than being entirely passive, women have to make themselves passive in
response to men's desire and action. She writes 'To *make* oneself an object, to
make oneself passive, is a very different thing from *being* a passive object:

a woman in love is neither asleep nor dead; there is a surge in her which unceasingly ebbs and flows: the ebb creates the spell that keeps desire alive' (II: pp. 156/400).

De Beauvoir says that young girls seem to have a desire to be dominated, which is often linked to masochism, but in fact women are not masochistic. Psychoanalysts distinguish three types of masochism: an alliance between pain and pleasure; erotic dependency; and self-punishment. Women are seen to be masochistic because pleasure and pain are allied and because women accept the passive role. But she argues that 'Pain has no greater and no less a place in woman's sexuality than in man's' and women do not really wish to be sexually dominated (II: pp. 185/419).[18] Furthermore, there is nothing masochistic about passivity. Instead, de Beauvoir defines masochism in a way she sees as similar to Sartre: 'Masochism exists when the individual chooses to be made purely a thing under the conscious will of others, to see herself as a thing, to play at being a thing' (II: pp. 186/419). She links this sense of masochism with the psychoanalytic notion of self-punishment. De Beauvoir says that women are tempted towards masochism of this kind due to their erotic situation. However, this is a mode of escape, not an authentic experience of sexuality (II: pp. 188/421).

De Beauvoir makes distinctive use of 'the look' in this context. She argues that it plays a special role in women's sexual lives, as women do not want to be looked at through masculine eyes and masculine judgement, or at least women want to be seen only in a positive light. Women are treated as objects in sex: in sexual desire the look is directed at them rather than being an attempt to unite subject and object, as Sartre claims. De Beauvoir argues that this is a crucial point and a misplaced word in a first sexual encounter can have lasting effects. In this case, the Other has looked at and made the woman into a certain kind of object: either beautiful and desirable or as somehow inferior. Here she cites Stekel again to show that a comment on the wedding night such as 'you're so skinny' can be enough to drive women to neuroses or frigidity (II: pp. 162/403). Suzanne L. Cataldi argues that de Beauvoir changes our understanding of frigidity by describing it as 'a symbolic use that women may make of their bodies', a description that is more useful than clinical and biomedical models (Simons, 2006, pp. 163–77).

Women experience how they are perceived and how sex is understood. Being beneath or lower in sex is experienced as a humiliation and alienation due to the association of the lower with inferiority. Gross perceptions of women are internalized; de Beauvoir writes: 'She is absorption, suction, humus, pitch and glue, a passive influx, insinuating and viscous: thus, at least, she vaguely feels herself to be' (II: pp. 167/407). Taboos and inhibitions of society combine with the sexual experience itself. Here it is not entirely clear whether de Beauvoir means that sexual experience is 'in itself' of a certain character or whether, given that women are seen as passive and so on, the sexual experience itself is coloured by and reflects and reinforces these other influences. Further on de Beauvoir writes: 'it is certainly true that woman's sex pleasure is quite different from man's' (II: pp. 181/415). Here she is referring to the idea that women are slower to reach orgasm than men, that vaginal orgasms are rare and vague, so the sexes' rhythms are not in harmony. She also returns to the notion that there is a definite end to sex for men that there is not for women, and the idea that sex is more psychological for women. These comments may appear to reinforce the notion that she is referring to 'eternal truths', but she maintains that 'women's experience is conditioned by the total situation' (II: pp. 183/417).

Men's attitudes to women and to sexuality are extremely important to the failure or trauma of heterosexual sex: de Beauvoir sees men as being too egoistic, or too violent or brutal or too detached, so that there is an asymmetry rather than reciprocity between the couple. Women also want men to be flesh, as Sartre claims is a general desire, but often find them too controlled and too distant. Men and women have different sexual desires. Women want to merge in sexuality; men seek domination and will not let themselves be passive (II: pp. 155/399). De Beauvoir writes: 'As we have seen, she wants to remain subject while she is made object' (II: pp. 183/417).

It should be noted that de Beauvoir affirms the view of sex that she attributes to women in general. This aim is a desire for reciprocity, or giving and receiving between both partners. What is needed is for both to be made flesh for the other and an abandonment to the pleasure of sex for both.[19] Men must become the prey for women so that women can reconcile being an object with subjectivity (II: pp. 177/413). In another passage, de Beauvoir argues that men deliberately ruin the 'bewitchment' of sex for women by asking questions such as 'Did you enjoy it?' as they want to assert domination rather than enjoy the fusion and reciprocity that women seek (II: pp. 184/418). De Beauvoir sums up her argument thus: the full development of feminine eroticism

> requires that – in love, affection, sensuality – woman succeeds in overcoming her passivity and in establishing a relationship of reciprocity with her partner. The asymmetry that exists between the eroticism of the male and that of the female creates insoluble problems as long as there is a battle of the sexes; they can easily be solved when woman finds in the male both desire and respect; if he lusts after her flesh while recognising her freedom, she feels herself to be the essential, her integrity remains unimpaired the while she makes herself object; she remains free in the submission to which she consents. (II: pp. 189/421–2)

This reciprocity is only possible if women are not oppressed. So in that sense the overcoming of the oppression of women is the key to a satisfying sexual life for women. There is a further complication to this satisfying experience, however, which concerns authenticity.

A More Authentic Sexuality

De Beauvoir uses the term 'authenticity' in two ways. One is to refer to the more authentic experience that will emerge when women are no longer oppressed. The other refers to the experience more authentic *than men* which she believes women already have under oppression. Neither sense of authenticity involves a search for a pure or true self. Rather, authenticity involves (in this case) a sense of not living in bad faith by avoiding sexual experience, the engagement with the other person this involves, and the insight sexuality gives us into the ambiguity of existence. First, for a more authentic experience, women have to overcome passivity and establish a relation of reciprocity with men for a 'normal and happy' eroticism to develop (II: pp. 189/421). Men should desire and respect women, and recognize women's freedom. If desire is linked to this acceptance of freedom, the alterity or otherness will not appear hostile and neither love nor sex will be based on conflict. There has to be a 'reciprocal generosity of body and soul' (II: pp. 190/422). Sexuality will not be reciprocal until women are no longer oppressed, because that reciprocity depends on the societal and economic situation as well as on the generosity that is needed from both men and women.

The second form of authenticity is interesting, as it also points the way to the kind of better sexual experience de Beauvoir has in mind. As I noted earlier, she argues that the erotic encounter is one that reveals the ambiguity between being body and spirit more than any other. However, de Beauvoir also contends that there is a more dramatic conflict for women because it is difficult for women to enjoy transcendence and freedom in the experience of being an object. She argues that 'Woman has a more authentic experience' of sexuality than men, as men succumb to the lure of a dominating role and the self-absorbed pleasures of orgasm (II: pp. 191/423). This description suggests that men also need to understand the way they are passive in sexuality and to experience sexual pleasure *with* the other person rather than to use the other person for their own satisfaction. Sara Heinämaa notes that both men and women experience their bodies as active and passive; the difference lies 'in their temporal organization, sequence, and succession' (2003, p. 133). In de Beauvoir's discussion of the erotic experiences of young American women, she also declares that they fail to realize an authentic erotic experience, because the young women are sexually immature and do not experience desire and pleasure properly and freely (II: pp. 175/411).

As I mentioned, de Beauvoir describes women's sexual pleasure as different from a man's, less localized and more overwhelming, and this may be one of the features of the 'special sensitivity' that she is thinking of in her final remarks in *The Second Sex*. One of the points stressed by Stekel is that women are rarely compensated for overcoming their inhibitions and moral concerns by great sexual pleasures. De Beauvoir concurs with him on this issue, claiming that women's bodies are unusually 'hysterical' (or 'psychosomatic', as Parshley has it), in that there is a close link between consciousness and bodily expression (II: pp. 176/412). Moral inhibitions may prevent pleasure, and the lack of pleasure reinforces the inhibition. Nevertheless, this aspect of female bodies may be subject to change when moral inhibitions dissipate. Conversely, men's embodiment could possibly change so that there is a greater link with psychological experiences.

De Beauvoir argues that the conflict that emerges in love and sexuality occurs due to women's oppression. Sexuality can only flourish in freedom, where we recognize the other as a unique individual. Sexuality will not be reciprocal unless women are no longer oppressed. De Beauvoir points the way towards a future in which sexuality would be a less troubling experience for all concerned, yet our present is still characterized by a double standard about sexuality, concern about the risk of pregnancy, inadequate contraception, childcare and an unequal division of parenting, as well as a perpetuation of myths concerning women's passivity in sexuality. Another aspect that would change women's experience is a movement away from the abrupt shift from virginity to sex, that the title of her chapter 'Sexual Initiation' refers to. Perhaps in the future women's sexuality will be more simple and men's sexuality more complex. Moreover, sensuality needs to be more closely linked with sexuality for women, as it is for men. Men need to accept a certain passivity in sexuality, and that will make the unity of freedom and transcendence, of subject and object, more possible for both.

What de Beauvoir argues about sexuality has to be connected with her account of love. Just as the sexuality influenced by myths is one that would be overcome, idolatrous love would be replaced by an authentic love that involved mutual respect and reciprocity. A friendship between the lovers will enable this ideal kind of relationship to flourish. Women may no longer experience love in a more authentic fashion than men once freedom can be experienced in sexuality, as men will also love in an authentic fashion. Men need love or generosity to give up their dominating role in sex (II: pp. 184/418). Debra Bergoffen stresses the theme of generosity in de Beauvoir's work and suggests that she has an ethic of the erotic that commends us to accept the risks of ambiguity and to respect the vulnerability of the other (Bergoffen, 1997, p. 217). In fact, de Beauvoir goes even further by suggesting that love and esteem or respect may lead to a happy sexual relationship even under oppression (II: pp. 178/414). So, all is not lost even if the revolution has not arrived, a point in de Beauvoir's work that is rarely emphasized.

In recent years, feminist philosophers have shown how de Beauvoir differed from the existential tradition (Le Doeuff, 2007; Lundgren-Gothlin, 1996; Bergoffen,

1997; Gatens in Card, 2003) or exploited possibilities in the phenomenological tradition (Heinämaa, 2003) to create a specifically feminist understanding of sexuality. Heinämaa has traced de Beauvoir's relation to the phenomenological tradition and argued that de Beauvoir develops the specificity of women's temporal experience of the body and sexuality (Card, 2003, pp. 66–86). Scholars have also taken de Beauvoir's work further in a number of different directions. Since the publication of *The Second Sex*, feminist philosophers such as Iris Marion Young have developed phenomenological accounts of different aspects of women's experience (Young, 2002), linked de Beauvoir's work on sexuality with issues of ageing and questions concerning race (Deutscher, 2008) and explored lesbian themes in de Beauvoir's life and work (Simons, 1994).

De Beauvoir's and Sartre's accounts of sexuality have been both criticized and defended by feminist philosophers. Not surprisingly, a great deal more feminist scholarly attention has been paid to de Beauvoir's work on love and sex than to Sartre's. Only relatively recently, as there has been more of a focus on de Beauvoir's work as philosophy, have the texts been rigorously and accurately interpreted and they still contain much potential for feminists to develop, use and apply in their work. The new translation of *The Second Sex* has received diverse reviews thus far, yet the existence of a complete and more accurate version of the text should be a stimulation to fresh de Beauvoir scholarship. The prospect of new work that will use de Beauvoir's overall framework of the complex relationship between facticity, social influences and experience in contemporary terms is exciting. Meanwhile, scholarly work on de Beauvoir continues to increase, and it is likely that we will see more feminist perspectives on Sartre too, as a wider range of his oeuvre is studied.

Notes

1. I would like to thank the audience at the Australasian Society for Continental Philosophy Conference at the University of Auckland, 2008 for a lively discussion of De Beauvoir's work, and Ashley Woodward and Felicity Joseph for thoughtful comments on an earlier version of the article.
2. Space constraints prevent me from discussing Camus's or Merleau-Ponty's work. See Jeffner Allen (1989) and Elizabeth Ann Bartlett (2004) for a discussion of Camus and feminism, and Olkowski and Weiss (2006) for feminist readings of Merleau-Ponty.
3. The page numbers refer to the French text and the Parshley translation respectively.
4. We cannot be/live both For-itself and In-itself simultaneously; that would be to be God.
5. One of the earliest articles to criticize Sartre from a feminist point of view is Margery Collins and Christine Pierce in their article 'Holes and Slime in Sartre's Psychoanalysis' (1976), which focuses on part 4 of *Being and Nothingness*, 'Having,

Doing and Being'. They find that Sartre uses feminine imagery to describe holes and slime and argue that he links the feminine, and so women, with the in-itself and men with the for-itself. Bustow (1992) defends Sartre against these criticisms.

6. Le Doeuff focuses on Sartre's use of oppressed figures to support his account of bad faith (2007, pp. 64–74). Sarah Hoagland is also critical of these examples (Murphy, 1999, p. 153).

7. Stekel is an Austrian psychoanalyst (1868–1940). For this essay I have used the English translation of Stekel's book.

8. Phyllis Morris discusses Sartre's concept of objectification, arguing that some forms of objectification, such as attentive awareness of an object and mutual recognition, are positive (Murphy, 1999). She also defends Sartre's general account of holes and slime, pointing out that they are intended to refer to qualities that apply equally to men and women (Murphy, 1999, pp. 70–1).

9. Iris Marion Young takes up Sartre's description of seriality in *Critique I* (2004) to explain how women form a group (Murphy, 1999).

10. Guillermine de Lacoste also argues that Sartre moves towards a recognition of the possibility of reciprocity in *Notebooks* (Murphy, 1999, pp. 284–5).

11. See, for example, Sonia Kruks (1990), Toril Moi (1999) and Sara Heinämaa (2003).

12. De Beauvoir is influenced by Freud in thinking that we go through oral, anal and genital stages in childhood. Nevertheless, from her discussion I would take it that they are not immutable structures, but subject to changes in society and child-rearing.

13. Deutscher says that De Beauvoir 'tends to privilege heterosexual sexuality and relationality in her work' (2008, 172).

14. In another chapter 'Childhood', De Beauvoir dismissed Freud's account of penis-envy, arguing that any such envy is due to men's greater freedom and power in an oppressive society, or is a trivial envy.

15. For De Beauvoir, man achieves what he wants and is fully in control; but for Sartre, sex in general is unsatisfying.

16. See La Caze (1994) for a more detailed discussion of this interpretation of De Beauvoir.

17. Men's desire may also be awakened by that of women, but because men are regarded as subjects, women don't look for the qualities of an object in them (pp. 154/398).

18. On Sartre's account of masochism, it is 'an attempt . . . to cause myself to be fascinated by my objectivity-for-others' (2003, p. 400).

19. See De Beauvoir (1966) for discussion of this view of sexuality in relation to Sade.

Bibliography

Allen, J. (1989), 'An Introduction to Patriarchal Existentialism: A Proposal for a Way Out of Existential Patriarchy', in Jeffner Allen and Iris Marion Young (eds), *The Thinking Muse: Feminism and Modern French Philosophy*. Bloomington, IN: Indiana University Press, pp. 71–84.

Bartky, S. L. (1990), *Femininity and Domination: Studies in the Phenomenology of Oppression*. New York: Routledge.

Bartlett, E. (2004), *Rebellious Feminism: Camus' Ethic of Rebellion and Feminist Thought*. New York: Palgrave Macmillan.

Bergoffen, D. (1997), *The Philosophy of Simone de Beauvoir: Gendered Phenomenologies, Erotic Generosities*. Albany, NY: SUNY Press.

Bustow, B. (1992), 'How Sexist is Sartre?' *Philosophy and Literature* 16 (1): 32–48.

Butler, J. (1990), *Gender Trouble: Feminism and the Subversion of Identity*. London: Routledge.

Card, C. (ed.) (2003), *The Cambridge Companion to Beauvoir*. Cambridge: Cambridge University Press.

Collins, M. L. and C. Pierce (1976), 'Holes and Slime: Sexism in Sartre's Psychoanalysis', in Carol C. Gould and Marx W. Wartofsky (eds), *Women and Philosophy: Towards a Theory of Liberation*. New York: Putnam's Sons.

De Beauvoir, S. (1966), 'Must We Burn Sade?' in the Marquis de Sade, *The 120 Days of Sodom and Other Writings*, trans. Annette Michelson. New York: Grove Press, pp. 11–82.

— (1976), *Le deuxième sexe*. II tomes. Paris: Gallimard.

— (1983), *The Second Sex*, trans. H. M. Parshley. Harmondsworth: Penguin.

— (2010), *The Second Sex*, New translation by Constance Borde and Sheila Malovany-Chevalier. New York: Knopf.

Deutscher, M. (2003), *Genre and Void: Looking Back at Sartre and Beauvoir*. Aldershot: Ashgate.

Deutscher, P. (1997), *Yielding Gender: Feminism, Deconstruction and the History of Philosophy*. London: Routledge.

— (2008), *The Philosophy of Simone de Beauvoir: Ambiguity, Conversion, Resistance*. New York: Cambridge University Press.

Fishwick, S. (2002), *The Body in the Work of Simone de Beauvoir*. Bern: Peter Lang.

Gatens, M. (1991), *Feminism and Philosophy: Perspectives on Difference and Equality*. Cambridge: Polity.

Greene, N. (1980), 'Sartre, Sexuality and the Second Sex'. *Philosophy and literature* 4 (2): 199–211.

Heinämaa, S. (2003), *Towards a Phenomenology of Sexual Difference: Husserl, Merleau-Ponty, Beauvoir*. Lanham, MD: Rowman & Littlefield.

Käll, L. F. (2010), 'Fashioned in Nakedness, Sculptured, and Caused to be Born: Bodies in Light of the Sartrean Gaze'. *Continental Philosophy Review* 43: 61–81.

Kruks, S. (1990), *Situation and Human Existence: Freedom, Subjectivity, and Society*. London: Unwin Hyman.

La Caze, M. (1994), 'Simone de Beauvoir and Female Bodies'. *Australian Feminist Studies* 20: 91–105.

Le Doeuff, M. (2007), *Hipparchia's Choice: An Essay Concerning Women, Philosophy, Etc.* 2nd edn. trans. Selous Trista. New York: Columbia University Press.

Lloyd, G. (1984), *The Man of Reason: 'Male and 'Female' in Western Philosophy*. London: Methuen.

Lundgren-Gothlin, E. (1996), *Sex and Existence: Simone de Beauvoir's The Second Sex*, trans. Linda Schenck. Hanover: Weleyan University Press.

Murphy, J. S. (ed.) (1999), *Feminist Interpretations of Jean-Paul Sartre*. University Park, PA: Pennsylvania State University Press.

Moi, T. (1994), *Simone de Beauvoir: The Making of an Intellectual Woman*. Oxford: Blackwell.

— (1999), *What is a Woman? And Other Essays*. Oxford: Oxford University Press.

Olkowski, D. and G. Weiss, (eds) (2006), *Feminist Interpretations of Maurice Merleau-Ponty*. University Park, PA: Pennsylvania State University Press,

Sartre, J-P. (1991), *Critique of Dialectical Reason: The Intelligibility of History*, vol. 2, trans. Quintin Hoare. London: Verso.

— (1992), *Notebooks for an Ethics*, trans. David Pellauer. Chicago: Chicago University Press.

— (1996), *Hope Now: The 1980 Interviews*, trans. Adrian van den Hoven. Chicago: Chicago University Press.

— (2003), *Being and Nothingness*, trans. Hazel Barnes. London: Routledge.

— (2004), *Critique of Dialectical Reason*, vol.1, trans. Alan Sheridan-Smith. London: Verso.

Sartre, J-P. and A. Elkaim-Sartre (1991), *Critique of Dialectical Reason: Volume 2*, trans. Q. Hoare. London: Verso.

Simons, M. A. (ed.) (1994), 'Lesbian Connections: Simon de Beauvoir and Feminism', in Claudia Card (ed.), *Adventures in Lesbian Philosophy*. Bloomington, IN: Indiana University Press, pp. 217–40.

— (2006), *The Philosophy of Simone de Beauvoir: Critical Essays*. Bloomington, IN: Indiana University Press.

Stekel, W. (1926), *Frigidity in Woman*. New York: Boni and Liveright.

Young, I. M. (2002), *Throwing Like a Girl and Other Essays in Feminist Philosophy and Social Theory*. Ann Arbor: UMI.

10 Existentialism and the Emotions

Suzanne L. Cataldi

Man was created a rebel; and how can rebels be happy?

Dostoevsky, *The Brothers Karamozov*

You can't imagine how low I felt, creeping along the hall in my pyjamas and peeping through the keyhole.

I know, passion is sordid, Francoise said.

Simone de Beauvoir, *She Came To Stay*

Existential themes of freedom, finitude and relations with human and divine others lend themselves especially well to discussions of emotions connected to personally transformative, ethically pertinent and ontologically significant experiences. Love. Anxiety. *Ennui.* Jealousy. Hate. *Ressentiment.* Envy. Outrage. Joy. Shame. Guilt. Compassion. Readers of existential texts can expect to be moved by provocative analyses and examples of emotional experiences that are often ambiguous. Open feelings of transcendence, idealistic aspirations and creative possibilities appear alongside portrayals of objective limitations, frustrating setbacks and worldly restrictions. Emotions are meaningful, and existentialists try to capture their social, metaphysical or psychological sense by examining them in concrete situational contexts.

Existentialism focuses on the accidental and the superfluous. In place of reassuring rationalistic or deterministic doctrines, it accommodates, even at great cost, 'the troublesome idea of a subjective caprice or an objective chance' (de Beauvoir, 1996, p. 109). Existentialists call the contingent sense of finding ourselves 'thrown' into a particular mood or set of circumstances 'facticity', and our bodily-being-in-the-world is part of it. Whether we are tapping our foot waiting impatiently for a friend to arrive, forging impetuously ahead with an ill-conceived plan or remorsefully fixated on a past action, existential analyses of emotions are sensitive to the ways we can be emotionally caught up in sensible surroundings, 'living' time and space.

Differentiating between what a person feels and what a person is may be impossible from an existential perspective. Since every person is always already and affectively being-in-the-world, emotions and moods are 'worldly' in a deep sense. That is, they affect more than our 'internal' subjective psychology. Through them we establish embodied relations with the world. They afford as well as block insight into the meaning of situations they 'colour' or infuse with their affective tones or ambiance. Because they shape and influence our perceptions of and behaviour in the world, it makes sense to speak, as some existentialists do, of a 'world' of anger or the 'world' of love. To Develop the meaning of a particular emotion is to illustrate its worldly 'side' or appearance. To inquire into the meanings of feeling lost, lonely or infatuated, for example, blissfully ecstatic or engulfed in melancholy, overwhelmed by a dizzying sense of insignificance or riddled by qualms over hard choices, is to ask how affectivity functions in human life or existence.

While it would be a stretch to go so far as one of de Beauvoir's fictional characters in remarking a 'keen zest for happiness' in existential literature (1990, p. 211), there is nevertheless something to be said, although often it is not, for its depictions of life-affirming, joyous experiences. Together with Sartre's stance that human beings are 'condemned' to be free, the emphasis by certain existential philosophers, Heidegger most notably, on temporality (and, therefore, mortality), darkens existential philosophy in a way that may overshadow some of its lighter, life-affirming and intensely pleasurable dimensions. We may wish to keep in mind, as Nietzsche does, the difference between what he called a 'wretched contentment' – the so-called happiness of the 'last man' – and the joy in folly one finds on the other side of the spirit of gravity.

Furthermore, while existentialism does indeed make room for absurdity and paradox, it is nonetheless important – perhaps in ways and for reasons existentialists themselves did not fully appreciate – that stark emotion/reason dichotomies be avoided in thinking about emotions. It is not simply the case that these lines are difficult to draw. As cognitive theories of emotions have been pointing out for years, emotions make rational and situational sense. Emotion/reason dichotomies should also be avoided because of the historical role that they, along with mind/body and other normative polarities have tended to play in the oppression of members of groups socially constructed or politically positioned as 'emotional'. This positioning is and has been used as a means to exclude and disempower people of colour and women, for example.

Routine stereotypes of existentialism as licensing an anything-goes type of irrationality have their limitations as well. We can appreciate this limitation in Sartre's portrait of the anti-Semite or indeed of any individual who chooses to live in a state of passionate hatred towards each and every member of a particular group. It is precisely the anti-Semite's imperviousness to reason, fear of its open and hesitant character that marks him out as racist (Sartre, 1995, p. 20).

Even Camus, with his philosophical focus on absurdity ('that divorce between the mind that desires and the world that disappoints' – 1955, p. 37) was critical of an absolute rationalism, commenting in *The Rebel* that it 'cannot be said too often, that absolute rationalism is not rationalism . . . The first drives the second beyond the limits that give it meaning and legitimacy' (1956, p. 289).

While certain existentialists may have been too quick to categorize emotions as irrational, we nonetheless can appreciate from an historical distance how their representation of moods as ontologically revelatory anticipated and expanded trends in contemporary European thought. Emotionally based or inspired 'cover-ups' in psychoanalytic, Marxist or deconstructive thought are cases in point. Nietzsche's theme of masking, Kierkegaard's indirect communications, de Beauvoir's 'mystifications', Sartrean 'bad faith' and the various inauthentic modes of existence set forth in Heidegger's early, existential philosophy all share a common theme of revealing hidden aspects of human reality.

Because this theme is threaded through a good portion of it, my approach to the topic of existentialism and the emotions will be through this notion of masking. Moreover, since they do tend to be underplayed or covered over in discussions and stereotypes of existential emotionality – and what more after all can be said about Heideggerian *Angst* that hasn't already been?, I will also highlight passages where the existential import of happiness, joy, compassionate solidarity and love of life can be found in the works of some representative thinkers. Finally, because human freedom, life and emotions are existentially and inextricably intertwined in ways that condition morality, some of what I have to say will naturally touch on ethics. In this regard, I concentrate on existential expressions and understandings of guilt and responsibility and other emotions related to moral judgements and self-assessments.

Jealous Rebels and Maniacally Passionate Persons: Emotions in Existential Fiction

Besides traditional philosophical texts and treatises, the emotional content of existential philosophy is portrayed in art. Many existential philosophers were talented playwrights and novelists. Existential characters, some drawn from mythico-religious as well as popular culture, embody specific types of emotional experiences and emotionally motivated behaviour. Seething spite, reprehensible behaviour, the humiliations of poverty, desires for vengeance, a hunger for respect and the need for self-esteem are all interwoven and exposed, for example, in *The Notes* of Dostoevsky's brooding Underground Man.

There are numerous crimes and punishments in existential literature; some are senseless, and some are heartless, the deliberately calculating stifling all compassion. In 'The Trial', Kafka's Joseph K knows he is on trial, but he does not know for what. The Underground Man confesses that his purposive and affected cruelty towards a prostitute, Liza, 'was not an impulse from the heart, but came from my evil brain . . . so completely a product of the brain, of *books*, that I could not keep it up for a minute' (Dostoevsky, 1960, p. 112). Raskolnikov, another one of Dostoevsky's intriguing characters, is plagued with guilt over at least one of the murders he commits in *Crime and Punishment*; we are never too sure about the second, however, and neither, it appears, is he. Both, however, result from a theory (1958, pp. 226–7). Camus's main character in *The Outsider*, Meursault, appears to be on trial for responding in emotionally unconventional ways to the death of his mother rather than for the murder he is accused of committing. As he becomes emotionally fleshed out in space and time, more self-conscious and less 'absorbed' in his surrounding after his own death sentence, this stranger becomes more familiar.

In Richard Wright's novel, *The Outsider*, Daemon Cross (the 'ethical criminal') is horrified at the end of his fictional life/story, not by guilt over the violence he perpetrates and the lives he killed and ruined, but because 'in my heart . . . I felt . . . I'm *innocent* . . . ' (2008, p. 586). Related to this strange feeling of innocence is Wright's chilling portrait of 'Jealous Rebels', intellectuals who 'will commit any crime, but never in passion'. Jealous of the power of existing rulers, they 'rise to challenge the rulers . . . these Jealous Rebels proceed to organize political parties, communist parties, nazi parties, fascist parties, all kinds of parties'. They manipulate the prejudices of others for their own purposes, mobilizing 'men into vast armies to fight and die for ideals that are transparently fraudulent' (2008, pp. 487–90). Wright goes on:

> They are jealous and uneasy, these men, of anyone who tries to lure their rats [those they exploit and coerce] away . . . The only real enemies of this system are not the rats themselves, but those outsiders who are conscious of what is happening and who seek to change the consciousness of the rats who are being controlled. (2008, p. 486)

Simone de Beauvoir's novel, *She Came to Stay*, examines jealousy from gendered and generational perspectives. This novel is historically as well as philosophically significant. It does not only illustrate male–female and (perhaps) de Beauvoir–Sartre relations and her existential views of nothingness in relation to being-for-others. It also portrays aspects of feminism developed in *The Second Sex* concerning the difficulties women may experience in forming healthy mother–daughter relationships or genuine female friendships when the 'shadow of the male . . . hangs darkly over them' (1989, p 519).

Francoise, the self-sacrificing female protagonist tries, unsuccessfully, to convince herself and others that she is 'pure' of 'base' feelings of jealousy; that she does not really mind sharing Pierre, whom she loves, with Xavière, her younger rival for his affections. Pierre, for his part, is lovesick over Xavière; his jealousy arouses his 'damned need of domination'. He hypocritically will not tolerate Xavière sleeping with another man. Recalling Sartre's view that 'in Love the Lover wants to be "the whole World" for the beloved' (1956, p. 367), all Pierre wants is for Xavière to look at him like 'nobody in the world existed for her but me' (de Beauvoir, 1990, p. 208). Self-centred Xavière, however, a proud and possessive 'emotional creature' (1990, p. 208), 'could not bear attention to be directed towards anyone but herself, even for a moment' (1990, p. 236). Xavière, who 'barred all dominance over her', represents 'absolute separateness' (p. 403) and also serves as a model 'for something worse than a childish or capricious hostility . . . true female hatred' (p. 388).

Pierre reminds Xavière that her possessiveness is 'not petty jealousy. It goes with your inflexibility, with the violence of your feelings' (p. 287). In a scene where Xavière takes voluptuous, masochistic pleasure in burning herself with a lighted cigarette, Francoise senses 'something horrible': 'Behind Xavière's maniacal pleasures, behind her hatred and jealousy . . . existed something like a condemnation with no appeal . . . an eternal absence and yet, by a staggering contradiction, this abyss of nothingness could make itself present to itself' (p. 291). This 'void' of an other's 'alien consciousness' is counterbalanced by Francoise's consciousness of creating a void within herself, contributing to her own annihilation by repressing her emotions. By disregarding her own dreams and desires, she realizes, she was letting Pierre and Xavière do to her what Xavière was doing with the cigarettes: 'letting them burn' her 'without feeling anything' (p. 293).

Xavière's 'maniacal' smile and pleasure (and Francoise's own joyful, developing taste for 'black and bitter' hatred) also appears connected to passages in *Ethics of Ambiguity*, where de Beauvoir distinguishes maniacally passionate persons from generous or genuinely free ones. The former exist 'enclosed in an injurious solitude', not in an engagement with others that has as its end one's own liberation and theirs in an open future. Because nothing exists outside of the continuously elusive object of her passion, the passionate subject's freedom is partially nihilistic and 'realized only as a separation'. Instead of cooperatively engaging freedoms, maniacal passion 'disunites' them, leading to struggle and oppression (1996, pp. 64–6). According to de Beauvoir's ethics of generosity, genuinely loving someone 'is to love him in his otherness and in that freedom by which he escapes'. Although dependence on others is frightening, 'no existence can be validly fulfilled if it is limited to itself' (1996, p. 67).

Self-Deception and Justifiable Outrage: Bad Faith and Mystifications

Existentialists are attuned to the various moods and manners in which we may lose, discover or relate to our selves, and the ways we may find ourselves

179

thrown, or driven, up against the walls of the unexpected. Karl Jaspers refers to encumbrances of uncontrollable and frequently incomprehensible natural, social and psychological forces as 'boundary situations': of war and subjugation; disease, despair and death; loneliness and isolation; guilt, shame and remorse. Existentialism is drawn to excessive, extreme situations of life: to times of momentous decision-making and crises of conscience, to steps outside of our ordinary ruts of routine and complacency and the dissatisfaction we may feel afterwards, when we step or sink back into them. Whatever we know or think we know about these experiences, existentialism tells us more, about human life and feeling *in extremis*.

We may of course question how universal its depictions of feelings and situations are; existentialists question this too. 'Speak for yourself', Dostoevsky's Underground Man imagines his readers saying to him, 'and for your miseries in your underground holes, but don't dare to say "all of us"' (1960, p. 115). While they may appear on the surface to be portraying '*the* human condition', because existential writers and their fictional protagonists privilege individuality over conformity, they consistently and persistently counsel their readers to become who they are or may potentially be and not contrive to be, as Dostoevsky puts it, 'some sort of impossible generalized' person (1960, p. 115). Adopting the general perspectives of 'humanity' or 'the public' is only, Kierkegaard remarks:

> a deceptive consolation, because the public is only there *in abstracto* . . . a kind of gigantic something, an abstract and deserted void which is everything and nothing . . . the most dangerous of all powers and the most insignificant: one can speak to a whole nation in the name of the public and still the public will be less than a single real man, however unimportant. (1946, p. 267)

Speaking 'for what concerns me in particular', the Underground Man says: 'I have only . . . in my life carried to an extreme what you have not dared to carry halfway, and what's more, you have taken your cowardice for good sense, and have found comfort in deceiving yourself' (1960, p. 115).

Unmasking self-deceptions in the form of escapist flights from wrenching decisions and the anguish associated with them – what de Beauvoir and Sartre call 'bad faith' – is another of existentialism's specialties. Existentialists do not aim to pacify or placate with logical abstractions or utopian ideals; they try to lift us out of complacency. They appeal to emotions to motivate us to act, to make changes in ourselves and the world. They exhort us to accept responsibility for 'the way things are', a past we both inherit and create, and to assume responsibility, in our own unique and imaginative styles, for realizing other possibilities. Emotionally speaking, existentialism has carefully crafted attitudes of daring and defiance in response to circumstances and situations we may encounter. Even in its religious and explicitly ethical incarnations, inspiring us to become more loving, compassionate or truthful with ourselves and others, existential philosophy can be irreverent and 'in your face'.

Like Dostoevsky's Underground Man, or in *The Dream of a Ridiculous Man*, existentialists rebel at least to some extent against philosophically privileging logic and reason. They tend to discount the importance of abstraction in favour of concrete life, embracing the passionate and paradoxical. Ethical injunctions may appear in this context, as Camus's ethic of revolt does in *The Myth of Sisyphus* under the heading 'An Absurd Reasoning' or as de Beauvoir's 'antimonies of action' do in her *Ethics of Ambiguity*. Because, as she argues, oppressors dishonestly refuse to renounce privileges and resist oppression as the demands of their own freedom require, because we cannot count on their collective conversion, ' "and since their subjectivity, by definition, escapes our control", . . . liberating actions, the ground of moral actions, cannot be "thoroughly moral" . . . "others will here have to be treated like things, with violence . . . in order to win the freedom of all" ' (1996, pp. 96–7). 'A freedom which is occupied in denying freedom is itself so outrageous that the outrageousness of the violence which one practices against it is almost cancelled out: hatred, indignation, and anger . . . wipe out all scruples' (1996, p. 97). Ethical behaviour is possible; dirty hands are inevitable.

Dostoevsky's Ridiculous Man, makes a different, but related paradoxical point concerning his dream of an earthly paradise: 'Suppose that this paradise will never come to pass (that I understand), yet I shall go on preaching it'. The dream can only be realized, he contends, if the 'old truth which has been told and retold a billion times' – to love others like yourself – would 'form part of our lives' (2010, p. 17). Kierkegaard gives this old truth, to love others like yourself, an unusual (for its pre-psychoanalytic times) twist; the difficulty, he helps us realize, may lie more in a lack in our ability to love our selves than an inability to love others, a lack that may be traceable to what Kierkegaard calls the 'sickness unto death' or despair, a will to be rid of the self one truly is (1954, p. 153).

In writing about our affective life, existentialism is methodically voyeuristic and exhibitionist. Its fiction shines a lurid light on base, disreputable and even brutal behaviour, but this is typically done in the interests of its clarifying, by way of contrast, an underlying ethos of freedom and responsibility, generosity and compassion. Emotional ups and downs and their attendant, sensuous pleasures and pains are true to life. Existentialists challenge us not just to think but also to feel as a mode or method of philosophizing. The bile is bait. The hook of existential literature is precisely its direct and unabashed appeal to our emotions and its depiction of them as disclosing murky aspects of ourselves and our embodied being-in-the-world in ways that reason, alone, cannot. Sartre's discussion of shame as a response to the philosophical problem of the existence of other minds is a clear case in point (cf. Sartre, 1956, p. 261).

Dramatic tension in existential literature frequently centres on clashes between individual freedoms, conflicts between happiness and freedom, or even, as in Kierkegaard's 'teleological suspension of the ethical', between the ethical and the religious. For characters in the grip of transformative emotional crises and experiences, these may appear mutually exclusive. The often excessive value placed on freedom typically costs something: entails sacrifice and suffering. As primary sources of *Angst*, remorse or guilt, freedom and responsibility condition emotional experiences and expressions.

In de Beauvoir's and Sartre's philosophy and literature, unhappiness stems from a disquieting inability to control how others see us. This failure explains why 'Hell is – other people!' and why there is 'no exit' in Sartre's famous play of that name (1955, p. 47). The diabolical character, Inez, taunts and tortures Garcin in hell not with red-hot pokers, but by viewing his earthly actions as cowardly and depriving him of the heroic image of himself he wishes to maintain in his own and another character's eyes. Similarly, by the end of *She Came to Stay*, de Beauvoir's protagonist progresses from a position of not caring what others think of her to being so troubled about appearing jealous, traitorous and odiously guilty in someone else's eyes that she is willing to resort to violence to try to put an end to it (1990, pp. 402–3).

Wright and de Beauvoir call important attention to mystification as a form of oppression, which strengthens oppressors by making accomplices of the oppressed. Mystifications mask violence by 'recourse to a new violence which even invades the mind' (de Beauvoir, 1996, p. 110). The 'cold rage' of Wright's outsider reminds us how socially and politically significant an emotion anger is. The freedom, and in some cases, even the possibility of expressing justifiable outrage depends on the socially constructed status of the insulted and injured relative to their persecutors.

Dostoevsky, Wright and de Beauvoir critique the 'reassuring doctrine' of historical materialism, where 'there is no longer any place for the anguish of choice, or for regret, or for outrage' (de Beauvoir, 1996, p. 109). Dostoevsky's Underground Man and the various role reversals that take place during the time span of the novel can productively be read as a treatise on outrageous and insulting conduct and against this historical backdrop. For example, attempting to apologize to a social 'superior', he is put down with the response: 'Insulted? You-u insulted me-e-e! Permit me to tell you sir, that you never under any circumstances, could possibly insult *me!*' (Dostoevsky, 1960, p. 71). Later, after patronizingly lording it over Liza in a brothel, he realizes that she is 'so crushed, poor girl; she considered herself infinitely beneath me; how could she feel anger or resentment?' (1960, p. 109). When she subsequently comes to his room out of love, he is ashamed of being seen in his own impoverished circumstances. Simultaneously hating and drawn to her, a vengeful outburst of passion and insulting gesture ensues because 'she was the heroine and I was just the crushed and humiliated creature she was earlier' (p. 110). She understands and so does he in that moment that he is 'incapable of loving her'. The novel opens 20 years later with this seemingly perverse character who has a 'sickness' he spitefully refuses to cure. Although he describes himself as 'morally rotting away in his corner' (p. 114), that is not exactly true. For he is of course remorseful; that is the disease he refuses to treat. At least, it would be a disease in the context of the deterministic ideology of 'The Crystal Palace', in the novel a socialist utopia.

Leaps of Faith and Over Men – from Kierkegaard's *Fear and Trembling* to Nietzsche's *Joyful Wisdom*

In *The Brother Karamozov*, Dostoevsky places his unforgettable depiction of the Grand Inquisitor, eyes gleaming with a 'sinister fire', alongside a radiant Jesus figure, with his 'gentle smile of infinite compassion'. The 'sun of love' burning in His heart is communicated through a silent kiss to burn in the Inquisitor's. This emotional gesture is not a kiss of death or betrayal. The silent message maintains a sense of mystery, keeping the freedom of faith alive.

'Faith is a miracle, and yet no man is excluded from it; for that in which all human life is unified is passion, and faith is a passion . . . the highest passion for man' (Kierkegaard, 1954, pp. 77, 131). As the 'knight of faith' makes his lonely and agonized trek up Mount Moriah, Abraham's trial embodies and animates *Fear and Trembling*. In Kierkegaard's retelling, Isaac is 'saved', along with a conception of faith that is not just blind, but entirely absurd. Here there is no pretense of understanding God's will or ways and no hope of making one's faith-based actions intelligible to others. Abraham cannot speak what 'he has at heart to say'. He 'is not what he is without' the dread, consisting in the contradiction between the ethical and the religious expression for what he would do: murder Isaac or sacrifice him (1954, p. 41).

Existence, grasped by faith, 'begins precisely there where thinking leaves off' (1954, p. 64). Paradox is the 'passion of thought' for Kierkegaard; the leap of faith that Abraham makes is a leap over the absurdity of a good God commanding or directing the murder of a/his own beloved son. Leaps of faith must be preceded by acts of 'infinite resignation', where one painfully recognizes one's contradictory desires are, from a finite, worldly perspective, impossible. One must be convinced, humanly speaking, of 'the impossibility with all the passion of his soul and with all his heart' (1954, p. 58). But one cannot humanly speak of this passion. If faith requires belief in the absurd, silence is its only mode of expression.

Kierkegaard's notion that the reality of religion and personal faith involves a leap over worldliness and absurdities 'into the arms of God' (1946, p. 269) stands in stark contrast to Nietzsche's earth-loving and earthly life-affirming 'overman', whom Nietzsche offers as a model for humanity's 'overcoming' what he saw as life-denying belief in God. For Nietzsche, the prodigious event, that 'God is dead! God remains dead! And we have killed him!' (1974, sec. 125) announced by a 'madman' is a type of joyful wisdom.

Despite radical differences in their views on the existence of God and other-worldly hopes, Nietzsche's free spirits and conception of the 'overman' are as excessively (although perhaps for Nietzsche not as metaphysically) individu-ated as Kierkegaard's knight of faith. Both philosophers are concerned with the destructive effects of 'levelling' on outstanding individuals. For Kierkegaard, the threat comes from 'the public' – a 'monstrous abstraction' – a 'nothing' of 'unreal individuals'. Nietzsche's free spirits are threatened by the mediocrity of the 'herd'.

Both thinkers can also be viewed in the context of 'boundary situations'. For Nietzsche, this would be the transgression of our (humanity's) murdering God; for Kierkegaard, it would be the transgression of murdering, 'sacrificing' a beloved son, on God's orders or instructions. They both describe situations where humanity is put to the test, up against and surpassing limitations, to consider how their characters – or ours – hold up, when 'we loosened this earth from its sun'. Can we bear 'the magnitude of this deed'? However much we may admire Abraham, we may still feel appalled, as even Kierkegaard admits to being, by Abraham's overstepping or 'suspending' the ethical bounds he does. If God is dead, are we not lost, Nietzsche and Dostoevsky ask, left with-out ethical mooring or sense of direction? 'Are we not straying as through an infinite nothing?' (Nietzsche, 1974, sec. 125).

'Not only cunning is found beneath a mask; there is much goodness in guile' (Nietzsche, 1955, sec. 40) – and guile in goodness, we might add. This is espe-cially the case in Nietzsche's thinking 'beyond good and evil', where they both appear on the same side of the will to power. Behind Nietzsche's account of the 'slave revolt in morality' is his speculative genealogy of the transvaluation of values, where the 'weak' and herd-like slaves come to esteem, and prescrip-tively require others to value, what nobility views as base or inferior. These transvaluations are effected through a process of creative *ressentiment* driven by 'the submerged hatred, the vengefulness of the impotent' (Nietzsche, 1969, sec. I, 10), an expression of their own will to dominance subversively enacted against the strong and powerful.

In *On the Genealogy of Morals* Nietzsche's traces the origin of the moral con-cept of guilt or the 'bad conscience' back through its (Germanic) linguistic roots to 'the very material concept *Schulden* [debts]' (1969, sec. II, 4). In his view, pun-ishment was not originally imposed to hold wrongdoers responsible for their deeds. Instead, it consisted in a vengeful venting of anger on someone who caused others harm. This anger, according to Nietzsche, was held in check by a 'primeval, deeply rooted . . . equivalence between injury and pain' that drew its power from 'contractual relationships between *creditor* and *debtor*' (as above). What is attained through punishment in Nietzsche's view is 'an increase in fear, a heightening of prudence, mastery of the desires: thus punishment *tames* men, but it does not make them "better"' (1969, sec. II, 15).

Extracting a kind of pleasure ('the exalted sensation of being allowed to despise and mistreat someone as "beneath him"') from this form of compensation (the 'lower the creditor stands in the social order' the greater the enjoyment), 'consists in a warrant for and a title to cruelty' (1969, sec. II, 5). Nietzsche acknowledges that his genealogy is conjectural, that these origins are 'difficult to fathom' and that his view is 'painful'. He seems, however, to believe that it provides insight into the problem: 'how can making suffer constitute a compensation'? – a question the concept of revenge 'does not enhance . . . but further veils and darkens' (1969, sec. II, 6). Pointing 'cautiously' in his critique of religion to an 'ever-increasing spiritualization and "deification" of cruelty' (as above) and a process of 'moralization' where what is later called a 'soul' develops, 'the animal "man" finally learns to be ashamed of all his instincts', evolving 'that queasy stomach and coated tongue through which not only the joy and innocence of the animal but life itself has become repugnant to him – so that he sometimes holds his nose in his own presence' (1969, sec. II, 7). Turning 'wild' and 'free' aggressive instincts, such as cruelty and joy in persecuting and attacking 'against the possessors of such instincts: *that* is the origin of the "bad conscience"' (1969, sec. II, 16).

Moralities that address themselves to making individuals 'happy' are recipes against passions, whether prescribed through Stoic indifference, Spinozistic analysis and vivisection, a toned down mediocracy of moral Aristotleanism or their restriction to intentionally spiritualized and 'adulterated' forms, 'as can be found in the symbolism of art or in music or in the love for God or in the love for mankind for God's sake' (Nietzsche, 1955, sec. 198). The desire behind these 'moralities of timidity' – what Nietzsche calls the 'imperative of herd-timidity' – is that 'someday there shall be *nothing more to fear*' (1955, sec. 201).

Fear is the 'mother of morality'; fear of one's neighbour is ultimately more important than love for one's neighbour, in Nietzsche's view. Once stabilized, a community's moral perspectives are decided by how much or how little a given state or passion endangers the common good or status quo. In these situations 'everything that lifts the individual above the herd' are felt as dangers and called evil; in situations where they are needed against common enemies and external dangers, 'strong and dangerous drives . . . for . . . revenge, cunning, rapacity, and love for domination . . . are actually cultivated and fostered' (1955, sec. 201). It is not possible in Nietzsche's philosophy, to systematically assign or categorize in any straightforward way 'positive' and 'negative' valuations to emotions.

That virtues grow, as Nietzsche contends, out of passions, is not philosophically novel. What is different and so provocative in Nietzsche's discussions is the way virtues grow or stem from emotions ordinarily thought of as vices – profound love out of equally profound hatred and desires for revenge.

Nietzsche depicts Dionysian frenzy and revelry in *The Birth of Tragedy* as providing, through a chorus of satyrs who live in a religiously acknowledged reality behind civilization a 'metaphysical comfort . . . that life is at the bottom of things . . . indestructibly powerful and pleasurable' (1967, pp. 58–9). Nietzsche's overman brings this frenzy back down to earth, away from otherworldly hope-mongering and priestly 'despisers of life'.

Nietzsche's sense of joy contrasts with the bland happiness of the last men. Their happiness is precautious, overly refined and dull, without longing or exertion, herd-like. One 'rubs against' one's neighbour for warmth. 'Everybody wants the same. Everybody is the same.' The last man is despicable to Nietzsche because he is wholly self-satisfied; a lacklustre dullard; he does not have enough 'chaos' within himself to reach beyond himself to create, 'to give birth to a dancing star'. No twinkle in his eye, the last man only blinks. Not even an occasional bit of 'poison' 'that makes for agreeable dreams' (Nietzsche, 1954, 18).

'The Drunken Song', Nietzsche's ode to joy, stands out against the last man's happiness and is connected to his theme of Eternal Recurrence and his ethic of life-affirmation. Here we find a euphoric Zarathustra dancing, full of the sweetness of wine and life. The world and worldly woes are deep, he exhorts, but 'even if woe is deep, *joy is deeper yet than agony*' (Nietzsche, 1954, sec. IV.19.8). Thirstier and hungrier than all woe, joy 'wants itself . . . wants agony . . . wants eternity'. 'Joy wants the eternity of *all* things' (Nietzsche, 1954, sec. IV.19.11). If you ever wanted happiness to abide, pleasurable moments to return, then, according to Nietzsche, because 'All things are entangled, ensnared, enamored', you wanted all back. To affirm earthly life and to love the world means for Zarathustra to embrace its eternal return, to embrace everything, even its woes – eternally.

On the other hand, in Kierkegaard's religiously existential view, what is gained is gained by *renouncing* everything, all earthly claims; that is: 'myself in my eternal consciousness, in blissful agreement with my love for the Eternal Being' (1954, p. 59).

The Call of Conscience and the Assertion of Nothing: Heidegger on Existential Guilt

Nietzsche's herd and Kierkegaard's public are precursors for Heidegger's conception of the 'they-self' (*das Man*). What Kierkegaard calls the 'sickness unto death' is similar to what Heidegger calls the being-guilty of conscience; that is, an awareness of a failure to live up to one's own potentialities.

In *Being and Time*, moral goodness and moral evil both presuppose an essential or primordial 'Being-guilty'. The Heideggerian call of conscience is a case of finding oneself 'as something which has failed to hear itself', finding that one's ownmost possibilities for Being have been covered over, lost in 'the publicness and idle talk of the "they"' (1962, sec. 55, p. 271).[1] This public or 'common sense . . . knows only the satisfying of manipulable rules and public norms and the failure to satisfy them' (1962, sec. 58, p. 288). The 'they-self' masks 'who' has 'really' chosen and even 'the manner in which it has tacitly relieved *Dasein* of the burden of explicitly choosing' the 'tasks, rules and standards' by which one abides (p. 268). Conscience is a calling away from 'public conscience', the 'voice of the they' (p. 278), and an appeal to one's own 'authentic' Self.

As Nietzsche observed and as Heidegger acknowledges, the notion of guilt can be traced linguistically back to a sense of 'owing' or having debts to others. However, guilt as a phenomenon is not for Heidegger necessarily related to coming to owe something to others through lawbreaking or 'a failure to satisfy some [other] requirement which applies to one's existent being with' them (p. 282). *Dasein*, he states, is not a 'household' whose infractions as indebtednesses need simply to be reckoned up and balanced off as a regulated business procedure (pp. 294, 288). Guilt as a 'debt' arising through deeds done or left undone is a derivative concept in Heidegger's ontological interpretation: 'Being-guilty does not first result from an indebtedness, . . . on the contrary, indebtedness becomes possible only "on the basis" of a primordial Being-guilty' (p. 284).

Heidegger connects the ordinary way of understanding a guilty conscience, guilt as an omission or a lack, 'when something which ought to be and which can be is missing' (p. 283), to an existential interpretation that makes the everyday experience intelligible. His existential definition of guilt – 'being-the-basis of a nullity' (p. 285) ontologically unveils a constitutive *in*capacity, a *not* at play at the very basis of *Dasein's* being as care.

Dasein as care is the entity whose being as thrown projection must take over being a basis. Taking hold of itself by standing in one possibility, it is constantly *not* others. 'Freedom . . . *is* only in the choice of one possibility – that is, in tolerating one's not having chosen the others and one's not being able to choose them' (p. 285). The call of conscience is the call of care – Being-guilty, *Dasein* is called forth and back: '*forth* to the possibility of taking over, in existing, even that thrown entity which it is; it calls *Dasein back* to its thrownness so as to understand this thrownness as the null basis which it has to take up into existence' (p. 287).

Heidegger relates his phenomenological sense of temporality as ecstatical unity and his ontological understanding of Being-guilty to the ordinary way we 'load' ourselves with guilt. We experience a bad conscience by turning back to a past lapse or instance of misconduct. As he points out, the call turns up *after* the transgression to which it refers back. 'Only by first positing that *Dasein* is an interconnected sequence of successive Experiences', can we understand the call or voice as something that comes later and refers us back. It calls us back, beyond the deed or misdeed, to a Being-guilty 'which is "earlier" than any indebtedness' (p. 291). This reference back can also be a calling forth to one's possibilities.

This voice, which may 'turn up' 'against our expectations and even against our will' has an unfamiliar (*unheimlich*) ring. It 'comes *from* me and yet from *beyond me and over me*' (p. 275). Called back to (its) thrownness as a null basis, *Dasein* is called out from its hiding place in the they-self and called back from idle public talk into reticence, its corresponding mode of discourse. The call of conscience asserts nothing. It simply 'calls *Dasein* forth to its possibilities' (p. 274); summons *Dasein* to existence, 'to its ownmost *potentiality*-for-Being-its-Self' (p. 273).

The 'assertion' of Nothing into which *Dasein* is 'called back' and 'thrown' is its own potential revealed in/as anxiety. 'Anxiety makes manifest in *Dasein* . . . its *Being-free for* the freedom of choosing itself and taking hold of itself . . . *Being-free for* . . . the authenticity of its being, and for this authenticity as a possibility which it always is' (p. 188).

Heidegger on Mood and Profound Affective States

The phenomenon of mood is a fundamental *existentiale* in Heidegger's ontology. Mood is 'a primordial kind of Being of *Dasein*, in which *Dasein* is disclosed to itself, *prior to* all cognition and volition, and *beyond* their range of disclosure' (p. 136). Arising out of our Being-in-the-world, that is, not from 'inside' or 'outside' us, *Dasein* always finds itself in one mood or another. Moods outline in advance how entities and encounters within the world will 'matter' to us, how we will be affected by them. Understanding belongs 'equiprimordially' to any mood. Moods disclose the manner in which *Dasein* is 'thrown' or delivered over to its facticity, its 'there'.

Thrownness is grasped affectively as a turning towards or turning away, not as a perceptual 'looking'. Moods may let the world matter to *Dasein* in a way that allows *Dasein* to evade its self, turning away particularly when 'the burdensome character of *Dasein*' is manifest in a mood (p. 135). Moods typically *close off* thrownness. The mood of anxiety genuinely discloses it.

Anxiety individualizes *Dasein*. In it *Dasein* feels uncanny, a sense of not-being-at-home. It is this uncanniness of *Dasein's* individualization, its sense that it is 'forsaken and abandoned to itself' that is typically covered up by absorption in the 'they' – and why the voice of conscience that calls us back can be heard as alien and unfamiliar. As an understanding of one's own uncanny 'thrownness' *into existence*, 'conscience manifests itself as the call of care . . . anxious about its potentiality-for-Being' (p. 277).

All moods for Heidegger are primarily grounded in having been and share an existential character of *'bringing* one *back to* something' (p. 340). This is as much the case for moods of elation, where burdens are alleviated and we feel uplifted, as it is for emotions like fear and hope that seem primarily oriented towards the future. For as we ourselves are brought along in moods' disclosures of how we are, we are related back to ourselves as thrown ground. Hence in fearfully or hopefully 'awaiting', that which threatens or the object of one's hope is 'awaited *right back to* the entity which I myself am' (p. 341).

While anxiety, with its 'peculiar indefiniteness' makes fear possible, there are important differences between these two phenomena. 'Fear is occasioned by entities with which we concern ourselves environmentally. Anxiety, however, springs from *Dasein* itself' (p. 344). In Being-towards-death, anxiety discloses a worldly insignificance; a worldly encounter might 'show itself in an empty mercilessness'. Heidegger adds, 'anxiety is anxious in the face of the "nothing" of the world' (p. 343) and the ever-impending possibility of *Dasein's* absolute impossibility in death.

According to Heidegger in 'What is Metaphysics?', only through 'projecting into Nothing' which is integral to what is, can we relate to what is (1949, p. 340), and *Dasein*, whose essence is to transcend or go beyond what is, is 'saturated' with nihilation. Nothing 'nihilates' and rational negation, the 'not', is only one of its modes. Heidegger mentions specific types of nihilating behaviour, such as loathing and renunciations. He also distinguishes real or profound affective states – 'the ground-phenomena of our *Dasein'* – which, as revelations of 'what-is-in-totality', hide the Nothing (p. 334). Heidegger mentions joy felt in 'the presence of the being – not merely the person – of someone we love' as an instance. Any mood 'in which, as we say, we "are" this or that (i.e. bored, happy, etc.)' would also qualify as real. In the mood of dread, we are kept 'in suspense' with something unfamiliar: with Nothing 'crowding round us' and Nothing to hold on to (p. 336). Nothing reveals the 'utter strangeness' of what is, in a way that may invite us to wonder.

Magical Transformations of the World: Sartre's Sketch of Emotions

Sartre takes up Heidegger's notion of Nothing in an existential ontology that identifies consciousness with Nothingness in opposition to – that is, as *not* Being – the Being upon which it remains dependent. Because consciousness is literally nothing in Sartre's view, there is no place for environmental conditioning to take deterministic 'hold'. Hence there is no authentic (predetermined) self to be in Sartre's existentialism, and it is 'bad faith' to pretend there is.

In his earlier work, *The Emotions*, Sartre regarded his outline of a theory of emotions as an experiment in phenomenological psychology; he wished to see if emotions could be treated as a truly significative phenomena (1975, p. 21). In his existential phenomenology, emotions 'cannot come to human reality from the outside' (1975, p. 17) for the same reason they cannot be classified as corporeal phenomena: neither the body nor the 'outside' can confer meaning upon their manifestations.

As a specific type of intentional consciousness, affective consciousness has a transcendental correlate: 'to hate Paul is to intend Paul as a transcendent object of consciousness' (Sartre, 2004, p. 69). While my emotional feelings exist only through their appearance and my consciousness of a feeling constitutes its meaning, 'my feeling of hate is not consciousness of hate'. That is, emotional consciousness is not for Sartre primarily a reflective state of consciousness; it is, at first, consciousness *of* or a way of apprehending the world.

Although ensembles of corporeal phenomena are associated with them, feelings are for Sartre 'something other than a simple physiological upheaval' (2004, p. 137). Neither are they purely subjective. Emotions 'feed' or are 'nurtured' on objects, as objects take on affective nuances or textures. Evocative qualities (the awesome, horrible, arousing, repugnant, etc.) appear at the heart of objects.

> [W]hen feeling is directed on at [*sic*] a real thing, currently perceived, the thing sends back to it, like a screen, the light that it receives from it. And so, by a game of back and forth, the feeling is constantly enriched, at the same time that the object imbibes affective qualities . . . each affective quality is so deeply incorporated in the object that it is impossible to distinguish between what is felt and what is perceived. (2004, p. 139)

Despite differences in the nature and depth of feelings, which depend on whether they are correlated with real or 'irreal' imaginary objects (2004, p. 143), the 'affected subject and the affective objective are bound in an indissoluble synthesis' (1975, p. 52). 'To like Pierre is to be conscious of Pierre as likeable' (2004, p. 28).

If we consider this deep incorporation or projection of likeability or other affectively nuanced senses onto persons or objects as quasi-observations, we can account for Sartre's contention that the 'affective-cognitive synthesis is . . . none other than the deep structure of the image consciousness' (2004, p. 73). Mental images are, for Sartre, ways that objects have of being absent within their very presence. The quasi-observational character of emotional perception allows us to link his discussion of affectivity in *The Imaginary* to his earlier thesis that emotions are magical transformations of a world.

Difficulty, for Sartre, is a quality of the world given in perception. In pragmatic intuition of the world's determinism and through the tug of exigencies experienced as originating there and as needing to be realized, apprehension of the means to achieve certain ends may appear 'as if it were furrowed with strict and narrow paths' (1975, p. 57). When there is no path or the paths become too difficult, the determined world is transformed into a magical one. Objective distances collapse. Tensions and conflicts created in being unable to sustain a particular behaviour or intention motivates or 'foists' a new perception that resolves them onto them. The body, 'directed by consciousness, changes its relations with the world in order that the world may change its qualities' (1975, p. 61). Consciousness tries to seize an impossible aim or object 'otherwise than what it is' by magically conferring another quality upon it. The magical world makes its appearance in emotional, non-reflective consciousness as a non-instrumental totality.

Sartre will sometimes speak of emotional consciousness as degraded; by this he means that it obscures a more rational or pragmatic approach to the accomplishment of some end. Confronted with a too-difficult task, emotions are a means of escaping worldly pressures and internal tensions. What consciousness 'cannot endure in one way it tries to grasp in another' (1975, p. 77). Their operation as a denial of the world and an evasion of its difficulties anticipates Sartre's more elaborated theme of consciousness as nihilating activity in *Being and Nothingness*. His view of emotional signification as purposeful and, more specifically, as functioning to obscure a more pragmatic, instrumental perspective on the world, is also related to this essay's theme of masking.

There is some aim or what Sartre calls 'finality' to emotional consciousness. As a form of behaviour, an 'in order to', structure is necessarily intended. Emotional forms of behaviour are 'inferior' in Sartre's view not only because they are not effective in achieving an originally desired end, but also because of an underlying 'in order *not* to' structure. Is it the case, Sartre asks, that I cannot talk because I am crying? Or do I sob 'precisely *in order not to say anything*?' (1975, p. 31). Emotional behaviour is, therefore, not 'disordered' conduct; it is still an 'organized system of means aiming at an end. And this system is *called* upon to mask, substitute for, and reject behaviour that one cannot or does not want to maintain' (1975, p. 32). Angry behaviour, for example, while not adapted to the precise, difficult or impossible solution called for in a situation, is well adapted to breaking the built-up tension resulting from it. When we are angry, we act upon, transform ourselves into beings with fewer needs, satisfied with 'crude and less well adapted solutions' (1975, p. 37).

The context-dependency in Sartre's view of emotions helps explain, as physiological theories of emotion cannot, the diversity of emotions, the various forms that emotions may take; they 'represent a particular subterfuge, a special trip, each one of them being a different means of eluding a difficulty' (1975, p. 32). Nevertheless, Sartre considered it of 'major importance' to separate the functional roles of emotions from their nature. Behaviour – or consciousness of behaviour – is not emotion. A true emotion is undergone; it runs its course. We cannot stop or abandon it at will. Emotion perpetuates itself by perpetuating the world in which consciousness holds itself captive. 'The qualities conferred upon objects are taken as true qualities' (1975, p. 73).

Emotions are serious. Belief is involved. The body is belief. This for Sartre is the import of their physiological accompaniments; the bodily disturbances attest to their 'weight'. They are, in Sartre's view, precisely what is needed 'in order to believe in magical behavior' and to grasp 'the essential point: emotion is a phenomenon of belief' (1975, p. 75). The emotional body–subject lives, is interested and believes, in the magical world it has established. Sartre likens emotional consciousness to dream consciousness, where one lives in an established world by believing in it.

Sartre also depicts how the body may be used as the means of incantation. Dancing for joy, for example, 'when the object of our desires appears near and easy to possess' (1975, p. 69) symbolically mimics possession of a desired object in an 'instantaneous totality' – short-circuiting the difficult or laborious behaviour that may be involved in actually reaping the benefits, over a long period of time, that the desired object signifies.

Bodily bearing and gestures are emotionally telling, expressively evocative. In Merleau-Ponty's *Phenomenology of Perception*, emotions are quasi-perceptible phenomena. He might hold, for example, that I can hear the gaiety in your laughter, the sorrow in your weeping or see the 'guilt written all over' your face. Emotions, in his view, are apprehended through a bodily 'grasp', 'in a kind of blind recognition which precedes the intellectual working out and clarification of the meaning' (Merleau-Ponty, 1962, pp. 184–5; cf. also Cataldi, 1993; Cataldi, 2008). While he recognizes, together with Sartre, that emotional experience is a distinct form of consciousness with voluntary dimensions, he doubted that frequently confirmed attitudes towards the world sedimented into bodily habits could be easily or 'magically' transformed (Merleau-Ponty, 1962, p. 441).

Consciousness, in Sartre's existential view, is transparent to itself. While his account of existential psychoanalysis rejects the existence of an unconscious psyche, substituting an 'original choice' of position in the world for an empirically psychoanalytic 'complex', both are total, prior to logic, and decisive of attitudes as 'the center of reference for an infinity of polyvalent meanings' (1956, p 570). Because of its founding on choice, existential psychoanalysis 'abandons the supposition that the environment acts mechanically on the subject under consideration' (1956, p. 572).

Alienation and Objectification: Sartre on Existential Guilt and Hatred

For Sartre, facticity or the existential sense of abandonment consists in being thrown into an inescapable and profound sense of responsibility. Through my freedom of choice and my freedom to project or assign meanings, I am wholly responsible for myself and my engagements in the world. Attempts to flee the freedom one has or to evade the anguish of personal responsibility for one's actions *and* passions is a type of guilty conduct, another form of bad faith.

Sartre also derives a notion of guilt as a type of original sin from the fact we perform in a world necessarily populated by others: 'I am guilty first when beneath the Other's look I experience my alienation and my nakedness as a fall from grace which I must assume' (1956 p. 410); I am guilty in the second place for causing others to have that same experience. In Sartre's ontology, self and other are never placed 'concretely on a plane of equality' (p. 408). Another's consciousness is inaccessible to me; 'I shall never touch the other save in his being-as-object' (p. 410).

Hatred is the attempt to abolish the alienation of being-as-object-for-the-Other, 'a *real* enslavement which comes to me through others' when I am put in the humiliating 'state of *being subject to* his freedom' (p. 411). Hatred, which aims to suppress this enslavement, is 'consciously projected against the disapproval of others' and has a symbolic aspect. 'The Other whom I hate represents all Others'. Suppressing or seeking the death of a particular hated other, 'is a project of suppressing others in general; that is, of recapturing my non-substantial freedom as for-itself' (p. 412).

'Hatred demands to be hated' in Sartre's view. It is doomed to failure in the sense that one's alienation is a permanent and irremediable possibility of being (trapped and tossed back-and-forth from subject to object) in the mode of being-for-others. *No Exit* and *L'Invitée* both deftly dramatize this link between existential guilt and hatred. While de Beauvoir did not share Sartre's pessimistic view of relations with others, it is worth noting that Sartre did gesture towards the possibility of an ethics of salvation or deliverance 'achieved only after a radical conversion' as a way out of the vicious circle he depicts (p. 412, n. 13), and which his *Notebooks for an Ethics* attempted to express. Had he in mind another 'original choice', one more accepting of a certain helplessness in relation to 'my upsurge in a world where there are others' and where my relations with them 'will be only variations on the original theme of my guilt'? (p. 410).

Metaphysical Guilt and the Logic of Creation: Nihilism and the Limits of Liberty in Jaspers and Camus

The Question of German Guilt is an ethical and historical self-examination that investigates both individual and group-based responsibility for war crimes and atrocities. In this series of lectures delivered in the aftermath of the horrors of Hitler's Germany, Karl Jaspers differentiates four types of guilt: criminal, political, moral and metaphysical. Criminal guilt involves law-breaking and punishment for it, along with the political liability Jaspers discusses is externally imposed. Political guilt is a type of guilt by association; a 'joint liability of all citizens for crimes committed by their state'. Political guilt is shared liability for letting 'such a regime rise among us' (Jaspers, 2000, p. 55). In Jaspers's schema, political guilt does not mean moral guilt, because so many Germans 'opposed all this evil' in their deepest hearts.

By underscoring how extraordinarily varied experiences of the ordeal were and differences in the type and extent of participation in the regime, Jaspers distinguishes this collective political liability from a mentality which judges a people collectively. This mentality is unfortunately common and viciously applied ('drilled into the heads with propaganda') to foster hatred among groups and nations. However, because it presupposes a false substantialization ('there is no such thing as a people as a whole'), collective condemnations of a people are always unjust in his view. 'A people cannot perish heroically, cannot be a criminal, cannot act morally or immorally; only its individuals can do so' (2000, p. 35).

Moral guilt is the type incurred by individuals whose own self-analysis reveals culpable errors; for example, 'conveniently closing one's eyes to events' or camouflaging oneself behind mendacious avowals of loyalty and self-deceptive rationalizations; neglecting to act or 'acting as if nothing had happened; succumbing to blind allegiance and the delusions of a false conscience' (2000, pp. 57–67).

Metaphysical guilt, a type of survivor's guilt, is 'the lack of absolute solidarity with the human being as such'. The invisible feeling of solidarity with humanity, the true collective in Jaspers view, 'is violated by my presence at a wrong or a crime' (p. 66), particularly if I stood silently by for the sake of my own survival. While Jaspers does not believe we are morally obligated to seek death when doing so would help no one, the fact that many persons spoke out in opposition and died as a result or in battling the regime, may weigh heavily on 'the ones who in utter impotence, outraged and despairing, were unable to prevent the crimes' (p. 67).

War destroys faith in humanity and moral realities in a way that matters metaphysically. 'All of us have somehow lost the ground under our feet; only a transcendently founded religious or philosophical faith' can restore it (p. 15). In the case of moral and metaphysical guilt, 'understood only by the individual in his community', the path of purification is 'a matter of our freedom', a liberating and never ending process of continuously becoming ourselves as we come 'again and again to the fork in the road, to the choice between the clean and the murky' (p. 114). Jaspers singles out for special reprobation intellectuals who 'went along in 1933' – one thinks of Heidegger here – 'who may be guilty of persisting in a mentality which, while not identical with party tenets and even disguised as metamorphosis and opposition, still clings in fact to . . . National-Socialism's inhuman, dictatorial, unexistentially nihilistic essence' (p. 63).

Jaspers does in any event speak personally of feeling 'co-responsible for what Germans do and have done' and of being German as a task, 'not a condition'. 'By our feeling of collective guilt we feel the entire task of renewing human existence from its origin – the task which is given to all . . . but which appears more urgently . . . when its own guilt brings a people face to face with nothingness' (p. 75).

It is critical to note that in spite of its many references to nothingness, existentialism is not nihilistic in the sense of a logic (or an illogic) that would lead to death camps and total destruction. Even for Camus, who considered absurdity 'the metaphysical state of the conscious man' (1955, p. 30), the world is unreasonable but not irrational; 'the absurd is lucid reason noting its limits' (1955, p. 36). In *The Rebel*, Camus contrasts the Nazi movement, whose 'systematic and scientific aspect really hides an irrational drive . . . of despair and arrogance' (1956, p. 184), with his notion of rebellion.

Just as a human being's power to rebel limits freedom, rebellion, too, 'demands a just limit'; 'the most extreme form of freedom, the freedom to kill, is not compatible with the sense of rebellion' (1956, p. 284). One cannot consistently demand freedom for oneself and the right to destroy the freedom of others: 'nihilistic passion . . . kills in the . . . conviction that this world is dedicated to death' (1956, p. 285).

Camus defines absurdity as a confrontation and an unceasing struggle between 'a world not in itself reasonable and a longing for clarity' (1955, p. 16). Unlike the 'bloodthirsty vanity of nihilism', absurdity and rebellion refuse to legitimize murder or suicide. They are 'in principle . . . a protest against death' (1956, p. 285). Camus is of course aware of the utter futility of this protest, but that is precisely his point: He does not want to 'mask the evidence'. Although it is 'the most harrowing passion of all' (1955, p. 17), we must, in Camus's view, learn to live with the feeling of absurdity, this absence of hope that is different to despair. He prefers an alert awareness of the 'basis of that conflict, that break between the world and my mind' to absurdity deified in mystical leaps of faith or to suicide which, 'like the leap, is acceptance at the extreme' (1955, p. 40). He imagines Sisyphus, his absurd hero, 'superior to his fate' and 'stronger than his rock' as he walks back down the mountain during an hour of conscious breathing space before returning to his useless labour.

In Camus's view, the most profound logic is the logic of creation, not destruction. While a certain progress towards their achievement might be made, he acknowledges that creative works – of art, love or commitment – are never done. But he also believes that the required discipline of the daily effort they demand may permit more freedom in their realization (1955, p. 87).

For Jaspers, 'the ideal of human existence as liberty' entails a modest resignation: 'before the transcendent we become aware of being humanly finite and incapable of perfection' (2000, p. 113). Along with a humility that allows us 'to struggle with love in discussing truth, and in truth to join with each other', for Jaspers seriousness and resolution spring from the work of clarifying a new life and its possibilities:

> [L]ife is no longer simply there to be naively, gaily enjoyed. We may seize the happiness of life if it is granted to us for intermediate moments, for breathing spells – but it does not fill out existence; it appears as amiable magic before a melancholy background. Essentially, our life remains permitted only to be consumed by a task. (2000, p. 113)

Whether this task consists in a lucid acknowledgement of the possibilities and limitations of earthly life, a recuperative overcoming of humanity or transcendent leaps of faith that ascribe to human life a superhuman significance, existentialists regard 'the struggle itself' – against servitude, falsehood and terror – as honourable and awe-inspiring, arduous but not necessarily devastating. 'The human heart has a tiresome tendency to label as fate only what crushes it. But happiness likewise is without reason, inevitable' (1955, p. 95). As Camus states and as his writing so eloquently and rigorously establishes: 'ironic philosophies produce passionate works' (1955, p. 86).

'One must imagine Sisyphus happy'.

Note

1. Pages references are to the German pagination of *Being and Time*, which all English translations also have on the margins of the page.

Bibliography

Camus, A. (1955), *The Myth of Sisyphus & Other Essays*, trans. J. O'Brien. New York: Vintage Books.
— (1956), *The Rebel: An Essay on Man in Revolt*, trans. A. Bower. New York: Vintage Books.
Cataldi, S. L. (1993), *Emotion, Depth and Flesh: A Study of Sensitive Space: Reflections on Merleau-Ponty's Philosophy of Embodiment*. Albany, NY: SUNY Press.
— (2008), 'Sense and Affectivity', in R. Diprose and J. Reynolds (eds), *Merleau-Ponty: Key Concepts*. Stocksfield: Acumen, pp. 163–73.

De Beauvoir, S. (1989), *The Second Sex*, trans. H. M. Parshley. New York: Vintage Books.

— (1990), *She Came to Stay*. New York: W. W. Norton.

— (1996), *The Ethics of Ambiguity*, trans. B. Frechtman. New York: Citadel Press.

Dostoevsky, F. (1958), *Crime and Punishment*, trans. C. Garnett. New York: Bantam Books.

— (1960), *Notes from Underground and the Grand Inquisitor*, trans. R. E. Matlaw. New York: E.P. Dutton.

— (2010), *The Dream of a Ridiculous Man*, trans. C. Garnett. LaVergne, TN: Kessinger Publishing.

Heidegger, M. (1949), 'What is Metaphysics?' in *Existence and Being*, trans. R. F. C. Hull and A. Crick. Chicago: Henry Regnery.

— (1962), *Being and Time*, trans. J. Macquarrie and E. Robinson. New York: Harper & Row.

Jaspers, K. (2000), *The Question of German Guilt*, trans. E. B. Ashton. New York: Fordham University Press.

Kierkegaard, S. (1946), *The Present Age* in R. Bretall (ed.), *A Kierkegaard Anthology*. New York: Modern Library.

— (1954), *The Sickness unto Death*, in *Fear and Trembling and The Sickness unto Death*, trans. W. Lowrie. New York: Doubleday.

Merleau-Ponty, M. (1962), *Phenomenology of Perception*, trans. C. Smith. London: Routledge.

Nietzsche, F. (1954), *Thus Spoke Zarathustra*, trans. W. Kaufmann. New York: Penguin Books.

— (1955), *Beyond Good and Evil*, trans. M. Cowan. Chicago: Henry Regnery.

— (1967), *The Birth of Tragedy*, trans. W. Kaufmann. New York: Vintage Books.

— (1969), *On the Genealogy of Morals*, trans. W. Kaufmann. New York: Vintage Books.

— (1974), *The Gay Science*, trans. W. Kaufmann. New York: Vintage Books.

Sartre, J-P. (1955), *No Exit and Three Other Plays*, trans. S. Gilbert. New York: Vintage Books.

— (1956), *Being and Nothingness*, trans. H. E. Barnes. New York: Philosophical Library.

— (1975), *The Emotions. Outline of a Theory*, trans. B. Frechtman. New York: Citadel Press.

— (1995), *Anti-Semite and Jew*, trans. G. J. Becker. New York: Schocken Books.

— (2004), *The Imaginary*, trans. J. Webber. New York: Routledge.

Wright, R. (2008), *The Outsider*. New York: HarperCollins.

11 Existentialism, Authenticity and the Self

Christopher Macann

'Become who you are!' is a slogan Nietzsche took from Pindar and employed on many occasions.[1] Heidegger's introduction of a theory of authenticity into *Being and Time* might be taken as the culmination of this same slogan. From Nietzsche's 'Death of God' to Heidegger's 'Finitude of *Dasein*', existential disenchantment deepens progressively, to the point that the authenticity of the self could even be taken as the only remaining salvational recipe, the last bulwark against nihilism. But in order for it even to be possible to raise the question of how a self might become who it is, we first need to come to terms with what it means to be a self, more particularly, what it means for a self to exist. In what concerns the conception of the self, we shall take Kierkegaard as our guide. Between the two poles of an examination of existence and the self, on the one hand, and the theory of authenticity, on the other, we shall interpose the two crucial themes of anxiety and conscience. By carefully reconsidering the doctrine of anxiety (derived by Heidegger and Sartre from Kierkegaard) and the doctrine of conscience (derived by Heidegger from Luther and by Sartre from Heidegger), we shall find ourselves in a position to correct the dangerous vacuity of the Heideggerian theory of authenticity (derived by Heidegger from Nietzsche).

Existence and the Self

As is well known, in *Being and Time* Heidegger developed an ontological alternative to Husserl's transcendental phenomenology, and so brought existentialism back into the centre of phenomenological philosophy. And this by drawing a radical distinction between entities which merely are, and entities that have their being 'to be'.

Heidegger never made a secret of his debt to Nietzsche; but he did make something of a secret of his debt to Kierkegaard, from whom he borrowed largely for his theory of anxiety (*Angst*), but whose name is only briefly noted in *Being and Time*. And yet it was Kierkegaard who gave philosophy its most

fruitful, existential definition of what it means to be a self. At the very beginning of his *Sickness unto Death*, Kierkegaard writes:

> A human being is Spirit. But what is spirit? Spirit is the self. But what is the
> self? The self is a relation that relates itself to itself. (1980, p. 13)

What it means to be human is defined in terms of our spiritual potential. And
our spiritual potential is then further defined in terms of what it means to be a
self. And precisely because the crucial last sentence sounds like a closed circle
of words, the circuit needs to be opened up to yield its wealth of meaning.

The self is a *relation*. This means that the self is not something substantial. At
one stroke, this phrase disqualifies all concepts of the self as an ego, whether
empirical or transcendental, as something that could be identified and reidenti-
fied as remaining one and the same throughout its changing states, for instance,
its thoughts, its experiences. But this does not imply that the self is, or ever
could be, nothing. Rather the contrary, for Kierkegaard: there is nothing more
real than the self, and no greater responsibility befalls the self than that it has to
make something of itself.

The self is not just a relation but a relation that actively *relates itself* (to itself).
This disqualifies any conception of the self as merely undergoing thoughts and
experiences, as being made up of the thoughts and experiences it *passively*
receives. So, too, any conception that would make of the relation an objective
relation that just happens to obtain between one thing and another, and which,
in so obtaining, makes no difference to that between which it obtains. For the
self actually makes itself be in and through just such a relational activity.

And to what does the self relate itself? In answer to this question, Kierkegaard offers the one word: 'self', and in so doing creates the impression that his
formula turns in a circle; worse, merely expresses a tautology: S = S. But how
could something so crucial to Kierkegaard's existentialism be reduced to a play
on words: the self, the solitary individual, the self that is called upon to indi-
vidualize itself in the face of itself and before God, how could this *existential*
definition of the self be reduced to a tautology?

Kierkegaard's answer to this objection is to be sought in his detailed descriptions of the way in which such a self does actually relate itself to itself. But
before trying to do justice to these descriptions, I would like first to propose a
threefold definition of the self derived from Kierkegaard's formula, and which
will make it possible to be much more specific with regard to that human spirituality which stands at the centre of Kierkegaard's philosophical investigation.

From the *relation itself*, or the relationality of the self, I derive an existential
category of *Reflexivity*. From that *to which* the self relates itself, when it relates
itself to itself, I derive an existential category of *Individuality*. And from the *being*
of that self which stands in such a relation (of itself to itself), I derive an

existential category of *Integrity*. From Kierkegaard's definition of the self we have now managed to derive three *existential* categories which, between them, can be taken to make up the being of the self – Reflexivity, Individuality and Integrity. But this seeming complication is only the beginning of further complications without which I find it difficult to come to terms with the existentialism of other figures, for example, Heidegger, Merleau-Ponty and Sartre. The best way to bring this out is with regard to the category of Individuality, that *to which* the self relates itself.

The simple answer to the question as to what it is that the self relates itself *to* originally is – its body. But this answer is quite simply *too* simple. For if the self is defined too straightforwardly in terms of its being a body, it becomes extremely difficult to do justice to what Kierkegaard meant by spirituality, the upward orientation of consciousness away from itself and towards – God. But what if the relation to the body were envisaged as *either* immediate *or* mediate and, if mediate, as *either* intermediately mediate *or* ultimately mediate? By drawing such a distinction between the three ways in which the self can stand in relation to its body, we not only do justice to such Cartesian conceptions of the self as depend upon a *distinction* (the *intermediately* mediate relation) of the self from its body but also to such conceptions as presuppose a further and final *abstraction* (the *ultimately* mediate relation) of the self from its body – without which it will prove difficult to do justice to what Kierkegaard had in mind when he talked of Man as Spirit.

To the objection that such a three-stage conception of the self runs counter to the spirit of the Heideggerian enterprise, and to his unrelenting opposition to Cartesianism, the answer is: yes, at least for the early Heidegger, the self has to be grasped in its concrete immediacy, and so against any tendency to posit consciousness in its *distinction*, or in its *abstraction*, from the body – and the same holds of Merleau-Ponty. But indirectly, both philosophers admitted these alternative possibilities, Heidegger in his offhand (because dismissive) repudiation of the ontic, Merleau-Ponty in his critique of empiricist and intellectualist conceptions of consciousness. Moreover, as I hope to show, it is impossible to do justice to Sartre's existentialism without allowing for a self that is *unable* to be itself. Worse, too simplistic a refusal of the detachment of the self from its body makes it impossible to come to terms with what Kierkegaard meant by Man as something other than a creature of flesh and blood, a creature condemned to living out its strictly finite existence between the two extreme limits of birth and death.

It was for reasons such as these that, in *Being and Becoming* (Macann, 2007), I defined the self in a threefold way, as existing itself in a relation of *coincidence* with its body, together with a relation of *distinction* and *abstraction* from its body. And precisely because I take it for granted that every way in which the self stands in relation to itself opens the way to a complementary relation to what is other than itself, this original, existential coincidence of the self with its body can be taken to *predetermine* an ontological relation of coincidence with the other (Heidegger's being-in-the-world), the derivative, existential distinction of the self from its body (Descartes's distinction of mind and body) can be taken to *predetermine* an equivalently ontological relation of distinction from the other (the Cartesian subject–object opposition), while the conclusive abstraction of the self from its body can be taken to open the way to the further distinction (in the transcendental philosophies of Kant and Husserl) of a transcendental from an empirical consciousness.

To sum up, human being stands in a twofold relation with what is, an existential relation of itself to itself and an ontological relation of itself to whatever is other than itself. Following Kierkegaard, the existential relation of the self to itself has been defined in a threefold way, in terms of a certain *Reflexivity, Individuality* and *Integrity*. And this threefold structure of the self is seen to undergo a threefold transformation, depending on whether the self stands in an original relation of *coincidence* with its body (and with the world) or in a derivative relation of *distinction* or *abstraction*. Moreover, these latter three ontological principles are set in an ordered progression so that the genetic development from one stage to the next represents a mark *both* of the development of consciousness *and* of a loss of the being relation.[2]

Existence and Authenticity

Given the crucial importance of the existential dimension Heidegger brings into phenomenological philosophy with *Being and Time*, it is surprising how infrequent and obscure are his references to existence (*Existenz*). The most valuable remarks are to be found early on in section 9: The Theme of the Analytic of *Dasein* (Heidegger, 1962, pp. 67–71). They can be brought under four connected heads:

1. Existence as opposed to essence: 'The "essence" of *Dasein* lies in its existence' – later to become Sartre's famous priority of existence over essence.
2. The distinction between an entity that has its being to be as opposed to one that simply is ('Accordingly, those characteristics which can be exhibited in this entity are not properties "present-at-hand" of some entity . . . they are in each case possible ways for it to be').
3. Possibilities of being are in turn rooted in the Mineness of the self ('That Being which is an *issue* for this entity in its very Being, is in each case mine').

4. Choosing or failing to choose one's ownmost possibilities of being brings with it the distinction of authenticity and inauthenticity ('and because *Dasein* is in each case essentially its own possibility, it *can*, in its very being, "choose" itself and win itself; it can also lose itself and never win itself; or only "seem" to do so').

Reading backwards, we find a theory of authenticity connected with the concept of existence from the very beginning: first, through the notion of choosing between possible ways of being; second, through the notion of mineness lying at the root of ownmost possibilities of being; and third, through the notion of existence, which lies at the root of the notion of mineness. Nor should the full force of the alternation between existence and essence be overlooked. It is not just a matter of contrasting an object whose universal properties stand out against the particular possibilities available to any individual *Dasein*, it is also a matter of differentiating a new phenomenology of existence from any (transcendental) phenomenology whose principal task is the resolution of objects into essences.

To sum up: *human being* is itself in such a way that it exists, that is, has its being 'to be'. Moreover, an *authentic* human being is an individual who accordingly chooses those possibilities of being which are its ownmost possibilities of being itself. Implied therein are three assumptions: (1) that each human being has a way of being (a nature) of its own; (2) that the task of life is to come to terms with who one is; and hence (3) to choose those authentic possibilities of being which will enable the self to become who it is.

And what of Sartre? Sartre's principal treatise *Being and Nothingness* is subtitled *An Essay on Phenomenological Ontology*. But *Being and Nothingness* is certainly not a contribution to transcendental phenomenology, given his refusal of the transcendental ego as voiced in his early paper 'The Transcendence of the Ego' (Sartre, 1957). However, neither is it ontological phenomenology, in the Heideggerian sense, given his abandonment of the search for a 'ground of the unity' in favour of the assumption of a dichotomy. And since one side of the dichotomy takes away from the self its constitutive power, the Nothingness of consciousness makes a phenomenological conception of the self difficult. In my view, *Being and Nothingness* is actually an essay in Cartesian dualism. Even if the nothingness of consciousness does at least avoid the error of according the self a substantial status, all that one gets by this admission is an alignment of Sartre's phenomenology with materialism, the sort of materialism that lies at the root of most analytic philosophy, and which brings Sartre's vision of the universe into line with that of Bertrand Russell. There is only *being-in-itself*, in other words, the material universe, consciousness being nothing more than a reaction, or response, to this fact on the part of an organism sufficiently sophisticated to be capable of furnishing a 'mirror of nature'.

But how could a materialist position ever possibly produce an existential philosophy? This is where Sartre's 'genius' makes itself known. He has done us the inestimable favour of bringing home the awfulness of the world-view that materialism implies. It is then up to us to decide whether there is nothing to be done about this (since that's the way it is) or, alternatively, to contest this vision.[3]

The dualisms with which Sartre operates change, but the philosophy remains unchangingly dualist. The initial duality of *Being* and *Nothingness* gives way to the duality of the *For-itself* and the *In-itself*, with, as a variant of the former, the duality of the *For-itself* and the *For-others*. The duality that interests us most in our existential examination of the self is that of the *For-itself* and the *In-itself*. At the beginning of part 2 on the *For-itself*, he asks 'what it means for consciousness that it must necessarily be what it is not and not be what it is'. And later on in the section on Temporality he goes on to tell us that the *For-itself* must meet the following requirement: 'to be what it is not and to not-be what it is' (Sartre, 1969, p. 137).

So how can the self (effectively, for Sartre, the *For-itself*) *be* itself, be *true* to itself, be itself *authentically?* Answer: it can't! And every attempt to do so inevitably commits the self to being in bad faith, to hypocrisy. The more a person insists upon his sincerity, the more certain you may be that he is acting in bad faith. All that the 'authentic' self can do is to recognize, in anguish, the *impossibility* of being itself.

And so what of Heidegger's critical alternative – to choose to be oneself or not to be oneself? (An alternative without which his theory of authenticity is meaningless.) Let us leave the answer to this question in abeyance for the moment and simply review the alternatives, insofar especially as they seem to confirm our three-stage conception of the genesis of the self.

1. Originally, the self cannot but *be* itself. This not being able to *not* be itself stems, I suggest, from the immediacy of the relation of the self with its body. Animals, and even children, simply are what their natures incline them to be; they *coincide* with their bodies in such a way that their behaviour is a spontaneous outcome of their very own nature.

2. Secondarily, the self cannot but *not be* itself. Not being able to be itself stems, I suggest, from the mediacy of the relation of the self with its body, that mediate relation enshrined in Descartes's distinction of mind and body. But why would the self ever let itself become so that it could not be itself? Because the complementary distance assumed by the self vis-à-vis the world makes possible an instrumental relation to the world, and to others. And this instrumental rationality brings its manipulative advantages, the negative implications of which the self is unable to see, due to its inescapable entrapment in bad faith.

3. So how is the self ever able to put itself in a position where being or not being itself can at least be seen as alternative possibilities? This alternative, I suggest, can only arise insofar as the self transforms itself, yet again, abstracts itself from its bodily being in such a way as to be able to consider what it means to be (or not to be) itself. Only a self that has detached itself from itself in this way is in a position to choose one or the other possibility authentically.

4. But, fourth, the realization of this possibility now also requires that the self be restored to itself again, to that self which it was originally, and which it has had to *stop* being in order to be able to develop itself. Resoluteness is not a matter of spontaneously acting out one's primordial nature but of holding to possibilities of being which, upon reflection, have been identified as ownmost possibilities *against* the temptation to not be oneself – with all its accompanying manipulative advantages.

Jaspers once reacted critically to Heidegger's theory with the question, 'resoluteness, but with respect to what?' (Jaspers, 1989, p. 179). By persistently refusing the structure of reflection, Heidegger makes it difficult for us even to understand what *he* meant by talking of an anxiety-ridden calling in question of self. What is lacking in Heidegger's ontological phenomenology are the genetic (dialectical?) resources needed to show how the self moves from stage to stage, transforming itself in such a way that it begins to conform, more and more, to what might be called its 'spiritual' potential. And no existential philosopher understood this better than Kierkegaard.[4] In order to bring this out, I want now to consider the two interconnected existential themes of *anxiety* and *conscience*.

Anxiety and Conscience

How strange that Sartre and Heidegger should both have seen the crucial importance, for existential philosophy, of Kierkegaard's theory of anxiety, and so have sought to integrate this category into the main body of their own ontological thinking, but without doing justice to its single most important feature, its upward orientation, the aspiration towards the heights.

Despair, Kierkegaard writes, 'is not depressing but instead is elevating, inasmuch as it views every human being under the destiny of the highest claim upon him, to be spirit' (1980, p. 22). 'Elevating', 'highest claim', 'spirituality': how could Heidegger and Sartre have failed to take note of this feature? Very simply, because it did not fit the format of their ontological presuppositions; in the case of Heidegger, the movement backward and downward against the Husserlian transcendental aspiration, and in the case of Sartre, Cartesianism without God, leading inexorably in the direction of realism and materialism.

No word can adequately convey the existential import of that calling in question of the self which the literature has tried to name with such words as 'anxiety', 'anguish', even 'despair', each one of which can so easily be interpreted as pathological states. That any psychological interpretation of anxiety fails entirely to come to terms with its philosophical (spiritual) significance is clear from Kierkegaard's own statements (as also from equivalent statements by Heidegger and Sartre). For instance, Kierkegaard's claim regarding the universality of this sickness, which, for him, does not mean that it is impossible to eradicate, only that the eradication can only come about through despair itself. For every attempt to get rid of despair only leads the self to 'labour itself into an ever deeper despair' (1980, p. 14). So that, in the end, the cure comes not from the self itself, still less from any other human being, but only – from God.

For Kierkegaard, despair is unavoidable because, although Man is a relation, he did not constitute this relation himself but exists this relation as constituted by a higher power. Basically, Kierkegaard was writing for Christians (whether nominal or real) and so assumed the theological premises of a God by whom each Soul was created. More, Kierkegaard assumed that God not only created each and every Soul but He then, as it were, left each created self *free* to be itself, to go its own way. Despair is my having to take responsibility for a self I did not constitute myself. 'If a human self had established itself, then there could be only one form: not to will to be oneself, to will to do away with oneself, but there could not be the form: in despair to will to be oneself' (1980, p. 13). So, the only way in which a self that wills to be itself can cease to be in despair is when it gives itself up and allows itself to be 'grounded transparently in the Power that established it' (p. 14).

The most interesting feature of Kierkegaard's theory of despair is the dialectical presentation of the stages along the way to the eradication of despair, which are developed (under the head of 'Despair as Defined by Consciousness') as the function of an ever-increasing intensification of consciousness, and whose several steps can be summarily presented as follows: (1) a self whose self-consciousness is of so low a level that it is not even aware of being in despair; (2) a self that has become conscious of being in despair and seeks to get rid of itself in order *not* to be in despair; (3) a self that despairingly wills to be itself. With the increase in consciousness goes an intensification of the will, which very wilfulness, so far from bringing the self nearer to a solution, only takes it ever further away from its goal, that of ceasing to be in despair.[5] The high point of this development brings the self to that paroxysm of despair which compels the self to make the leap of faith – inward and upward.

What use does Heidegger make of Kierkegaard's theory of anxiety? In section 29 of Chapter V, headed 'Being-in as such', Heidegger introduces an existentialia (*Befindlichkeit*) translated into English as 'state-of-mind', and then uses fear (sec. 30) to illustrate this existentialia in such a way as to mark the contrast with anxiety. It is in the following chapter VI, devoted to *Care*, and in a section (40) in which Care grounds the being-in-the-world of *Dasein* as a whole, that he tackles anxiety. Since the world figures as the field in which possibilities of being manifest themselves, 'being in the world itself is that in the face of which *Dasein* is anxious' (Heidegger, 1962, pp. 232/187). 'Anxiety', Heidegger tells us, 'individualizes *Dasein* and thus discloses it as *solus ipse*' (1962, pp. 233/188). Unlike fear, which flees in the face of some worldly danger, anxiety brings home to the self the fact that it flees from itself and into the world – in order not to have to come to terms with itself. Anxiety reveals to the self that in fleeing from itself into the arms of the world, it has lost its self.

Although Heidegger mostly deals with anxiety in chapter VI of part one division one (sec. 40) and deals with conscience mostly in chapter II of part one division two (secs 54–60), the two themes are nevertheless closely connected, as Heidegger makes clear when he tackles conscience later under the overall heading of *Dasein* and Temporality (division two). For conscience is presented as a call in which the self is called back to its authentic self and away from its lostness in the commonality of Man (*das Man*, usually translated as the 'They'). Such a call, which most often comes in the form of an imperative prohibition (Thou shalt not!, often rendered by Heidegger with the single word: 'Guilty!'), can only come to one who is open to the call, an openness which is attested in the state of mind of anxiety. The 'fear and trembling' of anxiety provokes in the self a response which finds concrete form in resolute commitment to ownmost possibilities of being. So conscience links anxiety, on the one hand, with resoluteness, on the other, and so also to authenticity, since by resoluteness Heidegger means the unswerving commitment of one's self to ownmost possibilities of being.

Unlike Heidegger, Sartre makes no secret of drawing his theory of anguish from Kierkegaard. Both Kierkegaard and Heidegger are mentioned by name as precursors of his own treatment of the theme. So basic is the concept of anxiety to Sartre's existential philosophy that it lies at the root of the nothingness which he defines consciousness as being. And this is why it appears right from the beginning of chapter one of *Being and Nothingness*. Sartre proceeds in a series of steps. He begins with the simple example of the negative judgement: 'Pierre is *not* in the café', in order to bring out the phenomenal relevance of the 'not' concealed in the judgement. It is the not-being-there of a Pierre whom I actively seek out that confers meaning upon the negative judgement – rather than the other way around. Sartre then passes over to the Hegelian concept of dialectical negation, which he has to reject since it presupposes the becoming of being – which Sartre cannot accept. Heidegger's phenomenological concept of nothingness is then in turn rejected by reversing the terms of the analysis. It is not by turning away from the transcendence of that world into which it is thrown that human being comes up against nothingness. For the transcendence of being-in-the-world would itself be impossible without that nothingness which consciousness is, and has to be, in order to posit a world as not being itself, that is, as a sphere of transcendence. This then leads Sartre straight over into his own conception of anguish as the fear of freedom, that freedom which consciousness is qua nothingness. 'We wished only to show that there exists a specific consciousness of freedom, and we wished to show that this consciousness is anguish. This means that we wished to establish anguish in its essential structure as consciousness of freedom' (Sartre, 1969, p. 33). From which he draws the conclusion: 'Anguish then is the reflective apprehension of freedom by itself' (1969, p. 39).

The next chapter, on 'Bad Faith', is designed to do two things: to show how the self tries to conceal from itself the fact of being free (psychological and even physiological determinism as so many ways in which the self pretends to itself that it couldn't help being and doing what it is and does), and also to show why these strategies in bad faith inevitably fail.

It would be tempting to take the opposite of bad faith in the direction of conscience. But of course, good faith or sincerity is, for Sartre, impossible, and precisely because the self can never *be* itself. Supposed sincerity is just the worst kind of bad faith, the bad faith that is incapable of comprehending the impossibility of good faith. For Sartre, there is no way out, save perhaps in the lucid recognition of the impossibility of being self. And so in the terms of his thought, there is no possibility of an existentialist Ethics.[6] Heidegger wants there to be a way out, and his theory of authenticity is designed to bring human being back to its very own self, and to authentic possibilities of being itself. And though both Sartre and Heidegger derived their concept of anxiety from Kierkegaard, neither took this theory in an 'upward' direction remotely resembling that advocated by their master.

What profiteth a man if he gains the whole world and loses his own soul? This biblical question puts the critical issue in the most extreme terms, and might even be taken as the only quake catastrophic enough to propel a man out of the comforting reassurance of what Heidegger calls *das Man*, and which brings with it all the advantages of instrumental rationality – manipulative control, whose deadly impact upon the self (let alone others) is concealed by hypocrisy. Our position is that good faith (as expressed in the phenomenon of conscience) is much more complicated than Heidegger would have us believe, but that it is not in principle impossible.

Let us try to reconstruct the theory of anxiety and conscience in line with our genetic conception of the self, and in such a way as to enable these two phenomena to be what Kierkegaard intended them to be, stepping stones along the way to a higher consciousness.

Sartre's theory of anxiety is developed on the only plane his philosophy recognizes, an objective universe where the self exists itself according to the formula: being what it is not and not being what it is. Heidegger's theory of anxiety and conscience manoeuvres between the ontic (objective) plane of the 'They' and a more primordial ontological plane covered over by *Fallenness*, and which has, therefore, to be recovered in resolute commitment to authentic possibilities of being. The movement is backward and downward, back to what I once was, and by becoming which again I shall succeed in being who I am.

The key to my genetic theory of anxiety and conscience is the use made of these two phenomena to precipitate the self out of the plane of an essentially objective (ontic) consciousness and onto the plane of an essentially reflective consciousness – but only in order to make possible, eventually, a reflective recuperation of the origin. Just as the phenomenological dimension of reflective consciousness is organized along two complementary lines, Reduction and Constitution, so the existential dimension of reflective consciousness is also organized in terms of a negative moment of Anxiety and a positive moment of Conscience.[7] However, whereas with the phenomenological reduction and constitution it is a matter of first *suspending* ('bracketing' in Husserl's words) and then *upholding* the relation to the *World*, here it is a matter of first suspending and then upholding the relation to the *Self*. This is the sense in which an existential reduction and constitution of the Self can be taken to prepare the way, and so to offer a motivation for, what would otherwise appear inexplicably mysterious – the calling in question of the World.

But this only pushes the critical question one step back. What could possibly prompt the self to call itself into question? Here, thanks to a deliberate deployment of Sartre's formula, an answer leaps to mind. Inasmuch as the self already is, and can only be, what it is *not* and *not* be what it is, the being of the self is already in question. The only remaining question being whether the self deliberately chooses to conceal from itself the truth of its (questionable) being. And this is where Kierkegaard comes to the rescue; for every attempt on the part of the self to conceal from itself its own questionable existence only brings the self that much more forcibly up against itself. I more or less follow Kierkegaard in his dialectical programming of the intensification of consciousness. We begin with a Self that is unaware of itself as being in despair, move on to a self that seeks to hide from itself the fact of being in despair, and conclude with a self that despairingly seeks to be itself. Each of these basic positions bring with it variations, but the thrust inward and upward not only holds but becomes ever more intense, forcing the self eventually to resituate its self upon a higher, reflective plane.

Conscience is the phenomenal attestation of this placement of the self upon the higher plane, of reflective consciousness. Following Heidegger, I treat conscience as a voice that calls to the self. The call of conscience is registered as a command that prohibits. And the call of conscience is received as coming 'from above'. Again, following Heidegger, and with much greater legitimacy, I treat the call of conscience as one that is addressed by the self to itself. In refusing the reflectivity of consciousness, Heidegger makes it difficult to show how the self could ever stand in relation to itself in the way required by the call of conscience. More, the genetic framework makes much better sense of conscience as a voice that calls 'from above'. To be sure, the genetic methodology makes it unnecessary to appeal to God (as per Kierkegaard) or even to a superego (as per Freud). For it is the higher (transcendental) self that can now be envisaged as calling to its own lower (empirical) self. And what, first and foremost, this higher self asks of its self is that it should be attuned to the ideal counterpart of its self, the other insofar as it is affected by the self's own actions. In an interpersonal context, any action affects others, and the higher self is that universal self capable of placing itself in the position of the other whose existence is affected by its own action. In acting, the self affects itself with the effects of its own actions on others, and is so motivated to abstain from actions that affect others adversely. The formula for conscience is, therefore, a negative formulation of the golden rule: *do not do to others what you would not have them do to you.* The conscienceless man is the man who disregards the effects of his actions on others – save only insofar as they might produce reactions favourable (or unfavourable) to himself. But, and this is the crucial point, only a self that has universalized itself, that has lost its specific anchorage in its self, in that body which is its own or that Ego it calls its 'I', is capable of allowing the other to emerge as the ideal counterpart of itself. With the phenomenon of conscience, I find myself haunted by myself in the form of an other who is the ideal counterpart of myself (cf. Macann, 2007, vol. 1, pp. 383–96).

This concept of conscience is much closer to that developed by Scheler in his essay 'Reue und Widergeburt' than it is to Heidegger, and we should give Scheler credit for linking the awakening of conscience to the emergence of a higher, more spiritual self (Scheler, 1954).

Heights and Depths

In a work titled *Reason and Existence*, Jaspers identified Kierkegaard and Nietzsche as *the* two original existential thinkers:

> The contemporary philosophical situation is determined by the fact that two philosophers, Kierkegaard and Nietzsche, who did not count in their times and, for a long time, remained without influence in the history of philosophy, have continually grown in significance. (Jaspers, 1955, p. 23)

There is a great deal of valuable material to be found in this introduction to existential philosophy, which uses Kierkegaard and Nietzsche as a way to get at the author's own existential position. But I want to focus on one single, and obviously central, theme: the relation of *Reason* to *Existence*. At the beginning, Jaspers seems to want to set them up in opposition to each other. When he says of his two archetypes: 'Both questioned reason from the depths of *Existenz*. Never on such a high level of thought had there been such a thorough-going and radical opposition to mere reason' (1955, p. 25), it seems that he is contrasting the sort of rational enterprise represented by the philosophies of Kant or Husserl with an entirely different enterprise that questions from the depths rather than the heights. Later on, however, and after having introduced his own notion of the 'Encompassing', he insists: 'The great poles of our being, which encounter one another in every mode of the Encompassing, are thus reason and Existence.' And a little later, this claim is further elucidated: '*Existenz* only becomes clear through reason; reason only has content through *Existenz*' (1955, p. 67).

It is, however, questionable whether Jaspers ever developed a methodology capable of negotiating the connection of heights (Reason) and depths (Existence), or whether his two key figures even fit the pattern of an essential complementarity of heights and depths. For Kierkegaard's thinking is unequivocally directed towards the heights, while Nietzsche spends a lot of his time attacking such philosophers of the heights as Plato and Kant, and has been interpreted by Heidegger as a philosopher of the depths.

It would take us too far out of our way to engage in an extensive discussion of Nietzsche. But something must be said, not just on account of Nietzsche himself, but of the enormous influence his thinking had on Heidegger. Heidegger preached the gospel of depths in opposition to heights;[8] and I would contend that, if there are 'barbaric' elements to be found in existential philosophy, they are to be attributed to what I have called an 'objective regression', the attempt to penetrate to the depths without having first scaled the heights (i.e. effected the 'reflective detour'). And there are 'barbaric' elements, more so in Nietzsche than in Heidegger.[9]

Consider this statement from *The Joyful Wisdom*:

What belongs to greatness

Who can attain to anything great if he does not feel in himself the force and will to inflict great pain? The ability to suffer is a small matter: in that line, weak women and even slaves often attain masterliness. But not to perish from internal distress and doubt when one inflicts great suffering and hears the cry of it – that is great, that belongs to greatness.[10]

The campaign against pity is conducted in book after book, for instance, here in a passage from *Dawn*, where he uses it to attack Schopenhauer and Mill:

It was Schopenhauer in Germany and John Stuart Mill in England who were the means of bringing into the greatest prominence this doctrine of sympathetic affections and of pity or utility to others as a principle of action.[11]

And the strangest thing is that it was from Schopenhauer that Nietzsche got his leading idea of the will. Early on, he stumbled across a copy of *World as Will and Representation*, absorbed and reproduced the message of the first book: The World as Will – First Aspect, and then 'forgot' to take account of the fourth book: The World as Will – Second Aspect. He hence overlooks the fact that Schopenhauer's master-work culminates not with wilfulness but with will-less-ness, the direction of the will against itself, the denial of the will by itself. Schopenhauer's treatment of Will and Representation undergoes a radical transformation in the transition from the First Aspect (books 1 and 2) to the Second Aspect (books 3 and 4). In the third book, Representation reappears, in sublimated form, as Art, and in the fourth, Will reappears, in sublimated form, as Ethics, or more simply as Saintliness. It is this 'spiritual' twist that marks Schopenhauer out as one of the greatest of modern Western philosophers, and one of the very few to have appreciated the spirit of Eastern philosophy – comparable perhaps only to Spinoza.

It would be absurd to try to capture the spirit of Nietzsche's philosophy in a few lines. It is, however, worth saying a few words on the relation of heights and depths in his most notorious work: *Thus Spoke Zarathustra*. Nietzsche begins with his prophet going up the mountain to dwell for a decade on the heights before coming back down. 'I must descend into the depths', . . . 'I must go down'. . . . 'Thus began Zarathustra's down-going'. And is it an accident that shortly after the first reference to his famous, if not infamous, claim: God is dead!, we find his first reference to the Overman? 'I teach you the Overman. Man is something that should be overcome. What have you done to overcome man?'[12] If God, the traditional creature of ultimate heights, has been deposed then Man has to take his place, not man in the ordinary, unexceptional sense of that word but in the sense of the Overman (*Übermensch*). In a section of part one titled: 'Of the Thousand and One Goals', we find the following: 'A table of values hangs over every people. Behold it is the table of its overcomings; behold it is the voice of its will to power'. This first reference to the will to power in the context of a table of the Overman's overcomings is initially presented neutrally as between the two alternatives of self-overcoming and overcoming others. But quickly this alternation is resolved in favour of overcoming others: 'Whatever causes it to rule and conquer and glitter, to the dread and envy of its neighbours, that it accounts the sublimest, the paramount, the evaluation and the meaning of all things'.

Admittedly, Nietzsche is also well aware of the need to deal with the civilizing mechanisms of self-overcoming.[13] But of the three mechanisms for self-overcoming he openly advocates – 'sublimation' (*Sublimierung*), 'spiritualization' (*Vergeistigung*) and 'command and obedience' – he makes it clear that the third is the real progenitor of the other two. For only he who has first learnt to obey, that is, has first been subjected to the command of others, can then learn to command himself – and so earn the right to command. (To be commanded, and so learn to command oneself, and so earn the right to command.) The crucially 'spiritual' relation of self-command is sandwiched between the two vitalistic (almost militaristic) relations of being commanded by others and commanding others.[14]

Nietzsche was simply not at the height of his own project: namely, to develop that idea of a higher man already anticipated by Schopenhauer, and confirmed by Kierkegaard, a man whose self-overcoming would precipitate him out of the vitalistic arena of strife and conflict and into the spiritual realm of compassion and comprehension. And this because he could not come to terms with the upward orientation implied by his own conception of self-overcoming and of the Overman.[15]

To the question, 'how the self can become who it is?', the answer is, 'only with great difficulty'. Originally, I cannot but *be* my self, so much so that my being-self is of little existential value. Socialization leads me to be who I am *not* and to *not be* who I am, to cultivate that *mask* built into the very meaning of the word 'person'. Only the self that is prepared to call itself in question, to free itself from the false *persona*, is in a position to determine which possibilities of being are authentic possibilities of becoming its self. It is this (desperate) search for self, typically represented in philosophy as a reaching upward and inward, away from the specious self and from the world, that enables the self to embark upon the corresponding process of self-actualization, the re-turn to self and to authentic possibilities of becoming who it is. In the words of the Buddha, reputedly his very last words: 'Work out your own salvation – with diligence'.

Notes

1. For instance, Nietzsche's last work, *Ecce Homo* is subtitled: *Wie man wird was man ist* (*How to Become What You Are*).
2. The word 'genetic' is taken from Piaget's child psychology and employed in *Being and Becoming* in a methodological sense to denote the stage-by-stage presentation of the growth and development of human consciousness. Heidegger's dictum: '*Je mehr Bewußtsein doch desto weinger Sein*' brings out the sense in which the gain in consciousness implies a loss of being.
3. Man is condemned to seek meaning in a world where no meaning is to be found. This, the most famous of Sartre's existential complaints, is reinforced by the bleak spirit in which he wrote the novel *Nausea*.
4. In his *Stages of Life's Way* Kierkegaard develops a three-stage theory of the spiritual evolution of human being from an Aesthetic, through a Moral, and on to a Religious stage. This trilogy is also present in his earlier work *Either-Or*.

5. In *Being and Becoming*, Anxiety (along with Conscience) features as the originary subdivision of Reflective Consciousness, and the dialectic of Anxiety is developed along Kierkegaardian lines as an ever-increasing intensification of Despair (see Macann, 2007, vol. 1, pp. 360–83).
6. The last words of *Being and Nothingness* talk of an Ethics to follow, which Ethics was never delivered, though notes towards such an ethics were published after Sartre's death. The philosophical poverty of the popular tract 'Existentialism is a Humanism' only confirms the incompatibility of Sartrean existentialism and ethics.
7. In *Being and Becoming*, Objective Spirit is presented in terms of Husserl's transcendental phenomenology and examined under two heads, the negative moment of the Reduction and the positive moment of Constitution. Along parallel lines, Anxiety is presented as a negative moment whose positive complement is Conscience. See Macann, 2007, vol. 1, pp. 397–421.
8. In his *Introduction to Metaphysics*, Heidegger rules Ethics out as a legitimate branch of philosophy on the grounds that whereas Ethics is oriented upward, ontology is oriented downward (see Heidegger, 1961, p. 164).
9. In *Beyond Good and Evil* section 257, we find Nietzsche using the word 'barbarian', not in a derogatory way but as a defiant slogan, and as an account of how every higher culture on earth has begun. 'Human beings whose nature was still natural, barbarians in every terrible sense of the word, men of prey who were still in possession of unbroken strength of will and lust for power, hurled themselves upon weaker, more civilised, more peaceful races.' In passages such as these, Nietzsche dares us to be – barbaric.
10. Friedrich Nietzsche, *Fröhliche Wissenschaft*, translated here as *The Joyful Wisdom*, IV 325.
11. Friedrich Nietzsche, *Morgenröthe*, translated here as *Dawn*, 132.
12. Friedrich Nietzsche, *Also Sprach Zarathustra*, translated here as *Thus Spoke Zarathustra*, Prologue 2.
13. Interpretations of Nietzsche which prefer to stress the element of self-overcoming often focus on those passages in which he singles out the Artist, the Philosopher and the Saint as the three ideal types of human being.
14. In a section of part 2 titled 'Of Self-Overcoming', Nietzsche develops this relation further. He begins by proclaiming: 'All living creatures are obeying creatures' and then goes on: 'He who cannot obey himself will be commanded.' The will to power is essentially the will to master others – to be the strongest. But all creatures begin by being commanded and have to learn self-command if they are to command others rather than being commanded by others. Despite the promising title, self-command is again conceived here primarily as a means of achieving command over others.
15. In my Ethics (volume IV, part 2 of *Being and Becoming*), I make use of Nietzsche to show how the 'lowest' system of 'vital' values can lay the foundations for the 'highest' system of 'religious' values. In both cases the values in question are 'values of the person'; but in the second case the very nature of the person has been transformed by the transition from 'vital' to 'physical' to 'spiritual' principles, thereby preparing the way for the conclusive system of 'religious' values.

Bibliography

Habermas, J. (1984), *The Theory of Communicative Action*, trans. T. McCarthy. Boston: Beacon Press.

Heidegger, M. (1961), *Introduction to Metaphysics*, trans. R. Manheim. New York: Doubleday.

— (1962), *Being and Time*, trans. J. Macquarie and E. Robinson. New York: Harper & Row.

Jaspers, K. (1955), *Reason and Existence*, trans. W. Earle. New York: Farrar Straus.

— (1989), *Notizen zu Martin Heidegger*. München/Zurich: Piper.

Kierkegaard, S. (1980), *The Sickness unto Death*, ed. and trans. H. V. Hong and E. H. Hong. Princeton: Princeton University Press.

Macann, C. (ed.) (1992), *Martin Heidegger: Critical Assessments*, vol. 4. London: Routledge.

— (2007), *Being and Becoming*. London and Bordeaux: Online Originals.

Sartre, J-P. (1957), *The Transcendence of the Ego*, trans. F. Williams and R. Kirkpatrick. New York: Farrar Srauss.

— (1969), *Being and Nothingness*, trans. H. E. Barnes. London: Routledge.

Scheler, M. (1954), 'Reue und Widergeburt', in *Vom Ewigen im Menschen*, GW, Band 5. Bern: Francke Verlag.

12 Existentialism and Latin America[1]

Roberto Domingo Toledo

Existentialism was a generative philosophical current in Latin America before the movement became influential in the United States and Europe. Since the birth of Latin America's first autonomous universities following the region's independence from Spain, Latin American philosophy and literature has been permeated with existentialist themes. A post-colonial identity crisis and Latin America's marginal situation led the region's nations to constantly question the beings that they are. Philosophers focused on the question of 'becoming' authentically Latin American and of 'authentic' versus 'inauthentic' philosophical practice. This self-interrogation, beginning as early as the fall of the Spanish empire, predated similar reflections among European existentialists like Martin Heidegger (1889–1976) and Jean-Paul Sartre (1905–1980).

The works of later European existentialists, such as Gabriel Marcel (1889–1973) and Sartre, were promptly translated into Spanish and incorporated into the Latin American Existentialist tradition. The Spanish translations of several major works, such as the 1943 translation of Heidegger's *Being and Time* and the 1957 translation of Merleau-Ponty's *Phenomenology of Perception*, preceded the first English versions. By the 1960s, the peak of existentialism in the United States, most Latin American philosophers had already proceeded to explore other tendencies, including analytic philosophy. The turn to analytic philosophy, as exchanges with North American Universities became more frequent, was sometimes understood as a purely assimilative move to gain access to North American philosophical circles. However, many contemporary Latin American philosophers creatively apply analytic tools to existentialist themes. Their existentialist heritage is also apparent in their self-conscious concern to authentically appropriate North American ideas in order to engage Latin America's concrete situation.

Latin American existentialism's focus on intersubjective relations and national and continental identity throughout its history has distinguished the movement from its European counterparts. The anguished solitary individual in a meaningless solipsistic world, often found in the thought of self-proclaimed European existentialists, has not been a common feature of Latin American

215

philosophy. Anticipating the post-existentialist thought of Maurice Merleau-Ponty (1908–1961), existentialism, phenomenology and historical hermeneutics have been intimately united in Ibero-American thought since José Ortega y Gasset (1883–1955) at the turn of the twentieth century.

The earliest readers of Husserl's phenomenology in Latin America, such as Antonio Caso (1883–1946) in Mexico, immediately abandoned the abstract character of Husserl's analysis of perception and intersubjectivity to address the existential situation of their nations. Vice versa, the existentialist thinker who most inspired Latin American thought, the Spaniard Miguel de Unamuno (1864–1936), was more concerned with community, the 'other', and national circumstances than were his sources of inspiration, Søren Kierkegaard (1813–1855) and Friedrich Nietzsche (1844–1900).

Ibero-American existentialism's precocious intersubjective focus has two historically intertwined roots: Ibero-American marginality and Ibero-American Catholicism. As Latin American communities searched for positive national identities within their marginal situation, they developed existential reflections concerned with the freedom of the individual, the relationship between the individual and the community, and the values that should ground this relationship. They sought for these values within their marginalized Catholic heritage and within the Catholic-inspired philosophy of values of Max Scheler (1874–1928), a German phenomenologist who addressed concrete existential and historical issues.

This essay does not aim to provide an exhaustive overview of recognized thinkers in Latin American existential phenomenology, which the Argentinean philosopher Clara Alicia Jalif de Bertranou has recently done (Jalif de Bertranou, 2010). Borrowing from her valuable work, this essay complements Jalif de Bertranou's article by elaborating on specific recurring themes and ideas in the works of key figures in Latin American existentialism, and especially within the Mexican tradition. Mexican anti-positivism and the Mexican Revolution were a fundamental source of inspiration for all Latin American existentialist philosophy. Moreover, Ortega's legacy was directly transplanted to the Mexican academy through the figure of José Gaos (1900–1969), who trained an entire generation of philosophers within Mexico and throughout Latin America.

Before arriving at the Mexican existentialist tradition, however, this essay will examine the earliest roots of Ibero-American existentialism in Miguel de Cervantes's novel *Don Quixote*, published in two parts in 1605 and the 1614. Considered to be the first modern novel, *Don Quixote* was the product of a period of decline and social unrest. A general economic, political and social crisis brought the Spanish empire into conflict with the modern world and its emerging market structures at the turn of the seventeenth century.[2] Unamuno's engagement with Cervantes and Quixotism placed the novel at the heart of the Ibero-American philosophical tradition that emerged with the fall of the empire at the end of the 1800s. Consequently, the novel form has been frequently used to express existentialist ideas throughout Latin America, and Latin American existentialism's home is found just as much in literature as in philosophy. The legacy of *Don Quixote* and existentialism has blurred the boundaries of literature and philosophy in Latin America, which explains some of the originality of Latin American thought.

Iberian Roots: Don Quixote, Don Miguel de Unamuno and José Ortega y Gasset

Following Milan Kundera, Eduardo Mendieta argues that *Don Quixote* (1605, 1614) is as central to the founding of modernity as Descartes. He observes four existentialist themes in Miguel de Cervantes's masterpiece: (1) freedom as self-realization through dreams and aspirations; (2) existence as fashioned through stories; (3) the importance of the values of honour and integrity; and (4) individual existence as involving an interweaving of psychological, moral and historical circumstances. In the early 1940s, Ortega's student Julián Marías (1914–2005) coined the term 'existentialist or personal novel', in contrast to ancient epics based on archetypes. Marías praised Unamuno for discovering the appropriate medium to express the truths of human existence and criticized Ortega for ignoring the importance of Unamuno's work. While Ortega's legacy in Latin America is more apparent than Unamuno's, Marías highlights the fundamental contribution of the latter. Cervantes and Unamuno are clearly the founders of Ibero-American existentialism in Marías' analysis.[3]

Miguel de Unamuno (1864–1936)

Unamuno was a Basque philosopher, novelist, playwright and poet. He was also one of the earliest readers of Nietzsche and Kierkegaard, the fathers of existentialism according to later self-proclaimed European existentialists. He is considered to be the ideological leader of the 'Generation of '98' movement, a group of intellectuals and artists who sought a positive Spanish identity after the loss of its colonies. In *Entorno al casticismo* (1895), Unamuno examines the greatness and misery of Spain, which he believed needed to embrace the rest of Europe without fear of losing its personality. At the same time, Unamuno wanted to 'hispanizar' Europe, praising 'the exaggerated individualism, the excessive imagination, the temperament and language of passion' of non-modern Spaniards (Masur, 1955, pp. 144–6).

Unamuno's work examines what he calls Spain's 'intrahistory', great personalities and expressions of national character that transcend transitory events in political history. Unamuno identifies the fictional figure of Don Quixote as the greatest expression of the Spanish soul. Inspired by Cervantes, Unamuno is the first philosopher to self-consciously appropriate the novel form to most effectively express existential truths. Unamuno viewed philosophy and poetry as 'twin sisters', and understood language as essentially creative rather than descriptive, anticipating Heidegger's *poesis*.[4]

Unamuno's early immersion in modern positivism led to a personal religious crisis in 1897, when he decided that rationalism was incompatible with his faith. He subsequently abandoned positivism for 'Quixotism': a radical affirmation of life, love and adventure. Unamuno develops Kierkegaard's critique of Kantian and Hegelian rationalism, yet he notes points in both philosophers where they too felt obliged to defend life, and not just reason, from their own will to live (Unamuno, 1912, pp. 5, 123). Moreover, he argues that Kierkegaard cannot escape rationalism. Unamuno celebrates the modern religious sentiment with its internal war, doubt and suffering.

In *The Tragic Sense of Life in Men and Nations* (1913), this anguished tension leads to compassion for each 'flesh and blood' individual's desire for perpetuation and for their suffering in the face of finitude. An ambiguity exists in Unamuno's response to modern circumstances. The battle between reason and faith leads us into an adventurous struggle to create a meaningful existence whose worth we can believe in. Unamuno thus partially embraces the rationalism and search for individual autonomy that Protestant society promotes.

However, in *Saint Manuel the Good, Martyr* (1933), Unamuno seems to envy those who successfully maintain a naïve faith in the afterlife to their deathbed. Unamuno challenges Nietzsche's implicit assumption that belief in an afterlife necessarily responds to a devaluation of this world. Whereas Protestantism focuses on consistent everyday actions in accordance with the moral law, Catholicism motivates individuals to commit great deeds and sacrifices to assure their place in an eternal order. For Unamuno, Don Quixote represents this Catholic sense of heroism. Unamuno himself is incapable of naïve faith, however. His heretical notion of God is born in doubt and is created out of a fundamental yearning for existence.

Modern anguished Quixotistas like Unamuno are driven to turn within and reach out to others in a dialectical fashion, perpetuating themselves by incorporating other personalities into their own without losing their own individuality (Unamuno, 1912, pp. 227–8). The intersubjective focus of Unamuno's existentialism is rooted both in his Catholicism and in his conviction that postcolonial Spain's identity can only be discovered through contact with other cultures that confront it (Venegas, 2009, p. 438). Unamuno sought to revive Spain's national identity in such a way that it would incorporate elements of Europe and of its African influences. He also believed that an alliance with Latin America was necessary for Spain's spiritual revival. He was one of the first Europeans to write on Latin American literature and philosophy and to maintain correspondence with thinkers from the New World.

José Ortega y Gasset (1883–1955)

Ortega is Spain's best know twentieth-century philosopher, part of the 'Generation of 1914', and leader of the 'Madrid School' of philosophy. His generation aimed to modernize the fallen colonial empire by embracing European rationalism. Ortega abandoned the 'reason is anti-vital' thesis of Kierkegaard, Nietzsche and his teacher Miguel de Unamuno. In *Meditations on Quixote* (1914) he follows Unamuno in examining the Quixotic character of Spanish culture, but does so in the context of accusing the country of ignorance. While accusing Unamuno of 'Africanism', Ortega nevertheless believed that Spain's lack of modernity and self-questioning of its identity could help overcome a crisis in modern rationalism and create a postmodern Europe.

In contrast to Unamuno's *tragic vitalism*, Ortega's philosophy of *ratiovitalism* places reason in the service of life and history. Criticizing scientific reason for treating humans like physical objects, Ortega developed Dilthey's philosophy of history and Scheler's philosophy of values. He left the anguished depths of Unamuno's inward-focused existentialism, uniting reason with Unamuno's existentialist drive for self-realization in order to create new values (Caponigri, 1969, p. 1972).

For Ortega, not only reason, but also technology, can serve life. 'Technique' is the capacity to self-transform, and modern technology heightens this human power. Modernity's crisis, however, has shown that scientific reason's development of means has often led people to 'lose the ability to will any ends at all' (Mitcham, 1994, pp. 48–9). *Meditación de la técnica* (1939), a more optimistic treatise than Heidegger's *The Question Concerning Technology* (1954), seeks to complement scientific rationalism and technology with an existentialist definition of life to motivate conscious self-creation in history. Ratiovitalism responds to the loss of ends in massified technological society, which Ortega analyses in the *Revolt of the Masses* (1930) and *The Dehumanization of Art* (1925).

In defining historical life, Ortega critiqued Husserlian phenomenology's focus on consciousness. Anticipating Merleau-Ponty as early as 1914, he argued that individuals are thoroughly penetrated by their historical situation (Mendieta, forthcoming). This 'happening' between historical things and individuals is preconscious life. Heidegger's similar concept of 'being in the world' came later, and lacked historicity before Ortega's influence (Graham, 1994, pp. 218, 261).

The Modern Theme (1923) argues that reason should help clarify the destiny of each age. Each individual of a generation has a different perspective on the happenings in life and each generation interprets reality differently, determining the direction of individual life projects at a given historical moment. The particular lineage and generational shifts that characterized Spanish philosophy since the empire's fall in 1898 motivated Ortega to reflect on 'generations'. Generations, which Ortega argues are generally 15 years long, are the underlying dynamic structure of historical reason uniting individual perspectives into larger social movements.

The legacy of Ortega and Unamuno in Latin America

Unamuno's and Ortega's reflections on post-colonial Spanish national identity resonated throughout Latin America. Contact with Ortega's ideas was increased when students from the influential School of Madrid fled Francisco Franco's regime during Spain's civil war. José Gaos, María Zambrano, José Gallegos Rocafull, Eugenio Imaz, y Luis Recaséns Siches, Manuel García Morente, José Ferrater Mora and Manuel Granell were all students of Ortega who impacted Latin American academic philosophy. Gaos, welcomed by Mexico's great nationalist president Lázaro Cárdenas, was especially important in promoting Ortega's ideas abroad. He published in the latter's *Revista del Occidente*, which diffused the works of Ortega and his School as well as Spanish translations of important works in European existentialism. Ortega's most cited phrase, 'I am myself plus my circumstance, and if I do not save my circumstance, I do not save myself' (Ortega, 1914, p. 30), inspired generations of Latin American philosophers to creatively engage their historical circumstance.

The nature of Unamuno's impact is harder to specify. Instead of transmitting an organized school of thought, he engaged the ideas of thinkers in a more singular manner through his personal correspondence with numerous philosophers throughout Latin America who interested him. What is certain, however, is that his existentialist reading of *Don Quixote* (1605, 1615) and his use of the novel for philosophical purposes profoundly influenced the direction of Latin American existentialism, blurring the boundaries between academic philosophy and literature.

Of Ortegas's students who immigrated to Latin America,[5] María Zambrano (1904–1991) was the most influenced by Unamuno. Her work is also rooted in the Catholic-inspired philosophy of her teacher Xavier Zubiri (1898–1983), a major figure in the School of Madrid who greatly impacted Latin American philosophy and liberation theology despite having remained in Spain. The first woman and the first philosopher to receive the 'Premio Cervantes' literature award, Zambrano was particularly interested in the truth in poetry and the poetic nature of existence. She also wrote on Cervantes's *Don Quixote* and the ambiguity inherent in the novel form (Gutierrez, 1984, pp. 121–33).

Catholic Values in Latin American Existentialism

Latin American existentialism has deep Christian roots, explaining the warm reception of Max Scheler (1874–1928) and the later Christian existentialist thought of Gabriel Marcel (1889–1973) and Maurice Blondel (1861–1941). However, Latin American existentialists employ Christianity in diverse ways.

Some have retained a strong connection to the Catholic Church and its precepts. These include the famous Peruvian Christian existentialist Alberto Wagner de Reyna (1915–2006), who offers a Christian interpretation of Heidegger, and the Chilean philosopher Clarence Finlayson (1913–1954) who criticized Sartre's atheistic existentialism. Existentialist ideas also influenced revolutionary Catholic philosophers like the Spanish priest and liberation theologian, Ignacio Ellacuría (1930–1989), who was a student of Zubiri before immigrating to El Salvador where he was assassinated.

Others have embarked on broader philosophies of religion, like the Heideggerian-influenced Vicente Ferreira da Silva (1916–1963). Considered to be the most important Brazilian existentialist, Ferreira da Silva examined the religious and mythological roots of all culture. He avoided reducing religion to anthropology by focusing on the mystery of being and the divine inherent in human life. Within his philosophy, he praised the Christian concept of 'spirit' that the ancients lacked.

Still others did not discuss the question of God or the divine. Nevertheless, the majority of Latin American existentialists, including those not primarily concerned with religious questions, directly or indirectly engaged Scheler's Catholic-inspired theory of values and the revisiting of these by his contemporary Nicolai Hartmann (1882–1950). Scheler's ideas resonated strongly with the particular form of individualism that characterizes Ibero-American existentialist thought.

In *La esencia de lo americano* (1971), the Mexican philosopher Leopoldo Zea distinguishes Latin America's Catholic-inspired individualism centred on 'personality' from North America's Protestant-inspired individualism concerned with 'security' necessary for material success:

> For the Latin American, it is important to be prominent in one's community, to serve others in serving oneself. The individual, far from respecting the proprieties of others strives to reach out and grow with others. When people do not possess the desired personality, they latch on to those who do and incorporate the goals of the desired personality into their own. In this way individuals complement one another and live together in communities which foster interaction. This type of individualism gave rise to rule by *caudillo* in Latin American countries, the person with the magnanimous personality looking out for the interests common to all. The North American

221

political leader is one who can bring about the greatest number of political, social, and economic advantages for other individuals. The Latin American *caudillo* is one who, through sheer force of personality, can rally support behind whatever cause. (Zea, 1971, p. 62)[6]

Zea's discussion of the Protestant work ethic in *The Role of the Americas in History* (1957) complements this analysis with a criticism of North America's lack of concern for community:

> Beginning with his sense of self-sufficiency, the Puritan limited his sense of solidarity. . . . The Puritan, therefore, did not see in the poverty of those around him a circumstance worthy of compassion and assistance, but rather as typical of a man's character, proof of his moral failure which, far from being pitied, ought to be condemned, because in that failure God has shown his condemnation of the unjust who have forsaken their mission. (pp. 120–1)[7]

In this way, Protestantism justified the 'Manifest Destiny' doctrine which was concerned with only the material success of North Americans.

In *Ressentiment* (1912), the German phenomenologist Scheler provides a theoretical basis for this difference in Latin American and North American values. Criticizing competition based on insecurity, he celebrates a noble confidence in one's person that permits one 'calmly to assimilate the merits of others' in the face of great people since such a person 'rejoices in their virtues and feels that they make the world more worthy of love' (Scheler, 1912, pp. 54–5). In face of those in need, he celebrates the nobility of Christian *caritas* that, out of an overabundance of life and desire to make the world worthy of love, values even the most downtrodden. He argues that Nietzsche mistakenly confuses recent Protestant varieties of Christianity with the essence of Christianity in the latter's analysis of the *ressentiment* in Christian love (1912, pp. 83–107).

For Scheler, Protestantism is influenced by a resentful attack on the nobility by the bourgeois and working classes who value individual effort rather than inherent worth. Thus, during the Reformation, Protestantism turned away from the Catholic notion of universal community and love became reduced to a biological sensation. Materialism was promoted instead of a Catholic sense of sacrifice with its celebration of freedom over mere biological life, implicit in acts of love.

Scheler's analysis explains why Unamuno still believed Spain's Counter-Reformation was important, despite its dogmatism, in the face of the Protestant ideals of science and rationalism (Unamuno, 1912, p. 322). That Latin American existentialists viewed Scheler as a kindred soul is not surprising. Scheler's hierarchy of values, which places spiritual values at the top, promotes resentment-free Catholic charity above all. The centrality of community in the development of the person in the Catholic heritage explains the alternative route of Latin American existentialism compared to some of the more solipsistic European versions.

Early Influences: Latin American Anti-Positivism

Positivism, primarily that of Auguste Comte (1798–1857) and Herbert Spencer (1820–1903), became the dominant philosophical movement in Latin America during the period surrounding the region's independence from Spain. The movement served a vital function in modernizing institutions and in loosening the grip of dogmatic Catholic doctrine on Latin American Universities. However, anti-positivist critiques in the first decades of the twentieth century began to emerge. They viewed positivism as Eurocentric and inadequate for Latin American circumstances.

The anti-positivists opposed modern determinism by celebrating human freedom and creativity, developing positions within the vitalism of Friedrich Nietzsche (1844–1900) and Henri Bergson (1859–1941). They also began promoting a Latin American identity based on Christian values through the aid of Scheler and Unamuno in opposition to European utilitarianism and materialism. Consequently, existentialist ideas were at the heart of the first independent Latin American philosophical movement. Francisco Romero, disciple of Alejandro Korn, called the major figures of anti-positivism the 'founders' of Latin American philosophy.

The Argentinean philosopher, Alejandro Korn (1860–1936) influenced generations of thinkers and helped establish Argentina as one of the poles of Latin American philosophy alongside Mexico through his university reforms. His famous work *La libertad creadora* (1920), influenced by Bergson, envisioned human life as a creative struggle to overcome material conditions.

The philosopher Raimundo de Farias Brito (1862–1917) introduced Bergson and European Spiritualism into Brazilian thought. He also aimed to unite philosophy and psychology. Considering him to be the precursor to Brazilian existentialism, Jalif de Bertranou argues that his critique of naturalism, his notion of consciousness and truth, and his tragic vision of existence predate similar ideas in Husserl and Heidegger (Jalif de Bertranou, 2010, p. 323).

The Uruguayan philosopher Carlos Vaz Ferreira was influenced by Bergson, Nietzsche and Unamuno. He described his philosophy of 'living logic' as a Quixotic struggle to clarify concrete problems while resting in uncertainty and tension, instead of falling into rigid systems. Unlike his personal correspondent Unamuno, his Quixotism embraced reason, bringing his thought closer to that of Ortega's ratiovitalism while retaining its own originality (Ardao, 2000, p. 52).

Ferreira's compatriot José Enriqué Rodó was the author of *Ariel* (1900), one of the most widely read books in Latin America. Based on Shakespeare's *Tempest*, in this work Rodó claims that Prospero's spirit servant Ariel represents Latin American nobility and the barbarous slave Caliban North American materialism. He thus inverts the colonial undertones of the play. Rodó draws on Nietzsche in his criticism of utilitarianism. Similarly to Scheler, however, he argues that the first Christian communities expressed a *'joie de vivre'*, which he opposes to the 'severity of the stoics' (Rodó, 1900, p. 36).

Of the anti-positivists, Rodó perhaps shared the most in common with Unamuno. Both writers in their personal correspondence critiqued abstract modern literature as well as philosophy In its stead, they promoted socially engaged philosophical literature in order to reach a broader public, much like Sartre did decades later. Rodó and Unamuno also identified with each other's religious sense, both having passed through personal crises as a result of their positivist education. The thinkers rejected dogmatism as a result, basing their faith in love, charity and solidarity instead – the basic values of the gospels (Gordo Piñar, 2009, pp. 110, 126).

The legacy of anti-positivism in Mexico is intimately connected to the Mexican revolution of 1910, which overthrew Porfirio Diaz's positivist regime. José Vasconcelos and Antonio Caso were products of Diaz's educational system, which was based on the Comte's social reformist ideas. The two philosophers founded the *Ateneo de la Juventud* in 1909, a cultural and intellectual institution that also aimed to reform Mexican education and society. However, the *Ateneo* promoted new national values that countered the deterministic and materialist ideals of Diaz's regime. Intellectuals from throughout Latin America were invited to participate, including Rodó. The Mexican Revolution and Mexican anti-positivist ideals were a source of inspiration for the rest of Latin America for decades to come.

José Vasconcelos (1882–1959), who served in Mexico's ministry of education, advocated an organic logic and saw life as a struggle to overcome entropy through the creation of harmonies. He is best known for his essay 'The Cosmic Race' (1925) that, despite its degrading stereotypes of non-whites, was progressive in its celebration of Ibero-American ethnic mixing compared to the Eurocentrism of the positivists and North American eugenic practices.

Antonio Caso (1883–1946) was influenced by the vitalism of Bergson and Scheler and by Nietzsche's anti-systematicity. Caso's most famous work, La 'Existencia como economía, como desinterés y como caridad' (1919), develops Scheler's analysis of the life-affirming quality of charity and sacrifice. He advocates action over contemplation, especially acts of freedom that resist the egoistic and Darwinistic tendencies of biological life. Despite his sympathy for Nietzsche's philosophy, in this essay, he notes Nietzsche's incapacity for charity and overcontemplativeness due to his weak and unhealthy state of being. Caso is also responsible for initiating decades of reflection on Mexico's national identity through his *El problema de México y la ideología nacional* (1924).

Mexican Existentialism: Marginality, Authenticity and the Question of Identity

Samuel Ramos (1897–1959)

Developing Caso's inquiries into Mexican culture, Caso's most recognized student Ramos became the first philosopher to establish a genuinely national philosophy. His *Profile of Man and Culture in Mexico* (1962/1934) introduced many central themes in Mexican and Latin American philosophy. The basic psychoanalytic thesis that post-colonial Mexico suffers from an inferiority complex inspired the works of later Mexican thinkers, including the existentialist writer Octavio Paz's world-renowned *Labyrinth of Solitude* (1950).

Existentialist reflections on authenticity permeate his discussion of the two phases of inauthentic philosophy following Mexico's independence from Spain in 1821. Ramos argues that, faced with the gap between Mexico's aspirations to equal Europe and the objective impossibility of doing so, Mexican philosophy blindly imitated European philosophy even if it was not appropriate for Mexican conditions (1962/1934, p. 11). With Mexico's 1910 Revolution and the First World War's discrediting of Europe, Mexican philosophy often went to the other extreme of resentfully rejecting everything foreign and even celebrating anti-intellectualism, according to Ramos (1962/1934, pp. 102–3).

Ramos broke with anti-positivism and his mentor's focus on intuition, adopting Ortega's ratiovitalism. His goal was to reform objective conditions by clarifying Mexico's historical situation as the latter aimed to do in Spain (Romanell, 1975, p. 82). Also like Ortega, Ramos wanted Mexicans to put technology in the service of life to avoid the errors of modern Europeans (1962/1934, p. 124).

Despite criticisms that Ramos's work is provincialist and that his characterology crude, he nevertheless makes interesting contributions to a phenomenology of culture that incorporates ambiguity into characterological analysis. He denies that specific Mexican characteristics can be simplistically linked to Spanish influences. For Ramos, Mexican Spanishness, like every component of the complex historical identity of Mexicans, is a 'generic kind of reaction to be found in all our tendencies, no matter how diverse they may be' (1962/1934, p. 28). Moreover, he offers ways of conceiving national identity that, instead of reducing it to objective legal criteria, involve 'nationality in a more vital, concrete sense: in a context of collective experiences – past and present – which are the result of collective undertakings' (Ramos, 1962/1934, appendix, p. 171).

Ramos's concern with national identity is linked to his understanding of the importance of a sense of community for individuals, which 'creates in each person a feeling of solidarity which in turn gives strength and inspiration to personal action' (1962/1934, appendix, p. 171). Adopting Ortega's notion of generations, Ramos argues that history is not driven by isolated individuals nor by masses, but by a community of individuals united by a 'strong spiritual bond' (p. 124). In an appendix added in 1958, he contrasts the resentful painful isolation of many Mexicans to the positive solitude of those with a rich inner life within a community. He explicitly refers to perhaps the most interesting chapter in Paz's work, 'The Dialectic of Solitude', which goes beyond the Mexican situation to address universal existential themes (Ramos, 1962/1934, appendix, pp. 175–6).

Underneath Ramos's ratiovitalism, Unamuno's influence can be seen in his disapproval of pure intellectualism and in his tragic understanding of the paralysing clash between European and Indian cultures, creating an almost insuperable situation (Romanell, 1975, p. 96). Ramos's focus on 'culture in action' in contrast to 'culture already objectified in works' (Ramos, 1962/1934, p. 117) reflects Bergson's enduring influence. In *Hacia un humanismo* (1940), Ramos explicitly adopts Scheler's philosophy of values and Heideggerian positions. In advocating charity, the text can be read as a return to Caso's anti-positivism as well.

José Gaos (1900–1969)

Gaos, disciple of Ortega and admirer of Ramos, was a major diffuser of existentialism and phenomenology in Mexico and the rest of Latin America. A Spanish civil-war exile, he called himself a *transterrado* instead of a *desterrado*, quickly making Mexico's circumstance his own. He became Mexican and wrote most of his philosophy in Mexico for Mexicans. Gaos saw many similarities in Spain and Mexico's situation involving a search for a post-colonial identity. He thought that Spain could learn from Mexico's more successful efforts to overcome an anachronistic past. At the same time, Gaos argued that the Americas could benefit from contemporary thought in Spain instead of simply rejecting everything connected to the colonial heritage (Zea, 1990, p. 197). Otherwise, Latin America risked imitating philosophies from the more powerful United States and Great Britain without these philosophies responding adequately to the concrete situation of Latin America.

Gaos was a prolific writer and, according to his student Luis Villoro, was responsible for introducing professional rigor into Mexican academic philosophy (Villoro, 1995, p. 77). He also translated many important works of existentialism and phenomenology. These include Scheler's *The Place of Man in the*

Cosmos in 1929, one of the most widely read books in Latin America for decades (Jalif de Bertranou, 2010, p. 324), and Heidegger's *Being and Time* in 1943, 19 years before the first English translation of the text.

After learning of Heidegger through Ortega, Gaos developed his own critique of existentialism at the moment when the movement first defined itself as such. In his essay 'Existencialismo y esencialismo' (1943), Gaos argues for a philosophy that does not fall into either extreme of essentialism or existentialism, of static being and meaningless nothingness. He sees this tendency in Aristotle and argues that Ortega's historical philosophy was a further step in this direction by refusing the extremes of pure rationalism and radical vitalism (Gaos, 1987/1943, p. 192; cf. Mendieta).

Gaos paid particular attention to the historical situatedness of philosophical activity, and he transmitted this sensitivity to his students. Besides Mexico's most recognized philosophers, he formed scholars throughout Latin America who came to Mexico to study with him. Worthy of mention is the Peruvian philosopher Augusto Salazar Bondy (1925–1974), best known for his *¿Existe una filosofía de nuestra América?* (1969), which combines existentialist and Marxist themes.

Leopoldo Zea (1912–2004)

Zea is the most important Mexican philosopher of the twentieth century and, according to the renowned Mexican politician Porfirio Muñoz Ledo, he is also the greatest philosopher of the Mexican Revolution and its implications. *El Positivismo en México* (1943), Zea's dissertation under Gaos, is his first major attempt to clarify Mexico's historical situation. He criticizes Mexican positivism for claiming to be an 'objective' and 'scientific' doctrine for the best management of society. Zea argues that it benefited a small elite who used it to defend the status quo before the anti-positivists and the Revolution discredited their positions. His analysis reflects his claim that all philosophy is born from concrete individuals in particular historical circumstances.

Along with other students of Gaos, Zea founded the Hyperion Group in 1949, modelled after the Ateneo de la Juventud at the dawn of the Revolution. The group applied the tools of existentialism and phenomenology to investigate *'mexicanidad'* and the question 'What is a Mexican?' (Zea, 1992/1957, pp. xii–xv). In *Posibilidad del mexicano* (1952), Zea ultimately argues that there is no Mexican essence. Instead, Mexico, Latin America and Spain share a particular historical circumstance, that of being marginal to Protestant Europe and North America (Zea, 1992/1957, pp. xv and xvii). In his culminating work on marginality, *Discurso desde la marginación y la barbarie* (1990), the continuation of *The Role of the Americas in History* (1957), Zea praises Gaos' project of an Ibero-American philosophy for allowing Mexico to seek a broader identity without sacrificing its own (Zea, 1990, p. 12).

Zea's analysis of marginality and his distinction between 'those who babble wanting to make the borrowed word their own versus those who own "the Word"' paved the way for later inversions of Rodó's *Ariel* that would assert Caliban as the true symbol of Latin America (Zea, 1992/1957, p. xxiii). Ultimately, Zea claims that a truly inclusive humanism will come from the margins because the centre typically has had no need to question itself or its originality. Zea uses Ortega's existentialist image of being 'shipwrecked' to describe the situation of the 'wretched' on the margins, an image that he borrows from Frantz Fanon (Zea, 1992/1957, pp. xxi–xxviii).

For Zea, marginality is no longer limited to the Third World alone but is becoming a globally shared circumstance. Decolonization and the presence of the 'other' in the metropoles of the centre have created an identity crisis for former colonial powers. The latter have been forced to recognize their incompleteness in the search for a new coexistence with other cultures. In Zea's words, Prospero is being Calibanized as well. Zea argues that Europe and North America can learn from the sense of solidarity in Latin America (Zea, 1992/1957, pp. 237–41). The new humanism that will emerge as a result will imply solidarity and equality without forced assimilation by the centre. Zea refers to the 'concrete universal' of Sartre, a philosopher whom Zea observes has begun to question the centre's identity as a result of decolonization (Zea, 1992/1957, pp. xxii, 243). Like Sartre's 'concrete universal', authentic solidarity recognizes all humans, not in the abstract, but in flesh and blood with their particular languages and customs (Zea, 1992/1957, p. 244).

As much as he incorporates Third World philosophy and contemporary self-critical perspectives from the centre, Zea privileges Ibero-American philosophy as a source for developing a new globally inclusive humanism. In *The Role of the Americas in History* (1957), Zea argues that Ibero-America possesses a rich tradition of Catholic-inspired humanism that has been marginalized since the Reformation when Protestant nations and values came to represent the 'modern age' (Zea, 1992/1957, p. xxxiv). Whereas the Protestant tradition has contributed valuable democratic legal structures, its societies only aim to secure individual profit. In contrast, marginal Catholic societies have a sense of community and *convivencia* (experiencing together) and are more likely to promote charity, the value that is currently missing in the neo-colonial world (Zea, 1992/1957, pp. xxix, xxxiv).

Zea's humanism, which promotes charity and anti-positivism, is influenced by Ramos's *Hacia un nuevo humanismo* (1940) and Caso's 'Existencia como economía, como desinterés y como caridad' (1919). However, Zea also takes into account the realities of exploitation, marginality and neo-colonialism that characterize Mexico's circumstance (Zea, 1992/1957, p. xxx). Two conflicting tendencies in Latin American philosophy, Latin America understood as Ariel versus Latin America understood as Caliban, are reconciled in Zea's philosophy. While being conscious of Latin America's state of dependency and marginality, Zea successfully resuscitates the idealism of Rodó's *Ariel* in promoting Latin American Catholic values, 'flesh and blood' humanism, and individualism that does not sacrifice interdependence. Moreover, Zea's philosophy clarifies the fusion of marginality and Catholicism in Latin America's existential values.

Zea's analysis has had a lasting impact on Latin American philosophy, as the Argentinean phenomenologist and analytic philosopher Francisco Miró Quesada (1918–) notes. Miró Quesada, known for helping develop a distinctly Latin American philosophy, considers Zea's analysis of dependency to be the precursor of the uniquely Latin American movement called liberation philosophy, which has been primarily developed in Argentina (Quesada Miró, 1981, p. 183). Zea successfully defended an existentialist-oriented liberation philosophy in his famous debate with Salazar Bondy in the late 1960s and early 1970s.

In *¿Existe una filosofía de nuestra América?* (1969), Bondy argues that Latin America has produced no authentic philosophical works, while using criteria from analytic philosophy to limit the scope of what counts as such. According to Bondy, this lack is a direct result of Latin America's dependent situation. Consequently, the only option is to negate this negative past through revolutionary action.

While Bondy usefully challenged complacency within philosophy in order to spur real action, Zea argued that rejecting Latin America's heritage is counter-productive. Instead, the past, with its deficiencies and contributions, must be integrated with the present to motivate creative developments. Zea also attacked the limits that Salazar Bondy placed on the domain of philosophy, defending the diversity of literary expression within the history of philosophical inquiry (Ofelia, 1993, pp. 103–6).

The Hyperion Group and the Rebel Luis Villoro (1922–)

Other members of the Hyperion Group have contributed to Mexico's rich existential–phenomenological tradition. Jorge Portilla (1919–1963) addressed existential questions with a phenomenological method and moral goals. He was also concerned with Mexican 'character', which he found lacking (Jalif de Bertranou, 2010, p. 361). In general, his philosophy attempted to synthesize Marxist humanism with Catholic notions.

Emilio Uranga (1921–1988) wrote *Análisis del ser del mexicano* (1952), which Mendieta considers to be 'one of the most original appropriations of Heidegger to develop a hermeneutical–ontological understanding of Mexican being', despite its close adherence to Ramos's thesis of inferiority (Mendieta, forthcoming). Uranga also translated Merleau-Ponty's *Phenomenology of Perception* in 1957. In his later work *De quién es la filosofía* (1977), Uranga turns to analytic philosophy in order to address existential questions concerning biography and Gaos' notion of 'philosophy as personal confession', using Bertrand Russell's theory of descriptions.

Luis Villoro (1922–), one of today's most important Mexican philosophers, deserves special mention for his controversial adoption of analytic philosophy. His work *Los grandes momentos del indigenismo en México* (1950) is a historical-based analysis influenced by existentialist concepts (Jalif de Bertranou, 2010, p. 362). He also translated works of Marcel, Sartre, Merleau-Ponty and Levinas. His later works, however, have led to frequent accusations that he adopted a North American ahistorical analytic philosophy in a purely imitative fashion in order to gain acceptance into Anglo-Saxon philosophical circles.

In *En México, entre libros. Pensadores del siglo XX* (1995), Villoro defends himself against Zea's attacks that he is imitating North American philosophy. He argues that Zea betrays his own definition of authentic philosophy in the process by suggesting that authenticity implies rejection of the foreign. In harmony with Zea's Gaosian definition of authentic philosophy as responding to one's circumstance, Villoro claims that he is using the tools of analytic philosophy to better clarify Mexico's political situation (Villoro, 1995, pp. 113–15).

Villoro incorporates existential–phenomenological understandings of identity into a pragmatic political philosophy characterized by analytic rigor. He thus exemplifies the tendency of Latin Americans not only to adopt, but to constantly surpass existentialism. A close reader of Zea, Villoro uses the tools of analytic philosophy to clarify Zea's various formulations of 'authenticity'. Villoro argues that Zea's Gaosian definition of authentic philosophy is Zea's most consistent and adequate definition of authenticity. Villoro explains this notion of authenticity as attention to one's concrete circumstance and as the creative appropriation of foreign ideas in such a way that it responds to genuine needs in one's own circumstance (1995, p. 95).

According to Villoro, Zea sometimes employs another inconsistent definition of authenticity as attention to one's own in opposition to the foreign (1995, p. 94). Villoro's *Estado plurial, pluralidad de culturas* (1999) clarifies that this latter definition is essentialist. It is based on 'an inaccurate understanding of cultural identity as a static entity, defined in exclusion to the identities of other cultures' (Villoro, 1999, p. 74).

Villoro thus distinguishes 'inauthentic' separatist movements from 'authentic' ethnic liberation movements. He argues that movements based on essentialist notions of culture often reinforce inherited privilege against the concrete needs of the rest of the community, preventing genuine autonomy: 'the blind repetition of inherited conventions is as powerful of a factor in alienation as the blind imitation of foreign ways of life' (1999, p. 119).

In contrast, Villoro argues that Mexico's Zapatista Liberation Movement defends an authentic notion of culture rooted in an existentialist understanding of identity. For Villoro, the communal identity that the Zapatistas defend is not based on 'characteristics that distinguish [the communities] from the rest', but rather on their 'concrete manner of expressing, in a given situation, their needs and desires, and manner of manifesting their projects, whether or not these are exclusive to them alone' (1999, p. 75).

For Villoro, the Zapatistas do not oppose 'elements coming from outside that respond to new historical needs' (1999, p. 76). They merely resist threats to their 'capacity to project and realize an ideal image of themselves in which they could recognize themselves [and] in which the past could be integrated with present reality' (p. 150).

Villoro uses analytic philosophy and existential phenomenology to clarify the present Zapatista rebellion, which Zea and others misperceived as being 'inauthentic'. He also defends a notion of individual rights that does not discount the importance of community and the right of individuals to participate in their community. Individual self-realization, Villoro argues, requires respect for the autonomy of one's culture and for one's ability to participate in that culture (p. 98). Unlike many North American varieties of analytic philosophy in respect to its context, Villoro's version remains existentially rooted in Mexico's concrete historical circumstance.

Existentialist Tendencies in the Rest of Latin America[8]

The question of national and Latin American identity, especially pronounced in Mexico, has characterized existentialism throughout Latin America. Consequently, Latin American existentialist thought has frequently engaged other fields to address pragmatic concerns. These include psychology and psychoanalysis, anthropology and philosophy of culture, philosophy of education, philosophy of law, Marxism and historical materialism, and philosophy of technology.

As in Mexico, the founders of Argentinean academic philosophy explored many of these directions. Carlos Astrada (1894–1970), one of the first philosophers to teach phenomenology and existentialism in Argentina, addresses the question of Argentinean national identity in his influential essay *El mito gaucho* (1948). As a result of his personal contact with Husserl, Heidegger, Scheler and Hartmann during his studies in Germany, his early philosophy addressed ethics and values from an existentialist perspective. *The Existential Revolution* (1952) initiates a later phase of Marxist-influenced humanist thought. Francisco

Romero (1891–1962), influenced by Korn, was interested in philosophical anthropology. His *Teoría del hombre* (1952) incorporates Scheler's and Hartmann's philosophies to develop an ontology of the spirit and of its objectification in culture.

Latin American philosophy of law frequently incorporates existentialist anthropology. The 'egological' legal philosophy of the Argentinean philosopher of law Carlos Cossio (1903–1987) had an international impact. His work incorporates the legal theory of the Austrian-American Hans Kelsen (1881–1973) with Husserlian, Schelerian and Heideggerian ideas. The 'tridimensional' legal theory of the Brazilian philosopher of law Miguel Reale (1910–2006) draws on Husserl, Scheler and Hartmann to critique substantialist notions of the person. His philosophy is based on existential values that are inseparable from culture as the objectification of human liberty and dignity. According to the Brazilian philosopher Aquiles Côrtes Guimarães, Reale's work represents the 'culminating point' in Brazilian phenomenology (Jalif de Bertranou, 2010, p. 332).

Like Ramos, many Latin American existentialists were interested in theories in psychology and psychoanalysis. Brazil in particular has a rich history of such crossovers. The well-known Brazilian existentialist Ernildo Stein (1934–) connected Heidegger and Freud in his work. Nilton Campos (1898–1963), who was director of the former University of Brazil's Institute of Psychology, was one of the first thinkers to apply phenomenology to the field of psychology and psychoanalysis. Existentialism and phenomenology were widely integrated into psychology departments, as well as other disciplines, throughout Latin America. Creusa Capalbo (1934–), who studied in Louvain and wrote his dissertation on Merleau-Ponty, brings together many fields that have interested Latin American existentialists in *Fenomenología e Ciências Humanas. Uma nova dimensão em antropologia, história e psicanálise* (1973).

One of the most influential movements in Latin America and on Latin American existentialists, due to the region's history of colonialism and neo-colonialism, is Marxism. The Peruvian José Carlos Mariátegui (1894–1930), Latin America's leading Marxist philosopher, was one of the first thinkers to bring Marxism and existentialism into a dialogue. He was critical of positivist and evolutionist brands of Marxism, including their anti-clericalism. Instead, he promoted the 'spirit of adventure', 'historical myths', 'romanticism' and 'Quixotism', a term he borrowed from Unamuno. Mariátegui sought to dialectically appropriate the spirit of pre-modern Incan communism into a postmodern Peruvian socialism, which he claimed would necessarily be a 'heroic creation' (Lowy and Penelope, 1998, pp. 78, 86). The recent work of the Spanish-born Marxist philosopher Gloria M. Comesaña-Santalices (1946–) continues the Latin American Marxist–existentialist tradition. She has written on Marxism and feminism as well as on the existential philosophies of Sartre and Zambrano.

In the midst of the technological development of post-colonial Latin American nations, Latin American existentialists have frequently addressed the issue of technology and society, relying on Heidegger and the more optimistic philosophy of Ortega. The Argentinean Eugenio Pucciarelli (1907–1995), part of Romero's and Korn's philosophical circle, was one of the earliest Latin Americans to write about the essence of science and technique. An example of creative applications of existential thought to technological issues in recent times is the work of the Puerto-Rican philosopher Elena Lugo. Lugo is especially known within the field of bio-ethics. Her ethics draws from Heidegger, Scheler's theory of values and the personalism of Emmanuel Mounier (1905–1950) with its concept of the 'unique dignity of the human being'. Her works include *Ética médica* (1984) and *Ética professional para la ingeniería* (1985). Like many Latin American existentialists before her, her philosophy of technology criticizes the loss of transcendental human ends in empiricist, utilitarian and materialist thought.

Borges, Carpentier and Quixotic existentialism in Latin American Literature

As Mendieta observes, existentialism was no longer a central concern of Latin American philosophy in the 1950s and 1960s when it became a vital movement in the United States and Europe. The major Latin American existentialists wrote many of their most influential works before the European thinkers Heidegger, Camus, Marcel and Sartre. They then proceeded to explore other currents, such as Marxism, Latin Americanism and analytic philosophy. The existentialist legacy is nevertheless present, even if only latently, in contemporary Latin American academic philosophy. For example, as Mendieta notes, contemporary liberation philosophy's focus on the 'fashioning of individuals with a concern with the historical and material conditions in which individuals determine their freedom thus fashioning their unique and irreplaceable selves' (Mendieta, forthcoming) resonates with the concerns of earlier Latin American existentialists.

An account of Latin American existentialism would not be complete, however, without addressing the impact of the movement on Latin American literature to the present day. The Argentinean Jorgé Luis Borges (1889–1986), an admirer of Cervantes and Unamuno, is arguably Latin America's most well-known existentialist. According to Mendieta, he has become the reference for a new generation of Latin American and Latino philosophers. One of Borges's most influential essays for philosophers and writers alike was 'Pierre Menard, Author of the Quixote' (1939). His literary and philosophical style was directly inspired by Cervantes's *Don Quixote*, which he analyses in 'Partial Magic in Quixote' (1952). Like Cervantes and Unamuno, Borges employs self-reflexive literary devices that question the boundaries between author and character and between fiction and reality.

Although Borges refused to identify himself with the contemporary European existentialist movement, Ion T. Agheana argues that his works address numerous existentialist themes: 'the contingency of the human being, the impotence of reason, the transcendence of the human being, the fragility of man, alienation, solitude, and so on' (Agheana, 1984, p. 31). Unlike other Latin American existentialists, however, Borges was not concerned with clarifying Argentina's historical circumstance.

He was nevertheless forced to position himself in respect to questions of national identity and authenticity in response to criticisms that his philosophy was inauthentic. In 'The Argentine Writer and Tradition' (1932), he argues that there is nothing 'un-argentine' about his attention to universal questions. Likewise, he claims the Koran is clearly an 'Arab' writing precisely for its lack of camels because only someone trying to fabricate an Arab text would feel obliged to add a camel.

In a contradictory fashion, Borges maintained that his individualism and his disbelief in the existence of nations and collectivities is an Argentinean trait. His reflections in 'Our Poor Individualism' (1946) more closely resemble those of other Latin American existentialists. In this essay, he claims that North American heroes, as represented in Hollywood films, are law-abiding citizens whereas Argentinean heroes are sentiment-driven individualists bound by passionate friendships.

Borges's work resonates with the magical realist tradition. While Borges clearly inspired the Colombian writer Gabriel García Márquez (1928–), the latter was also influenced by the other founder of magical realism Alejo Carpentier (1904–1980). Like Borges, the Cuban writer Carpentier drew his style directly from Cervantes. Carpentier openly engaged existential phenomenology and Gasset's thought as well (González Echevarría, 1985, pp. 127–34).

Unlike Borges, Carpentier was deeply concerned with Latin American identity. *El Reino de este Mundo* (1948) explores the question of how to express the identity of Latin America, the magical 'other' in the European imaginary. He also reflected on the nature of the novel, his primary tool of expression, which was a major theme of his famous interview with Sartre in 1961.

Philosophical descendents of the magical realism tradition include the Argentinean writer Julio Cortázar (1914–1984) who explicitly criticizes the inadequacy of Western rationalism for expressing reality. The characters in his collection *Bestiario* (1951) and in other works are frequently anguished and solitary. The Argentinean Luisa Valenzuela (1938–) is arguably today's most recognized Latin American woman writer. She is also an admirer of Borges and Cortázar, who in turn praised her contributions to the search for a Latin American Identity. Her widely translated mature work uses a magical realist style to address pressing political realities and patriarchal oppression, with which she feels a responsibility to engage as a writer. *The Lizard's Tail* (1983) examines the interconnection of patriarchy and torture in Argentina. The novel is characterized by ruptures through which the author inserts herself into the narrative.

Admirers of Borges outside of Argentina include the 'engaged' Paraguayan writer Augusto Roa Bastos (1917–2005). His first work *El Trueno entre las Hojas* (1953; Thunder among the Leaves) is an existentialist critique of the impacts of materialism and investigates Paraguayan identity. Valenzuela's reflections on Argentina's dictatorship was inspired by Roa Bastos's most famous work *I, The Supreme* (1974), which in turn has its roots in Carpentier's *El Recurso del Método* (1974). This 'dictator novel' genre abandons all idealism to examine the harsh realities that characterize Latin America's identity, an identity which includes the figure of the dictator (González Echevarría, 1980, pp. 205–28). Based historically on Paraguay's nineteenth-century dictator José Gaspar Rodríguez de Francia, *I, The Supreme* examines the connection between dictatorship and the modern in Latin America. It is also a reflection on the role of writing and documentation in modern bureaucratic nations.

As with Latin American existential philosophy, the themes of Latin American identity, heroic and passionate individualism, and engaging one's historical circumstance surface again and again in Latin American existentialist literature. Both Latin American philosophy and literature have appropriated existentialist tendencies to address these concerns since at least the end of the nineteenth century. Thanks to Cervantes and Unamuno, the boundaries between literature and philosophy have been challenged in Ibero-America, leading to a long tradition of literature directed to such philosophical ends. The profound impact of existentialism on Latin American culture can only be appreciated by recognizing the centrality of this fusion between philosophy and literature within Ibero-America's particular existentialist tradition.

Notes

1. I would like to thank Amy Oliver and Eduardo Mendieta for their important suggestions.
2. For an interesting discussion of the *Don Quixote*'s historical context, see P. Valir (1967), 'Don Quichotte et l'Espagne de 1600: Les fondements historiques d'un irréalisme', *Beitrage zur Romanischen Philologie*, Berlin: Rütten & Loening, pp. 207–16.
3. This paragraph summarizes content from E. Mendieta (forthcoming), 'Existentialisms in the Hispanic and Latin American Worlds: *El Quixote* and Its Existential Children' in Jonathan Judaken and Robert Bernasconi (eds), *Situating Existentialism*, New York: Columbia University Press.

4. For a discussion of Unamuno's philosophy of language, see Mendieta's *Quixote* article.
5. Jose Ferrater Mora (1912–1991), from the School of Madrid, who passed a brief period in Chile before immigrating to the United States, is another figure worth mentioning here for his writings on Unamuno as well as on Gasset.
6. Reference and translation drawn from Amy Oliver's introduction to L. Zea (1992, orig. 1957), *The Role of the Americas in History*, trans. S. Karsen. Savage, Lanham, MD: Rowman & Littlefield, p. 34. The content of this and the following paragraph summarizes her analysis.
7. Reference drawn from Oliver's introduction to the same book, p. xxxv.
8. Many of the biographical details in the following section are drawn from Jalif de Bertranou's and Mendieta's previously cited articles.

Bibliography

Agheana, I. T. (1984), *The Prose of Jorge Luis Borges: Existentialism and the Dynamics of Surprise*. New York: Peter Lang.

Ardao, A. (2000), *Lógica de la razón y de la inteligencia*. Montevideo: *Biblioteca de Marcha*, Facultad de Humanidades y Ciencias de la Educación.

Caponigri, R. (1969), 'Contemporary Spanish Philosophy'. *Modern Age* 12 (2).

Gaos, J. (1987), *Filosofía de la filosofia e historia de la filosofía* (2nd edn). Ciudad Universitaria, México: Universidad Nacional Autónoma de México, Coordinación de Humanidades.

González Echevarría, R. (1980), 'The Dictatorship of Rhetoric/The Rhetoric of Dictatorship: Carpentier, García Márquez, and Roa Bastos'. *Latin American Research Review* 2 (5).

— (1985), 'Borges, Carpentier y Ortega: Notas sobre dos Textos Olvidados'. *Quinto Centenario* (8).

Gordo Piñar, G. (2009), 'Unamuno y Rodó. Algo más que una mera correspondencia epistolar'. *Analogía*. 23 (1).

Graham, J. T. (1994), *A Pragmatist Philosophy of Life in Ortega* (Columbia, MO: University of Missouri Press.

Gutierrez, C. F. (1984), 'María Zambrano y la Hermenéutica del Quijote'. *Cuadernos Hispanoamericanos* (413).

Jalif de Bertranou, C. A. (2010), 'La fenomenología y la filosofía existencial', in E. Dussel, E. Mendieta and C. Bohórquez (eds), *El pensamiento filosofico Latinoamericano, del Caribe y 'Latino'(1300–2000): Historia, corrientes, temas y filósofos*. Mexico: Siglo XXI.

Lowy, M. and P. Penelope (1998), 'Marxism and Romanticism in the Work of Jose Carlos Mariategui'. *Latin American Perspectives* 25 (4).

Masur, G. (1955), 'Miguel de Unamuno'. *The Americas* 12 (2).

Mendieta, E. (forthcoming), 'Existentialisms in the Hispanic and Latin American Worlds: *El Quixote* and its Existential Children', in J. Judaken and R. Bernasconi (eds), *Situating Existentialism*. New York: Columbia University Press.

Mitcham, C. (1994), *Thinking through Technology: The Path between Engineering and Philosophy*. Chicago, IL: University of Chicago Press, 1994.

Ofelia, S. (1993), *Cultural Identity and Social Liberation in Latin American Thought.* Albany, NY: SUNY Press.

Ortega y Gasset, J. (1964, orig. 1914), *Meditaciones del Quijote e ideas sobre la novela.* Madrid: Espasa-Calpe.

Quesada Miró, F. (1981), *Proyecto y Realización del Filosofar Latinoamericano.* México, D.F.: Fondo de Cultura Económica.

Ramos, S. (1962, orig. 1934), *Profile of Man and Culture in Mexico*, trans. P. G. Earle. Austin, TX: University of Texas Press.

Rodó, J. E. (1988, orig. 1900), *Ariel*, trans. M. S. Peden. Austin, TX: University of Texas Press.

Romanell, P. (1975), 'Samuel Ramos on the Philosophy of Mexican Culture: Ortega and Unamuno in Mexico'. *Latin American Research Review* 10 (3).

Scheler, M. (2007, orig. 1912), *Ressentiment*, trans. William W. Holdheim Milwaukee, WI: Marquette University Press.

Unamuno, M. (1972, orig. 1912), *The Tragic Sense of Life in Men and Nations*, trans. Anthony Kerrigan. Princeton, NJ: Princeton University Press.

Venegas, J. L. (2009), 'Unamuno, Epistolarity, and the Rhetoric of Transatlantic Hispanism'. *MLN* 124 (2) (Hispanic Issue): 438–59.

Villoro, L. (1995), *En México, entre libros. Pensadores del siglo XX.* Mexico, D.F.: Fondo de Cultura Económica.

— (1999), *Estado plural, pluralidad de culturas.* Mexico, D.F.: Editorial Paídos Mexicana, S.A.

Zea, L. (1971), *La esencia de lo americano.* Buenos Aires: Editorial Pleamar.

— (1990), *Discurso Desde la Marginación y la Barbarie.* México, D.F.: Fondo de Cultura Económica.

— (1992, orig. 1957), *The Role of the Americas in History*, trans. S. Karsen. Savage, Lanham, MD: Rowman & Littlefield.

Part II

New Directions

13 Existentialism and Cognitive Science

Michael Wheeler and Ezequiel Di Paolo

The Trailer

In the broadest possible terms, cognitive science is the multidisciplinary attempt to explain psychological phenomena in a wholly scientific manner. Exactly which disciplines count as members of the cognitive–scientific community remains, to some extent, an open question, partly because the mix of disciplines one thinks of as contributing to the overall project will ultimately reflect the specific theoretical outlook on mind, cognition and intelligence, that one adopts. However, the interested bystander might typically glimpse some combination of artificial intelligence (AI) (including artificial life and certain areas of robotics), psychology (of various stripes), neuroscience, linguistics and philosophy. Traditionally, cognitive science has been dominated by the dual cognitivist principles of representationalism (intelligent systems work by building, storing and manipulating inner representations, where 'inner' standardly means 'realized in the brain') and computationalism (the processes by which those inner representations are built, stored and manipulated are computational in character). However, non-representational and non-computational approaches (e.g. some versions of the view that cognitive systems should be conceptualized as dynamical systems) are also part of the field's conceptual geography (see Clark, 2001; Boden, 2006.)

Now, according to one version of events, the story of the relationship between cognitive science and existentialism is rather like one of those Hollywood romances in which two people who start out hating each other, and who seem to be just about as ill-matched as anyone could possibly imagine, end up falling in love. In the present case, the happy couple still have some determined work to do before a discerning audience could be anywhere near confident that the match is one made to last, but, against the odds, there seems to be some genuine affection building, and who's to say how things might turn out. This is, we think, a story worth telling. In what follows, that's exactly what we shall endeavour to do.

Our story is best told by placing two historical plot-lines alongside each other. The first begins with Hubert Dreyfus's influential critique of orthodox (i.e. cognitivist) AI, a critique driven predominantly by existentialist insights (Dreyfus, 1990, 1992). If AI is taken to be the intellectual core of cognitive science (as advocated by, for example, Boden, 1990, p. 1; Boden, 2006, chapter 4), then Dreyfus's critique generalizes straightforwardly from orthodox AI to orthodox cognitive science, and that's the way Dreyfus thinks of it. In a perhaps unexpected plot twist, however, Dreyfus's existentialism-driven onslaught is later transformed into a debate over how certain kinds of existentialist insight might be used productively to shape, mould and interpret research in (so-called) *embodied* cognitive science. (Cognitive science is embodied in form when it takes the details of the specific bodily structures and bodily manipulative capacities that a thinker enjoys, plus the ways in which those capacities interlock with particular external factors such as artefacts, to play an essential and transformative role in generating intelligent action and other psychological phenomena.)

As will become clear, the prequel to our first plot-line would be the history of existentialist phenomenology, as represented by thinkers such as Heidegger in *Being and Time* (1927) and Merleau-Ponty in *Phenomenology of Perception* (1962). What makes this envisaged prequel especially interesting for us is that, in an intriguing example of common intellectual descent, our second plot-line starts precisely with one of Heidegger's students, Hans Jonas, and his existentialist phenomenology of life (Jonas, 1966). Jonas's central insight, as expressed recently by Evan Thompson, is that 'certain basic concepts needed to understand human experience turn out to be applicable to life itself', because 'certain existential structures of human life are an enriched version of those constitutive of all life' (Thompson, 2007, p. 57). As our second plot-line unfolds, we shall see that this existentially characterized deep continuity of life and mind, as revealed by Jonas, becomes one of the defining philosophical structures of one branch of (so-called) *enactive* cognitive science, an increasingly influential version of the embodied approach. So our two plot-lines, with their closely related points of intellectual departure, will ultimately reconverge.

As indicated already, the channel through which existentialism and cognitive science began to take proper notice of each other was opened up by phenomenology. In its existentialist manifestation, phenomenology may paradigmatically be depicted as a theoretical (or perhaps meta-theoretical) philosophical enterprise that, through an attentive and sensitive examination of ordinary experience, aims to reveal the transcendental yet historical conditions that give that experience its form. Because these target structures are transcendentally presupposed by ordinary experience, they must in some sense be present with that experience, but they are not simply available to be read off from its surface, hence the need for disciplined and careful phenomenological analysis to reveal them. And the historicality exhibited by the transcendental here is a consequence of (what, in this existentialist register, emerges as) the hermeneutic character of understanding in general, and thus of phenomenological understanding in particular. As an interpretative activity, phenomenological analysis is inevitably guided by certain historically embedded ways of thinking that the phenomenologist brings to the task, meaning that its results remain ceaselessly open to revision, enhancement and replacement. Beyond thinking of phenomenological analysis in this way, existentialist phenomenology is additionally conditioned by the characteristically existentialist conceptualization of human being as free and self-defining in (roughly) the following sense: *as a human being, I am capable of transcending my own facticity.* Here, 'my facticity' is understood as the physical, biological, psychological and historical features that might be established about me from the third-person perspective adopted by (among other explanatory practices) science. And transcendence is understood as the process of projection onto future possibilities in which I, in effect (although not necessarily reflectively), give value or meaning to those factical elements in terms of my projects and concerns, and thus bring forth a world of significance. Now, on the face of things, any research paradigm with this sort of profile is temperamentally bound to view cognitive science, which it is liable to interpret as being committed to an unobtainable-in-principle objective scientific explanation of human being, with a good deal of intellectual suspicion. Intellectual suspicion is one thing, of course. It is altogether another to provide the kind of detailed critical indictment that the cognitive scientists themselves might actually take seriously. It is with this thought that our opening credits finally roll.

Dreyfus, Phenomenology and the Problem of Relevance

Psychologically and behaviourally, human beings are extraordinarily proficient at homing in on what is contextually relevant in a situation, while ignoring what is contextually irrelevant. This remains true, even in the sort of dynamically shifting and open-ended scenarios in which we often find ourselves. In short, human beings display a remarkable (although often unremarked upon) capacity to think and act in ways that are fluidly and flexibly sensitive to context-dependent relevance. Among many other things, a truly successful cognitive science would need to explain this capacity, and do so in a wholly scientific manner (i.e. without appeal to some magical, naturalistically undischarged relevance detector). In cognitive-scientific circles, this explanatory challenge is sometimes known as the *frame problem*. We shall refer to it as the *problem of relevance*.

Viewed through the lens of an unreconstructed orthodox representational–computational cognitive science, the problem of relevance presents itself as the

dual problem of (1) how to retrieve just those behaviour-guiding internal representations that are contextually appropriate; and (2) how to update those representations in contextually appropriate ways. The natural thought, given the
lens through which we are currently looking, is that (1) and (2) can be achieved
if the intelligent agent specifies and tracks relevance, by systematically internally representing the key features of the contexts in which she finds herself.
These context-specifying inner representations will in turn determine which
first-order inner representations are relevant and so should be pressed into
behaviour-guiding service. This might seem like an intuitively promising
strategy. However, with the influence of existentialist phenomenologists such
as Heidegger and Merleau-Ponty firmly in the foreground, Hubert Dreyfus has
argued that, ultimately, it must fail (Dreyfus, 1990; see also Dreyfus,
2008; Wheeler, 2005, 2008, 2010b; Cappuccio and Wheeler, 2010; Rietveld,
forthcoming).

Dreyfus's critique has three strands. First, Heideggerian phenomenological
analysis reveals contexts to be complex, network-like semantic structures
defined with reference to the concerns and projects (or projections) of human
agents (Heidegger, 1927, p. 116). For example, my laptop is currently involved
in, or, as one might say, affords, an act of text-editing; that text-editing is
involved in writing a document; that document-writing is involved in meeting
a professional deadline; and that meeting of a professional deadline is involved
in (it is done for the sake of) my project of being a good academic. But phenomenology discloses human activity as sensitive not only to what Rietveld calls the
'figure-affordance we are currently directed at and responding to' but also to
what he calls 'a multiplicity of more marginally present ground-affordances
that solicit us as well' (Rietveld, forthcoming, p. 6). So the context-determining
links to which my activity is currently sensitive, either actively or potentially
(where 'potentially' signals the presence of a certain *priming for attention* rather
than the mere possibility of relevance – see below), might be traced not only, in
the active register, from laptops, to text-editing, to document-writing, to professional deadlines, to the project of being a good academic, but also, in the register of potentiality, from the post-it note reminder stuck to the laptop screen, to
the need to buy milk and bread on the way home, to the project of being a good
partner and father. In this way, contexts spread out, embed, overlap and combine to form the diffuse webs of relevance-determining relations that Heidegger (cf. 1927, p. 118) once called *totalities of involvements*. According to Dreyfus,
this has an important implication: because individual contexts inevitably leak
into these massively holistic structures, they resist any determinate specifica-
tion in the manner demanded by the orthodox representationalist strategy.

Secondly, Dreyfus interprets our fluid and flexible capacity for responding to
relevance as at root a *skill*, understood as a form of knowing-how. In the background here is Heidegger's concept of *circumspection*. 'Circumspection' is

Heidegger's term for (roughly) the adaptive sensitivity to context exhibited by our everyday skilled practical activity, a phenomenon which he identifies as the distinctive 'kind of sight' that action possesses (Heidegger, 1927, p. 99). Building on this idea of a distinctive kind of sight or knowledge, Dreyfus claims that the sort of skilled know-how at work in human sensitivity to relevance cannot be reduced to, and thus cannot be exhaustively accounted for by, the kind of knowledge-that-something-is-the-case paradigmatically associated with representational content.

Finally, Dreyfus predicts that, and explains why, a vicious regress will accompany any attempt to specify relevance through the introduction of inner representations whose function is to bind context-dependent features to entities. According to Dreyfus, any such second-order representational structures will need to have their own contextual relevance specified by third-order representations. But these new third-order structures will need to have *their* contextual relevance specified by fourth-order representations, and so on. One driver for this analysis is Heidegger's somewhat sketchy treatment of what he calls *value-predicates*, in effect Dreyfus's representations of context-dependent features (see Heidegger, 1927, p. 132; for discussion, see Dreyfus, 1990; Wheeler, 2005). Heidegger claims that adding value-predicates to context-independent primitives (e.g. raw sense data or, to give the argument a more contemporary tone, light-intensity gradients at the retina) can never be the ultimate source of relevance, since each such value-predicate requires further structures of the same kind to determine *its* contextual relevance.

On one reading of the foregoing set of considerations, Dreyfus's existentialism-influenced message is that representations cannot solve the problem of relevance. However, Dreyfus goes further, by suggesting that, from the perspective of existentialist phenomenology, the problem of relevance is, at least partly, an artefact of representationalism. As he put it recently, 'for Heidegger, all representational accounts are part of the problem' (Dreyfus, 2008, p. 358). Here there is an important subtlety to bring out. As Dreyfus has made clear, representations may sometimes figure in the phenomenology and the neural underpinning of skilled know-how, since while some cases of skilled know-how are cases of (what he calls) absorbed coping, in which representations play no part (Heidegger's domain of *readiness-to-hand*), others are cases in which absorbed coping breaks down and the agent confronts a context-embedded problem to solve (e.g. the failure of the laptop's internet connection that requires repair so that the activity of document preparation can continue; Heidegger's domain of *unreadiness-to-hand*). In cases like the latter, inner representations may form part of the cognitive response. For Dreyfus, however, the phenomenon that ultimately explains the relevance-sensitivity of human action, and thus neutralizes the problem of relevance, is ontologically more basic than non-representational ready-to-hand coping or representational practical problem solving. He dubs that phenomenon *background coping*, understood as a non-representational knowing how to get around one's world. As he puts it, the *'all coping, including unready-to-hand coping, takes place on the background of [a] basic nonrepresentational, holistic, absorbed, kind of intentionality, which Heidegger calls being-in-the-world'* (Dreyfus, 2008, pp. 345–6).

Despite Dreyfus's talk of background coping being a species of intentionality that is more fundamental than skilful coping, it should not be thought of as a wholly separate phenomenon (Cappuccio and Wheeler, 2010). Rather, as Merleau-Ponty (1962, p. 159) points out, 'movement and background are, in fact, only artificially separated stages of a unique totality'. Nevertheless, it is at the level of background coping that, to borrow an example from Gallagher (2008), the skilled climber's know-how first opens up the world as a familiar place of climbable mountains. When poised to engage in the action of climbing a mountain, the skilled climber does not build an inner representation of the mountain and then infer from that plus additionally represented knowledge of her own abilities that it is climbable by her. Rather, from a certain distance, in particular visual conditions, the mountain 'simply' looks climbable to her. Her climbing know-how is 'sedimented' in how the mountain looks to her. Background coping may thus be illuminated by Merleau-Ponty's (1962) notion of the intentional arc, according to which skills are not internally represented, but are realized as contextually situated solicitations by one's environment that tend to become more fine grained with experience (cf. Dreyfus, 2008, p. 340). Rietveld (forthcoming) provides a fuller phenomenological picture of background coping understood in terms of Merleau-Pontian solicitations, by drawing a distinction (referred to earlier) between different kinds of affordance (possibilities for action presented by the environment). Given a specific situation, some affordances are *mere* possibilities for action, where 'mere' signals the fact that although the agent *could* respond to them in some way, such a response would be contextually inappropriate. In the same situation, however, some affordances, precisely because they are either directly contextually relevant to the present task at hand, or have proved to be relevant in similar situations in the past, prime us for action and thus, as Rietveld (forthcoming) puts it, render us ready to act in appropriate ways by being *bodily potentiating*. Affordances of the latter kind are identified by Rietveld as a *solicitations*, divided into figure (relevant) affordances (those with which we are actively concerned) and ground (relevant) affordances (those with which we are not currently concerned but for which we are currently potentiated, and which are thus poised to summon us to act) (Rietveld, forthcoming, pp. 5–9).

Although Rietveld doesn't put things in quite the way that we are about to, his analysis of background coping suggests that acts of transcendence – concrete instances of projection onto possibilities (see above) – need to be understood more specifically as acts of projection onto *relevant* possibilities, interpreted as embodied potentiations or solicitations. The existentialist challenge to cognitive science to explain transcendence is thus fully revealed as being to show how naturalistically unmysterious states and mechanisms may causally underpin background coping, understood in terms of solicitations. At this point it is worth stressing that although Dreyfus is sometimes attributed with the view that AI, and by extension cognitive science, is impossible, this is to mis-state his position, which more accurately is that cognitive science as we (mostly) know it falls short of explaining human behaviour, with that shortfall explained in large part by the field's adherence to representationalism. So are there any cognitive–scientific models out there that might conceivably satisfy the Dreyfu-sian phenomenologist and the cognitive scientist? Perhaps there are. In recent work, Dreyfus (e.g. 2008) has cited with approval the neurodynamical frame-work developed by Walter Freeman (2000), in which the brain is conceptualized as a non-representational dynamical system primed by past experience to actively pick up and enrich significance, a system whose constantly shifting attractor landscape is identified as physically grounding Merleau-Ponty's intentional arc by causally explaining how newly encountered significances may interact with existing patterns of inner organization to create new global structures for interpreting and responding to stimuli.

We have just shifted philosophical key. The emerging idea is that existential-ist phenomenology might have a positive role to play in revealing phenomena and processes that cognitive science might profitably explore – indeed, that existentialist phenomenology might even become a member of the cognitive–scientific community and benefit from a collaborative engagement with the latter. This idea has also been explored by Wheeler (2005, 2008, 2010b) in his development and defence of (what he identifies explicitly as) a Heideggerian embodied cognitive science.[1]

Like Dreyfus, Wheeler takes the problem of relevance to be a central chal-lenge for cognitive science. His analysis differs from Dreyfus's, however, in drawing a distinction between two different dimensions to the problem of rele-vance, the *intracontext* problem, which challenges us to say how a naturalis-tically discharged system is able to achieve appropriate flexible and fluid action *within* a context, and the *intercontext* problem, which challenges us to say how a naturalistically discharged system is able to flexibly and fluidly switch *between* contexts in a relevance-sensitive manner. According to Wheeler, the intracon-text problem of relevance may be solved by what he calls *special-purpose adaptive couplings*. His favourite example is drawn from the domain of insect behaviour, which might set some alarm bells ringing in existentialist circles (and else-where), but the genuine differences between insect and human behaviour (not least in terms of the complexity of the contexts in which that behaviour is embedded) should not blind us to the fact that the context-sensitivity in ques-tion may be causally achieved by similar underlying mechanisms (for discussion, see Wheeler, 2008; see also below on the nature of animality). The example, then, concerns the female cricket's capacity to track a species-specific auditory advertisement produced by the male. Robotic modelling by Webb (1994) suggests that this is achieved through a combination of the basic anatomical structure of the female cricket's peripheral auditory system (which ensures that the amplitude of her ear-drum vibration will be higher on the side closer to a sound source) and the activation profiles of two interneurons that are tightly coupled with the specific temporal pattern of the male's song (such that only signals with the right temporal pattern will result in the female turning towards the sound source). Because this mechanism works correctly only in the presence of the right, contextually relevant input, context is not something that must be reconstructed by the mechanism once it is activated. Rather, context is something that is always automatically present in that mechanism at the point of triggering. Wheeler (2008) interprets this as a kind of intrinsic context-sensitivity that solves (or rather dissolves) the intracontext problem of relevance. So now what about the intercontext problem of relevance? Here is one possible model: fluid context-switching involves relevance-sensitive transitions between special-purpose adaptive couplings. It is here that Wheeler finds a place for the sort of shifting non-representational dynamical system explored by Freeman and endorsed by Dreyfus. Such systems support a capacity for large-scale holistic reconfiguration that seems ripe to explain how a system could self-organize so as to realize different sets of special-purpose adaptive couplings.

Given Merleau-Ponty's point (see above) that movement and background are only artificially separated, Wheeler's position, as just sketched, results in a disagreement with Dreyfus over the cognitive science of background coping. For Wheeler, but not for Dreyfus, the mechanistic basis of background coping has the dual character of Freeman-style dynamics and situated special-purpose adaptive coupling – the different species of mechanism that, according to Wheeler, might explain intercontext sensitivity to relevance and intracontext sensitivity to relevance, respectively. This dispute remains to be settled (although see Rietveld, forthcoming, for a discussion that finds in favour of Dreyfus). Whichever way it is resolved, however, the cognitive–scientific story here is incomplete, because the capacity for fluid systemic reorganization that arguably plays a key role in context-switching does not guarantee that the special-purpose adaptive couplings thereby brought on line (Wheeler) or the holistic reconfigurations of the system that transform its global dynamics (Dreyfus) will be the right (i.e. the newly contextually relevant) ones. All that is assured is that the system is a platform for the kind of flexibility that, *when harnessed appropriately* (i.e. in context-tracking ways), may help to generate fluid context-switching (see Wheeler, 2010b).

We have seen how the very same existentialist insights that shaped Dreyfus's critique of orthodox cognitive science are now helping in the development of a new kind of cognitive science. Interestingly, this sort of positive influence has been exerted via a different, although intimately related, channel.

Hans Jonas and the Enactive Approach to Life and Mind

In his introductory essay for a collection of his own papers translated from English into Spanish, Francisco Varela refers to his late discovery of Hans Jonas. He remarks on the surprising convergence of Jonas's philosophy with his own latest research directions (Varela, 2000). It is no small homage to Jonas that the title Varela chose for this collection was '*El fenómeno de la vida*', a literal translation of the title of Jonas's own collection of edited essays (written in the 1950s and early 1960s) sketching his ambitious philosophy of life from an existentialist, yet scientifically informed, perspective (Jonas, 1966). Varela's later work has been an attempt to engage with Jonas's bio-philosophy in an explicit dialogue with his own approach to life and cognition (Weber and Varela, 2002), exploring what Thompson (2007) and others have described as the deep continuity between life and mind.

It is curious, although not unheard of, for converging ideas to make an independent appearance (simultaneously or separated in time) in rather remote regions of human learning, represented in this case by an existentialist philosopher with an interest in ethics and theology and an unconventional biologist and neuroscientist interested in non-Cartesian approaches to the mind. What might have been a minor scholarly curiosity turned out to be, in fact, a productive well-spring of novel thinking. Often radical and controversial, the ideas that originate from this encounter are at the core of an important line of theorizing within embodied approaches in cognitive science around which much discussion has been generated.

Let us first focus in some detail on Jonas's existential bio-philosophy. The lack of philosophical attention devoted to the roots of human existence and experience in organic life demands some examination. Even today, as discourses on bio-politics, bio-ethics and the precariousness of life take centre stage, current interest lies less in making explicit the connections between life, values and existence than in highlighting the technological subjection of biological substrates to new forms of control or in measuring human beings against other life forms. Presumably, the latter ends would benefit from the former. It is in this context that Hans Jonas's 'existential interpretation of biological fact' stands out. While affinities may be found with thinkers like Kurt Goldstein, Helmut Plessner, Georges Canguilhelm and others, Jonas arguably provides a unique handle on a thorny issue: the problem of why existence should be accompanied by any form of interiority and caring at all.

In effect, this is the same worry that drove Dreyfus to his Heideggerian critique of AI, or rather its obverse side. Accordingly, norms cannot be captured in an artificial system without a real embeddedness in a world of significance (cultural and socially mediated in the human case). Jonas's enquiries are attempts to dig further into the question of why this embeddedness would happen at all, what kind of conditions must be put in place for anything to count as a world in the first place. To answer this question unavoidably implies, at least in hindsight, examining the sort of entity that can qualify as having some form of self-concerned existence. Jonas constructs his first move through the unorthodox pairing of two contrasting forms of thought: Darwinism and phenomenology. The tension thus created is not resolved. It is instead used as a springboard for a bold proposal: *all forms of life, even the simplest, have interiority and they all have a world.*

In building a bridge that connects the human organism with the evolution of life on earth, the supposed triumph of materialism (we are nothing but the result of the selective accumulation of random changes in chemical processes) presents us with 'the germ of its own overcoming' (Jonas, 1966, p. 53). The reason for this is that our own experience as concernful embodied beings with an interior life is not denied by arguments of continuity with a world of efficient causes. On the contrary, both the experience and the arguments direct us to the phenomenon of life itself as a good place to seek the roots of what is often claimed to be a unique human privilege. The Darwinian bridge, under this view, turns out to be a two-way street. It is our own living experience that allows us to know life in its full reality, according to Jonas. 'Only life can know life' is the evocative slogan that sums up this view; full knowledge of life is not to be achieved unless we acknowledge our own insider's perspective on the topic.

If we accept as plausible that the experience of concern is not exclusively human (although it may have some specific characteristics in humans) and that all other physical living beings may also be, rather than appear, intrinsically teleological and in possession of an inner life, is this because they are living or simply because they are physical? For Jonas, it is a question of selecting the most informative option, the one that is more revealing. For Whitehead's philosophy of the organism, Jonas argues (1966, pp. 95–6; 1968, pp. 235, 241), there is no useful concept of challenge to organic identity since this kind of identity is in this view extended to cover all cases of physical identity, even that of particles that simply endure. Yet it seems a pragmatically vacuous extension of vocabulary to say that atoms die or molecules get sick. Most versions of panpsychism are thus discarded since such precariousness is given to organisms by their singular mode of identity: not the identity of inert permanence ($A = A$) but that of a dynamical form made of an ever-changing material substrate.

The break with the substantial mode of identity is achieved in *metabolism*, a self-affirming precarious process of constant regeneration of form within a flux of matter and energy. This is a feature of all life. For Jonas, this level of physical organization seems to have the necessary existential credentials:

1. the establishment of a distinct 'self' for which being is its own achieve-ment and with organizational distinctions between inside and outside;
2. a precarious entity which is in constant environmental challenge, in *need* of material turnover and with the *freedom* to achieve it by regulating its exchanges with the environment; and
3. the establishment of norms following the logic of metabolism according to which otherwise neutral events, both internal and external, can be good or bad for the continuation of the organism.

Jonas's proposal is that metabolism is intrinsically teleological and all life pos-sesses an inward dimension, a statement that cannot be arrived at by the unpre-pared, disembodied observer. Without our own inner experience as unquestionable datum, this proposal would be at most regulative, providing some help to the student of nature but in itself not derivable by reason, as indi-cated by the Kantian analysis of the intrinsic teleology and self-organization of organisms in *The Critique of Judgement* (Kant, 1790). The fact that metabolism sustains a dynamic form of identity (not coinciding with its material constitu-tion at any given time except at the time of death) provides the possibility for the organism to become free. This freedom is expressed in the capability of the organism to engage with its medium in terms of the significance of a situation, thus contributing to its continuing dynamical autonomy and even opening up the possibility of novel value-making. However, this freedom is permitted by the meeting of very strict and specific material needs. It is a *needful freedom*. Rather than being paradoxical, this concept of freedom avoids the problems posed by determinism (and not solved by the inclusion of randomness) by operating on the relation of *mediation* between the self-sustaining, constantly becoming, identity and the 'target' of its worldly engagements. In this sense, the mode of realization of an autonomous process of identity generation (like metabolism) establishes the sort of access this identity has to the norms that describe its different modes of viability. This access may be less or more medi-ated (the difference, say, between reacting with aversion to contact with a hot surface and planning our movements so as to avoid touching it). Jonas's con-tention is that in the history of life and mind novel forms of increasingly medi-ated engagements have appeared allowing for more freedom at the cost of more precariousness.

Animals provide a clear example of such transitions. A new order of norms and values is founded in animality with the advent of self-generated motility and the coemergence of perception, action and emotion. By putting a distance and a lapse between the tensions of need and the consummation of satisfaction, the temporality of the inner life is spatialized. Animals can appreciate right now the danger that is impinging on them from a distance. The future event becomes a distant but present possibility. This is the origin of a special relation with the world, that of perception and action, which is charged with internal significance, and hence with the development of an emotional dimension (what might have been an inner life of just need and satisfaction now becomes rich in possibilities such as fear, desire, apprehension, distension, tiredness, curiosity, etc.). But this comes at a cost of more severe energetic demands (allowing the necessary fast and continuing movements across varying environmental conditions without replenishment for long periods) and novel forms of risk.

As an example of how mediation enables new forms of freedom, consider the behaviour of several species of insects, like the water boatman, that are able to breathe underwater by trapping air bubbles (plastrons) using tiny hairs in the abdomen. The bubbles refill with oxygen due to the differences in partial pressure provoked by respiration and are prevented from collapsing by the hairs, thus potentially working indefinitely (see Turner, 2000). These external lungs provide access to longer periods underwater thanks to a mediated regulation of environmental coupling (which is nevertheless riskier than normal breathing). The mediation in cases like this is so intimately connected with vital functions that the living system itself might be called extended. The issue at play in such reliable and conserved forms of mediation is, in each case, the question of the identity of such extended systems. New forms of life are built not so much 'on top' of existing ones but as possibilities for new forms of mediation and transformation of the relations between self-sustained identity and world.

Jonas recognizes other such transitions in modes of mediation in the history of life and mind, for instance, those afforded by a complex visual system or the capacity to make images that leads to the birth of eidetic human projects and the distinction between truth and falsehood. It is doubtful whether any intrinsic gain is implied at the metabolic level by expanding the realm of freedom at the cost of increased precariousness. As Jonas points out, 'the survival standard is inadequate for an evaluation of life' (1966, p. 106). He goes on:

> It is one of the paradoxes of life that it employs means which modify the end and themselves become part of it. The feeling animal strives to preserve itself as a feeling, not just a metabolizing entity, i.e., it strives to continue the very activity of feeling: the perceiving animal strives to preserve itself as a perceiving entity – and so on. Without these faculties there would be much less to preserve, and this less of what is to be preserved is the same as the less wherewith it is preserved. (p. 106)

Effectively, such transitions in mediacy inaugurate a domain that feeds back on itself; they imply a *new form of life*. Not just in a metaphorical sense, but in the strict sense of a novel process of identity generation underdetermined by metabolism.

The ideas in this landscape painted with broad strokes by Jonas are quite compelling and ripe for further exploration using the tools of systemic thinking and phenomenology. We can summarize the ideas that have the most direct and radical implications for cognitive science:

1. The use of a concept of identity whereby an individual is self-constructed by maintaining its own form in dynamic precarious conditions.
2. The implication from this form of identity that a living entity must thereby relate to the world with specific interests and norms, that is, the implication of an interior point of view.
3. The dialectics between living identity and the mediacy of its relation to the world leading to new forms of life of increased freedom and precariousness.

In cognitive science, the adoption of these ideas implies a radical break from traditional cognitivism (which we have earlier characterized as the dual principles of representationalism and computationalism) and possibly from other forms of functionalism as well. In contrast to (1), cognitivism does not have a theory of identity; the identity of a cognitive system is defined by convention or intuitive common-sense. In contrast to (2), cognitivism not only does not provide a good account of the origins of norms and values (as we have seen already), but also fails to see that such an account must inevitably involve the organization and identity of the cognitive system; in traditional cognitive terms, how an agent is organized, what it is, how it should behave, what it does and what it cares about, are all elements external to each other and brought together by a designer or an observer. And finally, in contrast to (3), cognitivism's way of understanding increasingly complex forms of mind is to measure their intuitive distance to the capabilities of an adult human being, as opposed to having a non-chauvinist method for understanding what is involved in the simultaneous transition to a new form of life and a new form of mind through the work of mediation.

Let us turn to how some of these ideas have influenced embodied approaches to cognition concerned with the deep continuity between life and mind. Towards the last decade of his life, Francisco Varela explored a line of argument linking his early work on the autonomy of living systems with new research directions on embodied cognition (Varela et al., 1991; Varela, 1991, 1997). One important lesson from his early work with Humberto Maturana on the theory of autopoiesis

(Maturana and Varela, 1980) was the reclaiming of the living organism as a well-defined term for scientific discourse and as a proper level for the analysis of biological and cognitive phenomena. Science in general is comfortable at levels of explanation below the organism (genes, brain patterns, drives) or above it (environmental triggers, selection history, social structures), but rarely do slippery terms like 'individual', 'subject' or 'organism', let alone 'experience', play anything more than intuitive role in scientific discourse. The theory of autopoiesis is an attempt to propose a definition of a living system in such a way that the term would articulate a series of useful implications for the scientist and, therefore, would become a practical tool for scientific usage – an objective that has not quite been achieved, which is a topic for a different discussion. The declared goal of this theory is to examine the logical relations between two questions: what is the organization of a living system and what are the possible ways in which a living system can relate to its world given this organization.

Varela felt that the more pressing issues in this endeavour had not been fully examined in the original theory. These include issues such as the natural purposefulness of organisms, whether their teleology is real or merely an ascription by the observer, the organism's relation to the world in terms of significance, the origin of the norms that guide its behaviour, and so on. He addressed these issues following a systemic approach (Varela, 1991, 1997): perhaps the purposefulness and sense-making of organisms are consequences of their organization as self-producing autonomous systems. This has led to the proposal that it is indeed the living organization that is responsible for the organism's capability to evaluate its encounters with the world. Sugar might be one of the many chemicals that we can observe surrounding a bacterium, but for the bacterium it is not a neutral presence. The value of sugar is manifested behaviourally by a biased swimming up the sugar gradient with its consequences for the continued conservation of life. In Varela's words, encounters with the world are not neutral for an organism; they are invested with a 'surplus of signification' as a consequence of their self-producing nature.

A refinement of this argument followed Varela's encounter with Jonas's work (Weber and Varela, 2002). For Varela, the element that Jonas's was lacking was a proper systemic approach to defining metabolism using systemic tools and the concept of self-organization; a framework like the theory of autopoiesis, in short. For the enactive project, Jonas provides a rough map and some tools to navigate an immense landscape connecting various forms of life and mind, including those of human beings.

In casting Jonas's ideas in the language of systems science, Weber and Varela set on a road of continued conceptual refinement that is still transited today. As an example, the attempt to derive sense-making (the organism's capacity of relating to the world in terms of meaning, norms and values) from simple autopoiesis (the ongoing self-construction of the organism) actually fails in its first instance. The reason for this is simple: if autopoiesis is all that is needed for a living system to be able to relate to its world in meaningful terms, then how are we to account for the graded nature of this relation, the fact that some things are appreciated by an organism as better than others, some risks are worth taking while others are not, some days as more full of struggle while others are more comfortable and relaxed? Across all of these graded differences the organism remains indistinctively alive; its autopoiesis does not change. Something else apart from an organization that establishes an all-or-nothing distinction between life and death is needed for sense-making if this graded nature is to be explained. This extra characteristic is *adaptivity* (Di Paolo, 2005), in short: a capacity that the organism has, in some cases, to revert the tendencies that, if allowed to continue, would result in its death. With this capacity (which comes in a large variety of forms and may be transformed during the organism's lifetime), it is possible to recover both the graded nature of our experience in making sense of the world as well as the spirit of Varela's starting intuitions. The refined argument now reads: sense-making implies both the presence of a self-sustained precarious organization (like autopoiesis) and some form of adaptivity.

Jonas's key contributions are thus given a solid basis by the enactive approach (without implying that this endeavour is yet finished). This basis enables the conceptual articulation needed to examine several of the blind spots of cognitivism, and this has led to a series of new proposals and critiques (see, Stewart et al., 2010). For instance, enactive ideas have provided a new angle to debates on the extended mind hypothesis (Wheeler, 2010a; Di Paolo, 2009; Thompson and Stapleton, 2009) where, enactivists argue, the concepts of autonomy, precariousness and sense-making elaborated above throw new light into how to determine what constitutes a cognitive system. Similar concerns have motivated more precise definitions of agency based on Jonasian arguments of continuity between life and mind (Barandiaran et al., 2009). Computer models based on this approach to agency have provided insights on the relation between metabolism and behaviour in protocells and bacteria (Egbert and Di Paolo, 2009; Egbert et al., 2010).

The concepts of autonomy and sense-making have been applied to a theory of social cognition less concerned with postulating mentalizing capabilities for understanding others' mental states and more focused on the processes of embodied interaction and participatory understanding (De Jaegher and Di Paolo, 2007; De Jaegher, 2009; De Jaegher et al., 2010; Di Paolo et al., 2008; Fuchs and De Jaegher, 2009; Froese and Di Paolo, 2009; McGann and De Jaegher, 2009). The concern with experience and identity alerted researchers to problems with otherwise embodied proposals, like the sensorimotor approach to perception and consciousness (O'Regan and Noë, 2001). Thompson (2007) has critiqued this approach for lacking a proper place for the autonomy of the cognitive system, which is phenomenologically translated as a lack of a good account of the subjectivity of personal experience. Other offshoots of enactive thought include a non-representational perspective on mental imagery (Thompson, 2007), neurophenomenological accounts of the dynamics of first-person time-consciousness (Varela, 1999), the fine time-structure of neural self-organization in perception (Varela et al., 2001), elucidations of the role of goal-directedness in action (McGann, 2007), refinements to notions of skills and perceptual modalities (McGann, 2010), and work on developmental robotics (Vernon, 2010) and evolutionary robotics (Di Paolo and Iizuka, 2008; Rohde, 2010).

It may be too early to fully evaluate these new developments – many of which are still making their way into more mainstream regions of cognitive science. It is, however, already remarkable that they all seem to derive from the encounter between Varela and Jonas's existential bio-philosophy. It is as if Jonas's insights, precisely because they originate in concerns that are far removed from mainstream cognitive science, may have served to unblock some of the most resilient impasses the field has had to deal with over the past 50 years. Remarkably, the very same thing could be said in relation to the insights of Heidegger and Merleau-Ponty, insights that, as we saw earlier, have been shaping recent cognitive–scientific approaches to the problem of relevance. Our two plot-lines have finally reconverged.

Note

1. For further examples, not mentioned elsewhere in this piece, in which existentialist phenomenology has been used to make a positive contribution to embodied cognitive science, see, for example, Gallagher (2005), Kiverstein (forthcoming) and Rowlands (2010), among others. For an innovative empirical study in embodied cognition that seeks to isolate the psychological signature of Heidegger's distinction between readiness-to-hand and unreadiness-to-hand, see Dotov et al. (2010). For recent arguments which conclude that the project of positive integration will be thwarted, unless cognitive science can divest itself of the kind of naturalism that Wheeler, for example, takes to be at the philosophical heart of the field, see Ratcliffe (forthcoming) and Rehberg (forthcoming).

Bibliography

Barandiaran, X., E. Di Paolo and M. Rohde (2009), 'Defining Agency Individuality, Normativity, Asymmetry and Spatio-Temporality in Action'. *Adaptive Behavior* 17 (5): 367–86.
Boden, M. A. (1990), 'Introduction', in M. A. Boden (ed.), *The Philosophy of Artificial Intelligence*. Oxford: Oxford University Press.

— (2006), *Mind as Machine: A History of Cognitive Science* (2 vols). Oxford: Oxford University Press.

Cappuccio, M. and M. Wheeler (2010), 'When the Twain Meet: Could the Study of Mind be a Meeting of Minds?' in J. Reynolds, E. Mares, J. Williams and J. Chase (eds), *Postanalytic and Metacontinental: Crossing Philosophical Divides*. London: Continuum.

Clark, A. (2001), *Mindware: An Introduction to the Philosophy of Cognitive Science*. Oxford: Oxford University Press.

De Jaegher, H. (2009), 'Social Understanding through Direct Perception? Yes, by Interacting'. *Consciousness and Cognition* 18 (2): 535–42.

De Jaegher, H. and E. Di Paolo (2007), 'Participatory Sense-Making: An Enactive Approach to Social Cognition'. *Phenomenology and the Cognitive Sciences* 6 (4): 485–507.

De Jaegher, H., E. Di Paolo and S. Gallagher (2010), 'Does Social Interaction Constitute Social Cognition?' *Trends in Cognitive Sciences* 14 (10): 441–7.

Di Paolo, E. A. (2005), 'Autopoiesis, Adaptivity, Teleology, Agency'. *Phenomenology and the Cognitive Sciences* 4: 429–52.

— (2009), 'Extended Life'. *Topoi* 28: 9–21.

Di Paolo, E. A. and H. Iizuka (2008), 'How (Not) to Model Autonomous Behaviour'. *BioSystems* 91: 409–23.

Di Paolo, E., M. Rohde and H. Iizuka (2008), 'Sensitivity to Social Contingency or Stability of Interaction? Modelling the Dynamics of Perceptual Crossing'. *New Ideas in Psychology* 26 (2): 278–94.

Dotov, D. G., L. Nie and A. Chemero (2010), 'A Demonstration of the Transition from Ready-to-Hand to Unready-to-Hand'. *PLoS ONE* 5 (3): e9433. doi:10.1371/journal.pone.0009433

Dreyfus, H. L. (1990), *Being-in-the-World: A Commentary on Heidegger's Being and Time, Division I*. Cambridge, MA: MIT Press.

— (1992), *What Computers Still Can't Do: A Critique of Artificial Reason*. Cambridge, MA: MIT Press.

— (2008), 'Why Heideggerian AI Failed and How Fixing It Would Require Making It More Heideggerian', in P. Husbands, O. Holland and M. Wheeler (eds), *The Mechanical Mind in History*. Cambridge, MA: MIT Press, pp. 331–71.

Egbert, M. and E. A. Di Paolo (2009), 'Integrating Behavior and Autopoiesis: An Exploration in Computational Chemo-Ethology'. *Adaptive Behavior* 17: 387–401.

Egbert, M., X. Barandiaran and E. A. Di Paolo (2010), 'A Minimal Model of Metabolism-Based Chemotaxis'. *PLoS Computational Biology* 6 (12): e1001004. doi:10.1371/journal.pcbi.1001004.

Freeman, W. (2000), *How Brains Make Up Their Minds*. New York: Columbia University Press.

Froese, T. and E. A. Di Paolo (2009), 'Sociality and the Life-Mind Continuity Thesis'. *Phenomenology and the Cognitive Sciences* 8 (4): 439–63.

Fuchs, T. and H. De Jaegher (2009), 'Enactive Intersubjectivity: Participatory Sense-Making and Mutual Incorporation'. *Phenomenology and the Cognitive Sciences* 8 (4): 465–86.

Gallagher, S. (2005), *How the Body Shapes the Mind*. Oxford: Oxford University Press.

— (2008), 'Are Minimal Representations Still Representations?' *International Journal of Philosophical Studies* 16 (3): 351–69.

Heidegger, M. (1927), *Being and Time*, trans. J. Macquarrie and E. Robinson. Oxford: Basil Blackwell.

Jonas, H. (1966), *The Phenomenon of Life: Towards a Philosophical Biology*. Evanston, IL: Northwestern University Press.

— (1968), 'Biological Foundations of Individuality'. *International Philosophical Quarterly* 8: 231–51.

Kant, I. (1790), *The Critique of Judgement*, trans. J. C. Meredith. Oxford: Oxford University Press (this edition first published in 1952).

Kiverstein, J. (forthcoming), 'Subjectivity without a Subject-Object Distinction?' in J. Kiverstein and M. Wheeler (eds), *Heidegger and Cognitive Science*. Basingstoke: Palgrave Macmillan.

McGann, M. (2007), 'Enactive Theorists Do It on Purpose'. *Phenomenology and the Cognitive Sciences* 6 (4): 463–83.

— (2010), 'Perceptual Modalities: Modes of Presentation or Modes of Action?' *Journal of Consciousness Studies* 17: 72–94.

McGann, M. and H. De Jaegher (2009), 'Self-Other Contingencies: Enacting Social Perception'. *Phenomenology and the Cognitive Sciences* 8 (4): 417–37.

Maturana, H. and F. J. Varela (1980), *Autopoiesis and Cognition: The Realization of the Living*. Dordrecht, Holland: D. Reidel Publishing.

Merleau-Ponty, M. (1962), *Phenomenology of Perception*, trans. C. Smith. London: Routledge.

O'Regan, J. K. and A. Noë, (2001), 'A Sensorimotor Account of Vision and Visual Consciousness'. *Behavioral and Brain Sciences* 24 (5): 883–917.

Ratcliffe, M. (forthcoming), 'There Can Be No Cognitive Science of *Dasein*', in J. Kiverstein and M. Wheeler (eds), *Heidegger and Cognitive Science*. Basingstoke: Palgrave Macmillan.

Rehberg, A. (forthcoming), 'Heidegger and Cognitive Science – Aporetic Reflections', in J. Kiverstein and M. Wheeler (eds), *Heidegger and Cognitive Science*. Basingstoke: Palgrave Macmillan.

Rietveld, E. (forthcoming), 'Context-Switching and Responsiveness to Real Relevance', in J. Kiverstein and M. Wheeler (eds), *Heidegger and Cognitive Science*. Basingstoke: Palgrave Macmillan.

Rohde, M. (2009), *Enaction, Embodiment, Evolutionary Robotics. Simulation Models for a Post-Cognitivist Science of Mind*. Amsterdam and Paris: Atlantis Press.

Rowlands, M. (2010), *The New Science of the Mind: From Extended Mind to Embodied Phenomenology*. Cambridge, MA: MIT Press.

Stewart, J., O. Gapenne and E. A. Di Paolo (eds) (2010), *Enaction: Towards a New Paradigm for Cognitive Science*. Cambridge, MA: MIT Press.

Thompson, E. (2007), *Mind in life: Biology, Phenomenology, and the Sciences of Mind*. Cambridge, MA: Harvard University Press.

Thompson, E. and M. Stapleton (2009), 'Making Sense of Sense-Making: Reflections on Enactive and Extended Mind Theories'. *Topoi* 28: 23–30.

Turner, J. S (2000), *The Extended Organism: The Physiology of Animal-Built Structures*. Cambridge, MA: Harvard University Press.

Varela, F. J. (1991), 'Organism: A Meshwork of Selfless Selves', in A. I. Tauber (ed.), *Organism and the Origin of the Self*. Netherlands: Kluwer Academic, pp. 79–107.

— (1997), 'Patterns of Life: Intertwining Identity and Cognition'. *Brain and Cognition* 34: 72–87.

— (1999), 'The Specious Present: A Neurophenomenology of Time Consciousness', in J. Petitot, F. J. Varela, B. Pachoud and J.-M. Roy (eds), *Naturalizing Phenomenology*. Stanford, CA: Stanford University Press, pp. 266–314.

— (2000), *El Fenómeno de la Vida*. Editorial Dolmen, Santiago de Chile.

Varela, F. J., E. Thompson and E. Rosch (1991), *The Embodied Mind: Cognitive Science and Human Experience*. Cambridge, MA: MIT Press.

Varela, F. J., J.-P. Lachaux, E. Rodriguez and J. Matinerie (2001), 'The Brainweb: Phase Synchronization and Large-Scale Integration'. *Nature Reviews. Neuroscience* 2: 229–30.

Vernon, D. (2010), 'Enaction as a Conceptual Framework for Developmental Cognitive Robotics'. *Paladyn Journal of Behavioral Robotics* 1 (2): 89–98.

Webb, B. (1994), 'Robotic Experiments in Cricket Phonotaxis', in D. Cliff, P. Husbands, J.-A. Meyer and S. W. Wilson (eds), *From Animals to Animats 3: Proceedings of the Third International Conference on Simulation of Adaptive Behavior*. Cambridge, MA: MIT Press, pp. 45–54.

Weber, A. and F. J. Varela (2002), 'Life after Kant: Natural Purposes and the Autopoietic Foundations of Biological Individuality'. *Phenomenology and the Cognitive Sciences* 1: 97–125.

Wheeler, M. (2005), *Reconstructing the Cognitive World: The Next Step*. Cambridge, MA: MIT Press.

— (2008), 'Cognition in Context: Phenomenology, Situated Robotics and the Frame Problem'. *International Journal of Philosophical Studies* 16 (3): 323–49.

— (2010a), 'Minds, Things, and Materiality', in C. Renfrew and L. Malafouris (eds), *The Cognitive Life of Things: Recasting the Boundaries of the Mind*. Cambridge: McDonald Institute for Archaeological Research Publications.

— (2010b), 'The Problem of Representation', in S. Gallagher and D. Schmicking (eds), *Handbook of Phenomenology and Cognitive Science*. Dordrecht: Springer, pp. 319–36.

14 Existentialism and Poststructuralism: Some Unfashionable Observations[1]

*Jack Reynolds and
Ashley Woodward*

This chapter challenges the received *doxa* that the generation of 'poststructural-ist' philosophers broke decisively with existentialism and rendered it out of date, a mere historical curiosity. Drawing on recent research in the area, it draws some lines of influence, and even argues for some surprising points of com-monality, between existentialism and poststructuralism. At least some of the core philosophical ideas of poststructuralists such as Michel Foucault, Jacques Derrida and Gilles Deleuze bear more in common with existentialism than is often supposed. Furthermore, it addresses a common resistance to poststructur-alism by committed existentialists by showing that poststructuralism does not abandon concern with responsibility and decision, but in fact develops these themes in ways that are proximate to existentialist concerns. Finally, it argues that some of the needs that some prominent contemporary philosophers find lacking in poststructuralism – in particular, the need for subjective agency – are already met in significant ways in existentialism. These three points serve to throw new light on the contemporary relevance of existentialism, and to open up new directions for research.

Is Existentialism Passé?

It is hard to think of many contemporary European philosophers who would not endorse the denunciation of existentialism as passé. For example, Gianni Vattimo (whose own teacher, Luigi Pareyson, was the primary representative of existentialism in Italy), has written that 'today's philosophical climate shows little interest in [the existentialist] subject and is in general unreceptive to the themes of "classic" existentialism, such as the individual, freedom to choose, responsibility, death, and *Angst*' (1993, pp. 40–1). Even more bluntly, Jean

260 Even more bluntly, Jean

Baudrillard has remarked: 'We have thrown off that old existential garb . . . Who cares about freedom, bad faith and authenticity today?' (2001, p. 73). This denunciation was influenced by Heidegger in his 'Letter on "Humanism"' (Heidegger, 1998), and has been perpetuated in the anti-humanism of structuralists like Louis Althusser and Roland Barthes.

In the 1960s structuralism took over from existentialism both academically and perhaps even in terms of public attention in France, and to a lesser extent elsewhere in Europe. Structuralism sought to provide a new, 'scientific' methodology for the human sciences that aimed at producing a stable and secure knowledge of a system or a structure. It viewed anything that can be considered meaningful as a system of signs produced by the 'differences' between the elements of an underlying structure. Significantly, it sought to do so without any reference to subjectivity and consciousness, except to the extent that it argued that both languages and systems *precede* and *produce* individuals as subjects. As such, structuralism displaced the *humanism* – understood in this, sense, as the view that human beings are the source and masters of meaning in the world – which was a significant part of existential phenomenology. (A second sense of 'humanism' to which poststructuralism is frequently opposed is the use of the category 'human' as a foundation for all thought.)

However, it wasn't long before structuralism was itself being challenged by poststructuralism in France in the late 1960s. Philosophers like Lyotard, Deleuze, Derrida and Foucault were all important in this regard, challenging the 'centrist' assumption of structuralism that an understanding of one key or central element of the structure – whether it be kinship laws, the workings of language, the educational system or the devices employed in a literary text – allows for an explanation of the entire system. Poststructuralism also cast into question structuralism's strict determinism, instead insisting upon the role of unpredictable and random forces in the genesis of any structure, law or norm. Opposing structuralism's quasi-scientific claims to objectivity, rationality and intelligibility, poststructuralism instead pointed to certain moments, or 'events', that disrupt any stable and secure sense of meaning and identity.

Despite this problematization of structuralism's simple determinism, and despite their concern to show the way in which the event resists and exceeds all of our attempted reconstructions of it, it has generally been assumed that poststructuralist concerns have remained at a distance from the existentialist's wartime preoccupations with freedom, death, responsibility, anguish, and the like. This is largely because poststructuralists have continued to endorse much of the structuralist view of meaning as extrasubjective, and have mobilized versions of this idea to dismiss existentialism. In addition, they have continued to highlight problems with, and the limits to, humanism, arguing that it is spurious to begin from the assumption that consciousness and subjectivity are fundamental when they are in fact socio-culturally produced, albeit not in as overdetermined a way as the structuralists might have thought. In that respect, it is unsurprising that theorists like Jean-Luc Nancy, Foucault, Derrida, and many others, have continued to directly associate existentialism with human-ism and 'the philosophy of the subject'. Although we will argue that the oppos-ition between poststructuralism and existentialism is not as stark as these theorists would have us believe, let us consider some indicative remarks, remarks that might incline one to think that there might be a killing of the father at stake here, an anxiety of influence going on in regard to their predecessors on the French scene, and particularly Sartre.

Famously, Foucault once characterized Sartre's *Critique of Dialectical Reason* as 'the magnificent and pathetic attempt of a man of the nineteenth century to think the twentieth century' (Foucault, 2001, pp. 541–2; trans. Jon Roffe), and in general treated him as the embodiment of all that is wrong with what he takes to be an outmoded conception of the intellectual. While Sartre, like Foucault, was a great critic of bourgeois society, Foucault thought that he partook in the grand tradition of what he dubbed the 'universal intellectual', one who judges a society from the basis of some set of transcendent or ahistorical principles, insufficiently grounded in local practices.[2] Foucault also included criticisms of Sartre in the original draft of his major book *The Order of Things* (Foucault, 1989), which he removed from the proofs prior to publication (Miller: 44).

In the introduction to his doctoral thesis on Husserl, Derrida began by stri-dently distancing himself from Sartre and Merleau-Ponty, and their versions of existential phenomenology, and he also criticized Sartre in *Margins of Phil-osophy* (1985, pp. 109–36). In the process, he posited a gap between his deconstructive position and existentialism that arguably wasn't breached for over 20 years.

Lyotard's perhaps somewhat ironically titled paper 'A Success of Sartre's' (1986) is in fact mostly a statement of Sartre's failures. The 'success' alluded to in the title may be understood as Sartre's apparent later realization that human beings are not independent originators of meaning (in Sartre's terms, 'transcend-ences') who communicate these meanings transparently with each other, but rather that language has the power to constitute meanings and condition the subjects who use it (as the structuralists and poststructuralists had argued). Lyotard writes that 'in capitalism (and this is one of the issues at stake in the Flaubert study) prose has ceased being, for Sartre, the medium within which transcendences communicate' (1986, p. xx). Instead, according to Lyotard, Sar-tre realized 'that words could not be dissipated in the transparency of a signify-ing intention, that capitalist modernity, but perhaps also the being of language itself, was part and parcel of pure communication and freedom' (p. xxii). He argues that Sartre's humanist thesis on the subjective control of meaning gives way to an 'ontological' recognition of the 'thickness' of words, and their power over the subject who is 'spoken by' them (pp. xxi–xxii). In other words, to put the point bluntly, according to Lyotard, Sartre's one success was in realizing that his existentialist philosophy was wrong.

In his retrospective *Passwords*, Baudrillard indicated that the entire trajectory of his thought can be understood as an examination of 'the object', in direct reaction to the phenomenological and existentialist 'philosophies of the subject' that dominated the previous generation of thinkers. (However, it is curious to note that the primary source of inspiration he cites for this investigation of the object is Antoine Roquentin's famous encounter with the excrescent existence of the tree root in Sartre's novel *Nausea*) (Baudrillard, 2003, p. 3).

Rapprochement?

Although there are some valid reasons for this critical reception of existentialism, especially in terms of the now widely accepted rejection of narrowly humanistic and subjectivistic theories of meaning, this way of thinking nevertheless obscures two key points:

1. The resources within existentialism that do not admit of humanism, even if it is the case that consciousness is prioritized (and this later clause is also called into question by major aspects of the works of Nietzsche, Merleau-Ponty and Heidegger. As the above-cited remarks indicate, much of the poststructuralist reaction to existentialism has in fact been a reaction not to existentialism *tout court*, but to Sartre with the intent of accentuating their differences from him. Moreover, much of this critical reaction also seems to centre on Sartre's perhaps most famous text, 'Existentialism is a Humanism' (1975) and the suggestion that   existentialism is committed to a problematic form of humanism. But, not only are some existentialists not humanists, there is a strong *anti*-humanistic tradition of existentialism, one that is even present in Sartre himself, particularly in *Nausea*, (in his chapter in this *Companion* Colin Davis hence indicates something like the form that a deconstruction of Derrida's oppositional relationship to Sartre and humanism might take). More generally, while taking the meaning of human existence as a central concern, many existentialists have nevertheless been opposed to humanism in both senses previously indicated – 'man' as the origin of meaning, and as foundation. For example, Kierkegaard is strongly critical of humanism for its assumption that human existence does not rely for its sense of meaning on something greater (i.e. God). Moreover, Nietzsche takes humanism to task for its hubris in assuming that the current human state is the 'highest form' of life, and criticizes its attempt to replace the dead God with the category 'man'. Furthermore, despite his heroic individualism, Nietzsche anticipated (and inspired) many aspects of the poststructuralist theses on language and

the critique of the subject.

It might thus be possible to distinguish humanistic/anti-humanistic existentialism just as it is possible to distinguish theistic/atheistic existentialism. One common move which has tended to obscure the anti-humanistic dimension of existentialism has been to assert that thinkers such as Nietzsche and Heidegger, crucial to poststructuralism, were never really existentialist at all, creating a neat (although we would argue, illusory) divide between existentialism, understood as essentially humanistic, and anti-humanistic 'proto-poststructuralist' thinkers. This tendency over the past several decades to interpret Nietzsche and Heidegger in such a way as to disavow their association with existentialism explains why the centrality of these two figures for *both* existentialism and poststructuralism has failed to complicate the distinction between these two traditions as much as it might. While this disavowal is arguably unsustainable (see Ansell-Pearson's chapter in this *Companion* on Nietzsche's existentialism), we will largely focus our attempts at rapprochement here on Sartrean existentialism, since this seems to be the core kernel of resistance to such attempts.

2. Also neglected by this putative opposition are the significant similarities between aspects of existentialism and some contemporary poststructuralist thinkers. We will briefly explore some points of contact between particular poststructuralists and particular existentialists below. But first, it will be useful to schematize some general points:

a. Existentialists and poststructuralists frequently share a search for the conditions and limits of rationality (including the way in which events and existence exceed our rational reconstructions of them); and a concern to defend the 'others' of reason – such as the emotions, desire and the body – as philosophically significant. For both traditions, this is frequently associated with an opposition to the philosophy of Hegel, albeit in differing ways: while for the existentialists it is the 'existing individual' which cannot be fully incorporated into a rational system, for poststructuralists it is 'the event'.

b. There is an important sense in which the poststructuralist dynamic between 'structure' and 'event' is anticipated by the existentialist dynamic between 'facticity' and 'transcendence'. Against ontologies which understand reality as fundamentally stable or as fundamentally changing, many existentialists and many poststructuralists view reality as consisting of a dynamic between tendencies towards stability and immutability, and tendencies towards disruption and change. Both dynamics can be generalized as a dynamic between 'essence' and 'existence', where essence indicates stability, and existence, change. Moreover, just as poststructuralists arguably often seem guilty of overvaluing the event, so the existentialists often seem guilty of overvaluing transcendence – to the extent that critics often forget the dimension of facticity entirely, understanding existentialism as a philosophy of unbounded free transcendence. However, in both traditions, both poles are asserted as necessary.

c. Following on from this ontological proximity, there are also some points of resonance in regard to their objections to determinism, including scientific determinism. Existentialists typically argued for the freedom and openness to possibility of the existing individual, in contrast to the determinism of the material world suggested by Newtonian laws, as well as to social or psychological determinisms. Structuralism placed this existentialist freedom in question by pointing to deep, conditioning structures of various kinds (myths, the unconscious, language, social codes), which they believed determined human behaviour at a level beneath our conscious intentions. While continuing to eschew the existentialist individual and support many of the insights of structuralism, the poststructuralists rejected determinism by arguing in various ways that structures are subject to disruption through unpredictable, undetermined occurrences or 'events'. Derrida, for example, frequently invokes the future and the 'to come' in many of his late writings, pointing to the way in which all laws, or norms, need to be open to revision and open to that which might come (but not to that which *must* come), rather than closing themselves off from change.

d. Existentialism and poststructuralism share a frequent rejection of foundationalism. Modern philosophy, beginning with Descartes's *cogito*, is frequently understood as attempting to find an adequately secure foundation for all rational inquiry and human projects. Existentialists and poststructuralists generally deny that such a foundation is possible or desirable. Existentialists assert the ultimate incapacity of reason to fully grasp our existential situation, and insist on the intractability of faith, decision, or some other confrontation with radical contingency as central to human life. Poststructuralists likewise assert the intractable nature of events, unpredictable occurrences that attest to an unavoidable contingency haunting every attempt to pin things down in terms of necessary structures.

e. Both existentialism and poststructuralism frequently entertain a decentred and anti-foundational conception of the subject. While structuralists and poststructuralists frequently dismissed existentialism as a 'philosophy of the subject', it has increasingly been realized that poststructuralism develops a decentred notion of the subject, and one which was anticipated in important respects by existentialist thinkers (see below for more on this). A key issue here is that dismissals of the 'existentialist subject' have, arguably, frequently conflated this subject with the Cartesian subject (understood as a permanent substance which acts as a foundation). The source of this conflation is likely Sartre's invocation of Descartes's *cogito* as the starting-point and 'firm foundation' for existentialism in the 'Existentialism is a Humanism' lecture. However, this is unfortunately misrepresentative: not only do many other existentialists, such as Kierkegaard, Nietzsche and Heidegger, develop a radically non-Cartesian notion of the subject, but Sartre's own earlier work *The Transcendence of the Ego* (Sartre, 1960) also points radically in this direction.

f. Both of these theoretical trajectories also partake in a probing inquiry into freedom and responsibility that explores the limits of ethical reasoning. We treat this in more detail below in regard to the comparison of Sartre and Derrida on responsibility and 'undecidability', but for now perhaps it suffices to note that to differing extents the 'usual suspects' associated with existentialism and poststructuralism are both concerned with describing and enumerating transcendental conditions for ethics and politics, rather than any normative ethics itself, particularly one of a cognitivist variety that emphasizes reason. There is a sense in which the very attempt to offer a prescriptive ethics is akin to a transcendental mistake, in that it undermines the very meaning of responsibility and decision-making as they enumerate it. Indeed, even de Beauvoir, the most explicit proponent of an existentialist ethics, was not prescribing any kind of universal recipe for action or a single monistic theory of what is valuable. As she comments:

> It will be said that these considerations remain quite abstract. What must be done, practically? Which action is good? Which action is bad? To ask such a question is also to fall into a naive abstraction . . . Ethics does not furnish recipes any more than do science and art. One can merely propose methods. (1976, p. 134)

In this sense, she offers a method for questioning that is said to be necessary for ethical action, but which would be undermined by prescriptions or, arguably, even any liberal principles of a negative variety, which risk, for de Beauvoir, amounting to being 'a curator of the given world', who sides 'with what has been over what has not yet been' (1976, p. 91). Philosophy of time is important here, since de Beauvoir's ongoing insistence upon the importance of an 'open future' bears some significant similarities to the transcendental import that Derrida accords to that which is 'to come' and most of the other major poststructuralist thinkers have also exalted the importance of the future in related ways. Both the existentialists and poststructuralists also reject transcendent and other-wordly determinants of success or value (such as wealth, religion, but also philosophical systems), as well as any meta-ethical realism, in which moral values are thought to be like real properties awaiting our discovery if only all of us were reasonable enough to recognize them.

This list does not pretend to be exhaustive, but rather is offered as a provocation to further research. We shall now consider some particular poststructuralists in their relation to existentialism. Despite the kind of strident remarks about existentialism that we have rehearsed above, we can read some of the post-structuralist thinkers otherwise, and show that some of their work does in fact owe a lot to their existential predecessors, more than they are usually prepared to avow. We will now take a selective look at three examples: Foucault, Derrida and Deleuze.

Foucault

Some important work has already been done to draw out the commonalities between Sartre and the intellectual who from a certain perspective usurped his place, simultaneously supplanting existentialism with the new paradigms of structuralism and poststructuralism: Michel Foucault. The most obvious point of contact between the two thinkers is their views on the self. In 'Self-Creating Selves: Sartre and Foucault', Phyllis Sutton Morris compares the two thinkers on this issue, noting both differences and similarities between the early Sartre and the late Foucault. For Sartre, she argues, the agent that creates the self differs from the self that is created: the agent is the 'lived body', as it is engaged in practical activity in the world. The created self, ego, or what Sartre calls 'essence', is the pattern built up by the various 'actions, utterances, and emotional responses one enacts in the world' (Morris, 1997, p. 540). By contrast, when Foucault becomes interested in problems of the self in his late works, it is not the lived body that is the agent of self-creation, but the conscious relation of the self to itself. Drawing on ancient Greek and Roman practices such as attention to diet, writing letters and journals, and meditational practices, Foucault emphasizes the role of conscious self-mastery in the creation of the self. Perhaps surprisingly, then, Morris highlights that it is Foucault who gives a greater role to the conscious self in its own creation than Sartre, for whom the agency of creation is the spontaneous, pre-reflective actions of the lived body in its encounters with the world. Nevertheless, Morris also points out the strong commonalities between their interests:

> In his later work Foucault not only shares with the early Sartre the view that there is no fixed original essence of an individual, but also shares the view that instead of seeking to discover a nonexistent, original, true self, one might engage in actively forming the self as a work of art. (p. 544)

Moreover, she suggests that their differences of view on how the self is to be created might best be understood as differences of emphasis, and that both approaches – pre-reflective and reflective – 'do not appear to be mutually incompatible if combined sequentially by someone who hopes to shape his life more carefully' (p. 549).

A significant contribution to the revision of our views on Sartre has been Nik Farrell Fox's *The New Sartre: Explorations in Postmodernism*. Fox presents an analysis that traces 'the strands of opposition and convergence between Sartre's work and poststructuralist theory across a broad range of study' (2003, p. 3). While other poststructuralists are also discussed, an important point of departure for Fox's study was the recognition of similarities between Sartre and Foucault, occluded by the debates between them. Fox argues that Sartre and Foucault cannot be starkly differentiated in their views of the subject (as is sometimes done) by viewing Sartre's subject as entirely free, while Foucault's subject is entirely constrained by the effects of power that produce it. Rather, both Sartre and Foucault recognize and are concerned to think the relation between the poles of freedom and constraint that mark the subject (pp. 34–5). More broadly, against what he notes is a common view of Sartre's existentialist subject as antithetical to the poststructuralist decentring of the subject, Fox argues that 'Sartre's idea of a contingent, non-essential subject (which he argues consistently for throughout his work) has much in common with, and indeed prefigures, the decentred subject theorised by poststructuralists and postmodernists' (p. 7). In a related vein, although one that focuses upon Sartre's later work and in particular *Critique of Dialectical Reason*, Thomas Flynn has also written an important two-volume text on Sartre and Foucault titled *Sartre, Foucault, and Historical Reason* (1997, 2005).

Derrida

It is obvious enough that there can have been no deconstruction without Heidegger, notwithstanding the many problems Derrida has with *Being and Time*. Beyond this, however, Derrida observes in the interview published in *A Taste for the Secret* that although he did distance himself from the 'philosophy of existence', as well as a certain existentialist interpretation of Husserl, his 'intention was certainly not to draw away from the concern for existence itself, for concrete personal commitment, or from the existential pathos that, in a sense, I have never lost . . . In some ways, a philosopher without the ethico-existential pathos does not interest me very much' (Derrida and Ferraris, 2001, p. 40). He then goes to on to affirm the importance of Kierkegaard to his own work, adding that, 'the resistance of existence to the concept or system – this is something I attach great importance to and feel very deeply, something I am always ready to stand up for' (p. 40).

Derrida's 'quasi-existential' affirmation of the resistance of existence to conceptual system-building is very important here, as it links on to a broader tendency of virtually all poststructuralist thought. After all, it is not only Derrida, but also Deleuze, Lyotard and, others more recently, Alain Badiou, who exalt the importance of the event and the way in which it is irreducible to, and exceeds, particular rational representations of it. Although these poststructuralist characterizations of the event are not univocal in their mean-ing, their use of the concept of the event is closely related to that of existence (or *Existenz*), as it is employed by Sartre, de Beauvoir, Jaspers and Heidegger. Both the poststructuralists and the existentialists are keen to point to certain limits to knowledge (e.g. the way in which it can never fully grasp the event, or existence).

In addition to his endorsement of Kierkegaard, it is important to note that Derrida's view of his immediate existential predecessors in France also grad-ually became more positive. For example, *Memoirs of the Blind* discusses Mer-leau-Ponty in a largely positive manner, and his essay 'Salut, Salut: Dead Man Running' (which can be found in *Negotiations*) talks about Sartre, again in a positive light. (However, this latter text on Sartre doesn't involve much explicit philosophical negotiation with Sartre's key ideas.) Derrida did finally turn to devote sustained attention to the work of Merleau-Ponty, in one of his last major books, *On Touching*. As Reynolds has argued elsewhere, the engagement with the work of Merleau-Ponty is notable in Derrida's *oeuvre* for its lack of charity and a sort of bluntness about the criticisms he expresses (Reynolds, 2008), and this is perhaps because there are actually some important connections between their works, perhaps particularly in *The Visible and the Invisible* (see Reynolds, 2004). Indeed, since existentialism's heyday, Merleau-Ponty's importance has increasingly been recognized, and his place 'between' existentialism and (post-) structuralism complicates the identification of existentialism *tout court* with cli-chés about Sartre's philosophy, such as radical freedom (on this point, see also Keith Ansell-Pearson's chapter in this *Companion*).

Christina Howells has indicated some significant proximities between Sartre and Derrida (1998). She notes that '"Derrideans" and "Sartreans" have tended to inhabit very different, even opposed camps, either side of the structuralist divide', but notes her own interest in both thinkers around theories of the subject. She points to what she believes is 'Derrida's influential and arguably wilful misreading of Sartre' in the essay 'The Ends of Man' (Howells, 1998, p. 27). Derrida reads Sartre's 'phenomenological ontology' as a kind of philosophical anthropology, and accuses him of never questioning the history of the concept 'Man'. However, Howells notes that in seeming opposition to his main thesis, Derrida has two footnotes that indi-cate the proximity of Sartre's and his own concerns. Here Derrida discusses Sartre's 'ironic dismantling of humanism in the person of the Autodidacte' in *Nausea* and 'the importance of the notions of lack, negativity and non-self-identity' in both *Being and Nothingness* and the *Critique of Dialectical Reason* (p. 27).

Howells then argues that Sartre's analysis of the 'self-presence' of the for-itself anticipates Derrida's work in *Speech and Phenomena*, precisely in its asser-tion of the impossibility of full presence. Like Derrida after him, Sartre draws on Husserl, and in particular the analysis of the temporality of consciousness, to 'deconstruct' the notion of a self-present subject. For Sartre, consciousness is always non-self-identical because it is always transcending itself; it is a 'transcendental field' without a subject, which brings a subject into being through its own self-reflection (pp. 27–8). Howells concludes that Derrida's criticisms of Sartre erroneously obscure their similarities, and that 'in the caße of Husserl, Derrida's own analyses are strikingly close to Sartre's and the foundations of his critique of phenomenology almost identical' (p. 28). (Derrida never responded adequately to Howells on this issue, albeit not considering a longish private letter to her.) Other scholars have also noted striking continuities between Sartre and Derrida (cf. Rajan, 2002).

Deleuze

In an essay written in 1964, a month after Sartre's refusal of the Nobel Prize for literature, and titled 'Il a été mon maître' ('He was My Master') (Deleuze, 2004a, p. 77), Deleuze writes sympathetically of the Sartre of *Being and Nothingness*, along with his insistence on conflictual relations and a certain inevitability of violence, over and against the Sartre of 'Existentialism is a Humanism'. The latter text was Sartre's (in)famous public lecture, attended by thousands including Deleuze, that attempted to reconcile his existentialist convictions with an ethics of respect for the other's freedom (in *Being and Nothingness*, on the other hand, he famously states that respect for the other's freedom is an empty word; p. 49), somewhat along the lines of Simone de Beauvoir's subsequent book, *The Ethics of Ambiguity*. For Deleuze, however, it is the earlier work that is described as a tough, penetrating existentialism, whereas 'Existentialism is a Humanism' is seen as a Kantianism that verges on re-enacting a spurious kingdom of ends.

Moreover, Deleuze repeatedly endorses the Sartre of the *Transcendence of the Ego*, crediting his analysis of Husserl with discovering a 'pure immanence' of the transcendental field. In this text, Sartre shows how phenomenology need not, and should not, posit a transcendental ego that is inside *all* experience; any ego is literally transcendent to, or not part of phenomenological experience, which involves nothing more than what Sartre calls nonthetic self-awareness (we are aware that we are *not* that object that we are intending or negating). At the same time, Deleuze suggests in *The Logic of Sense* that there is no value in insisting upon the priority of consciousness (as Sartre does), since consciousness always makes reference to 'synthes[es] of unification' (2004b, p. 102) and ends up reintroducing a type of ontological transcendence. On this analysis, Sartre betrays his discovery of the immanence of the transcendental field by reintroducing the *form*, if not the content (since, for Sartre, consciousness has no *content* and is literally no-thing-ness), of the subject in its Cartesian–Husserlian formulation (see Reynolds and Roffe, 2006).

The relations of Deleuze to Sartre have as yet received less attention than the relations of Foucault and Derrida to his work, but it is a topic that deserves further research. Moreover, another topic that deserves further investigation is the role played by Jean Wahl's notion of 'existential empiricism' in the development of Deleuze's 'transcendental empiricism'. Wahl was a key 'background' figure in the historical development of existentialism, both through having done work on Hegel that contributed to the development of French existentialism, and through crystallizing it as a movement in some seminal studies of existentialist thinkers.

It would not only be misleading, but also pointless, to argue too insistently or pervasively for commonalities between poststructuralism and existentialism. But by showing here that there are many more such commonalities than is generally assumed, we hope to open up paths to further research which are frequently blocked by the unquestioned assumption that poststructuralism has somehow simply rendered existentialism 'passé' (invalid, because outmoded).

Responsibility and Decision

The points made above mostly speak to the relevance of existentialism from the point of view of poststructuralism. However, a rapprochement between the two traditions has also met some resistance from the other direction; that is, committed existentialists have been critical of poststructuralism. One of the most central of these criticisms involves the accusation that poststructuralist philosophies void the important ethical category of responsibility. This criticism is expressed clearly by Robert C. Solomon, a well-known Nietzschean and Sartrean, in his appearance in the film *Waking Life* (2001). Here, he explains to a student:

> I've read the postmodernists with some interest, even admiration, but when I read them I always have this awful nagging feeling that something absolutely essential is getting left out. The more you talk about the person as a social construction or as a confluence of forces, or as fragmented or marginalized, what you do is you open up a whole new world of excuses. And when Sartre talks about responsibility he's not talking about something abstract, he's not talking about the kind of self or soul that theologians would argue about, it's something very concrete, it's you and me talking, making decisions, doing things, and taking the consequences.

The view, then, is that poststructuralism (or postmodernism) lacks engagement with the crucial issues of responsibility and decision.

If we probe this view a little, however, things are not as cut and dried as one might think. In fact, it can be coherently argued that the issue of responsibility is an important one for poststructuralism generally; in different ways, a concern with responsibility to otherness is evident in the work of Derrida, Lyotard and Foucault. In fact we would argue that a rapprochement of existentialism and poststructuralism can be effected around the locus of responsibility. Nor, to head off a possible objection, can it be argued that the existentialist emphasis is more clearly concerned with responsibility to the self, rather than with responsibility to other(s), since Buber, Levinas and other theistic existentialists already emphasized this theme. While it would be possible to detail the theme of responsibility in the works of the other poststructuralists mentioned above, to make our case we will focus on the themes of responsibility and decision in the later Derrida.

Drawing on the work of Kierkegaard, in multiple different texts Derrida argues that the instant of the decision must be mad, provocatively telling us that a decision requires an undecidable leap beyond all prior preparations and rational calculations for that decision (1996, p. 77). According to him, this applies to all decisions and not just those regarding the conversion to religious faith that preoccupies Kierkegaard. This is one place that his work seems to meet up with Sartre's, for whom any decision must be equally unjustifiable and equally mad. This is dramatically evinced in Antoine Roquentin's existential struggles in *Nausea*, but also throughout the entirety of *Being and Nothingness*. Derrida and Sartre come together in their rejection of any Kantian categorical imperative that claims that all moral decisions can and should be based on reason. This understanding of the decision also has clear consequences for issues to do with responsibility and it is on such a theme that this surprising proximity between Sartre and Derrida is reaffirmed.

Notwithstanding his complicated account of fundamental projects, Sartre disavows the possibility of providing any rational justification for our choices. The most famous example of this is recounted in both *Being and Nothingness* and 'Existentialism is a Humanism'. Sartre recalls a student of his who came to see him with an ethical dilemma, basically to seek guidance about whether he should look after his sick and dying mother on her deathbed, or join the resistance movement to fight his country's Nazi oppressors. Sartre not only refused to give an answer but he also intimated that this kind of conflict is involved in all attempts to be responsible. Responsibility is never easy on Sartre's understanding; there is no risk of being self-satisfied, with a good conscience and complacent with the choices that we have made. On the contrary, assuming responsibility is very intimidating and liable to induce the experience of anguish, because all such decisions are ultimately unjustifiable.

While questions remain regarding whether or not Derrida thinks that responsibility can ever be assumed, as Sartre's analysis at least sometimes implies,

Derrida nevertheless (re)stages an analogous dilemma in his reading of Abraham's biblical sacrifice of his son, Isaac, upon Mount Moriah. In *The Gift of Death*, Derrida points to a fundamental tension between responsibility for all others (e.g. freeing the world from the Nazi party in Sartre's example) and responsibility for a singular loved one (e.g. the sick mother). Responsibility involves enduring this trial of the 'undecidable decision', where attending to the call of a particular other (such as God in Abraham's case) will inevitably demand an estrangement from the 'other others' and the more general ethical demands of a community, who were horrified by Abraham's willingness to sacrifice his son. Whatever decision one may take, whether it be to prefer a singular other or to prefer all others, it can never be wholly justified (1996, p. 70). For both Derrida and Sartre, to have a good conscience, to assume that one's hands are clean and that one is acting on the side of the good and the just, is to inevitably presage a greater violence.

While Sartre is rightly famous in the history of philosophy for his many and varied arguments for freedom, and it is also true that Derrida has rarely discussed freedom, any simple opposition between them on this issue of freedom would also, we think, be misleading. After all, Sartre's concept of 'the situation' refers to the necessary intermingling of facticity and freedom, and he insists that there is freedom only in a situation and there is a situation only through freedom. He also goes on to claim that situation and motivation for pursuing certain projects are indistinguishable, suggesting that, 'the situation, the common product of the contingency of the in-itself and of freedom, is an ambiguous phenomenon in which it is impossible for the for-itself to distinguish the contribution of freedom from that of the brute existent' (1958, p. 487). Taking this ambiguity of the 'situation' into account, Sartre doesn't seem to be as committed to a conception of the free and sovereign subject who decides as is often suspected, even if he is nevertheless closer to such a conception than Derrida. For Derrida, any theory of the subject is incapable of accounting for the slightest decision, because such a view would necessarily involve 'the unfolding of an egological immanence, the autonomic and automatic deployment of predicates or possibilities proper to a subject, without the tearing rupture that should occur in every decision we call free' (1999, p. 24). In other words, if a decision is envisaged as simply following from certain character attributes, then it would not genuinely be a decision. Clearly, however, a decision, for Sartre, does not flow from any egological immanence – recall that there is no character trait of 'cowardice' that dictates that the hiker will give in to their fatigue, in one of the great examples that populate *Being and Nothingness* – and his philosophy does not constitute a theory of the subject in that sense. Rather, the subject is literally no-thing, except in reflection, and this ensures that, for Sartre, decisions are always characterized by a radical rupture with immanence and the past.

Of course, it would be difficult to deny that there are some significant points of difference between Sartre's and Derrida's conceptions of the decision. In *Politics of Friendship*, for example, Derrida argues that far from returning us to any sovereign conception of free will, what needs to be considered is the fundamentally 'passive' aspect of a decision that is always made for the other, and he insists that there is no freedom without the other. He eventually concludes: '*in sum, the decision is unconscious* – insane as that may seem, it involves the unconscious but is nevertheless responsible' (1997, p. 69). This suggestion that the decision is always passive, partially unconscious, and for the other, highlights that Derrida is not returning us to a Sartrean paradigm of the activity and projects of the for-itself. Nevertheless, while Sartre criticizes the concept of the unconscious, his insistence that choices are not ones that we are reflectively conscious of (his is not a philosophy of free *will*) blurs the difference between them on decision-making and responsibility.

The Return of the Subject

The place of the subject in existential philosophies, and the eclipse of the subject by structuralism, is one of the decisive factors accounting for existentialism long having been considered passé. But the subject has made a slow return, first as brought back into play but in a decentred way (as something to be explained, rather than as a principle of explanation) in poststructuralism, and more strongly in the 'late' poststructuralism of philosophers like Foucault and Lyotard.[3] More recently, however, the 'new wave' of continental philosophers who oppose themselves to poststructuralism have done so at least in part by resurrecting the philosophy of the subject (albeit in a new form). Of most significance here are Slavoj Žižek's *The Ticklish Subject* (1999) and Alain Badiou's *Theory of the Subject* (as well as later works, such as *Being and Event*). Žižek's book *The Ticklish Subject* 'endeavours to reassert the Cartesian subject, whose rejection forms the silent pact of all the struggling parties of today's academia' (1999, p. 2). However, Žižek clarifies, 'the point, of course, is not to return to the *cogito* in the guise in which this notion has dominated modern thought (the self-transparent thinking subject), but to bring to light its forgotten obverse' (p. 2). For Žižek, this 'forgotten obverse' is the kernel of political resistance offered by the subject, which he argues is lacking in poststructuralist philosophies such as Foucault's. He argues against the political adequacy of Foucault's late conception of the subject, asserting that it cannot pose an effective resistance to power because Foucault understands the subject, as well as any resistance which issues from it, as thoroughly produced and conditioned by the structures of power:

The problem here is that, after insisting that the disciplinary power mechanisms produce the very object on which they exert their force (the subject is not only that which is oppressed by the power but emerges himself as the product of this oppression) . . . it is as if Foucault himself tacitly acknowledges that this absolute continuity of resistance to power is not enough to ground effective resistance to power, a resistance that would not be 'part of the game' but would allow the subject to assume a position that exempts him from the disciplinary / confessional mode of power. (Žižek, 1999, p. 249)

In their general introduction to the philosophy of Badiou in *Infinite Thought*, Justin Clemens and Oliver Feltham position his work on the subject in direct opposition to poststructuralism. They argue that there are two basic problems of the subject, *identity* and *agency*. Poststructuralists tended to focus on the first issue, theorizing the subject within a general ontology, and problematizing its unity and identity. However, they argue, this treatment had the perhaps unintended consequence of undermining agency, a problem which they did not tend to foreground. As they put it:

> [A]s for agency – philosophy's second fundamental problem in the thought of the subject – the consequence of poststructuralism's almost exclusive concentration on the first problem has been that the critics of poststructuralism have had an easy pitch: all they have had to do is to accuse the poststructurlaists of robbing the subject of agency: if there is no self-identical subject, then what is the ground for autonomous rational action? (Feltham and Clemens in Badiou, 2003)

One of Badiou's major contributions to contemporary philosophy, then, is the reassertion of the agency of the subject as an issue of central importance.

There is, then, in influential currents of contemporary continental philosophy, a breaking-down of one of the central barriers to a reconsideration of existentialism: its characterization (rightly or wrongly) as a 'philosophy of the subject'. Indeed, because of both his own and Sartre's emphasis on the category of the subject, Badiou has remarked that one day, perhaps a new division will be recognized in twentieth-century French philosophy, 'a possible regrouping of Lacan, Sartre, and myself, on the one hand, and on the other, of the Heideggerians and, in some ways, Deleuze and Lyotard' (Badiou, quoted in Hallward, 2003, p. xxviii).

This 'return of the subject' in recent continental philosophy, along with Badiou's admiration for Sartre, admits of the possibility of a new interest in existentialist theories of the subject. What is perhaps immediately noticeable as a possible topic of interest here is the fact that many existentialist theories of the subject evince a deep engagement with both problems of the subject noted above: identity and agency. As the work of Christina Howells, Nik Farrell Fox, Thomas Flynn, and others have shown, while the 'deconstruction' of the identity of the subject was radicalized by the poststructuralists, it was well underway in the works of the existentialists. However, the existentialists, far more so than the poststructuralists, were concerned to try to think agency in relation to the 'non-self-identical' subject. Existentialism, we then suggest, admits of resources for thinking the problems which were grappled with both by the poststructuralists, and by recent thinkers such as Žižek and Badiou. A reconsideration of these resources offers a different light on this complex of problems concerning the subject, and is a further reason that existentialism should not be dismissed as 'passé' in the contemporary context.

Much of the resistance to existentialism as a 'philosophy of the subject' is due to Sartre's invocation of the Cartesian cogito in 'Existentialism is a Humanism'. This is then suggestive of Descartes's own view of the subject as substance and as foundation. However, this construal flies in the face of Sartre's own earlier arguments, as well as that of other existentialists (Kierkegaard, Nietzsche, Heidegger, etc.). As Christopher Macann explains in his chapter in this *Companion*, for Kierkegaard the self is a (self-)relation, which means first that it is not a substance. Moreover, Sartre presents a displacement of the ego in his early writings, such that consciousness becomes a flux without a secure foundation. The very notion of 'existence' developed by existentialism implies that the self is always 'outside itself', or 'ecstatic'. If poststructuralism decentres the subject, we need to ask if a theory of the subject as decentred is not already the principle trait of the existentialist theory of the subject. However, a key difference is that for the existentialists, this decentred subject is accorded a far greater degree of agency, and plays an essential role in the constitution of meaning. This is what some philosophers criticize poststructuralism for lacking, and it is this concern for agency (especially political) which is the basis of the 'return of the subject' in recent continental philosophy. We might then suggest that the existentialist theories of the subject or self are worth reviewing, with respect to the promise that they might combine the best insights of both the poststructuralists and some of the more recent 'continentals': a theory of the subject which is decentred, but has agency.

Conclusion: Existentialism after Poststructuralism

Of course, to advocate new research in existentialism today is not to suggest ignoring philosophical developments of the past 50 or more years. Any reconsideration of existentialist themes, we assert, must take place in the critical light of poststructuralism (as well as of other recent thinkers and traditions). While we defend the continuing relevance of much existentialist philosophy, it remains the case that structuralism and poststructuralism have problematized some key existentialist ideas in compelling ways. What, then, might new directions in existentialist research learn from poststructuralism? Again, the following is far from intended as an exhaustive list, but briefly indicates a few key points we consider to be worth further consideration and investigation.

- *Theories of meaning.* One of the most compelling insights of structuralism has been to show the extrasubjective character of meaning, the fact that systems of meaning pre-exist individual subjects, and shape the meanings available to those subjects. We would agree that the exclusive focus on the constitution of meaning by the intentional consciousness of the individual does appear inadequate in this light. Nevertheless, we would also argue that the structuralist theory does not invalidate the results of the phenomenological reduction, which shows that the intentionality of consciousness is a *necessary* condition for the *experience* of meaning, even if not a sufficient condition. Research in this direction might investigate how extrasubjective systems of meaning make up the 'background' from which subjects draw in the intentional construction of meaning.
- *The philosophical role of human existence.* There is an important sense in which, at least in its most popular strand, existentialism was bound up with the optimistic phenomenological project to give a new foundation to, and solve many of the problems of, philosophy, associated with phenomenology. The developments of 'existential phenomenology' began to undermine the foundational project of phenomenology, while, in turn, the further development of Heidegger's thinking, and the rise of structuralism contributed to the decline of existentialism. The result of these developments is that human existence can no longer have the central and foundational role it was accorded in the 'golden age' of existentialism and phenomenology. Nevertheless, we assert, human existence is a crucially important 'regional ontology' to study, even if it can no longer be understood as the basis of a foundational ontology. How to study human existence in a way which recognizes both its philosophical decentring and its special relevance is a possible topic of further investigation.
- *The ontological scope of 'existence'.* For most existentialist philosophers, the term 'existence' is delimited to human beings, and its features of dynamism, openness and possibility are contrasted with the fixed,

'essential', and objective features of everything else in the world. As Andrew J. Mitchell's chapter for this *Companion* discusses, however, Heidegger moved away from this position in works after *Being and Time*, extending features reserved for the essence of *Dasein* (characterized as 'existence') to essence in general. Mitchell suggests this is a necessary development, as *Dasein* cannot exist in a world of objects. Similarly, poststructuralism has in general extended the dynamism the existentialists reserved for human existence to cover *all* existence. Thus, these developments would suggest a necessary rethinking of what sometimes appears as a clear-cut distinction between human being and all other modes of being in existentialist ontologies (and in this respect Merleau-Ponty's work appears as central).

- *Theories of the subject and consciousness.* Another area of further research concerning existentialism is the subject and consciousness. While we have argued that the existentialist subject is far more decentred than is often recognized, it needs now to be considered in the light of the radical decentrings and displacements suggested by poststructuralism, as well as of the new theories of the subject recently gaining currency. Consciousness has generally been all but ignored by poststructuralists, and so a key question for further research might be, what would a 'poststructuralist theory of consciousness' look like? How would it differ from that of Sartre's, or of other existentialists? However displaced the role of consciousness might be in contemporary philosophy, it remains an intriguing feature of existence worth deep philosophical consideration.
- *Freedom and constraint.* Arguably one of the greatest resistances to existentialism today is the apparent implausibility of Sartre's radical views on the scope of human freedom, especially in *Being and Nothingness*. Again the work of structuralists, poststructuralists, and others has made us acutely aware of the limitations of this view. However, not only did many existentialists not share Sartre's radical views on freedom here (e.g. Nietzsche, Merleau-Ponty and de Beauvoir), but Sartre himself later came to realize the extent to which constraints, particularly the constraints of exploitative social and political structures, limit human freedom, and attempted to negotiate freedom and constraint in a more adequate way in his existential Marxist philosophy (cf. Flynn, 1997, 2005). New research in existentialism today must take a similarly critical view of the often-exaggerated views of human freedom in 'classic' existentialism.

Like all profound developments in the history of philosophy, the tradition of existentialism is far from exhausted. Rather than existentialism being passé, it is such a dismissal which is itself passé: it was in large part the symptom of a generation of thinkers trying to ward off the 'anxiety of influence'. It is typical of philosophers of each generation – perhaps especially in France – to oppose themselves to the ideas of the previous generation; typically what happens is that they remain in important respects influenced by the generation who taught them and whose books they grew up reading, but this influence is something they strive to cover over. We hope to have charted some of these possible hidden influences in the preceding pages. Moreover, for a number of decades now it has been common for scholars of Nietzsche, Heidegger, and other figures associated with existentialism to emphatically denounce this association, sometimes through a vocal opposition to Sartre. Such a move served to shore up the respectability of their philosophical concerns against the potential discrediting effects of 'popular' existentialism.

We assert that such a time has passed. The separation from such anxieties, which time has now allowed (time may not heal all wounds, but it allows a certain scarification to take place), enables us to attend once again to the existentialist tradition with a more serious, and less ideological, eye, and to mine its rich resources for engaging with current and persistent philosophical problems. From the degree of distance we have now gained, we may make a fairer assessment of the ideas of both the existentialist and poststructuralist generations, and the patterns of both resonance and dissonance that are revealed in comparisons between them.

Notes

1. Some parts of this chapter reprise, and transform, elements of the final chapter of Jack Reynolds, *Understanding Existentialism* (Durham, UK: Acumen, 2006).
2. Of course, it is arguable that this opposition is an exaggerated one and that Foucault protests a little too much (Gutting, 2008). Certainly both differently partake in a certain French tradition of the engaged public intellectual that derives from Voltaire and Zola, among others.
3. The most well-known expression of this is Foucault's interest in the subject in the last period of his works, as discussed above. For a discussion of a renewed interest in the subject in the late Lyotard, see Williams (2000).

Bibliography

Badiou, A. (2003), *Infinite Thought*, trans. and ed. O. Feltham and J. Clemens. London: Continuum.
Baudrillard, J. (2001), *Impossible Exchange*, trans. C. Turner. London: Verso.
— (2003), *Passwords*, trans. C. Turner. London: Verso.
De Beauvoir, S. (1976), *The Ethics of Ambiguity*, trans. B. Frechtman. New York: Kensington Publishing.

Deleuze, G. (2004a), *Desert Islands and Other Texts*, trans. F. Guillame. New York: Semiotext(e).
— (2004b), *The Logic of Sense*, trans. M. Lester and C. Stivale. London: Continuum.
Derrida, J. (1985), *Margins of Philosophy*, trans. A. Bass. Chicago: University of Chicago Press.
— (1996), *The Gift of Death*, trans. D. Wills. Chicago: University of Chicago Press.
— (1997), *Politics of Friendship*, trans. G. Collins. London: Verso.
— (1999), *Adieu to Emmanuel Levinas*, trans. P.-A. Brault and M. Naas. Palo Alto, CA: Stanford University Press.
Derrida, J. and M. Ferraris (2001), *A Taste for the Secret*. Cambridge: Polity.
Flynn, T. (1997, 2005, 2 vols), *Sartre, Foucault, and Historical Reason*. Chicago: University of Chicago Press.
Foucault, M. (2001), *Dits et Écrits*, vol. 1. Paris: Gallimard.
— (1989), The *Order of Things*. London: Routledge.
Fox, N. F. (2003), *The New Sartre: Explorations in Postmodernism*. New York: Continuum.
Gutting, G. (2008), 'Michel Foucault', *Stanford Encyclopedia of Philosophy*. http://plato.stanford.edu/entries/foucault/
Hallward, P. (2003), *Badiou: A Subject to Truth*. Minneapolis and London: University of Minnesota Press.
Heidegger, M. (1998), 'Letter on "Humanism"', in W. McNeill (ed.), *Pathmarks*. Cambridge: Cambridge University Press.
Howells, C. (1998), *Derrida: Deconstruction from Phenomenology to Ethics*. Cambridge: Polity.
Lyotard, J.-F. (1986), 'A Success of Sartre's', foreword in D. Hollier, *The Politics of Prose: Essay on Sartre*. Minneapolis: University of Minnesota Press.
Miller, James (1993), *The Passion of Michel Foucault*. Cambridge, MA: Harvard University Press.
Morris, P. S. (1997), 'Self-Creating Selves: Sartre and Foucault'. *American Catholic Philosophical Quarterly* 70 (4): 537–49.
Rajan, T. (2002), *Deconstruction and the Remainders of Phenomenology*. Stanford: Stanford University Press.
Reynolds, J. (2004), *Merleau-Ponty and Derrida: Intertwining Embodiment and Alterity*. Athens, OH: Ohio University Press.
— (2008), 'Touched by Time: Some Critical Reflections on Derrida's Reading of Merleau-Ponty in *Le Toucher*'. *Sophia* 47 (3): 311–25.
Reynolds, J. and J. Roffe (2006), 'Merleau-Ponty and Deleuze: Immanence, Univocity and Phenomenology'. *Journal of the British Society of Phenomenology* 37 (3): 228–51.
Sartre, J- P. (1958), *Being and Nothingness*, trans. H. Barnes. London: Routledge.
— (1960), *The Transcendence of the Ego: An Existentialist Theory of Consciousness*, trans. F. Williams and R. Kirkpatrick. New York: Hill and Wang.
— (1975), 'Existentialism is a Humanism', in W. Kaufmann (ed.), *Existentialism from Doestoevsky to Sartre*. New York: Meridian.

Vattimo, G. (1993), 'The Decline of the Subject and the Problem of Testimony', in *The Adventure of Difference: Philosophy After Nietzsche and Heidegger*, trans. C. Blamires with T. Harrison. Baltimore, MD: Johns Hopkins University Press.

Williams, J. (2000), 'The Last Refuge from Nihilism'. *International Journal of Philosophical Studies* 8 (1): 115–24.

Žižek, S. (1999), *The Ticklish Subject*. London: Verso.

15 Recent Developments in Scholarship on Key Existentialists

I. Kierkegaard

William McDonald

Søren Kierkegaard is now a global phenomenon. His work has been translated into dozens of languages, Kierkegaard societies have sprung up on almost every continent, international conferences on his work are held frequently, and his work is discussed widely on the internet.[1] He has been anthologized, bowdlerized, abridged, put in a nutshell, reduced to 90 minutes, and even turned into a comic book (see Bretall, 1973; Van De Weyer, 1997; Strathern, 2001; Robinson and Zarate, 2006). In addition, Kierkegaard's work continues to attract serious scholarship.

The most extensive developments in recent scholarship are due to the activities of the Søren Kierkegaard Research Centre in Copenhagen. The centrepiece of these activities is the production of a new Danish edition of Kierkegaard's writings, consisting of 28 volumes of Kierkegaard's writings plus 27 volumes of commentary (Cappelørn et al., 1997–). Each volume of Kierkegaard's writings, meticulously reconstructed from earlier editions, notebooks and journals, is accompanied by its own volume of commentary, in which line-by-line comment is made on textual variations, literary allusions, contemporary historical events and other material deemed relevant to textual critique, philological accuracy and historical realism. The new edition corrects mistakes in the first three editions of Kierkegaard's *Samlede Værker* [Collected Works] and thoroughly revises, regroups and corrects the earlier edition of Kierkegaard's *Papirer* [Papers]. It is set to become the standard primary source for Kierkegaard scholarship.

The new edition is supplemented by a multivolume reference work in English, titled *Kierkegaard Research: Sources, Reception and Resources*, under the general editorship of Jon Stewart, comprising a projected 41 books (Stewart, 2007b). The first tranche of volumes in this series consists of interdisciplinary essays which identify the sources of Kierkegaard's thought, together with their importance and influence on his work. The sources include ancient Greek and Roman, biblical, patristic, medieval, renaissance and modern traditions, as well as Kierkegaard's German and Danish contemporaries. The second set of volumes documents Kierkegaard's global reception, on the one hand geographically, in tomes devoted to 'Northern and Western Europe', 'Southern, Central and Eastern Europe' and 'The Near East, Asia, Australia and the Americas'; on the other hand thematically, in tomes devoted, respectively, to Kierkegaard's influences on existentialism, theology, philosophy, literature, social sciences and social–political thought. The *Resources* section of the *Kierkegaard Research* series includes volumes on *Kierkegaard's Concepts, Kierkegaard's Literary Figures and Motifs, Kierkegaard Organizations and Publication Series, Kierkegaard Secondary Literature,* a *Kierkegaard Bibliography* and *The Auction Catalogue of Kierkegaard's Library.* The aim of the series is that 'the articles will constitute the natural point of departure for any future investigation into the issue in question'.[2]

Another contribution from the Søren Kierkegaard Research Centre is a series of English translations of key texts by Kierkegaard's contemporaries (Stewart, 2005–).[3] These include five volumes of works by J. L. Heiberg, Copenhagen's literary doyen in the Danish 'Golden Age' and the person most responsible for popularizing Hegel's philosophy among Danish intellectuals. They also include works by J. P. Mynster, Bishop Primate of the Danish People's Church, F. C. Sibbern, professor of philosophy at Copenhagen University, Poul Martin Møller, Kierkegaard's closest philosophical and literary mentor and Hans Christian Andersen. The availability of these texts in English translation greatly enhances the capacity of English-language readers to understand Kierkegaard's response to his Danish contemporaries.

These translations are supplemented by a series of monographs and edited collections on themes from the Danish 'Golden Age' (Stewart, 2007a). The series includes the following: K. Brian Söderquist, *The Isolated Self: Truth and Untruth in Søren Kierkegaard's* On the Concept of Irony; Robert Leslie Horn, *Positivity and Dialectic: A Study of the Theological Method of Hans Lassen Martensen;* Jon Stewart, *A History of Hegelianism in Golden Age Denmark;* Curtis L. Thompson, *Following the Cultured Public's Chosen One: Why Martensen Mattered to Kierkegaard;* Jon Stewart (ed.), *Johan Ludvig Heiberg: Philosopher, Littérateur, Dramaturge, and Political Thinker;* and Jon Stewart (ed.), *Hans Lassen Martensen: Philosopher and Speculative Theologian.*

In addition, the Søren Kierkegaard Research Centre produces a series of monographs and yearbooks (Cappelørn and Deuser, 1997– ; Cappelørn and Deuser, 1996–). The most recent monographs, all published by Walter de Gruyter, are as follows: Heiko Schulz, *Aneignung und Reflexion: Studien zur Rezeption Søren Kierkegaards* (2010); Jürgen v. Stolzenberg and Smail Rapic, *Kierkegaard und Fichte* (2010); Karsten Harries, *Between Nihilism and Faith* (2010); Michael O. Bjergsø, *Kierkegaards deiktische Theologie* (2009); Daniel Greenspan, *The Passion of Infinity* (2008); Andreas Kirchbaum, *Kierkegaard und Schleiermacher* (2008); Marius Mjaaland, *Autopsia: Self, Death and God After Kierkegaard and Derrida* (2008); Smail Rapic, *Ethische Selbstverständigung* (2007); Joseph Westphal,

The Kierkegaardian Author (2007); Jochen Schmidt, *Vielstimmige Rede vom Unsagbaren*, (2006); and Joachim Boldt, *Kierkegaards 'Furcht und Zittern' als Bild seines ethischen Erkenntnisbegriffs* (2006). The *Kierkegaard Studies Yearbooks* consist of articles written on themes relevant to the volume of *Søren Kierkegaards Skrifter* published in the corresponding year.

The Søren Kierkegaard Research Centre also hosts a project on 'Self, Identity, and Reflexive Cognition' (see Stokes, 2010). The project is being undertaken by Patrick Stokes, and 'seeks to bring Kierkegaard's work on selfhood and reflexive thought into dialogue with contemporary analytic philosophy of self and personal identity'.[4] Stokes brings Kierkegaard's insights into relation with, among others, Derek Parfit, Galen Strawson, Kim Atkins, Daniel Hutto, David Velleman, Dan Zahavi, Shaun Gallagher and with neo-Lockean conceptions of selfhood. Stokes's project focuses on 'the relationship between imagination and self, the role of reflexive thought in self-constitution, and the role of narrative in the creation of the self' (2010).

Danish speakers are not the only beneficiaries of the new Danish edition of *Søren Kierkegaards Skrifter*, the whole edition is also being translated into German, Spanish and Dutch (Cappelørn et al., 2005–). The volumes of *Søren Kierkegaards Skrifter* devoted to his notebooks and journals are being translated into English and French (Cappelørn et al., 2007–).

English-language readers already have *Kierkegaard's Writings* (Kierkegaard, 1978–). Each volume has an historical introduction, comprehensive notes and supplementary texts derived from Kierkegaard's journals and provisional manuscripts. The English translations are supplemented by the series, *International Kierkegaard Commentary* (Perkins, 1984–2010), with each volume in the series devoted to essays on the corresponding volume of *Kierkegaard's Writings*. The articles are multidisciplinary, and broad-ranging in their approaches, scope and concerns.

Kierkegaardiana is a multilingual journal published under the auspices of the Danish Kierkegaard Society and the Department of Søren Kierkegaard Research, University of Copenhagen.[5] Kierkegaard conferences, events and publications are notified in the *International Kierkegaard Newsletter*. Founded and edited by the late Julia Watkin from 1980 until 2004, its publication has now been taken over by the Hong Kierkegaard Library at St Olaf College, Minnesota, where the *Søren Kierkegaard Newsletter* is also published.[6] The latter also contains articles and reviews.

The Hong Kierkegaard Library is another major centre for Kierkegaard studies. It houses the world's best single collection of Kierkegaard resources, in readily accessible form. It hosts a continuing stream of international Kierkegaard researchers and postgraduate students, as well as a series of *International Kierkegaard Conferences*. Although the Hong Kierkegaard Library and the Søren Kierkegaard Research Centre are the main drivers, there are other productive

Kierkegaard centres around the globe. A new series of scholarly volumes called *Acta Kierkegaardiana* has appeared. Its editorial board is spread between Slovakia, Canada, the United States and the United Kingdom. Its brief is to 'enrich our understanding of Kierkegaard in relation to his cultural and historical context, while also exploring how his ideas relate to contemporary concerns in philosophy, theology and literature'.[7]

Some recent scholarship focuses on understanding Kierkegaard's work in its historical context, while at the same time showing how Kierkegaard's engagement with broadly post-Kantian themes is still relevant and cogent (see, for example, Knappe, 2004; Kosch, 2006). Other recent scholarship seeks to show how Kierkegaard's work continues to be important by assimilating it to themes, arguments and strategies in the work of more recent thinkers. Monographs on this theme include Mulhall (2003), Schönbaumsfeld (2007), Davenport and Rudd (2001), Llewelyn (2009) and Westphal (2008). This aim is not confined to comparisons of Kierkegaard's work with that of other European thinkers. It also extends to religious and philosophical traditions from Asia. Most of these comparisons have been with Buddhist traditions, from Pure Land Buddhism to Mādhyamika and Zen, but also with Bushido, Shinto, Daoism and Confucianism (see Mortensen, 1996; Giles, 2008). They include comparisons with Dōgen, Hakuin, Nishida, Tsongkhapa and Zhuangzi.

Other recent scholarship pursues Kierkegaard's insights on narrative notions of the self, divine command ethics, moral psychology based on character, and analyses of particular virtues and passions (see, for example, Lippit, 2007; Evans, 2004; Stokes, 2010). The latter includes several studies of particular moods, affects and passions in Kierkegaard's work, particularly boredom, anxiety, despair and love (see, for example, McDonald, 2009b; Grøn, 2008; Theunissen, 2005; Mooney, 2008; Ferreira, 2001; Furtak, 2005). There has also been renewed interest in Kierkegaard's *Edifying Discourses*, which aim to build up in their readers positive affective states such as patience, hope, perseverance, devotion, resolve, faith and love (see Pattison, 2002; Walsh, 2006; Cappelørn et al., 2000).

Kierkegaard's concern for the existing individual, and his conviction that each of us has an urgent task to become an ethical–religious self in the face of anxiety, suffering and despair, still prompts passionate engagement in his readers. As temporal creatures driven by desire, constrained by finitude and fallibility, and vulnerable to our herd instincts, it is difficult to attain spiritual equilibrium. According to Kierkegaard, in modern humanism our hubris has grown to monstrous proportions, yet the task of selfhood requires humility, patience, faith, devotion, resignation, renunciation, repentance and inner strength. In particular, Kierkegaard was concerned to combat the bombastic claims of speculative philosophy to achieve absolute reason, and thereby to be conscious of all reality. He demonstrated the emptiness of such claims, and the hollow promises upon which they were based. His critiques of speculative philosophy and his careful portrayals of existential types – fictional characters, who embody life-views (*Livsanskuelser*) and life-developments (*Livsudviklinger*) – fed into the search in existentialism for authenticity. Although Adorno's critique of Heidegger in *The Jargon of Authenticity* (Adorno, 1973) undermines this existentialist project, as do postmodern and poststructuralist announcements of 'the death of man', recent Kierkegaard scholarship continues to explore questions of the constitution of the self, its psychological and social obstacles and resources, and its ethical and spiritual goals. This scholarship, however, focuses on unpacking particular notions such as inwardness, anxiety, despair, happiness, imagination, freedom and love,[8] rather than pursuing the question of authenticity – a question never at the centre of Kierkegaard scholarship anyway. It also continues to provide critiques of philosophical pretension, whether in the guise of analytic scientism or continental obscurantism.[9]

Although Kierkegaard was assimilated to existentialist philosophy, especially because of his influence on Heidegger, relatively little Kierkegaard scholarship has focused on his existentialism as such. So the flux in philosophical fashion affecting the popularity of existentialism has barely touched Kierkegaard scholarship.[10]

However, there is considerable interest in comparing Kierkegaard's work with that of French philosophers of religion, including Emmanuel Levinas, Jacques Derrida, Michel Henry, Gabriel Marcel and Jacques Maritain, whose work has at least some elements which might be construed as existentialist.[11] This interest also underpins the radical theology of writers such as John D. Caputo and Mark C. Taylor, whose work continues to engage with Kierkegaard (see Caputo, 2007; Caputo and Vattimo, 2007; Taylor, 2007). Scholars are also still finding inspiration in what Kierkegaard has to say on the central existentialist themes of temporality, death and everyday life (see Stokes and Buben, 2010; Kylliänen, 2009).

Kierkegaard scholarship was split in the last two decades of the twentieth century over pro- and anti-postmodern interpretations of his work. The postmodern interpretations tended to sideline existentialist interpretations, which found more of a home in theological and analytic Kierkegaard scholarship – or were ignored altogether. The postmodernists in the debate have mainly moved on to radical theology and to recuperating themes from recent Continental philosophers other than postmodern eclecticism, semantic scepticism and ironic iconoclasm.[12] This has freed some space for renewed consideration of Kierkegaard and existentialism. The most recent scholarship explicitly on Kierkegaard and existentialism generally takes an historical perspective, looking particularly at the existentialist reception of Kierkegaard. This includes his reception in existential theology and literature, as well as philosophy. It connects Kierkegaard with Dostoevsky, Shestov, Berdyaev, Kafka, Camus, Buber, Rosenzweig, Jaspers, Unamuno, de Beauvoir, Sartre, Wahl, and others (see Nagy, 1997;

Stewart, forthcoming; Hubben, 1997). No attempt is made to distance Kierkegaard from existentialism, since Kierkegaard's influence on existentialism is incorporated as only one strand of Kierkegaard reception.

Recent Kierkegaard scholarship is booming around the world, not least in South America, Central Europe and Asia. Although Kierkegaard's Christian existentialism remains at the centre of interest in his work, recent scholarship is by no means bound by the concerns of twentieth-century European existentialism. It also extends to Asian existentialism (see Giles, 2008). The breadth of research is impossible to capture in an essay of this length. Despite all the scholarship, Kierkegaard's work lives with all its original passion and insight for 'that single individual' – his heartfelt reader.

Notes

1. See Hubert L. Dreyfus, 'Kierkegaard on the Internet: Anonymity vs Commitment in the Present Age', http://socrates.berkeley.edu/~hdreyfus/html/paper_kierkegaard.html; The Søren Kierkegaard Research Centre Copenhagen, www.sk.ku.dk/eng.asp; articles in *The Stanford Encyclopedia of Philosophy*, http://plato.stanford.edu/entries/kierkegaard/, and *The Internet Encyclopedia of Philosophy*, www.iep.utm.edu/kierkega/
2. www.sk.ku.dk/KRSRR/section1.htm
3. The series comprises a projected ten volumes.
4. Patrick Stokes, www.sk.ku.dk/stokes/about.htm
5. For a full list of contents of *Kierkegaardiana* volumes 1–23, 1955–2004, see www.sk.ku.dk/selskab/kierkegaardiana.htm
6. Søren Kierkegaard Newsletter, 1980–2009 (www.stolaf.edu/collections/kierkegaard/newsletters/); Julia Watkin (ed.), International Kierkegaard Newsletter, 1979–2005 (www.stolaf.edu/collections/kierkegaard/watkin/newsletters.html).
7. Acta Kierkegaardiana: www.actakierkegaardiana.com/
8. On inwardness, see Carlisle (2005). On anxiety, see Grøn (2008). On despair, see Theunissen (2005). On happiness, see Kahn (1985). On imagination, see Ferreira (1991). On love, see Ferreira (2001).
9. For an extended discussion of Kierkegaard's critique of 'chatter' see Fenves (1993). See also Hale (2002), for discussions of Kierkegaard on the limits of language and science.
10. In some parts of the world, the assimilation to existentialism was the initial vehicle for the discovery of Kierkegaard, and interest in Kierkegaard suffered when existentialism was displaced by the French poststructuralists. See McDonald (2009a).
11. On Kierkegaard and Levinas, see Westphal (2008). On Derrida, see Llewelyn (2009). On Henry, see Stan (forthcoming). On Marcel, see Knox (forthcoming). On Maritain, see Kramer (forthcoming).
12. Mark C. Taylor and Louis Mackey edited a series for Florida State University Press called 'Kierkegaard and Postmodernism'. See also Matuštík and Westphal (1995), and Jegstrup (2004). For a critique of postmodern interpretations of Kierkegaard, see Walsh (1991).

Bibliography

Adorno, T. W. (1973), *The Jargon of Authenticity*, trans. K. Tarnowski and F. Will. London: Routledge.

Bretall, R. (ed.) (1973), *A Kierkegaard Anthology*. Princeton: Princeton University Press.

Cappelørn, N. J. and H. Deuser (eds) (1996–), *Kierkegaard Studies Yearbook*. Berlin: Walter de Gruyter.

— (eds) (1997–), *Kierkegaard Monograph Series*. Berlin: Walter de Gruyter.

Cappelørn, N. J., H. Deuser, H. Anz and H. Schulz (eds) (2005–), *Deutsche Søren Kierkegaard Edition*. Berlin: Walter de Gruyter; *Escritos de Soeren Kierkegaard*, Editorial Trotta; *Kierkegaard Werken Redaktieraad*, Damon (2008).

Cappelørn, N. J. et al. (eds) (1997–), *Søren Kierkegaards Skrifter*. København: G.E.C. Gads Forlag.

— (eds) (2000), *Kierkegaard Studies Yearbook 2000*. Berlin: Walter de Gruyter.

— (eds) (2007–), *Kierkegaard's Journals and Notebooks*. Princeton: Princeton University Press; *Journaux et cahiers de notes*. Editions Fayard/Editions L'Orante.

Caputo, J. D. (2007), *How to Read Kierkegaard*. London: Granta Books.

Caputo, J. D. and G. Vattimo (2007), *After the Death of God*. New York: Columbia University Press.

Carlisle, C. (2005), *Kierkegaard's Philosophy of Becoming: Movements and Positions*. Albany, NY: SUNY Press.

Davenport, J. and A. Rudd (eds) (2001), *Kierkegaard after McIntyre: Essays on Freedom, Narrative and Virtue*. Chicago: Open Court.

Evans, S. (2004), *Kierkegaard's Ethic of Love: Divine Commands and Moral Requirements*. London: Oxford University Press.

Fenves, P. (1993), *'Chatter': Language and History in Kierkegaard*. Stanford: Stanford University Press.

Ferreira, M. J. (1991), *Transforming Vision: Imagination and Will in Kierkegaardian Faith*. Oxford: Clarendon Press.

— (2001), *Love's Grateful Striving: A Commentary on Kierkegaard's* Works of Love. London: Oxford University Press.

Furtak, R. (2005), *Wisdom in Love: Kierkegaard and the Ancient Quest for Emotional Integrity*. Notre Dame, Indiana: University of Notre Dame Press.

Giles, J. (ed.) (2008), *Kierkegaard and Japanese Thought*. Basingstoke: Palgrave Macmillan.

Grøn, A. (2008), *The Concept of Anxiety in Søren Kierkegaard*, trans. J. B. L. Knox. Macon: Mercer University Press.

Hale, G. A. (2002), *Kierkegaard and the Ends of Language*. Minneapolis and London: University of Minnesota Press.

Hubben, W. (1997), *Dostoevsky, Kierkegaard, Nietzsche and Kafka*. New York: Simon & Schuster.

Jegstrup, E. (ed.) (2004), *The New Kierkegaard*. Bloomington, IN: Indiana University Press.

Kahn, A. (1985), Salighed *as Happiness: Kierkegaard on the Concept* Salighed. Waterloo, ON: Wilfred Laurier University Press.

Kierkegaard, S. (1978–), *Kierkegaard's Writings*, ed. H. V. Hong and E. H. Hong. Princeton: Princeton University Press.

Knappe, U. (2004), *Theory and Practice in Kant and Kierkegaard*. Berlin: Walter de Gruyter.

Knox, J. B. L. (forthcoming), 'Gabriel Marcel: The Silence of Truth', in Stewart (forthcoming).

Kosch, M. (2006), *Freedom and Reason in Kant, Schelling, and Kierkegaard*. London: Oxford University Press.

Kramer, N. (forthcoming), 'Jacques Maritain: Kierkegaard as "Champion of the Singular"', in Stewart (forthcoming).

Kylliänen, J. (2009), *Living Poetically in the Modern Age: The Situational Aspects of Kierkegaard's Thought*. Philosophical Studies from the University of Helsinki 24.

Lippit, J. (2007), 'Getting the Story Straight: Kierkegaard, MacIntyre and Some Problems with Narrative'. *Inquiry* 50: 34–69.

Llewelyn, J. (2009), *Margins of Religion: Between Kierkegaard and Derrida*. Bloomington, IN: Indiana University Press.

McDonald, W. (2009a), 'Australia: An Archaeology of the Silence of Kierkegaard's Philosophical Reception', in J. Stewart (ed.), *Kierkegaard Studies: Sources, Reception, and Resources* vol. 8. Aldershot: Ashgate.

McDonald, W. (2009b), 'Kierkegaard's Demonic Boredom', in C. Salzani and B. dalla Pezza (eds), *Essays on Boredom and Modernity*. Amsterdam and New York: Rodopi.

Matuštík, M. J. and M. Westphal (eds) (1995), *Kierkegaard in Post/Modernity*. Bloomington, IN: Indiana University Press.

Mooney, E. F. (ed.) (2008), *Ethics, Love, and Faith in Kierkegaard*. Bloomington, IN and Indianapolis: Indiana University Press.

Mortensen, F. H. (1996), *Kierkegaard Made in Japan*. Odense: University Press of Southern Denmark.

Mulhall, S. (2003), *Inheritance and Originality: Wittgenstein, Heidegger, and Kierkegaard*. London: Oxford University Press.

Nagy, A. (1997), 'The Ultimate Paradox: Existentialism at the Crossroads of Religious Philosophy and Bolshevism', in N. J. Cappelørn and J. Stewart (eds), *Kierkegaard Revisited: Proceedings of the Conference 'Kierkegaard and the Meaning of Meaning It'*. Berlin: Walter de Gruyter.

Pattison, G. (2002), *Kierkegaard's Upbuilding Discourses: Philosophy, Literature and Theology*. London: Routledge.

Perkins, R. L. (ed.) (1984–2010), *International Kierkegaard Commentary*, 24 vols. Macon: Mercer University Press.

Robinson, D. and O. Zarate (2006), *Introducing Kierkegaard*. London: Icon Books.

Schönbaumsfeld, G. (2007), *A Confusion of Spheres: Kierkegaard and Wittgenstein on Philosophy and Religion*. London: Oxford University Press.

Stan, L. (forthcoming), 'Michel Henry: The Goodness of Living Affectivity', in Stewart (forthcoming).

Stewart, J. (ed.) (2005–), *Texts from Golden Age Denmark*. Copenhagen: Museum Tusculanum Press.

— (ed.) (2007a), *Danish Golden Age Studies*. Copenhagen: Museum Tusculanum Press.

— (ed.) (2007b), *Kierkegaard Research: Sources, Reception and Resources*. London: Ashgate.

— (ed.) (forthcoming), *KRSRR Volume 9: Kierkegaard's Influence on Existentialism*. Aldershot, etc.: Ashgate, (forthcoming).

Stokes, P. (2010), *Kierkegaard's Mirrors: Interest, Self, and Moral Vision*. Basingstoke: Palgrave Macmillan.

Stokes, P. and A. Buben (eds) (2010), *Kierkegaard and Death*. Bloomington, IN: Indiana University Press.

Strathern, P. (2001), *Kierkegaard in 90 Minutes*. Lanham, MD: Ivan R. Dee.

Taylor, M. C. (2007), *After God*. Chicago: University of Chicago Press.

Theunissen, M. (2005), *Kierkegaard's Concept of Despair*, trans. B. Harshav and H. Illbruck. Princeton: Princeton University Press.

Van De Weyer, R. (ed.) (1997), *Kierkegaard in a Nutshell*. London: Hodder & Stoughton.

Walsh, S. (1991), 'Kierkegaard and Postmodernism'. *International Journal for Philosophy of Religion* 29 (2): 113–22.

— (2006), *Living Christianly: Kierkegaard's Dialectic of Christian Existence*. University Park, PA: Pennsylvania State University Press.

Westphal, M. (2008), *Levinas and Kierkegaard in Dialogue*. Bloomington, IN: Indiana University Press.

II. Nietzsche

Keith Ansell-Pearson

It has long been customary to identify Nietzsche, along with Kierkegaard, as a nineteenth-century precursor of existentialism. His links with existentialism have been established on the basis of his celebration of radical individual freedom and his general campaign against all beliefs and philosophies which ascribe to the world, human existence and history a purpose or goal other than the meaning imposed by man himself (Copleston, 1965, p. 194; see also Blackham, 1961). However, as a number of recent commentators have pointed out, Nietzsche's denial of free will – at least as conceived as a metaphysical *causa sui* – and his biological naturalism places him at a distance from existentialism (Reynolds, 2006, p. 9; see also Cooper, 1999, p. 9; for new research on Nietzsche and free will see Gemes, 2006). As Reynolds notes, Nietzsche is an enigmatic figure in the history of philosophy, one not easily reducible to *any* school or movement of philosophy.

The current climate in Nietzsche scholarship is largely hostile to construing Nietzsche as an existentialist. For example, even someone like Robert C. Solomon, who has long read Nietzsche as an existentialist, felt compelled in his final study to ask the question, 'Is Nietzsche an existentialist?' (Solomon, 2003, p. 206). Richard Schacht, one of the most eminent Anglo-American commentators on Nietzsche, has gone so far as to advise that we 'try to forget about existentialism' if we wish to get Nietzsche aright on matters concerning morals and normativity (Schacht, 2001, p. 151). There have been several notable trends in recent scholarship that in their different ways call into question the value of approaching Nietzsche as an existentialist. I regard these efforts as misguided and am keen to defend Nietzsche's project as one of authenticity. Some commentators on Nietzsche express an antipathy towards existentialism on account of its alleged idealistic and romantic claims for independence and self-expression or self-assertion (informing Schacht's judgement above is the view that existentialism is a form of radical individualism). Thus, in his instructive reading of Nietzsche as an ethicist, Simon May contends that Nietzsche is not an existentialist at all since the latter presupposes a voluntaristic break with tradition, history and the past that Nietzsche does not entertain. Freedom presupposes, as its condition – as 'fate' or 'necessity' – 'the reality of our nature, nurture, and life-circumstances, and hence of our individual past . . . . "Freedom of the will" – which, for him, means mastery of ourselves and thus of circumstances – is unattainable without maximally expressing what he calls the "necessity" of our own nature' (May, 1999, p. 21). This point does not rest on a denial of contingency; it is rather the recognition that what may be contingent as one's history is necessity as one's fate; 'only by maximally expressing – i.e. "willing" – that necessity can one be free' (p. 22).

Arguably this rests on a caricature of existentialism, and certain self-proclaimed existentialists, such as Merleau-Ponty, never construed freedom in the way suggested here (Merleau-Ponty, 1989, III: 3). Moreover, as Heidegger would point out, fate requires, as the ontological condition for its possibility, the state of Being of care or temporality: 'Only if death, guilt, conscience, freedom, and finitude reside together equiprimordially in the Being of an entity as they do in care, can that entity exist in the mode of fate' (Heidegger, 1980, pp. 436–7). For Heidegger, as Mulhall points out, the heritage of one's culture, into which one is thrown and dispersed, and the heritage of oneself, as the potentiality for authentic individuality, 'fuse in a mutually revivifying way' (Mulhall, 1996, p. 170). Only by grasping the finitude of my existence, which serves to make it something fateful, am I 'snatched back', Heidegger says, from an endless multiplicity of possibilities and in fact brought into contact with the simplicity of *Dasein*'s fate. As Mulhall notes, what Heidegger is offering is a vision of freedom peculiar to a finite and conditioned being (mortal freedom): '*Dasein*'s capacity to choose how to live and who to be is real and distinctive. But it cannot choose not to have this capacity, and it must exercise it in circumstances that it has not freely chosen and upon a range of possibilities that it has not itself defined' (Mulhall, 1996, p. 171). This can only mean that my freedom comes to fulfilment not through an attempted transcendence of limits and constraints, but through a 'resolute acceptance of them as they really are – through a clear-sighted acknowledgement of the necessities and accidents of one's situation and one's fate' (p. 171).

The dominant trend in recent scholarship is to interpret Nietzsche as a naturalist. However, Nietzsche has been linked with several different naturalisms: methodological (Leiter, 2002), existential (Hatab, 2005) and artful (Acampora, 2006a; see also Acampora, 2010). In some cases Nietzsche's naturalism is seen to conflict with existentialism, in other cases not. Hatab construes Nietzsche's project as one of 'existential naturalism' which is, he says, not a reductive naturalism in terms of the categories of science, 'but an embrace of the finite limit conditions of worldly existence as the new measure of thought' (2005, pp. 7, 14). With the death of God we are left with a choice of either a nihilistic collapse of meaning or a revaluation of meaning in terms of the immanent conditions of finite life. Leiter, by contrast, develops his interpretation of Nietzsche as a naturalist and fatalist by contesting the so-called existentialist reading developed by the likes of Alexander Nehamas (1985) and Richard Rorty (1989), and which, it is alleged, has its source in Karl Jaspers's 1936 interpretation of Nietzsche as an ethicist of self-creation (Jaspers, 1965, pp. 151–62). For Leiter, Nietzsche is a naturalist in the sense of someone who holds that the claims of philosophy should be continuous with the methods and insights of natural science, and he is a fatalist because for him the basic character of an individual's life is fixed in advance by virtue of the largely immutable physiological and psychological facts that make the person who s/he is (Leiter, 2001). Leiter has been taken to task by Owen and Ridley, who seek to demonstrate the roots of Nietzsche's thinking on fate in the writings of Ralph Waldo Emerson (1803–1882), for whom there is no fatal opposition between fate and the assumption of creative agency (Owen and Ridley, 2003). When they point out that for Emerson the strong human being views fate – the inevitable appearance of chance and necessity in our lives – not simply as a negative constraint but as providing the materials and means for freedom, one gets the distinct impression that this is an anticipation on Emerson's part of the well-known dialectic of facticity and transcendence that lies at the centre of existentialist thinking on agency and our being in the world. For Owen and Ridley the self is never a fully developed fact but something that works out 'possibilities' (2003, p. 67). Indeed, a stress on there being 'possibilities of life' is a recurring refrain of Nietzsche's thought and famously he describes man as the as-yet-undetermined animal (*Beyond Good and Evil* 62).

The key point is that constraints are not opposed to freedom, but are its condition. As Guay has noted in an article on 'Nietzsche and Freedom': 'Constraints are thus productive: they create the possibility of novel activities' (2002, p. 308). 'Morality' in Nietzsche's eyes is that mode of thought which fantasizes about a metaphysical subject that bootstraps itself into existence and so encourages 'a quite peculiar conception of autonomy' (Ridley, 2005, p. xiii). On this conception the self is only properly self-governing and responsible for its actions to the extent that what it does is the product of freedom of the will in the superlative metaphysical sense, the sense that Nietzsche takes to task, for example, in *Beyond Good and Evil* (e.g. sec. 21) as the desire to pull oneself into existence by the hair and out of the swamps of nothingness. This supposes a freedom that makes it independent of our nature – be it a first or second nature – and of our circumstances. As Ridley further points out, for Nietzsche 'necessities' have to be acknowledged and worked over and considered 'as material to be exploited and, where possible, affirmed' (2005, p. xiii; see, for example, *The Gay Science* 290 and *Beyond Good and Evil* 188). This explains why Nietzsche famously says that to become creators we must also become 'the best learners and discoverers of everything that is lawful and necessary in the world: we must become *physicists* in order to be able to be *creators*' (*The Gay Science* 335). We may note that the early Nietzsche conceived of education as first and foremost an instruction in what is necessary (nature) and then in the changing and the variable (civil society). It is here that the question arises concerning whether things must be as they are (e.g. are the laws of civil society invariable?). History is the inquiry into how things have become what they are and shows that things could be different. The task is to ascertain how much power the human being has. The Greeks, for example, show us how different human existence can be, while the Romans show us how things became what they are for us (*KSA* 8, 5 [64]). The aim of education is not to teach submission to necessity, since we have to know first what is necessary and there might be many necessities (*KSA* 5 [21]).

Although Leiter has pertinent criticisms to make of the overly voluntarist readings of Nietzsche we encounter in Nehamas and Rorty, when the attempt is made to then discredit Nietzsche's credentials as an existentialist it is more often than not a straw man of existentialism that is being denounced. As several commentators have pointed out, existentialism does not rest on a disavowal of contingency, the past, history, and so on, since in a condition of pure possibility nothing would motivate or compel us with any degree of urgency (Reynolds, 2006, p. 33). Although 'possibility' has an ontological priority in existentialist thinkers such as Heidegger and Sartre, it is not thought independently of the dimensions of facticity and actuality (Reynolds, 2006, p. 34; Gorner, 2007, p. 79), and thus to portray existentialism as advocating romantic self-creation – self-creation in the bootstrapping sense – is to produce something of a wild caricature. As Jaspers points out, Nietzsche's thinking suffers when he denies 'transcendence' or the domain of existential possibilities and reduces living to the domain of biological or natural actualities. At the level of existence, he notes, it is impossible to separate the physiological or causal – as well as the psychological and sociological – from 'Existenz', so that whatever we come to know of ourselves through the investigation of science is so intimately bound up with us that we could not exist without it. At the same time it is important we recognize that existential possibility and physiological and psychological actuality are involved with each other. He notes that Nietzsche himself denies the doctrine of the unchangeability of character and condemns the average man's belief in himself as a fully developed state of affairs (see D 560). Nietzsche's adherence to Pindar's maxim, 'become what you are!', is rendered meaningless if it is made to refer merely to 'an innate just-being-so as a psychological state of affairs' (Jaspers, 1965, p. 159). This is arguably what Leiter's naturalist and fatalist reading of Nietzsche on how one becomes what one is does. As Jaspers astutely notes, in the maxim it is not a definite law or objectively derivable obligation that decides, but rather 'reliance on the "creative" source in me', which may be lacking (1965, p. 159). We should also note the placing of 'creative' in scare quotes (which Leiter does not acknowledge), since, as Jaspers also observes, 'creation' is one of those 'signs' of Nietzsche's philosophizing that, like life, eternal recurrence, and will to power, is never fully or adequately conceptualized (1965, p. 152). In addition, as Janaway has noted, although the precise extent to which Nietzsche is successful in seeking to combine his naturalistic accounts of the human being with an account of 'creative agency' may be subject to debate, 'it is wrong to think that he wishes to exclude creative agency from his picture of humanity' – without it his critique of moral values and task of learning to think and feel differently (D 103) makes little sense (Janaway, 2007, p. 123).

In the rest of this entry I want to focus on what I see as the core issue in considering Nietzsche's relation to existentialism, namely, the extent to which, and the ways in which, he anticipates existentialism's search for an authentic mode of existence. In thinking through this question, I am influenced by the claim that existentialism introduces into philosophical discourse a *new* norm – that of authenticity – for understanding what it means to be human, and that this is different to the norm of truth championed by natural science and the norms of the good and the right that lie at the heart of moral theory (see Crowell, 2010, p. 2). This norm is tied to a distinctive, post-Cartesian concept of self as practical, embodied, being-in-the-world (2010, p. 25). I find it uncontroversial that Nietzsche is a thinker of such embodied agency. Moreover, as David E. Cooper has stressed, a persistent theme in the writings of existentialists is the contrast between the life of the authentic individual and the life immersed in the anonymous crowd, herd, or mass (1999, p. 110). Along with Kierkegaard, Nietzsche is one of the first modern writers to paint such a contrast and to do so by making *explicit* reference to the task of the authentic human being. In the literature to date this has not been sufficiently demonstrated (but see Guay, 2002, for a good attempt).

Today notions of autonomy and sovereign individuality have been placed under suspicion in many quarters of philosophy and in some quarters of

Nietzsche studies (see Acampora, 2006b). Although a postmodern audience appears embarrassed by such notions, it remains the case that they inform Nietzsche's thinking on the tasks of philosophy at a very deep level. Sometimes it is flatly stated that Nietzsche denies the self without further investigation or any deep appreciation of his oeuvre (see Sorabji, 2006, p. 17). Other arguments offered against construing Nietzsche as a thinker of sovereign agency and autonomy include construing him as a thinker of fate, which he clearly is, though I see no good reason why he cannot have both a doctrine of fate and of sovereignty (on fate and freedom in Nietzsche see Richardson, 1996, pp. 208–9, and Acampora, 2010). The two concepts run throughout Nietzsche's oeuvre. Moreover, Nietzsche thinks that for us moderns existence often assumes the site of a tragic equivocation, structured as it is by an antinomy of fate and freedom (see *Thus Spoke Zarathustra*, 'On Old and New Tablets', p. 9). The sovereign individual is depicted by Nietzsche as an agent that has an awareness (the conscience) of power and freedom; it is master of a 'free will' (the power to make an independent decision, *Beyond Good and Evil* 208); it has an 'enduring, unbreakable will' and 'its own standard of value', and is 'strong enough to stand upright in the face of fate (*Schicksal*)' (note: it does not conquer fate, which is impossible) (*On the Genealogy of Morality* II, 2). In a notebook from 1873–1874 he says that the aim of wisdom is 'to enable a human being to face all the blows of fate (*Schicksalsschläge*) with equal firmness, to arm him for all times' (*KSA* 7, 30 [25]).

Nietzsche, I would contend, is a strong thinker of authenticity, which is arguably the core notion – and value – espoused by existentialism. Nietzsche opposes all attempts to define the human being through abstract or general categories, maintaining 'that the life of the individual cannot have its meaning in something historical, in his disappearance into some category' (*KSA* 7, 34 [32]). He first uses the expression 'authentic human being' in the *Unfashionable Observations* (1873–1876), although I think his overall free-spirited philosophy can, if one pays attention to its most essential tasks, be construed as a unified search for an authentic mode of existence. In the unfashionable observation on history Nietzsche draws a contrast between 'the common human being' who clutches at their animal existence with greed and gloomy earnestness, and those noble natures who live life heroically, bequeathing to posterity 'the signature of their most authentic being' (*das Monogramm ihres eigensten Wesens*), be it a work, a deed, or a creation (*UO* II: 2, p. 98; *KSA* p. 260). In the search for genuine or authentic (*Aechtheit*) personality Nietzsche subjects to criticism the cult of inwardness, the machine-like existence demanded by contemporary culture, and uniformity. Our age prides itself not on being the era of 'harmonious personalities' who are complete and mature, but of common, utilitarian labour: 'That simply means: human beings must be broken in to serve the purposes of the age, so they can be put to work' (*UO* II: 7). In the unfashionable observation on Schopenhauer as educator Nietzsche invites us to encounter, 'the fundamental law' of our 'authentic self' (*eigentlichen Selbst*) and seeks to awaken the individual to engage in a battle with everything that prevents it from achieving self-liberation: fear, cowardice, laziness, herd opinions, and custom and convention (*UO* III: 1). For Nietzsche each individual is confronted with a 'task' but finds it necessary to flee from it and drug itself with sociability (*UO* III: 5). Nietzsche attacks the 'morality' (*Sittlichkeit*) of education that holds sway in his time – 'a speedy education so that one quickly becomes a moneymaker' – which looks upon the education that makes human beings solitary and sets them goals beyond money and acquisition, as nothing more than refined egoism or immoral cultural Epicureanism (*UO* III: 6).

In *The Gay Science* 335 (1882) Nietzsche advises us as follows: 'Let us therefore *limit* ourselves to the purification of our opinions and valuations and to the *creation of our own new tables of what is good.*' In the unfashionable observation on Schopenhauer this works as the 'law' of the authentic self and higher life: 'your true being does not lie deeply hidden within you, but rather immeasurably high above you, or at least above what you commonly take to be your ego' (*UO* III: 1). In *Schopenhauer as Educator* it is the job of conscience to awaken the self to its task: ' "Be yourself! You are none of those things that you now do, think, and desire" ' (*UO* III: 1). In *The Gay Science* 335 it is the job of the 'intellectual conscience', the form of conscience superior to the moral conscience: what Nietzsche calls the conscience behind our conscience. Whatever the name of this conscience, the end is the same: to become what one 'is', where this refers to that which is 'unique, singular, incomparable'.

This preoccupation with identifying an authentic mode of existence, against the claims of common utilitarian morality, continues into Nietzsche's later texts. Let me take as my example *Dawn* (*D*) from 1881, part of Nietzsche's 'free-spirit' trilogy of 1878–1882 and also part of his so-called positivist or naturalist phase (see Abbey, 2000, pp. 7–10). Here Nietzsche argues that hitherto individuals have lived in fear and as conforming herd animals; they have concealed themselves in the communal generality of the concepts 'human being' and 'society'. Today the prejudice holds sway in Europe that the sympathetic affects, compassion and actions deemed to be congenial, disinterested or of general utility, define the moral. Although Nietzsche mentions Schopenhauer and Mill as famous teachers of this conception of morality, he holds that they merely echo doctrines that have been sprouting up in both fine and crude forms since the French Revolution (*D* 132). Central to modernity, as Nietzsche perceives it, is the idea that the ego must deny itself and adapt itself to the whole and as a result the 'individual' is debilitated and cancelled: 'one never tires of enumerating and excoriating everything evil and malicious, prodigal, costly, and extravagant in the prior form of individual existence . . . compassion for the individual and passion for society here go hand in hand' (*D* 132).

In an aphorism on 'pseudo-egotism' Nietzsche notes how most people live their life by doing nothing for their ego but live in accordance with the 'phantom ego' that has been formed in the opinions of those around them and is conveyed to them. The result is that we live in a fog of impersonal or half-personal opinions and arbitrary evaluations: 'one person always in the head of another and then again this head in other heads: a curious world of phantasms that nonetheless knows how to don such a sensible appearance!' (*D* 105). Even the modern glorification of work and talk of its blessings can be interpreted as a fear of everything individual. The subjection to hard industriousness from early until late serves as 'the best policeman' since it keeps everyone in bounds and hinders the development of reason, desire and the craving for independence. It uses vast amounts of nervous energy which could be given over to reflection, brooding, dreaming and working through our experiences: 'a society in which there is continuous hard work will have more security: and security is currently worshipped as the supreme divinity' (*D* 173). Nietzsche claims that it is the moral fashion of a commercial society to value actions aimed at common security and to cultivate above all the sympathetic affections. At work here he thinks is a collective drive towards timidity which desires that life be rid of all the dangers it might have once held: 'Are we not, with this prodigious intent to grate off all the rough and sharp edges of life, well on the way to turning humanity into *sand*!' (*D* 174). In place of the ruling ethic of sympathy and self-sacrifice, which can assume the form of a 'tyrannical encroachment', Nietzsche invites individuals to engage in self-fashioning, cultivating a self that the other can behold with pleasure, a 'lovely, peaceful, self-enclosed garden . . . with high walls to protect against the dangers and dust of the roadway, but with a hospitable gate as well' (*D* 174). Before an individual can practise benevolence towards others he has to be beneficently disposed towards himself, otherwise he is running from and hating himself, and seeking to rescue himself from himself in others (*D* 516).

Nietzsche notes that we typically adopt the evaluations which guide our actions out of fear and only pretend that they are our own; we then grow accustomed to the pretence that this ends up being our nature. To have one's own evaluation of things is something exceedingly rare (*D* 104). It is necessary to contest the idea that there is a single moral-making morality; every code of ethics that affirms itself in an exclusive manner 'destroys too much valuable energy and costs humanity much too dearly' (*D* 164). In the future, Nietzsche hopes, the inventive and fructifying person shall no longer be sacrificed and numerous new attempts at living life and creating community shall be undertaken. When this takes place we will find that an enormous load of guilty conscience has been purged from the world. Humanity has suffered for too long from teachers of morality who wanted too much all at once and sought to lay down precepts for everyone (*D* 194). Clearly, Nietzsche is not advocating the abolition of all possible types or forms of morality. Where morality centres on 'continual self-command and self-overcoming . . . in great things and in the smallest', Nietzsche is a champion of it (*The Wanderer and His Shadow* 45). His concern is that 'morality' in the forms it has assumed in the greater part of human history, right up to Kant's moral law, has opened up an abundance of sources of displeasure and with every refinement of morals the human being has only become more discontented with itself, its neighbour, and its lot (*D* 106). The individual in search of happiness, and who wishes to become its own lawgiver, cannot be tended with prescriptions for the path to happiness, simply because individual happiness springs from one's own unknown laws and external prescriptions only serve to obstruct and hinder it: 'The so-called "moral" precepts are, in truth, directed against individuals and are in no way aimed at promoting their happiness' (*D* 108). Up to now, Nietzsche notes, the moral law has been supposed to stand above our personal likes and dislikes; we did not want to impose this law upon ourselves but preferred to take it from somewhere or have it commanded to us. Nietzsche looks ahead to a possible future lawgiving, 'founded on the idea "I submit only to the law which I myself have given, in great things and in small"', and observes: 'There are so many experiments still to make! There are so many futures still to dawn!' (*D* 187).

Nietzsche, it should be clear, is a thinker of authenticity and one who paved the way for some radical currents in existentialist thought. However, this should not be taken to mean that he advocates a romantic kind of isolated individualism (see Hicks and Rosenberg, 2008, p. 152). As one commentator has recently pointed out, at stake for Nietzsche are not a few individuals but the future of humankind. This is his perfectionist demand that we do all we can to enhance the level of the species by extending the range of human possibilities: 'Exceptional or singular individuals figure *not* as the exclusive beneficiaries but as the great experimenters, as the key to realizing a perfectionist demand that has a *generic* or *general* orientation towards humankind' (Siemens, 2009, p. 30).

Abbreviations

D   *Dawn*, trans. Brittain Smith (Stanford: Stanford University Press, forthcoming).

KSA   *Sämtliche Werke: Kritische Studienausgabe in 15 Bänden* (Berlin and New York: Walter de Gruyter, 1977).

UO   *Unfashionable Observations*, trans. with an afterword, Richard T. Gray (Stanford: Stanford University Press, 1995).

Bibliography

Abbey, R. (2000), *Nietzsche's Middle Period*. Oxford and New York: Oxford University Press.

Blackham, H. J. (1961), *Six Existentialist Thinkers*. London: Routledge & Kegan Paul.

Cooper, D. E. (1999), *Existentialism* (2nd edn). Oxford and Malden, MA: Basil Blackwell.

Copleston, F. (1965), *A History of Philosophy: Schopenhauer to Nietzsche*, vol. 7, part II. New York: Image Books, Doubleday.

Crowell, S. (2010), 'Existentialism'. *Stanford Encyclopedia of Philosophy*, pp. 1–31 (http://plato.stanford.edu/entries/existentialism/).

Davis Acampora, C. (2006a), 'Naturalism and Nietzsche's Moral Psychology', in Keith Ansell-Pearson (ed.), *A Companion to Nietzsche*. Oxford and Malden MA: Basil Blackwell.

— (2006b), 'On Sovereignty and Overhumanity: Why It Matters How We Read Nietzsche's *Genealogy* II: 2', in Christa Davis Acampora (ed.), *Nietzsche's On the Genealogy of Morals: Critical Essays*. Lanham, MD and Oxford: Rowman & Littlefield.

— (2010), 'Beholding Nietzsche: Ecce Homo, Fate, and Freedom', in Ken Gemes and John Richardson (eds), *The Oxford Handbook to Nietzsche*. Oxford and New York: Oxford University Press.

Gemes, K. (2006), 'Nietzsche on the Sovereign Individual, Free Will and Autonomy'. *Proceedings of the Aristotelian Society*, Supplementary Volume 80: 321–39.

Gorner, P. (2007), *Heidegger's Being and Time: An Introduction*. Cambridge and New York: Cambridge University Press.

Guay, R. (2002), 'Nietzsche on Freedom'. *European Journal of Philosophy* 10 (3): 302–27.

Hatab, L. J. (2005), *Nietzsche's Life Sentence: Coming to Terms with Eternal Recurrence*. London and New York: Routledge.

Heidegger, M. (1980), *Being and Time*, trans. J. Macquarrie and E. Robinson. Oxford: Basil Blackwell.

Hicks, S. V. and A. Rosenberg (2008), 'Nietzsche and the Transfiguration of Asceticism: An Ethics of Self-Fashioning', in Hicks and Rosenberg (eds), *Reading Nietzsche at the Margins*. West Lafayette: Purdue University Press.

Janaway, C. (2007), *Beyond Selflessness: Reading Nietzsche's Genealogy*. Oxford and New York: Oxford University Press.

Jaspers, K. (1965), *Nietzsche: An Introduction to the Understanding of His Philosophical Activity*, trans. C. F. Wallraff and F. J. Schmitz. Chicago: Henry Regnery.

Leiter, B. (2001), 'The Paradox of Fatalism and Self-Creation in Nietzsche', in J. Richardson and B. Leiter (eds), *Nietzsche*. Oxford and New York: Oxford University Press.

— (2002), *Nietzsche on Morality*. London and New York: Routledge.

May, S. (1999), *Nietzsche's Ethics and His War on Morality*. Oxford and New York: Oxford University Press.

Merleau-Ponty, M. (1989), *Phenomenology of Perception*, trans. C. Smith. London and New York: Routledge.

Mulhall, S. (1996), *Heidegger and Being and Time*. London and New York: Routledge.

Nehamas, A. (1985), *Nietzsche. Life as Literature*. Cambridge, MA: Harvard University Press.

Owen, D. and A. Ridley (2003), 'On Fate'. *International Studies in Philosophy* 35 (3): 63–78.

Reynolds, J. (2006), *Understanding Existentialism*. Chesham: Acumen Press.

Richardson, J. (1996), *Nietzsche's System*. Oxford and New York: Oxford University Press.

Ridley, A. (2005), 'Introduction' to F. Nietzsche, *The Anti-Christ, Ecce Homo, Twilight of the Idols and Other Writings*, trans. J. Norman. Cambridge and New York: Cambridge University Press.

Rorty, R. (1989), *Contingency, Irony, and Solidarity*. Cambridge: Cambridge University Press.

Schacht, R. (2001), 'Nietzschean Normativity', in R. Schacht (ed.), *Nietzsche's Postmoralism*. Cambridge: Cambridge University Press.

Siemens, H. (2009), 'Nietzsche's Critique of Democracy'. *Journal of Nietzsche Studies* 38: 20–38.

Solomon, R. C. (2003), *Living with Nietzsche: What the Great 'Immoralist' Has to Teach Us*. Oxford and New York: Oxford University Press.

Sorabji, R. (2006), *Self: Ancient and Modern Insights about Individuality, Life, and Death*. Oxford: Clarendon Press.

III. Heidegger

Andrew J. Mitchell

Heidegger's importance for existentialism is nowhere clearer than in the famed claim from *Being and Time*, 'the essence of *Dasein* lies in its existence' (*GA* 2: 56/41). Here one finds an insistence on *Existenz* as the mode of being of *Dasein*, a mode that is to be distinguished from that of tools (*Zuhandenheit*) or other objects (*Vorhandenheit*). But while essence may be an inappropriate term for *Dasein*, Heidegger does not question its appropriateness for these other beings in the world. Ten years later this has changed. In the *Contributions to Philosophy (from Enowning)*, Heidegger's notebooks from 1936–1938, first published posthumously on the centennial of Heidegger's birth in 1989, he undertakes a rethinking of essence that is not restricted simply to *Dasein*, but extends now to all beings qua beings. The publication of the *Contributions*, hailed as Heidegger's 'second magnum opus',[1] has shaped all recent developments in Heidegger scholarship and is obviously of great relevance for any existentialism that would claim a Heideggerian influence.

Across the history of philosophy, essence has served both epistemological and ontological roles. As the 'whatness' or *quidditas* of an object, essence determines 'what' a thing is and what it means to know that thing. This whatness is nothing peculiar to the particular thing in question, however, but something held in common by other things of the same sort. Epistemologically this means that to know what the thing is one must know its essence. Due to the general nature of this essence, however, one never knows the thing as a particular, but always only comprehends it in its 'essentials'. Ontologically, essence is identified (some would say conflated) with the substantial basis for the thing, whether this basis stands beneath the thing supporting its properties (*substantia*) or simply underlies the thing in its appearance (*hypokeimenon*).

Heidegger's mature sense of essence differs from these traditional views at almost every point. Essence for Heidegger is nothing substantial, it is an 'event' or 'occurrence'; essence does not lie beneath or below the object in question, but is found at the 'limit' of the object; essence is nothing general, but what makes the thing a unique singularity. Traditional conceptions of essence have tried to undergird the *presence* of the thing by means of a similarly present essence, while Heidegger views the essence that grants the thing as a matter of *withdrawal*, one of the key ideas of the *Contributions* as a whole. Withdrawal orients us towards the non-present character of essence and leads to a consideration of the thing not as present object, but as 'remainder' or as 'abandoned'.

In the *Contributions to Philosophy*, Heidegger draws the reader's attention to the transitional (verbal) character of essence through his use of the strange nominalization 'essencing' (*Wesung*). The 'action' of essence, however, is quickly termed by Heidegger an 'occurrence of the truth of beyng' (*GA* 65: 288/202–3; translation mine).[2] Here by considering essence as an occurrence (*Geschehnis*), Heidegger could be said to 'temporalize' essence. Essence is no longer anything eternal and abiding, but something that takes place historically, an occurrence at a particular place and time within an historical context. But essence is also an occurrence of the 'truth of beyng'. The understanding of truth operative here is the Greek conception of truth as *alêtheia*, as unconcealment (*Unverborgenheit*). The concern of the *Contributions* is to think beings apart from oppositional terms like presence and absence or even, as would appear to be the case here, concealment and unconcealment. In keeping with this line of thought, what appears in 'truth', or rather what is 'unconcealed' is nothing other than concealment itself. The truth of beyng brings to light the ineradicable persistence of concealment. This is in keeping with how Heidegger refers to the 'truth of beyng' elsewhere in the *Contributions*, as the 'clearing for self-concealment' (*Lichtung für das Sich-verbergen*; *GA* 65: 346/242; translation mine). Two points follow from this determination.

First, in regards to the relationship between the essencing of the thing and the clearing, the clearing constitutes the space of appearance for things in the world. It is an area beyond the boundaries of the thing wherein the thing appears. By essencing, the thing exists in such a manner that it is opened onto this clearing. The thing exists, in other words, in need of and in an essential relation to the clearing. The idea of a completely encapsulated object is here abandoned in favour of a conception of things whereby they open onto what lies beyond them *so thoroughly that this beyond, the clearing, is involved in their very essence*. In the occurrence of the truth of beyng, a clearing is opened through the essencing of the thing. But essence does not open the clearing by protruding into a pre-established reality. Essence does not *present* itself in this clearing, nor does its *presence* open this clearing. Instead, essence enters the clearing through withdrawal.

The second point to be understood from the determination of essence as an occurrence of the 'clearing for self-concealment' turns upon the notion of self-concealment itself. This should not be understood too quickly in terms of the commonplace that all appearance appears against the backdrop of concealment. Instead, the idea that Heidegger struggles to formulate throughout these pages of the *Contributions* is that precisely what appears in the appearance of the thing is concealment. But this does not mean that the appearing thing conceals the departure of something else. The situation here is one of 'self-concealment', where the thing conceals through its own self-presentation the departure that is inherent to essence, withdrawal. With essencing as withdrawal, what it means for a thing to 'be' essentially is for it to occur in such a way that there is simultaneously a self-concealment. Essencing is a way of *not* showing oneself. Essencing is the occurrence of a thing whereby it announces its self-concealment. The essence of a thing is nothing general, it *is* nothing at all; instead, essence marks withdrawal.

Both of these clarifications require us to think further into the role of withdrawal in essencing. For Heidegger, what withdraws is beyng. But this does not mean that beings are without beyng. Instead, withdrawal serves to connect beings all the more strongly (essentially) to beyng. What the logic of withdrawal struggles to articulate is the difficult thought that beings would be in relation to beyng without being identical to or coincident with beyng. Essencing is the way that beings remain *near* to beyng. Essence describes the surface of contact and separation between appearance and withdrawal, where beings touch beyng. It draws the limit between concealment and revelation. This liminal structure of essence requires a seemingly paradoxical formulation, in terms which themselves divide upon both sides of this line: essence is the appearing of a self-concealing. The self-enclosed object of modern metaphysics knows no withdrawal. The thing of Heidegger's determination, however, exists as thing on account of a withdrawal which interrupts the self-enclosure of the thing, holds it open and spills it out onto the world (essencing as occurrence of clearing). Essence brings the thing into community and communication with the world and others. Withdrawal extends things beyond themselves and connects them with what is not present, with what is no thing, with the other, with beyng. Withdrawal makes room for what lies beyond the being.

For these reasons, withdrawal cannot be identified with lack. Withdrawal does not mean that a portion of the object is missing. In fact, withdrawal does not take anything away from the thing at all. It is not a reserve into which a portion of the object would steal away, absent in regard to what remained. In other words, withdrawal is never partial, it affects the whole of the thing. There is no missing piece of the being that would be lacking here or hiding somewhere else.

That which withdraws into its essence lacks nothing, even though the thing does not appear in its entirety. That which essences cannot be identified with that which is present. For this reason, withdrawal reveals the thing, not as stock at our disposal – the culmination of presence – but simply as thing. Withdrawal lets the thing remain a thing. This determination of the very being of the thing as a matter of withdrawal has nothing to do with absence.

Withdrawal is consequently nothing negative. It does not leave the being lacking anything. The withdrawal of being is just as much an abandonment of being, where it is the whole being, not just a piece, that is abandoned. But to be abandoned, *to be* in an abandoned manner, is to have belonged once at an *earlier* point. In the same way, withdrawal is a severance and an attachment, the positive character of which Heidegger terms a giving: the essence of self-concealing is a 'giving self-withdrawing' (*GA* 65: 249/176; translation mine). In concealing itself, the thing gives itself as the marker of withdrawal. Withdrawal is a positive event of appearing. Withdrawal is a way of naming the fact that things exist contextually.

The appearance of what essences is thus an announcement of self-concealing. The same withdrawal that opens the clearing *places* the thing in the clearing as well. Withdrawal conceals itself, but this withdrawal must nevertheless give itself to view and occur in the clearing. If concealment passed unremarked, there would be no relation between it and ourselves, between it and the world. Concealment would be an utter absence, the necessary complement to a metaphysics of presence. A non-appearing concealment would be a pure concealment, and this purity would annihilate it. Therefore, concealment must *appear* in order that it might announce itself *as concealed*. Such a thought of essence is a matter neither of presence nor absence, but of singularity.

The remainder (the being understood as opened by withdrawal) is singular. The withdrawal of being that lets the thing remain and opens the clearing for its self-concealment singularizes the thing. Essence is just this way of being of the singular: 'The essence [*Wesen*] is not the general, but instead precisely the essencing [*Wesung*] of the respective singularity [*jeweiligen Einzigkeit*]' (*GA* 65: 66/46; translation mine). The particular being, in essence, is never fully present; it is marked by withdrawal. Because it is not all here, it cannot be accounted for in an inventory of stock at our disposal or comprehended within the bounds of a concept. Because the thing remains to this extent unaccounted for and unknown, it cannot be replaced by another thing identical to it. The thing is not present for comparison and equation with another present entity. In withdrawing the thing from replacement, essencing acts as a singularizing force, whereby the thing is each time unique. With this thinking of singularity, Heidegger has not abandoned the thought of commonality that is endemic to essence. There can be no community of individuals when these are considered identical in essence. What results from such a grouping is a homogeneity, an increase of the same (*das Gleiche*). Instead, by opening the thing onto the clearing, the thing is placed in communication and irreducible community with others while maintaining its singularity. It entertains relations and is itself constituted through such relations with others unique in their own way and different from it, including relations with us, with *Dasein*.

A few conclusions can be drawn from this renewed thinking of essence on Heidegger's part. First, with the thinking of essence found in the *Contributions*, Heidegger corrects an omission from *Being and Time*. There can be no transformation of the subject if it remains within a world of objects. *Dasein* cannot be *Dasein* in a world of objects. Subject and object are metaphysically the same. Heidegger's renewed thinking of essence begins the work of rethinking thing and world, a task completed in his later thought.

Second, it is this notion of essence that we should also bear in mind as the positive counter-concept when we read Heidegger's explicit criticisms of existentialism in the 'Letter on "Humanism"'. Recall that one of Heidegger's objections to Sartre's adoption of the motto 'existence precedes essence' (see Sartre, 2007, p. 20) was that it simply reversed the traditional view that essence precedes existence without rethinking the terms themselves. As Heidegger famously noted, 'the reversal of a metaphysical statement remains a metaphysical statement' (*GA* 9: 328/250). Sartre – and by implication, all 'existentialism' – would have simply adopted the medieval determinations of *existentia* and *essentia* without further ado. These determinations are thought on the basis of a production model through an analogy with the activity of the craftsperson. A craftsman or creator God would have an idea in their mind, the essence, before producing an existing object. On this count, '[e]xistentia is the name for the realization of something that is as it appears in its Idea', that is, in the mind of God or the craftsperson, and *essentia* is accordingly understood as the 'possibility' for this realization (*GA* 9: 326/249, 325/248). Sartre even keeps to this craftsperson analogy in seeing human essence as a production of human existence ('man is nothing other than what he makes of himself. This is the first principle of existentialism'; Sartre, 2007, p. 22). Heidegger's statement in *Being and Time* avoided any such claims of precedence or production ('the essence of *Dasein* lies *in* its existence'; *GA* 2: 56/41; emphasis mine) and thus was no mere reversal. Heidegger's conception of essence, then, as developed in the middle period of his work (i.e. in the *Contributions* and related texts), breaks with the traditional view and any 'existentialism' that would moor itself to such a conception.

Lastly, however, we might see in Heidegger's conception of essence a provocation for existential thought rather than an out and out rejection of it. Ultimately, if existentialism can be viewed as taking its departure from a sense of human finitude then Heidegger could be seen as an ally in this. When that finitude is subsequently used to justify the actions of a Cartesian subject that, like a God, would bestow meaning on an otherwise meaningless world and in so doing create itself in the process, then the fragility of that finitude is betrayed.

Heidegger's thinking of essence should return us to a thought of the finitude of existence, not the position of a master that of its own accord would decide the meaning of both itself and its world. Heidegger provides us with the opportunity to think a more humble and patient existentialism. Heidegger's thinking of essence calls us back to fragility, finitude and our relations with things in the world. Surely this is the starting-point for any philosophy that would bear the name existentialism.

Notes

1. '*zweite Hauptwerk*', Friedrich-Wilhelm von Herrmann, jacket flap to *GA* 65.
2. I will render *Seyn* as 'beyng' to distinguish it from *Sein* ('being'), a crucial distinction for the *Contributions*. Beyng names being as both distinct from particular beings and from traditional conceptions of 'being' itself, as beyng is the withdrawal which grants beings in the first place (and metaphysical notions of 'being' are   only the abstraction from these abandoned beings).

Bibliography

Heidegger's texts are cited parenthetically in the text by German/English pagination according to *Gesamtausgabe* (*GA*) volume number as listed below:

Heidegger, M. (1977), *Sein und Zeit*, ed. F.-W. von Herrmann. *Gesamtausgabe* vol. 2. Frankfurt am Main: Vittorio Klostermann. English translation: *Being and Time*, trans. J. Stambaugh and D. J. Schmidt. Albany, NY: SUNY Press, 2010.

— (1989), *Beiträge zur Philosophie (vom Ereignis)*, ed. F.-W. von Herrmann. *Gesamtausgabe* vol. 65. Frankfurt am Main: Vittorio Klostermann. English translation: *Contributions to Philosophy (from Enowning)*, trans. P. Emad and K. Maly. Bloomington, IN: Indiana University Press, 1999.

— (1996), 'Brief über den "Humanismus"', in F.-W. von Herrmann (ed.), *Wegmarken. Gesamtausgabe* vol. 9 (3rd edn). Frankfurt am Main: Vittorio Klostermann. English translation: 'Letter on "Humanism"', in W. McNeill (ed.), *Pathmarks*, trans. F. A. Capuzzi, rev. W. McNeill and D. F. Krell. Cambridge: Cambridge University Press, 1998.

Sartre, J-P. (2007), *Existentialism is a Humanism*, ed. J. Kulka, trans. C. Macomber. New Haven: Yale University Press.

IV. Sartre

Peter Gratton

For some decades, philosophers in France and elsewhere have suffered under a Sartrean anxiety of influence. Clearly influential – each major thinker of the past two generations has read and commented on his work – Sartre had long been depicted as a relic of a bygone era of heroic individualism, marked by his depictions of a free subject choosing its own manner of existence. At the height of his fame in the decade or so after the Second World War, Sartre was already being challenged by incipient movements in structuralism that depicted existentialism as a naïve account of freedom that ignored the effect of linguistic and cultural formations on subjectivity. Worse, Sartre's specific political engagements, including his public polemics over communism, were seen to devalue his philosophical positions in the back-and-forth of ephemeral political debates. Thus, when Sartre published his thousand-page *The Critique of Dialectical Reason* at the end of the 1950s, the best-known French thinkers of the 1960s (Claude Lévi-Strauss, Jacques Lacan, Michel Foucault, Gilles Deleuze, Julia Kristeva and Jacques Derrida, among others) looked on the author, when they regarded his work at all, with something like profound embarrassment. Existentialism had given way to structuralism and then poststructuralism, and Sartre's work was dubbed either too individualistic or, contrarily, too devoted to a fossilized form of Marxist historicism to be of any use. In *The Order of Things* (1966), Foucault declared the 'death of man', and, soon after, he labelled Sartre the last great thinker of the *nineteenth* century.

But philosophers coming of age in the 1990s and turn of the century have seen Sartre less as a father figure to be killed off by an Oedipal horde than as one of the last thinkers who simply mattered. Of course, these later philosophers were taught Sartre by a previous generation of professors who often proffered the moral that Sartre was to be studied by poetry-spouting 18-year-olds taking an existentialism class to appear edgy, but few others. Those interested in phenomenology were directed to Husserl, Heidegger or Merleau-Ponty, not to Sartre, whose version of the subject was deemed too Cartesian, ahistorical and disembodied to account for genuine modes of access to the 'things themselves'. In fact, this dominant view of Sartre was critiqued long ago by the philosopher himself, and the Sartre championed by new generations of philosophers was the one who had abandoned the voluntarism of *Being and Nothingness*. He had in fact been discovered anew through his *Critique of Dialectical Reason* and his anti-colonial writings of the 1960s – works that had previously been almost written out of the history of contemporary European philosophy. Building on those who kept the flame of Sartre's work alive in the 1970s and 1980s, including Frederic Jameson, Thomas Flynn and William McBride, such thinkers as Robert J. C. Young, Bill Martin, Robert Bernasconi, Nik Farrell Fox, along with all those attending various national conferences on Sartre's work, argued for a radical Sartre who was not simply the 'last thinker of the nineteenth century', but rather an essential thinker for confronting existence in the twenty-first.

One important strand of this work has been the 'poststructuralist' Sartre propounded by Christina Howells, Hugh J. Silverman and Nik Farrell Fox, among others.

This approach argues not just that Sartre influenced later movements, but that in crucial ways he was 'deconstructionist', 'postmodern', and so on, *avant la lettre*. In this, such thinkers as Howells looked to be almost standing athwart history, since the waves of French structuralism and poststructuralism smothered serious discussions of Sartre's work for several decades. It is impossible to summarize these movements, but it's enough to say that figures ranging from Lacan to Derrida to Irigaray agreed with Foucault in calling for the 'death of man' and of the humanism Sartre linked with existentialism in his famed lecture of 1946. Jacques Derrida, a student reading Sartre at the time of that lecture, captures this ambivalence about Sartre, depicting him as both 'harmful' and 'catastrophic', but nevertheless all the same 'an enormous influence', even 'a model' for philosophers like him (Peeters, 2010, pp. 45–50). The poststructuralists were not, as some suggest, arguing that human beings were disappearing or that subjectivity itself was simply *passé*, but we can identify several shared hypotheses challenging a version of Sartre viewed simply as a thinker of human freedom: (1) that societal and political contexts are productive of forces of subjectification; (2) that the history of Western metaphysics, including, they argued, Sartre, tends to reduce all being to a God or one strata of reality, a view dubbed the 'metaphysics of presence'; and (3) that the texts of history and even the narratives one tells about oneself carry multiple meanings in increasingly fragmented societies. Moreover, if Sartre's descriptions of the free subject of his early work were inimical to these context-driven philosophers, his later descriptions of historical 'totalization' in the *Critique of Dialectical Reason* were even more strongly anathema to a postmodern era of fragmented narratives. Nevertheless, one clear direction in Sartre studies has been to demonstrate that it was because of Sartre, not despite him, that later thinkers recognized the problem of the split subject. It was Sartre, as Howells, Fox and Silverman argue, who announced an anti-essentialist account of subjectivity and, along with it, attempted to invent a politics that answered to this loss of subjective, patriarchal or racialist views founded upon a supposed human nature. It was also Sartre who produced biographies such as *The Family Idiot*, depicting the various internal divisions of its subject, the novelist Gustave Flaubert; and it was Sartre who presaged later descriptions of a subject creatively drawing itself while embedded in complex and mobile frameworks. Finally, Sartre was not unaware of the import of language, as some philosophers writing after the linguistic turn in philosophy might suggest. As he put it in *Search for a Method*, 'it is the individual who is inside culture and inside language' (1968, p. 113), not vice versa, and this was the starting-point for his analyses.

What stands out, though, in recent discussions of Sartre's legacy is his championing of 'praxis' or engaged action that arises to shift these cultural and linguistic systems. Even while critiquing his view of history as a 'totality', the contemporary poststructuralist Jean-Luc Nancy and others (to be discussed below) stress the importance of Sartre's efforts 'to formulate a new way of thinking the subject of social *praxis*' (Nancy, 2010, p. 9). This is particularly apparent in his early accounts of the engaged subject in *Being and Nothingness*, but also stands as the centrepiece of the later *Critique* and *Search for a Method*, which served as its preface. In those works, Sartre argued that human beings act in the context of their material circumstances. There is an inherent tension between human praxis and what he called the 'practico-inert', which is not just the things of nature but also the sedimented institutions left over from previous forms of praxis. In the dialectical relation between praxis and these historical and material givens, Sartre argues, human beings are thus made by history. But he argues that this is not the end of the story, since it is in groups that individuals, joined with others, can erupt in collective struggle to overcome this history. Sartre's depictions of *le groupe en fusion*, which he opposed to 'seriality', the alienated, everyday existence in which we are passive to what comes, has become central to generations of the Left looking for an 'abrupt resurrection of liberty', as Sartre depicted the freedom of collective action, in an era when true political action has been on retreat. For these thinkers, Sartre has been taken as not simply providing a theoretical counter to deterministic forms of poststructuralist or Marxist theories, but also as providing something of a method for activists confronting corporatist forms of seriality. While politics is often depicted in terms of state action, or even in the production of selves, as in the work of Michel Foucault, Sartre's fundamental insight for a new generation of Marxists such as Peter Hallward and Nina Power, has been to work out a politics of groups acting at a distance *from* and often in the face *of* state action.

This is most apparent in the writings of Alain Badiou, who is best known for his application of set theory to considerations of political events, but who has also often noted the inheritance of his thought from Sartre. Badiou argues that Sartre 'invites us to look again at the question of the political subject' (understood by Badiou not as individuals, but the masses engaged in action), and for this reason 'remains one of those who re-awakened Marxism' (2009, p. 35). While following Sartre in many key aspects, Badiou critiques Sartre for thinking of revolutionary groups as at odds with the 'serial' masses around them. However, arguing on Sartrean ground, Badiou himself has faced criticism for not being able to account for how events that reshape the political landscape can occur. How do collectivities unite? What is the status of their shared goals? Why do they tend to solidify into hierarchical institutions? To these questions, along with outstanding analyses of such revolutionary moments as the storming of the Bastille, Sartre thus offers a corrective to Badiouian theory by depicting the manner in which the type of revolutionary struggles championed by Badiou can be brought about.

One such set of revolutionary struggles was the anti-colonial movement of the 1950s and 1960s. In a preface to the English translation of a collection of Sartre's anti-colonial writings, Robert J. C. Young rightly notes that Sartre 'constituted one of the major philosophical influences on Francophone anti-colonial thinkers and activists' (Young, 2002, p. vii). It's worth noting that Sartre was one of the few prominent French intellectuals of the period who was active early and often against French and other forms of colonialism. While the diminutive intellectual with thick glasses makes something of a comic sight next to military-garbed revolutionaries in pictures from the period, there is no doubting his real political influence at the time. In any case, Sartre's influence on Francophone African philosophy and post-colonial theory derived less from his direct political interventions than his early phenomenological analyses of the Other, his writings on black literature, and his timely and theoretically astute studies of the political philosophy of Patrice Lumumba, a major anti-colonial thinker and the first president of the Congo. The most prominent example of Sartre's influence on anti- and post-colonial thinking is through Frantz Fanon's phenomenology of the 'racial gaze', which he argued reduced blacks to one object among others. Fanon's *Black Skin/White Masks* (1951) remains a foundational text for critical race theory and is avowedly indebted to Sartre's accounts of subjectivity in *Being and Nothingness* and *Anti-Semite and Jew* (1946). In these writings, Young notes, 'Fanon recognised an insight into the mechanics of how colonialism was able to produce a sense of inferiority in colonial subjects' (2002, p. xiii). For this and a number of other reasons, Sartre is an 'African philosopher', as Young provocatively calls him (2002, p. xxii; cf. Mudimbe, 1988, pp. 82–6), having sparked generations doing work in what has come to be called Africana existential thought (see, for example, Gordon, 2000).

One final direction in Sartre studies is exemplified by thinkers who, while interested in his powerful accounts of the manner in which human beings are treated as objects, have used his work to upend traditional conceptions of what it means to be an object in the first place. In one famous scene in *Nausea* (1938), for example, the character Roquentin considers the brute facticity of a tree root, which is simply there 'in excess [*de trop*]', just as Roquentin himself is (see Morin, 2009, pp. 35–53). This scene has long been read in terms of its depiction of the absurd, but new movements in realism, materialism and ecological thought have questioned the anthropocentric basis of much of Western philosophy, with a consequence that Sartre's meditations on the agency of 'things', in multiple senses, takes on new life (Kaufman, 2011). The brute facticity of things became the 'practico-inert' of his later work, which itself produced an 'anti-praxis' befuddling human enterprise. 'Nature is not exclusively the in-itself', he noted in a late interview, 'A plant that is growing is no longer altogether in-itself. It is more complex. It is alive' (Schilpp, 1981, p. 40). In a similar manner, so too is the 'practico-inert' of Sartre's many books, which, in their own form of anti-praxis, have held off attempts to turn the last page on his work, which continues to remain alive to those needing an existential antidote to today's philosophical ennui.

Bibliography

Badiou, A. (2009), *Pocket Pantheon: Figures of Postwar Philosophy*. London: Verso.

Gordon, L. (2000), *Existentia Africana: Understanding Africana Existential Thought*. New York: Routledge.

Kaufman, E. (2011), *Rocks, Plants, and Objects in French Phenomenology*. New York: Columbia University Press.

Morin, M.-E. (2009), 'Thinking Things: Heidegger, Sartre, Nancy'. *Sartre Studies International* 15/2 (Winter): 35–53.

Mudimbe, V. Y. (1988), *The Invention of Africa*. Indianapolis, IN: Indiana University Press.

Nancy, J.-L. (2010), *The Truth of Democracy*, trans. P.-A. Brault and M. Naas. New York: Fordham University Press.

Peeters, B. (2010), *Derrida*. Paris: Flammarion.

Sartre, J-P. (1968), *Search for a Method*, trans. H. Barnes. New York: Vintage.

Schilpp, P. A. (ed.) (1981), 'An Interview with Jean-Paul Sartre'. *The Philosophy of Jean-Paul Sartre*. La Salle, IL: Open Court.

Young, R. J. C. (2002), 'Sartre: The "African Philosopher"', in Jean-Paul Sartre, *Colonialism and Neo-Colonialism*. New York: Routledge.

V. De Beauvoir

Laura Hengehold

When Michele le Doeuff published *Hipparchia's Choice* in 1989, de Beauvoir was primarily regarded as a novelist, as the unconventional life partner of Jean-Paul Sartre, and as an activist who had written a historic work on women's oppression. Moreover, both French and American feminists believed changes in gender politics during the 1970s had rendered *The Second Sex* (1949) obsolete (Delphy, 1995; Moses, 2003 ; de Beauvoir, 1952). Admittedly, more intellectuals than activists feared de Beauvoir held women to masculinist norms, as Julia Kristeva did in her 1979 essay 'Women's Time' (Kristeva, 1986). But because the philosophical complexity of her non-fiction was largely ignored, de Beauvoir was often caricatured in debates over marriage and motherhood.

By the mid-1980s, de Beauvoir's writing was less and less likely to be interpreted, whether positively or negatively, in terms of her private life (Moi, 1994). Margaret Simons revealed that Parshley's English translation had systematically obscured technical terms that would have made *The Second Sex* recognizable as the work of a professionally trained philosopher (1983). Judith Butler cited de Beauvoir as a source for her hugely influential understanding of gender as performativity (1989), and in a special 1985 issue of *Hypatia*, Linda Singer challenged Kristeva by identifying resources for a robust philosophy of sexual difference in *The Second Sex* (Singer, 1990). Meanwhile, Elizabeth Fallaize (1988) argued that de Beauvoir's literary voice was less Sartrean than previously accepted.

Michèle le Doeuff identified a pluralist epistemology resisting the hierarchical and socially detached character of much academic French philosophy in *The Second Sex*. Asking what unacknowledged role the philosopher's *image* plays in organizing the tradition and teaching of philosophy, her influential study *Hipparchia's Choice* linked de Beauvoir's hypotheses about social knowledge concerning women to the difficulty of working as a woman philosopher in a country where female education, work opportunities and self-image were weighed down by historical opposition to birth control and abortion.

During the 1990s, *Hipparchia's Choice* was followed by a flurry of books and articles establishing de Beauvoir's intellectual independence from Sartre (Kruks, 1990; Fullbrook and Fullbrook, 1994; Simons, 1999; see the summary of this by Daigle and Golumb, 2009). Some of this work, well documented elsewhere, was done by academic societies such as the Simone de Beauvoir Circle of the American Philosophical Association and the society and journal for Simone de Beauvoir Studies (McBride, 2003; Kruks, 2005; Tidd, 2008; Simons, 2010). In 2003, the latter met with the Groupe d`Études Sartriennes to break down de Beauvoir's philosophical invisibility in France. At this conference, one of several to result in a special journal issue, Kristeva gave de Beauvoir far more credit than she had in 1979 (*Simone de Beauvoir Studies* 2003–2004).[1]

Today, de Beauvoir is recognized for contributions to existentialism and phenomenology that go far beyond 'supplementing' Sartre's thought with reflections on intersubjectivity or ethics (Kruks, 1990; Arp, 2001; Bergoffen, 1997). These include themes in the philosophy of social science, politics and history. Recent scholarship has addressed challenges posed to philosophical notions of disciplinary, sexual and psychological identity by the many genres and translations of de Beauvoir's work, and examined her debts to figures in the history of philosophy. It has also considered de Beauvoir's relevance for debates about maternity, racism and the situation of women in the post-colonial world; political commitment and violence; and the nature of aging and history.

Textuality

De Beauvoir communicated with her public through a number of imperfectly compatible media – essays, journalism, novels and memoirs, as well as letters which were eventually compiled for posthumous publication. A single text might contain different genres, disciplines and vocabularies, and this complexity may have been responsible for some of the early negative judgements of de Beauvoir's philosophical work (Deutscher, 2008) . As an international phenomenon, de Beauvoir's work also differs from translation to translation – many based on the flawed English version of *The Second Sex* from 1954 (Simons, 1983; Antonopolous, 1997; Moi, 2004).[2]

The de Beauvoir Series by Illinois University Press represents an Anglophone effort to collect and translate de Beauvoir's philosophical works with systematic attention to their philosophical terminology.[3] But de Beauvoir's writing also has an irreducibly anti-systematic dimension, reflecting her admiration of Kierkegaard. It suggests that personal and philosophical identity, including sexual identity, depend unsettlingly on textuality, scholarly institutions and public recognition. Readers must wonder: is the consistency of our identity possible only through the rigid perceptions of others? Is there any such thing as the 'original language' of a philosophy? And what ethical stance should existentialists take towards the public record: should they resist the potential 'bad faith' of an identity or risk its rigidity in the effort to preserve relationships?

These questions became quite concrete when letters published after de Beauvoir's death appeared to contradict her published memoirs on topics including bisexuality, truthfulness in personal relationships, and opinions on the relative value of philosophy and literature. Lesbian scholars ambivalent about her description of female romantic relationships in *The Second Sex* were forced to contend with evidence that de Beauvoir was not exclusively heterosexual (e.g. see essays in Al-Hibri and Simons, 1990). This resulted in nuanced reflections on the importance of women's friendships, erotic or platonic (see essays in Simons, 1995; Ward, 2006). Discovering discrepancies between the memoirs, interviews, letters and diaries also required scholars to find value in de Beauvoir's writing apart from their idealization of de Beauvoir as feminist role model. Pilardi (1999), Tidd (1999), Fraser (1999) and Bainbrigge (2005) explored possible de Beauvoirian responses to such questions about identity.

Literature

Although de Beauvoir's novels had always been of interest to literary critics, especially feminists, publication of the letters led to new interest in her philosophy of literature, which viewed the novel as an attempt to create lived experiences shared by strangers.[4] The multiple versions of her public and private self showed that de Beauvoir's corpus as a whole blurred the lines between philosophy, literature and 'real life' (Fallaize, 1988; Holveck, 2002; Scholz and Mussett, 2005). De Beauvoir conceived of philosophy *as* literature and refused to distinguish thinking from experiencing to the same extent as Sartre. In de Beauvoir's novels, Eleanore Holveck (2002) found subtle arguments against (and experimental variations on) the understanding of experience put forward by phenomenologists and aesthetic theorists including Hegel, Husserl and Breton.

Although de Beauvoir disagreed strongly with poststructuralist notions of philosophy, literature and the novel, by the end of the decade scholars were using them to re-read de Beauvoir's *oeuvre* (Kruks, 2001; Deutscher, 2008; Holland, 2009). Her existentialism was compared to Foucauldian discipline, to his ethic of care for the self and to *parrhesia* (Butler, 1990, 1994; Kruks, 2001; Vintges, 1996; Hengehold, 2006) and Derrida's critique of the metaphysics of presence in literary and philosophical representation was applied to her work (Heath, 1989; Deutscher, 2008; Holland, 2009). In 1998, British editors put *The Second Sex* in dialogue with feminists influenced by poststructuralism and queer theory (Evans, 1998; see also Wilkerson, 2007).

Epistemology

Once Le Doeuff cut through de Beauvoir's public identification with Sartreanism, scholars quickly began looking for other influences on her thought, especially her epistemology. The 1996 translation of *Sex and Existence*, Eva Lundgren-Gothlin's study of de Beauvoir's debt to Hegelian and Marxist ideas about intersubjectivity and production, marked an important transition. Not long after, Nancy Bauer (2001) explored resemblances between de Beauvoir's starting-point in *The Second Sex* and that most canonical of French epistemologists, Descartes.

Many other efforts to unearth the connections between de Beauvoir and other thinkers focus on twentieth-century phenomenology, especially Merleau-Ponty, Husserl, Heidegger and Hegel (Kruks, 1990; Bergoffen, 1997; Holveck, 2002; Bauer, 2006). Such studies read *The Second Sex* as a critique of knowledge about women's experience, biological and social–scientific (especially Holveck, 2002). Toril Moi, finally, has worked to bring de Beauvoir's ideas about womanhood into dialogue with the Anglophone tradition of ordinary language philosophy (Moi, 2001). By changing the *way* in which de Beauvoir is imagined to have argued against women's entrapment as Other in the masculinist imaginary, Moi hopes feminists will stop believing they must choose decisively between poststructuralism and classical rationalism – a dichotomy, she argues, reflecting a mistaken hope that political legitimacy can be guaranteed through theoretical complexity and correctness.

313

Female Embodiment

Scholarship re-evaluating and reinterpretating de Beauvoir's ideas about maternity, aging and biology continues to expand. De Beauvoir's treatment of maternity in *The Second Sex* was notoriously negative and alienated many younger scholars during the 1970s, including Kristeva (1986). Since then, Ward (1995), Fishwick (2002) and Heinämaa (2003) have made clear in different ways that de Beauvoir considers the female body non-naturalistically as the site of existential and cognitive *ambiguity*, since it is both the vehicle of a personal project and one's immersion in a collective situation. Embodiment may be liberating as well as oppressive. However, lines such as 'the female, to a greater extent than the male, is the prey of the species' have led to biologistic and masculinist misreadings (e.g. Evans, 1985). Linda Zerilli (1992) argues that de Beauvoir's scepticism about maternity was a reaction to postwar French pronatalism. She asks how de Beauvoir's complex rhetorical strategies in that chapter reveal her views on female *subjectivity* rather than anatomy. Similarly, Moi (2001) situates *The Second Sex* with respect to early twentieth-century medical discourses in which reproductive biology was considered 'pervasive' of female attitudes and behaviour.

In *The Second Sex* and earlier essays, de Beauvoir argued that women are tempted to live through their children or justify their existence through maternal devotion (1952, 2004). These ethical failures lead to conflict and failed developmental opportunities for both generations, and are especially damaging for daughters.[5] Fredrika Scarth (2004) regards motherhood as a test case for de Beauvoir's ethical, as well as metaphysical claims that human beings are fundamentally relational. Emily Grosholz (2004) suggested that Colette's mother Sido offered a valid portrait of a 'good' de Beauvoirian mother. Lisa Guenther, finally, shows how common Western cultural myths about selfless motherhood allowed male philosophers like Levinas to embrace maternity as a metaphor for ethical devotion (2006). Guenther neither dismisses ethical devotion nor wishes that women should be physically and emotionally sacrificed to an abstract version of this goal. From an existentialist perspective, the effort to establish abstract principles regarding abortion or the simple opportunity to bear children should never overshadow the ethical quality of mother–child relationships.

Political Thought

De Beauvoir's concepts of the *Other* (formed in dialogue with Hegel, Husserl and Sartre) and of *Mitsein* (in dialogue with Heidegger) are enormously provocative for sociological and psychological research. Her uniquely social notion of Otherness may have emerged as a result of encountering anti-black racism in the United States (Simons, 1999; Ruhe, 2006). During the 1990s, however, de Beauvoir's relative inattention to the issue of racial politics and global diversity was strongly criticized (Spelman, 1990; Nzegwu, 2004). Some authors have responded by investigating her debts to the analyses of racism proffered by Richard Wright and Gunnar Myrdal (Simons, 1999; Ruhe, 2006; Deutscher, 2008). De Beauvoir's activism during the Algerian war has also been documented, along with the possibility of her influence on Fanon's ideas regarding the corporeality of the Othered body and Hegel's master–slave dialectic (Moi, 1994; J. Murphy, 1995; Ruhe, 2006; A. Murphy, 2006).[6] Like Fanon, de Beauvoir believed that conflict was a constant threat or potential for interpersonal and intergroup relations. However, this did not mean she believed groups were *incapable* of facilitating one another's freedom.

Outside of the Anglophone and Francophone world, de Beauvoir was primarily read as the author of *The Second Sex*. Marxists often considered her style of feminism to be 'bourgeois' because it emphasized individual self-development and rights, although she supported socialist causes in France, argued that women's liberation was impossible without economic independence, and reported as a journalist on Communist societies such as China and Cuba (Whitmarsh, 1981; Marso and Moynagh, 2006; Weiss, 2006; A. Murphy, 2006). A special issue of the Bulletin of the Societé Américaine de la Langue Française includes essays on de Beauvoir's ambivalent reception in Communist China and the former GDR, where governments claimed feminism as official policy but discouraged women from researching their own situation (see Hervé, 2003; Jinhua 2003).[7] Some feminists from African societies with a strong tradition of institutionalized female power believe de Beauvoir promotes unnecessary conflict between the sexes; but others, especially African women from an urban milieu, have stated that despite her ethnocentrism (shared by almost all French writers of the time) de Beauvoir had a profound impact on their personal efforts to grapple with gendered power (Nzegwu, 2004; Chiwengo, 2003).

In *Pyrrhus and Cinéas* and *Ethics of Ambiguity*, de Beauvoir proposed that human freedom could only be preserved insofar as people refused to confirm or congeal themselves *as beings* in order, rather, to *disclose* being, including the being of human values (de Beauvoir, 2004, 2000). Following the Second World War, de Beauvoir acknowledged that it was difficult to establish or defend political and economic structures capable of promoting the capacity of all human beings to disclose and create value. Moreover, the ambiguity of human existence extends to tensions between collectives and individuals. In her essays on the meaning and proper punishment of 'crimes against humanity', in novels like *The Mandarins*, in her introductions to literary works by new authors, and in her public defence of Algerian militant Djamila Boupacha, de Beauvoir demonstrated multiple ways in which political conflict could be ethically apprehended and assumed.[8] *The Second Sex* problematized solidarity among the oppressed and the temptation to collude with oppressors. Not least, de Beauvoir concerned herself with the artist's proper role in political conflict; while in *The Mandarins* (1999), Henri elects to write works that cannot be used by any party, de Beauvoir also criticized the 'aesthetic attitude' of treating suffering as a spectacle rather than a situation in which the artist is morally implicated (2000).

Aging and History

Such reflections make it inevitable that de Beauvoir's implicit and explicit contribution to philosophy of history and temporality would come under scrutiny. History as lived experience was an important theme in novels like *All Men are Mortal* and *The Mandarins*. Lundgren-Gothlin approached this theme by way of de Beauvoir's debt to Hegel and Marx (1996). Michel Kail (2006) uses de Beauvoir's statement that women's oppression did not 'happen' at a specific moment in history to suggest that the relationship between human history and natural history cannot be reduced to biology. Women's oppression is both a critical standpoint and a *virtual* rather than historical event.[9]

During her adult life, de Beauvoir also witnessed an enormous change in the status of the elderly, who ceased to be revered (and were sometimes resented) in the extended family home. With lengthening life spans and access to social insurance, the aged had more positive social contact with each other but faced cultural marginalization. *The Coming of Age* was the result of de Beauvoir's phenomenological reflections and empirical research on these topics. Oliver Davis (2006) believes this text reveals the fundamental confusion within gerontology between the political struggle against ageism and the existential task of coming to terms with human vulnerability and death.[10] Deutscher suggests that if women are the Other in intimate space, and racialized peoples are the Other to Europeans in geography, de Beauvoir may have regarded the elderly as Other in time (2008).

De Beauvoir's ambivalence towards aging and towards sexual and political power between different generations is a pressing existential issue for the independent women who have become daughters and granddaughters of second wave feminism (Chaperon, 2000; Celestin et al., 2003). De Beauvoir observed that gender hierarchy, if not sexuality and intimacy, become less significant as people age – at least in affluent societies. However, women often outlive men. How can they avoid loneliness? How can both sexes relate to historical change in a way that makes them participants in a vibrant and conflicted present rather than relics of the political and cultural past? Finally, what kind of emotional and technical care are they owed in a just society? These questions inform ongoing debates about migration, fertility and the international division of labour in industrialized countries where anxiety about an aging population often gives rise to racist resentment.

De Beauvoir also witnessed the profound transformation of French and other older democracies from an industrial to a service-based mode of production. She was enormously critical of the ways in which women could be trapped in a rigid self-image or forced to compete endlessly for individuality by the repetitive nature of much care work (Veltman, 2004; Deutscher, 2008; Virno, 2004). Today it is more obvious that the meaning and potential of biology change in relation to production methods, medical technology and the human life span. Although the birth rate has fallen since 1949 and more men help care for their own children, both sexes, especially from racial minorities, risk being 'othered' in the paid workforce of the service economy. It remains to be seen how well de Beauvoir's political philosophy, developed during the heart of the cold war and decolonization, will make the leap into a world where biological categories of 'normal' and 'Other' become less important than cultural categories of 'carers', 'cared-for' and those who are denied such care.

Notes

1. For the French Cinquantenaire of *The Second Sex* (1999), see Ingrid Galster (2004), as well as *Les Temps Modernes* (Kail, 2002), *Simone de Beauvoir Studies* (2003–2004) and *SAPLF* (2003); on de Beauvoir's centennial conference see Tidd (2008).
2. A new unabridged translation was published by Knopf (De Beauvoir, 2010) but controversy about philosophical content remains.
3. *The Beauvoir Series*, 7 vols, ed. Margaret A. Simons and Sylvie Le Bon de Beauvoir, Carbondale: Illinois University Press.
4. See 'Metaphysics and the Novel', 'My Experience as a Writer' and 'What Can Literature Do' in de Beauvoir 2011.
5. Despite the protests of Lacanian feminists that de Beauvoir neglected to value female sexual difference and maternal capacities, it was an analyst influenced by the object relations tradition, Jessica Benjamin (1988), who best used de Beauvoir's ideas about immanence and transcendence to understand the lopsided effects of gendered parenting on children's overvaluation of masculinity.
6. Algerian feminist Marnia Lazreg appealed to de Beauvoir in an effort to broaden Western views on North African women's lives, and de Beauvoir served playwright Alek Toumi as an emblematic figure for understanding their changing situation in the face of fundamentalism.
7. Additional articles by Tania Roy and Ngwarsungo Chiwengo address reception in India and the Democratic Republic of Congo.
8. For example, 'An Eye for an Eye' and 'Moral Idealism and Political Realism', in de Beauvoir (2004). See also Scholz and Mussett (2005).

9. His thesis receives unexpected backing from Simons' discovery of Bergson's importance in her 1927 diary (Simons 1999, 2003; de Beauvoir, 2006). Simons suggests that de Beauvoir draws on Bergson's ideas about speciation and individuation in *Creative Evolution* for much of her argument that women's struggle for *individuation* is more difficult than that of men.
10. Many scholars have noted de Beauvoir's personal horror of death, and some people reacted with horror to her description of her mother's and Sartre's deaths. See Marks (1973) and Bainbrigge (2005).

Bibliography

Al-Hibri, A. and M. A. Simons (eds) (1990), *Hypatia Reborn: Essays in Feminist Philosophy*. Bloomington, IN: Indiana University Press.

Alexander Antonopoulos, A. (1997), 'The Eclipse of Gender: Simone de Beauvoir and the *Différance* of Translation'. *Philosophy Today* 41 (1/4) : 112-22.

Arp, K. (2001), *The Bonds of Freedom: Simone de Beauvoir's Existential Ethics*. Chicago: Open Court.

Bainbrigge, S. (2005), *Writing against Death: The Autobiographies of Simone de Beauvoir*. Amsterdam and New York: Rodopi.

Bauer, N. (2001), *Simone de Beauvoir, Philosophy, and Feminism*. New York: Columbia University Press.

— (2006), 'Beauvoir's Heideggerian Ontology', in Margaret A. Simons (ed.), *The Philosophy of Simone de Beauvoir: Critical Essays*. Bloomington, IN: Indiana University Press. : 65-91

Benjamin, J. (1988), *The Bonds of Love: Psychoanalysis, Feminism, and the Problem of Domination*. New York: Pantheon.

Bergoffen, D. (1997), *The Philosophy of Simone de Beauvoir: Gendered Phenomenologies, Erotic Generosities*. Albany, NY: SUNY Press.

Butler, J. (1990), 'Recovery and Invention: The Projects of Desire in Hegel, Kojève, Hyppolite, and Sartre'. Ph.D. Dissertation, Yale University. Abstract in *Dissertation Abstracts International* 46 (3A) (September 1985): 727A.

— (1994), *Gender Trouble: Feminism and the Subversion of Identity*. New York: Routledge.

— (1996), 'Gendering the Body: Beauvoir's Philosophical Contribution', in A. Garry and M. Pearsall (eds), *Women, Knowledge, and Reality: Explorations in Philosophy*. Boston: Unwin Hyman : 253-62.

— (2006), *Gender Trouble*. New York: Routledge.

Celestin, R., E. DalMolin and I. De Courtivron (eds) (2003), *Beyond French Feminisms: Debates on Women, Politics, and Culture in France, 1981–2001*. New York: Palgrave MacMillan.

Chaperon, S. (2000), *Les Annees Beauvoir (1945–1970)*. Paris: Fayard.

Chiwengo, N. (2003), 'Otherness and Female Identities'. *Bulletin of the Société Américaine de Philosophie de la Langue Française* 13 (1) : 167-76.

Daigle, C. and J. Golumb, (eds) (2009), *Beauvoir and Sartre: The Riddle of Influence*. Bloomington, IN: Indiana University Press.

Davis, O. (2006), *Age Rage and Going Gently: Stories of the Senescent Subject in Twentieth-Century French Writing*. Amsterdam and New York: Rodopi.

De Beauvoir, S. (1966), *Les Belles Images*. Paris: Gallimard.

— (1949), *Le Deuxième Sexe*, 2 vols. Paris: Gallimard.

— (1952), *The Second Sex*. Trans. H. M. Parshley. New York: Alfred A. Knopf.

— (1999), *The Mandarins*, trans. L. Friedman. New York: W. W. Norton.

— (2000), *The Ethics of Ambiguity*, trans. B. Frechtman. New York: Citadel.

— (2004), *Simone de Beauvoir: Philosophical Writings*, ed. M. A. Simons with M. Timmermann and M. B. Mader. Chicago: University of Illinois Press.

— (2006), *Diary of a Philosophy Student. The De Beauvoir Series*, ed. B. Klaw, S. Le Bon De Beauvoir, M. Simons, M. Timmerman. Chicago: University of Illinois Press.

— (2010), *The Second Sex*, trans. C. Borde and S. Malovany-Chevalier. New York: Alfred A. Knopf.

— (2011), *'The Useless Mouths' and Other Literary Writings. The De Beauvoir Series*, ed. M. Timmerman and M. A. Simons. Chicago: University of Illinois Press.

Delphy, C. (1995), 'French Feminism: An Essential Move'. *Yale French Studies* 87: 190–221.

Deutscher, P. (2008), *The Philosophy of Simone de Beauvoir: Ambiguity, Conversion, Resistance*. Cambridge: Cambridge University Press.

Evans, M. (1985), *Simone de Beauvoir: A Feminist Mandarin*. London: Tavistock Press.

— (ed.) (1998), *Simone de Beauvoir's The Second Sex: New Interdisciplinary Essays*. Manchester: Manchester University Press.

Fallaize, E. (1988), *The Novels of Simone de Beauvoir*. London and New York: Routledge.

Fishwick, S. (2002), *The Body in the Work of Simone de Beauvoir*. Bern: Peter Lang.

Fraser, M. (1999), *Identity Without Selfhood: Simone de Beauvoir and Bisexuality*. Cambridge: Cambridge University Press.

Fullbrook, K. and E. Fullbrook. (1994), *Simone de Beauvoir and Jean-Paul Sartre: The Remaking of a Twentieth Century Legend*. New York: Basic Books.

Galster, I. (2004), *Les Deuxieme Sexe de Simone de Beauvoir*. Paris: Presse del'Université Paris-Sorbonne.

Grosholz, E. (2004), "The House We Never Leave: Childhood, Shelter, and Freedom in the Writings of Beauvoir and Colette." In The *Legacy of Simone de Beauvoir*, ed. by Emily R. Grosholz. Oxford: Oxford University Press, 173–92.

Guenther, L. (2006), *The Gift of the Other: Levinas and the Politics of Reproduction*. Albany, NY: SUNY Press.

Heath, J. (1989), *Simone de Beauvoir*. Hempstead, UK: Harvester Wheatsheaf.

Heinämaa, S. (2003), *Towards a Phenomenology of Sexual Difference: Husserl, Merleau-Ponty, Beauvoir*. Lanham, MD: Rowman & Littlefield.

Hengehold, L. (2006), 'Beauvoir's Parrhesiastic Contracts: Frank-Speaking and the Philosophical-Political Couple', in M. A. Simons (ed.), *The Philosophy of Simone de Beauvoir: Critical Essays*. Bloomington: Indiana University Press , 178–200.

Hervé, F. (2003), 'Regards d'Allemagne: Le Cinquantenaire du *Deuxieme Sexe*'. *Bulletin of the Société Américaine de Philosophie de la Langue Française* 13 (1).

Holland, A. (2009), *Excess and Transgression in Simone de Beauvoir's Fiction; The Discourse of Madness*. Farnham, UK and Burlington, VT: Ashgate.

Holveck, E. (2002), *Simone de Beauvoir's Philosophy of Lived Experience: Literature and Metaphysics*. Lanham, MD: Rowman & Littlefield.

Jinhua, D. (2003), 'Traces of Time: Simone de Beauvoir in China', trans. H. Wang. *Bulletin of the Société Américaine de Philosophie de la Langue Française* 13 (1) : 177–91.

Kail, M. (ed.) (2002), *Les Temps Modernes. Presences de Simone de Beauvoir* 619: 5–252.

— (2006), *Simone de Beauvoir Philosophe*. Paris: Presses Universitaires de France.

Kristeva, J. (1986), 'Women's Time', in T. Moi (ed.), *The Kristeva Reader*. New York: Columbia University Press, pp. 187–213.

Kruks, S. (1990), *Situation and Human Existence: Freedom, Subjectivity, and Society*. London: Unwin Hyman.

— (2001), *Retrieving Experience: Subjectivity and Recognition in Feminist Politics*. Ithaca: Cornell University Press.

— (2005), 'Beauvoir's Time/Our Time: The Renaissance in Simone de Beauvoir Studies'. *Feminist Studies* 31 (2): 286–309.

Le Doeuff, M. (1989), *L'Etude et le Rouet*. Paris: Seuil; trans. as *Hipparchia's Choice: An Essay Concerning Women, Philosophy, etc.* ed. T. Selous. London: Blackwell.

Lundgren-Gothlin, E. (1996) *Sex and Existence: Simone De Beauvoir's 'The Second Sex'*. Hanover: Wesleyan University Press.

McBride, W. (2003), 'Philosophy, Literature, and Everyday Life in *The Second Sex: The Current Beauvoir Revival'*. *SAPLF* 13 (1).

Marks, E. (1973), *Simone de Beauvoir: Encounters with Death*. New Brunswick, NJ: Rutgers University Press.

Marso, L. J. and P. Moynagh. (2006), *Simone de Beauvoir's Political Thinking*. Urbana-Champaign: Illinois University Press.

Michielsens, M. (1999), 'Fiftieth anniversary of *The Second Sex'*. *The European Journal of Women's Studies* 6 (3): 363–8.

Moi, T. (1994), *Simone de Beauvoir: The Making of an Intellectual Woman*. Oxford: Blackwell.

— (2001), *What is a Woman?: And Other Essays*. New York: Oxford University Press.

— (2004), 'While We Wait: Notes on the English Translation of *The Second Sex'*, in E. R. Grosholz (ed.), *The Legacy of Simone de Beauvoir*. Oxford: Oxford University Press.

Moses, C. (2003), 'Made in America: French Feminism in Academia', in R. Celestin, E. DalMolin and I. Decourtivron (eds), *Beyond French Feminisms: Debates on Women, Politics, and Culture in France, 1981–2001*. New York: Palgrave MacMillan, pp. 261–84.

Murphy, A. (2006), 'Between Generosity and Violence: Towards a Revolutionary Politics in the Philosophy of Simone de Beauvoir, in M. A. Simons (ed.), *The Philosophy of Simone de Beauvoir: Critical Essays*. Bloomington, IN: Indiana University Press,

Murphy, J. S. (1995), 'Beauvoir and the Algerian War: Toward a Postcolonial Ethics', in M. A. Simons (ed.), *Feminist Interpretations of Simone de Beauvoir*. University Park, PA: Pennsylvania State University Press.

Nzegwu, N. U. (2004), *Family Matters: Feminist Themes in African Philosophy of Culture*. Albany, NY: SUNY Press.

Pilardi, J. (1999), *Simone de Beauvoir Writing the Self: Philosophy Becomes Autobiography*. Westport, CT: Praeger.

Ruhe, D. (2006), *Contextualiser Le Deuxieme Sexe: Index Raisonné des Moms Propres*. Bern: Peter Lang.

Sanday, P. R. and R. Gallagher Goodenough (1990), *Beyond the Second Sex: New Directions in the Anthropology of Gender*. Philadelphia: University of Pennsylvania Press.

Scarth, F. (2004), *The Other Within: Ethics, Politics, and the Body in Simone de Beauvoir*. Lanham, MD: Rowman & Littlefield.

Scholz, S. and S. M. Mussett (2005), *The Contradictions of Freedom: Philosophical Essays on Simone de Beauvoir's The Mandarins*. Albany, NY: SUNY Press.

Simone de Beauvoir Studies (2003–2004), *The Talk of the Town: Beauvoir and Sartre*. General Editor Y. Astartita Patterson. Vol. 20.

Simons, M. A. (1983), 'The Silencing of Simone de Beauvoir: Guess What's Missing from *The Second Sex*?' *Women's Studies International Forum* 6 (5): 559–64.

— (ed.) (1995), *Feminist Interpretations of Simone de Beauvoir*, University Park, PA: Pennsylvania State University Press.

— (1999), *Simone de Beauvoir and The Second Sex: Feminism, Race, and the Origins of Existentialism*. Lanham, MD: Rowman & Littlefield.

— (2003), 'Bergson's Influence on Beauvoir's Philosophical Methodology', in C. Card (ed.), *The Cambridge Companion to Simone de Beauvoir*. Cambridge: Cambridge University Press.

— (ed.) (2006), *The Philosophy of Simone de Beauvoir: Critical Essays*. Bloomington, IN: Indiana University Press.

— (2010), 'Confronting an Impasse: Reflections on the Past and Future of Beauvoir Scholarship'. *Hypatia* : 25(4) 909–26.

Singer, L. (1990), 'Interpretation and Retrieval: Re-Reading Beauvoir', in M. A. Simons and A. Y. al-Hibri (eds), *Hypatia Reborn: Essays in Feminist Philosophy*. Bloomington, IN: Indiana University Press.

Spelman, E. V. (1990), 'Simone de Beauvoir and Women: Just Who Does She Think "We" Is?' in *Inessential Woman: Problems of Exclusion in Feminist Thought*. Boston: Beacon Press.

Tidd, U. (1999), *Simone de Beauvoir, Gender, and Testimony*. Cambridge: Cambridge University Press.

— (2008), 'État Présent: Simone De Beauvoir Studies'. *French Studies* 62 (2): 200–8.

Veltman, A. (2004), 'The Sisyphean Torture of Housework: Simone de Beauvoir and Inequitable Divisions of Domestic Work in Marriage'. *Hypatia* 19 (3): 121–43.

Vintges, K. (1996), *Philosophy as Passion: The Thinking of Simone de Beauvoir*, trans. Anne Lavelle. Bloomington, IN: Indiana University Press.

Virno, P. (2004), *A Grammar of the Multitude*, trans. J. Cascaito. New York: Semiotext(e).

Ward, J. K. (1995), 'Beauvoir's Two Senses of "Body" in "The Second Sex"' in Margaret A. Simons (ed.), *Feminist interpretations of Simone de Beauvoir*. University Park, PA: Pennsylvania State University Press.

— (2006), 'Reciprocity and Friendship in Beauvoir's Thought', in Margaret A. Simons (ed.), *The Philosophy of Simone de Beauvoir: Critical Essays*. Bloomington, IN: Indiana University Press : 146–62.

Weiss, G. (2006), 'Challenging Choices: An Ethic of Oppression' in *The Philosophy of Simone de Beauvoir: Critical Essays*. Ed. by Margaret A. Simons. Bloomington: Indiana University Press, 241–61.

Whitmarsh, A. (1981), *Simone de Beauvoir and the Limits of Commitment*. Cambridge: Cambridge University Press.

Wilkerson, W. (2007), *Ambiguity and Sexuality: A Theory of Sexual Identity*. New York: Palgrave MacMillan.

Zerilli, L. M. G. (1992), 'A Process without a Subject: Simone de Beauvoir and Julia Kristeva on Maternity'. *Signs* 18 (1): 111–35.

Part III

Resources

16 A–Z Glossary

Abbagnano

Nicola Abbagnano (1901–1990) was an Italian philosopher who played an important role in the introduction of existentialism to Italy. His writings in the 1930s present an account of philosophy as a search for Being and, at the same time, a rejection of both **Heidegger**'s definition of authentic existence as 'being-towards-death' and Jaspers's conception of Being as unattainable, which Abbagnano regarded as marked with 'dread' and 'failure' respectively. Conversely, Abbagnano proposed what he called *positive existentialism*, that is, a philosophical approach that emphasizes the notion of possibility, while at the same time stressing human finitude. During the 1940s, he focused on science, asserting its cognitive value and suggesting an account of philosophy as epistemological enquiry able to complement science. Subsequently, he relied on Dewey's pragmatism and on neopositivism to support the idea of a 'new Enlightenment', a revaluation of reason considered 'as a human force endeavouring to make the world more human'. However, he later considered the new Enlightenment a failure because of the success of Marxism (which he regarded as a development of idealism), and he developed an increasing interest in the contribution that philosophy can offer to the solution of everyday problems. From 1936 to 1976 he taught history of philosophy at the University of Turin. His essays on art, science, sociology, and so on, are collated in several books, including *Il problema dell'arte* (1925), *La Fisica Nuova* (1934), *La struttura dell'Esistenza* (1939), *Esistenziulismo Positivo* (1948) and *Possibilità e Libertà* (1956). He was also the author of an excellent history of philosophy textbook, used by several generations of students in Italy.

Paolo Diego Bubbio

Absurdity

Absurdity is a key notion in the early thought and literature of **Camus**. By the absurd, Camus did not mean to express the nihilistic view that human life or experience is meaningless. Camus's notion of absurdity aims to describe the human predicament as he saw it, or, as he later commented, as his generation found it in the streets. This is a predicament wherein humans find themselves torn between an ineradicable desire for a unified explanation for their experiences, and the unavailability of such an explanation. This absurdity confronts us in a host of experiences Camus describes in *The Myth of Sisyphus* (1942) and dramatizes in *The Outsider* (1942) and the early play *Caligula* (1958/1944). These include, most prominently, facing one's own mortality, but Camus cites a host of other manifestations of the absurd, from not recognizing oneself momentarily in one's mirror image, to the inescapably metaphoric nature of even the most advanced scientific notions.

Significantly, Camus denies that the 'decent' or truthful response to absurdity involves despair or **suicide**, or licenses philosophical positions (like those he attributes to **Kierkegaard** or Chestov) that celebrate the arationality of the human condition. The flipside of rationalist denials of our inability to account for the whole (in this camp Camus places Plato, **Husserl**, and others), such positions involve what he terms a 'leap' out of the absurd predicament, by denying one of its poles (the drive to a unified meaning, or the impossibility of such unity). Living with the absurd involves what Camus terms a 'tension' or 'rebellion' against the inescapable temptation of making such leaps into total explanations. In his early work, this leads to a 'quantitative' aesthetics of living, which would multiply experiences in full awareness of their transitoriness (the actor, Don Juan, the conqueror). After 1941 and Camus's involvement in the French resistance, it becomes the basis for his post-nihilistic political ethics of human solidarity founded on the impossibility of giving a defensible, post-religious justification for murder.

Mathew Sharpe

Ambiguity

In **de Beauvoir**'s work 'ambiguity' describes the nature of human existence, which is characterized by an irreducible tension and irrevocable connection between our ontological **freedom** (our **transcendence**) and our 'embeddedness' in the world (our **facticity**). This means that, while being ultimately 'free' from any fixed or inherent 'nature' that might exhaustively define us, we are *at the same time* situated and embodied beings whose materiality is significant to (and affected by) our experience of the world (our history, social location, age, sex, class, etc.) and the others with whom we share this world.

The term 'ambi' means an 'encompassing of both', or, 'being both ways'. Encapsulated in the term ambiguity is our existence as *both* self and **other**, subject and object, a life that is dying from the moment of conception. In *The Ethics of Ambiguity* (1947), de Beauvoir's description of the constant play and tension between what are usually seen as mutually exclusive facets of our being has led to what is often seen as a contradiction in her account of freedom and existence. This is because she argues that we are always ontologically free (we have no essence that determines us) but *at the same time* we are always situated – historically, physically, temporally and psychologically located – in the world with others, which impacts upon our practical freedom and our capacity to act. De Beauvoir does not want us to try to 'overcome' this tension, however, but to *accept* it in order to live *authentically*.

Our ethical actions should be based on a willingness to *engage* with this ambiguity, to maintain the tension that ambiguity implies, and to ensure that others also have the opportunity to engage with their freedom by refusing to see them as 'things'. The maintenance of this tension is crucial to de Beauvoir's ethics and she argues that it needs to be preserved rather than collapsed, both in a theoretical account of ethics and in our practical relation to the world. Neither the transcendent nor the immanent aspect of human existence should be privileged, and the indeterminacy and lack of clarity that ambiguous phenomena are traditionally condemned for become characteristics that are celebrated in an ethics that has its foundations in the acknowledgement of paradox and tension. In *Phenomenology of Perception* (1945), Merleau-Ponty also offers a sustained account of the necessary ambiguity of embodied subjectivity, with some related ethical implications.

Tessa Saunders

Angst/Anguish/Anxiety

Angst (also variously translated as anguish, anxiety or dread) is not fear, which focuses on a particular being. The term is central to the works of **Kierkegaard**, **Heidegger**, **Sartre** and **Camus**. For Kierkegaard, angst (sometimes translated as dread or anxiety) is not an emotion, but a deep-seated strife at the heart of human being over its existence. The course of history need not have been this way, and angst is a reaction to the fundamental choices we have to make in the face of our mortality. In his writings of the 1920s, Heidegger took up Kierkegaard's term (but often translated as *anxiety*) to argue that human beings for the most part ramble on in 'idle talk', repeating clichés about everything from the weather to **death** to cover over their angst over finitude. Like Kierkegaard, Heidegger argued that angst was not directed towards fearsome beings or situations, but instead was 'nothing other than the pure and simple experience of being in the sense of **being-in-the-world**'. In angst, we are struck by a fundamental **mood** of uncanniness (*Unheimlichkeit*) that presses home, so to speak, the fact of our **thrownness** into the world (you didn't choose *this* life) while bringing to the fore our possibilities to be something other than what we've made of ourselves. Camus would later link angst to the absurdity of existence, the mismatch between the cause-and-effect nature around us and our consciousness of the choices before us. For Sartre, angst (translated as *anguish*) is the human awareness of not just our inherent **freedom**, but also our **responsibility** for our own free choices. Sartre argues that for the most part, we evade this responsibility, since we are devoted instead to a 'bad faith' that denies the freedom of an engaged existence.

Peter Gratton

Authenticity

The existentialist credo that 'existence precedes essence' does not seem to leave much room for normative claims about what one ought to do. Yet, 'authenticity' is an ethical term central to existentialism. **Heidegger** uses 'authenticity' (*Eigentlichkeit*) to describe when the being that we ourselves are (*Dasein*) is most its 'own' (*eigen*). But if what is one's own is precisely one's possibilities, then how can one choice be more 'authentic' than others? For Heidegger and later existentialist writers, such as **Sartre**, authenticity is not acceding to a pregiven identity (to be authentically 'urban' or 'hipster' or some other identity), but the opposite. Heidegger contrasts authenticity to the inauthentic existence of *das Man* (the '**they**'), the public persona we take on when immersed in the clichés of everyday life, when we simply go along with what comes along. Here, *Dasein* 'loses itself', and Sartre termed this loss '**bad faith**'. This state of 'fallenness and inauthenticity' is a stupor that requires, for a Heidegger, the 'call of conscience'. Thus, the ethic of authenticity can't give you a set of norms to follow, since the point precisely is to act from out of one's own **freedom**, not merely to conform to the crowds around us. Sartre's account of authenticity, as he argues in *Notebooks for an Ethics* (1947–1948), is not just about our relation to ourselves, but is an assumption of our responsibility to affirm the freedom of others through sustained practical engagements.

Peter Gratton

Bad Faith

Bad faith (*mauvaise foi*) is a form of existential self-deception theorized by **Sartre** in *Being and Nothingness* (1943). Sartre's analysis of **nothingness** suggests that the for-itself's power of negation can be turned against the in-itself (see **Being-in-itself/Being-for-itself**): reflective consciousness negates the pre-reflective consciousness it takes as its object because it cannot grasp what is pre-reflective without thematizing it. Thus the self is torn in reflection between being posited as a unity and being reflexively grasped as a duality. This instability at the heart of the self opens up the possibility of a project of self-deception through which the for-itself attempts to evade **anguish**. Anguish arises from the awareness of the nothingness at the heart of the for-itself. The project of bad faith thus involves a self-interpretation that does not recognize the for-itself for what it is. Either by singling out one of the two poles of **freedom** and **facticity**, or by misunderstanding their nature, the for-itself is viewed in terms of some in-itself being. Sartre gives a number of examples. Famously, a café waiter who fully identifies with his facticity views himself as an in-itself waiter. The woman who is ambivalent about being seduced interprets her body as an in-itself she can freely rise above. Even sincerity involves an identification with an in-itself, that of the sincere individual. Although in each case, the for-itself also relates to this in-itself in a way that betrays its nature as always lying beyond any fixed interpretation of itself, the resulting interpretative instability hides behind that of all self-reflection. Unlike **Heidegger**'s understanding of inauthenticity, this is condemned by Sartre as fundamentally immoral.

Christian Onof

Barth, Karl

Swiss Reformed theologian, Karl Barth (1886–1968) is widely regarded to have been the most significant Protestant theologian of the twentieth century. Barth was an 'existentialist theologian' in the minds of his contemporaries because of his early works, particularly his celebrated second edition of *The Epistle to the Romans* (1922) and *Christian Dogmatics* (1927).

Barth is indebted to **Kierkegaard** and his concept of the 'infinite qualitative difference' between **God** and humanity, a relationship that Barth claims 'is for me the theme of the Bible and the essence of philosophy'. Following Kierkegaard, Barth bases his theological method upon the understanding that God is 'Wholly Other': transcendent to humanity. Religious knowledge is understood to be totally dependent upon God's self-revelation, the Word of God, notably in Jesus Christ. This stood as a strong challenge to the prominent liberal Protestantism of his education, which Barth argues had ceded theological method to anthropology and religious philosophy, thus losing Christocentric particularity.

In his later work *The Church Dogmatics* (4 vols, 1939–1957) Barth begins to eschew existentialism, declaring that he will now avoid 'the slightest appearance of giving theology a basis, support, or even a mere justification in the way of existential philosophy'. However, Barth does not reject existentialism as a theological dialogue partner. He critically engages both **Heidegger** and **Sartre** on the question of **nothingness**, but seeks to give the concept a decidedly theological significance. Barth's turn away from existential philosophy famously led him into conflict with Rudolf **Bultmann**.

Bret D. Stephenson

Beckett

Samuel Beckett (1906–1989), Irish writer best known for the incendiary twentieth-century play *Waiting for Godot* (1948), was most of all interested in human beings' apprehension of basic experience under constraint. From Beckett's first published story *Assumption* (1929) to his final play *What is the Word* (1989), human existence is exposed in exhaustive detail through everyday action and thought pushed to staggering extremes. Writing poetry, plays and prose for 60 years, Beckett's exhaustive approach to life's constraints mirrors the progressively spare nature of his writing, typified by the basic social hierarchy of the play *Catastrophe* (1982) and the repetitions of his final play, *What Where* (1983). In an interview from 1961, Beckett famously stated: 'I wouldn't have had any reason to write . . . novels if I could have expressed their subject in philosophic terms.' This is Beckett's virtue: his texts have a distilled *availability* to existential interpretation, different indeed from expository existential texts. As with philosopher **Heidegger**'s existential analytic of everydayness, Beckett's work mines life at its most primordial. His plays take place on single sets, often barren rooms, and novels like *The Unnamable* are recounted by narrators dying or unsure of ever having existed. As for Heidegger too, 'authentic' being can only be encountered in anticipation of **death**, as in the play *Krapp's Last Tape* (1958). Beckett's profundity is in approaching the liminal ambiguity of 'being' through writing as spare as the tremulous existences actualized within it.

Corey Wakeling

Being-in-Itself/Being-for-Itself

In his *Cartesian Meditations* (1931), **Husserl** distances himself from the Cartesian view that to exist as a conscious human being is to be a substance. The key difference between our way of being and that of other things (being-in-itself) is that we are not *in* the world in the same way as things are *in* space. This leads **Heidegger** to reinterpret our existence as defined through its being in-a-world, thereby completely rejecting the Cartesian framework of subjectivity. **Sartre** takes this difference as showing that we are not in the world in the spatial mode of being characterizing things, but in a different mode, the mode of *not being* *what one is.* This characterizes the spontaneity of consciousness, which is always beyond any property that could characterize it.

Sartre's *Being and Nothingness* thus differentiates between two types of being that cannot be reduced to the phenomenon we experience: the being of the object of consciousness, and consciousness itself. *Being-in-itself* characterizes entities that are complete in themselves. *Being-for-itself* is a lack of being that is intentionally directed towards being-in-itself through negation. It is a 'hole of being at the heart of Being'. **Nothingness** separates these two beings.

This lack of being defines a *fundamental project* for the for-itself: to transcend itself towards being in-itself. But the goal of this project, which is the desire to be God, that is, a being-for-itself-in-itself, is an impossibility. Being-for-itself is authentic when it grasps that the gap to the in-itself is unbridgeable.

Christian Onof

Being-in-the-World

A key feature of our way of being as humans, according to the tradition of Western metaphysics, is that we are subjects. This characterizes us as beings who encounter a world of objects through a cognitive relation. **Heidegger** challenges both this notion of subjectivity and the nature of our relation to the world. His complaint stems from the need to re-examine the central question of Being. To be human is to be the kind of being for which there is Being, that is, for which things are intelligible. As a result, existence is not to be understood in terms of a subject posited independently of objects.

Heidegger proposes rather to understand human existence as a way of being that is defined *through its relation* to things that are intelligible to it. That is, it cannot be isolated as subject from this environment: its way of being is 'being-in-the-world'. The relation to the world that is implied here is not one of spatial location as for objects, but that of being-in.

Heidegger characterizes this as a relation of concern. That is, the intelligibility of things for me is not that of cognition, but of what is meaningful to my existence. This meaning is essentially practical and reflects my involvements with things. The primacy of being-in-the-world implies that we are to understand our existence as a **facticity**. We are not primarily subjects who happen to encounter things as objects, but rather primordially find ourselves in a world.

Christian Onof

331

Berdyaev

Nikolai Berdyaev (1874–1948) was the best-known of the Russian religious philosophers of the first half of the twentieth century. Although strongly influenced
by German idealism and Jacob Boehme, the distinctive Russian character of his
work was reflected in the influence of **Dostoevsky**, to whom he devoted an
important book, and in his lifelong preoccupation with the historical destiny of
Russia and 'the Russian idea'. Berdyaev placed an especially high value on
human **freedom** (or 'Spirit') and the **transcendence** of personality over biology,
culture, politics and ontology. He also attacked the reification of religious values in the Church, an attack he saw as prefigured in Dostoevsky's 'Legend of the
Grand Inquisitor'. His emphasis on freedom is already marked in his *The Meaning of the Creative Act* (1908), where he proposes a high view of human creativity
as reflecting the image of the creator **God**. Although he had suffered internal
exile under Tsarist rule and was sympathetic to some of the social aims of the
Revolution, he was expelled from the Soviet Union in 1922. He finally settled in
Paris, where he forged close friendships with thinkers such as Jacques Maritain
and edited the journal *Put'* (*The Way*), one of the most influential organs for
philosophical reflection among Russian émigrés. In this period his thought
became more markedly dualistic as he saw totalitarian systems tightening their
grip on European life, a dualism reflected in such book titles as *Slavery and Freedom* and *The Realm of Spirit and the Realm of Caesar*.

George Pattison

Binswanger

Ludwig Binswanger (1881–1966). See the chapter 'Existentialism, Psychoanalysis and Psychotherapy'.

Body

Existential approaches to the body are attuned to the fact that we live as bodily
beings. Rather than account for the human body in purely objective terms,
existential and phenomenological accounts of the body acknowledge its lived
dimension. The German term *Lieb* (living body/organism) is distinguished
from *Körper* (physical body/matter) to underscore this point. It is said that
medical and scientific orientations do not take sufficient account of this fact,
which concerns the difference between one's own experience of illness and its
objective existence 'for others' (**Sartre**). The lived body is not always thought
positively, however. **De Beauvoir** feels that feminine corporeality played an

ambivalent role, and suggests that it hinders the **transcendence** that inheres less problematically in masculine forms of agency.

The body plays a consistently pivotal role in **Merleau-Ponty**'s philosophy, which focuses on matters of perception and movement. For him, it is through our bodies that we are open and available to the world. Posture, for example, is conceived as a permeable orientation towards the world and others rather than some static physical fact. Although Merleau-Ponty's later work suggests a complex relation between human sentience and the perceived world, beyond any simple subject–object distinction, the body still features as key to human experience.

There is another strand of corporeal thinking which resists the phenomenological 'lived body'. Rather than smoothly integrate the body with subjectivity, Nietzsche affirmed the potential of the body to exceed the perspective of conscious agency. Georges Bataille and Pierre Klossowski developed Nietzsche's suggestion, inaugurating a French reading of the body's singular potential in the mid-twentieth century that was more or less contemporaneous with Merleau-Ponty's phenomenological philosophy of the body.

Philipa Rothfield

Boredom

Boredom became a noticeable feature of modern cultural attitudes in the later eighteenth century. In the Romantic period the beginnings of a cult of boredom are witnessed by, for example, Byron's *Don Juan* and Pushkin's *Eugene Onegin*. By 1843, **Kierkegaard** is able to write of it as a characteristic feature of aesthetic **nihilism**. Written under the guise of one of his aesthetic pseudonyms, Kierkegaard's essay 'The Rotation Method' (in *Either/Or*) offers a mini-history of the world as a history of boredom. The topic had already been addressed in philosophy by **Schopenhauer**, who depicted human life as oscillating between the pain of unfulfilled desire and the boredom consequent on its fulfilment. Only those with higher intellectual endowments were able to escape this vicious circle.

Kierkegaard, however, sees boredom not as inevitable but as a result of adopting a particular view of life. Like other mental states, boredom belongs within the domain of **freedom** and **responsibility**. The negative effects of boredom and its association with crime were explored extensively by **Dostoevsky** in characters such as Svidrigailov (*Crime and Punishment*) and Stavrogin (*Demons*), while Baudelaire gave paradigmatic expression to the ennui of modern urban existence. In *What is Metaphysics?* and *The Basic Concepts of Metaphysics* **Heidegger** portrayed deep boredom as leading to a loss of the sense of Being that could provoke the individual into a heightened reflection on the question of the meaning of Being as such. Postwar, boredom was frequently seen as an aspect of modern disenchantment, as in Alberto Moravia's novel *Boredom*.

George Pattison

Boss

Medard Boss (1903–1990). See 'Existentialism, Psychoanalysis and Psychotherapy'.

Buber

Born in Vienna but having spent most of his life in Germany and then Israel, Martin Buber (1878–1965) is most well known for his 'dialogic philosophy', which was influenced by Kant, **Kierkegaard**, **Nietzsche**, Simmel and Dilthey. Dialogic philosophy argues that it is the task of each person to fully actualize his or her uniqueness by developing a unified personality. This process occurs through the dual acts of distancing and relating in encounters with others. In Buber's 'ontology of the between' each partner in a relation exists as a polarity of that relation, so that the relation or the 'between' is what is 'real'. Although often labelled an existentialist, Buber rejected the label, arguing that existentialism does not fully acknowledge otherness. His placement of meetings with others at the centre of human reality was a major influence on Emmanuel Levinas.

Buber's most widely read book is the 1923 *I and Thou* (*Ich und Du*), which distinguished between 'I–Thou' and 'I–It' modes of existence. In an 'I–It' relation the other is a static object that is classified under universal categories, experienced and used. In an 'I–Thou' relation each participates in the dynamic process of the other, who is encountered as a unique subject. 'I–It', or 'monologic', relations are necessary for scientific and practical activity, but the development of the person occurs through 'I–Thou', or 'dialogic', relations. 'I–Thou' relations can occur with nature, between people, and with spirit, or the 'eternal Thou'.

Buber was especially interested in pedagogic and therapeutic 'I–Thou' relations, in which one partner helps the other to actualize their self, and he developed a philosophy of education based on education of character. His dialogic philosophy also fits into a larger program of cultural criticism. He was a cultural Zionist who advocated a binational Israeli–Palestinian state and the renewal of society through decentralized, communitarian socialism. He rejected material determinism and believed social change occurs from the ground up as interpersonal relations are altered.

In his studies of the relation between religion and philosophy, Buber criticized philosophy for assuming that the mind experiences a detached world and locating truth in universals. He criticized the isolation and instrumentality of self-consciousness in phenomenology, the suspension of the ethical in Kierkegaard, and Marx, Nietzsche and Freud for treating the other's truth as mere ideology. Buber preferred religion, which locates truth in subjective experience and has an exemplary encounter with otherness in the relation with **God**. However, he was critical of both the legal aspect – which rejects the particularities of each situation – and the mystical aspect of religion. He showed that mysticism follows the same dynamic as collectivism. In both, absorption of the self in the all turns into an individualistic lack of engagement with others. Buber's rejection of religious law and mysticism was controversial in religious circles, while his disdain for systemization made him an outsider in philosophy.

Sarah Scott

Bultmann

German theologian and New Testament scholar, Rudolf Bultmann (1884–1976) is among the foremost of the existentialist theologians and best remembered for his projects of 'demythologizing' and the existentialist interpretation of scripture. In the 1920s Bultmann came under the influence of his Marburg colleague **Heidegger**, and after reading *Being and Time*, he sought to apply Heidegger's existentialist notion of human being as '**being-in-the-world**' to the task of biblical interpretation. For Bultmann, existential analysis provides the theologian with the conceptual categories necessary for understanding the human condition of the believer as addressed in the *kerygma*, or proclamation of the gospel, not only in the mythologized past of scripture, but also in the present age. As outlined in his essay 'New Testament and Mythology' (1941), Bultmann's project of demythologizing did not advocate the excision of mythical elements from Christian texts, but instead called for their careful reinterpretation 'in terms of their understanding of existence'. For example, faith in Jesus Christ is, for Bultmann, based not in a series of judgements concerning the historical veracity of scripture, but rather, in the existential orientation of the believer who is personally confronted by the gospel message in the present day. The twin projects of demythologizing and the existential interpretation of scripture is, for Bultmann, a necessary means for making the message of the New Testament intelligible to a scientific age that is unable to penetrate the mythological language of the gospel writers. Bultmann was, however, frequently criticized by **Barth** and others for having ceded theological autonomy to existential philosophy.

Bret D. Stephenson

335

Camus

Albert Camus (1913–1960) was an author, thinker, essayist, dramatist, political journalist and Nobel Prize Winner. Camus was born and raised in French-occupied Algeria, 'poor but happy', as he would later describe it. Camus's work is structured in three phases, in each of which Camus wrote a framing play, a novel and an extended philosophical essay. Camus's name will forever be popularly associated with the short novel, *The Outsider* (1942). The novel is a dispassionate description of a man, Meursault, whose only defence for shooting an Arab is 'the sun' and 'the sea'. It is aligned with the play *Caligula* (1944) and philosophical essay *The Myth of Sisyphus* (1942), which examined the famous idea of **absurdity**.

From 1943, Camus became associated with the newspaper *Combat*, which was involved with the French resistance to the Nazi occupiers. The experience had a decisive effect, which can be tracked in a series of lyrical essays such as 'The Almond Trees', 'Prometheus in the Underworld' and 'Letters to a German Friend'. Camus's thinking passed from a broadly ethical focus on individual experiences and attitudes to a political philosophy of solidarity. Camus claims in 1942 that an authentic response to the absurd involves a rebellion against the impulse to 'leap' to metaphysical conclusions. Following 1943, Camus begins to argue that 'I rebel, therefore we are'. According to the later Camus, the inalienable individual demand for a unifying meaning to life examined in his first work embodies and points towards a community (the 'we are') with our contemporaries that does not rest on any, unavailable, metaphysical teachings. Camus's 1947 novel *The Plague* dramatizes this position in a plague-stricken, quarantined city, and it is developed philosophically at length in *The Rebel* (1950), a sustained critique of fascism and Stalinism. Camus's criticism in *The Rebel* of the Marxist heritage, and advocacy of a broadly social–democratic politics, put him at odds with his contemporaries **Sartre**, **Merleau-Ponty** and **de Beauvoir**. The 1950s were indeed a difficult period for Camus, as his second marriage collapsed, his hopes for France's reform from the immediate post-resistance period were quashed, and his attempts to mediate in the French–Algerian conflict met hostility from both sides. Camus's disillusionment at this time is reflected in the dark fictional monologue *The Fall* (1956), and the captivating pieces in *Exile and the Kingdom* (1957), which immediately preceded his award of the Nobel Prize for literature. At the time of his untimely death by car accident in 1960, Camus had begun work on a third phase of writings, including the posthumously published draft of the novel *The First Man*.

Mathew Sharpe

Cioran

Emil M. Cioran (1911–1995) was a Romanian born essayist and aphorist, who lived and wrote for the most part in Paris, where he lived from 1937 until his death. His early years involved a frequently remarked commitment to right-wing political views, and during this time he penned pieces in favour of Hitler and Franco. After moving to Paris in 1937, this orientation in his work declined before being criticized by Cioran himself. Cioran's writings, which tend towards the short form, deal with many of the great concerns of existentialism (suffering, **death** and despair, alienation and the lack of a given meaning in life), while also dwelling on topics of a more pronounced phenomenological nature, like insomnia, solitude and the experience and nature of music.

Cioran is often compared to **Nietzsche**, with whom he shares not only the same genres of writing, and many of his most well-known themes, but also his mercilessly critical gaze. Nonetheless, the tone of Cioran's work is darker, and he criticizes Nietzsche for his optimism, his naïvety and frivolity especially with respect to metaphysical themes, and the breathlessness of his later prose. Cioran is the more measured of the two, but also the more fatalistic. There is nonetheless a strain of refined, minimal humanism in Cioran's writings, which sees the incurably pointless, comical and horrifying strivings of human beings, alone and collectively, through the eyes of a certain pity and occasional muted amazement. Underlying this humanism is a modern form of Stoic ethics: a methodical and rigorous expulsion of metaphysical investment and naïve hope engendering a noble form of human existence.

Jon Roffe

Dasein

The term *Dasein* arises in response to **Heidegger**'s question: 'what is the being that will give access to the question of the meaning of Being?' The answer is the being for whom Being matters; human existence, or more literally, the being defined by its 'being-there'. *Dasein* is, therefore, *nothing other* than 'Man', inasmuch as being-there describes the state of human existence in terms of its **being-in-the-world**.

The method pursued in *Being and Time* may be said to consist in the attempt to elucidate the character of *Dasein*, through understanding *Dasein* within the bounds of temporality. An interpretation of its temporality would allow us in turn to approach the meaning of Being itself. Heidegger holds that this must lead us to confront the existential matters of mortality, and thus by extension, **angst**. This raises the problem of **authenticity** – the possibility for *Dasein* to exist in its fullness such that it might comprehend Being. In turn, Heidegger's understanding of authenticity as contextualized by its historical quality means that *Dasein*'s being finds its expression both in, and *as* time. This mutuality between *Dasein* and temporality was only intended as but one aspect of a broader, never-completed project of Heidegger's: to deconstruct the history of philosophy itself in relation to temporality.

Steven Churchill

Das Man

Das Man is the German, third-person singular meaning 'they' or 'one', as in 'one just doesn't dress that way'. *Das Man* plays an important role in Martin **Heidegger**'s *Being and Time* (1927). *Das Man*, the 'they', is the public persona we tend to take on when following the masses, and is thus opposed to the authentic recognition of our ownmost possibilities beyond what 'they say' one should be. Heidegger's analysis is influenced by the work of **Kierkegaard**, who argued that singular individuals lose themselves in the 'crowd', and **Nietzsche**, who excoriated 'herd moralities' always out to destroy the freest spirits among us. For Heidegger, *Dasein*, the being that we ourselves are, dwells constantly in the 'they'. We chit-chat about the weather or lose ourselves in vain discussions about sports, all because that's what 'people do'. We do this even as we conform to the paradoxical dictum that we shouldn't conform. For Heidegger, though, *das Man* is not new to modern mass man, but derives from our **being-in-the-world** as mortal beings. In the face of **angst** over our ownmost possibilities, including our being-towards-death, *das Man* 'tranquilizes' us with regard to 'all possibilities of Being'. Despite these negative portrayals of *das Man*, the lesson is not that we can escape to some ideal place where such a public persona is not created and maintained. Rather, our existence is marked by a struggle to rise out of the crowd, to orient our ownmost possibilities in ways not directed by the whims of what 'one says'.

Peter Gratton

Death

For existentialist thinkers, the theme of death is central in the context of meaning, **authenticity** and **freedom**: that is, the inevitability of death rebounds on the understanding of *what* it means to live, and *how* one can best live. Contemplation of death points to the deep paradox of human existence: that we are both contingent and transcendent; that we are finite creatures with a taste for and anticipation of the infinite. Death is, as **Jaspers** put it, the archetypal 'limit situation' that we are powerless to comprehend or change. However, there are radical differences among existentialist thinkers about the interpretation of death, and these are largely traceable to the decisive differences between atheistic and theistic branches of the movement.

According to **Heidegger**, who is arguably neutral on the question of **God**, death is the unsurpassable possibility that is the ultimate context for all other possibilities: that is, *Dasein* exists *as* 'being-towards-death'. Far from being an 'external' threat, death is the intrinsic and constantly present potentiality that lies at the heart of the structure of *Dasein*'s existence. Consequently, facing up to the

existential meaning of death – a recognition that involves **anxiety** – is the definitive mark of authentic being, for it has a uniquely individualizing effect on *Dasein*;
one's death is uniquely one's own. Of course, in our immersion in 'the they' (*das
Man*) we commonly trivialize death, seeking comfort in practices and assumptions that impersonalize and sanitize death, making it inconspicuous and irrelevant to the task of living. Such practices have the result of cutting us off from the
very horizon within which authenticity is possible.

The strident atheism of **Sartre** and **Camus** strongly challenge Heidegger's
approach to death. For Sartre, there is nothing distinctly 'mine' about my death,
as if 'my death' were some kind of unique and personally forged creation. To the
contrary, meaning is a function of the temporal structure of human freedom that
is terminated or truncated by death. The meaninglessness of death is further
underlined by the arbitrariness and abruptness of its arrival, breaking in on the
process of free unfolding. Far from being the principal possibility *within* the life
of an individual, death is entirely 'other' to the possibility-driven ontological
structure of human beings as free agents. Given all this, death is literally an
absurdity. Indeed, it ultimately reduces life itself to an absurdity: 'It is **absurd**
that we are born, and it is absurd that we die.' A similar approach led Camus to
claim that **suicide** is the only serious philosophical question, although he argued
against it as an option. For him, suicide is a defeatist act; instead he urges us to
rise – Sisyphus like – in scorn and revolt against the cruelty of death by defiantly
embracing life even in the midst of its absurdity.

Among the theistic existentialists, **Marcel** and **Unamuno** drew a clear trajectory between the contemplation of death and belief in God. According to Marcel, far from being absurd, death underlines the transcendent and immortal
essence of human being. On the one hand, human **transcendence** emerges most
strongly in the experience of faithful love which is itself made possible by the
primal human urge for communion with God. But on the other hand, it is in the
death of a loved one that the transcendent nature of human being is most
acutely revealed, for intimate love itself affirms the immortality of the beloved.
Unamuno comes to a similar conclusion on the basis of a consideration of the
creature's stubborn will to persist in being (Spinoza's *conatus essendi*), which he
reads as an insatiable appetite for immortality and an implicit affirmation of
belief in God as the source of all life.

Richard Colledge

De Beauvoir

Simone de Beauvoir (1908–1986) was born in Paris and studied philosophy at the
Sorbonne. For several years, de Beauvoir taught philosophy at high schools in the
country and in Paris, but she soon focused on literary and philosophical writing.

She published her first novel *She Came to Stay* in 1943. This was followed by several essays developing existentialism, and *The Ethics of Ambiguity* (1947). In *The Ethics of Ambiguity* de Beauvoir emphasizes the **ambiguity** of human life: 'to say that [existence] is ambiguous is to assert that its meaning is never fixed, that it must be constantly won'. On her account, this ambiguity implies that we have to create our own values and projects. She links the idea of a basic ontological **freedom** with an ethics that acknowledges and values that freedom, and examines ethical attitudes and antinomies of action.

Her most famous work of philosophy is *The Second Sex* (1949), which develops an existential–phenomenological account of the oppression of women. Existentialism is the view that there is no predetermined human nature, that we are all absolutely free to determine how we shall live, and must, therefore, be held responsible for all our actions. De Beauvoir made fundamental alterations to the theory as initially expounded by **Sartre**, outlining a theory of oppression, a notable lack in Sartre's formulation of existentialism. De Beauvoir's view is that women are materially oppressed in lacking the concrete means to form a group and be free, and psychologically oppressed in having internalized a sense of self as the **Other** – that is, as strange and inferior. One of her most controversial claims is that women are sometimes in **bad faith**, or willingly pursue their own lack of freedom, something she considers a moral fault. Her view is that 'every time **transcendence** falls back into immanence, stagnation, there is a degradation of existence into the "in-itself" – the brutish life of subjection to given conditions – and of liberty into constraint or contingence. This downfall represents a moral fault if the subject consents to it; if it is inflicted upon him, it spells frustration and oppression. In both cases it is an absolute evil.'

The second volume of *The Second Sex* provides a detailed phenomenological description supporting her contention that 'one is not born, but rather becomes, a woman'. De Beauvoir's recommendations for change are multiple: economic independence for women, a refusal to accept the limited roles for women endorsed by society, and an alteration in the myths and stories about women. De Beauvoir's ideas have had an enormous influence on women's liberation movements as well as inspiring a vast and growing body of scholarship. Her later work, *Old Age* (1970), uses her central conception of the Other to interrogate the experience of aging and **death**.

De Beauvoir's novels include *All Men are Mortal* (1946), *The Mandarins* (1954) and *The Woman Destroyed* (1967). She was editor of and writer for the journal *Les Temps Modernes* with Sartre and **Merleau-Ponty** for many years, and wrote four volumes of memoirs. In 2004 de Beauvoir's early philosophical essays were published for the first time in English in the collection *Philosophical Writings*. In 2009 the first complete translation of *The Second Sex* was published, an event likely to further enhance philosophical understanding of her thought.

Marguerite La Caze

Dostoevsky

In the novels *Notes from Underground, Crime and Punishment, The Idiot, Demons* and *The Brothers Karamazov*, Fyodor Dostoevsky (1821–1881) created a range of characters, scenarios and questions that anticipated many of the themes of twentieth-century existentialism. Shortly after his first novel appeared, he was arrested for involvement in a radical discussion group. Following many months of solitary confinement, culminating in a mock execution, he spent four years in a prison camp, followed by five years compulsory military service. These experiences provided rich material for novels that explored the extremes of human emotion, and Dostoevsky was from early on familiar with the criminality and **nihilism** of many of his characters. The irrationalism of the Underground Man and the atheism of Ivan Karamazov were seen as expressing the author's own views, although it is clear that Dostoevsky was concerned to expose modern nihilism as a form of human self-deification and, as such, rebellion against **God**. This is particularly clear in his depiction of such characters as Raskolnikov (*Crime and Punishment*), Kirillov (*Demons*) and Ivan Karamazov himself, whose atheism was summed up in the statement that 'If God does not exist, everything is permitted.' Although his 'legend' of an encounter between Christ and the Grand Inquisitor can be seen as an attack on ecclesiastical Christianity and although he confessed to never definitively escaping the crucible of doubt in which his **faith** was formed, Dostoevsky extolled a form of Christian life marked by love of Christ, universal compassion and absolute humility.

George Pattison

Dread (see Angst/Anguish/Anxiety)

Ecstases

Rooted in the Greek *ekstasis*, meaning 'to stand outside', the *ecstases* are the focal point of **Heidegger**'s investigations into the being of time. We generally think of time in terms of the stable ticking of the clock from past to present to future, with each of our experiences anchored in some present 'now'. Heidegger argues, however, that this is an 'inauthentic' conception of time and that temporality is the '*ekstatikon* pure and simple', a 'primordial "outside-of-itself" in and for itself'. As 'possibility', *Dasein*, the being that we ourselves are, is never *in* time standing at some now-point. Rather, *Dasein* is always out-ahead-of-itself in its future, which Heidegger considered the primary ecstasis. But this projection carries along our historicity and the meaning that the past has made possible. Thus, the second 'ecstasis' is 'having been', with the third being the present, which for Heidegger is not the 'now-point' of clock-time, but instead marks our being-alongside other beings, including other *Daseins*. But although we can separate these ecstases through reflection, they form a 'unity', an unstable timing or rhythm of existence that provides for our openness towards a future not wholly written from the past or present. This Heideggerian discussion becomes important later to **Sartre** in *Being and Nothingness*, where he argues that each ecstasis is united with the others, such that the past is always a 'past-future', the future is a 'future-past', and the present is not a 'now', but the attentiveness of the self to its existence.

Peter Gratton

Facticity

In twentieth-century existentialism, 'facticity' (*Faktizität* – a term coined by Fichte and the neo-Kantians) came to stand for concrete, situated, 'given' subjectivity. In **Heidegger**'s early Marburg writings, *facticity* simply designates the character of the Being of **Dasein** in its temporal particularity. In *Being and Time*, however, it is used in a more specific sense as one of the three dimensions of care (*Sorge*) along with understanding or projection (or sometimes 'existentiality') and falling. As such, it is often used in ways that are largely synonymous with **thrownness** (*Geworfenheit*). Heidegger unpacks the meaning of facticity largely via his analysis of 'states-of-mind' (*Befindlichkeit*). His contention here is that *Dasein* always and already has its way of **being-in-the-world** according to a **mood** 'into which it has been delivered over'.

For **Sartre**, facticity comes to mean 'determinedness' in the sense of the 'weight' of the past and the demands of the present that stand opposed to the realization of the individual's **freedom**. In this context, facticity means something quite close to what **Kierkegaard** referred to as 'necessity' (*Nødvendighed*). Here, where the term is open to more '**ontic**' elaboration than in Heideggerian thought, one may speak of facticity as relating to a sense of the 'givenness' of life through which horizons are narrowed and one performs one's 'received' roles and functions, rather than exercising one's freedom in its dizzying absoluteness.

Richard Colledge

Faith

It is generally acknowledged that arguments for religious beliefs such as the existence of **God**, an afterlife, and so on, are not compelling. Many people with religious beliefs, however, continue to hold their beliefs claiming simply to have faith. In the existential tradition **Kierkegaard** is the philosopher who has dealt most with giving an account of faith. For Kierkegaard, faith has little to do with believing in something because there is good evidence. It is rather an unwavering determination to believe passionately in something despite, or even because of, its absurdity. This approach has the result that the objective truth of one's beliefs becomes irrelevant. Faith is solely a way of believing something or a way of existing. It is this aspect of faith – focusing on the individual's existence rather than the object of belief – that ties it to existentialism.

The problem is that here the distinction between a reasonable faith and an unreasonable or blind faith is lost. Consequently, a person with such faith has no rational arguments for his or her faith. This means that there are no rational grounds for choosing one faith over another. Thus, the faith that God became a man is on par with the faith that Zeus became a swan. For many people such a view of faith is unacceptable. However, to go the other way and hold that faith should be based on good evidence is to make faith into the conclusion of an argument. And, as mentioned, arguments for religious beliefs are not rationally compelling.

James Giles

Frankl

Viktor Frankl (1905–1997). See the chapter 'Existentialism, Psychoanalysis and Psychotherapy'.

Freedom

Freedom is the quintessential existentialist value. It lies at the heart of most existential philosophies. For example, for **Sartre** in *Being and Nothingness* the human being is a free upsurge of consciousness thanks to which there is a world. Most existentialists, except notably **Nietzsche**, insist that the human being is free. The freedom of human intentional consciousness allows for the world to be born and for values to be erected. Ontological freedom allows the creation of the world through the conscious being's perception of objects. By the same token, it is a moral freedom since it allows the free valuing of things in the created world. It is also, for most existentialists, a freedom from the illusions of an afterlife and an otherworldly realm. For theistic existentialists, freedom means insisting that the relation to **God** and the values He posits is one that is freely chosen by the individual. For atheistic existentialism, the human being is understood as entirely responsible for his or her own fate, choices and values. In *The Brothers Karamazov* (1880), **Dostoevsky** suggested: 'If God does not exist, everything is permitted.' However, the freedom gained from the absence of

God is not to be equated with moral licence. If existentialists posit the human being as free, they also insist that the human is, therefore, responsible for himself, his actions and the world he creates through action, a world with or without God. For existentialists like **de Beauvoir** and Sartre, the philosophy of freedom entails a social and political stance that requires the commitment of individuals to make the world one in which freedom may flourish. And, therefore, individuals ought to work towards liberation.

Christine Daigle

God

God is a problematic figure for existentialism, theistic or atheistic. **Kierkegaard**, a theist existentialist, speaks of God as an unknown that stands beyond the reach of our reason. It is through introspection that the subject will discover this unknown, a 'something' of which we may say nothing. A similar problem arises for **Marcel**, who locates the relation of the individual with God at the pre-reflective level of consciousness (which supports the reflective, that is, rational, consciousness). God is the bearer of existence and gives meaning to the world and the existents living therein. But the relation with God, or God himself, may never be reflectively illuminated. The relation is what sustains intersubjectivity and the relation between consciousnesses and objects in the world, but is one that will escape our reflective inquiries. Atheistic existentialism's problem with God is very different. According to the atheist existentialist, the problem with believing that God exists is that the individual will relinquish his **responsibility** to Him. This is unacceptable for existentialists who want the human being to be responsible for his own choices and actions. Some suggest that God has been invented by human beings so they can escape moral responsibility. Others, in the same vein as Aristotle, will rather claim that it does not matter whether God exists or not since the individual has to decide whether this God has any value for him. Most, however, will prefer to echo **Nietzsche** and declare the death of God and of all accompanying transcendent values to focus on the human being and his world.

Christine Daigle

Guilt

The category of guilt is of great importance for existentialist thought, in which the everyday notion of responsibility for one's actions is often transformed such that the individual is understood to be in some sense irredeemably or constitutionally guilty.

Kierkegaard sets his reflections on guilt in the context of the Christian doctrine of original sin, which is for him part of the structure of human being. In the process, he sets the notion of guilt in dialectical relation not with innocence but with **anxiety**. In contrast, **Nietzsche** offers a genealogy of guilt in which he suggests that the moral notion had its origins in reprisal against loan defaulters (*Schuld* carrying connotations of guilt and/or debt). A 'bad conscience', then, is essentially a turning inward of the same logic of reprisal.

Heidegger's analysis of guilt takes the concept in a radically new direction, arguing that guilt is not the product of either sinfulness or indebtedness; rather all such notions are themselves only possible on the basis of a prior primordial Being-guilty. Heidegger links this ontological sense of guilt to *Dasein*'s **thrownness**: that is, its not being its own basis or ground. *Dasein* is guilty (or in debt) insofar as it either resides in a ground not of its own making, or resolutely 'takes it over' *as* its own. But in either case, *Dasein* never has power 'over [its] ownmost Being from the ground up'.

Later existentialist thinkers developed the notion in related diverse ways. For **Marcel**, for example, an intrinsic guilt resides in the impossibility of mutually upholding faithfulness to oneself and to others, including the Divine other.

Richard Colledge

Hegel

G. W. F. Hegel (1770–1831) is the most influential of the post-Kantian philosophers, having integrated elements from the idealist philosophies of both Fichte and Schelling. Hegel's system included a *phenomenology* that reconstructed the cognitive experiences of consciousness in its historical journey towards self-consciousness; a *'logic'* of the basic categories of thought about reality; a *philosophy of history* that conceptualized the events of world history as stages in the realization of **freedom**; and a *political philosophy* that outlined the development of free modern subjects as depending upon the spheres of family, civil society (economy) and the political state. An essential reference point for Karl Marx, Hegel was also significant for **Kierkegaard**, who pitted the singular existence of the authentic individual against Hegel's abstract system of reason.

Hegel's *Phenomenology of Spirit* (1807) is best known for its account of the 'master/slave' dialectic. Self-consciousness is presented as commencing with a life-and-death struggle between protagonists who each seek recognition of their own independence. The protagonist who risks his life for freedom becomes 'master', while the one who experiences the 'fear of **death**' becomes a 'slave'. The master, however, does not enjoy genuine recognition from an equal, whereas the slave develops his capacities through work and comes to recognize himself via the fruits of his labours. This unequal recognition is eventually superseded by mutual recognition within modern social and cultural institutions.

Hegel's 'master/slave' dialectic was taken up by French Hegelians (Alexandre Kojève and Jean Hyppolite) and significantly influenced French existentialism, for example in **Sartre**'s accounts of the self-divided subject and of relations with others, and **de Beauvoir**'s analysis of gender relations.

Robert Sinnerbrink

Heidegger

The influence of Martin Heidegger (1889–1976) on existentialism cannot be overstated. In his magnum opus, *Being and Time* (1927), Heidegger sought to return philosophy to the meaning of the Being of beings. But the route that he took, by first explicating the meaning of the being that we ourselves are, for which he used the German term *Dasein*, provided the very path that later existentialists, including **Sartre**, would tread in plumbing the depths of human subjectivity. The irony, given his renown as an existentialist, is that Heidegger later published his 'Letter on "Humanism"' (1947) as a direct counter to existentialist appropriations that he deemed too focused on subjective experience. This reading of Heidegger arose because *Being and Time* did not make the full turn to the question of the meaning of Being, ending instead with a conception of the temporality of *Dasein*, not of Being as such. Nevertheless, his arguments in that work were crucial for all later existentialist thinkers.

Philosophy, Heidegger argued, should not be about what we can know, but about our practical engagements with the world around us, that is, 'how' we exist prior to any conscious reflection. Fundamentally, Heidegger argued that we are future-oriented beings who have a certain 'care' for the world. By this Heidegger does not mean an emotional response to existence, but rather that the world is always already imbued with meaning for us. This 'care' is always structured towards the future and the possibilities of each *Dasein*. To use a Sartrean term, we each have a set of 'projects', and thus we are not defined by our past or some human essence, but instead by the possibilities that leave each existence open. According to Heidegger, this openness to the future is finite, however, and each *Dasein* is 'thrown' into existence having 'being-towards-death' as part of the structure of its being. Hence, whether we wish to evade our mortality or not, **death** is an ever-present possibility, not a theoretical or abstract point.

After the publication of *Being and Time*, Heidegger's task was to further his 'deconstruction' (*Destruktion* or *Abbau*) of previous ways of thinking Being as one stable entity among others, which he argued was also a linguistic task. He thus championed poets such as **Rilke** and Goethe as taking up the charge of thinking in an age when technological efficiency was stifling what was left of all creativity. The fundamental claim of Heidegger, from his earliest writings to his last, is that Being, and hence beings, does not have a stable essence, but is a 'how', a 'manner' or a 'way'. Our existence is not reducible to biological accounts of our bodily matter, just as our being-towards-death has a meaning beyond evolutionary accounts of the survival instinct. In this way, our existence always precedes any supposed essence of the human being, and indeed to exist means to be open to a future not yet written by the techno-scientific accounts of the present age.

Peter Gratton

Husserl

The influence of the phenomenology of Edmund Husserl (1859–1938) upon philosophers who have been characterized as existentialist, including **Heidegger, Sartre** and **Merleau-Ponty**, is uncontroversial; the more difficult question is whether such influence is best understood in terms of the development of ideas in Husserl's thought or as formed predominately in opposition to his thought.

An instructive programmatic statement of Husserl's philosophical project is found in the 1910 essay 'Philosophy as Rigorous Science'. Here Husserl explains his project as aiming to provide the conceptual underpinnings of a 'science of science', an aspiration which has echoes of the Aristotelian notion of a 'first philosophy'. Husserl's concern with the origins and meaning of formal sciences such as arithmetic and logic is, from the outset, motivated by an awareness of the generality and universality of these disciplines in the sense that they form the inferential and conceptual framework for all other branches of knowledge. Husserl's 'transcendental turn' at the time of the *Ideas 1* (1913) represents less a departure from his earlier investigations than a new-found conviction that it is through a transcendental phenomenology, concerned with questions of essence, that the origin and meaning of the sciences can best be understood. This direction of thought appears to subordinate problems of 'human existence' to the project of articulating the essential structures of pure consciousness and the role such structures play in the development of the sciences.

How does such a project, then, relate to existentialism? Consideration of Heidegger's attempt to recapture the 'true' meaning of phenomenology in *Being and Time* (1927) can help point in the direction of a more nuanced understanding of Husserl's relation to existential philosophy. Heidegger's claim in *Being and Time* is that phenomenology is best conceived as an attempt to disclose the things themselves as they show themselves in our concerned dealings with them. This suggests an analysis which sets out from our experience of the world as it discloses itself in practical interactions made possible by our 'situatedness' and the structure of phenomenological time-consciousness. The key insight here, from the perspective of understanding Husserl's complex relation to existentialism, is that an adequate understanding of the origin and meaning of the sciences depends upon an account of our concrete situation as practically oriented and embodied, or, to adopt Heidegger's own terminology, on the status of scientific 'assertion' (*Aussage*) as derivative of the more originary modes of discourse found in understanding (*Verstehen*) and interpretation (*Auslegung*).

George Duke

Intentionality

Intentionality is a characteristic of consciousness. To be conscious is always to be conscious *of* something: to 'intend' (or refer to, or be directed towards) a particular object. As such, consciousness is not itself a 'thing', but is rather the *directedness towards* things. This theme was revived (in a refined form) in the 1870s by Franz Brentano from medieval Scholasticism, and it subsequently became a central axiom of **Husserl**'s phenomenological method, and thereafter existentialist thought.

For Husserl, intended 'objects' are discrete meanings or awarenesses *immanent* to consciousness, including awareness of material objects, illusions, ideas, inner emotional responses, and so on. Phenomenology, unlike the natural sciences, 'brackets out' the vexed question of whether and how objects exist independently of the contents of consciousness. **Heidegger** developed Husserl's doctrine of intentionality in ways that moved still further away from the residue of Cartesian metaphysics. He vastly broadened the scope of Husserl's subject–object intentional structure to encompass the complex multilayered whole of *Dasein*'s **being-in-the-world**. In this way, the focus shifted from an emphasis on the privileged vantage point of Husserl's isolated ego that 'constitutes' the world and its meaning to a view in which *Dasein* is always already in a meaning-saturated world, in which *Dasein* and world interpenetrate each other.

Sartre continued the decentring of the subject in its world-constituting role by arguing that far from the ego being the source of consciousness (with some kind of sovereign oversight of the process), it is rather itself constituted *by* consciousness. **Merleau-Ponty** took this tradition of thought in a strongly 'bodily' direction by charting the psychophysical dimensions and expressions of intentionality through such diverse phenomena as the sense of the **body** in space, our reaching for and contacting worldly objects, the various modes of intersubjectivity, bodily gesture, and so on.

Richard Colledge

Jaspers

The philosophy of Karl Jaspers (1883–1969), along with that of **Heidegger**, gave rise to the German existentialist movement in the early part of the twentieth century. Jaspers, who now stands in the shadow of Heidegger's philosophical stature, was first trained as a psychologist prior to transitioning to philosophy. As a psychologist he adopted **Husserl's** phenomenological method and produced one major work called *General Psychopathology* (1913), which is still in print. Jaspers's foray into existentialism is marked by his juxtaposition of **Kierkegaard** and **Nietzsche**, which first appeared in his early work *Psychology of World Views* (1919). This comparison resulted in the development of his 'philosophy of existence' (*Existenz-Philosophy*), which is predicated on an always unfinished goading of human inquiry beyond the limits of cognition towards Being-itself. This fundamental concept was reworked and eventually appeared in what is commonly considered the major work of his later period, *Of Truth* (1947), which remains untranslated in its entirety. While the influences of Kierkegaard and Nietzsche reappear throughout Jaspers's oeuvre, his major philosophical underpinnings are inextricably tied to Kant's theory of Ideas and his transcendental deduction.

Jaspers claims his philosophical and existential identity through his anti-systematic approach to the pervasive ontological question: What is Being? His response to the question of Being is grounded in a rich architectonic structure he calls 'the Encompassing'. Following Kant, Jaspers rejects the possibility of a formal ontology and works to identify various realms of being through the construct of the Encompassing, which manifests itself in immanent and transcendent, as well as subjective and objective, modes. Jaspers argues that the Encompassing is not itself the horizon of our knowledge, nor is it something we actually encounter qua object. Rather, the Encompassing can be understood as the ground of Being from which new horizons emerge. In Jaspers's own words, 'the Modes of the Encompassing illuminate a basic feature of man's possibility'.

In addition to Jaspers's primary work as an existentialist, he made significant contributions to the fields of political philosophy and the philosophy of religion. In particular, his text *Philosophical Faith and Revelation* (1967) offers a compelling critique of revelation and religious dogma while arguing that moments of transcendence are possible through what he describes in technical terms as 'philosophical faith'. Jaspers's first of two major works, *Philosophy* (1932), is a three-volume set covering his philosophy of Being. It includes his 'Philosophical World Orientation' (vol. 1), 'Existential Elucidation' (vol. 2) and 'Metaphysics' (vol. 3). Between the publication of *Philosophy* and his second major work, the aforementioned *Of Truth*, Jaspers was removed from his professorship at the University of Heidelberg by the Nazi regime and his relationship with Heidegger was subsequently and irreconcilably damaged over Heidegger's political affiliation with National Socialism. Jasper's small text *Philosophy of*

Existence is a record of the last lectures given by him before leaving Germany in 1937 and serve as a brief introduction to his existentialism. After the Second World War, Jaspers moved to Switzerland where he served as a professor at University of Basel until his death in 1969.

Nick Wernicki

Kafka

Franz Kafka (1883–1924) was an Austrian writer, the author of three unfinished novels and numerous works of short fiction, generally considered to be among the greatest of modernist literature. Relative to the strain of existentialism that promotes an heroic and self-asserted mode of subjectivity, Kafka is far from being an existentialist writer. On the other hand, he is unmatched in the canon of modern fiction in invoking the absurdity of the human situation in a meaningless world.

In Kafka's work, this world lacking in its own ultimate significance nonetheless appears to his various protagonists (whether human, animal or the other peculiar animates of Kafka's thought) as having a *hidden* meaning. Their situation is at once eccentric and unfounded. In 'Investigations of a Dog', the titular character recalls how, as a young dog, he was 'filled with a premonition of great things – a premonition that may well have been delusional, for I always had it'.

The principle theme of Kafka's work is the interminable search or process, the attempt to arrive at the locus of meaning that does not exist. The friction between the attempt and the lack of a real goal, the dynamic of an investment that is confounded, though not entirely, at every point, is what gives force to much of his work.

The correlate of this theme is that of a baroque and, since ultimately ungrounded, necessarily cruel set of laws, customs and bureaucracies, whose significance and authority remains mysterious to those trapped within them.

Jon Roffe

Kierkegaard

Among the epithets bestowed on Søren Kierkegaard (1813–1855) have been 'the master of irony', 'the melancholy Dane' and 'the father of existentialism'. All are in some respects valid, but also potentially misleading. His Master's thesis on Socratic irony witnesses to his fascination with the theme of irony and he proved an able exponent of it in his own writing. Yet he insisted that his central concerns called for a serious or 'earnest' approach to life. For many readers, Kierkegaard is all too serious, since themes of melancholy, **anxiety**, **boredom** and despair pervade such works as *Either/Or*, *Repetition*, *The Concept of Anxiety*, *Stages on Life's Way* and *The Sickness unto Death*. His portrayal of Romantic aestheticism shows a form of existence in which such moods dominated and eventually extinguished the self. However, he also argued that the self was capable of choosing itself in such a way as to escape these states and, in a decisive 'moment of vision', of realizing its potential **freedom**.

A preliminary form of such choice is seen in the 'ethical' view of life promoted in the second part of *Either/Or*. Yet Kierkegaard regarded this as inadequate for dealing with the extreme form of despair that Christianity calls sin and from which we can only be redeemed by **faith** in Christ as Saviour. Thus, while Kierkegaard speaks of the three stages of the aesthetic, the ethical and the religious, the religious stage is further subdivided between a kind of religiousness ('religiousness A') that is compatible with general human experience and the specifically Christian religiousness ('religiousness B') that depends on faith. Kierkegaard himself did not use the expression 'leap of faith' often ascribed to him but he did understand faith as involving a leap beyond the intellectual horizon of any merely immanent philosophical system. One of his principle complaints against Hegelianism is precisely that it tries to think of **God** in concepts drawn from immanence and thus reduces theology to anthropology – as became explicit in Feuerbach. These religious themes are particularly developed in such pseudonymous works as *Philosophical Fragments* (or *Crumbs*), *Concluding Unscientific Postscript*, *Training in Christianity* and *The Sickness unto Death* as well as in the so-called upbuilding or Christian discourses that he published alongside the pseudonymous works.

In all his writings Kierkegaard was clear that the decisive issues in human life could not be adequately dealt with at the theoretical level but had to be engaged with existentially, as matters of urgent concern to the existing human being, whom he portrayed as thoroughly temporal and confronted by the ineluctable yet unthinkable reality of **death**. In the 1920s it was precisely this Kierkegaardian sense of 'existence' that would give its title to the philosophical movement associated with **Jaspers** and **Heidegger**, who also made extensive use of such Kierkegaardian concepts as anxiety, concern, **guilt**, repetition and the moment of vision. However, Heidegger rejected Kierkegaard's religious conclusions and the extent to which existentialism can also be Christian remains debatable. For Kierkegaard himself, it couldn't be anything else.

George Pattison

Laing

R. D. Laing (1927–1989). See the chapter 'Existentialism, Psychotherapy and Psychoanalysis'.

Look

Sartre argues in *Being and Nothingness* (1943) that there is an original relation with the **Other**, which he calls 'the look'. The look is not just visual: it can be 'a rustling of branches . . . or the slight opening of a shutter, or a light movement of a curtain'. In apprehending a look of the Other we become aware of being looked at. Sartre's best-known example concerns the phenomenon of shame. He writes: 'Let us imagine that moved by jealousy, curiosity, or vice I have just glued my ear to the door and looked through a keyhole. . . . But all of a sudden I hear footsteps in the hall. Someone is looking at me!' The sound transforms the relation to the self by revealing the presence of the Other. When looking through the keyhole the person is totally involved in the **situation**, but when they are looked at by the Other they are judged. In shame, pride or fear, we experience ourselves as objects and experience the subjectivity of the Other. Phenomena like these show that there are other consciousnesses. Through the look, we live the situation of being looked at, while gaining object-ness, which is a kind of being. However, this is an unhappy consciousness, Sartre argues, because the individual loses the **freedom** that depends upon their transcendent subjectivity. The look leads to conflict in relations with others as we try to affirm ourselves at their expense. Thus, for Sartre, the structure of the look governs our concrete relations with others, as in relating to others one is either looker (subject) or looked at (object).

Marguerite La Caze

Marcel

Widely considered to be the first French existentialist, Gabriel Honoré Marcel (1889–1973) was a unique voice among existentialists. Marcel was a true intellectual who enjoyed professional success as a philosopher, playwright, literary critic and concert pianist. Marcel's lifelong fascination with death was impacted especially by the loss of his mother prior to his fourth birthday, as well as by his experiences as a non-combatant soldier in the First World War. Marcel's philosophical training was overseen at the Sorbonne by Henri Bergson, although Marcel's early writing also reveals a particular attraction to William James's pragmatism, the synthetic philosophy of Herbert Spencer, and Spinoza. He flirted with idealism throughout his career, and although he bristled at attempts to categorize his philosophy, he often referred to his thinking as neo-Socratic.

As Marcel developed philosophically, his work was marked by an emphasis on the concrete, on lived experience. He argued that life was absurd, but that no person was qualified to argue (as he thought **Heidegger** did) that the entire created system was tragic. Meaninglessness instead comes from the human propensity towards materialism and self-destruction. The individual buys into the idea that she is only a natural machine, and so is nothing more than the functions she can perform. People are thereby degraded by understanding the human condition as accidental and merely functional. Human despair is a by-product of living a rational – rather than a reflective – life. The role of the philosopher should not be to offer systematic justification for a life of indifference, but rather to testify that the 'logic of death' (as Marcel called it) could be overcome through proper reflection, creative acts and relationships that are committed to defeating injustice in the world.

Effective philosophical practice will lead, on Marcel's view, to religious commitment and, indeed, Marcel's existentialism suffered the label of 'Christian existentialism' – a label he came to revile. Even prior to his conversion to Catholicism at the age of 40, however, Marcel had become a noted opponent of atheistic existentialism, especially that of **Sartre**. Although their relationship as young adults was amicable, as Sartre grew in fame, Marcel became more vocal in his dissent towards Sartre's characterizations of the isolated self, of the death of **God**, and of lived experience as having 'no exit'. Marcel agreed that humans are naturally and tragically alienated from others, but he ultimately rejected Sartre's conception of man. Sartre's existentialism leads to the simultaneous exaltation and abasement of the self, since a person must be self-dependent like a god and, at the same time, the refuse of an inconceivable universe.

Marcel's conception of **freedom** is the most philosophically enduring of all of his themes, although the last decade has seen a resurgence of attention paid to Marcel's metaphysics, epistemology and ethics. It can be difficult to systematize Marcel's work, in large part because the main Marcelian themes are so interconnected. A close read, however, shows that in addition to that of freedom, Marcel's important philosophical contributions were on the themes of **problem and mystery**, participation, reflection, creative fidelity and presence.

Jill Graper Hernandez

May

In 1958, Rollo May (1909–1994), Ernst Angel and Henri F. Ellenberger introduced existential psychology and psychiatry to America in the ground-breaking text *Existence*. May's work initiated a turn from clinical, behavioural psychology relying on technical reason towards a psychology that recognizes human beings as **being-in-the-world** through the integration of existential philosophy, ontology and phenomenological psychology. May distinguishes three interrelated 'modes of being' in which human beings live simultaneously: (1) the *Umwelt*, about which traditional psychoanalysis of the period was primarily concerned, is categorized by instinctual drives and biological determinism and is the mode in which Freud makes his most important contributions; (2) the *Mitwelt*, which May argues is underconceptualized by traditional psychoanalysis, is categorized by the interrelationships between human beings; (3) the *Eigenwelt*, which May argues is largely ignored in modern and depth psychology, is categorized by the self in relation to itself.

May argues that existential psychotherapy moves beyond traditional psychotherapy by penetrating all three 'modes of being', thus responding to **Nietzsche** and **Kierkegaard**'s claim that the well-spring of **anxiety** for human beings is the loss of a sense of self and a loss of world. May's Columbia University dissertation, published as *The Concept of Anxiety* (1950), illustrates the relationship between anxiety and the development of selfhood. The dissertation was supervised by the famous philosophical theologian **Tillich**, who became May's lifelong mentor. After Tillich's death May wrote *Paulus: A Spiritual Teacher* (1973), a devotional biography of Tillich; his influence can be recognized throughout May's work. May co-authored his last major text *The Psychology of Existence: An Integrative Clinical Perspective* (1995) before his death in 1994.

Nick Wernicki

Merleau-Ponty

Maurice Merleau-Ponty (1908–1961) was a leading figure in the movement of existentialist phenomenology. His major work, *Phenomenology of Perception* (1945) criticizes both the intellectualist and empiricist traditions. Merleau-Ponty argues that both traditions misconstrue the subject's relation to the world. For the intellectualists, the subject is able to discover knowledge of the world through thought alone, independent of the subject's interpretations and individual concerns. For the empiricists, knowledge about the world can be discovered through experience. Both these accounts lead to a radical bifurcation between the knower and the known and distort the way we experience the world. For Merleau-Ponty, these accounts are mistaken because our subjective embodiment – our sensory and cognitive make-up – structure the way the world appears to us in a fundamental way.

Drawing on **Husserl** and **Heidegger**'s works on phenomenology, Merleau-Ponty demonstrates how phenomenology is able to offer a more unified account between objectivity and consciousness. Merleau-Ponty's most significant contribution was to emphasize the mediating role of the **body** in perception, and the way in which our background subjective assumptions are involved in all acts of understanding and interpretation. For Merleau-Ponty, we are not as disengaged and unaffected by the world and others as Descartes's theory of the subject implies. Nor do we experience our bodies as extensions of our minds. As Merleau-Ponty writes: 'Descartes and particularly Kant *detached* the subject . . . they presented consciousness, the absolute certainty of my existence for myself, as the condition of there being anything at all.' The problem here is that experience of the world is conceived as something separate from the subject that experiences it.

Phenomenology, by contrast, and by virtue of its very method of describing experiences, demonstrates the way in which the subject is already embedded in and affected by the world and others by virtue of its embodiment. For Merleau-Ponty, the aim of phenomenology is to reach an undistorted 'pure' description of experience: 'it tries to give a direct description of our experience as it is, without taking account of its psychological origin and the causal explanations which the scientist, the historian or the sociologist may be able to provide.' This 'manner or style of thinking' discloses to us certain existential facts: that 'our fate is in our hands', that we are 'responsible for our history through reflection' and by the 'decisions on which we stake our life'. Phenomenology thus aims to demonstrate the manner in which our existence is meaningfully lived.

Merleau-Ponty also wrote about a number of other subjects including politics, aesthetics, psychology, history and biology. His first book, *Structure of Behaviour* (1942) engaged with and criticized the 'Gestalt' school of psychology. In 1947, he published *Humanism and Terror*, revealing a conflict between his commitments to Marxist socialism and revelations of Soviet repression. Other works include *Sense and Nonsense* (1948), *Adventures of the Dialectic* (1955) and *Signs* (1960). His final work, *The Visible and the Invisible*, was published after his sudden death in 1961.

Sarah Sorial

Mood

Kierkegaard was pivotal in the emergence of mood as a key philosophical theme and not simply a psychological curiosity. In Kierkegaardian thought, the centrality of the individual's emotional life flows from his emphasis on spirit in the context of subjective innerness, and this is a theme of great importance for his ontology of the self and his explorations of its various stages of existence. His pseudonymous works explore such key moods as the melancholy of the aesthete, the centrality of **anxiety** (which was critically important for later existentialist thought) and the ontological misrelation (imbalance) of despair. For

Kierkegaard, such moods are at the heart of the nobility and the tragedy of human being, and are of central importance for the awakening of spirit.

Mood (*Stimmung*) is no less central for **Heidegger**, albeit in a different key. Ontologically, he characterizes the everyday phenomenon of mood as 'state-of-mind' (*Befindlichkeit*: that is, the state in which one finds oneself). For Heidegger, moods are not incidental emotional states that impact on mental faculties; rather they are primordial and ubiquitous modes of **being-in-the-world** *through which* the world is disclosed to *Dasein*. Insofar as we always already find ourselves opened out on the world in a given state of mind, our moods are a basic aspect of our thrownness into the world. Two states-of-mind receive particular attention as 'basic moods': **anxiety** and **boredom**. Unlike moods such as fear or loathing, anxiety and boredom have no particular objects, and as such they transcend **ontic** importance and reveal the existential structure of *Dasein*'s being-in-the-world. In anxiety, for example, *Dasein* finds itself in an uncanny state that paradoxically opens the possibility of authentic existence.

Richard Colledge

Mystery (see Problem and Mystery)

Nausea

Sartre tackles the notion of nausea in his novel of the same name published in 1938. Its main character, Antoine Roquentin, suffers from nausea as things have lost their meaning for him. He says that the world has lost its veneer. That means that when he looks at things, they do not make sense anymore. Things begin to 'exist' rather than to 'be', and he is confronted with their incomprehensibility. Being faced with the absurdity of the world, devoid of human meaning, is a trigger for nausea. For human consciousness, it is nauseating to suddenly be faced with the being that supports the world we are familiar with. For example, when Roquentin is sitting on a bench in a public park, probably the most famous passage of the novel, the garden disappears from his view and he then becomes conscious of the being that lies behind the humanly ordered and meaningful 'garden'. The garden is such because human consciousnesses have given this portion of being that particular meaning. But, as Roquentin notes, the realm of being is not that of words and reasons. Suffering from nausea is an indication that a human being has had a glance at the fundamental contingency of the world. It is the outcome of the confrontation between the human desire to give meaning to things and the fundamental absence of such meaning. In that sense, the nausea suffered by Roquentin is similar to what Albert Camus describes as absurdity in *The Myth of Sisyphus* (1943).

Christine Daigle

Nietzsche

Friedrich Nietzsche (1844–1900) is one of the most influential philosophers in modern culture as well as a significant thinker in the existentialist tradition. His work was initially regarded as that of a literary stylist and cultural critic, and then as a forerunner of German existential thought (Max Scheler, **Jaspers**, **Heidegger**) and French existentialism (**Camus** and **Sartre**). The Nazis tried to appropriate Nietzsche, despite his prescient criticisms of German nationalism and anti-Semitism. Postwar philosophers, especially in France, turned to Nietzsche as an alternative to prevailing currents of phenomenology, Hegelian–Marxism and positivism. There is lively current interest in Nietzsche from a wide range of perspectives.

Deeply influenced by **Schopenhauer** and romantic composer Richard Wagner, Nietzsche's first book, *The Birth of Tragedy* (1872), argued that art was the product of two dynamic drives: towards form and individuation (expressed by the Greek god Apollo); and towards formlessness and disintegration (expressed by the god Dionysus). Tragic art is born of the union of Apollonian and Dionysian impulses, but is superseded by more reflective kinds of drama. According to Nietzsche, modern culture is in need of a rebirth of tragic art (like Wagner's operas) because it is suffering from an excess of 'Socratic optimism' (the view that existence is rationally knowable and thus morally meaningful). If we are to overcome the crisis of meaning in modernity, we should renew the Greek 'tragic view' of life (that existence lacks intrinsic meaning, and so must be given value through philosophy, art and culture).

In *On the Genealogy of Morality* (1887), Nietzsche argued that Western culture has inherited two opposing modes of moral–ethical evaluation. There is *master morality*, in which the dominant masters affirm their own goodness (their power and nobility), while devaluing slaves and inferiors as 'bad'. And there is *slave morality*, in which the slaves designate the masters as 'evil', and thus redeem themselves (the weak or inferior) as the 'good'. Nietzsche argued that master morality (Greek virtue ethics) was overthrown by slave morality (Christianity), and that modern secular culture was still governed by Christian morality and Platonic metaphysics, which together foster *ressentiment* (resentment) against life, time and robust flourishing.

Nietzsche is most famous for his reflections on *nihilism*, expressed in the well-known phrase, 'God is dead'. He was the first thinker to give 'nihilism' a philosophical interpretation that combined a critical diagnosis of modern culture with a critique of 'Platonic' (two-world) metaphysics and (Christian) morality. For Nietzsche, nihilism means *'that the highest values devalue themselves'*. It arises because of the attempt to find meaning in existence by means of a life-negating metaphysics. Once religion is challenged by science, and human nature is shown to be contingent, the ultimate sources of morality are undermined ('God is dead'). Various substitute 'idols' are then posited to fill the void (belief in science, progress, humanity, reason or **freedom**) but these too are sceptically devalued over time. Nietzsche attacked Christian morality and modern 'democratic' culture for being nihilistic: destructive of the dynamics of human vitality and cultural creativity. We need, therefore, to overcome nihilistic forms of morality, culture and metaphysics, in favour of life-affirming perspectives that would make possible a post-metaphysical form of life.

Robert Sinnerbrink

Nothingness

One of the key questions motivating existentialism is: what is it to have our kind of being? Existentialism draws our attention to a fundamental difference of our being to other kinds of beings: we are 'existing' entities, which are essentially always outside and beyond themselves, and as such, are not grounded. **Dostoyevsky**, **Kierkegaard** and **Camus** understand that which is not grounded as facing an *abyss of nothingness*. This is meaninglessness, and being aware of it typically takes the form of an experience such as *angst*.

The ontological significance of nothingness is analysed by **Heidegger** and **Sartre**. Heidegger understands our existence as **being-in-the-world**. *Anxiety* arises when the background of all the meaningful involvements, that is, the world itself, comes into view. This reveals that there is nothing beyond the world. Anxiety is, therefore, the fear of no-thing. This experience is the key to **authenticity**. For Sartre, it remains to be explained how nothingness as the negation of the whole of being can come into existence. He observes that negations such as 'Pierre's absence' are, in fact, located among beings, and as such constitutive of reality. They originate from the for-itself which Sartre describes as its own nothingness. Nothingness is thus what separates the for-itself from the fullness of being of the in-itself (see **being-in-itself/being-for-itself**). In negation, the for-itself dissociates itself from the order of causality and reveals itself as free. *Anguish* arises from the awareness of this freedom. It is not fear, as it has no object, but rather the experience of confronting the nothingness within the for-itself.

Christian Onof

Nihilism

The term 'nihilism' (from the Latin, *nihil*, meaning 'nothing') refers to the doctrine that existence lacks meaning, that truth is illusory, or that morality is groundless. It was introduced into philosophy by Friedrich Jacobi in his *Letter to Fichte* (1799). For Jacobi, Kantian idealism led to the sceptical self-undermining of knowledge and morality. If all of our claims are dependent upon reason, and reason is grounded in self-consciousness, our knowledge and morality lack an absolute foundation. Idealism thus leads to transcendental egoism or nihilism (all claims reduce to our own arbitrary positing).

Hegel elaborated this insight into the sceptical consequences of Enlightenment reason. In the *Phenomenology of Spirit* (1807), Hegel remarks that traditional religious faith can no longer provide an authoritative source of meaning and value in a rational, historically self-conscious world. Alienated modern subjects experience this loss of divine substance and substantial selfhood as the 'death of God'. The task of reconciliation formerly played by religion is now taken over by rational self-reflection.

Nietzsche developed the concept of nihilism most fully, famously expressed in the phrase, 'God is dead'. For Nietzsche, nihilism is a cultural, moral and philosophical condition in which 'the highest values devalue themselves'. It arises when we devalue this-worldly existence in favour of an (unavailable) transcendent source of truth (God). Once religion is challenged by science, and human nature is shown to be contingent, these transcendent sources of morality are undermined. Nietzsche argued that we must, therefore, traverse modern nihilism in order to overcome nihilistic forms of morality, culture and metaphysics via life-affirming perspectives, heralding a post-metaphysical form of life. Nihilism became a central theme for many later existential philosophers, including **Heidegger**, **Sartre** and **Camus**.

Robert Sinnerbrink

Ontic/Ontological

Heidegger distinguishes two levels of analyses: the ontic and the ontological. What is 'ontological' (*Ontologisch*), for Heidegger, are the structures of Being that make particular beings possible. In *Being and Time* (1927), these are *Dasein*'s 'care' (*Sorge*), its **being-in-the-world**, and the finitude and temporality of Being itself. The 'ontic' (*ontisch*), on the other hand, is akin to the empirical occurrences that make up our existence. Heidegger refers to the ontological structures of *Dasein* as 'existential' (*existenzial*), while referring to its ontic doings as 'existentielle' (*existenziell*). Thus, while *Dasein*, the being that we ourselves are, has the ontological–existential structure of care – it is always involved in the world whether or not it cares about people or things in the everyday sense – ontically it may be indifferent or engaged, withdrawn, or attentive. For the most part, Heidegger argues, *Dasein* is ensnared in its everyday concerns, but nevertheless 'the ontical distinction of *Dasein* lies in the fact that it is ontological'. Thus one of our ontic concerns – one of paramount importance to Heidegger – is the ability of *Dasein* to ask after the meaning of its existence. In this way, the ontological and the ontic are not two levels of reality: *Dasein* is never wholly 'ontic' (it is never just what it does, since it is always on the way towards further possibilities), nor is *Dasein* wholly 'ontological', since its 'care' is always turned towards its 'ontic' concerns. **Sartre** late takes up this distinction in *Being and Nothingness* in terms of the 'ontological level' of human being in the world and the 'phenomenological' considerations of the ontic particulars of our lives.

Peter Gratton

Ortega

José Ortega y Gasset (1883–1955). See the chapter 'Existentialism and Latin America'.

Other

The other is a term in existential philosophy that refers to any individual other than oneself. It is meant to capture the experience of radical separation that one can feel when encountering another person. The other presents himself or herself to me as beyond my awareness and beyond my control. This view has its roots in Descartes and gives rise in analytic philosophy to what is known as the problem of other minds. But in existential thought it also implies that the other is a threat. For the other is always free to construe me in any way. I can never know how the other is construing me, nor can I have control over this construal.

Sartre, who is best known for this line of thought, describes this situation by saying that conflict is the meaning of 'being-for-others'. This conflict arises because in any encounter there is the attempt both to see the other as an object (rather than a person) and to escape being seen as an object by the other. The basis of this conflict is the desire to maintain one's sense of **freedom**, something one finds it difficult to do when one is aware that one is being seen as an object. Also, by seeing the other as an object I achieve the sense that the other is not free to construe me as an object; for if the other is seen as an object then he or she is experienced as something that cannot construe me in any sense.

James Giles

Problem and Mystery

The basic distinction grounding the method of **Marcel** is between *problem* and *mystery*. Marcel grew wary of systematic philosophy that dislocates the existential character of experience from philosophical issues, because it makes the question of being a problem to be solved, rather than a mystery with which to be engaged.

Problems are objective and detached, and are the sorts of things that can (at least in principle) be solved. Problems are defused by analysing facts, sharpening the language used to assess the issues, and detaching the self from the problem at hand. Since the distinctive feature of problems is that they can be completely met and defeated, they can also be reduced or minimized. In addition, when answers are sought for problems we come across, the solutions we find become common property, so that they can be verified and rediscovered by any person.

Due in part to materialism, technology, and the dominance of philosophical and scientific methodology, Marcel contends that the question of being has been reduced to the level of a problem. The self and all of its relationships, goals and desires are treated as obstacles to be conquered. When life dissolves into a series of opportunities to problem-solve, however, the result is that the body is alienated from the self and becomes yet another object. This alienation allows people to either be possessed as objects or viewed in terms of mere functionality. If the only aspect of being that the self knows is the fact of existence, the question of what it means to be in the world is answered by asserting that the self exists. Such a person – the 'problematic person' – invariably is shut out of meaningful experiences by the reduction of everything in life to the fact of existence.

Mystery, however, collapses the gap between experiences and what is essential to the self. Whereas problems are characterized by solvability, a mystery must be thought of as something in which the self is caught up and whose fundamental nature is, therefore, not entirely accessible. That is not to say that the mysterious is unknowable, however, since unknowability is a limiting feature of a problem. Conversely, the recognition of mystery is a positive act of the mind, apprehended through intuition without an immediate knowledge that the self possesses it. Mystery is intuited when experiences slowly illuminate it. Marcel does not mean to bring a vague literary floweriness to the discourse on mystery; rather, the *mystery of our being* involves the situations we are concerned with – our experiences   and as such, the nature of mystery can only be grasped, acknowledged or recognized from the inside.

In order to illuminate (rather than clarify, as we would a problem) the mystery of being, we must start with the experiences of the individual and gradually move out to the individual's experiences with other persons. Experiences provide a resource for a phenomenological exploration that allows us to achieve what Marcel calls 'plenitude', or the full life. Plenitude, of course, can never be achieved by the abstractions and objectifications of the problematic person. Instead, the full life is a goal accessible only to individuals who break out of problematicity.

Jill Graper Hernandez

Pareyson

Luigi Pareyson (1918–1991) was a seminal Italian philosopher who introduced existentialism to Italy (*La filosofia dell'esistenza e Carlo Jaspers*, 1939). According to Pareyson, the main features that characterize the philosophy of existence are 'the revaluation of the singular, ontologicity, and the concept of **situation**'. In his elaboration of these themes, Pareyson mainly refers to **Jaspers** and **Marcel**. The singular, or *person*, is conceived as a paradoxical coincidence of a relation with the self and a relation with Being. This is the reason why Pareyson names his philosophy of existence *ontological personalism*. Maintaining the relation with Being is an existential commitment, and this commitment is fidelity to Being.

In 1971 Pareyson published *Verità e Interpretazione*, which represents the evolution of his existentialism into one of the most impressive hermeneutic theories in contemporary philosophy. If reality is accessible only through personal existence, every human act or thought is an interpretation. Interpretation is not only a particular kind of knowledge but the constitutive feature of all human activity, and thus it can be extended from the problem of the knowledge of things to the problem of interpersonal relationships: interpretation is 'knowledge of forms by persons'. The relation with truth is a hermeneutic relation, in which the link with truth is total and the formulation is personal, so that the interpretation necessarily entails an ontological feature. Pareyson's theory of interpretation culminates in the principle of the inexhaustibility of truth, thus founding the possibility of a pluralistic – but not relativistic – conception of truth: 'there is nothing but interpretation of truth and there is no interpretation of anything but truth'.

The core of the hermeneutic relation is **freedom**, as the possibility of fidelity to Being and at the same time as the possibility to break the bond with Being. In Pareyson's late writings, his personalistic existentialism, his anti-relativistic hermeneutics and his ontology of freedom are combined and elaborated in light of his reading of **Heidegger** and Schelling to form a reflection on the problem of evil. His last unfinished work, *Ontology of Freedom*, was published posthumously in 1995. As a professor of philosophy at the University of Turin, he had many famous students, including Gianni Vattimo and Umberto Eco. A collection of Pareyson's selected writings has been recently translated into English, under the title *Existence, Interpretation, Freedom*.

Paolo Diego Bubbio

Pascal

Blaise Pascal (1632–1662) was a French mathematician, physicist and philosopher. His interests in philosophy and religion took a turn when as an adult he nearly lost his life in an incident in which his carriage almost fell off a bridge. After this event he devoted his life to Christianity and produced religious and philosophical writings such as *Provincial Letters* (1656–1657) and his famous *Pensées* (1656–1658).

Pensées is a collection of personal thoughts on topics like religion, fear, **death**, despair and hope. It is a work that is a forerunner to modern existential philosophy. Probably the best-known section in the work is where Pascal argues that since there is neither definitive proof for or against the existence of **God**, one must gamble and make a choice of whether to believe or not to believe. He then argues that if one chooses to believe in God and God exists, then one has everything to gain (eternal happiness in heaven), whereas if one chooses not to believe and God exists, then one has everything to loose (eternal damnation in hell). Therefore, one ought to believe.

This argument, known as Pascal's wager, ushers in the existential approach to religion – one that was taken up by **Kierkegaard** – by shifting the focus away from the objective existence of God and towards the individual's belief. The main problem with the argument, however, is that it is unclear how someone can choose to believe in something that he or she might see as obviously false.

James Giles

Rilke

Rainer Maria Rilke (1875–1926) was a German poet and novelist whose often exquisite and sometimes disquieting presentations of existential necessities has lent his works to an existentialist interpretation. The interpretation was first suggested by Otto Friedrich Bollnow in *Rilke* (1951), with the most notable example being Walter Kaufmann's *From Shakespeare to Existentialism* (1959). Kaufman compares Rilke to **Nietzsche** on four shared motifs: the acute awareness of their own embeddedness in a historical situation; the redirection of piety away from traditionalist mores and towards an open future; the resolve to affirm life and with it the identity of 'terribleness and bliss'; and their repudiation of otherworldliness. Rilke's repudiation was neither positivistic nor atheistic, but a subtle treatment of desire and despair, accompanied by an affirmation of the creative potentials therein.

The *Duino Elegies*, which together with the *Sonnets to Orpheus* is often considered the zenith of Rilke's work, opens with: 'If I cried out, who would hear me up there, among the angelic orders?' A central theme of Rilke's poetry is human longing for communion with the ineffable, a longing frustrated by doubt and **anxiety**, but which ultimately addresses future potentials as divine. His *Ninth Elegy* poses the question: 'why then still insist on being human?' He responds: 'because to be here means so much', and because 'it's *one* time for each thing and *only* one. Once and no more. And the same for us: *once.*' Rilke calls on us to be responsible for our **authenticity** through a recollection of our finitude. One of the consequences of this recognition is that we choose to live 'abandoned and exposed' to the 'blissfully earthly', the earth which regains for Rilke the attributes that he once assigned to **God**.

To do justice to the existential depth and potential of Rilke's poetry it is best to resist extracting philosophical theses and instead focus on the moods and experiences his poetry manifests (of homelessness, of **anguish**, of the recognition of the necessity of one's own **death** and the importance of solitude) and how they incite existentialist insights. Rilke's non-fiction works *Letters to a Young Poet* and the *Notebooks of Malte Laurids Brigge* (often thought to anticipate **Sartre**'s *Nausea*) will give the reader another avenue to his thoughts. But the eloquence and intricacy with which Rilke expressed the consequences of these thoughts in his poetry made him an influence on existentialists, such as **Heidegger**, and encourages us to include him in the existentialist tradition.

Sherah Bloor

Responsibility

In general existentialist terms, responsibility may be defined as the conscious awareness of the freely choosing self as the sole author of a given project or moment. Responsibility is, therefore, potentially understood from this perspective as weighing upon existence, insofar as it inescapably attends our efforts and projects, but responsibility also reveals itself as a transcendence. We are forced to confront the extent to which we are responsible for our freely chosen transcendence, thereby leaving us open to experiencing **angst**.

Friedrich **Nietzsche** imbued the concept with a typically elevated sensibility, seeking in particular to position 'heavy' responsibilities taken on in a life-affirming spirit and in pursuit of a 'unifying project' as befitting (and indeed, indicative of) the capabilities of Higher Men. **Kierkegaard** understood responsibility in terms of his Christian **faith**. For Kierkegaard, Christian faith is a matter of individual subjective passion; only on the basis of faith is an individual able to become an authentic self. This self is the sum of our creative efforts, which **God** judges for eternity.

Initially, Sartre held that we are responsible insofar as meaning and value in the world are assigned by virtue of our life-orienting fundamental 'project'. Later, he would come to incorporate individual responsibility into class relationships, thereby adding an existentialist dimension of ethical responsibility to a Marxist emphasis on collective creativity. **De Beauvoir** understood responsibility in a more 'immediate' collective sense, such that we would deliberately will ourselves and others free.

Steven Churchill

Ressentiment

Ressentiment (resentment) features in **Nietzsche**'s account of the emergence of human subjectivity in *On the Genealogy of Morality*. *Ressentiment* is a slow poison that permeates the perspective of the weak in relation to the strong. It fuels the hatred of the powerless towards the powerful, ultimately leading to 'their' dubious victory and construct – the moral subject. *Ressentiment* is absent from the carefree pleasures of the powerful, who have no need to resent anything outside themselves.

The distinction between those who experience *ressentiment* and those who do not is borne out in two different modes of creating value. The powerful exercise a 'noble' way of arriving at value, through the affirmative ascription of goodness to themselves. A consequence of this active way of creating value is that its **other** (the bad) is secondary and contingent. The powerless, by contrast, depend upon negation and denigration of the other in order to create value. The notion of goodness in the 'slave morality' of the weak is parasitic on damning amorality as evil. Virtue arises from (moral) restraint, from *not* doing something that others do.

The goodness of slave morality thus depends upon the construction of evil, whereas noble goodness depends only upon itself. Nietzsche sees the invention of (slave) morality as an imaginary revenge, for the uncensored exercise of power is called evil by those who are by definition unable to exercise power. It is the hollow victory of *ressentiment*.

Philipa Rothfield

Sartre

Jean-Paul Sartre (1905–1980) was a philosopher, novelist, playwright and political activist. He was responsible for popularizing existentialism and for expanding the scope of phenomenological reflection to include descriptions of ordinary human action. Sartre's most significant contribution is his analysis of the nature of human **freedom** and how human relationships are structured by it. Sartre's fundamental insight is the concept of contingency. The recognition that there is no **God** or deity means that there is no overarching plan to the world and no intrinsic meaning to events. Being just *is*, but it does not have to be. Moreover, there is no essence to being a human being, no predetermined or fixed human nature. Sartre defines existence in terms of freedom. His major philosophical work, *Being and Nothingness* (1943) and his plays and novels seek to explore the psychological and moral implications of the fact that there is no intrinsic meaning to existence.

In *Being and Nothingness* Sartre gives an account of three fundamental types of being: **being-in-itself, being-for-itself** and being-for-others. Being-in-itself refers to non-conscious entities or brute matter. Sartre describes it as being 'glued to itself' because unlike consciousness, being-in-itself cannot transcend itself. In Sartre's words: 'it is an immanence which cannot realize itself, an affirmation which cannot affirm itself, an activity which cannot act, because it is glued to itself.' The world of the in-itself is superfluous because it has no meaning independent of consciousness. Being-for-itself refers to consciousness. It is being-for-itself that gives meaning to things by virtue of the projects that it pursues. Unlike the in-itself, the for-itself is temporal, and defined in terms of possibility and transcendence. The for-itself is characterized as nothingness, and thus, as absolute freedom. Because there is no essence to existence, the for-itself must make itself what it is, or it must choose its condition. It is able to do this because human consciousness is free, in the sense that it can be anything. But consciousness can never be reduced to its choice or limited by its condition. The for-itself must transcend itself towards a particular possibility, becoming something that has not yet been realized. The failure to own up to this freedom and the failure to thus choose oneself is, for Sartre, an act of **bad faith** or self-deception.

The third type of being is being-for-others. This refers to the realm of intersubjective relations. Unlike the relationship between the for-itself and the in-itself, the relationship between the for-itself and others is inherently conflicted. The conflict arises because the **other** is also a consciousness with its own possibilities; that is, the other is also an absolute freedom. In the encounter with the other, the freedom of the for-itself is at stake, because the other can make the for-itself an object, thus limiting its freedom. The antagonism that lies at the heart of all human relations is depicted in one of Sartre's most famous plays, *No Exit* (1944). The political and ethical implications of Sartre's existentialism are also explored in *The Flies* (1942), in a series of lectures presented in 1945 and published under the title *Existentialism and Humanism* and in *Anti-Semite and Jew* (1946), among many others.

Sarah Sorial

Schopenhauer

Arthur Schopenhauer (1788–1860) is one of the world's great philosophers, whose influence in modern philosophy has been greatly underappreciated. His fundamental work *The World as Will and Representation* (1818) can be seen as a precursor to important ideas in contemporary psychology, psychoanalysis, evolutionary theory and postmodernism, as well as in existentialism. His views on love, **death**, **suicide**, happiness and suffering have influenced many of the great writers of the world, including **Dostoevsky**, **Beckett** and Leo Tolstoy, yet during his lifetime his work was almost entirely ignored or rejected.

Scholarly analysis of the influence of Schopenhauer's work on the thinkers he inspired is strangely lacking, despite the enormity of his influence on some of the great thinkers of modern philosophy, such as **Nietzsche**, Sigmund Freud and Ludwig Wittgenstein. Existentialism has been significantly influenced by Schopenhauer, mainly through Nietzsche. But to find the influence of Schopenhauer on these twentieth-century thinkers is no easy task, and one must look deep into the work of Schopenhauer, particularly his ethics, to find such connections. While perhaps not in agreement with everything they would say (the Sartrean motto 'existence precedes essence' would not feature in a Schopenhaurian philosophy), Schopenhauer's philosophy resonates with that of the existentialists in grappling with the role of the individual, and with the suffering and gloom that life seems to place on us.

William Hebblewhite

Situation

Nowhere is the general existentialist project of 'personalizing' the world more evident than in the fundamental concept of situation. To talk of one's situation is to announce one's perspective *on* their existence as it is lived *in* the midst of a personally meaningful site of existence. The situation serves, then, as an ambiguous ground for **freedom**. In *Being and Nothingness* (1943), **Sartre** states: 'The *situation* is an ambiguous phenomenon in which it is impossible for the for-itself to distinguish the contribution of freedom from that of the brute existent.' Consider Sartre's example of the mountain climber: his apprehension of the crag as 'too tall' to scale is understood by him as a feature of the situation. In fact, he has neglected to consider the role of freedom in giving rise *to* the situation now confronting him, and the freedom he has *in* his situation to regard it differently, and so to give up, or to persist, and so on. Freedom-in-situation is thusly differentiated from freedom-of-consciousness, since transcending the immanence of one's situation involves unavoidable consideration of the freedom of others in shaping one's experience *of* immanence. Therefore, Sartre holds, 'there is freedom only in a situation, and there is a *situation* only through freedom'. Further, for Sartre this 'antimony' provides the exact relation between freedom and **facticity**. Of course, the 'exact' relation at issue here is properly revealed as one of **ambiguity**.

Sartre's postwar Collective politics re-employs the concept of situation in the service of a 'philosophy of revolution'. In his essay 'Materialism and Revolution'

(1946) Sartre argued that 'revolutionary behaviour' is facilitated by, and through, 'new [that is, recast or reconsidered] ideas of "situation" and "being in the world"'. For Sartre, materialism (as represented by scholastic Marxism at the time) could not accommodate and explain **transcendence**, as it viewed the 'unfolding' of a new order out of the present state of affairs as inevitable. He felt transcendence to be crucial to analysing, and then implementing, the human **subject**'s movement towards a new social order, and saw that the concept of situation allowed for this to be articulated, since transcendence presupposes situation, as the ground for its realization. As such, situation serves as a major bridging concept between Sartre's 'apolitical' existentialism and his 'committed' perspective.

Steven Churchill

Suicide

Suicide is a theme that is of concern to existentialism. For **Marcel**, suicide takes a prominent position because of an inevitable attraction to 'the void' that must occur in any philosophy that affirms the entirety of being. For existentialists like **Camus** and **Sartre** suicide becomes an issue because of the absurdity of existence. An obvious response to this awareness is suicide. For if my existence is **absurd**, there seems no point in my continuing to exist. So pressing is this issue that, for Camus, the question of whether one ought to commit suicide becomes the 'one truly serious philosophical question'.

For Marcel, the solution to suicide is to see that the same **freedom** that enables me to choose this attraction also enables me to choose the ontological-counter-weight to suicide, namely, love. Camus's answer is that the way of dealing with the absurdity of life is to accept it with dignity and to draw strength from it. For Sartre, the response is to see suicide itself as an absurdity. This is because it is both the project that destroys all my projects and thus itself, and also because it allows the viewpoint of the other person to take precedence over mine.

James Giles

Tillich

Paul Tillich (1886–1965) is best categorized as a philosophical theologian, underscoring his commitment to the dialogue between the two disciplines. Tillich's ongoing engagement with German Idealism is evident throughout his work. However, his encounter with **Heidegger** while at Marburg and the later work of Schelling forged the existentialism that characterizes his thinking. Tillich's liberal Christian theology is founded on the concept of 'ultimate concern', through which he broadens the category of religion to include any form of 'being ulti-mately concerned about one's own being, about one's self and one's world, about its meaning and its estrangement and its finitude'. Within the context of ultimate concern, the concept of **God** lies beyond any theistic or symbolic Chris-tian God as the objectless and infinite Ground of Being from which finite human beings are fundamentally estranged; therefore, there is no necessity for a proof of God in Tillich's theology. In his best-known work of ontology and existential philosophy, *The Courage to Be* (1952), Tillich argues that the awareness of the ever-present threat of non-being, which is contained in being, is manifest in **anxiety** over **death**, meaninglessness and condemnation. Anxiety and courage are ontologically interdependent in the sense that courage is essential for the self-affirmation of being in spite of the threat of non-being. Tillich argues that the Ground of Being is the ultimate source of the courage to be over against the threat of non-being, a courage that requires **transcendence** beyond theism. Pre-supposing that the self is grasped by 'ultimate concern', the concept of God qua object must be overcome for the anxiety of meaninglessness and doubt to be taken into the courage to be. He argues that there can be Christian existential-ists, insofar as they ask existential questions, but there can be no Christian exis-tentialism because Christians answer as theists, not as existentialists. Tillich thus rejects the distinction between atheistic and theistic existentialisms.

Tillich spent nearly two decades lecturing on philosophy and theology in Ger-many before joining Max Horkheimer and Theodor W. Adorno at the University of Frankfurt am Main. There he wrote *The Socialist Decision* (1933), which, along with his outward opposition to the Nazi party, led to his dismissal from the Uni-versity. Through the help of Reinhold Niebuhr he fled to the United States, where he accepted a professorship at Union Theological Seminary (1933–1955) before moving to Harvard University (1955–1962) and University of Chicago (1962–1965). Tillich is best known for his three-volume work *Systematic Theology* (1951, 1957, 1963), in which he traces the rise of existentialism and the problem of estrangement back to Hegel within the larger context of his Christian theology. In his lecture *Existentialist Aspects of Modern Art* (1956) Tillich offers a short but powerful treatment of modern art and existentialism. He posits Picasso's *Guer-nica* as religious art *par excellence* and argues that in order for art to be considered existentialist it must reflect 'ultimate concern'. Marking his death in 1965, the *New York Times* called him 'one of Christianity's most influential theologians'.

Nick Wernicki

Throwness

Heidegger coined the term 'throwness' (*Geworfenheit*) to indicate the way in which **Dasein** finds itself always already in the world immersed in situations and meanings not of its own making or choosing. As such, it indicates 'the **facticity** of [*Dasein's*] being delivered over'. By far the dominant existential sense in which Heidegger discusses thrownness relates to his analysis of state of mind. Accordingly, *Dasein* is always in-the-world under the sway of one **mood** or another; we simply find ourselves in these states through which the world is opened for us, and we to it. In more **ontic** ways of speaking, it is also possible to develop Heidegger's notion of thrownness to speak of the inevitability of our always already finding ourselves formed by a vast array of factors such as our family of origin, genetic characteristics, culture, language, place in history and society, the influence of our past actions and those of others on us, and so on. All such factors contribute to a complex matrix that constitutes and opens (as well as limits) our present possibilities.

Dasein never escapes its thrownness, although a genuine transformation is possible in terms of the way it relates to it. Heidegger presents *Dasein's* fallenness as essentially a continuation of its thrownness: that is, being-fallen is a way that 'facticity lets itself be seen phenomenally', for falling is essentially a matter of '*remaining in the throw*'. Remaining in this 'default position' is characterized by Heidegger as inauthentic. **Authenticity** (as 'anticipatory resoluteness') involves 'taking over' our thrownness as our ownmost (*eigentlich*) project. Nonetheless, the 'nullity' of our thrownness 'permeates' care 'through and through', so that all possibilities are thrown and therefore 'null'.

Richard Colledge

Transcendence

In general existentialist terms, human existence is revealed as transcendent against the backdrop of the immanence, or 'passive' existence, of all other objects with which we share a physical space and which delineate our **situation**. Our existence is marked-out as 'active' to the extent that we transcend the immanence of our situation in pursuit of our freely chosen projects. On this account, we are both immanent and transcendent at once, since our situation, and our relation to it, is defined (at least in part) by our **facticity**.

Transcendence is perhaps most often referred to in discussions of the existentialism of **Sartre** and **de Beauvoir**, but was also employed by both their predecessors and their contemporaries. **Kierkegaard** understands transcendence in terms of a 'leap', which would allow one to realize the 'lie of character' that he claims characterizes the existence of the great majority of subjects, and to instead become a self-realized person. This 'leap' is of course a 'leap to **faith**' in its fuller sense, given that self-realization for Kierkegaard would also involve accepting, with recourse to faith alone, the paradox of **God** moving from the noumenal realm into the worldly realm, Christ's human form. **Heidegger** uses the term in discussing the relationship between our human being and Being, as well as the problem of the unity of **being-in-the world**.

Often, when Sartre invokes transcendence, he refers simply to the for-itself's going beyond the given in projecting itself, while at other times he actually calls the for-itself a transcendence. If I turn the **Other** into an object for me, then they are for me a transcendence-transcended on Sartre's terms. On the other hand, **being-in-itself** which overflows all its appearances and thus falls outside all of my attempts to grasp it, is called a transcendent being. On this account, Sartre may be said to view transcendence as both purely substantive, and as a process. **De Beauvoir** understands transcendence in a different sense; intrinsic to her view is a rejection of Sartre's ontological **freedom** for 'ethical freedom' instead. Freedom rendered in this way is to be imbued from the outset with an Other-oriented concern that is expressed as we embrace it, such that we deliberately will ourselves and others free. We do so by undertaking 'constructive movements', such that we realize our transcendence not merely through the mundane activities comprising day-to-day life, but through activities that lend life meaning; mundane activity fades into relative immanence, with meaningful activity assuming transcendent status.

Steven Churchill

Übermensch

Nietzsche introduces the notion of the *Übermensch* in his book *Thus Spoke Zarathustra* (1883 and 1885). This term has been variously translated as 'superman', 'overman', 'overperson' and 'overhuman'. The latter is the most appropriate translation. In German, the term is gender neutral and Nietzsche uses it to refer to a way of being that human beings ought to aspire to. The *Übermensch* has often been understood as some final stage at the end of an evolutionary ladder. Some statements by Nietzsche may lead readers on that path, for example, when he says that the *Übermensch* is to man what man is to the ape. However, a metaphor like this merely intends to show the distance that separates the human being of Nietzsche's days from the *Übermensch*. One will be an *Übermensch* once one has freed oneself from the belief in **God** and an otherworldly realm, once one has accepted the 'truth' of the eternal return and once one has understood the world and oneself as **will to power**. This is not easy, and these 'truths' might in fact crush weaker human beings. Nietzsche hints that the way to *Übermenshlichkeit* (overhumanness) might be reserved for only those strong spirits who will be able to handle these 'truths'. The handling of such truths requires an *active* value-creation on the part of the individual. Accepting the world and one's place therein means to posit oneself as a creator of values rather than passively receiving them from a transcendent beyond. This, however, does not necessarily lead to an elitism, and the *Übermensch* should not be understood as some kind of aristocratic power figure. Rather, Nietzsche offers it as a moral ideal human beings ought to aspire to.

Christine Daigle

Unamuno

Miguel de Unamuno (1864–1936). See the chapter 'Existentialism and Latin America'.

Will to Power

The will to power is a pivotal concept in **Nietzsche**'s philosophy. Nietzsche sees it as the primary drive underlying all behaviour. Although there is a sense in which the will to power expresses 'an insatiable desire to manifest power', there are important differences between its various manifestations. Nietzsche makes much of these differences. He is particularly critical of the ways in which certain forms of the will to power conspire against life, inhibiting the latter's growth and expansion. These 'nihilistic' manifestations of the will to power cluster around the feeling of **ressentiment** and the creation of 'slave morality'. Nihilistic diminutions of the will to power can be contrasted with those affirmative manifestations of the will to power that embrace and enhance life. Were human inhibitions to be overcome, life would simply grow and expand, giving way to new impositions, new and creative urges which Nietzsche idealizes through the figure of the *Übermensch*.

Understood ontologically, the will to power is Nietzsche's vision of reality understood as becoming, rather than being. It is a principle of explanation which is immanent, rather than transcendent. It is the generative principle that inheres in all that occurs, the driving force behind all events. The will to power is neither an act of human will nor a scientific form of causality. Rather, it is embedded within events as their organizing principle. Nietzsche understands reality as, at bottom, a clash of forces in an endless flux of becoming. The will to power is that which imposes itself in the midst of these forces. It is interpretative, formative and creative, working between and among forces, gauging their relative strengths and resistances, shaping the chaotic forces of the world into temporarily stable structures, and disrupting these structures through the production of new events, in an endless cycle of eternal return.

Philipa Rothfield

17 A Chronology of Key Events, Texts and Thinkers

1807	Hegel, *The Phenomenology of Spirit*.
1819	Schopenhauer, *The World as Will and Representation*.
1827–1854	The later philosophy of F. W. J. von Schelling, which critiqued Hegelian idealism and developed the special concept of 'existence' influential on Kierkegaard and later existentialists.
1843–1855	In various texts, the Danish philosopher Søren Kierkegaard (1813–1855) challenged the religious orthodoxy of his time, as well as the enlightenment emphasis on rationality and Hegel's systematizing ambitions that he felt left no place for the individual. He instead called for a lived commitment and 'a leap of faith' that he insisted involved facing up to the prospect of 'dread'.
1843	Kierkegaard, *Either/Or* (2 vols). Kierkegaard, *Fear and Trembling*.
1844	Kierkegaard, *The Concept of Dread*. Kierkegaard, *Philosophical Fragments*.
1845	Kierkegaard, *Stages on Life's Way*.
1846	Kierkegaard, *Concluding Unscientific Postscript*. Marx and Engels, *The German Ideology*.
1848	Marx and Engels, *The Communist Manifesto*.
1849	Kierkegaard, *The Sickness unto Death*.
1872	Nietzsche, *The Birth of Tragedy*. German philosopher Friedrich Nietzsche (1844–1900) argued for a more Dionysian and excessive relation to the world, in opposition to the Apollonian rationality that he thought unduly dominant. In his later books, he diagnosed the *ressentiment* and slave morality afflicting his times, and tried to encourage a more life-affirmative relation to the world through provocative ideas such as the will to power, the eternal return of the same, and the *Übermensch*.

1874	Dostoevsky, *Crime and Punishment* and *The Idiot*. Tolstoy, *War and Peace*.
1878	Nietzsche, *Human All Too Human*.
1880	Dostoevsky, *The Brothers Karamazov*.
1881	Nietzsche, *Daybreak*.
1882	Nietzsche, *The Gay Science*.
1883	Dilthey, *The Introduction to the Human Sciences*.
1883–1885	Nietzsche, *Thus Spoke Zarathustra*.
1885	Marx, *Capital* vol. 2.
1886	Nietzsche, *Beyond Good and Evil*.
1887	Nietzsche, *On the Genealogy of Morals*. Tolstoy, *The Death of Ivan Ilych*.
1888	Nietzsche, *The Case of Wagner, Twilight of the Idols, Ecce Homo* and *The Anti-Christ*.
1896	Bergson, *Matter and Memory*.
1900–1901	Husserl, *Logical Investigations*. Edmund Husserl (1859–1938) was the founder of phenomenology, a way of thinking that focuses on our experiences and tries to discern the essences of such experiences. Husserl's work, and particularly his *Logical Investigations* and *Ideas* (1913), were taken up in very different ways by Heidegger (who was his student and assistant for a time), Sartre, Merleau-Ponty, and many other philosophers associated with existential phenomenology.
1913	Freud, *Totem and Taboo*. Husserl, *Ideas Pertaining to a Pure Phenomenology and to a Phenomenological Philosophy* book 1. Basque philosopher Unamuno published his *The Tragic Sense of Life in Men and Nations*.
	Jaspers, *General Psychopathology*. Writing his early works around the time of the First World War, German philosopher Karl Jaspers (1883–1969) developed the notion of *Existenz*, arguing that we have no fixed or essential self; the self is instead only its possibilities and what it might become. The revelation of the lack of any essential self is best revealed in 'limit situations', which include death, suffering and guilt.
1925	Kafka, *The Trial*.

1927	Martin Heidegger (1889–1976) published his famous existential work, *Being and Time*, which immediately attracted great interest in Germany, concerned as it was with moods, facing up to the prospect of one's own death, and with how these phenomena shed light on a question that he thought Western philosophy had forgotten – the question of Being. Gabriel Marcel's *Metaphysical Journal* was published, arguably the first work of French existentialism.
1929	Mexican philosopher Jose Gaos's translation of Scheler's *The Place of Man in the Cosmos* into Spanish – it became one of the most widely read books in Latin America. Fritz Heinemann's *New Paths in Philosophy*, in which (he later claimed) he was the first to use the term 'philosophy of existence' (*Existenzphilosophie*).
1930	Jean Wahl, *The Unhappiness of Consciousness in the Philosophy of Hegel*. This book began to popularize Hegel in France and influenced the view of human being as unhappy consciousness found in Sartre and other existentialists. Emmanuel Levinas's translation of Husserl's *Cartesian Meditations* into French, which made the methods of phenomenology available to philosophers like Sartre and Merleau-Ponty.
1932	Jaspers, *Philosophy* (3 vols).
1933	Heidegger was made Rector of the University of Freiburg. At the time he was a supporter of Nazism and made several controversial comments (and introduced policies) that seem to many to have been anti-Semitic.
1935	Jaspers, *Reason and Existenz*. Marcel, *Being and Having*.
1932–1939	Alexandre Kojève lectured on Hegel in France, bringing the notion of the 'master–slave' dialectic to prominence in this country, along with a more 'existential' understanding of Hegel that emphasized, in a Heideggerian manner, the importance for human freedom of confronting the prospect of one's own death. His seminars were attended by almost all of the major French intellectual figures of the time, although possibly not Sartre.
1936	Jaspers, *Nietzsche: An Introduction to the Understanding of His Philosophical Activity*. This book is an important source for the 'existentialist' interpretation of Nietzsche.

1937	Sartre, *The Transcendence of the Ego*. Here Sartre (1905–1980) distances himself from aspects of Husserlian phenomenology and begins to develop his own original account of phenomenology.
1938	Sartre's remarkably evocative novel *Nausea* was published to widespread acclaim. Publication of Jean Wahl's *Kierkegaardian Studies* helped to popularize the little-known Danish philosopher in France.
1939 1939–1944	Borge's essay 'Pierre Menard, Author of Quixote' – a major influence on Latin America's existentialist philosophers and writers. The Second World War and the German occupation of France. Both Maurice Merleau-Ponty (1908–1961) and Sartre did military service, and in 1940 Sartre was captured and imprisoned and there he continued to study Heidegger's *Being and Time*.
1940s	Jose Ortega y Gasset's student, Julian Marius, coined the term 'existentialist or personal novel'.
1941–1949	Sartre quickly attained a greater fame on the basis of his novels, as well as plays like *Flies* (1943) and *No Exit* (1944) but also because of his political engagement. He, de Beauvoir and Merleau-Ponty were the founders and co-editors of the influential political, literary and philosophical magazine, *Les Temps Modernes*.
1942	Albert Camus (1913–1960) published his philosophical treatise on the absurd, *The Myth of Sisyphus*, which argued, among other things, that the only truly serious philosophical question is whether or not to commit suicide. Published in the same year, his compelling novella, *The Outsider*, was, however, more significant in bringing the mood of existentialism to a wider audience.
1943	Sartre's philosophical magnus opus, *Being and Nothingness*, was completed, and it quickly became the core text of French existentialism, preoccupied as it is with freedom, responsibility and authenticity. Gabriel Marcel coined the term *existentialiste* to describe Sartre in his review of *Being and Nothingness* in *Les Tempes Modernes*. Heidegger's *Being and Time* translated into Spanish by Mexican philosopher Jose Gaos, thus making it available to Latin America 19 years before the English translation. De Beauvoir's 'metaphysical novel' *She Came to Stay* (contains a version of the phenomenological proof of other minds).
1944	Sartre's play *No Exit* (contains the famous line 'Hell is other people').

1945	Merleau-Ponty published his very important book, *Phenomenology of Perception*, which both endorsed and subtly refined Sartrean existentialism by focusing upon the significance of our embodiment. De Beauvoir's novel, *The Blood of Others*.
	Sartre's public lecture 'Existentialism is a Humanism' at the Club Maintenant helped to popularize existentialism when it was later published in an inexpensive volume. It also gave existentialism a more optimistic tenor – one which Heidegger later rebuffed.
1946	De Beauvoir's novel, *All Men are Mortal*. Jean Wahl's lecture 'A Short History of Existentialism' at the Club Maintenant, with responses by Nikolai Berdyaev, Georges Gurvitch and Emmanuel Levinas.
1947	Simone de Beauvoir (1908–1986) published *The Ethics of Ambiguity*, which developed the ethical significance of existentialism. Heidegger's essay, *Letter on Humanism* (reply to Sartre). Buber, *Between Man and Man*. Levinas, *Existence and Existents*. Merleau-Ponty, *Humanism and Terror*. Camus, *The Plague*.
1948	Sartre, *Dirty Hands*.
1949	De Beauvoir published her enormously influential treatise on the situation of women, *The Second Sex*.
	Heidegger, 'The Question Concerning Technology'.
1950	Marcel, *The Mystery of Being* (2 vols). Walter Kaufmann, *Nietzsche: Philosopher, Psychologist, Antichrist*. This book is generally taken as a classic existentialist reading of Nietzsche, despite Kaufmann's protestations.
1951	The release of Camus's *The Rebel* in 1951 created a furore at *Les Temps Modernes* because Camus refused to countenance any kind of Marxist revolution. This dispute resulted in Camus and Sartre acrimoniously ending their friendship.
	Marcel, *Man against Mass Society* – deals with existentialist themes of freedom. Beckett, *Malone Dies* and *Molloy*.
1952	Fanon, *Black Skin, White Masks* – extends and criticizes aspects of Sartrean existentialism in relation to situations of oppression.

	Carlos Astrada, one of the first to teach phenomenology and existialism in Argentina, published *The Existentialist Revolution*.
1953	Samuel Beckett's *Waiting for Godot* was performed for the first time, having been written in 1949.
1954	De Beauvoir, *The Mandarins* – novel dealing with issues of postwar ethics wins the prestigious French literature prize the *Prix Goncourt*.
	Jean Wahl, *Philosophies of Existence*.
1956	Walter Kaufmann (ed.), *Existentialism from Dostoevsky to Sartre*, an anthology which played a major role in introducing European existentialists to North America.
	Camus, *The Fall*.
1957	Mexican philosopher Emilio Uranga translated Merleau-Ponty's *Phenomenology of Perception* into Spanish, making it available to Latin America.
Late 1950s, early 1960s	The structuralism of theorists like Roland Barthes, Claude Levi-Strauss, Louis Althusser, Michel Foucault (his early work), and others, began to assume the limelight in French intellectual life.
1960	Camus died tragically in a car accident.
	Sartre published volume 1 of *Critique of Dialectical Reason*, which sought to bring together existentialism and Marxism.
1961	Merleau-Ponty died, before completing his great work, *The Visible and the Invisible*.
	The Algerian struggles for independence from France became fiercer.
	Levinas, *Totality and Infinity*.
	Fanon, *The Wretched of the Earth*.
	Cuban writer Alejo Carpentier conducted a famous interview with Sartre on 'the nature of the novel'.
1962	First translation of Heidegger's *Being and Time* into English (by John Macquarie and Edward Robinson).
1964	Theodor W. Adorno published a scathing critique of Heidegger called *The Jargon of Authenticity*. Sartre turned down the Nobel Prize for literature.
	Sartre published his existentialist autobiography *Words*.
	Merleau-Ponty's unfinished *The Visible and the Invisible* published posthumously.
1965	Jean Wahl's *Metaphysical Experience*, which analyses and defends the religious dimension of transcendence.

1966	De Beauvoir, *Les Belle Images.* Heidegger interviewed in German magazine *Der Spiegel*, with requirement that the interview not be published until after his death.
1967	Jacques Derrida (1930–2004) published three very influential books that have been associated with poststructuralism – *Of Grammatology, Writing and Difference* and *Speech and Phenomena.* Along with philosophers like Gilles Deleuze, Jean-François Lyotard and Michel Foucault, his work problematizes certain structuralist assumptions and continues to be influential.
May 1968	Student uprisings in Paris and around the world.
1970	De Beauvoir published *The Coming of Age*, a critique of society's prejudice against the elderly.
1976	Heidegger died. His 1966 *Der Spiegel* interview was published in accordance with his wishes.
1980	Sartre died and 50–100,000 people flocked to his funeral in the streets of Paris.
1986	De Beauvoir died.
2009	New English translation by Borde and Malovany-Chevallier of de Beauvoir's *The Second Sex* published in the United Kingdom, fuelled by belief that there were deep flaws in the original (H. M. Parshley) translation.

18 Research Resources in Existentialism

The following is a list of journals, societies and websites that will be helpful in researching existentialism. Some online resources are listed, but in addition many of the societies have affiliated websites with useful links to other existentialism sources.

Journals

The following journals, although not dedicated exclusively to existentialism, regularly publish articles on existentialist and phenomenological philosophy.

- *The Agonist* (A Nietzsche Circle journal)
- *Bulletin de la Société Américaine de Philosophie de Langue Française*
- *Chiasmi International: Trilingual Studies Concerning the Thought of Merleau-Ponty*
- *Continental Philosophy Review* (formerly *Man and World*)
- *European Journal of Philosophy*
- *European Journal of Women's Studies*
- *Existenz: An International Journal in Philosophy, Religion, Politics, and the Arts Journal* (focuses on the work of Karl Jaspers as well as existentialism and phenomenology generally)
- *Heidegger Studies*
- *History and Theory: Studies in the Philosophy of History*
- *History of European Ideas*
- *Hypatia* (often features feminist discussions of phenomenology and existentialism)
- *International Journal of Philosophical Studies*
- *Journal of Nietzsche Studies*
- *Journal of the Albert Camus Society*
- *Journal of the British Society of Phenomenology*
- *New Nietzsche Studies*
- *Nietzsche-Studien*
- *Phaenex* (Electronic journal, interdisciplinary)
- *Philosophy and Literature*
- *Philosophy Today*

- *Research in Phenomenology*
- *Review of Existential Psychology*
- *Sartre Studies International*
- *Signs: Journal of Women in Culture and Society*
- *Simone de Beauvoir Studies* (published by the Simone de Beauvoir Society)
- *Sophia: International Journal for Philosophy of Religion, Metaphysical Theology and Ethics*
- *Symposium: Canadian Journal of Continental Philosophy*
- *Yale French Studies* (includes articles on French existentialism)

Existential Philosophy Societies and Associations

- Albert Camus Society of the United Kingdom
- Albert Camus Society of the United States
- Australasian Existential Society (focuses on psychotherapy)
- Australasian Nietzsche Society
- Australasian Society of Continental Philosophy
- British Society for Phenomenology
- Camus Studies Association
- Canadian Society for Continental Philosophy
- Existential and Phenomenological Theory and Culture
- Existentialist Society (Melbourne, Australia)
- Friedrich Nietzsche Society
- Gabriel Marcel Society
- Heidegger Circle
- Karl Jaspers Society of North America
- Kierkegaard Society of the United Kingdom
- Melbourne School of Continental Philosophy
- Merleau-Ponty Circle
- Nietzsche Circle
- Nietzsche Society
- North American Heidegger Conference
- North American Nietzsche Society
- North American Sartre Society
- Simone de Beauvoir Society (international, based in America)
- *Société Américaine de Philosophie de la Langue Française* (SAPLF)
- Society for Continental Philosophy and Theology
- Society for European Philosophy
- Society for Existential Analysis (focuses on psychotherapy)
- Society for Existential and Phenomenological Theory and Culture/Théorie et culture existentialistes et phénoménologiques (EPTC/TCEP) (Canada)
- Society for Iberian and Latin American Thought

- Society for Phenomenology and Existential Philosophy (SPEP)
- Society for Women in Philosophy (SWIP)
- Søren Kierkegaard Society (USA)
- UK Sartre Society (formerly the UK Society for Sartrean Studies)

Websites

Centre for Advanced Research in Phenomenology
  www.phenomenologycenter.org/phenom.htm (includes a useful 'What is Phenomenology' article, as well as complete online bibliography of Simone de Beauvoir's works and good list of secondary sources)
Epistemelinks
  www.epistemelinks.org (database of philosophy links)
Ereignis
  www.beyng.com/ (links to Heidegger pages in English)
Existential Christianity
  www.existentialchristianity.net/
Existential Psychotherapy
  www.existentialpsychotherapy.net/
Existentialism: Continental Philosophy Bulletin Board
  www.continental-philosophy.org/category/existentialism/ (useful for up-to-date information on what's going on in existentialism)
Existentialism Primer
  www.tameri.com/csw/exist/
Hong Kierkegaard Library
  www.stolaf.edu/collections/kierkegaard/
Hubert L. Dreyfus
  http://socrates.berkeley.edu/~hdreyfus/ (links to podcasts of his lectures on Heidegger and existentialism)
Internet Encyclopedia of Philosophy
  www.iep.utm.edu/ (comprehensive entries on all the main existentialist figures)
Kierkegaard Studies in Australasia
  http://home.vicnet.net.au/~kierk/
The Merleau-Ponty Circle
  www.uri.edu/artsci/phl/impc/ (website of this American society includes a link to a very useful bibliography of secondary works on Merleau-Ponty)
The Nietzsche Circle
  www.nietzschecircle.com/index.html
Nietzsche Source
  www.nietzschesource.org/ (contains Nietzsche's collected works and archival documents in German)
Phenomenology Online
  www.phenomenologyonline.com/home.html (contains links to some interesting articles on the phenomenology of 'real-life' situations)
Sartre exhibition

http://expositions.bnf.fr/sartre/ (an interesting virtual exhibition containing archival images, manuscripts and features from the life of Jean-Paul Sartre)
Sartre society website
    www.sartreuk.org/site/view.php?page_name=1999 (website includes extensive searchable bibliography of secondary literature 1999–present)
Sartre sources online
    www.sartre.org/
Society of Existential Analysis
    www.existentialanalysis.co.uk
Søren Kierkegaard Research Center (SKC)
    www.sk.ku.dk/
Stanford Encyclopedia of Philosophy
    http://plato.stanford.edu/ (respected online encyclopedia)

19 Annotated Guide to Further Reading

This annotated guide to the secondary literature associated with existentialism is comprised of 10 sections:

    I. General Texts on Existentialism
   II. Camus
  III. De Beauvoir
  IV. Heidegger
   V. Jaspers
  VI. Kierkegaard
 VII. Marcel
VIII. Merleau-Ponty
  IX. Nietzsche
   X. Sartre

I. General Texts on Existentialism

There are a lot of general texts on existentialism that are worthy of consideration. Of recent texts, David Cooper's *Existentialism* (London: Routledge, 2001) is a good thematic study that is unusual in emphasizing the closeness between Heidegger and Sartre's philosophies. Jack Reynolds' *Understanding Existentialism* (Chesham: Acumen, 2006) pays more attention to Merleau-Ponty's and Sartre's work, and Thomas Flynn's *Existentialism: A Very Short Introduction* (Oxford: Oxford University Press, 2006) is admirably clear and succinct. Sonia Kruks' *Situation and Human Existence: Freedom, Subjectivity and Society* (London: Unwin Hyman, 1990) focuses more on the work of de Beauvoir and has some interesting reflections on Sartre's later work, most notably his often neglected book, *Critique of Dialectical Reason*.

    Also worth considering are introductory books on phenomenology, which often offer helpful elucidations of the work of Heidegger, Sartre and Merleau-Ponty, in particular. In this respect, we recommend two: Christopher Macann's *Four Phenomenological Philosophers: Husserl, Heidegger, Sartre, Merleau-Ponty* (London: Routledge, 1993), and Dermot Moran's *Introduction to Phenomenology* (London: Routledge, 2000). The latter has a companion volume, an anthology:

The Phenomenology Reader (London: Routledge, 2002). Together these give the reader a high-level introduction to, and overview of, the topic without shying away from the more difficult texts and concepts. Two recently released collections of essays that also contain some very useful essays on both phenomenology and existentialism are Hubert L. Dreyfus and Mark A. Wrathall, eds, *A Companion to Phenomenology and Existentialism* (London: Wiley-Blackwell, 2009), and Sebastian Luft and Søren Overgaard, eds, *Routledge Companion to Phenomenology* (London: Routledge, 2011).

If one is looking for more detail on the link between some early existential thinkers, such as Nietzsche and Kierkegaard, and their twentieth-century developments, books on existentialism released in the 1960s and early 1970s are the best bet, including the early, classic study by Jean Wahl, *Philosophies of Existence* (London: Routledge, 1969), and John Macquarrie's *Existentialism* (London: Penguin, 1973).

In regard to shorter articles on existentialism, Steven Crowell's entry on existentialism for *The Stanford Encyclopedia of Philosophy* is a perceptive summary, as is Mark Wrathall's essay, 'Existential Phenomenology' (in *A Companion to Phenomenology and Existentialism*).

Also of interest is the forthcoming *Situating Existentialism* (ed. Jonathan Judaken and Robert Bernasconi, New York: Columbia University Press), which seeks to examine Sartre's ideas in a broader existential perspective, including that of religious existentialism, Hispanic and Africana existentialism and feminism. Beyond this, we list below some other texts of potential interest.

Other Useful Works

Barrett, W. (1961), *Irrational Man: A Study in Existential Philosophy*. London: Heinemann.

Blackham, H. J. (1952), *Six Existentialist Thinkers*. London: Routledge and Kegan Paul.

Deutscher, M. (2003), *Genre and Void: Looking Back at Sartre and Beauvoir*. Ashgate: Aldershot.

Grene, M. (1959), *Introduction to Existentialism*. Chicago: University of Chicago Press.

Luijpen, W. A. M. (1960), *Existential Phenomenology*. Duquesne Studies Philosophical Series 12. Pittsburgh: Duquesne University.

Olson, R. G. (1962), *An Introduction to Existentialism*. New York: Dover Publications.

Wahl, J. (1949), *A Short History of Existentialism*, trans. F. Williams and S. Mason. New York: Philosophical Library.

Warnock, M. (1970), *Existentialism*. London and New York: Oxford University Press.

Zaner, R. M. and D. Ihde (1973), *Phenomenology and Existentialism*. New York: Putnam (Capricorn Books).

Existentialism Anthologies

Friedman, M. S. (ed.) (1964), *The Worlds of Existentialism: A Critical Reader*. New York: Random House.

Guignon, C. and D. Pereboom (eds) (1995), *Existentialism: Basic Writings*. Indianapolis: Hackett.

Kaufmann, W. (ed.) (1975), *Existentialism from Dostoevsky to Sartre*. New York: Meridian [1956].

Langiulli, N. (ed.), (1971), *The Existentialist Tradition*. New York: Anchor Books.

MacDonald, P. S. (ed.) (2000), *The Existentialist Reader: An Anthology of Key Texts*. Edinburgh: Edinburgh University Press.

Marino, G. (ed.) (2004), *Basic Writings of Existentialism*. New York: Modern Library.

Oaklander, N. L. (1992), *Existentialist Philosophy: An Introduction*. Englewood Cliffs, NJ: Prentice Hall.

Solomon, R. C. (ed.) (1974), *Existentialism*. New York: Modern Library.

Special Topics in Existentialism

Fallico, A. B. (1962), *Art and Existentialism*. Englewood Cliffs, NJ: Prentice Hall.

Gordon, L. R. (ed.) (1997), *Existence in Black: An Anthology of Black Existential Philosophy*. New York: Routledge.

Gordon, L. R. (2000), *Existentia Africana: Understanding Africana Existential Thought*. New York: Routledge.

McBride, W. L. (ed.) (1996), *The Development and Meaning of Twentieth-Century Existentialism*. London: Routledge.

Tuttle, H. (1996), *The Crowd is Untruth: The Existential Critique of Mass Society in the Thought of Kierkegaard, Nietzsche, Heidegger, and Ortega y Gasset*. New York: Peter Lang.

Reference Works

Gordon, H. (ed.) (1999), *Dictionary of Existentialism*. Westport: Greenwood Press.

Michelman, S. (ed.) (2008), *Historical Dictionary of Existentialism*. Maryland: Scarecrow Press.

II. Camus

Albert Camus's complete works in French (*Œuvres completes*) have recently been published in a new Pléiade edition by Gallimard, in four volumes, under the editorial direction of Jacquelline Lévi-Valensi and Raymond Gay-Crosier (2006–2008). Most of Camus's works are available in English in various, non-standardized translations. For a representative selection, see *Albert Camus: The*

Essential Writings (New York: Harper Colophon Books, 1979). Camus's most significant philosophical works are *The Myth of Sisyphus*, trans. J. O'Brien (London: Penguin, 2000) and *The Rebel*, trans. A. Bower (London: Penguin, 1972). His thesis has been published as *Christian Metaphysics and Neoplatonism*, trans. R. D. Srigley (Columbia and London: University of Missouri Press, 2007). Essay collections include *Lyrical and Critical Essays*, ed. P. Thody, trans. E. C. Kennedy (London: Vintage, 1970) and *Resistance, Rebellion, and Death: Essays* (London: Vintage, 1995). Some of his journalistic writings have been published in *Camus at* Combat: *Writing 1944–1947*, ed. J. Lévi-Valensi, trans. A. Goldhammer (Princeton: Princeton University Press, 2006). Various editions of Camus's novels, plays, notebooks and other writings are also available in English translations.

Many biographical treatments of Camus are available, including Herbert R. Lottman's *Albert Camus: A Biography* (Garden City, NY: Doubleday, 1979), Oliver Todd's *Albert Camus: A Life*, trans. B. Ivry (London: Vintage, 1998), Robert Zaretsky's *Albert Camus: Elements of a Life* (Ithaca: Cornell University Press, 2010) and Elizabeth Hawes' *Camus, A Romance* (New York: Grove Press, 2010). On Camus's relation to Sartre, see the collection of their critical exchanges *Sartre and Camus: A Historic Confrontation*, ed. and trans. D. A. Sprintzen and A. Van Den Hoven (New York: Humanity Books), and Ronald Aronson's biographical account *Camus and Sartre: The Story of a Friendship and the Quarrel That Ended It* (Chicago: University of Chicago Press, 2004).

The secondary literature has demonstrated a revival of interest in Camus over the last decade or so, although much of it is biographical, literary or political – rather than philosophical – in orientation. An exception to this is David Sherman's *Camus* (Stafford: Wiley-Blackwell, 2008), a recent study that establishes Camus's important contributions to existential philosophy. John Foley's *Albert Camus: From the Absurd to Revolt* (Montreal: McGill-Queens University Press, 2008) is a thorough contemporary study. For a recent study of Camus's fiction, see Moya Longstaffe, *The Fiction of Albert Camus* (Bern: Peter Lang, 2007), and on his plays, see Michael Y. Bennett, *Reassessing the Theatre of the Absurd: Camus, Beckett, Ionesco, Genet, and Pinter* (Basingstoke: Palgrave Macmillan, 2011). On Camus's politics, see Fred H. Willohite's *Beyond Nihilism: Albert Camus' Contribution to Political Thought* (Baton Rouge, LA: Louisiana State University Press, 1968) and Jefferey C. Isaac's *Arendt, Camus, and Modern Rebellion* (New Haven: Yale University Press, 2009). Camus's import for feminism is studied by Elizabeth Ann Bartlett in her *Rebellious Feminism: Camus' Ethic of Rebellion and Feminist Thought* (Basingstoke: Palgrave Macmillan, 2004), and his relation to post-colonial issues is explored in David Carroll's *Albert Camus the Algerian: Colonialism, Terrorism, Justice* (New York: Columbia University Press, 2008).

General collections of critical essays on Camus include *Camus: A Collection of Critical Essays*, ed. G. Brée (Englewood Cliffs, NJ: Prentice Hall, 1962) and *Critical Essays on Albert Camus*, ed. B. L. Knapp (Waterville, Maine: Thorndike Press, 1988).

Other Useful Works

Bronner, S. E. (1999), *Camus: Portrait of a Moralist*. Minneapolis: University of Minnesota Press.

Cruikshank, J. (1962), 'Albert Camus', in J. Cruikshank (ed.), *The Novelist as Philosopher*. London: Oxford University Press.

Davison, R. (1997), *Camus: The Challenge of Dostoevsky*. Exeter: University of Exeter Press.

Hansen, K. W. (1993), *Tragic Lucidity: Discourse of Recuperation in Unamuno and Camus*. Frankfurt am Main: Peter Lang.

Hughes, E. J. (ed.) (2007), *The Cambridge Companion to Camus*. Cambridge: Cambridge University Press.

McCarthy, P. (1982), *Camus: A Critical Study of His Life and Work*. London: Hamilton.

Novello, S. (2010), *Albert Camus as Political Thinker: Nihilisms and the Politics of Contempt*. Basingstoke: Palgrave Macmillan.

Rizzuto, A. (1998), *Camus: Love and Sexuality*. Gainesville: University Press of Florida.

Sessler, T. (2008), *Levinas and Camus: Humanism for the Twenty-First Century*. London and New York: Continuum.

Solomon, R. C. (2006), *Dark Feelings, Grim Thoughts: Experience and Reflection in Camus and Sartre*. London: Oxford University Press.

Sprintzen, D. (1991), *Camus: A Critical Examination*. Philadelphia: Temple University Press.

Thody, P. (1957), *Albert Camus: A Study of His Work*. London: Hamilton.

III. De Beauvoir

There are more recent secondary texts on de Beauvoir than on many of the other figures with which this book is concerned, and that is partly because her work remains a significant site of contestation within the various different 'schools' of feminism. Some of the most useful recent texts on her work are the following: Kristana Arp, *The Bonds of Freedom* (Chicago: Open Court, 2001); Nancy Bauer, *Simone de Beauvoir, Philosophy and Feminism* (New York: Columbia University Press, 2001); and Debra Bergoffen, *The Philosophy of Simone de Beauvoir: Gendered Phenomenologies, Erotic Generosities* (Albany, NY: SUNY Press, 1997). The last offers another level of interpretation of de Beauvoir's work, identifying a 'muted voice' that calls for a renewed generosity of being. The many works of Margaret A. Simons on de Beauvoir are well researched and explore the historical and material background to de Beauvoir's work, for instance, Margaret A. Simons, *Beauvoir and The Second Sex: Feminism, Race and the Origins of Existentialism* (Lanham, MD: Rowman & Littlefield, 1999). Of course, unlike Heidegger, Sartre and Merleau-Ponty, de Beauvoir's own writings are admirably clear and *The Ethics of Ambiguity* should itself be read from beginning to end, as with her famous book, *The Second Sex*. Michele Le Doeuff's *Hipparchia's Choice: An Essay Concerning Women, Philosophy, etc.*, trans. T. Selous (Oxford: Blackwell, 1991) is a highly influential text which seeks to understand de Beauvoir's work on its own terms, disentangling it from Sartre's influence, with an emphasis on de Beauvoir's contribution to ethics. Toril Moi's *The Making of an Intellectual Woman* (Oxford: Blackwell, 1994) examines de Beauvoir's politics and sociology and strategies for liberation. Joseph Mahon's *Existentialism, Feminism and Simone de Beauvoir* (London: Macmillan, 1997) offers a useful guide to the main feminist evaluations of de Beauvoir's philosophy as well as drawing out the philosophical positions extant in her work. For an illumination of the influence of Husserlian phenomenology in de Beauvoir's work, see Sara Heinämaa's *Towards a Phenomenology of Sexual Difference: Husserl, Merleau-Ponty, Beauvoir* (Lanham, MD: Rowman & Littlefield, 2003). In addition, the 'de Beauvoir Series' at Illinois University Press (ed. Margaret A. Simons and Sylvie Le Bon de Beauvoir) is an ongoing project of new translations of de Beauvoir's philosophical works with particular attention to their philosophical terminology.

Other Useful Works

Daigle, C. and J. Golumb (eds) (2009), *Beauvoir and Sartre: The Riddle of Influence*. Bloomington, IN: Indiana University Press.

Deutscher, P. (2008), *The Philosophy of Simone de Beauvoir: Ambiguity, Conversion, Resistance*. Cambridge: Cambridge University Press.

Evans, R. (ed.) (1998), *Simone de Beauvoir's* The Second Sex: *New Interdisciplinary Essays*. Manchester: Manchester University Press.

Fullbrook, K. and E. Fullbrook (1994), *Simone de Beauvoir and Jean-Paul Sartre: The Remaking of a Twentieth Century Legend*. New York: Basic Books.

Holveck, E. (2002), *Simone de Beauvoir's Philosophy of Lived Experience: Literature and Metaphysics*. Lanham, MD: Rowman & Littlefield.

Lundgren-Gothlin, F. (1996), *Sex and Existence: Simone de Beauvoir's 'The Second Sex'*, trans. Schenck. Hanover: Wesleyan University Press.

Marso, L. J. and P. Moynagh (2006), *Simone de Beauvoir's Political Thinking*. Urbana-Champaign: Illinois University Press.

Simons, M. (ed.) (1995), *Feminist Interpretations of Simone de Beauvoir*. University Park, PA: Pennsylvania State University Press.

Vintges, K. (1996), *Philosophy as Passion: The Thinking of Simone de Beauvoir*, trans. Lavelle. Bloomington, IN: Indiana University Press.

IV. Heidegger

Heidegger's complete works in German are the *Gesamtausgabe* (Frankfurt am Main: Vittorio Klostermann). This is an ongoing project, and not all of the projected one hundred volumes have yet appeared in publication. Of these, many, but not all, have been translated into English.

The focus of the existentialist interpretations of Heidegger revolve around his book *Being and Time*, of which there are two main English translations: one by John Macquarrie and Edward Robinson (Oxford: Blackwell, 1962), and one by Joan Stambaugh (Albany, NY: SUNY Press, 1996) that has recently been updated by Dennis Schmidt. There are several commentaries on this notoriously difficult text. Four helpful such works are Hubert Dreyfus, *Being-in-the-world: A Commentary on Heidegger's Being and Time, Division 1* (Cambridge, MA: MIT Press, 1991); Stephen Mulhall, *Routledge Philosophy Guidebook to Heidegger and Being and Time* (London: Routledge, 1996); Michael Gelven, *A Commentary on Heidegger's Being and Time* (Illinois: Northern Illinois University Press, 1989); and William Blattner, *Heidegger's Being and Time: A Reader's Guide* (London and New York: Continuum, 2007). It is Dreyfus's that has been the more influential in bringing Heidegger's thought to a wide Anglophone audience, despite Dreyfus's reluctance to consider Division 2 of *Being and Time* (and the material on death) in much detail. Also from this period, before his apparent 'turn' away from existential phenomenology, and notable for its discussion of anxiety, is the lecture 'What is Metaphysics?' that is found in *Basic Writings*, ed. D. F. Krell (San Francisco: Harper, 1993).

One of Heidegger's most approachable introductions to his own philosophical development and interests is the essay 'My Way to Phenomenology' in Walter Kaufmann's edited volume *Existentialism from Dostoevsky to Sartre* (New York: Meridian, 1975). Heidegger's 'Letter on Humanism' not only contains his criticisms of Sartrean existentialism, but is one of the clearest and most concise statements of his philosophical concerns. This essay is contained along with many of his other best-known short articles in *Basic Writings*, which makes a good introduction to his work through a combination of primary material and commentary. Another useful sampling of primary texts is *The Heidegger Reader*, ed. G. Figal, trans. J. Veith (Bloomington, IN: Indiana University Press, 2009). Among the many other translations of Heidegger's works available, we may note two relatively recent works which present new translations of some of his best-known collections of shorter writings: *Pathmarks*, a translation of *Wegmarken* by W. McNeill (Cambridge: Cambridge University Press, 1998) and *Off the Beaten Track*, a translation of *Holzwege* by J. Young and K. Haynes (Cambridge: Cambridge University Press, 2002). Also requiring mention here is Heidegger's *Contributions to Philosophy: From Enowning*, trans. P. Emad and K. Maly (Bloomington, IN: Indiana University Press, 1999). Sometimes touted as Heidegger's 'second *magnum opus*' and major work of the post-*Being and Time* era, the *Contributions* is a highly esoteric work with which scholars are still grappling.

There is a great deal of exegetical and interpretative literature on Heidegger. Good secondary introductory texts to Heidegger are Richard Polt's *Heidegger:*

An Introduction (Ithaca: Cornell University Press, 1999) and Miguel de Beistegui's *The New Heidegger* (London: Continuum, 2005). A classic and monumental interpretation of Heidegger's philosophy is William Richardson's *Heidegger: Through Phenomenology to Thought* (New York: Fordham University Press, 2003). In terms of critical contributions and collections of essays on Heidegger, there are several worthy of consideration, including Hubert L. Dreyfus and Harrison Hall, eds, *Heidegger: A Critical Reader* (Oxford: Oxford University Press, 1992) and Charles Guignon, ed., *The Cambridge Companion to Heidegger* (Cambridge: Cambridge University Press, 1993). Also worth examining because of their focus upon the existential significance of Heidegger's thought is John Richardson's *Existential Phenomenology: A Heideggerian Critique of the Cartesian Project* (Oxford: Oxford University Press, 1986) and John Haugeland's essay 'Truth and Finitude: Heidegger's Transcendental Existentialism', which can be found in *Heidegger, Authenticity and Modernity*, ed. Mark Wrathall and Jeff Malpas (Cambridge, MA: MIT Press, 2000). There are several biographies of Heidegger, including Hugo Ott's *Martin Heidegger: A Political Life*, trans. A. Blunden (London: Harper Collins, 1993) and Rüdiger Safranski's *Martin Heidegger: Between Good and Evil*, trans. E. Osers (Cambridge, MA: Harvard University Press, 1998).

While free web resources are not always to be trusted, there is a good introduction to Heidegger (and in fact to all of the thinkers considered in this book), available on the Internet Encyclopedia of Philosophy –www.iep.utm.edu/h/ heidegge.htm

Other Useful Works

Blattner, W. (1999), *Heidegger's Temporal Idealism*. Cambridge: Cambridge University Press.

Denker, A. (2000), *Historical Dictionary of Heidegger's Philosophy*. Lanham, MD: Scarecrow Press.

Frede, D. (1993), 'The Question of Being: Heidegger's Project', in C. Guignon (ed.), *The Cambridge Companion to Heidegger*. Cambridge: Cambridge University Press.

Harman, G. (2007), *Heidegger Explained: From Phenomenon to Thing*. Chicago: Open Court.

Holland, Nancy J. and P. Huntington (eds) (2001), *Feminist Interpretations of Martin Heidegger*. University Park, PA: Pennsylvania State University Press.

Inwood, M. (1997), *Heidegger*. Oxford: Oxford University Press.

— (1999), *A Heidegger Dictionary*. Stafford: Wiley-Blackwell.

Kleinberg, E. (2005), *Generation Existential: Heidegger's Philosophy in France, 1927–1961*. Ithaca: Cornell University Press.

Kockelmans, J. J. (ed.) (1986), *A Companion to Martin Heidegger's 'Being and Time'*. Washington, DC: Centre for Advanced Research in Phenomenology and University Press of America.

Krell, D. F. (1992), *Daimon Life: Heidegger and Life-Philosophy*. Bloomington, IN: Indiana University Press.

Löwith, K. (1995), *Martin Heidegger and European Nihilism*, ed. R. Wolin, trans. G. Steiner. New York: Columbia University Press.

Malpas, J. (2003), 'Martin Heidegger', in R. C. Solomon and D. Sherman (eds), *Blackwell Guide to Continental Philosophy*. Oxford: Basil Blackwell.

Pöggeler, O. (1987), *Martin Heidegger's Path of Thinking*, trans. D. Magurshak and S. Barber. Atlantic Highlands, NJ: Humanities Press International.

Petzet, H. W. (1993), *Encounters and Dialogues with Martin Heidegger, 1929–1976*, trans. P. Emad and K. Maly. Chicago: University of Chicago Press.

Steiner, G. (1992), *Heidegger*. London: Fontana Press.

Strauss, L. (1989), 'An Introduction to Heideggerian Existentialism', in T. L. Pangle (ed.), *The Rebirth of Classical Rationalism: An Introduction to the Thought of Leo Strauss*. Chicago: University of Chicago Press.

Waterhouse, R. (1981), *A Heidegger Critique: A Critical Examination of the Existential Phenomenology of Martin Heidegger*. Brighton, Sussex: Harvester Press; Atlantic Highlands, NJ: Humanities Press.

Wolin, R. (ed.) (1993), *The Heidegger Controversy: A Critical Reader*. Cambridge, MA: MIT Press.

Zimmerman, M. E. (1986), *Eclipse of the Self: the Development of Heidegger's Concept of Authenticity*. Athens, OH: Ohio University Press.

V. Jaspers

Many of Jaspers works have been translated into English, but there remain some notable exceptions (such as *Psychology of Worldviews* and *Of Truth*). For a selection of Jaspers's texts, see *Karl Jaspers: Basic Philosophical Writings*, ed. and trans. E. Ehrlich, L. H. Ehrlich and G. B. Pepper (New York: Humanities Press, 1994). Good introductions to his philosophy are provided by the texts *Reason and Existence*, trans. W. Earle (New York: Farrar Straus, 1955) and *Philosophy of Existence*, trans. R. F. Grabau (Philadelphia: University of Pennsylvania Press, 1971). His major philosophical work available in English translation is *Philosophy*, 3 vols, trans. E. B. Ashton (Chicago: Chicago University Press, 1969–1971). Jaspers's *Nietzsche: An Introduction to the Understanding of His Philosophical Activity*, trans. C. F. Wellraff and F. J. Schmitz (Tucson: University of Arizona Press, 1965) was key to Nietzsche's reception as an existentialist.

There has been less work on Jaspers in English, especially in recent years, than on many of the other major existentialist figures. The collection *The Philosophy of Karl Jaspers*, ed. P. A. Schilpp (La Salle, IL: Open Court, 1981) remains a valuable secondary text, while more recent is Kurt Salamun and Gregory J. Walters (eds), *Karl Jaspers' Philosophy: Expositions and Interpretations* (New York: Humanity Books, 2008). A notable recent study is Chris Thornhill's *Karl Jaspers: Politics and Metaphysics* (London: Routledge, 2002).

Other Useful Works

Bormuth, M. (2011), *Life Conduct in Modern Times: Karl Jaspers and Psychoanalysis*. New York: Springer.

Ehrlich, L. H. (1975), *Karl Jaspers: Philosophy as Faith*. Amherst: University of Massachusetts Press.

Ehrlich, L. H. and R. Wisser (eds) (1988), *Karl Jaspers Today: Philosophy at the Threshold of the Future*. Lanham, MD: University Press of America.

Kirkbright, S. (2004), *Karl Jaspers: A Biography – Navigations in Truth*. New Haven: Yale University Press.

Koterski, J. W. and R. J. Langley (eds) (2003), *Karl Jaspers on Philosophy of History and History of Philosophy*. New York: Humanity Books.

Olson, A. M. (1979), *Transcendence and Hermeneutics: An Interpretation of the Philosophy of Karl Jaspers*. Dordrecht: Kluwer Academic Publishers.

— (ed.) (1993), *Heidegger and Jaspers*. Philadelphia: Temple University Press.

Peach, F. (2008), *Death, 'Deathlessness' and Existenz in Karl Jaspers' Philosophy*. Edinburgh: Edinburgh University Press.

Young-Bruehl, E. (1981), *Freedom and Karl Jaspers' Philosophy*. New Haven: Yale University Press.

VI. Kierkegaard

William McDonald's chapter on Kierkegaard in the New Directions section of this book provides an extensive guide to recent literature. In addition, the beginner is well advised to take a look at John Caputo's *How to Read Kierkegaard* (London: Granta Books, 2007). George Pattison's *The Philosophy of Kierkegaard* (Montreal: McGill-Queens University Press, 2005) is also recommended.

In relation to Kierkegaard's own texts, those with the most distinctively existential flavour include *Fear and Trembling*, *The Concept of Anxiety* and *Sickness unto Death*. His much longer *Either/Or* (2 vols) remains a classic. William McDonald's *Stanford Encyclopedia* entry on Kierkegaard also provides a helpful overview of his various works and core philosophical contributions.

VII. Marcel

Gabriel Marcel remains outside the circle of the more well-known existentialists but there is a body of significant scholarship available to the interested student. A good starting-point is the Gabriel Marcel volume in the Library of Living Philosophers series, *The Philosophy of Gabriel Marcel* (La Salle, IL: Open Court, 1984); it includes Marcel's interesting 'Autobiographical Essay' as well as critical discussions of his ideas, to which Marcel provides short responses. For a deeper level of discussion of Marcel's ontology, see the collection of essays edited by W. Cooney, *Contributions of Gabriel Marcel to Philosophy: A Collection of Essays* (Lewiston, NY: E. Mellen Press, 1989). For discussion of Marcel's dramatic–philosophical output, see Katherine Rose Hanley's *Dramatic Approaches to Creative Fidelity* (Lanham, MD: University Press of America, 1987) and Denis Moran's *Gabriel Marcel: Existentialist Philosopher, Dramatist, Educator* (Lanham, MD: University Press of America, 1992). For a translation of a selection of his plays, see *Gabriel Marcel: 3 Plays* (New York: Hill & Wang, 1965). Marcel's response to Sartrean existentialism is scattered throughout various short works, but see in particular *The Philosophy of Existentialism* (New York: Citadel Press, 2002). Marcel devotes a chapter of this work to analysing some of Sartre's famous examples, such as the person spying through a keyhole. Also in this collection is one of his most important essays: 'On the Ontological Mystery'.

Other Useful Works

Anderson, T. C. (2006), *A Commentary on Gabriel Marcel's* The Mystery of Being. Milwaukee, WI: Marquette University Press.

Busch, T. W. (ed.) (1987), *The Participant Perspective: A Gabriel Marcel Reader*. Lanham, MD: University Press of America.

Gallagher, K. T. (1962), *The Philosophy of Gabriel Marcel*. New York: Fordham University Press.

Peccorini, F. (1987), *Selfhood as Thinking Thought in the Work of Gabriel Marcel: A New Interpretation*. Lewiston, NY: E. Mellen Press.

Sweetman, B. (2008), *The Vision of Gabriel Marcel: Epistemology, Human Person, the Transcendent*. New York: Rodopi.

VIII. Merleau-Ponty

There are many good books on Merleau-Ponty, among them Martin Dillon's *Merleau-Ponty's Ontology* (Bloomington, IN: Indiana University Press, 1988), Stephen Priest's *Merleau-Ponty* (London: Routledge, 1998), Monica Langer's *Merleau-Ponty's Phenomenology of Perception: A Guide and Commentary* (Hampshire: MacMillan Press, 1989), and the *Cambridge Companion to Merleau-Ponty*, eds, Taylor Carman and Mark Hansen (Cambridge: Cambridge University Press, 2005). Not all of these are overly attentive to Merleau-Ponty's significance for existentialism, however, and in this respect probably the best text to look at is Jon Stewart, ed., *The Debate between Sartre and Merleau-Ponty* (Evanston, IL: Northwestern University Press, 1998). It contains all of the key texts in the debate between Sartre and Merleau-Ponty, including some of those written by de Beauvoir. It is also complemented by some of the most perceptive secondary commentaries on their interrelation, including John Compton's 'Sartre, Merleau-Ponty, and Human Freedom' and Martin Dillon's 'Sartre on the Phenomenal Body and Merleau-Ponty's

Critique'. Also important in this regard is Thomas W. Busch's 'Existentialism: The New Philosophy', which can be found in *Merleau-Ponty: Key Concepts*, ed. R. Diprose and J. Reynolds (Chesham: Acumen, 2008). Another recent work of note is Lawrence Hass's *Merleau-Ponty's Philosophy* (Bloomington, IN: Indiana University Press, 2008), which focuses on Merleau-Ponty's methodology and relates his work to more recent theory such as contemporary physicalism, feminist theory and poststructuralism.

While most commentaries on Merleau-Ponty's interactions with Sartre focus on his two main philosophical texts – *Phenomenology of Perception* and *The Visible and the Invisible* – there are also several other texts by Merleau-Ponty the existence of which it is important to be aware. What follows is a brief summary of these.

'Hegel as Existentialist', in *Sense and Nonsense*, trans. H. Dreyfus and P. Dreyfus (Evanston, IL: Northwestern University Press, 1964).

In this essay, Merleau-Ponty suggests that Hegel can be redeemed as an important existentialist figure, and he points out that it was Hegel who first emphasized that 'man is a place of unrest', a theme that is common from Kierkegaard to Sartre. Merleau-Ponty also endorses the young Hegel's focus upon death, and in this text there are also some comments on Heidegger. In particular, Merleau-Ponty suggests that Heidegger 'lacks not historicity but, on the contrary, an affirmation of the individual: he does not mention that struggle of consciousnesses and that opposition of freedoms without which co-existence sinks into anonymity and everyday banality' (p. 69). This repeats Sartre's criticism of Heidegger's notion of *Mitsein* in *Being and Nothingness*.

'The Battle over Existentialism', in *Sense and Nonsense*.

Here Merleau-Ponty discusses his relationship with Sartre in more positive terms, and defends Sartre against certain caricatures of his work, although he nevertheless argues that he remains too dualist, 'too exclusively antithetic' (p. 72).

'The Philosophy of Existence', in *Texts and Dialogues: On Philosophy, Politics, and Culture*, ed. H. Silverman and J. Barry, trans. M. Smith et al. (Amherst, NY: Humanity Books, 1992).

Merleau-Ponty retrospectively presents a historical overview of the milieu and development of French existentialism, considering the contribution that the idealism of Leon Brunschvicg and Henri Bergson had on Sartre and himself.

'The Child's Relations with Others', in *The Primacy of Perception*, ed. and trans. James Edie (Evanston, IL: Northwestern University Press, 1964).

In this text, Merleau-Ponty uses both psychoanalytic and ontological arguments to suggest that there is something missing with Sartre's argument that conflict is the primary mode of relating to others. In particular, he argues that this mode of conflict is dependent on, and presupposes, a more primordial self-other union – a 'transitivism' – of the infant with their mother, as well as the external world, more generally.

'Sartre and Ultra-Bolshevism', in *Adventures of the Dialectic*, trans. J. Bien (Evanston, IL: Northwestern University Press, 1973).

In this long essay, Merleau-Ponty contends that Sartre's consciousness/thing distinction gives him political troubles, particularly in regard to his attempted rapprochement of existentialism with Marxism, the latter of which ultimately seeks to overcome any kind of subject–object mode of relation. According to Merleau-Ponty, Sartre effectively posits the Communist Party as the subject, while the workers assume a position equivalent to the object, and the result is that the party is envisaged as holding the proletariat in existence; Sartre's position hence constitutes a renewed Leninism, or an ultra-Bolshevism. For Merleau-Ponty, the deterministic versions of Marxism constitute a philosophy of objectivity, and Sartre's position remains a philosophy of subjectivity. Both are envisaged as ultimately terroristic.

Other Useful Works

Carman, T. (2008), *Merleau-Ponty*. London: Routledge.
Coole, D. H. (2007), *Merleau-Ponty and Modern Politics after Anti-Humanism*. Lanham, MD: Rowman & Littlefield.
Olkowski, D. and J. Morley (eds) (1999), *Merleau-Ponty, Interiority and Exteriority, Psychic Life, and World*. Albany, NY: SUNY Press.
Olkowski, D. and G. Weiss (eds) (2007), *Feminist Interpretations of Maurice Merleau-Ponty*. Philadelphia: Pennsylvania State University Press.
Toadvine, T. and L. Lawlor (2007), *The Merleau-Ponty Reader*. Evanston, IL: Northwestern University Press.

IX. Nietzsche

Reading Nietzsche's own writings[1] is, of course, absolutely indispensable in coming to terms with his thought. The standard edition of the complete works in Nietzsche's original German is the *Kritische Gesamtausgabe: Werke*, edited by Giorgio Colli and Mazzino Montinari (Berlin: Walter de Gruyter, 1967–). In the case of most of Nietzsche's books, there are several English translations to choose from. The first, and to date only, full English translation of his complete works, edited by Oscar Levy (Edinburgh and London: T.N. Foulis, 1909–1913), is now considered unreliable and is generally avoided. A translation of the complete works based on a shorter version of the Colli and Montinari edition, the *Complete Works of Friedrich Nietzsche*, edited by Bernd Magnus, Keith Ansell-Pearson and Alan D. Schrift, is currently underway, but so far only three volumes of the projected twenty have appeared (Stanford: Stanford University Press, 1995–). Cambridge University Press has recently published good critical editions of all Nietzsche's major works. Penguin also publishes inexpensive editions of most of

Nietzsche's major works, many in classic translations by Walter Kaufmann or R. J. Hollingdale.

There are also several popular collections of selected works by Nietzsche. Kaufmann's *The Portable Nietzsche* (London: Penguin, 1977) contains translations of several full-length books and a selection of letters, while his *Basic Writings of Nietzsche* (New York: Modern Library, 1968) contains several more complete books. Hollingdale's *A Nietzsche Reader* (London: Penguin, 1977) contains thematically organized selections from works Nietzsche published (nothing from the *Nachlass* is included). Keith Ansell-Pearson and Duncan Large's *The Nietzsche Reader* (Oxford: Blackwell, 2006) contains a wide selection, including many early unpublished writings, as well as an excellent commentary.

Many short introductions to Nietzsche's thought are also available, of which we will mention two as particularly recommended. Ansell Pearson's *How to Read Nietzsche* (London: Granta, 2006) brings to bear the author's extensive scholarly knowledge on the topic, but is short, engaging and accessible to the reader new to Nietzsche. Gianni Vattimo's *Nietzsche: An Introduction* (Stanford: Stanford University Press, 2001) is a good introductory overview of Nietzsche's thought which contains a useful historical overview of the history of Nietzsche reception.

Several biographies of Nietzsche are also available, which also serve as introductions to his thought. The classic in English is R. J. Hollingdale's *Nietzsche: The Man and His Philosophy* (New York: Cambridge University Press, 1999). More recent biographies are Ronald Hayman's *Nietzsche: A Critical Life* (London: Weidenfeld and Nicolson, 1980), Rüdiger Safranski's *Nietzsche: A Philosophical Biography* (London: Granta, 2003) and Julian Young's *Friedrich Nietzsche: A Philosophical Biography* (Cambridge: Cambridge University Press, 2010). Safranski's book is a particularly good introduction to Nietzsche's thought, focusing more on his philosophical development than the events of his life and drawing on recent research.

There is a plethora of exegetical material on Nietzsche. The classic 'existentialist' interpretations of Nietzsche are Karl Jaspers's *Nietzsche: An Introduction to the Understanding of His Philosophical Activity*, trans. C. F. Wellraff and F. J. Schmitz (Tucson: University of Arizona Press, 1965) and Walter Kaufmann's *Nietzsche: Philosopher, Psychologist, Antichrist* (Princeton: Princeton University Press, 1974). For historical and thematic overviews of Nietzsche's reception and influence, see Ashley Woodward's *Understanding Nietzscheanism* (Durham: Acumen, 2011), which contains a chapter on existentialism, and his edited volume *Interpreting Nietzsche* (London: Continuum, 2011). For guidance on recent trends in Nietzsche scholarship, see *A Companion to Nietzsche*, ed. K Ansell-Pearson (Cambridge, MA: Blackwell, 2007) and *The Oxford Handbook to Nietzsche*, ed. K. Gemes and J. Richardson (Oxford: Oxford University Press, forthcoming).

Notes

1. Some of this material also appears in a different form in Ashley Woodward (2011), *Understanding Nietzscheanism*. Durham: Acumen.

Other Useful Works

Allison, D. B. (ed.) (1985), *The New Nietzsche: Contemporary Styles of Interpretation*. Cambridge, MA: MIT Press.

Bataille, G. (2004), *On Nietzsche*, trans. B. Boone. London: Continuum.

Danto, A. (2005), *Nietzsche as Philosopher*, expanded edn. New York: Columbia University Press.

Deleuze, G. (1983), *Nietzsche and Philosophy*, trans. H. Tomlinson. New York: Columbia University Press.

Derrida, J. (1979), *Spurs: Nietzsche's Styles*, trans. B. Harlow. Chicago: University of Chicago Press.

Diethe, C. (2006), *Historical Dictionary of Nietzscheanism*, 2nd edn. Maryland: Scarecrow Press.

Fink, E. (2003), *Nietzsche's Philosophy*. London and New York: Continuum.

Heidegger, M. (1979–1987), *Nietzsche*, trans. David Farrell Krell. 4 vols. San Francisco: Harper & Row.

Irigaray, L. (1991), *Marine Lover of Friedrich Nietzsche*, trans. G. C. Gill. New York: Columbia University Press.

Klossowski, P. (2005), *Nietzsche and the Vicious Circle*, trans. D. W. Smith. London and New York: Continuum.

Kofman, S. (1993), *Nietzsche and Metaphor*, trans. Duncan Large. Stanford: Stanford University Press.

Leiter, B. and J. Richardson (eds) (2001), *Nietzsche*. Oxford: Oxford University Press.

Löwith, K. (1997), *Nietzsche's Philosophy of the Eternal Recurrence of the Same*, trans. J. Harvey Lomax. Berkelely: University of California Press.

Magnus, B. (1978), *Nietzsche's Existential Imperative*. Bloomington, IN: Indiana University Press.

Müller-Lauter, W. (1999), *Nietzsche: His Philosophy of Contradictions and the Contradictions of His Philosophy*, trans. D. J. Parent. Urbana and Chicago: University of Illinois Press.

Nehamas, A. (1985), *Nietzsche: Life as Literature*. Cambridge, MA: Harvard University Press.

Oliver, K. and M. Pearsall (eds) (1998), *Feminist Interpretations of Friedrich Nietzsche*. University Park, PA: Pennsylvania State University Press.

Schacht, R. (1983), *Nietzsche*. London and Boston: Routledge & Kegan Paul.

X. Sartre

Joseph S. Catalano's book, *A Commentary on Sartre's Being and Nothingness* (Chicago: Midway Reprints, 1986), remains one of the best introductory books on Sartre's major existentialist text, *Being and Nothingness*, although some new and important commentaries have appeared in the past few years by well-respected scholars. These include Sebastian Gardner's *Sartre's Being and Nothingness: A Reader's Guide* (London: Continuum 2010), Jonathan Webber's *The Existentialism of Jean-Paul Sartre* (London: Routledge, 2008), Webber's edited collection *Reading Sartre: On Phenomenology and Existentialism* (London: Routledge, 2010), Anthony Hatzimoysis's *The Philosophy of Sartre* (Durham: Acumen, 2010) and Katherine Morris' *Sartre* (Stafford:Wiley-Blackwell, 2008). It is interesting that all of these books have recently been commissioned, suggesting either that the publishers are making a mistake or that there is a distinct revival of interest in Sartre, especially in the United Kingdom.

Some of the first English-language books on Sartre can be helpful, such as those by Mary Warnock, *The Philosophy of Sartre* (London: Hutchinson University Library, 1965) and Hazel E.Barnes, *Sartre* (Philadelphia: Lippincott, 1973). In terms of ethics, Hazel Barnes' *Existentialist Ethics* (Chicago: University of Chicago Press, 1985) and Thomas C. Anderson's *Sartre's Two Ethics: From Authenticity to Integral Humanity* (La Salle, IL: Open Court, 1993) and *The Foundation and Structure of Sartrean Ethics* (Lawrence: University Press of Kansas, 1979) are both very useful. However, neither give much attention to Sartre's *Notebooks for an Ethics* (Chicago: University of Chicago Press, 1992), a text that was unpublished during his own lifetime which attempts to work out the ethics promised in the odd place in *Being and Nothingness*. Juliette Simont's essay on 'Sartre's Ethics', in Christina Howells (ed.), *The Cambridge Companion to Sartre* (Cambridge: Cambridge University Press, 1992) is also acute, as are many of the other essays in this volume. For reflections on the connection between Sartre's literature and his philosophy, see Iris Murdoch's *Sartre: Romantic Rationalist* (London: Fontana, 1977) and Rhiannon Goldthorpe, *Sartre: Literature and Theory* (Cambridge: Cambridge University Press, 1986).

There are also more systematic expositions of his ontology available, including Peter Caws' *Sartre* (London: Routledge, 1979) and Klaus Hartmann's *Sartre's Ontology* (Evanston, IL: Northwestern University Press, 1966). Christina Howells' article on Sartre in the *Routledge Encyclopedia of Philosophy* is a good place to begin further research, and Christian Onof's entry on Sartre for the Internet Encyclopedia of Philosophy is admirably clear:www.utm.iep.edu/s/sartre.htm. On a more difficult and critical level is Maurice Natanson's rejection of Sartre's ontology in his book: *A Critique of Jean-Paul Sartre's Ontology* (The Hague: Martinus Nijhoff, 1973). Probably the most systematic collection of material on Sartre that is available in the English language is the eight-volume collection edited by William McBride, *Sartre and Existentialism: Philosophy, Politics, Ethics, the Psyche, Literature, and Aesthetics* (London: Routledge, 1996).

The central role of a Husserl-inspired phenomenology in Sartre's existentialism is sometimes misunderstood or downplayed. A good corrective introduction to this topic is Thomas W. Busch's article 'Sartre's Use of the Reduction: *Being and Nothingness* Reconsidered', in H. J. Silverman and F. A. Elliston (eds), *Jean-Paul Sartre: Contemporary Approaches to his Philosophy* (Pittsburgh: Duquesne University Press, 1980), while a challenging study is undertaken by David Reisman, in *Sartre's Phenomenology* (London: Continuum, 2007), where the look of the Other plays a central role.

Some interesting work has also been done recently by Thomas W. Busch exploring some of the nuances of Sartre's conception of freedom in *The Power of Consciousness and the Force of Circumstances in Sartre's Philosophy* (Bloomington, IN: Indiana University Press, 1990). In a related vein, although one that focuses upon Sartre's later work and in particular the *Critique of Dialectical Reason*, Thomas R. Flynn has also written an important book examining Sartre's relation to Marxism – *Sartre and Marxist Existentialism* (Chicago: University of Chicago Press, 1990) – and since then a two-volume text on Sartre and Foucault titled *Sartre, Foucault, and Historical Reason* (Chicago: University of Chicago Press, 1997, 2005).

Other Useful Works

Coombes, S. (2008), *The Early Sartre and Marxism*. Oxford: Peter Lang.

Cox, G. (1999), 'Heidegger and Sartre on Death'. *Cogito* 3: 171–5. (A short but clear account of their differences.)

Cox, G. (2008), *The Sartre Dictionary*. London: Continuum.

Cox, G. (2009), *Sartre and Fiction*. London: Continuum.

Fourny, J.-F. and C. D. Minahen (eds) (1997), *Situating Sartre in Twentieth Century Thought and Culture*. New York: St Martins Press. (Focuses on situating Sartre within the contexts of feminism, postcolonialism and gender studies.)

Fox, N. F. (2003), *The New Sartre: Explorations in Postmodernism*. London: Continuum.

Howells, C. (2009), *Sartre: The Necessity of Freedom*. Cambridge: Cambridge University Press.

Judaken, J. (2009), *Jean-Paul Sartre and the Jewish Question*. Lincoln, NE: University of Nebraska Press.

Judaken, J. (ed.) (2008), *Race after Sartre: Antiracism, Africana Existentialism, Postcolonialism*. Albany, NY: SUNY Press.

Levy, N. (2002), *Being Up-to-Date: Foucault, Sartre and Postmodernity*. Berne: Peter Lang.

Murphy, J. S. (ed.) (1999), *Feminist Interpretations of Jean-Paul Sartre*. University Park, PA: Pennsylvania State University Press.

Wider, K. (1997), *The Bodily Nature of Consciousness: Sartre and Contemporary Philosophy of Mind*. New York: Cornell University Press.

INDEX

Note: numbers in **bold** designate the corresponding A–Z Glossary entry

Abbagnano, Nicola **325**
Abraham 43, 101, 132, 183–4, 273
absence, Pierre in the café (Sartre) 52, 179, 206
absurdity 64, 77–8, 86, 125, 127, 147, 176–7, 181, 183, 195, 211, 309, **325**
Adorno, Theodor 21, 71, 286
aging 311, 314
  and history 316–17
alterity 102, 169 *see also* Other
Althusser, Louis 261
ambiguity 23, 25, 28, 30, 33, 101–3, 139, 218, 220, 225, 273, 314, **326**
  between Merleau-Ponty and Sartre 22
  Ethics of Ambiguity (de Beauvoir) 98–9, 101, 149, 179, 181, 270, 315
  paradox of 107–11
Angst/anxiety 15, 19, 49, 64, 66, 83, 103–4, 108, 113, 121–3, 135, 148, 175, 188–9, 198, 204, 213n.5, 213n.7, 262, 279, 285–6, 287n.8, 305, **327**
  and conscience 204–9
anguish 16, 19, 25, 139, 182, 205, 215, 218–19, 234, 261, 272, 327–8, 329, 358, 364, **327**
  in Sartre 52, 54, 150, 180, 193, 203, 206–7
Artificial Intelligence 241–60
authenticity/inauthenticity 15, 20, 21, 58n. 4, 64, 86, 144, 156, 161, 164, 167, 169–71, 170, 198, 212, 234, 261, 286
  and existence 201–4
  in Heidegger 49–50, 73–4, 124–7, 133, 177, 187–8, 206–8, 291
  Jargon of Authenticity (Adorno) 286
  in Kierkegaard 66
  and Latin American identity 215
  and Mexican existentialism 225–31
  in Nietzsche 294–8
  in Sartre 55, 135n.5, 155, 189

bad faith 20, 27, 29, 55, 87, 92, 103, 105, 155, 161, 169, 172n.6, 177, 189, 193, 203, 207, 261, 312, **328**
  and mystifications 179–83
  of women 156–8
Badiou, Alain 274, 308
Barthes, Roland 261, 378
Barth, Karl 128, **329**
Beckett, Samuel **330**
Being/beyng (as opposed to beings) 4, 18, 20, 21, 31, 39, 40, 44, 46, 47, 48, 50, 51, 52, 53, 58, 72, 73, 74, 121, 125, 126, 131, 134, 187, 188, 189, 301, 302, 305n.2, 325, 331, 333, 337, 346, 347, 349, 359, 362, 369
  being-for-itself 26, 92, 156, **330**
  being-in-itself 92, 156, 202, **330**
  being-for-others 156, 160, 163, 178
  being-in-the-world 18, 20–1, 24, 46–51, 73, 98, 120, 133, 175–6, 181, 188, 201, 205–7, 246, 294 **331**
  being-towards-death 20, 50, 121, 124–5, 133, 189
Being and Nothingness (Sartre) 3, 15, 18, 20–3, 27–8, 30, 45, 51–8, 79–80, 85–7, 92–3, 103–7, 136, 156–62, 191–3, 202–7, 213n.6, 272–4, 328–9, 331, 342, 366, 398–400.
Being and Time (Heidegger) 3, 16, 18–21, 44, 47–8, 50–1, 56, 72–5, 120–1, 124–6, 187, 198, 201, 215, 227, 242, 268, 278, 300, 304
Berdyaev, Nikolai 6, 117, 131, 286, **332**
Binswanger, Ludwig 6, 84–5, **332**
body 17, 24, 30, 84–5, 91–2, 98, 102–3, 105, 145, 156, 176, 190–2, 200–1, 203, 209, **332**
  biological 12, 85–9, 91, 121–2, 163–6, 249
  body-subject 12, 192
  gendered 155, 158, 163, 165–6, 314
  lived 12, 19, 45, 108, 267, **332–3**
  sexual 103–7, 160–1, 169, 171, 264

boredom 4, 19–20, 40, 56, 285, **333**
Borges, Jorge Luis 233–5
Boss, Medard 84, **334**
boundary situation *see* limit situation
Buber, Martin 6, 84, 112–15, 131–3, 272, 286, **334–5**
Bultmann, Rudolf 120, **335**
Butler, Judith 12, 163

Camus, Albert 2–3, 5, 43, 63, 86, 138–40, 147–53, 171, 177–8, 286, **336**
care (*Sorge*) 48, 50, 53, 117, 120, 187, 189, 206, 291
Carpentier, Alejo 233–5
Christian existentialism 15, 117–37, 221, 287
    Catholic existentialism (Latin America) 221–3
Cioran, Emil **336–7**
cogito 18, 25–6, 51, 56, 77–9, 265–6, 274, 276 *see also* Descartes
cognitive science 241–60
conscience 121, 180, 186–9, 194, 198, 204, 272–3, 291, 296–7
    and anxiety 204–9, 213n.5, 213n.7
    bad conscience 184–5
    call of conscience 186–8
consciousness
    reflective, pre-reflective 18–19, 22, 24–5, 56, 59n.9, 99, 267–8
contingency 23, 28, 108, 125, 139, 160, 234, 265

Dasein 20, 21, 52, 56, 58, 73–4, 84, 120–2, 131, 133, 135, 187–9, 201–2, 206, 278, 291, 300, 305, **337**
    freedom of 49–50
    and reality 50–1
    and transcendence 48–9
    and truth 46–8
das Man, the many, the herd, "the one" 20, 65, 73–4, 184–6, 206–7, 285, 294, 296, **338**
death 2, 3, 15–16, 25, 83, 117–18, 123, 125, 127, 130, 139, 149, 160, 180, 189, 193, 195, 260, 261, 273, 286, 291, 316, **338–9** *see also* being-towards-death and God, death of
    authentic/inauthentic apprehension of in de Beauvoir 143–6, 318n.10

in Heidegger 4, 20, 21, 133
de Beauvoir, Simone 2–3, 5, 11–13, 15–18, 25, 32–3, 75, 77, 103, 106–8, 112, 115, 138–40, 266, 269–70, 278, 286, **339** *see also* ambiguity, reciprocity, *The Second Sex*
    current scholarship about 310–22
    on emotions 175–82, 193
    ethics 98–103
    literature 143–9
    method 26–30
    on sexuality 162–71, 278, 286
decision 15, 21, 55, 85, 87–8, 93–4, 101, 104, 112, 123, 130, 140, 150–1, 157–8, 180, 260, 265–6, 295
    and responsibility 271–4
Deleuze, Gilles 261, 270
Derrida, Jacques 21, 141, 261–74, 286
Descartes, René 26, 77, 85, 201, 217, 265–6
desire 103–7, 160–1, 169, 171, 264
despair 117, 145, 147, 180–1, 195, 204–5, 208, 213n.5, 285–6, 287n. 8
Dostoevsky, Fyodor 4, 42, 100, 117, 120, 126–30, 135, 138, 147, 149, 175, 177–8, 180–4, 286, **341**
dread 15, 105, 107–8, 117, 157, 183, 189, 211 *see also Angst*
Dreyfus, Hubert 242–9

ecstases 7, **341**
ego 19, 21–3, 44, 51, 53, 54, 56, 58, 59, 90, 199, 202, 209, 266, 267, 270, 276, 296, 297, 348 *see also* transcendental ego, *Transcendence of the Ego*
embodiment 45, 102–3, 105, 107–8, 162 *see also* body
    female 314
emotions 9, 13, 165, 52, 147, 175–97, 251–2, 264, 267, 314, 316
    Sketch for a Theory of the Emotions (Sartre) 189–92
empiricism 24, 271
eternal return 68, 186, 294, 371–3
ethics 13, 26, 43, 50, 51, 55, 59n. 11, 74, 83, 98–116, 149, 152, 177, 179, 193, 207, 211, 213, 233, 249, 266, 270, 285, 297, 311, 326, 327, 337, 340, 353, 357, 367
Existenz 5, 119, 201, 210, 269, 293, 300, 349, 359, 374–5, 380, 393.

experience, lived 3, 16, 27, 41, 44, 83, 138–9, 150, 153, 162, 312, 316

facticity 12, 22, 25, 29, 54, 106, 120, 156, 157–8, 162, 171, 175, 188, 192, 234, 264–5, 273, 292–3, 309, **342**
faith 40, 43, 49, 67, 100–1, 194, 218, 224, 265, 272, 283, 285, **342** *see also* bad faith, leap of faith, religion)
fallenness (Heidegger) 20, 208, 328
Fanon, Frantz 228, 309, 315, 377–8.
fear 20, 104, 127, 132, 133, 159, 165, 176, 183, 185, 189, 205, 206, 207, 217, 252, 296, 297, 327, 345, 352, 356, 358, 363
feminism 10–13, 75, 155–74, 178, 232, 315–21, 387–9 *see also* gender
freedom **343**
 Dasein's 49–50
 of the for-itself 54–6
 ontology of 42–3
 Sartre and 156
French philosophy 2, 5, 13–14, 15, 22, 71, 88, 119, 126, 262, 271, 275, 279n. 2, 286, 306–7, 309–11, 313–15, 317
 and cold war politics 75–80
 Free French 55
 Revolution 66, 296
Foucault, Michel 260–2, 267–8, 271–2, 274–5, 306–8, 378–9, 400
Frankl, Viktor 84
Freud, Sigmund 84–96, 160, 172, 209, 232, 335, 354, 367, 374
future 7, 20, 26, 48, 72, 83, 84, 86, 87, 93, 96, 99, 108, 109, 111, 114, 120, 121, 128, 152, 156, 163, 170, 179, 189, 243, 252, 265, 266, 283, 297, 298, 341, 342, 346, 347, 363

Gaos, Josè 216, 220, 226–7, 230
gender 102, 155, 310–11, 316 *see also* feminism
German philosophy 2, 19, 65, 72, 74–5, 78, 120, 216, 222
God 4, 16, 40–3, 49, 54, 66, 77–9, 86, 96, 100–4, 112–14, 117–21, 126–35, 139, 171, 183–5, 198–200, 204–5, 209, 211, 218, 221–2, 263–4, 273, 304, 307, **344**
 death of 78, 96, 114, 119, 126–7, 198, 292, **344**

guilt 15, 50, 117, 121, 124, 136, 150, 165, 175, 177–88, 192–5, 206, 265, 291, 297, 344–5.

habit 8, 17, 19, 24, 102, 192
hate 160, 175, 190, 193
Hegel, GWF 5, 10, 16, 26, 39, 43, 63, 65–7, 78, 81, 105, 123–4, 138, 149, 206, 218, 264, 271, 283, 313–16, **345–6**
Heidegger, Martin **346–7** *see also* Angst / anxiety, authenticity/inauthenticity, *Being and Time*, being-towards-death, *Dasein*, das Man, fallenness, guilt, idle talk, resoluteness, throwness, they-self
 current scholarship about, 300–4
 fundamental ontology 19–21
 Nazism and the crisis of modernity 71–5
 rejection of 'existentialist' label 20, 261, 304
hermeneutics 17, 21, 46, 47, 216, 362
Hitler 193, 337 *see also* Nazism
humanism 63, 75–9, 108–11, 114, 226, 228–9, 231, 261–70, 285, 307
 "Existentialism as a Humanism" (Sartre) 15, 55, 85, 88, 91, 104, 135n. 5, 142, 213n.6, 265, 270, 272, 275
humanism–(Continued)
 "Letter on Humanism" (Heidegger) 20, 261, 304
 "Humanism and Terror" (Merleau-Ponty) 75–9, 108–11
Husserl, Edmund 8–10, 12, 16–19, 30, 32, 44–6, 51, 53, 56, 99–100, 102, 119, 121, 126, 138, 198, 201, 204, 208, 210, 213n.7, 216, 219, 223, 231–2, 262, 268, 270–1, 306, **347–8**
 and de Beauvoir 26–9, 162
 and Heidegger 19–21
 and Merleau-Ponty 23–5, 107–8
 and Sartre 21–3
Hyperion Group 227, 229–31
idealism 5, 24, 43, 44, 50, 51, 57, 59, 120, 229, 235, 325, 332, 353, 358, 359, 368

idle talk 187, 188, 327 *see also* das Man
immanence 25, 27, 28, 162, 163, 166, 270, 273, 317n.5, 340, 351, 366, 367, 370, 371

indifference 160, 185
intentionality 17, 19, 23–4, 46, 99–103, 106–7, 112, 246, 277, **348**

Jaspers, Karl 5, 15–16, 45, 49, 83, 180, 193–7, 204, 209–10, 269, 286, 292–4, 325, 338, **349–50**
Jonas, Hans 14, 242, 249–56

Kafka, Franz 4, 138, 147, 178, 286, **350**
Kant, Immanuel 17, 40, 43–4, 51, 53, 55, 57, 59, 62. 64, 70, 135, 201, 210, 218, 251, 270, 272, 285, 298
Kierkegaard, Søren 5, 15–16, 39–41, 43, 64–8, 100–1, 121–5, 132–3, 183–4, 198–201, 205, **350–1**, 355–6, 373
    see also Angst, dread, leap of faith, *Sickness Unto Death*
    current scholarship about 282–9
Kojève, Alexandre 16, 346, 375.

Lacan, Jacques 90, 275, 306–7, 317
Laing, R D 83–9, **352**
Latin America
    existentialism in 215–38
leap of faith (Kierkegaard) 15, 101, 183, 195, 196, 205, 272, 351, 370
Le Doeuff, Michèle 26, 29, 157, 170, 172–3, 310–11, 313
Les Temps Modernes 2, 15, 75, 77, 79, 317, 319, 340, 376–7
Levinas, Emmanuel 21–2, 50, 131–2, 135–6, 230, 272, 286–7, 314, 334, 375, 377–8
limit situation/boundary situation 15, 184, 338
literature, existentialist use of 7, 107, 138–54, 175–97, 215–38, 312–13
    as ethical investigation 148–53
    Latin American existentialist 233–5
lived body *see* body
lived experience 3, 16, 27, 41, 44, 83, 138–9, 150, 153, 162, 312, 316
look 156, 158–9, 167, **352**
    countering of 103–7
love 10, 26, 66, 89, 95, 105–6, 130–5, 150, 155–6, 158–61, 167–71, 175–7, 179, 181–3, 185, 189, 195–6, 218, 222, 224, 241, 285–6

Lyotard, Jean-François 68, 261–3, 269, 274–5, 379.

Marcel, Gabriel 3, 5–6, 15, 18, 30–3, 49, 54–5, 58–9, 104, 117, 131, 135, 138, 215, 221, 230, 233, 286–7, 339, 344–5, **352–3** *see also* problem and mystery
Marcuse, Herbert 73
marriage 124, 125, 165, 166, 310
Marx, Karl 10, 62, 76, 78–80, 119, 177, 227, 229, 231–3, 278, 306, 308, 313, 315–16, 325, 335–6, 345, 355, 357, 364, 368, 373–4, 377–8, 396
masochism 160–1, 167, 179
master-slave dialectic 105, 315, 375
May, Rollo 83–4, **353–4**
memory 16, 22, 92
Merleau-Ponty, Maurice 2, 3, 5–6, 9, 12–14, 15–19, 21–3, 30, 32, 45, 51, 85, 91, 98, 103, 112, 162, 192, 200, 215–16, 219, 230, 232, 242, 244, 2468, 256, 262–3, 269, 278, 291, 306, 313, **354–5**
    paradox of ambiguity 107–11
    Phenomenology of Perception 23–6
    politics 75–81
    and Sartre 21–3
metaphysics of presence 307, 313
mood 84, 99, 107–8, 175, **355–6** *see also* emotions
    Heidegger on 188–9
mortality 3, 58, 150, 176
mystery *see* problem and mystery
Nancy, Jean-Luc 262, 308
nausea 2, 4, 19, 23, 56, 142, 212n.3, 263, 269, 272, 309, **356**
    Nausea (novel by Jean-Paul Sartre) 2, 23, 142, 212n.3, 263, 269, 272, **356**

Nazism 55, 71–3, 75, 77, 84, 178, 195, 272–3, 336, 349, 357, 369, 375
negation 52, 147, 189, 206
Nietzsche, Friedrich 41–3, 63–4, 68–71, 183–6, 198, 209–12, 263–4, 266, 333, 345, **357–8**, 359, 365, 371–2 *see also* eternal return, God, *ressentiment*, values, will to power
    current scholarship about 290–9
nihilation 56, 59 n.11, 189, 191, 135n.5
nihilism 68, 128, 130, 193–6, 198, 283, **358–9**

nothingness 40, 43, 45, 52–8, 99, 105, 117, 121, 125, 127, 131, 178–9, 189, 195, 202, 206–7, 227, 293, **358**

ontic-ontological difference 19–21, 50, 156, 358, **359–60**
oppression 11–12, 28, 101–3, 155–6, 162, 169–70, 176, 179, 181–2, 235, 275, 310, 316
 sexuality under 162–4
Ortega y Gasset, Josè 216–36, **360**
Other 17, 83, 99–103, 114, 118–19, 127, 131–5, 141, 144, 146–7, 149–50, 156, 158–9, 167–8, 187–93, 198, 201, 209, 270, 274, 302, 309, **360**
 de Beauvoir's concept of 314–16
 and the Look 103–6, 158–9
 in sexuality 160–2, 169–71
 woman as other 102

Pareyson, Luigi 260, **362**
Pascal, Blaise 3–4, 117, **362–3**
Passion(s) 40, 65, 68, 101, 124, 129, 175, 178, 179, 182, 183, 185, 186, 193, 195, 196, 217, 285, 287, 296, 364
past 7, 48, 74, 83, 84, 93, 96, 105, 121, 143, 156, 163, 180, 225, 229, 231, 246, 273, 291, 293, 316, 335, 341, 342, 346
phenomenology 8–10, 15–36, 43–58, 86, 98, 102, 104, 108, 126, 139, 162, 190, 198, 201–4, 227, 243–9, 262, 270, 277 *see also* Husserl and other philosophers associated with phenomenology
Plato 68, 138, 210, 312, 326, 357.
politics *see also* Hitler, Nazism
 and existentialism 10–13, 62–82, 98–116.
poststructuralism 14, 80, 260–79, 306, 307, 313
present-at-hand (Heidegger) 18, 201
problem and mystery (Marcel) 31–2, **360–1**
projection 53, 156, 187, 190, 243, 244, 246, 341, 342
psychoanalysis 1, 6, 83–97, 192, 232, 354, 366

psychology 51, 55, 83–97, 176, 190, 212n.2, 223, 231, 232, 241, 285, 353, 355, 366
psychotherapy 83–97, 354

questioning 30, 32, 46, 266
Quixote, Don 216–20, 233–6

Ramos, Samuel 225–6, 232
rationalism 24, 43, 65, 177, 218, 219, 222, 227, 234, 313
ready-to-hand (Heidegger) 18, 20, 21, 245
rebellion (Camus) 77, 78, 128, 195, 231, 326, 336, 341
reciprocity (de Beauvoir) 103, 106, 107, 115, 132, 133, 165, 168, 169, 170, 172n.10
religion / religious experience 3, 13, 31, 43, 49, 63, 65–70, 83, 88, 95, 117–37, 177, 180–3, 185, 194, 213n.15, 218, 224, 2666, 272, 285–6 *see also* Christian existentialism
resoluteness (Heidegger) 21, 49, 124, 125, 136, 204, 206, 370
responsibility 4, 21, 55, 87, 92, 98, 100–1, 107, 132, 149, 157, 180–1, 192–3, 199, 205, 266, 271–4, **364–5**
ressentiment (Nietzsche) 175, 184, 222, 357, 365, 372
Rilke, Rainer Maria 346, **363–4**

sadism 160–1
Sartre, Jean-Paul **365** *see also* absence, anguish, authenticity/inauthenticity, bad faith, *Being and Nothingness*, look, negation, nothingness, others, responsibility, shame
 current scholarship about 305–10
 and freedom 156
 and Husserl 21–3
 and Merleau-Ponty 21–3
Schopenhauer, Arthur 41, 63, 68, 210–2, 295–6, **366–7**
Second Sex, The (de Beauvoir) 2, 11, 26–30, 75, 101–2, 143, 155, 162, 170–1, 178, 310, 316
 new translation of 28, 171, 389, 310–1
self 28, 30–3, 198–214 *see also* subject
sexual difference 158, 166, 311, 317n.5

sexuality 83, 90, 92, 155–74 *see also* body, desire
  authentic 169–74
  homosexuality 105,157, 164, 171, 312
  masochism 160–1, 167, 179
  sadism 160–1
  under oppression 162–4
  women's 164–9
shame (Sartre) 22, 159, 181, 352
Sickness Unto Death (Kierkegaard) 181, 186, 199, 351
Sisyphus, the myth of (Camus) 2, 34, 77, 147, 195–6, 326, 336, 339, 356, 376, 387.
situation **367–8**
structuralism 1, 80, 261, 265, 267, 274, 277, 306, 307
subject 6, 7, 12, 17, 23, 24, 30, 32, 39, 44, 47, 52, 56, 57, 58, 59n.13, 62, 73, 85, 87, 96, 98, 100–5, 109, 112, 121, 122, 134, 135, 141, 143, 144, 145, 146, 159, 163, 164, 167, 170, 172n.17, 179, 190, 192, 193, 201, 254, 260, 262–6, 268, 269–71, 273–8, 279n.3, 292, 304, 306, 307, 308, 309, 326, 330, 331, 333, 334, 340, 344, 345, 348, 350, 352, 354, 355, 359, 365, 368, 370, 396
subjectivity 20, 31, 39–46, 63, 65, 81, 83, 98–103, 105, 108, 111, 112, 113, 134, 135n.3, 146, 159, 160, 168, 181, 216, 256, 261, 306, 307, 309, 311, 314, 327, 330, 333, 344, 352, 365, 396
  and truth 39–41
suicide 2, 77, 127, 151, 164, 195, **368**

technology 73, 219, 225, 231, 233, 317, 361
they-self 186–8
thrownness 187–9, **369–70**
Tillich, Paul 6, 117, **368–9**
transcendence 27, 39–42, 45, 55, 58, 158–9, 161–3, 166, 169–70, 175, 206–7, 234, 243, 246–7, 262, 264–5, 270, 291–3, 317n.5, **370–1**
  Dasein as 48–9
  and the for-itself 52–4
Transcendence of the Ego (Sartre) 21–3, 202, 266, 270
transcendental ego 19, 22, 24, 44, 56, 59, 199, 201–2, 270
transcendental method/reasoning 4, 17, 24, 28–9, 44, 48, 51, 53, 56, 59, 108, 198–9, 201–2, 242–3, 266, 270–1, 347, 349
truth 39–61, 79, 102, 132, 168, 218, 252, 294, 301, 335, 343, 349, 362, 371

Ubermensch 41, 211, 214, **371–2**
Unamuno, Miguel de 216–24, 232–3, 235, 286, **372**
unconscious 92–5, 157, 192, 265, 274

values 12, 41, 43, 55, 63, 70, 76, 78, 86, 100, 104, 110, 123, 126, 184, 211, 213, 216, 217, 219, 221–4, 226, 228, 229, 231, 232, 233, 249, 251, 253, 254, 266, 294, 315, 340, 343, 344, 357, 359, 371
Varela, Francisco 249, 253–4, 256
Villoro, Luis 226, 229–31
violence 13, 43, 67, 76, 77, 111, 149, 150, 151, 152, 178, 179, 181, 182, 270, 273, 311

war *see also* violence
  Algerian 88, 149, 315
  cold war 75–80, 317
  Korean 79
  World War II *see also* Nazism 2, 15, 20, 22, 55, 71, 76, 149–50, 306, 315
will to power (Nietzsche) 84, 184, 211, 213n.14, 294, **372**

Zea, Leopoldo 221–2, 226–31

CPSIA information can be obtained at www.ICGtesting.com
Printed in the USA
LVOW100043150912

298931LV00007B/24/P